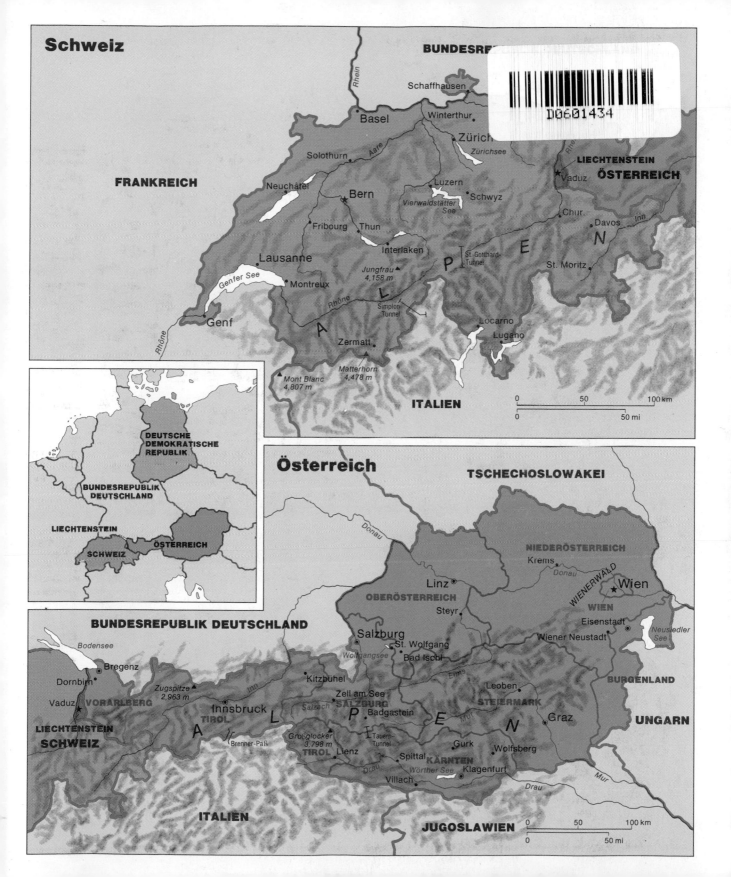

Deutsch heute

Grundstufe

Deutsch heute

Grundstufe/Fourth Edition

Jack Moeller
Oakland University

Helmut Liedloff
Southern Illinois University

Houghton Mifflin Company   Boston

Dallas   Geneva, Illinois   Palo Alto   Princeton, New Jersey

Cover photo by J.H. Neumann / Bildarchiv Bucher, Munich, West Germany

The authors and editors would like to thank the following authors and publishers for granting permission to use copyrighted material:

Mani Matter, "Heidi," from *Us emer lääre Gygechaschte*, Zürich: Benziger Verlag, 1972, and LP Zyt 24, *I han es Zündhölzli azünd*, Produktion + Copyright: Zytglogge Verlag, Gümligen.
Helga M. Novak, "Schlittenfahren," from *Palisaden. Erzählungen*, © 1980 by Hermann Luchterhand Verlag, Darmstadt und Neuwied.
Werner Schmidli, "Als ich noch jung war," from *Sagen Sie nicht, beim Geld hört der Spaß auf*, Zürich: Benziger Verlag, 1971. Reprinted by permission of the author.
Christa Wolf, "Ich geh' da nicht mehr hin," from *Kindheitsmuster*, © Aufbau-Verlag Berlin und Weimar 1976.

Credits for photos and illustrations may be found at the end of the Reference Section in this book.

Printed in the U.S.A.

Library of Congress Catalog Card Number: 87-80878
Student Text ISBN: 0-395-35948-1
Instructor's Annotated Edition ISBN: 0-395-44872-7

EFGHIJ-D-96543210

Contents

Reference Section

Introduction

Deutsch heute: Grundstufe, Fourth Edition is an introductory program in German designed for college students and other adult learners. The basic intention of *Deutsch heute* is to provide students with a sound basis for learning German as it is used in spoken and written communication today within the context of German-speaking culture. The *Deutsch heute* program offers systematic practice in the four basic language skills of listening, speaking, reading, and writing, along with materials geared to provide a firm foundation in the basic elements of German grammar. Building on the previous editions of *Deutsch heute*, the Fourth Edition provides more activities that guide students in employing their skills in active personal communication. By the end of the course, students should have mastered the basic features of the sound and writing system, be familiar with the communicative functions of the language, be able to use actively many basic grammatical structures in everyday conversation and writing, and be in control of an active vocabulary of approximately 1200 words and a passive vocabulary of considerably larger dimension.

Another goal of the Fourth Edition of *Deutsch heute* is to familiarize students with contemporary life and culture in the four primary German-speaking countries. The dialogues and readings convey important information on everyday life and culture of the Federal Republic of Germany, the German Democratic Republic, Austria, and Switzerland, often focusing on specific topics. The readings are mature in content but simple in structure. Cultural notes throughout the textbook provide more in-depth information. In combination with the photographs, realia, and drawings included in the Fourth Edition of *Deutsch heute*, the readings help convey to students what life is like in the German-speaking countries today.

A further aim of *Deutsch heute, Fourth Edition* is to have students experience the relationship between culture and language, thereby making them more aware of their own native language and culture.

Organization of the Student Text

The student text contains an introductory unit (*Einführung*) and fourteen chapters (*Kapitel*). The *Einführung* is designed to get students speaking and using German for active, personal communication from the very start. It introduces students to the German sound system by means of a short dialogue (*Bausteine für Gespräche*), the German alphabet, and numbers. Students learn to give information about themselves, to spell words, to use numbers in simple arithmetic, to give the day of the week, and to describe the contents of their rooms by size and color.

Each of the *Kapitel* centers on a cultural theme such as the geography of the two German states, university life, shopping, German attitudes toward privacy, the German economy, leisure time, or the social position of women and foreign workers. There are also specific readings on the German Democratic Republic, Austria, and Switzerland.

A typical chapter is composed of the following seven sections:

1. *Lernziele* are chapter objectives that summarize the content of each chapter and provide the student with categorized learning goals in four areas: communicative functions (*Sprechakte*), grammar (*Grammatik*), vocabulary (*Vokabeln*), and culture (*Landeskunde*).

2. *Bausteine für Gespräche* introduce idiomatic and colloquial phrases presented in dialogue format. Communication practice and vocabulary development continue in the oral activities that follow, which include *Fragen* (questions on the dialogues), and *Sie haben das Wort* (activities offering choices so that students can formulate their own responses). A list of *Vokabeln* follows the *Bausteine*, and most chapters contain sections of vocabulary expansion exercises and activities (*Erweiterung des Wortschatzes*).

3. *Lesestücke*, the core cultural readings, present the cultural theme of each chapter, beginning in

Kapitel 2. Each *Lesestück* is preceded by pre-reading activities to aid and direct students toward a successful experience in second language reading: *Zum Thema (About the Topic)* contains questions that help familiarize students with the topic of each reading by letting them discover what they may already know about the topic through brainstorming, and *Leitfragen (Questions to Consider While Reading)* give direction to students' reading by focusing on main points and asking students to search for specific information as indicated by key words and phrases *(Stichworte)*. Readings are then followed by a number of written and oral exercises including *Fragen zum Lesestück, Sie haben das Wort, Erzählen Sie! (Talk About It!), Vokabeln,* and *Erweiterung des Wortschatzes.*

4. *Übungen zur Aussprache (Exercises for Pronunciation)* practice pronunciation through contrastive drills and representative words in sentence context. The illustrated proverbs offer additional practice, as well as an enjoyable way to learn set phrases that are an integral part of the culture of German-speaking countries.

5. *Grammatik und Übungen (Grammar and Exercises)* explain grammatical concepts in concise, lucid terms and contain illustrative examples, often with equivalents in English. Grammar is explained in English to ensure immediate comprehension, and basic terms are regularly defined for the novice language learner. German structure is often contrasted with English to clarify the structure of both languages. The exercises can be completed in writing or orally in class; they can also be used by students for review and additional practice in combination with the student audio cassettes for home or language lab study.

6. *Wiederholung (Review)* activities practice the content, structure, and vocabulary of the chapter in new formats and reintroduce material from earlier chapters. The responses in the activities progress from controlled to free.

7. *Grammatik zum Nachschlagen (Grammar for Reference)* summarizes grammar topics introduced in the chapter. This is a reference section that is useful for review.

Sie haben das Wort activities occur throughout the chapter, in the *Bausteine* and *Lesestück* sections, as well as

in the *Grammatik und Übungen.* In addition, **Deutsch heute, Fourth Edition** is illustrated with numerous photographs, realia, and line drawings. Since many of the photographs and pieces of realia are closely related to the cultural notes and themes of the dialogues and core reading selections, they can be effectively used as the basis for many class activities or out-of-class assignments. The line drawings are used to introduce word sets and to demonstrate grammatical concepts and semantic differences explained in the grammar section. Maps of the German-speaking countries are found on the inside cover leaves at both the front and back of the book; a map of Europe can be found opposite the Introduction included in the *Einführung* on page 3.

The short stories by Helga Novak, Werner Schmidli, and Christa Wolf introduce students to literary prose. In style and content, these selections offer students a change of pace from the regular chapters and the satisfaction of reading German as written by established authors. Side glosses and notes clarify unfamiliar vocabulary and structures, and questions aid student comprehension and discussion.

The Reference section contains the following elements:

Pronunciation and Writing Guide: This sound-symbol section gives three or four key words and simplified phonetic symbols for each German sound. Each section provides hints on how to pronounce the sound, and where useful, contrasts it with English.

Grammatical Tables: The tables in the Reference section include the following charts: (1) paradigms for pronouns, articles, adjectives, and nouns; (2) comparisons of irregular adjectives and adverbs; (3) lists of prepositions governing the accusative, dative, or genitive case; (4) special verb + preposition combinations; (5) dative verbs; (6) examples of regular, irregular, and stem-changing verbs in various tenses of the indicative, passive, and subjunctive; and (7) a list of the strong and irregular weak verbs used in the Fourth Edition of **Deutsch heute** with principal parts and English meanings.

Supplementary Expressions: This reference list of supplementary expressions helps students increase the number of things they can say and write during the course of a chapter. The list of expressions is organized according to functions and notions, for example, stalling for time; expressing skepticism, regret, or admiration; asking for favors; and making requests.

Supplementary Word Sets: This reference list of supplementary word sets offers students another opportunity to personalize vocabulary. These word lists, arranged by theme and chapter, are helpful to students with special interest in a topic who wish to expand their vocabulary. Many of the *Sie haben das Wort* personalization activities indicate where these lists may be useful, and they are often correlated with topics presented in the *Erweiterung des Wortschatzes* sections.

Supplementary Dialogues: This list of specific, functional phrases in dialogue format is useful for students traveling or living in German-speaking countries. These dialogues for "survival German" take place in settings such as the airport, the post office, and the hotel.

German-English Vocabulary: The German-English end vocabulary lists all words used in *Deutsch heute, Fourth Edition* except numbers. Numerals after the English definitions indicate the chapter in which words and phrases are introduced in the *Vokabeln* lists for the *Bausteine für Gespräche* and *Lesestücke*. Recognition vocabulary from readings and exercises not intended for active mastery is also included.

English-German Vocabulary: The English-German end vocabulary contains the words listed in the *Vokabeln* lists of the *Einführung* and all fourteen *Kapitel*. This list of approximately 1200 words constitutes the active vocabulary of a student who has successfully completed the *Deutsch heute* program.

Index: The index indicates the pages on which grammatical features and topics in the *Erweiterung des Wortschatzes* are introduced. References to the pronunciation sections and cultural notes are also included.

Workbook/Lab Manual

The workbook/lab manual consists of four sections: (1) a lab manual that requires students to react orally or in writing to material on the recordings; (2) a workbook with writing exercises coordinated with each chapter of the text; (3) a set of self-tests with an answer key for correction; and (4), new to the Fourth Edition, a set of proficiency cards, which provide tasks and problem-solving activities for in-class use. Exercises in the workbook/lab manual parallel the presentation of content, structure, and vocabulary in the student text. Many workbook chapters contain short reading passages based on familiar material to give students extra practice in reading German. The Fourth Edition of the *Deutsch heute* workbook/lab manual contains many communicative exercises that allow students greater freedom of expression, and several new realia-based exercises.

Pages are perforated so that students can hand in their assignments to the instructor. Answers to the exercises in the workbook/lab manual are printed in the tapescript and answer key to the workbook/lab manual, a booklet provided to the instructor upon adoption of the program. However, if the instructor wishes to have students correct their own work, the tapescript and answer key to the workbook/lab manual can be made available for student purchase upon arrangement with the publisher. At the end of the workbook/lab manual, self-test exercises for each chapter allow students to test their mastery of the chapter material; immediate reinforcement is provided by the answer key.

The all-new proficiency cards coordinated with each chapter allow students to synthesize their acquired knowledge of communicative function, vocabulary, grammar, and culture in simulations of culturally authentic situations. Intended as free activities for students in which the instructor refrains from correcting and providing any information or feedback until their completion, the proficiency cards allow students to employ their acquired knowledge and demonstrate to themselves and their peers their growing language proficiency and ability to use German for active and personal communication in creative, culturally relevant contexts.

Recordings

The recordings that accompany *Deutsch heute, Fourth Edition* were made in the Federal Republic of Germany to provide the best possible models of German speech. Using a cast of young adult and adult actors and actresses, the recordings provide recorded versions of printed material from the *Einführung*; the *Bausteine*; the *Lesestücke*, followed by true-false and multiple-choice questions; the *Übungen zur Aussprache*; exercises from the *Grammatik und Übungen*, some with additional items appearing only in the recordings; and the three short stories in the textbook. In addition, the recordings include the listening comprehension exercises called *Übungen zum Hörverständnis* from the workbook/lab manual.

Sentences from the *Bausteine* are spoken once at normal speed, then modeled phrase by phrase with pauses for student repetition, and finally modeled again with pauses for repetition of complete utterances. The phrases in the *Sie haben das Wort* sections are also modeled for student repetition. The core reading selections (*Lesestücke*) are recorded without pauses. Pronunciation exercises are recorded in two phases: cue and pause for student response. The grammar exercises are recorded in three phases: cue, pause for student response, and confirmation response. Activities from the *Wiederholung* section are not on tape. The *Übungen zum Hörverständnis* from the lab manual are followed by a pause to allow students to respond in writing. Longer reading passages are read twice.

The recordings are available for student purchase in boxed sets of Studio Audio Cassettes.

Acknowledgments

The authors and publisher would like to thank the following people for their valuable contributions to the creation of the Fourth Edition of *Deutsch heute:* Constanze Kirmse, Ruth Maxwell, Marianne Richert, and Cynthia Westhof.

Special thanks also go to Professor Renate Gerulaitis of Oakland University for her on-going suggestions in shaping the program, and to Professor John Barthel of Oakland University for his valuable suggestions throughout the preparation of the Fourth Edition.

Finally, we would like to thank the following instructors for their thoughtful reviews and response to various surveys. Their input has proved invaluable in the development of the Fourth Edition of *Deutsch heute:*

Jerome Bakken, University of North Dakota (Grand Forks, ND)

Carol J. Bander, Saddleback College (Mission Viejo, CA)

Benjamin Blaney, Mississippi State University (Mississippi State, MS)

Barbara Bopp, University of California at Los Angeles (Los Angeles, CA)

Peter F. Brueckner, University of Oklahoma (Norman, OK)

Heidi Byrnes, Georgetown University (Washington, DC)

Jeannette Clausen, Indiana University—Purdue University (Fort Wayne, IN)

Hannelore Crossgrove, University of Rhode Island (Kingston, RI)

Linda DeMeritt, Allegheny College (Meadville, PA)

Dina Dodds, Lewis & Clark College (Portland, OR)

Bruce Duncan, Dartmouth College (Hanover, NH)

Edward Fichtner, Queens College, City University of New York (Flushing, NY)

Henry Fullenwider, University of Kansas (Lawrence, KS)

Henry Geitz, University of Wisconsin (Madison, WI)

Rolf Goebel, University of Alabama (University, AL)

Beverly Harris-Schenz, University of Pittsburgh (Pittsburgh, PA)

Ronald Hauser, State University of New York, Buffalo (Buffalo, NY)

Peter Herzog, College of St. Thomas (St. Paul, MN)

Ernst Hoffmann, Hunter College, City University of New York (New York, NY)

Barbara Hyams, Boston University (Boston, MA)

Brian Lewis, University of Colorado (Boulder, CO)

Paul Luckau, Brigham Young University (Provo, UT)

Charles Lutcavage, Harvard University (Cambridge, MA)

Manfred Prokop, University of Alberta (Canada)

James Reece, University of Idaho (Moscow, ID)

Michael Resler, Boston College (Boston, MA)

Lee Stavenhagen, Texas A&M University (College Station, TX)

Chris Stevens, University of Michigan (Ann Arbor, MI)

Gerhard Strasser, Pennsylvania State University (University Park, PA)

Special thanks to Goetz Seifert of the University of Tennessee at Martin for his in-depth review and comments.

Einführung

Lernziele

Sprechakte [Functions]

Asking for and giving personal information:
  name, age, address, telephone number
Introducing oneself
Thanking people
Spelling
Doing simple calculations
Asking what day it is
Asking about colors

Grammatik [Grammar]

Gender of nouns
Noun-pronoun relationship

Vokabeln [Vocabulary]

The alphabet
Numbers
Objects in a student's room
Colors

Landeskunde [Culture]

Writing German addresses
Registering and studying at a German
  university
Making and receiving telephone calls
The telephone system in the Federal Republic
  of Germany

Zürich – Hier spricht man deutsch.

1

Introduction

In this introductory unit you will learn to give some information about yourself, to count and spell in German, and to name the days of the week. You will also learn the colors and some common nouns.

The best way to learn to pronounce German is to imitate speakers of German, as completely and accurately as you can. Some of the sounds of German are just like those of English and will cause you no trouble. Others may sound strange to you at first and be more difficult for you to pronounce. With practice, you will be able to master the unfamiliar sounds as well as the familiar ones.

Though imitation is the one indispensable way of learning to pronounce any language, there are two things that should help you in your practice. First, you should learn how to manipulate your vocal organs so as to produce distinctly different sounds. Second, you should learn to distinguish German sounds from the English sounds that you might be tempted to substitute for them.

As you learn to pronounce German, you will also start to read and write it. Here a word of caution is in order. The writing system of German (or any language) was designed for people who already know the language. No ordinary writing system was ever designed to meet the needs of people who are learning a language. Writing is a method of reminding us on paper of things that we already know how to say; it is not a set of directions telling us how a language should be pronounced.

The Pronunciation and Writing Guide in the Reference section will give you some help with the German sound system. Further practice with specific sounds will be given in the pronunciation section of each chapter.

Europa

ISLAND
Reykjavik

Europäisches
Nordmeer

Atlantischer
Ozean

NORWEGEN
Oslo

SCHWEDEN
Stockholm

FINNLAND
Helsinki

Ostsee

Moskau

IRLAND
Dublin

GROSSBRITANNIEN
London

Nordsee

DÄNEMARK
Kopenhagen

SOWJETUNION

Amsterdam
Den Haag
NIEDERLANDE
Brüssel
BELGIEN
Bonn
LUXEMBURG
Luxemburg
Paris
BUNDESREPUBLIK
DEUTSCHLAND

Berlin
DEUTSCHE
DEMOKRATISCHE
REPUBLIK

POLEN
Warschau

Prag
TSCHECHOSLOWAKEI

0   200   400   600 km
0   200   400 mi

LIECHTENSTEIN
Vaduz
Wien
FRANKREICH
Bern
SCHWEIZ
ÖSTERREICH
Budapest
UNGARN

RUMÄNIEN
Bukarest

Schwarzes
Meer

PORTUGAL
Lissabon
Madrid
SPANIEN

ANDORRA

ITALIEN
Rom

JUGOSLAWIEN
Belgrad

BULGARIEN
Sofia

Tirana
ALBANIEN

GRIECHENLAND
Athen

TÜRKEI

MAROKKO

ALGERIEN

TUNESIEN

Mittelmeer

Mittelmeer

Bausteine für Gespräche

(Building Blocks for Conversation)

The dialogues in this section will help you acquire a stock of idiomatic phrases that will enable you to participate in conversations on everyday topics.

Wie heißen Sie?   What is your name?

Im Sekretariat   *At the registrar's office*

Sekretärin: Wie heißen Sie?   What is your name?
Gisela Riedholt: Ich heiße Gisela   My name is Gisela Riedholt.
  Riedholt.
Sekretärin: Wie buchstabiert man   How do you spell that?
  das?
Gisela Riedholt: R-i-e-d-h-o-l-t.   R-i-e-d-h-o-l-t.
Sekretärin: Ihre Adresse bitte, Frau   Your address, please, Ms. Riedholt.
  Riedholt.
Gisela Riedholt: Gartenstraße 15,   15 Garden Street, Bremen 1.
  Bremen 1.
Sekretärin: Und Ihre Telefonnum-   And your telephone number?
  mer?
Gisela Riedholt: 50 56 55.   50 56 55.
Sekretärin: Danke.   Thank you.
Gisela Riedholt: Bitte.   You're welcome.

Sie haben das Wort (You have the floor)

The material in this section gives you the opportunity to talk about your personal feelings and experiences. Substitute your own words for those in brackets.

A   Wie heißen Sie? Get acquainted with members of your class. Introduce yourself to your fellow students and ask what their names are.

| Getting acquainted |

Sie (You) | *Gesprächspartner/in (Partner)*

Ich heiße [Dieter]. Wie heißen Sie? | Ich heiße [Barbara].

B   Heißen Sie Inge? See how well you remember the names of at least four fellow students. If you're wrong they will correct you.

Sie (You) | *Gesprächspartner/in (Partner)*

Heißen Sie [Mark Schmidt]? | Ja.°
Sie heißen [Monika], nicht°? | Nein.° Ich heiße [Karin].

In a German address, the zip code (*Postleitzahl*) precedes the name of the city. Zip codes have a maximum of four numbers and indicate the geographic area within the Federal Republic of Germany. Hamburg, in northern Germany, has the zip code 2000; Bremen, also in northern Germany, has the zip 2800. The names of large cities are often followed by an additional number indicating the postal district: 6000 Frankfurt 1.

Die Briefträgerin bringt die Post.

Erweiterung des Wortschatzes
(Vocabulary Expansion)

1   Das Alphabet

The German alphabet has 26 regular letters and 4 special letters. They are pronounced as follows:

a	ah	**g**	geh	**l**	ell	**q**	kuh	**v**	fau	**ä**	äh (a-Umlaut)
b	beh	**h**	hah	**m**	emm	**r**	err	**w**	weh	**ö**	öh (o-Umlaut)
c	tseh	**i**	ih	**n**	enn	**s**	ess	**x**	iks	**ü**	üh (u-Umlaut)
d	deh	**j**	jot	**o**	oh	**t**	teh	**y**	üppsilon	**ß**	ess-tsett
e	eh	**k**	kah	**p**	peh	**u**	uh	**z**	tsett		
f	eff										

Capital letters are indicated by **groß: großes B, großes W.** Lower-case letters are indicated by **klein: kleines b, kleines w.**

A   Buchstabieren   Ask your instructor or a fellow student for her/his name. Then ask how to spell it.

▶   Wie heißen Sie?   *Fischer.*
▶   Wie buchstabiert man das?   *Eff-ih-ess-tseh-hah-eh-err.*

B   Abkürzungen (Abbreviations)   Pronounce the following abbreviations:

1. VW (= Volkswagen)
2. USA (= U.S.A.)
3. BMW (= Bayerische Motorenwerke)
4. DDR (= Deutsche Demokratische Republik)
5. CDU (= Christlich-Demokratische Union)
6. FDP (= Freie Demokratische Partei)
7. SPD (= Sozialdemokratische Partei Deutschlands)

**Volkswagen –
da weiß man,
was man hat**

**Freude am
Fahren**

The academic year at a German university has two terms: the *Wintersemester,* from mid-October to mid-February; and the *Sommersemester,* from mid-April to mid-July. Students must register each semester. The first time a student registers is called *Immatrikulation;* any subsequent registration is a *Rückmeldung.* Courses taken by the student are listed in an official transcript book (*Studienbuch*), which the student is responsible for, along with certificates signed by a professor to acknowledge the student's presence and success in the seminar (*Seminarscheine*). German students do not pay tuition, but they are required to have health insurance (*Krankenversicherung*). An ID card (*Studentenausweis*) enables a student to use university facilities such as the library and the cafeteria (*Mensa*) and to get reductions on theater and museum tickets, certain club memberships, and public transportation.

———————————

Stefans Studentenausweis

FREIE UNIVERSITÄT BERLIN

Studenten-Ausweis   WINTER -Semester 86/87
      Gultig vom: 01.10.86   bis   31.03.87
Gilt in Verbindung mit dem Personalausweis bzw. Reisepaß.

Name, Vorname:
KRAUTH STEFAN

Geburtsdatum: 09.02.59   Matrikelnummer: 1312182

      V1312182

— — — bitte nur hier falten — — —

Studiengang/Teilstudiengänge   Fachsemester
Germanistik/Deutsch   18
Theaterwissenschaft   18
Publizistik   18
Fachbereich bzw. Zentralinstitut   WE
FB Germanistik
Weiterer Studiengang   Fachsemester

Diese Bescheinigung wurde per Computer erstellt und ist ohne Unterschrift der ausstellenden Behörde gültig. Zusätzliche Änderungen bedürfen der Bestätigung durch das Immatrikulationsbüro.
Die Unterschrift des Ausweisinhabers schließt die Anerkennung der gültigen Benutzungsordnungen der FU-Bibliotheken mit ein.

BVG   BVG   Unterschrift des Ausweisinhabers

C   **Wie buchstabiert man das?**   Spell the following words aloud in German.

Sekretärin, ich, Adresse, danke, bitte

2   Die Zahlen von 1 bis 1.000

0 = null	11 = elf	21 = einundzwanzig
1 = eins	12 = zwölf	22 = zweiundzwanzig
2 = zwei	13 = dreizehn	30 = dreißig
3 = drei	14 = vierzehn	40 = vierzig
4 = vier	15 = fünfzehn	50 = fünfzig
5 = fünf	16 = sechzehn	60 = sechzig
6 = sechs	17 = siebzehn	70 = siebzig
7 = sieben	18 = achtzehn	80 = achtzig
8 = acht	19 = neunzehn	90 = neunzig
9 = neun	20 = zwanzig	100 = hundert
10 = zehn		101 = hunderteins
		1.000 = tausend

Note the following irregularities:

1.   **Eins** (*one*) becomes **ein** when it combines with the twenties, thirties, and so on: **einundzwanzig, einunddreißig.**
2.   **Dreißig** (*thirty*) ends in **-ßig** instead of the usual **-zig.**
3.   **Vier** (*four*) is pronounced with long [ī], but **vierzehn** (*fourteen*) and **vierzig** (*forty*) are pronounced with short [i].
4.   **Sechs** (*six*) is pronounced [şeks], but **sechzehn** (*sixteen*) and **sechzig** (*sixty*) are pronounced [şeç-].
5.   **Sieben** (*seven*) ends in **-en,** but the **-en** is dropped in **siebzehn** (*seventeen*) and **siebzig** (*seventy*).
6.   **Acht** (*eight*) is pronounced [axt], but the final **t** fuses with initial **ts** in **achtzehn** (*eighteen*) and **achtzig** (*eighty*).
7.   Numbers in the twenties, thirties, and so on follow the pattern of the nursery rhyme "four-and-twenty blackbirds":
     21 = einundzwanzig (*one-and-twenty*)
     32 = zweiunddreißig (*two-and-thirty*)
8.   German uses a period instead of a comma in numbers over 999. German uses a comma instead of a period to indicate decimals.

German	English
1.000 g (Gramm)	1,000 g
4,57 m (Meter)	4.57 m

9. Simple arithmetic:
    Addition (**+** = **und**): **Fünf und drei ist acht.**
    Subtraction (**−** = **weniger**): **Fünf weniger drei ist zwei.**
    Multiplication (**×** or **·** = **mal**): **Fünf mal drei ist fünfzehn.**
    Division (**:** = **[dividiert] durch**): **Fünfzehn durch drei ist fünf.**

D   Rechnen (Doing arithmetic)   Find a partner. Each of you takes a piece of paper and writes out five simple mathematical problems. Read your five problems to your partner and let her/him solve them; then solve your partner's five problems.

▶   Wieviel° ist drei und zwei [3 + 2]?   *Drei und zwei ist fünf.*

E   Ihre Adresse? Ihre Telefonnummer?   Obtain the address and telephone number of four fellow students. Write them down. If you don't know their names, ask them first. Be sure to say "thank you" and "you're welcome."

Sie (You)	*Gesprächspartner/in (Partner)*
Wie ist Ihre Adresse?	[Gartenstraße 15.]
Wie ist Ihre Telefonnummer?	[652-9846].
Danke.	Bitte.

F   Wie alt sind Sie°?   Find out the ages of four fellow students. Be sure you know their names. Write down the information.

Sie (You)	*Gesprächspartner/in (Partner)*
Wie alt sind Sie?	Ich bin [19] Jahre alt.

G   Ich heiße ...   Give the class some information about yourself. Follow the model.

▶   Ich heiße _____ . Ich bin _____ Jahre alt. Meine° Adresse ist _____ .
     Meine Telefonnummer ist _____ .

Public telephones in Germany are usually installed in bright yellow booths. They operate on a coin-operated message-unit system that automatically calculates charges for local or long-distance calls. Local calls cost a minimum of 20 Pfennig. Calls outside the immediate area require both an area code (*Vorwahl*) and additional 10 Pfennig, 50 Pfennig, or 1 Mark coins. When time and money are running out, a warning sign reminds the person on the phone to insert more coins. The telephone system is run by the Federal Post Office (*Bundespost*). Every post office maintains public telephones, which are either coin operated or billed through a postal clerk.

Germans usually identify themselves at once when they answer the phone. Callers also give their names before asking for the person they are trying to reach.

Whereas people who want to end a telephone conversation formally say *Auf Wiederhören* (literally: "until we hear each other again"), friends typically use an informal *Tschüß* ("So long") or *Bis dann* (" 'Til later") to say good-by. For example:

— Ingrid Breimann.
— Hier ist Gerda. Kann ich bitte mit Thomas sprechen?
— Hallo, Gerda. Thomas ist nicht zu Hause. Er spielt heute Fußball.
— Ach ja, richtig. Ich rufe später wieder an. Bis dann, Ingrid.
— Tschüß.

— Ingrid Breimann.
— This is Gerda. Can I speak to Thomas, please?
— Hi, Gerda. Thomas is not at home. He is playing soccer today.
— Oh, that's right. I'll call later. Till later, Ingrid.
— So long.

Die Telefonzellen sind gelb. Gelb ist die Farbe der Bundespost.

3 Wochentage

Welcher Tag ist heute?	What day is it today?
Heute ist Montag.	Today is Monday.
Dienstag	Tuesday
Mittwoch	Wednesday
Donnerstag	Thursday
Freitag	Friday
Samstag (*in southern Germany*)	Saturday
Sonnabend (*in northern Germany*)	
Sonntag	Sunday

H **Welcher Tag ist heute?** Ask a fellow student what day it is today.

▶ Welcher Tag ist heute? *Heute ist [Mittwoch].*

I **Nein, heute ist Montag.** Practice correcting people who are always a day behind.

▶ Ist heute Dienstag? *Nein, heute ist Mittwoch.*

1. Montag?
2. Sonntag?
3. Mittwoch?

4. Freitag?
5. Donnerstag?
6. Samstag?

Nichtstun erquickt.

4 Gender of nouns

Masculine	Neuter	Feminine
the man ← he	the baby ← it	the woman ← she
	the word ← it	

Every English noun belongs to one of three genders: masculine, neuter, or feminine. The gender of a singular English noun shows up in the choice of the pronoun that is used to refer back to it.

The English type of gender system is one of natural gender. Nouns referring to male beings are masculine. Nouns referring to female beings are feminine. Nouns referring to young beings (if thought of as still undifferentiated as to sex) are neuter, and all nouns referring to inanimate objects are also neuter. (*Neuter* is the Latin word for *neither*, i.e., neither masculine nor feminine.)

Like English, German generally uses a system of natural gender for nouns that refer to living beings. Unlike English, however, German also makes gender distinctions in nouns that do not refer to living things. This type of gender system is one of grammatical gender.

Masculine	Neuter	Feminine
der Mann° ← er	das Kind° ← es	die Frau ← sie
der Junge° ← er	das Mädchen° ← es	
der Tag ← er	das Wort° ← es	die Adresse ← sie

In German there are three groups of nouns: masculine (**der**-nouns), neuter (**das**-nouns), and feminine (**die**-nouns). The definite articles **der, das,** and **die** function like the English definite article *the*. Most nouns referring to males are **der**-nouns (**der Mann** = *man*, **der Junge** = *boy*), most nouns referring to females are **die**-nouns (**die Frau** = *woman*), and nouns referring to young beings are **das**-nouns (**das Kind** = *child*). **Mädchen** (= *girl*) is a **das**-noun because all words ending in **-chen** are **das**-nouns. Other nouns may belong to any of the three groups: **der Tag, das Wort, die Adresse.**

• *Signals of gender*

Like English, German signals the gender of a noun in the choice of the pronoun that is used to refer back to it: **er** is masculine, **es** is neuter, and **sie** is feminine. Unlike English, however, German also signals gender in the choice of the definite article that precedes a noun: **der** is masculine, **das** is neuter, and **die** is feminine.

The article is the most powerful signal of gender. You should always learn a German noun together with its definite article, because there is no simple way of predicting the gender of a particular noun.

5   Ein Studentenzimmer (A student's room)

Learn the following nouns:

1. der Bleistift	5. das Bett	14. die Büchertasche

2. der Kugel-
     schreiber
     (der Kuli)
	6. das Bild	15. die Gitarre

	7. das Buch	16. die Lampe
	8. das Fenster	17. die Pflanze
3. der Stuhl	9. das Heft	18. die Tür
4. der Tisch	10. das Papier	19. die Uhr
	11. das Poster	20. die Wand
	12. das Radio	
	13. das Zimmer	

J   Groß oder klein?   Sabine ist going to help you arrange your room. She asks whether certain pieces of furniture are large (**groß**) or small (**klein**). Respond.

▶   Ist das Zimmer groß oder klein?   *Das Zimmer ist [groß].*

1.   Ist das Fenster groß oder klein?
2.   Ist das Bett groß oder klein?
3.   Und der Tisch?
4.   Wie ist der Stuhl?

5. Ist das Radio groß oder klein?
6. Wie ist die Uhr?
7. Und die Lampe?

K   Alt oder neu?   Tell Ilse whether various things in your room are new (**neu**) or old (**alt**).

▶   Tisch   *Der Tisch ist [neu].*

1. Stuhl	6. Büchertasche
2. Bett	7. Buch
3. Lampe	8. Kugelschreiber
4. Uhr	9. Bild
5. Radio	10. Poster

L   Groß, klein, alt   You and Erik are sitting in a snack bar watching people. Make comments about them using the cues.

▶   Kind / groß   *Das Kind da° ist groß!*

1. Mann / groß	5. Junge / klein
2. Frau / groß	6. Frau / alt
3. Mann / alt	7. Mädchen / klein
4. Kind / klein	

6   Pronouns

Wie alt ist Mark?	How old is Mark?
Er ist zwanzig.	He is twenty.

A **pronoun** is a part of speech that designates a person, place, thing, or concept. It functions as nouns do. A pronoun is capable of replacing a noun or a noun phrase.

7   Noun-pronoun relationship

Der Mann ist groß.	**Er** ist groß.	He is tall.
Der Stuhl ist groß.	**Er** ist groß.	It is large.
Das Kind ist klein.	**Es** ist klein.	She/He is small.
Das Zimmer ist klein.	**Es** ist klein.	It is small
Die Frau ist groß.	**Sie** ist groß.	She is tall.
Die Lampe ist groß.	**Sie** ist groß.	It is large.

In German the pronouns **er, es,** and **sie** may refer to persons or things. In English the singular pronoun referring to things (it) is different from those referring to persons (she, he).

M Wie ist das Zimmer?   Tanja is seeing your room for the first time since you made some changes. She's trying to sort out which things are new and which are old. Respond, using a pronoun instead of the noun.

▶   Ist der Tisch neu?   *Ja, er ist neu.*

1. Ist der Stuhl alt?
2. Ist die Uhr neu?
3. Ist das Radio alt?
4. Ist die Pflanze neu?
5. Ist die Lampe alt?
6. Ist die Büchertasche neu?
7. Ist das Poster neu?

8   Die Farben (Colors)

The cognates in the following sentences should help you guess the English equivalents of these colors.

blau	Die See ist blau.
braun	Die Schokolade ist braun.
gelb	Die Banane ist gelb.
grau	Die Maus ist grau.
grün	Das Gras ist grün.
rot	Die Tomate ist rot.
schwarz	Die Kohle ist schwarz.
weiß	Das Papier ist weiß.

DPD
Deutscher Paket Dienst

Die schnellen, sicheren Pakete.

N   Welche Farbe?   Describe the colors of various items in your room or in the classroom. You may want to refer to the Supplementary Word Sets on page R-24 of the Reference Section.

▶   Welche Farbe hat der Tisch?   *Der Tisch ist [braun].*

1. Stuhl
2. Lampe
3. Bett

4. Radio
5. Deutschbuch
6. Heft

7. Kugelschreiber
8. Bleistift
9. Wand

O   Wie ist das Studentenzimmer?   Use your imagination to describe the objects in the picture of the student room on page 12. Use a variety of adjectives.

▶   Die Tür ist **groß, alt** und **grün.**

Vokabeln (Vocabulary)

In English, proper nouns like *Monday* or *America* are capitalized, but not common nouns like *address* or *street*. In German, all nouns are capitalized: proper nouns like **Montag** or **Amerika** as well as common nouns like **Adresse** and **Straße.** Unlike English, German does not capitalize proper adjectives.

Compare the following:　**amerikanisch**　　American
　　　　　　　　　　　　englisch　　　　English
　　　　　　　　　　　　deutsch　　　　German

The German pronoun **Sie** (you *formal*) and the possessive adjective **Ihr** (your *formal*) are capitalized in writing. The pronoun **ich** (I) is not capitalized in German.

_ Substantive (Nouns) _

die **Adresse** address
das **Bett** bed
das **Bild** picture; photo
der **Bleistift** pencil
die **Büchertasche** book bag
das **Buch** book
der **Dienstag** Tuesday
der **Donnerstag** Thursday
die **Farbe** color
das **Fenster** window
die **Frau** woman; **Frau** Mrs., Ms. (*term of address for married women, and, officially, for all adult women*)
das **Fräulein** young lady; **Fräulein** Miss
der **Freitag** Friday
der **Garten** garden
die **Gitarre** guitar
das **Heft** notebook
das **Jahr** year
der **Junge** boy
das **Kind** child
der **Kugelschreiber** (der **Kuli**, *colloquial*) ballpoint pen
die **Lampe** lamp
das **Mädchen** girl
der **Mann** man
der **Mittwoch** Wednesday
der **Montag** Monday

die **Nummer** number
das **Papier** paper
die **Pflanze** plant
das **Poster** poster
das **Radio** radio
der **Samstag** (*in southern Germany*) Saturday
der **Sekretär** (*m.*) / die **Sekretärin** (*f.*) secretary
der **Sonnabend** (*in northern Germany*) Saturday
der **Sonntag** Sunday
die **Straße** street
der **Student** (*m.*) / die **Studentin** (*f.*) student
der **Stuhl** chair
der **Tag** day
das **Telefon** telephone
die **Telefonnummer** telephone number
der **Tisch** table
die **Tür** door
die **Uhr** clock, watch
die **Wand** wall
die **Woche** week
das **Wort** word
die **Zahl** number, numeral
das **Zimmer** room

Verben (Verbs)

bin / ist / sind   am / is / are
buchstabieren   to spell
hat / haben   has / have
heißen   to be named

Andere Wörter (Other words)

alt   old
bitte   please; you're welcome
blau   blue
braun   brown
da   there
danke   thanks
das   that; the (*neuter*)
der   the (*masculine*)
die   the (*feminine*)
[dividiert] durch   divided by
  (*in division*)
er   he, it
es   it
gelb   yellow
grau   gray
groß   large, big; tall (*people*)
grün   green
heute   today
ich   I
Ihr(e)   your

ja   yes
klein   small; short (*people*)
mal   times (*in multiplication*)
mein(e)   my
nein   no
neu   new
nicht? (*tag question*)   don't you? isn't
  it? **Sie heißen Monika, nicht?**
   Your name is Monika, isn't it?
rot   red
schwarz   black
sie   she, it
Sie   you
und   and; plus (*in addition*)
weiß   white
welch (-er, -es, -e)   which
weniger   minus (*in subtraction*)
wie   how
wieviel   how much

EBERHARD-KARLS-UNIVERSITÄT TÜBINGEN

Ein Student und eine Studentin in Münster

Besondere Ausdrücke (Special expressions)

Ich bin 19 Jahre alt. I'm 19 years old.

Sie heißen [Mark], nicht? Your name is [Mark], isn't it?

Welche Farbe hat ... ? What color is ...?

Welcher Tag ist heute? What day is today?

Wie alt sind Sie? How old are you?

Wie ist Ihre Adresse? What's your address?

Wie heißen Sie? What's your name?

Kapitel 1

Lernziele

Sprechakte

Greeting people formally
Greeting friends
Saying good-by
Asking people how they are
Asking about personal plans
Asking what kind of person someone is
Describing people
Expressing agreement and disagreement
Expressing likes and dislikes
Telling time

Grammatik

Pronouns and nouns as subjects
Three forms for *you:* **du, ihr, Sie**
The verb **sein**
Regular verbs
Expressing likes and dislikes with **gern**
Negation with **nicht**
Expressing future time with the present tense
Asking specific and general questions
Tag questions

Vokabeln

Descriptive adjectives
Sports

Landeskunde

Regional greetings and farewells
Appropriate use of **du** and **Sie**
The role of sports in the Federal Republic of
  Germany

Studenten an der Freien Universität Berlin

19

| Bausteine für Gespräche

Wie geht's?

Im Seminar

Professor Müller: Guten Morgen, Frau Schneider! Wie geht es Ihnen?

Professor Schneider: Guten Morgen, Herr Müller! Gut, danke. Und Ihnen?

Professor Müller: Danke, ganz gut.

Im Hörsaal

Gisela: Tag, Jürgen! Wie geht's?

Jürgen: Tag, Gisela. Mir geht's schlecht.

Gisela: Was ist los? Bist du krank?
Jürgen: Ich glaube ja.
Gisela: Oh, das tut mir leid.

How are you?

In the seminar

Good morning, Mrs. Schneider. How are you?

Good morning, Mr. Müller. Fine, thanks. And you?

Thanks, not bad.

In the lecture hall

Hi, Jürgen. How are you [How's it going]?
Hi, Gisela. I'm not well.

What's wrong? Are you sick?
I think so.
Oh, I'm sorry.

People who live in German-speaking countries often greet each other with a handshake; they always do so when they are introduced. Greetings and farewells vary. *Tag* and *Morgen* are less formal than *Guten Tag* and *Guten Morgen*. In southern Germany or in Austria one might hear *Grüß Gott* or *Grüß dich, Servus* or *Ade*. In Switzerland one often hears *Grüetzi* or *Salut*. To say good-by one says *Auf Wiedersehen* (which can be shortened to *Wiedersehen*). In some areas *Auf Wiederschauen* and *Adieu* are also used to say good-by. Both *(Auf) Wiedersehen* and *(Auf) Wiederschauen* mean literally "Until we see each other [meet] again." In the small shops the customer as well as the store owner says *Auf Wiedersehen*. *Tschüß* and *Tschau* are reserved for friends and family, and *Gute Nacht* (good night) is used at bedtime.

Auf Wiedersehen! Gute Reise!

Sie haben das Wort

A   Guten Tag!   Greet different people in the class. Choose a time of day   Greeting someone
and greet your partner, who responds appropriately.

Sie	*Gesprächspartner/in*
Guten Morgen!	Morgen!
Guten Tag!	Tag!
Guten Abend°!	Abend°!
	Hallo°!
	Grüß dich°!

Hallo, wie geht's?

B   Wie geht's?   Find a partner and role-play a scene between you and a   Asking people how
they are
friend or a professor. Assume you haven't seen your friend or the professor
for several days and you run into her/him in the cafeteria. Say hello and ask
how she/he is.

Sie	*Gesprächspartner/in*
Hallo, [Tanja]! Wie geht's?	Gut, danke.
Guten Tag, Herr/Frau Professor, wie	Danke, ganz gut.
geht es Ihnen?	Nicht so gut.
	Schlecht.
	Ich bin krank.
	Ich bin müde°.

Was machst du gern?

Lutz: Was machst du heute abend?
Ute: Nichts Besonderes. Ich höre
  vielleicht Musik.
Lutz: Spielst du Tennis?
Ute: Ja. Tennis spiele ich sehr
  gern.
Lutz: Wirklich? Ich auch. Spielst
  du heute abend mit mir?
Ute: Gern! Um sieben Uhr?
Lutz: Gut.

What do you like to do?

What are you doing tonight?
Nothing special. Maybe I'll listen to
  some music.
Do you play tennis?
Yes, I like to play tennis a lot.

Really? Me, too./So do I. Will you
  play [a set] with me this evening?
I'd love to! At seven?
Fine.

Sie haben das Wort

When sample sentences have one or more words in **boldface type**, you should replace those words in subsequent sentences with the new words provided.

C   **Was spielen Sie gern?**   Find out which activities your instructor or a fellow student likes to do. Then respond to her/his questions. You may want to refer to the Supplementary Word Sets on page R-24 of the Reference Section.

Expressing likes and dislikes

Sie

Spielen Sie	**gern**	**Schach°?**
Spielst du	gut	Karten°?
	oft°	Fußball°?
	viel°	Tennis?
		Tischtennis°?
		Basketball°?
		Volleyball°?
		Videospiele°?

Gesprächspartner/in

Ja. Und Sie?
Ja. Du auch, nicht?
Nein. Und du?
Nein. Aber° du, nicht?

D   **Treiben Sie gern Sport?**   Your instructor or a fellow student asks whether you like to engage in sports. Respond as in the model.

Asking about personal plans

Gesprächspartner/in

Treiben Sie° gern Sport°?
Treibst du

Machen Sie viel Sport?
Machst du

Sie

Ja. Ich **schwimme°** gern.
      wandere° gern
      spiele gern Tennis
Nein. Ich mache nicht viel Sport.
Nein, nicht viel.

E   **Was machst du?**   Think about what you are going to do today. Ask a few classmates what they are going to do in their free time. They will ask you in turn.

Sie

Was machst du **heute morgen°?**
                nachmittag°?
                abend°?

Gesprächspartner/in

Ich	arbeite°.
	mache Deutsch°
	spiele Tennis
	höre Musik
	gehe ins Kino°
	gehe tanzen°

F   **Ich mache das.**   Report to the class four things you do or don't do. Use **gern, viel, oft, nicht gern, nicht viel, nicht oft.**

Reporting

▶   *Ich spiele [nicht] viel Schach.*

Erweiterung des Wortschatzes

1 Was für ein Mensch sind Sie?

fleißig

faul

intelligent

dumm

lustig

ernst

konservativ

progressiv

nett

doof

ruhig

nervös

A   Was für ein Mensch?   Ask three students what kind of person they are. Then report on your findings.

Sie	*Gesprächspartner/in*
Was für ein Mensch bist du? [Frank] ist lustig.	Ich bin lustig.

B   Und Sie, Frau/Herr Professor?   Ask your instructor what kind of person she/he is.

▶   Was für ein Mensch sind Sie?

C   Ja oder nein?   In groups of three, ask your partners whether they agree with your opinions of certain people. One of them agrees, but the other doesn't and corrects your opinions with an opposite adjective. You may want to refer to the Supplementary Word Sets on page R-24 of the Reference Section.

Sie	*Gesprächspartner/in*
[Margit] ist sehr ernst, nicht?	A: Ja, sehr°. B: Nein, ich glaube nicht ... Sie° ist sehr lustig.

D   So bin ich.   Tell the class what kind of person you are. Use five adjectives.

▶   *Ich bin [ernst].*

far out
DISCO-BAR
Universitätsstraße 3
7800 Freiburg
Telefon 0761/26673

22.00 – 3.00 Uhr

2   Telling time

The following methods are used to express clock time.

Wieviel Uhr ist es? ⎫
Wie spät ist es?   ⎬   What time is it?

	Method 1	Method 2
1.00 Uhr	Es ist eins.	Es ist eins.
	Es ist ein Uhr.	Es ist ein Uhr.
1.05 Uhr	Es ist fünf (Minuten) nach eins.	Es ist ein Uhr fünf.
1.15 Uhr	Es ist Viertel nach eins.	Es ist ein Uhr fünfzehn.
1.25 Uhr	Es ist fünf (Minuten) vor halb zwei.	Es ist ein Uhr fünfundzwanzig.
1.30 Uhr	Es ist halb zwei.	Es ist ein Uhr dreißig.
1.35 Uhr	Es ist fünf nach halb zwei.	Es ist ein Uhr fünfunddreißig.
1.45 Uhr	Es ist Viertel vor zwei.	Es ist ein Uhr fünfundvierzig.
1.55 Uhr	Es ist fünf (Minuten) vor zwei.	Es ist ein Uhr fünfundfünfzig.
2.00 Uhr	Es ist zwei Uhr.	Es ist zwei Uhr.

Note that German uses a period instead of a colon in time expressions.

German has two ways to indicate clock time. With a few exceptions, they parallel the two ways English indicates clock time.

Method 1   Es ist Viertel nach acht.   It's a quarter past eight.
Method 2   Es ist acht Uhr fünfzehn.   It's eight-fifteen.

In conversational German, method 1 is used to indicate time. Notice that the **-s** of **eins** is dropped before the word **Uhr.** The expression with **halb** indicates the hour to come, not the preceding hour: **halb zwei = 1.30 Uhr.**

In official time, such as train and plane schedules and concerts, method 2 is used.

Mein Zug fährt um **7.30 Uhr [7 Uhr 30].**   My train leaves at 7:30 A.M.
Das Konzert beginnt um **19.30 Uhr [19 Uhr 30].**   The concert begins at 7:30 P.M.

Official time is indicated on a 24-hour basis.

Um wieviel Uhr spielen wir Tennis?   (At) what time are we playing tennis?
Um halb neun.   At 8:30.

German uses **um** + a time expression to ask or speak about the specific hour that something will or did take place.

E   Wie spät ist es?   A friend asks you what time it is. Respond using the times listed below, in German.

▶   2.00 Uhr   *Es ist zwei.*

1.	3.00 Uhr	4.	1.20 Uhr
2.	6.15 Uhr	5.	4.55 Uhr
3.	11.45 Uhr	6.	2.30 Uhr

F   Nein, später°!   Say that it is ten minutes later than your friend thinks it is.

▶   Ist es 8 Uhr?   *Nein, später! Es ist zehn nach acht.*

1.	12.00 Uhr	5.	5.20 Uhr
2.	1.05 Uhr	6.	8.40 Uhr
3.	2.05 Uhr	7.	9.40 Uhr
4.	4.20 Uhr		

G   Fahrplan (Train schedule)   On a train schedule **Ankunft** indicates when a train arrives and **Abfahrt** when it departs. Using the train schedule, say when the trains arrive at: **Köln, Bonn, Nürnberg**

1. bis 30. Mai 1987

IC 667
Meistersinger
Dortmund – Nürnberg

Ankunft	km	Abfahrt	Anschlüsse
	Dortmund Hbf	17.48	
18.09	**Hagen** Hbf	18.10	
18.25	**Wuppertal-Elberfeld**	18.26	
18.54	**Köln** Hbf	18.58	intercity **hotel ibis köln** Tel. 02 21/13 20 51
19.16	**Bonn** Hbf	19.18	
19.49	**Koblenz** Hbf	19.51	HOTEL **Hohenstaufen** 100 m v. Hbf. Tel. (02 61) 3 70 81
20.40	**Mainz** Hbf	20.42	
20.58	**Frankfurt** (Main) Flughafen	21.00	
21.13	**Frankfurt (Main)** Hbf	21.21	
21.49	**Aschaffenburg** Hbf	21.50	
22.39	**Würzburg** Hbf	22.41	
23.35	**Nürnberg** Hbf		**hotel ibis nürnberg** Tel. 09 11/23 71-0

Now say when the trains depart from: **Dortmund, Koblenz, Würzburg**

H   Rollenspiel (Role playing)   You and a friend have planned some activities for the weekend, but you can't remember when you're supposed to do what. Even though it's embarrassing, you have to ask. Your partner takes the role of your friend and responds with an appropriate time.

Sie	*Gesprächspartner/in*
Um wieviel Uhr/Wann ...	Wir [gehen] um [halb neun] ...

1. gehen wir heute abend ins Kino?
2. gehen wir Samstag abend tanzen?
3. spielen wir Samstag nachmittag Tennis?
4. hören wir heute Musik?
5. gehen wir Sonntag wandern?
6. gehen wir schwimmen?
7. machen wir Deutsch?

Vokabeln

— Substantive

der **Abend**   evening
der **Basketball**   basketball
(das) **Deutsch**   German language
der **Fußball**   soccer
der **Herr**   gentleman; **Herr**   Mr.
die **Karte**   card; postcard; die **Karten**
   (*pl.*)   (playing) cards
das **Kino**   movie theater
der **Mensch**   person, human being
die **Minute**   minute
der **Morgen**   morning

die **Musik**   music
der **Nachmittag**   afternoon
der **Professor** (*m.*)/die **Professorin** (*f.*)
   professor
das **Schach**   chess
der **Sport**   sport
das **Tennis**   tennis
das **Tischtennis**   table tennis, Ping-
   Pong
das **Videospiel**   video game
der **Volleyball**   volleyball

— Verben

arbeiten   to work; to study
gehen   to go
glauben   to believe
hören   to hear
machen   to do; to make
schwimmen   to swim

sein   to be
spielen   to play
tanzen   to dance
treiben   to engage in
wandern   to hike; to go walking

Andere Wörter

aber but, however
auch also
doof silly, dull
du you (*familiar sg.*)
dumm dumb, stupid
ein(e) a, an
ernst serious
faul lazy
fleißig industrious, hard-working
ganz complete, whole; very; **ganz gut** not bad, O.K.
gern gladly, willingly; *used with verbs to indicate liking, as in* **Ich spiele *gern* Tennis.**
gut good, well; fine
halb half
hallo hello
heute abend this evening
heute morgen this morning
heute nachmittag this afternoon
ihr you (*familiar pl.*)
intelligent smart, intelligent
konservativ conservative
krank sick, ill
lustig merry, cheerful
mit with

müde tired
nach after
nervös nervous
nett nice
nicht not
nichts nothing
oder or
oft often
progressiv progressive
ruhig calm, easy-going, quiet
schlecht bad, badly
sehr very
sie she, they
so so
spät late; **später** later
um at; **um zehn Uhr** at ten o'clock
viel much
vielleicht maybe, perhaps
vor before
wann when
was what
was für (ein) what kind of (a)
wer who
wir we
wirklich really

Besondere Ausdrücke

auf Wiedersehen good-by
Das tut mir leid. I'm sorry.
Grüß dich! Hi!
Guten Abend!/Abend! Good evening!
Guten Morgen!/Morgen! Good morning!
Guten Tag!/Tag! hello
halb half past; **halb zwei** one-thirty
Ich auch. Me too. So do I.
Ich mache Deutsch. I'm doing German homework.
ins Kino to the movies
Mir geht's schlecht. I'm not well.

mit mir with me
nicht? (*tag question*) don't you? isn't he? isn't that so?, etc.
nichts Besonderes nothing special
O.K. okay
tschüß so long, good-by (*informal*)
Um wieviel Uhr? At what time?
um [sieben] Uhr at [seven] o'clock
Was ist los? What's wrong?
Wie geht's? How are you?
Wie geht es Ihnen? How are you?
Wie spät ist es? What time is it?
Wieviel Uhr ist es? What time is it?
Viertel nach quarter after
Viertel vor quarter of, quarter to

Übungen zur Aussprache

Review the pronunciation of long and short **u** and **o** in the Reference section at the end of the book. Read aloud the words in each column from top to bottom. Then read each set of word pairs across. Check your pronunciation by listening to your instructor or the tape.

long ū	short u	long ō	short o
Mus	muß	Moos	Most
buk	Buckel	bog	Bock
Schuster	Schuß	Schote	Schotte
Stuhle	Stulle	Ofen	offen
tun	Tunnel	Tone	Tonne

Read the sentences aloud, paying special attention to the way you pronounce long and short **u** and **o** in the boldfaced words.

1. Spielt **Monika oft Rockmusik?**
2. Ist heute **Mittwoch oder Donnerstag?**
3. Es ist **Montag**.
4. Geht es Ihnen **gut?**
5. Ja, danke. **Und** Ihnen?

Doof bleibt doof, da helfen keine Pillen!

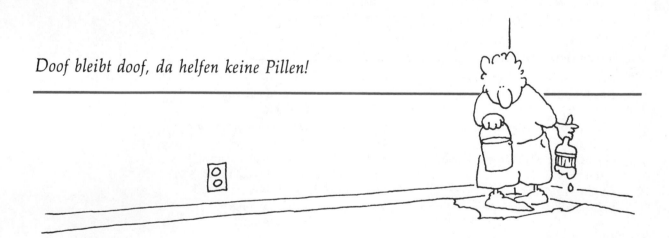

Grammatik und Übungen

1 Subject pronouns

Singular		Plural	
ich	I	**wir**	we
du	you (*familiar*)	**ihr**	you (*familiar*)
er	he/it		
es	it	**sie**	they
sie	she/it		
	Sie you (*formal*)		

2 The subject pronouns *du, ihr, Sie*

Tag, Elke! ... Was machst **du**?
Tag, Inge! Tag, Gerd! ... Was macht **ihr**?

The familiar forms **du** and **ihr** are used when addressing relatives, close friends, and persons under approximately fifteen years of age. **Du** and **ihr** are also used frequently among members of a group such as students, athletes, laborers, and soldiers. **Du** is singular, **ihr** is plural.

Tag, Herr Wagner! ... Was machen **Sie**?
Tag, Frau Braun! Tag, Fräulein Schneider! ... Was machen **Sie**?

Sie is a more formal form of address, and is used when addressing one or more strangers or adults with whom the speaker is not on intimate terms. **Sie** is both singular and plural.

A   Ich, du, er   Give the subject pronouns you would use in the following situations.

▶   You're talking about a female friend.   *sie*

1. You're talking about a male friend.
2. You're talking to either a male or a female friend.
3. You're talking about yourself.
4. You're talking about yourself and a friend.
5. You're talking to your parents.
6. You're talking to a clerk in a store.
7. You're talking about your father.
8. You're talking about your sister.
9. You're talking about a child.
10. You're talking to your professor.

Historically speaking, *sie sind* (they are) and *Sie sind* (you are) are the same form. It was considered polite to address someone in the third person plural and to capitalize the pronoun in writing.

The development of formal pronouns to address a person was a phenomenon common to most European languages. English used to distinguish singular *thou / thee* from plural *ye/you; thou/thee* was restricted to informal usage, and *ye/you* was used both as informal plural and formal singular and plural. Today only *you* survives as our all-purpose pronoun. In German (as well as in other European languages such as French, Spanish, and Italian) there are still distinctions between the formal and informal pronouns for *you.*

The formal pronoun *Sie* is used for everyday communication outside the realm of family and friends. Even neighbors and coworkers address each other as *Sie* (they *siezen*). *Du* (along with its plural form *ihr*) is traditionally a form of address used among relatives or close friends. An older person usually decides on the appropriateness of this form in speaking to someone younger. Most young people address each other with *du* (they *duzen*) nowadays. A step somewhere between *du* and *Sie* is to use a first name and *Sie*. This form of address expresses intimacy and respect at the same time, and is often a "warm up" for the less formal, more friendly *duzen.*

Im Supermarkt sagt man „Sie" zueinander.

3   Present tense of *sein*

sein	
ich **bin**	wir **sind**
du **bist**	ihr **seid**
er/es/sie **ist**	sie **sind**
Sie **sind**	

to be	
I am	we are
you are	you are
he/it/she is	they are
you are	

The verb **sein,** like its English equivalent *to be,* is irregular in the present tense.

B   Nein, so bin ich nicht.   Gisela is asking frank questions about what kind of person you are. Say you're the opposite of what she is suggesting, even when it contradicts what you previously said.

▶   Was für ein Mensch bist du? Bist du ruhig?   *Nein, ich bin nervös.*

1. Bist du fleißig?
2. Bist du dumm?
3. Bist du heute ernst?
4. Bist du konservativ?
5. Bist du doof?
6. Bist du heute faul?

C   Nein, so sind sie nicht.   Benno is talking about your friends. Say they're the opposite of what he thinks.

▶   Frank ist progressiv, nicht?   *Nein, er ist konservativ.*

1. Gisela ist konservativ, nicht?
2. Alex ist ruhig, nicht?
3. Andrea ist nett, nicht?
4. Bruno ist lustig, nicht?
5. Beate und Christl sind dumm, nicht?
6. Dietmar und Mark sind doof, nicht?
7. Inge und Erika sind faul, nicht?

D   Progessive Menschen   Say that the persons listed below are progressive in their political views.

▶   Ingrid   *Ingrid ist progressiv.*

1. Gerd
2. du
3. wir
4. ihr
5. ich
6. Monika und Günter
7. Jens und Ute

4   Infinitive

Infinitive	Stem + ending	English equivalents
glauben	glaub + en	*to believe*
heißen	heiß + en	*to be named*
arbeiten	arbeit + en	*to work; study*
wandern	wander + n	*to hike; go walking*

The basic form of a German verb (the form listed in dictionaries and vocabularies) is the infinitive. German infinitives consist of a stem and the ending **-en** or **-n**.

5   The finite verb

Andrea **arbeitet** viel.   Andrea works a lot.
Arbeitest du viel?   Do you work a lot?

The finite verb is the verb form that agrees with the subject.

6   Present tense of regular verbs

glauben
ich glaub**e**   wir glaub**en**
du glaub**st**   ihr glaub**t**
er/es/sie glaub**t**   sie glaub**en**
Sie glaub**en**

to believe
I believe   we believe
you believe   you believe
he/it/she believes   they believe
you believe

In the present tense, most English verbs have two different forms; most German verbs have four different forms.

The present tense of regular German verbs is formed by adding the endings **-e, -st, -t,** and **-en** to the infinitive stem. The verb endings change according to the subject.

In informal spoken German, the ending **-e** is sometimes dropped from the **ich**-form: **Ich glaub' das wirklich nicht.**

arbeiten: to study; work
ich arbeit**e**   wir arbeit**en**
du arbeit**est**   ihr arbeit**et**
er/es/sie arbeit**et**   sie arbeit**en**
Sie arbeit**en**

In regular English verbs, the third-person singular ending is usually *-s: she works.* After certain verb stems, however, this ending expands to *-es: she teaches, he dances.*

German also has verb stems that require an expansion of the ending. If a verb stem ends in **-d** or **-t,** the endings **-st** and **-t** expand to **-est** and **-et.** The other endings are regular.

heißen: to be called	
ich heiße	wir heißen
du heißt	ihr heißt
er/es/sie heißt	sie heißen
Sie heißen	

If a verb stem ends in a sibilant (**s, ss, ß, z**), the **-st** ending contracts to a **-t: du heißt, du tanzt.** The other endings are regular.

7   The construction *gern* + verb

Ich spiele **gern** Tennis.   I like to play tennis.
Ich spiele **nicht gern** Golf.   I don't like to play golf.

The most common way of saying in German that you like doing something is to use **gern** + verb. To say that you don't like doing something, use **nicht gern.**

E   Ja, das mache ich.   Sabine is trying to find out more about you and your plans. Answer her questions in the affirmative.

▶   Treibst du gern Sport?   *Ja, ich treibe gern Sport.*

1.   Arbeitest du heute morgen?
2.   Arbeitest du gern?
3.   Spielst du heute nachmittag Tennis?
4.   Spielst du auch Volleyball?
5.   Machst du viel Sport?
6.   Schwimmst du gern?
7.   Hörst du auch gern Musik?
8.   Wanderst du viel?
9.   Spielst du oft Videospiele?

F   Und du, Uwe?   Uwe is telling about the things his friend Lore does. Ask whether he enjoys the same things. Begin your question with the verb.

▶   Lore treibt gern Sport.   *Treibst du auch gern Sport?*

1.   Sie macht viel Sport.
2.   Sie spielt auch gern Volleyball.
3.   Sie schwimmt gern.
4.   Lore spielt gut Schach.
5.   Und sie hört gern Musik.
6.   Sie arbeitet auch viel.
7.   Sie wandert gern.
8.   Sie geht gern ins Kino.
9.   Sie tanzt gern.

Sie haben das Wort

Choose four things that some people like to do. Find four students who like to do the activities — one for each activity. Report to the class. You may want to refer to the Supplementary Word Sets on Page R-24 of the Reference Section.

▶   Spielst du gern Schach?   *Ja, sehr gern und oft.*
Nein, Schach ist dumm.

German people of all ages engage in sports and they especially enjoy soccer (*Fußball*) and gymnastics (*Turnen*). School sports are intramural rather than intermural. A person who wishes to participate in competitive sports can join a sports club (*Sportverein*). In the Federal Republic there are about 60 thousand such clubs, with approximately 18 million members. Even the smallest village has its own *Verein,* which also plays an important part in the social life of the town. *Fußball* is played by over 3 million Germans, of whom 75 thousand play on a thousand women's teams. Not only does the local *Sportverein* often sponsor a *Fußball* team that may compete at an international level, but it provides for many other popular sports like *Handball, Tischtennis, Turnen, Leichtathletik,* and *Schwimmen.*

Am Wochenende spielen viele Leute Fußball.

TSV Bayer 04 Leverkusen

Bayer Leverkusen
Fünf Spieler schossen fünf Tore

Eintracht Frankfurt
Daheim endlich wieder stabil

Fortuna Düsseldorf
Eine Mannschaft der offenen Tür

Hamburger SV
1:0 reicht nicht mehr zum Sieg

8   Position of *nicht*

The position of **nicht** is determined by various elements in the sentence.

Herr Wagner *arbeitet* **nicht.**	Mr. Wagner doesn't work.
Mark glaubt *Inge* **nicht.**	Mark doesn't believe Inge.
Ich glaube *es* **nicht.**	I don't believe it.
Arbeitest du *heute* **nicht?**	Aren't you working today?

Nicht always follows:

1. the finite verb (e.g., er **arbeitet**)
2. nouns used as objects (e.g., **Inge**)
3. pronouns used as objects (e.g., **es**)
4. specific adverbs of time (e.g., **heute**)

Benno ist **nicht** *faul*.
Das ist **nicht** *Frau Wagner*.
Wir wandern **nicht** *oft*.
Wir gehen heute **nicht** *ins Kino*.

Benno is not lazy.
That is not Ms. Wagner.
We don't hike much.
We're not going to the movies today.

Nicht precedes most other kinds of elements:

1. predicate adjectives (a predicate adjective completes the meaning of a linking verb; the most frequently used linking verb is **sein,** *to be*: e.g., Mark ist nicht **faul.**)
2. predicate nouns (a predicate noun is a noun that completes the meaning of a linking verb: e.g., Das ist nicht **Frau Wagner.**)
3. adverbs, including general time adverbs (e.g., nicht **oft**, nicht **sehr**, nicht **gern**)
4. prepositional phrases (e.g., nicht **ins Kino**)

Ich gehe **nicht** *oft ins Kino*.   I don't often go to the movies.

If several of the elements occur in a sentence, **nicht** usually precedes the first one.

G   Ich nicht.   A new acquaintance has a number of questions about you and your friends. Unfortunately you have to answer all in the negative. Use **nicht** in the proper place.

▶   Treibst du gern Sport?   *Nein, ich treibe nicht gern Sport.*

1. Spielst du gern Schach?
2. Wanderst du viel?
3. Spielst du oft Fußball?
4. Gehst du oft ins Kino?
5. Gehst du heute abend ins Kino?
6. Bist du müde?
7. Ist das Klaus Braun?
8. Ist es Klaus Meier?
9. Arbeitet Frau Schmidt in Hamburg?

H   Wir nicht.   Jutta, a new acquaintance, has some questions for you and Hans-Dieter. Answer in the negative.

▶   Macht ihr viel Sport?   *Nein. Wir machen nicht viel Sport.*

1.   Spielt ihr viel Basketball?
2.   Spielt ihr oft Tennis?
3.   Schwimmt ihr gern?
4.   Arbeitet ihr viel?
5.   Arbeitet ihr gern?
6.   Hört ihr gern Musik?
7.   Wandert ihr viel?
8.   Spielt ihr gern Tischtennis?
9.   Tanzt ihr gern?

I   Aber macht ihr es gern?   Your friends tell you what they're doing today. Ask whether they like to do those things. Begin your questions with the verb.

▶   Wir spielen heute morgen Tennis.   *Spielt ihr gern Tennis?*

1.   Wir spielen auch Fußball.
2.   Wir gehen heute schwimmen.
3.   Wir arbeiten heute abend.
4.   Wir spielen auch Karten.
5.   Wir hören heute abend Musik.
6.   Wir wandern heute nachmittag.
7.   Wir gehen heute abend ins Kino.
8.   Wir gehen auch tanzen.

J   Detlev aber nicht.   Veronika makes some observations about Detlev and Inge. Say that she's right about Inge, but not Detlev.

▶   Detlev and Inge treiben gern Sport, nicht?   *Inge treibt gern Sport, Detlev aber nicht.*

1.   Detlev und Inge machen viel Sport, nicht?
2.   Sie schwimmen gut, nicht?
3.   Sie arbeiten viel, nicht?
4.   Sie arbeiten gern, nicht?
5.   Sie spielen oft Schach, nicht?
6.   Sie spielen sehr viel Videospiele, nicht?
7.   Sie hören gern Musik, nicht?
8.   Sie machen auch Musik, nicht?
9.   Sie tanzen gern, nicht?

K   Und das machen sie gern.   Nicole and Gustav lead an active life. Say what they like to do.

▶   Arbeiten Nicole und Gustav viel in   *Ja, und sie arbeiten gern in*
     Bremen?   *Bremen.*

1. Treiben Nicole und Gustav viel   5. Hören sie oft Radio?
    Sport?   6. Spielen sie viel Tischtennis?
2. Sind sie oft in Basel?   7. Tanzen sie oft?
3. Spielen sie viel Schach?   8. Gehen sie viel ins Kino?
4. Hören sie viel Musik?   9. Spielen sie oft Videospiele?

L   Das ist gesund. (It's healthy.)   Many Germans believe that fresh air is especially healthy. Say that the following people believe it.

▶   Wir glauben das. (Sie)   *Sie glauben das.*

1. ich   5. wir
2. sie (*pl.*)   6. Herr Müller
3. er   7. Frau Schneider
4. sie (*sg.*)   8. Gabi und Jürgen

Sie haben das Wort

Was machst du gern?   Take a partner and try to find five things you have in common with her/him and five things you don't have in common. When you are ready, introduce your partner to the class and tell everyone a little about her/him.

Sie	Gesprächspartner/in
Ich schwimme gern. Schwimmst du auch gern?	[Ja.]
Das hier ist Inge. Sie schwimmt gern.	

Finding common likes and dislikes

9   Present-tense meanings

Sie **arbeitet** gut. = $\begin{cases} \text{She } works \text{ well. (plain)} \\ \text{She } does\ work \text{ well. (emphatic)} \\ \text{She } is\ working \text{ well. (progressive)} \end{cases}$

German uses a single verb form to express ideas or actions that may require one of three different forms in English.

Du **gehst** heute nachmittag schwimmen, nicht?	You*'re going* swimming this afternoon, aren't you?

German, like English, may use the present tense to express action intended or planned for the future.

M   Wie sagt man das? (How do you say that?)   Give the German equivalents of the following sentences.

▶   Frank does not work well.   *Frank arbeitet nicht gut.*

1.   Karla does work a lot.
2.   I do believe that.
3.   Stefan does play soccer well.
4.   You're working tonight, Ute.
5.   You do that well, Ursula.
6.   I'm playing tennis today.

7.   We're playing basketball today.
8.   I believe so.
9.   Detlev is going to the movies.
10.   I'm going dancing.

10   Specific questions

Wann gehst du schwimmen?   ⌒   When are you going swimming?
Wer arbeitet heute nachmittag°?   ⌒   Who is working this afternoon?

A specific question asks for a particular bit of information. It begins with an interrogative expression such as **wann** (*when*), **was** (*what*), **welch** (*which*), **wer** (*who*), and **wie** (*how*). The interrogative is followed by the verb, then the subject. The voice normally falls at the end of a specific question, just as it does in English.

N   Wie bitte?   Klaus is talking to you, but you don't quite understand what he says. Ask for more information using the cued interrogative words to begin the question.

▶   Frank spielt heute Fußball. (wer)   *Wer spielt heute Fußball?*

1.   Wir spielen um halb sieben Basketball. (wann)
2.   Frau Schneider ist sehr nett. (wer)
3.   Barbara spielt gern Volleyball. (was)
4.   Professor Wagner macht heute nichts Besonderes. (was)
5.   Ute arbeitet heute nachmittag. (wann)

Wo bekommt man was
am besten...?
   Gelbe Seiten –
ist doch klar.

6. Lutz geht heute um Viertel vor elf. (wann)
7. Es geht Jürgen schlecht. (wie)
8. Sie heißt Meike. (wie)
9. Veronika spielt gern Tennis. (was)
10. Werner hört gern Musik. (wer)
11. Detlev ist oft müde. (wer)
12. Veronika ist 19 Jahre alt. (wie alt)
13. Lutz hört gern Western und Rock. (was für Musik)

11 General questions

Gehst du nicht schwimmen? ⌵⌃ Aren't you going swimming?
Treiben Sie gern Sport?   ⌵⌃   Do you like to play sports?

A general question requires a yes-or-no answer. It begins with the verb. A general question in English often requires a form of the auxiliary verb *to be* or *to do* plus the main verb. A general question in German uses only the main verb. The voice normally rises at the end of a general question, just as it does in English.

O Wirklich, Beate? Beate makes some comments about her plans and about your friends. Ask whether her statements are really correct.

▶   Ich arbeite heute abend.   *Arbeitest du wirklich heute abend?*

1. Ich schwimme gut.
2. Ich spiele oft Basketball.
3. Ich treibe gern Sport.
4. Kurt und ich spielen heute Schach.
5. Wir spielen gut.
6. Klaus spielt gut Fußball.
7. Petra spielt viel Volleyball.
8. Rita macht viel Sport.
9. Wir wandern gern.
10. Wir gehen heute abend ins Kino.

12 Tag questions

Du hörst gern Musik, **nicht?**   You like to listen to music, don't you?

Mark geht heute abend ins Kino,   Mark is going to the movies to-
  nicht?   night, isn't he?

A tag question is literally "tagged on" to the end of a statement. In English the tag equivalent to **nicht?** depends on the subject of the sentence: *don't you?, aren't you?, isn't he?,* and *doesn't she?,* etc.

P Nicht? In a conversation with a friend, ask for confirmation that what you think is correct. Use the tag question **nicht?**

▶ Frau Meier ist sehr nett.   *Frau Meier ist sehr nett, nicht?*

1. Professor Wagner arbeitet viel.
2. Sie und ihr Mann wandern gern.
3. Jürgen ist oft müde.
4. Rita macht viel Sport.
5. Sie schwimmt gut.
6. Sie ist auch sehr intelligent.
7. Wir gehen heute abend ins Kino.
8. Wir gehen um sieben.

Q Wie sagt man das? You overhear someone on the phone talking with Ursula. Translate the questions for Dieter, your German friend.

▶ Ursula, how are you?   *Ursula, wie geht's?*

1. What are you doing, Ursula?
2. Are you working?
3. Are you going swimming today?
4. Is Rudi going also?
5. When are you playing tennis, Ursula?
6. Does Rudi play well?
7. What kind of person is Rudi?
8. Do you like to play chess?
9. Rudi likes to play, too, doesn't he?
10. You really believe that, don't you?
11. When are Rudi and Beate going to the movies?

| Wiederholung

A Kurze Gespräche (Short conversations) Read the conversations and answer the questions.

Lutz: Wie heißt der Junge?
Ute: Er heißt Klaus.
Lutz: Und das Mädchen?
Ute: Sie heißt Gabi.

1. Wie heißt der Junge?
2. Wie heißt das Mädchen?

Gabi: Wie geht's Jürgen?
Klaus: Gut.
Gabi: Spielt er heute morgen Fußball?
Klaus: Ich glaube ja.

3. Wie geht es Jürgen?
4. Wer spielt heute morgen Fußball?

Christel: Was machst du heute abend?
Michael: Ich spiele Tennis.
Christel: Um wieviel Uhr?
Michael: Um halb acht.

5. Was macht Michael heute abend?
6. Um wieviel Uhr spielt er?

B   Ja, Veronika.   Confirm Veronika's information about you and your friends.

▶   Gabi arbeitet in Basel, nicht?   *Ja, sie arbeitet in Basel.*

1. Du arbeitest in Zürich, nicht?
2. Wolf hört gern Musik, nicht?
3. Renate und Paula spielen gut Rock, nicht?
4. Wir spielen gut Basketball, nicht?
5. Trudi macht viel Sport, nicht?
6. Du und Regina, ihr spielt gern Tennis, nicht?

C   Was machen sie?   Construct sentences using the following cues.

▶   was / machen / du / heute / ?   *Was machst du heute?*

1. er / heißen / Konrad
2. wie / heißen / du / ?
3. wie / arbeiten / er / ?
4. wann / gehen / Martha / ins Kino / ?
5. was / machen / Martha und er / heute abend / ?
6. Martha / schwimmen / gut und viel
7. ich / glauben / das / nicht
8. wer / treiben / gern / Sport / ?
9. Lore / spielen / gut / Fußball // nicht / ?

D   Ergänzen Sie. (Complete.)   Complete the sentences below with appropriate words.

1. Wie _____ es Ihnen?
2. Arbeitest _____ heute nicht?
3. Ich _____ heute Tennis.
4. Arbeiten _____ heute abend?
5. _____ heißen Sie?
6. _____ geht Ulrich ins Kino?
7. _____ du viel Sport?
8. _____ spiele gern Volleyball.

E   Wie sagt man das?   Give the German equivalents of the sentences below.

1. What's your name?
2. How are you?
3. What are you doing today?
4. Do you like to listen to music?
5. Do you play chess well?
6. Are you going to the movies tonight?
7. When do you work?

F   Wie sind sie?   Describe five people, using the adjectives you know. You may want to refer to the Supplementary Word Sets on page R-24 of the Reference Section.

▶   *Robert ist doof.*
    Marie ist oft krank.

G   Wie ist Ihr Zimmer?   Describe various objects in your room, using at least two adjectives for each object.

H   Wie bitte?   For each one of the questions below, give as many responses as will logically follow. Select the responses from the list, and add a few of your own.

Ich arbeite. Und Sie? □ Schillerstraße 59. □ Nein, nicht gut. □ Ich glaube ja. □ Ja, gern und oft. □ Nicht so gut. □ Ich bin krank. □ Ute Bauer. □ Ich spiele Volleyball. □ Nein, ich bin müde. □ Ich höre Musik. □ Ich gehe ins Kino.

1. Wie heißen Sie?
2. Wie ist Ihre Adresse?
3. Wie geht es Ihnen?
4. Was ist los?
5. Sind Sie krank?
6. Was machen Sie heute abend?
7. Hören Sie gern Musik?
8. Spielen Sie gut Tischtennis?

I   Was sagen Sie? (What do you say?)   Respond appropriately to the expressions or questions below.

1. Guten Tag!
2. Wie ist Ihre Telefonnummer?
3. Welcher Tag ist heute?
4. Welche Farbe hat Ihre Zimmertür?
5. Wie spät ist es?

6. Wie geht's?
7. Was ist los?
8. Was machen Sie heute abend?
9. Hören Sie gern Musik?
10. Treiben Sie gern Sport?
11. Was für ein Mensch sind Sie?

J   Anregung (Idea) Introduce yourself to a classmate you don't know well. Be prepared to ask for and provide information in German that answers the questions below.

Wie heißen Sie? □ Wie alt sind Sie? □ Wie ist Ihre Adresse? □ Wie ist Ihre Telefonnummer? □ Was für ein Mensch sind Sie? □ Was machen Sie gern?

Grammatik zum Nachschlagen

The letters in parentheses following grammatical headings refer to the corresponding exercises in the **Übungen.**

Sentence types

A language is a communication system, a device for conveying information from one person to another. The basic communicative unit in language is the sentence.

Both English and German have four major sentence types:

1. statements, which make an assertion

   Ruth spielt gut Tennis.   *Ruth plays tennis well.*

2. specific questions, which contain a question word and ask for specific information

   Wann spielt sie Volleyball?   *When does she play volleyball?*

3. general questions, which ask for a yes-or-no answer

   Spielt Kirk auch gut?   *Does Kirk also play well?*

4. commands, which ask the hearer to do something

   Ruth, spiel nicht soviel Tennis!   *Ruth, don't play so much tennis.*

In this chapter statements and questions are discussed. Commands will be discussed in *Kapitel 3.*

Subject pronouns (A)

Singular		Plural	
1.	**ich** I	**wir** we	
2.	**du** you	**ihr** you	
	(*fam. sg.*)	(*fam. pl.*)	
	er he, it		
3.	**es** it	**sie** they	
	sie she, it		
	Sie you (*formal*)		

A personal pronoun is said to have "person," which indicates the identity of the subject.

1. First person refers to the one(s) speaking *(I, we)*.
2. Second person refers to the one(s) spoken to *(you)*.
3. Third person refers to the one(s) or thing(s) spoken about *(he/it/she, they)*.

The subject pronouns *du, ihr,* and *Sie* (A)

There are three ways to express *you* in German: **du, ihr,** and **Sie.** The familiar forms **du** and **ihr** are used in addressing relatives, close friends, or persons under approximately fifteen years of age. **Du** and **ihr** are also used frequently among members of a group such as students, athletes, laborers, and soldiers.

Sie is a more formal form of address. It is used when addressing one or more strangers or adults with whom the speaker is not on intimate terms.

EDUSCHO

Kaffee wie Sie ihn lieben.

The meanings and use of *sie* and *Sie*

Glaubt **sie** das?	Does she believe that?
Glauben **sie** das?	Do they believe that?
Glauben **Sie** das?	Do you believe that?

In spoken German, the meanings of **sie** *(she)*, **sie** *(they)*, and **Sie** *(you)* can be distinguished by the corresponding verb forms and by context.

> sie + singular verb form = *she*
> sie + plural verb form = *they*
> Sie + plural verb form = *you* (formal)

In written German, **Sie** *(you)* is always capitalized.

Present tense of *sein* (B–D)

ich **bin**	wir **sind**
du **bist**	ihr **seid**
er/es/sie **ist**	sie **sind**
Sie **sind**	

Infinitive and infinitive stem

Infinitive	Stem + ending
glauben	glaub + en
wandern	wander + n

The basic form of a German verb is the infinitive. Most German infinitives end in **-en**; a few end in **-n,** such as **wandern.** In vocabularies and dictionaries, verbs are listed in their infinitive form.

Present tense of regular verbs (E–L)

	glauben	arbeiten	heißen
ich	glaube	arbeite	heiße
du	glaubst	arbeitest	heißt
er/es/sie	glaubt	arbeitet	heißt
wir	glauben	arbeiten	heißen
ihr	glaubt	arbeitet	heißt
sie	glauben	arbeiten	heißen
Sie	glauben	arbeiten	heißen

1. German verb endings change, depending on what the subject of the verb is. The verb endings are added to the infinitive stem. There are four basic endings in the present tense of most regular verbs: **-e, -st, -t, -en**.
2. If a verb stem ends in **-d** or **-t,** the endings **-st** and **-t** expand to **-est** and **-et**.
3. If a verb stem ends in a sibilant (**s, ss, ß, z**), the **-st** ending contracts to **-t**.

The finite verb

Kannst du das buchstabieren?   Can you spell that?

The finite verb form agrees with the subject. In the sentence above, **kannst** (*can*) is finite and agrees with the subject **du. Buchstabieren** (*to spell*) is not a finite form. It is an infinitive and does not agree with the subject.

The construction *gern* + verb (E, F, I–K)

Lore schwimmt **gern**.	Lore likes to swim.
Peter schwimmt **nicht gern**.	Peter doesn't like to swim.

Gern + verb is used to say that one likes doing something.
Nicht gern is used to express a dislike.

Position of *nicht* (G, H)

The position of **nicht** is determined by the various elements in the sentence. Because of the great flexibility of **nicht**, its use is best learned by observing its position in sentences you hear and read. Here are several guidelines:

1. **Nicht** always follows:
   a. the finite verb

   Bernd arbeitet **nicht**.   Bernd is not working.

2. **Nicht** generally follows:
   a. noun objects

   Ich glaube *Bernd* **nicht**.   I don't believe Bernd.

   b. pronoun objects

   Ich glaube *es* **nicht**.   I don't believe it.

   c. specific time expressions

   Bernd spielt *heute* **nicht**.   Bernd is not playing today.

3. **Nicht** precedes other elements:
   a. predicate adjectives

   Uwe ist **nicht** *nett*.   Uwe isn't nice.

   b. predicate nouns

   Das ist **nicht** *Herr Schmidt*.   That isn't Mr. Schmidt.

   c. adverbs

   Er spielt **nicht** *gut* Tennis.   He doesn't play tennis well.

   d. expressions of general time

   Er spielt **nicht** *oft* Tennis.   He doesn't play tennis often.

   e. prepositional phrases

   Ute geht **nicht** *ins Kino*.   Ute isn't going to the movies.

4. If several of the elements occur in a sentence, **nicht** usually precedes the first one.

   Ich gehe **nicht** *oft ins Kino*.   I don't often go to the movies.

Specific and general questions   (N, O, Q)

1	2	3		
Wann gehen Sie? ⌃		When are you going?		
Wo arbeitest du? ⌃		Where do you work?		

A German speaker signals the meaning "specific question" by using an interrogative in first position and the finite verb in second position. The voice normally falls at the end of a specific question, just as it does in English.

Notice that the German signal for "specific question" is simpler than the corresponding English signal. In German, the finite verb is in second position. In English, a form of the auxiliary verb *to be* or *to do* is often used.

1	2	3		
Bist du müde? ↘↗		Are you tired?		
Spielt Andrea gut? ↘↗		Does Andrea play well?		
Arbeitest du heute? ↘↗		Are you working today?		

A German speaker signals the meaning "general question" by putting the finite verb in the first position. The voice normally rises at the end of a general question, just as it does in English.

Notice that the German signal for "general question" is simpler than the corresponding English signal. In German, the verb is in first position. English often has to use a form of the auxiliary verb *to do* or *to be* plus *-ing*.

Tag questions   (P, Q)

Du kommst um vier, **nicht**?   You're coming at four, aren't you?
Gisela spielt gut Schach, **nicht**?   Gisela plays chess well, doesn't she?

A tag question is literally "tagged on" to the end of a statement. In English, the "tag" expressed by the German **nicht**? depends on the subject: aren't you?, doesn't she?, etc.

Kapitel 2

Lernziele

Sprechakte

Talking about the weather
Summarizing information
Inquiring about someone's birthday
Asking for personal information
Expressing agreement and disagreement

Grammatik

Past tense of **sein**
Present tense of **haben**
Position of the finite verbs in statements
Nominative case
Plural of nouns
Indefinite article **ein**
Expressing negation by **kein** and **nicht**
Possession with proper names
Possessive adjectives
Demonstrative pronouns **der, das, die**

Vokabeln

Months and seasons
Weather expressions
Names of countries
Suffixes -**er** and -**in**
Understanding the flavoring particle **aber**

Landeskunde

Geography and climate of the Federal Republic of Germany and the DDR
Development of the standard German language
Birthday customs and greetings

Das Wetter ist oft kühl im Sommer und es regnet viel.

51

| Bausteine für Gespräche

Wie ist das Wetter?	How's the weather?
Im Sommer	*In the summer*
Frau Schmidt: Schönes Wetter, nicht?	Nice weather, huh?
Herr Braun: Ja, aber es ist zu trocken.	Yes, but it's too dry.
Frau Schmidt: Vielleicht regnet es morgen.	Maybe it'll rain tomorrow.
Herr Braun: Hoffentlich.	I hope so.
Im Herbst	*In the fall*
Herr Jung: Heute ist es wirklich kalt, nicht?	It's really cold today, isn't it?
Frau Hofer: Ja, leider, und gestern war es noch so schön.	Yes, unfortunately. And it was still so nice yesterday.
Herr Jung: Jetzt bleibt es bestimmt kalt.	Now it'll certainly stay cold.
Im Winter	*In the winter*
Dieter: Was für ein Wetter!	What weather!
Ingrid: Der Wind ist furchtbar kalt. Ich glaube, es schneit bald.	The wind is awfully cold. I think it's going to snow soon.

Sie haben das Wort

A   Schönes Wetter, nicht?   A fellow student comments on the weather. Agree with her/him.

> Discussing the weather

Gesprächspartner/in	*Sie*	
Schönes Wetter, hm?	Ja, es ist wirklich	**schön.**
Gutes		gut
Schlechtes		schlecht
Furchtbares		furchtbar
		warm°
		kalt

B   Das Wetter   Ask a fellow student about the weather. Then ask how it was on three previous days. You may want to refer to the Supplementary Word Sets on page R-25 of the Reference Section.

Sie	*Gesprächspartner/in*

Wie ist das Wetter?

Es ist	**kalt.**
	schlecht
	naß°
	warm
	schön
	heiß°

Wie war das Wetter **gestern?**
        am Montag

Der Wind	war	**furchtbar**	**kalt.**
Die Sonne		zu	heiß
Das Wetter		sehr	warm
Es			schön

C   Vielleicht morgen.   Make a prediction about the weather to three fellow students. Each should respond differently to your prediction.

Sie	*Gesprächspartner/in*

Vielleicht **regnet es** morgen.	Ja, vielleicht.
schneit es	Ich glaube nicht.
scheint° die Sonne°	Hoffentlich nicht.

D   Was für ein Wetter!   A fellow student is unhappy with the weather. Respond by commenting on the weather yesterday.

Gesprächspartner/in	*Sie*

Was für ein **Wetter!**	Ja, und gestern war es **noch schön warm°**.
Wind	auch schlecht
Regen°	auch kalt
Schnee°	noch trocken

E   Was sagen Sie?   For each of the comments below give as many responses as will logically follow. Select the responses from the list, and add a few of your own.

Hoffentlich. □ Leider. □ Vielleicht. □ Jetzt bleibt es so. □ Vielleicht schneit es bald. □ Vielleicht regnet es. □ Ja, leider. □ Nein, noch nicht.

1. Heute ist es schön warm.
2. Heute ist es wirklich heiß.
3. Es ist zu trocken.
4. Was für ein Wetter!
5. Der Wind ist furchtbar kalt.
6. Schneit es?
7. Jetzt bleibt es bestimmt kalt.

Erweiterung des Wortschatzes

1 Die Monate

Januar	April	Juli	Oktober
Februar	Mai	August	November
März	Juni	September	Dezember

2 Die Jahreszeiten

der Frühling   spring

der Sommer   summer

der Herbst   autumn, fall

der Winter   winter

A   Wann ist es ... ?   Tell in what months the following weather conditions occur.

▶   Wann ist es oft kalt?   *Im Januar und im Februar.*

1.   Wann regnet es viel?
2.   Wann schneit es viel?
3.   Wann ist es oft heiß?
4.   Wann scheint die Sonne nicht viel?
5.   Wann ist es schön warm?
6.   Wann ist es sehr trocken?
7.   Wann ist der Wind kalt? warm? heiß?
8.   Wann ist das Wetter gut — nicht heiß und nicht kalt?

B   Wie heißen sie?   Answer the following questions about the seasons.

1.   Wie heißen die Wintermonate? die Sommermonate?
2.   Wie heißen die Herbstmonate? die Frühlingsmonate?

Sie haben das Wort

A   Wie ist das Wetter ... ?   Respond to a fellow student's questions about the weather in different seasons. You may want to refer to the Supplementary Word Sets on page R-25 of the Reference Section.

Gesprächspartner/in	*Sie*
Wie ist das Wetter im [Herbst]?	Es ist [schön].

Talking about seasonal weather

B   Das Wetter in ... ?   Form a group of four students. Student No. 1 names a month or season. Student No. 2 makes a comment or asks a question from pages 52 and 53. Students Nos. 3 and 4 respond. Repeat the procedure with four different months or seasons.

▶   Student Nr. 1: *der Juli*
    Student Nr. 2: *Wie ist das Wetter?*
    Student Nr. 3: *Es ist heiß.*
    Student Nr. 4: *Es ist schön.*

C   Wann hast du Geburtstag°?   Interview four students to find out the month of their birthday.

Sie	*Gesprächspartner/in*
Wann hast du Geburtstag?	*Im [Mai].*

D   Du auch?   Find another student who has a birthday the same month you do.

Sie	*Gesprächspartner/in*
Ich habe im [März] Geburtstag. Und du?	Im [April]. Auch im [März].

Woche	JANUAR 1 2 3 4 5	FEBRUAR 5 6 7 8 9	MÄRZ 9 10 11 12 13	APRIL 14 15 16 17 18	MAI 18 19 20 21 22	JUNI 22 23 24 25 26	JULI 27 28 29 30 31 31	AUGUST 32 33 34 35	SEPTEMBER 36 37 38 39 40	OKTOBER 40 41 42 43 44	NOVEMBER 44 45 46 47 48	DEZEMBER 48 49 50 51 52 1
Mo	7 14 21 28	4 11 18 25	4 11 18 25	1 8 15 22 29	6 13 20 27	3 10 17 24	1 8 15 22 29	5 12 19 26	2 9 16 23 30	7 14 21 28	4 11 18 25	2 9 16 23 30
Di	1 8 15 22 29	5 12 19 26	5 12 19 26	2 9 16 23 30	7 14 21 28	4 11 18 25	2 9 16 23 30	6 13 20 27	3 10 17 24	1 8 15 22 29	5 12 19 26	3 10 17 24 31
Mi	2 9 16 23 30	6 13 20 27	6 13 20 27	3 10 17 24	1 8 15 22 29	5 12 19 26	3 10 17 24 31	7 14 21 28	4 11 18 25	2 9 16 23 30	6 13 20 27	4 11 18 25
Do	3 10 17 24 31	7 14 21 28	7 14 21 28	4 11 18 25	2 9 16 23 30	6 13 20 27	4 11 18 25	1 8 15 22 29	5 12 19 26	3 10 17 24 31	7 14 21 28	5 12 19 26
Fr	4 11 18 25	1 8 15 22	1 8 15 22 29	5 12 19 26	3 10 17 24 31	7 14 21 28	5 12 19 26	2 9 16 23 30	6 13 20 27	4 11 18 25	1 8 15 22 29	6 13 20 27
Sa	5 12 19 26	2 9 16 23	2 9 16 23 30	6 13 20 27	4 11 18 25	1 8 15 22 29	6 13 20 27	3 10 17 24 31	7 14 21 28	5 12 19 26	2 9 16 23 30	7 14 21 28
So	6 13 20 27	3 10 17 24	3 10 17 24 31	7 14 21 28	5 12 19 26	2 9 16 23 30	7 14 21 28	4 11 18 25	1 8 15 22 29	6 13 20 27	3 10 17 24	1 8 15 22 29

Vokabeln

Substantive

der **Frühling** spring	der **Sommer** summer
der **Geburtstag** birthday	die **Sonne** sun
der **Herbst** autumn, fall	das **Wetter** weather
der **Monat** month	der **Wind** wind
der **Regen** rain	der **Winter** winter
der **Schnee** snow	

Verben

bleiben to remain	**schneien** to snow
regnen to rain	**war** was (*past tense of* **sein**)
scheinen to shine	

Andere Wörter

bald soon	**leider** unfortunately
bestimmt certain(ly)	**morgen** tomorrow
furchtbar horrible, horribly	**naß** wet
gestern yesterday	**noch** still; in addition
heiß hot	**schön** nice, beautiful
hoffentlich I hope	**trocken** dry
jetzt now	**warm** warm
kalt cold	**zu** too

Besondere Ausdrücke

Was für ein Wetter ... ! What weather . . . !	**schön warm** nice and warm

Kühl und klein? — Ja und nein! _____

Vorbereitung auf das Lesen

Before every reading (**Lesestück**) you will find series of questions or statements that will help you read and understand the text. Questions included under the title **Zum Thema (On the topic)** will help you discover what you may already know about the topic, while **Leitfragen (Study questions)** give direction to your reading by suggesting things to look for as you work through the text. As preparation for this reading passage on the size of Germany and its weather, answer as many of the questions below as you can.

● *Zum Thema*

1. Large and small are relative terms. Name some other relative terms.
2. Do you think the concept of cold means the same thing to inhabitants of Florida as to those of Toronto, Canada?
3. Where do you think winters are colder: Minnesota U.S.A.; Ontario, Canada; or northern Germany?
4. Where do you think winters are colder: in northern Germany (Hamburg) or in southern Germany (Munich)?
5. Locate the following countries and cities on the maps at the front of this book and on page 3:

Belgien	die DDR (Deutsche Demo-	Hamburg	Österreich
Berlin	kratische Republik)	Luxemburg	Polen
Bonn	Dänemark	Magdeburg	die Schweiz
die Bundesrepublik	Frankfurt	München	die Tschechoslowakei
Deutschland	Frankreich	die Niederlande	

● *Leitfragen*

1. Which is farther north: Bonn, the capital of the Federal Republic of Germany, or Washington, D.C.?
2. You will find data on the number of inhabitants of the two Germanies relative to their size. In order to establish a comparison, find out how many people live in Illinois and Indiana (or in Nova Scotia and New Brunswick). How many people live in Ohio (or Nova Scotia or New Brunswick)?
3. In order to compare distances, find out how many kilometers it is from Washington, D.C., to Los Angeles. How many kilometers is it from Minneapolis to Miami?
4. How many countries border the U.S.A.? Canada?
5. How many countries border the Federal Republic of Germany? How many can you name?

Ein Deutscher in Deutschland sagt: „Heute ist es aber° heiß. Es ist schon   *really*
richtig Sommer." Ein Amerikaner hört das und denkt: „Heiß? Hier? Jetzt?
Nein! Schön warm."

    Wörter wie „heiß" und „warm" sind also relativ. Denn in Deutschland
5 ist der Sommer anders. Deutschland liegt nämlich° weiter nördlich als   *after all*
Amerika. Nehmen wir° zum Beispiel die Hauptstädte. Bonn ist die   **nehmen wir:** *let's take*
Hauptstadt der° Bundesrepublik Deutschland. Washington ist die ame-   *of the*
rikanische Hauptstadt. Bonn liegt circa° 1300 Kilometer weiter nördlich   *approximately*
als Washington. Ost-Berlin* ist die Hauptstadt der° Deutschen Demo-   *of the*
10 kratischen Republik. Es liegt noch zweihundert Kilometer weiter nördlich
als Bonn.

    Auch der Atlantische Ozean beeinflußt das Klima. Er beeinflußt es
mehr in der Bundesrepublik als in der DDR. Und er beeinflußt es mehr im
Norden als im Süden. So ist das Wetter oft kühl im Sommer und nicht so
15 kalt im Winter.

---

*In the West, the capital of the *DDR* is called *Ost-Berlin*; in the East it is referred
to as *Berlin*.

Auch die Wörter „groß" und „klein" sind relativ, wenigstens° in der   *at least*
Geographie. Für Deutsche ist Amerika sehr groß. Für Amerikaner sind die
Bundesrepublik und DDR sehr klein. Die Bundesrepublik hat etwa
sechzig Millionen Einwohner, aber sie ist nur etwa so groß wie Illinois
20 und Indiana zusammen (oder doppelt so groß wie Neuschottland° und   *Nova Scotia*
Neubraunschweig° zusammen). Die DDR hat circa siebzehn Millionen   *New Brunswick*
Einwohner, und sie ist etwa so groß wie Ohio (oder doppelt so groß wie
Neuschottland). In der DDR sind es von Magdeburg im Westen nach
Frankfurt im Osten zweihundert Kilometer. Von Hamburg im Norden der
25 Bundesrepublik nach München im Süden sind es nur sechshundert Kilometer. In Deutschland haben „groß" und „klein" also andere Dimensio-
nen als in Amerika.

Die zwei deutschen Staaten liegen im Zentrum° Europas. Sie haben   *center*
neun Nachbarn: Das Nachbarland im Norden ist Dänemark, die Nachbar-
30 länder im Süden sind Österreich und die Schweiz; im Osten liegen Polen
und die Tschechoslowakei, und im Westen Frankreich, Luxemburg,
Belgien und die Niederlande.

Fragen zum Lesestück
(Questions on the reading passage)

1. Was sagt ein Deutscher in Deutschland im Sommer?
2. Was denkt der Amerikaner?
3. Welche Wörter sind relativ?
4. Warum° ist der Sommer anders als in Amerika?
5. Wie ist der Sommer in Deutschland?
6. Wie heißt die Hauptstadt der Bundesrepublik? Wie heißt die Hauptstadt der DDR?
7. Welche Stadt° liegt weiter nördlich — Bonn oder Washington?
8. Wo° beeinflußt der Atlantische Ozean das Wetter mehr — in der
   Bundesrepublik oder in der DDR?
9. Wie groß ist die Bundesrepublik? die DDR?
10. Wieviel° Einwohner hat die Bundesrepublik? die DDR?
11. Wieviel Kilometer sind es von Magdeburg nach Frankfurt?
12. Wieviel Kilometer sind es von Hamburg nach München?
13. Wieviel Nachbarn haben die zwei deutschen Staaten zusammen?

Erzählen Sie! (Talk about it!)   Use the following questions as guides to
briefly talk about the Federal Republic of Germany.

Erzählen Sie von° der Bundesrepublik Deutschland!   *about*
Wie groß ist die Bundesrepublik? Wieviel Einwohner hat sie? Wo liegt
   sie? Wieviel Nachbarn hat sie? Wie ist das Klima? Was beeinflußt das
   Klima?

| Schleswig-Holstein | Hamburg | Niedersachsen | Bremen | Nordrhein-Westfalen | Hessen | Rheinland-Pfalz | Baden-Württemberg | Bayern | Saarland | Berlin (West) |

Vokabeln

Nouns are listed with their plural forms: die **Stadt, ⁼e = die Städte.**

— Substantive

(das) **Amerika** America
der **Amerikaner, -** / die **Amerikanerin, -nen** American person
das **Beispiel, -e** example
die **Bundesrepublik Deutschland** Federal Republic of Germany (West Germany)
die **DDR** (die **Deutsche Demokratische Republik**) German Democratic Republic (East Germany)
der **Deutsche** (*m.*) / die **Deutsche** (*f.*) / die **Deutschen** (*pl.*) German person
ein **Deutscher** (*m.*) / eine **Deutsche** (*f.*) a German person
(das) **Deutschland** Germany
der **Einwohner, -** / die **Einwohnerin, -nen** inhabitant
das **Europa** Europe
die **Hauptstadt, ⁼e** capital

der **Kilometer, -** kilometer
das **Klima** climate
das **Land, ⁼er** country, land
die **Million, -en** million
der **Nachbar, -n** / die **Nachbarin, -nen** neighbor
der **Norden** north
der **Osten** east
(das) **Österreich** Austria
der **Österreicher, -** / die **Österreicherin, -nen** Austrian person
der **Ozean** ocean
die **Schweiz** Switzerland
der **Schweizer, -** / die **Schweizerin, -nen** Swiss person
der **Staat, -en** country; state
die **Stadt, ⁼e** city
der **Süden** south
der **Westen** west
das **Wort, ⁼er** word

— Verben

beeinflussen to influence
denken to think
erzählen to tell, narrate

haben to have
liegen to lie, be situated
sagen to say, tell

_ Andere Wörter _____

als than	**nördlich** to the north
also therefore, so	**nur** only
amerikanisch American (*adj.*)	**richtig** correct, right; real
andere other	**schon** already
anders different(ly)	**so ... wie** as . . . as
denn (*conj.*) because, for	**von** from; of
deutsch German (*adj.*)	**warum** why
etwa approximately, about	**weiter** farther, further
für for	**wie** like; **ein Wort wie heiß**
hier here	a word like hot
in in	**wieder** again
kühl cool	**wo** where
mehr more	**zusammen** together
nach to (*with cities and countries, e.g.,*	
nach Berlin)	

_ Besondere Ausdrücke _____

zum Beispiel (*abbrev.* **z.B.**) for example

Erweiterung des Wortschatzes

1 Flavoring particle *aber*

"Flavoring" particles are little words used to express a speaker's attitude about an utterance. These flavoring particles relate the utterance to something the speaker or the listener has said or thought. Depending on the choice of the particle and sometimes on the tone of voice, the speaker expresses interest, surprise, impatience, denial, and so on. Because a particle has various shades of meaning that depend on the context, a dictionary can give only the approximate English meaning. With experience you will gain a "feel" for the meaning and use of these words, which are very characteristic of colloquial German.

Der Wind ist **aber** kalt.	The wind is really cold.
Heute ist das Wetter **aber** furchtbar.	I think the weather is horrible today, don't you?

In addition to its usual meaning of *but*, **aber** can be used as a flavoring particle. **Aber** often indicates a situation that is somewhat unexpected, or it gives added emphasis to the speaker's feelings about an utterance.

A   Was bedeutet das? (What does that mean?)   How would you express the following sentences in idiomatic English?

1. Das Wetter ist aber furchtbar.
2. Der Wind ist aber kalt.
3. Der Sommer ist aber schön.
4. Heute ist es aber heiß.
5. In Kanada ist der Winter aber kalt.
6. Der Wind ist aber furchtbar.

2   Names of countries

Wie groß ist **Deutschland?**	How large is Germany?
Existiert **das romantische Deutschland** noch?	Does romantic Germany still exist?

The names of most countries are neuter; for example **(das) Deutschland** and **(das) Amerika.** However, articles are not used with names of countries that are neuter, unless the name is preceded by an adjective.

Die Schweiz ist schön.	Switzerland is beautiful.
Die USA sind groß.	The United States is large.

The names of a few countries are feminine (e.g., **die Schweiz**); some names are used only in the plural (e.g., **die USA**). Articles are always used with names of countries that are feminine or plural.

B   Andere Länder   Try to guess the English names for the countries listed below.

1. Italien
2. Spanien
3. Griechenland
4. Schweden
5. Rumänien
6. Rußland
7. Norwegen
8. Jugoslawien
9. die Türkei
10. die Niederlande

3   The suffix -in

Masculine	der Nachbar
Feminine	die Nachbar**in**
Feminine plural	die Nachbar**innen**

The suffix **-in** added to the singular masculine noun gives the feminine equivalent. The plural of a noun with the suffix **-in** ends in **-nen.**

C   Mann oder Frau?   Give the other form — feminine or masculine — of the words listed below.

▶   die Professorin   *der Professor*

1.   die Sekretärin
2.   der Student
3.   die Amerikanerin
4.   der Einwohner

4   The noun suffixes -*er* and -*er* + -*in*

| England | der Engländ**er** | die Engländ**erin** |
| Berlin | der Berlin**er** | die Berlin**erin** |

The noun suffix **-er** is added to the name of a city, state, or country to indicate a male inhabitant. Some names take umlaut. The additional suffix **-in** indicates a female inhabitant.

ICK BIN EEN BERLINA
DA KIKSTE WA, IS WAT?

D   Welche Länder? Welche Städte?   The following people come from (*kommen aus*) certain cities and countries. Complete the sentences.

▶   Anton kommt aus Berlin. Er ist _____ .   *Er ist Berliner.*
▶   Astrid kommt aus Hamburg. Sie ist _____ .   *Sie ist Hamburgerin.*

1.   Benno kommt aus der Schweiz. Er ist _____ .
2.   Heike kommt aus Frankfurt. Sie ist _____ .
3.   Herr Klee kommt aus Österreich. Er ist _____ .
4.   Heidi kommt aus der Schweiz. Sie ist _____ .

▶   Thomas ist Amerikaner. Er kommt aus _____ .   *Er kommt aus Amerika.*

5.   Barbara ist Münchnerin. Sie kommt aus _____ .
6.   Luigi ist Italiener. Er kommt aus _____ .
7.   Trudi ist Norwegerin. Sie kommt aus _____ .
8.   Carlos ist Spanier. Er kommt aus _____ .

Übungen zur Aussprache

Review the pronunciation of long and short **o** and **ö** in the Reference section at the end of the book. Read aloud the words in each column from top to bottom. Then read the sets of word pairs across. Check your pronunciation by listening to your instructor or the tape.

long ē	long ȫ	short e	short ö	long ō	long ȫ	short o	short ö
Hefe	Höfe	Gent	gönnt	schon	schön	konnte	könnte
Lehne	Löhne	helle	Hölle	Ofen	Öfen	Frosch	Frösche
Sehne	Söhne	kennen	können	losen	lösen	Koch	Köche
beten	böten	Beller	Böller	hohe	Höhe	Bock	Böcke
hehle	Höhle	Bäcker	Böcke	tot	töten	Kopf	Köpfe

Read the following sentences aloud, paying special attention to the way you pronounce long and short **o** and **ö** in the boldfaced words.

1. Wie ist der **Sommer** in **Österreich?**
2. Im **Sommer** ist es **oft schön.**
3. Deutschland liegt weiter **nördlich** als Amerika.
4. Warum ist Peter heute **so nervös?**
5. Er **hört** die **Wörter** nicht.

Viele Köche verderben den Brei.

| Grammatik und Übungen

1   Simple past tense of *sein*

Present	Heute ist das Wetter gut.	The weather is good today.
Simple past	Gestern war es schlecht.	It was bad yesterday.

The simple past tense of **sein** is **war**.

ich **war**	wir waren	
du warst	ihr wart	
er/es/sie **war**	sie waren	
Sie waren		

I was	we were
you were	you were
he/it/she was	they were
you were	

In the simple past, the **ich-** and **er/es/sie**-forms have no verb endings.

A   Nicht gut   Everybody had a bad day yesterday. Tell how the people mentioned below were. Use the past tense of *sein.*

▶   Günter / nervös   *Günter war nervös.*

1. Nicole / müde
2. ich / krank
3. wir / faul
4. Bernd und Eva / nicht sehr nett
5. du / sehr müde
6. ihr / wirklich dumm

Sie haben das Wort

Ask a fellow student what the weather was like on four previous days. Record the answers. You may want to refer to the Supplementary Word Sets on page R-25 of the Reference Section.

Inquiring about the weather

Sie	*Gesprächspartner/in*
Wie war das Wetter am [Samstag]?	Es war [schön].
	[Samstag] war es [schön].

2   Present tense of *haben*

haben: to have	
ich habe	wir haben
du **hast**	ihr habt
er/es/sie **hat**	sie haben
Sie haben	

The verb **haben** is irregular in the **du-** and **er/es/sie**-forms of the present tense.

B Wann hast du Geburtstag? Frank and his friends are comparing birthdays. Say that the people mentioned were born in the same months as their friends. Change the form of **haben** to agree with the subject. Add **auch**, as in the model.

▶ Du hast im März Geburtstag. (Jens)   *Jens hat auch im März Geburtstag.*

1. Petra hat im Juni Geburtstag. (ich)
2. Wir haben im Februar Geburtstag. (Karin und Urs)
3. Jürgen hat im Mai Geburtstag. (ihr)
4. Ulrike und Thomas haben im September Geburtstag. (wir)
5. Anke hat im März Geburtstag. (du)
6. Ich habe im November Geburtstag. (Ellen)

In German-speaking countries birthdays are celebrated in different ways. The "birthday child" (*Geburtstagskind*) may have an afternoon coffee party (*Geburtstagskaffee*) with family members and friends or a more extensive birthday party in the evening. At the *Geburtstagskaffee* candles are placed around the edge of a birthday cake (*Geburtstagskuchen*) and blown out by the person whose birthday it is. Although the *Geburtstagskind* is often taken out by family members or friends, he or she usually invites friends to a party or brings a cake to work. Besides giving presents (*Geburtstagsgeschenke*) it is common to send a birthday card. Common greetings are: *Herzlichen Glückwunsch zum Geburtstag!* (Happy birthday!) or *Alles Gute zum Geburtstag!* (All the best on your birthday!), and *Ich gratuliere zum Geburtstag!* (Congratulations on your birthday!).

Herzlichen Glückwunsch zum Geburtstag!

3   Position of the finite verb in statements

1		2	3		4
Der Sommer		ist	in Deutschland		anders.
In Deutschland		ist	**der Sommer**		anders.

In a German statement, the finite verb is always in second position, even when an element other than the subject (for example, an adverb or a prepositional phrase) is in first position. When an element other than the subject is in first position, the subject follows the verb.

C   Morgen spielen wir Tennis.   You and Sonja are talking about a possible tennis game. Agree with her by restating her comments, beginning with the word in parentheses. Follow the model.

▶   Wir spielen morgen Tennis, nicht? (morgen)   *Ja, morgen spielen wir Tennis.*

1.   Es ist hoffentlich warm. (hoffentlich)
2.   Das Wetter war gestern schlecht, nicht? (gestern)
3.   Es ist heute schön, nicht? (heute)
4.   Das Wetter war auch am Mittwoch gut, nicht? (am Mittwoch)
5.   Das Wetter bleibt jetzt bestimmt gut, nicht? (jetzt)
6.   Die Sonne scheint hoffentlich. (hoffentlich)

FOR MONDAY

D   Wie sagt man das?   Give the German equivalents of the following statements. Begin your responses with the adverbial element given in parentheses. Be sure the verb is in second position.

1.   The sun is shining today. (*heute*)
2.   The weather was also nice yesterday. (*gestern*)
3.   I hope the weather remains nice. (*hoffentlich*)
4.   In Germany the summer is often cold. (*in Deutschland*)
5.   In America the summer is often warm. (*in Amerika*)
6.   It was cold on Thursday. (*am Donnerstag*)
7.   Maybe it'll rain tomorrow. (*vielleicht*)
8.   We're playing tennis tomorrow, aren't we? (*morgen*)

Sie haben das Wort

Explain when your birthday is and what the weather is usually like at that time of year. Make a brief report to a group of four or to the whole class.

Describing seasonal weather

▶   *Ich habe im Februar Geburtstag. Im Februar ist es kalt. Es schneit oft, und die Sonne scheint nicht viel.*

4   The nominative case

That woman plays tennis well.
She doesn't play volleyball very well.

English uses word order to signal different grammatical functions of nouns or pronouns. In a statement in English the subject precedes the verb.

Die Frau spielt gut Tennis.
Volleyball spielt **sie** aber nicht sehr gut.

German uses a different type of signal to indicate the grammatical function of nouns and pronouns. German uses a signal called *case*. When a noun or pronoun is used as the subject of a sentence, it is in the nominative case.

Masculine	Neuter	Feminine
der	das	die

In the nominative case, the German definite article has three forms. They are all equivalent to "the" in English.

Subject	Predicate Noun
Herr Lange ist **Professor.**
Das Mädchen heißt **Gabi Fischer.**
Das ist nicht **der Junge.**

Subject	Predicate Noun
Mr. Lange is a professor.
The girl's name is Gabi Fischer.
That is not the boy.

The nominative case is also used for a *predicate noun*. A predicate noun designates a person, concept, or thing that is equated with the subject. A predicate noun completes the meaning of linking verbs such as **sein** and **heißen.** In a negative sentence **nicht** precedes the predicate noun.

E   Wie ist das Wetter?   Practice making comments about the weather. Use the cues provided. Make the comments in the past tense.

▶   Wetter / schön   *Das Wetter war schön.*

1. Morgen / kalt
2. Tag / warm
3. Wind / warm
4. Sonne / heiß
5. Abend / kalt
6. Tag / naß

Zum Valentinstag!
y bunte Frühlings-
primeln im Weiden-
körbchen 6,95

Wunderbar:
der Februar. Da gibt's bei
WERTKAUF*noch fast alles für den Winter.
Und schon fast alles für den Sommer.
Alles zu den berühmten W*Preisen.

F   Wie heißen sie?   Your friend can't keep people's names and objects straight. Say that she/he is wrong about each one. In your response use **nicht** before the predicate noun.

▶   Heißt der Junge Mark?   *Nein, er heißt nicht Mark.*

1. Heißt das Mädchen Meike?
2. Heißt das Kind Dieter?
3. Heißt die Frau Meier?
4. Heißt der Professor Schmidt?
5. Heißt die Professorin Nagel?
6. Heißt die Sekretärin Neumann?

▶   Ist das der Tisch?   *Nein, das ist nicht der Tisch.*

1. Ist das der Stuhl?
2. Ist das die Lampe?
3. Ist das das Radio?

4. Ist das das Buch?
5. Ist das die Uhr?

5   Plural of nouns

A thousand years ago English had a variety of ways to signal the plural of nouns. With some nouns it used stem change: *mann — menn (man, men); fōt — fēt (foot, feet);* with other nouns it used endings: *stān — stānas (stone, stones); oxa — oxun (ox, oxen);* and with still other nouns it used no signal at all: *scēap — scēap (sheep, sheep).* Over the centuries the ending *-as* gradually replaced most other plural endings, and its modern development *-(e)s* is now the almost universal signal for the plural of English nouns.

Type	Plural signal	Singular	Plural
1	-	das Fenster	die Fenster
	̈	der Garten	die Gärten
2	-e	der Tisch	die Tische
	̈e	der Stuhl	die St**ü**hle
3	-er	das Kind	die Kind**er**
	̈er	das Buch	die B**ü**cher
4	-en	die Frau	die Frau**en**
	-n	die Lampe	die Lampe**n**
	-nen	die Studentin	die Studentin**nen**
5	-s	das Radio	die Radios

German uses five basic types of signals to mark the plural of nouns: the endings **-, -e, -er, -(e)n,** and **-s.** Some of the nouns of types 1, 2, and 3 add umlaut in the plural. Nouns of type 4 that end in **-in** add **-nen** in the plural. German makes no gender distinctions in the plural; the definite article **die** is used with all plural nouns.

When you learn a German noun, you must also learn its plural form because there is no sure way of predicting to which plural-type the noun belongs. You will, however, gradually discover that there is a kind of system to the various types. This "system" depends partly on whether the noun is a **der-**, **das-**, or **die**-noun, and partly on how many syllables it has.

Die Kinder sind nett. **Sie** sind nett.
Die Lampen sind alt. **Sie** sind alt.

The personal pronoun **sie** (they) may refer to persons or things.

G   Alt oder neu?   Alex wants to know whether the things in your room are new or old. Tell him that the one is new and the other is old. Use the adverb **da** after the singular noun.

▶   Sind die Stühle neu?   *Der Stuhl da ist neu. Der da ist alt.*

1.   Sind die Lampen neu?
2.   Sind die Tische neu?
3.   Sind die zwei Radios neu?
4.   Sind die zwei Betten neu?
5.   Sind die zwei Bücher neu?
6.   Sind die zwei Uhren neu?

H   Der, das, die   State the noun with the definite article and then give the plural with the definite article.

▶   Tisch   *der Tisch / die Tische*

1.   Stuhl   5.   Heft
2.   Buch   6.   Lampe
3.   Bleistift   7.   Radio
4.   Kugelschreiber

I   Machen Sie Sätze! (Form sentences.)   Make up sentences in the singular and then in the plural. Be sure the subject and verb agree.

▶   Stadt / liegen / im Norden   *Die Stadt liegt im Norden.*
                                   Die Städte liegen im Norden.

1.   Nachbarin / sein / nett
2.   Straße / sein / schön
3.   Frau / arbeiten / viel
4.   Student / arbeiten / nicht viel
5.   Mann / spielen / viel Fußball
6.   Kind / spielen / gern Volleyball
7.   Zimmer / sein / kalt
8.   Garten / sein / klein

A thousand years ago there was no standard form of the German language. The large central European area from the North Sea and the Baltic Sea to the Alps in the south was inhabited by many different types of "Germans" who spoke many different kinds of "German."

Seit Martin Luther gibt es eine deutsche Sprache.

Martin Luther in the sixteenth century played an important role in the development and refinement of German. For his Bible translation and other works, Luther used a form of the language spoken in east central Germany; eventually it became the spoken and written standard for all of Germany as well as Austria and Switzerland. This single standard language is called *Hochdeutsch*. It is used professionally and officially (e.g., in newspapers and on radio and TV).

A recent reaction to the standard use of *Hochdeutsch* in all domains of public life has been the revival of interest in local dialects in many regions. Realizing that dialects are often neglected and that a few of them are dying out, authors, journalists, and pop musicians are making local dialects popular again.

Dialects are often incomprehensible to people from different regions and may even differ significantly from town to town. Complete words, intonation, and pronunciation can vary dramatically. (Different ways to say *sprechen*, for example, include *schwätzen, schnacken, talken*). However, the speakers from different areas within the German-speaking countries such as *Bayern, Sachsen, Burgenland* or *Tirol* can always communicate with each other in *Hochdeutsch*. This way, the different German-speaking countries are linguistically unified.

Eine niederdeutsche Karte: Das tut mir aber leid, daß du krank bist. Werde schnell wieder gesund. Gute Besserung.

6   The indefinite article *ein*

Ist das **ein** Radio oder **eine** Uhr?   Is that a radio or a clock?

The German indefinite article **ein** is equivalent to English *a* or *an*.

Masculine	Neuter	Feminine
ein Mann	ein Kind	eine Frau

In the nominative case the German indefinite article has two forms: **ein** for masculine and neuter, and **eine** for feminine. The indefinite article has no plural form.

J   Was ist das?   Jan is taking his first drawing course and is showing some of his first attempts to draw things. You're a little doubtful about the results. Use an indefinite article in the response.

▶   Das Kind ist nicht schlecht, nicht?   *Das ist ein Kind?*

1.   Die Frau ist schön, nicht?
2.   Der Mann ist gut, nicht?
3.   Das Kind ist schön, nicht?
4.   Der Stuhl ist nicht schlecht, nicht?
5.   Die Lampe ist lustig, nicht?
6.   Die Uhr ist nicht schlecht, nicht?
7.   Der Tisch ist schön, nicht?

7   The negative *kein*

Ist das **ein** Radio?   Is that a radio?
Nein, das ist **kein** Radio.   No, that's not a radio.

Sind die Studenten Amerikaner?   Are the students Americans?
Nein, sie sind **keine** Amerikaner.   No, they are not Americans.

The negative form of **ein** is **kein.** It is equivalent to English *not a, not any,* or *no*. It negates a noun that in the positive would be preceded by a form of **ein** or no article at all.

Masculine	Neuter	Feminine	Plural
kein Tisch	**kein** Radio	**keine** Uhr	**keine** Radios

In the nominative case **kein** has two forms: **kein** for masculine and neuter, and **keine** for feminine and plural.

K   Das ist es nicht.   To get back at you Jan pretends he can't figure out what you have drawn. Tell him his guesses are wrong. Use a form of **kein** in your responses.

▶   Ist das eine Frau?   *Nein, das ist keine Frau.*

1. Ist das ein Mann?
2. Ist das ein Mädchen?
3. Ist das ein Kind?
4. Ist das eine Lampe?

5. Ist das eine Tür?
6. Ist das ein Zimmer?
7. Ist das ein Tisch?

L   Das ist es aber nicht.   Gabi compliments you on your drawings, but unfortunately she mistakes what they represent. Use a form of **kein** in the response.

▶   Der Mann ist gut.   *Das ist aber kein Mann.*

1. Die Frau ist schön.
2. Das Kind ist gut.
3. Die Uhr ist gut.
4. Die Tür ist gut.
5. Der Stuhl ist gut.
6. Das Zimmer ist schön.

8   *Kein* vs. *nicht*

Ist das **eine** Uhr?   Nein, das ist **keine** Uhr.
Ist das **die** Uhr?   Nein, das ist **nicht die** Uhr.

Kein is used to make negative a noun that would be preceded by **ein** or no article at all in an affirmative sentence. **Nicht** is used in a negative sentence when the noun is preceded by a definite article.

M   Nicht oder kein?   Answer the following questions in the negative. Use **nicht** or **kein** before the predicate noun, as appropriate.

▶   München ist die Hauptstadt von   *Nein, München ist nicht die*
     Deutschland, nicht?   *Hauptstadt von Deutschland.*
▶   Das ist ein Kugelschreiber, nicht?   *Nein, das ist kein Kugelschreiber.*

1. Ist er Student?
2. Ist das die Gartenstraße?
3. Ist sie Studentin?
4. Ist das ein Stuhl?
5. Ist das das Buch?
6. Ist Berlin die Hauptstadt der Bundesrepublik?
7. Ist das eine Straße?

9   Proper names showing possession

Das ist Giselas Buch.	That is Gisela's book.
Das ist Jens' Kuli.	That is Jens's ballpoint pen.

In German, an **-s** is usually added to a proper name to show possession or other close relationship. If the name already ends in an **s**-sound, no **-s** is added. In written German, an apostrophe is used after a name ending in an **-s** sound.

N   Ist das Gerds Buch?   After a club meeting you and a friend are straightening up. Tell your friend to whom the various things belong. Use the possessive form of the proper name.

▶   Gerd / Buch   *Das ist Gerds Buch.*

1. Beate / Kuli
2. Bruno / Lampe
3. Petra / Radio
4. Regina / Heft
5. Thomas / Büchertasche
6. Sylvia / Uhr

10   Possessive adjectives

Mein Zimmer ist groß.	My room is large.
Ist **dein** Zimmer groß?	Is your room large?
Ist **sein** Zimmer groß?	Is his room large?
Ist **ihr** Zimmer groß?	Is her room large?
Unser Zimmer ist groß.	Our room is large.
Ist **euer** Zimmer groß?	Is your room large?
Ist **ihr** Zimmer groß?	Is their room large?
Ist **Ihr** Zimmer groß?	Is your room large?

German possessive adjectives are equivalent in meaning to the English possessive adjectives, such as *my*, *his*, and *her*. Context usually makes clear whether **ihr** is the subject pronoun *you*, the adjective *her* or *their*, or the adjective *your*. Note that **Ihr** (your) is capitalized, just as the corresponding subject pronoun **Sie** (you) is.

der Bleistift	Wo ist ein Bleistift?
	Wo ist **mein** Bleistift?
das Heft	Wo ist ein Heft?
	Wo ist **mein** Heft?
die Uhr	Wo ist eine Uhr?
	Wo ist **meine** Uhr?
die Bücher	Wo sind **meine** Bücher?

Since possessive adjectives take the same endings as **ein**, they are frequently called **ein**-words.

Wo ist **euer** Radio? Wo sind **eure** Bücher?

When **euer** has an ending, the **-e-** preceding the **-r-** is usually omitted.

O   So ist es.   You are discussing several persons' things. Say that the things are similar. Use the cued possessive adjectives.

▶   Ingrids Zimmer ist groß. (dein)   *Dein Zimmer auch.*

1. Daniels Lampe ist schön. (ihr)
2. Ingrids Stühle sind neu. (euer)
3. Ingrids Tisch ist sehr alt. (sein)
4. Daniels Garten ist klein. (mein)
5. Brunos Bilder sind furchtbar. (unser)
6. Brunos Poster sind anders. (dein)

P   Wie sagt man das?   Complete the sentences with the German equivalents of the cued words.

▶   _____ Mann arbeitet nicht. (*her*)   *Ihr Mann arbeitet nicht.*

1. _____ Kind heißt Dieter. (*their*)
2. _____ Frau ist lustig. (*his*)
3. Barbara, Frank, was für ein Mensch ist _____ Nachbar? (*your*)
4. Wo sind _____ Kinder, Frau Neumann? (*your*)
5. Ich glaube, das ist _____ Kuli. (*my*)
6. Ist das _____ Uhr, Gisela? (*your*)

11   Demonstrative pronouns *der, das, die*

Lore spielt viel Tischtennis, nicht?	Lore plays a lot of table tennis, doesn't she?
Ja, **die** spielt wirklich gut.	Yes, she plays really well.
Mark spielt viel Fußball.	Mark plays a lot of soccer.
Ja, **der** spielt aber schlecht.	Yes, but he plays poorly.

Der, das, and **die** are often used as demonstrative pronouns to replace nouns. A demonstrative pronoun is used instead of a personal pronoun (**er, sie, es**) when the pronoun is to be emphasized. Demonstrative pronouns usually occur at or near the beginning of a sentence. The English equivalent is usually a personal pronoun (*he, she, it, they*).

Q   Ja, so sind die.   Dieter is speaking on the phone with Renate. They're discussing friends and agreeing with each other. Use a demonstrative pronoun as the subject.

▶   Barbara ist intelligent, nicht?   *Ja, die ist wirklich intelligent.*

1. Thomas war gestern lustig, nicht?
2. Professor Müller ist alt, nicht?
3. Die Kinder sind heute lustig, nicht?
4. Gerd und Dieter sind faul, nicht?
5. Frau Professor Dörflinger ist konservativ, nicht?
6. Max und Christine waren gestern doof, nicht?

| Wiederholung

A   Singular, Plural   Give the singular and plural forms of each noun. Give the appropriate form of the definite article with each noun.

▶   Einwohner   *der Einwohner, die Einwohner*

1. Mädchen
2. Stadt
3. Wort
4. Monat
5. Tag
6. Woche
7. Mann
8. Frau
9. Nachbarin
10. Stuhl
11. Kugelschreiber
12. Fenster
13. Garten

B   Machen Sie Sätze!   Form sentences, using the cues provided.

▶   Wer / sagen / das / ?   *Wer sagt das?*

1. Jens / arbeiten / heute abend / nicht / ?
2. warum / ihr / spielen / heute / wieder / Tennis / ?
3. er / glauben / das / nicht
4. du / gehen / morgen / ?
5. sie (*pl.*) / schwimmen / gern
6. ich / sagen / nichts
7. wo / liegen / Deutschland / ?
8. Deutschland / liegen / weiter nördlich / als Amerika
9. vielleicht / es / regnen / morgen
10. hoffentlich / die Sonne / scheinen

C   Wer, wie, wo, was?   Form questions that elicit the responses given. Begin the questions with the cued words.

▶   Danke, gut. (Wie)   *Wie geht es Ihnen?*

1.   Das Wetter ist schön. (Wie)
2.   In Deutschland ist das Wetter im Sommer oft kühl. (Wo)
3.   Nein, es regnet heute nicht. (Regnet)
4.   Ja, der Tag war schön. (War)
5.   Das Wetter ist furchtbar. (Wie)
6.   Herr Braun sagt das oft. (Wer)
7.   Die Studenten gehen heute abend. (Wann)
8.   Dieter spielt gern Tennis. (Was)
9.   Gabi arbeitet in München. (Wo)

D   Wie sagt man das?   Give the German equivalents of the sentences below.

▶   It's raining.   *Es regnet.*

1.   It's not raining.
2.   Does she believe that?
3.   What do you think?
4.   Is she saying that?
5.   Do you swim well?
6.   What are you saying?
7.   Who's going tomorrow?
8.   How often does he do that?
9.   Is Dieter working today?
10.   We play a lot of tennis.

E   Ihre Meinung (Your opinion)   Answer according to your own personal experience.

1.   Wie ist das Wetter heute?
2.   Regnet es heute?
3.   Ist es kalt oder warm?
4.   Wann regnet es viel? Im Sommer? Im Frühling?
5.   Wie war das Wetter am Samstag? Gestern?

F   Farben   Name the colors of some of the objects in your room.

▶   *Der Kugelschreiber ist [rot].*

G   So sind meine Freunde.   Pick three friends and describe them with three adjectives each.

▶   *Tanja ist groß, konservativ und nett.*

H   Anregung

1. Make up ten sentences about the weather in German.
2. Using a newspaper map, write a weather report for the United States,
    Canada or the Federal Republic of Germany. Be sure to give tempera-
    ture readings for at least five cities and the weather conditions for sev-
    eral different regions.

▶   *In Chicago sind es fünf Grad°. Es regnet.*   *degrees*

| Grammatik zum Nachschlagen ──────────

Simple past tense of *sein*   (A)

ich **war**	wir waren
du warst	ihr wart
er/es/sie **war**	sie waren
Sie waren	

Present tense of *haben*   (B)

ich habe	wir haben
du **hast**	ihr habt
er/es/sie **hat**	sie haben
Sie haben	

Position of the finite verb in statements   (C, D)

	1	2	3	4
	Subject	**Verb**	**Adverb**	**Adjective**
Normal	**Der Sommer**	ist	in Deutschland	anders.
	Adverb	**Verb**	**Subject**	**Adjective**
Inverted	In Deutschland	ist	**der Sommer**	anders.

In a German statement, the verb is always in second position. In so-called
normal word order, the subject is in first position. In so-called inverted word
order, something other than the subject (for example, an adverb, an adjective, or indirect object) is in first position, and the subject follows the verb.

Plural of nouns (G–I)

In the vocabularies of this book, the plural of most nouns is indicated after the singular forms. For example:

das Zimmer, - indicates that there is no change in the plural form of the noun: **das Zimmer, die Zimmer**

die Stadt, ⸚e indicates that an **-e** is added in the plural, and an umlaut is added to the appropriate vowel: **die Stadt, die Städte**

Type	Plural signal	Singular	Plural
1	**0** (no change)	das Zimmer	die Zimmer
	⸚	der Garten	die Gärten
2	**-e**	das Heft	die Hefte
	⸚**e**	die Stadt	die Städte
3	**-er**	das Kind	die Kinder
	⸚**er**	der Mann	die Männer
4	**-en**	die Tür	die Türen
	-n	die Lampe	die Lampen
	-nen	die Studentin	die Studentinnen
5	**-s**	das Radio	die Radios

Nominative case (E, F)

Der Mann arbeitet heute nicht.   The man is not working today.
Spielt **das Kind** gern Tennis?   Does the child like to play tennis?

German nouns show different cases depending on how they are used in a sentence. When a noun is used as the subject of a sentence, it is in the nominative case.

Subject	Predicate Noun
Frau Lange ist	Professorin.
Der Junge heißt	Gerhard Meier.

A noun that designates a person, concept, or thing that is equated with the subject and completes the meaning of the linking verbs **sein, heißen,** or **werden** (*to become*) is called a predicate noun. It is in the nominative case.

Nominative case of definite articles, indefinite articles, and *kein* (J–L)

der Stuhl	Da ist **ein** Stuhl.	Hier ist **kein** Stuhl.
das Radio	Da ist **ein** Radio.	Hier ist **kein** Radio.
die Lampe	Da ist **eine** Lampe.	Hier ist **keine** Lampe.
die Bücher	Da sind Bücher.	Hier sind **keine** Bücher.

The indefinite article **ein** is equivalent to English *a* or *an*. **Ein** has no plural form. **Kein** is the negative form of **ein** and is equivalent to *not a, not any,* or *no*. **Kein** has plural forms.

Kein vs. *nicht* (M)

Ist das **eine** Uhr?   Nein, das ist **keine** Uhr.
Ist das **die** Uhr?   Nein, das ist **nicht die** Uhr.

Kein is used to make negative a noun that would be preceded by **ein** or no article at all in an affirmative sentence. **Nicht** is used in a negative sentence when the noun is preceded by a definite article. (For other uses of **nicht,** see *Kapitel 1,* pages 36–37 and 48.)

Possession with proper names (N)

Das ist Ingrids Buch.   That is Ingrid's book.
Das ist Jens' Buch.   That's Jens's book.

A proper name is a word that designates a specific individual or place (e.g., Ingrid, Berlin). In German as in English, possession and other close relationships are expressed by adding **-s** to the proper names. If the name already ends in an **s-** sound, no **-s** is added. In written German, an apostrophe is used only when no **-s** is added (e.g., Jens' Buch).

Possessive adjectives (O, P)

- *Forms and meanings*

Singular			Plural		
ich:	**mein**	my	wir:	**unser**	our
du:	**dein**	your	ihr:	**euer**	your
er:	**sein**	his, its			
es:	**sein**	its	sie:	**ihr**	their
sie:	**ihr**	her, its			
	Sie: **Ihr**	your			

- *Nominative of possessive adjectives*

Masculine		Neuter		Feminine		Plural	
ein		ein		eine		—	
mein	Tisch	**mein**	Radio	**meine**	Uhr	**meine**	Bücher
unser		**unser**		**unsere**		**unsere**	

The possessive adjectives are often called **ein**-words because they take the same endings as the indefinite article **ein**.

Uns(e)re Stadt ist nicht groß. Wie groß ist **eure** Stadt?

When **unser** has an ending, the form may contract: **unsere** > **unsre**.
When **euer** has an ending, the form usually contracts: **euere** > **eure**.

Demonstrative pronouns *der, das, die* (Q)

Karin arbeitet viel.	Karin works a lot.
Ja, **die** arbeitet viel.	Yes, she works a lot.

Thomas ist nett.	Thomas is nice.
Ja, **der** ist wirklich nett.	Yes, he's really nice.

Der, das, die are often used as demonstrative pronouns to replace nouns.

Kapitel 3

Lernziele

Sprechakte

Shopping and buying groceries
Telling someone to do something
Expressing likes and dislikes
Discussing meals
Expressing and inquiring about need
Expressing expectation of a positive or of a negative response

Grammatik

Verbs with stem-vowel change **e** > **i**
Word order: time and place expressions
Imperatives
Accusative case
Direct objects
Expressing likes and dislikes with **gern**
Es gibt

Vokabeln

Flavoring particles: **denn** and **ja**
Use of **doch**
Common foods
Noun compounds
Days of the week as adverbs
Units of weight, measurement, and quantity

Landeskunde

Apotheke and **Drogerie**
Shopping for groceries
Specialty stores vs. supermarkets
Typical German breakfast
Currency in German-speaking countries

Frische Sachen auf dem Markt in Lüneburg

| Bausteine für Gespräche _____

Was brauchst du?

Jochen: Gibt es hier keine
  Apotheke?
Heike: Doch. Was brauchst du
  denn?
Jochen: Ich brauche etwas gegen
  Kopfschmerzen.
Heike: Ich habe noch ein paar
  Aspirin hier. Nimm die!

What do you need?

Isn't there a pharmacy around
  here?
Why sure there is. What do you
  need?
I need something for a headache.

I still have a few aspirin here. Take
  these.

Gehst du jetzt einkaufen?

Jürgen: Gehst du jetzt einkaufen?
Petra: Ja, warum fragst du?
Jürgen: Wir brauchen Spaghetti.
  Ich mache morgen Spaghetti.
Petra: Sonst noch etwas?
Jürgen: Ein Graubrot und ein
  Schwarzbrot! Kauf das aber bei
  Müller! Da ist das Brot besser.

Are you going shopping now?

Are you going shopping now?
Yes, why do you ask?
We need spaghetti. I'm making
  spaghetti tomorrow.
Anything else?
A rye bread and a pumpernickel.
  Buy that at Müller's. The bread
  is better there.

Sie haben das Wort

A   Was suchen Sie?   Think of three things you need to buy. Your instructor or a fellow student asks what kind of store you're looking for. Respond. You may want to refer to the Supplementary Word Sets on page R-25 for names of specialty shops.

Gesprächspartner/in	*Sie*
Was suchst°du?	Eine Apotheke. Gibt es hier eine Apotheke?
Was suchen Sie?	Eine Bäckerei°. Gibt es hier eine Bäckerei?
	Eine Metzgerei°. Gibt es hier eine Metzgerei?
	Einen Supermarkt°. Gibt es hier einen Supermarkt?
	Eine Drogerie°. Gibt es hier eine Drogerie?

> Inquiring about shopping possibilities

An *Apotheke* sells prescription and non-prescription drugs. In every town and in each section of a large city, one *Apotheke* offers emergency service (*Notdienst*) at night and on Sunday. A pharmacist (*Apotheker*) is a university graduate. A *Drogerie* sells a wide variety of toilet articles and many other items found in American drugstores. It is being replaced gradually by the bigger and cheaper self-service drugstore (*Drogeriemarkt*), which also sells nonprescription drugs. A druggist (*Drogist*) is trained in a three-year apprenticeship.

There are generally fewer prescription-free drugs in Germany than in the U.S., and they cannot be found in supermarkets.

Aspirin gibt es in der Apotheke.

B   Geh doch!   Your friend needs some things. Tell her/him to go to the store that sells them.

Expressing needs

Gesprächspartner/in		*Sie*	
Ich brauche	**etwas gegen Kopfschmerzen.**	Geh doch°	**in die Apotheke!**
	Brot für morgen		zum Bäcker!
	Wurst° für heute abend		zum Metzger!
	Spaghetti		in den Supermarkt!
	ein Heft		ins Kaufhaus°!
	ein Buch über° Schach		in die Buchhandlung°!

C   Sonst noch etwas?   You've been telling a friend what you need, but there's something you've forgotten. What is it? When she/he asks whether there's anything else you need, say what it is.

Gesprächspartner/in	*Sie*	
Brauchst du sonst noch etwas?	Ja, wir haben	**kein Brot** mehr°.
		keine Spaghetti
		kein Bier°
		keinen Kaffee°
		keine Butter°

D   Kopfschmerzen   Your instructor or fellow student asks you whether you have a headache. Respond appropriately.

Gesprächspartner/in	*Sie*
Haben Sie Kopfschmerzen? Hast du	Ja, furchtbar. Ja, ich brauche Aspirin. Ja, es geht mir schlecht. Ja, leider. Nein, warum fragst du/fragen Sie? Nein, ich habe keine Kopfschmerzen.

E   Rollenspiel   In groups of three, prepare an original skit using the questions and responses in **A–D** above. You may follow the outline below.

1. What are you looking for?   [A drugstore.]
2. Why?   [I need something for my headache.]
3. Do you need anything else?   [Yes. We have no more bread.]
4. Go to the [bakery.]

F   Gespräche   Construct two dialogues based on the elements provided.

1. *Michael:* wo / hier / sein / Apotheke / ?
   Lore: warum / fragen / ?
   Michael: brauchen / etwas / gegen / Kopfschmerzen
2. *Frau Schmidt:* Wetter / furchtbar // haben / Kopfschmerzen
   Herr Braun: das / leid tun // hoffentlich / Sonne / morgen
   Frau Schmidt: glauben / nicht // regnen / bestimmt / wieder

Vokabeln

— Substantive

das **Abendessen, -** evening meal
die **Apotheke, -n** pharmacy
das **Aspirin** aspirin
der **Bäcker, -** baker
die **Bäckerei, -en** bakery
das **Bier, -e** beer
das **Brot, -e** bread
die **Buchhandlung, -en** bookstore
die **Butter** butter
die **Drogerie, -n** drugstore
das **Frühstück** breakfast
das **Haus, ̈er** house

der **Kaffee** coffee
das **Kaufhaus, ̈er** department store
die **Kopfschmerzen** (*pl.*) headache
der **Metzger, -** butcher
die **Metzgerei, -en** butcher shop, meat market
das **Mittagessen** midday meal
die **Spaghetti** (*pl.*) spaghetti
der **Supermarkt, ̈e** supermarket
die **Tasche, -n** bag; pocket
die **Wurst, ̈e** sausage, lunch meat

— Verben

brauchen to need	**kaufen** to buy
einkaufen to shop	**nehmen (nimmt)** to take
essen (ißt) to eat	**suchen** to look for
fragen to ask	

— Andere Wörter

bei at; at a place of business (**beim [Metzger]**); at the home of (**bei [Ingrid]**)

besser better

doch yes (*after a negative question or statement*)

ein paar a few

gegen against

kein not a, not any

sonst otherwise

über about

— Besondere Ausdrücke

beim Bäcker at the bakery

beim Metzger at the butcher shop

es gibt there is; there are

in die Apotheke to the pharmacy

in den Supermarkt to the supermarket

kein ... mehr no more . . .

Sonst noch etwas? Anything else?

zum Abendessen for the evening meal, for dinner

zum Bäcker to the bakery

zum Frühstück for breakfast

zum Metzger to the butcher shop

zum Mittagessen for the midday meal, for lunch

Germans do most of their food shopping in supermarkets. These supermarkets tend to be smaller than American ones, and most of them are within walking distance of residential areas. Most people go shopping several times a week. Although the markets are self-service stores, fresh foods such as cheeses, sausages and cold cuts, bread, and vegetables are sold mostly by shop assistants at separate counters. Many prepackaged foods are also available. Customers carry their own shopping bags (*Einkaufstaschen*) to the supermarkets or buy plastic bags (*Plastiktüten*) at the check-out register. They pay with cash, not by check or by charging.

Im Supermarkt – man bringt eine Einkaufstasche oder man kauft eine Plastiktüte.

Erweiterung des Wortschatzes

1   Flavoring particle *denn*

"Flavoring" particles are little words used to express a speaker's attitude about an utterance. These flavoring particles relate the utterance to something the speaker or the listener has said or thought. Depending on the choice of the particle and sometimes on the tone of voice, the speaker expresses interest, surprise, impatience, denial, and so on. Because a particle has various shades of meaning that depend on the context, a dictionary can give only an approximate English meaning. With experience you will gain a "feel" for the meaning and use of these words, which are very characteristic of colloquial German.

Detlev: Was brauchst du **denn**?
Ute: Spaghetti.
Detlev: Machst du **denn** wieder Spaghetti?

Denn is used frequently in questions to show the personal interest of the speaker. It softens the speaker's question and makes it less abrupt. **Denn** also refers back to a previous utterance of the speaker or listener or to a topic familiar to both.

2   Flavoring particle *doch*

The flavoring particle **doch** is used in unstressed position to express several shades of meaning.

Du machst **doch** heute Spaghetti, nicht?

You're making spaghetti today, aren't you?

Das glaubst du **doch** nicht.

{ You surely don't believe that.
  You can't really believe that!

The speaker uses **doch** to ask the listener for corroboration. "This is really true, isn't it?"

Geh **doch** in den Supermarkt!   Why don't you go to the supermarket?
Machen Sie es **doch**!   Go ahead and do it.

The speaker uses **doch** to persuade the listener to do something.

Das ist **doch** dumm.   You must know that that's stupid.

The speaker uses **doch** to express slight impatience: "Come on, really. . . ."

3 *Doch* as positive response to negative statements or questions

Jochen: Gibt es hier keine Apotheke?

Isn't there a pharmacy around here?

Heike: **Doch.**

Why, sure there is.

Jochen: Es regnet heute nicht.

It's not going to rain today.

Heike: **Doch.**

Yes, it will.

In addition to its function as a flavoring particle, stressed **doch** may be used as a one-word positive response to a negative statement or question. By using **doch**, the speaker contradicts the assumption contained in a previous assertion or question.

A   Was bedeutet das? (What does that mean?)   Give an English equivalent of the conversation below.

Paula: Arbeitest du denn nicht?
Gerd: Nein, ich habe doch Kopfschmerzen.
Paula: Dann nimm doch Aspirin!
Gerd: Wir haben aber kein Aspirin mehr.
Paula: Gehst du denn nicht einkaufen?
Gerd: Doch.
Paula: Kauf doch etwas Aspirin!

B   Doch oder ja?   Respond in the positive, using **doch** or **ja** as appropriate.

▶   Arbeitest du heute nicht?   *Doch.*
▶   Gehst du um sieben?   *Ja.*

1. Brauchen wir Brot?
2. Gehst du nicht zum Bäcker?
3. Hast du kein Aspirin?
4. Gibt es hier eine Apotheke?
5. Klaus spielt gut Tennis, nicht?
6. Treibst du auch viel Sport?
7. Andrea spielt nicht gut Tennis.
8. Du glaubst das nicht.

4 Lebensmittel

1. der Käse
2. der Wein, -e
3. der Kuchen, -
4. der Fisch, -e
5. der Tee
6. das Brot, -e
7. das Obst
8. das Gemüse
9. das Ei, -er
10. das Fleisch
11. die Butter
12. die Milch
13. die Kartoffel, -n

Sie haben das Wort

Interview fellow students to learn what they eat at various meals.

Sie	Gesprächspartner/in
Was ißt du zum Frühstück°? zum Mittagessen°? zum Abendessen°?	Ich esse [zwei Brötchen].

> Talking about meals and food

In towns and cities of the German-speaking countries it is very common to shop at outdoor markets that are held either daily or once or twice a week on market day (*Markttag*). There farmers from the region sell fresh vegetables, fruit, flowers, eggs, herbs, and teas. In smaller towns, these markets are often integrated into the medieval town architecture (e.g., in Freiburg). In bigger cities Turkish or Italian markets, which have sprung up with the presence of foreign workers, sell their specialties from home. Hamburg's famous *Fischmarkt* in the *St. Pauli* harbor district opens very early on Sunday mornings and sells not only fish but a great variety of fresh products from all over the world. Some of these outdoor markets are famous for their colorful arrangements of products, others for atmosphere or beautiful location or even for the people selling there, who have become local personalities.

Frisches Obst auf dem Markt in Offenbach.

I Einkaufen in Deutschland

Vorbereitung auf das Lesen

- *Zum Thema*

1. Where do you think people in this country do most of their food shopping? In supermarkets? Or in small stores (for example, buying bread in a bakery, meat in a butcher shop, fish in a fish market)? How about you?
2. Do most people in this country open a can of coffee or grind their own coffee beans? How about you?
3. Would people in this country be likely to buy cut flowers every weekend? How about you?
4. Name some other shopping habits you think are common in this country.

● *Leitfragen*

1. What is the role of small specialty stores in Germany (die **Bäckerei**, bakery / die **Metzgerei**, butcher shop) versus supermarkets (der **Supermarkt**)?
2. Many Germans shop at open-air markets. Are they more like supermarkets or specialty stores?
3. Would Germans be likely to buy cut flowers for the weekend?
4. How does the German pharmacy (die **Apotheke**) differ from the drugstore (die **Drogerie**)?

Es ist Samstag. Monika macht Frühstück. Sie macht es besonders schön, denn Diane und Joan aus° Amerika sind da. Ihre° Schwester Andrea   *from / her* kommt in die Küche°, und Monika sagt: „Du, Andrea, wir haben keinen   *kitchen* Kaffee und keine Marmelade mehr. Geh bitte zu Meiers und kauf Kaffee
5 und Marmelade." Andrea nimmt Einkaufstasche und Geld und geht. Nebenan° ist noch ein Tante-Emma-Laden°. Da kauft sie manchmal   *next door / mom-and-pop* morgens. Da kennt man sie. Hoffentlich schließt der nicht auch bald,   *store* denkt Andrea. Viele Leute gehen jetzt in den Supermarkt, denn da ist es natürlich billiger. Aber hier ist es viel persönlicher°.   *more personal*
10   Herr Meier sagt: „Guten Morgen, Fräulein Stamer. Was bekommen Sie denn heute?"

„Ich brauche Kaffee, ein Pfund."

„Ungemahlen°, wie immer?"   *unground*

„Ja, natürlich. Und dann brauche ich noch Marmelade. Ich nehme zwei
15 Sorten°."   *kinds*

„Haben Sie denn Besuch?"

„Ja, Freundinnen aus Amerika sind da. — Gut, das ist alles für heute."
Andrea nimmt noch eine Morgenzeitung und bezahlt.

„Auf Wiedersehen, Fräulein Stamer, und schönes Wochenende!"
20   „Danke. Tschüß, Herr Meier."

Der Bäcker ist gegenüber°. Da riecht es immer so gut. Andrea kauft   *across from here* Brötchen. Die sind noch ganz warm. Und ein Schwarzbrot von gestern nimmt sie auch noch.

Das Frühstück ist wirklich sehr gut. Joan und Diane finden die Brötchen
25 und den Kaffee besonders gut. Monika sagt: „Wir mahlen° ihn° ja auch   *grind / it* selbst und kochen ihn dann gleich. So verliert er kein Aroma." Joan denkt: Wirklich?

Später gehen die Vier zusammen auf° den Markt. Sie kaufen ein Kilo   *to* Erbsen° und Kartoffeln fürs° Mittagessen. Der Fischmann ist auch da.   *peas / = für das*
30 Hier kaufen sie frischen Fisch. Den essen sie zum Abendessen. Joan sagt: „Das Einkaufen° hier ist nicht schlecht. Nur die Einkaufstaschen sind   *shopping* etwas schwer." Dann gehen sie auf den Blumenmarkt. Für wenig Geld

Hier ist der Fisch frisch.

bekommen sie einen sehr schönen Strauß°. Monika kommt oft samstags   *bouquet*
mit Blumen nach Hause.

35   Auf dem Weg nach Hause gehen sie noch in eine Drogerie. Monika
braucht einen Kamm° und Andrea einen Lippenstift.° Diane fragt: „Wo   *comb / lipstick*
ist denn hier das Aspirin? Ich brauche Aspirin und Vitamintabletten."
Monika fragt: „Bist du denn krank?" — „Nein, ich nehme immer   *stand, are*
Vitamintabletten." Monika denkt: Wirklich? Und sie sagt: „Hier, die
40   Vitamintabletten stehen° hier. Aber Aspirin hat eine Apotheke." So
gehen sie noch in die Apotheke. Dann haben sie endlich alles, wenigstens bis Montag.

Fragen zum Lesestück

1. Welcher Tag ist es?
2. Warum macht Monika das Frühstück besonders schön?
3. Was brauchen Monika und Andrea?
4. Was für ein Laden ist nebenan?
5. Warum schließen Meiers vielleicht bald?
6. Wo ist es persönlicher, bei Meiers oder im Supermarkt?
7. Und wo ist es billiger?
8. Warum kauft Andrea zwei Sorten Marmelade?
9. Was kauft Andrea noch?

10. Von wann ist das Schwarzbrot? Und die Brötchen?
11. Was finden Joan und Diane besonders gut? Warum?
12. Was glaubt Monika — warum verliert der Kaffee kein Aroma?
13. Was machen die Vier später?
14. Was gibt es auf dem Markt?
15. Für wann kaufen sie den Fisch?
16. Joan findet das Einkaufen nicht schlecht. Warum findet sie es dann doch nicht so gut?
17. Was kauft Monika oft samstags?
18. Wer hat Vitamintabletten, die Drogerie oder die Apotheke?
19. Wer hat Aspirin?

A German breakfast (*Frühstück*) can be quite extensive. Usually it consists of a hot beverage, fresh rolls (*Brötchen*) or bread, butter, and jam; often there are also cold cuts, an egg, cheese or perhaps yogurt, whole grain granola (*Müsli*), and juice or fruit. Pancakes (*Pfannkuchen*) are not a common breakfast food. Eggs for breakfast are usually soft-boiled (*weichgekochte Eier*). Scrambled eggs (*Rühreier*) and fried eggs (*Spiegeleier*) are more often served for the evening meal (*Abendessen*). The main warm meal of the day is usually eaten at noon (*Mittagessen*).

Zum Frühstück gibt es Brot, Butter, Marmelade, Kaffee und Milch.

Bilder aus der Bundesrepublik Deutschland

Oben: **Die Fahne der Bundesrepublik** Schwarz, Rot, Gold. *Unten:* **Bonn am Rhein** Die Hauptstadt der Bundesrepublik — das Regierungsviertel.

Futuristische Designstudie
Fahrzeug-Interieur Limousine

Ganz links oben: **München**
BMW-Museum — Ein Auto
der Zukunft. *Ganz links unten:*
Hamburg an der Elbe Der
größte Hafen der Bundes-
republik. *Diese Seite oben:*
Hamburger Philharmonie
Der Staat subventioniert die
Orchester. *Diese Seite unten:*
Elzach im Schwarzwald
Umzug am Fastnachts-
sonntag.

Oben: **Schaftlach** Volkskunst an einem bayrischen
Haus. *Unten:* **Schwabing**
Wenn das Wetter warm ist,
sitzt man gern draußen.

Vokabeln

— Substantive

der **Besuch, -e**   visit; **wir haben Besuch**   we have company
die **Blume, -n**   flower
das **Brötchen, -**   roll
die **Einkaufstasche, -n**   shopping bag
der **Freund, -e**/die **Freundin, -nen**   friend
das **Geld**   money
das **Glas, ¨er**   glass
das **Gramm**   gram (*abbrev.* **g**)
das **Kilo(gramm)**   kilogram (*abbrev.* **kg**)

der **Liter, -**   liter (*abbrev.* **l** = 1.056 U.S. quarts)
die **Leute** (*pl.*)   people
die **Marmelade**   marmalade, jam
der **Markt, ¨e**   market
das **Pfund**   pound (= 1.1 U.S. pounds; *abbrev.* **Pfd.**)
die **Schwester, -n**   sister
die **Tablette, -n**   tablet, pill
der **Weg, -e**   way
das **Wochenende, -n**   weekend
die **Zeitung, -en**   newspaper

— Verben

bekommen   to receive
bezahlen   to pay (for); **sie bezahlt das Essen**   she pays for the meal
finden   to find; **wie findest du das Brot?**   how do you like the bread?
geben (gibt)   to give
kennen   to know, be acquainted with

kochen   to cook
kommen   to come
riechen   to smell
schließen   to close
stehen   to stand, be located
verlieren   to lose

— Andere Wörter

alles   everything, all
besonders   especially, particularly
billig   cheap; **billiger**   cheaper
bis   until
dann   then
endlich   finally
etwas   some, somewhat
frisch   fresh
gleich   immediately; same; similar
immer   always
man   one, people

manchmal   sometimes
morgens   in the morning
natürlich   natural(ly); of course
samstags   on Saturdays
schwer   heavy; difficult
selbst   oneself, myself [etc.]
viele   many
wenig   little, few
wie   as
zu   to

— Besondere Ausdrücke

auf dem Weg   on the way
Besuch haben   to have company
nach Hause   (to go) home
wie immer   as always
zu Abend essen   to have the evening meal

zu Mittag essen   to have the noontime meal
Schönes Wochenende!   Have a nice weekend!

Erweiterung des Wortschatzes

5   Noun compounds

die **Blumen** + der **Markt** = der **Blumenmarkt**
flowers + *market* = *flower market*

kaufen + das **Haus** = das **Kaufhaus**
to buy + *building* = *department store*

A characteristic of German is its ability to form noun compounds easily. Where German uses compounds, English often uses separate words. Your vocabulary will increase rapidly if you learn to analyze the component parts of compounds.

der Kopf + **die** Schmerzen = **die** Kopfschmerzen
der Fisch + **der** Mann = **der** Fischmann

The last element of a compound determines its gender.

A   Was bedeutet das? (What does that mean?)   The compounds listed below are made up of cognates and familiar nouns. Give the English equivalent of each.

1.   der Winterabend
2.   der Sommertag
3.   die Marktfrau
4.   der Sonnenschein
5.   die Tischlampe
6.   die Morgenzeitung
7.   die Zimmertür

6   Days of the week as adverbs

Noun	Adverb	English equivalent
Montag	montags	Mondays
Samstag	samstags	Saturdays
Morgen	morgens	mornings
Abend	abends	evenings

A noun that names a day of the week or a part of a day may be used as an adverb to indicate repetition or habitual action. An **-s** is added to the noun. In writing, adverbs are not capitalized.

Sie haben das Wort

Ein Interview   Interview a partner. Record her/his responses.

Wann essen Sie mehr — mittags oder abends?
Wann sind Sie sehr müde — morgens oder abends?
Wann arbeiten Sie mehr — samstags oder sonntags?
Wann gehen Sie einkaufen — freitags, samstags, oder wann?
Gehen Sie morgens oder abends einkaufen?

> Inquiring about personal habits

7   Units of weight

1 Kilo(gramm)	= 1000 Gramm
1 Pfund	= 500 Gramm
1 *(American) pound*	= 454 Gramm

In the United States a system of weight is used in which a pound consists of 16 ounces. In German-speaking countries the metric system is used: the basic unit of weight is the **Gramm**, and a thousand grams are a **Kilo(gramm)**. German speakers also use the older term **Pfund** for half a **Kilo(gramm)**, or 500 (**fünfhundert**) **Gramm**. The English-language *pound* equals 454 **Gramm**.

8   Units of measurement and quantity

Geben Sie mir zwei **Pfund** Kaffee!   Give me two pounds of coffee.
Ich nehme zwei **Glas** Milch.   I'll take two glasses of milk.
Er kauft zwei **Liter** Milch.   He's buying two liters of milk.

In German, masculine and neuter nouns expressing measure, weight, or number are in the singular.

B   Einkaufen   Answer the questions affirmatively, as in the model.

▶ Wieviel Pfund Kaffee kaufen Sie? zwei?   *Ja, ich kaufe zwei Pfund Kaffee.*

1. Wieviel Pfund Fisch kaufen Sie? drei?
2. Wieviel Pfund Butter kaufen Sie? zwei?
3. Wieviel Liter Milch kaufen Sie? vier?
4. Wieviel Gramm Tee kaufen Sie? 250?
5. Wieviel Gramm Käse kaufen Sie? 200?
6. Wieviel Kilo Kartoffeln kaufen Sie? fünf?
7. Wieviel Glas Marmelade kaufen Sie? zwei?

9 Flavoring particle *ja*

Wir mahlen ihn ja selbst. We grind it ourselves, of course [as we both know].

Ja may be used by a speaker to express the belief that an utterance is related to a condition that both the speaker and the listener are aware of, or should be aware of.

C Was bedeutet das? Give the English equivalents of the sentences below. Pay special attention to the flavoring words in italics.

1. Gehen Sie *denn* heute nicht einkaufen?
2. Hier gibt es *ja* keinen Tante-Emma-Laden.
3. Im Tante-Emma-Laden kennt man Andrea *doch*.
4. Die Wurst ist *ja* nicht frisch.
5. Haben Sie *denn* kein Brot von gestern?
6. Das Brot von gestern schmeckt *ja* besser.
7. Das ist *ja* furchtbar!
8. Das macht man *doch* nicht.

While German-speaking countries are similar in many ways, they do not share a common monetary system. The Federal Republic's basic unit is the *Deutsche Mark (DM)*. It contains 100 *Pfennig (Pf)*. The *DDR* also uses a *Mark*, although its value is somewhat different from that of the Federal Republic. Switzerland's basic unit, the *Franken (sFr.)*, is roughly equal in value to the *Mark* of the Federal Republic. There are 100 *Rappen (Rp.)* in a *Franken*. Austria's basic unit is the *Schilling (S)*. The *Schilling* is a much smaller unit than the *Mark*: a piece of cake costs about 28 *Schilling*, the equivalent of 4 *DM*. There are 100 *Groschen (g)* in a *Schilling*.

Übungen zur Aussprache

Review the pronunciation of long and short **ü** and **u** in the Reference section at the end of the book. Then read the words in each pair of columns across. Check your pronunciation by listening to your instructor or the tape.

long $\bar{\imath}$	long $\bar{\ddot{u}}$	short i	short $\ddot{u}$
Biene	Bühne	Kiste	Küste
diene	Düne	Lifte	Lüfte
Kiel	kühl	Kissen	küssen
liegen	lügen	missen	müssen
fielen	fühlen	Binde	Bünde

long $\bar{\ddot{u}}$	short $\ddot{u}$	long $\bar{u}$	long $\bar{\ddot{u}}$	short u	short $\ddot{u}$
Füße	Flüsse	Huhn	Hühner	Fluß	Flüsse
Mühle	Müll	Hut	Hüte	Bund	Bünde
Sühne	Sünde	Fuß	Füße	Kuß	Küsse
Blüte	Bütte	Zug	Züge	Luft	Lüfte
Düne	dünne	Blut	Blüte	Kunst	Künste

Read the following sentences aloud, paying special attention to the way you pronounce long and short **ü** and **u** in the boldfaced words.

1. **Für** ihren Mann kauft sie einen **Butterkuchen**.
2. Der **Student** kann seine **Bücher** nicht finden.
3. **Jürgen sucht** ein **Buch** über **Musik**.
4. Im **Frühling** sind die **Blumen** auf dem Markt besonders schön.

In der Kürze liegt die Würze.

| Grammatik und Übungen

1   Verbs with stem-vowel change *e>i*

essen: to eat	
ich esse	wir essen
du **ißt**	ihr eßt
er/es/sie **ißt**	sie essen
Sie essen	

geben: to give	
ich gebe	wir geben
du **gibst**	ihr gebt
er/es/sie **gibt**	sie geben
Sie geben	

nehmen: to take	
ich nehme	wir nehmen
du **nimmst**	ihr nehmt
er/es/sie **nimmt**	sie nehmen
Sie nehmen	

English has only two verbs with stem-vowel changes in the third-person singular, present tense: *say > says (sezz)*, and *do > does (duzz)*.

German, on the other hand, has a considerable number of verbs with a stem-vowel change in the **du-** and **er/es/sie-**forms. Some verbs with stem vowel **e** change **e** to **i**. The verbs of this type that you know so far are **essen**, **geben**, and **nehmen**. The stem of **essen** ends in a sibilant; the ending **-st** therefore contracts to a **-t = du ißt** (see page 35). **Nehmen** has an additional spelling change: **du nimmst, er/es/sie nimmt**. In the chapter vocabularies in this book, stem-vowel changes are indicated in parentheses: **geben (gibt).**

A   Was geben wir Inge?   Inge needs things for her room at college. Tell what various friends are giving her. Use the proper form of **geben**.

▶   Walter / zwei alte Stühle   *Walter gibt Inge zwei alte Stühle.*

1.   Claudia / zwei Hefte
2.   Dietmar und Jens / ein Radio
3.   wir / eine Lampe
4.   ihr / eine Uhr
5.   Frau Hauff / eine Büchertasche
6.   du / ein Buch über Musik
7.   ich / zwei Kugelschreiber

B   Was nehmen wir?   You're in a restaurant with a group of friends. Indicate what you think each person will eat or drink. Use the proper form of **nehmen**.

▶   Grete / Kaffee   *Grete nimmt Kaffee, nicht?*

1. du / Tee
2. Franz / Milch
3. ihr / etwas Obst
4. wir / Wurst und Brot
5. Volker und Inge / Käse und Brot
6. Tanja / Kuchen

C   Was essen sie gern?   You are planning a picnic. Ask what the people listed below would like to eat. Use the proper form of **essen**.

▶   Frank   *Was ißt Frank gern?*

1. du
2. Barbara
3. Alex und Dieter
4. ihr
5. Paula

Sie haben das Wort

Was ißt du?   A friend asks questions about your eating habits.

Gesprächspartner/in		Sie	
Nimmst du	Vitamintabletten?	Ja,	**viel.**
			immer
Nimmst du	oft Aspirin?	Ja, aber nicht viel.	
Ißt du viel	**Brot?**	Nein, nicht sehr	**oft.**
	Kuchen		viel
	Obst		gern
	Gemüse	Warum fragst du?	
	Käse		
Ißt du gern	[Schwarzbrot]?		

> Answering questions about eating habits

2   Word order with expressions of time and place

Time	Place
Sie geht heute in die Buchhandlung.	

Place	Time
She's going to the bookstore today.	

When a German sentence contains both a time expression and a place expression, the time expression precedes the place expression.

D Wann gehst du? Your friend is trying to guess when you're going to do various errands. Confirm the guesses.

▶ Wann gehst du in die Stadt? Heute morgen? *Ja, ich gehe heute morgen in die Stadt.*

1. Wann gehst du in den Supermarkt? Um neun?
2. Wann gehst du in die Buchhandlung? Morgen?
3. Wann gehst du zum Bäcker? Später?
4. Wann gehst du in die Apotheke? Heute morgen?
5. Wann gehst du ins Kaufhaus? Jetzt?
6. Wann gehst du zum Metzger? Heute?

3 Imperatives

The imperative forms are used to express commands. In both German and English, the verb is in first position.

In written German, an exclamation mark is generally used after an imperative. If there is no special emphasis, a period is used.

• *du-imperative*

Erna! { **Frag(e)** Frau Müller! / **Arbeite** jetzt, bitte! / **Gib** mir bitte das Brot!

Erna! { Ask Mrs. Müller. / Work now, please. / Give me the bread, please.

The **du**-imperative consists of the stem of a verb plus **-e**, but the **-e** is often dropped in informal usage: **frage!** > **frag!** If the stem of the verb ends in **-d** or **-t**, the **-e** may not be omitted in written German: **arbeite!** If the stem vowel of a verb changes from **e** to **i**, the imperative has this vowel change and never has final **-e: geben** > **gib! essen** > **iß! nehmen** > **nimm!**

E Mach das jetzt! You've dropped some hints on what you want your friend to do. Now restate your requests, using the **du**-imperative.

▶ Du gehst jetzt einkaufen, nicht? *Geh jetzt einkaufen!*

1. Du machst das jetzt, nicht?
2. Du kaufst das Brot bei Müller, nicht?
3. Du nimmst nur Schwarzbrot, nicht?
4. Du kaufst noch sechs Brötchen, nicht?
5. Du gehst auch zum Metzger, nicht?
6. Du kommst gleich nach Hause, nicht?
7. Du gibst mir das Geld, nicht?
8. Du ißt etwas Obst, nicht?

• **ihr**-*imperative*

Günter! Peter! { **Fragt** Frau Müller!   Günter! Peter! { Ask Mrs. Müller.
       Gebt mir bitte   Give me the
       das Brot!   bread, please.

The **ihr**-imperative is identical with the **ihr**-form of the present tense.

F   **Ja, macht das.**   You're planning a surprise party for Jürgen. Tell your
friends what to do, following the model. Use the **ihr**-imperative.

▶   Gehen wir in die Buchhandlung?   *Natürlich. Geht in die Buchhandlung.*

1. Machen wir das jetzt?
2. Kaufen wir ein Buch über Tennis?
3. Geben wir Jürgen das Buch morgen?
4. Kochen wir heute abend Spaghetti?
5. Gehen wir einkaufen?
6. Kaufen wir alles im Supermarkt?

- ## *Sie-imperative*

Herr Schmidt! $\left\{ \begin{array}{l} \textbf{Fragen Sie} \text{ Frau} \\ \text{Müller!} \\ \textbf{Geben Sie} \text{ mir} \\ \text{bitte das Brot!} \end{array} \right.$ Mr. Schmidt! $\left\{ \begin{array}{l} \text{Ask Mrs. Müller.} \\ \text{Give me the} \\ \text{bread, please.} \end{array} \right.$

The **Sie**-imperative is identical with the **Sie**-form of the present tense. The pronoun **Sie** is always stated and follows the verb directly. In speech, one differentiates a command from a question by the inflection of the voice. The voice rises at the end of a question and falls at the end of a command.

- ## *Imperative of* **sein**

Sei nicht so nervös!   Don't be so nervous.
Seid ruhig!   Be quiet.
Seien Sie so gut!   Be so kind.

Note that the **du-** and **Sie**-imperatives of **sein** are different from the **du-** and **Sie**-forms of the present tense.

G   **Schön, gehen Sie!**   Encourage your indecisive acquaintance to go ahead with her/his plans. Use the **Sie**-imperative.

▶   Ich glaube, ich gehe jetzt einkaufen.   *Schön°, gehen Sie jetzt einkaufen!*   O.K.

1.   Ich glaube, ich kaufe Kaffee.
2.   Ich glaube, ich kaufe auch Marmelade.
3.   Ich glaube, ich bezahle alles selbst.
4.   Ich glaube, ich mache das heute nachmittag.
5.   Ich glaube, ich gehe auch in die Apotheke.
6.   Ich glaube, ich kaufe Aspirin.
7.   Ich glaube, ich komme heute abend wieder nach Hause.

H   **Wie sagt man das?**   Give the German equivalents of the commands below. The use of first and last names will indicate whether you should use **du-, ihr-** or **Sie**-imperatives.

▶   Stay here, Sylvia.   *Bleib hier, Sylvia!*
▶   Don't ask, Mr. Braun.   *Fragen Sie nicht, Herr Braun!*

1.   Don't work too much, Inge.
2.   Say something, Udo.
3.   Go to the supermarket, Gisela and Tanja.
4.   Don't believe that, Jörg and Thomas.
5.   Buy bread and sausage, Mr. Jahn.
6.   Please spell that, Mrs. Koch.
7.   Eat the bread now, Tanja.
8.   Take aspirin, Alex.
9.   Be so kind, Mrs. Schulz, and stay here.
10. Alex, be quiet.

Sie haben das Wort

You are with a friend in Germany who needs to buy some food for dinner and some other items for her/his room. Tell her/him where to go to get them. You may want to refer to the Supplementary Word Sets on page R-25 for names of specialty shops.

Giving directives

Gesprächspartner/in	*Sie*

▶   Ich brauche [Aspirin].   *Geh doch [in die Apotheke]!*

Brot □ Wurst □ Blumen □ Papier □ ein Buch über Jazz

4   Direct object

Kennst du **Lotte Schneider?**   Do you know Lotte Schneider?
Frank ißt gern **Kuchen.**   Frank likes to eat cake.

The direct object is the noun or pronoun that receives or is affected by the action of the verb. The direct object answers the question whom (**Lotte**) or what (**Kuchen**).

5   Accusative of the definite articles *der, das, die*

	Nominative	Accusative
Masculine	**Der** Kaffee ist billig.	Nehmen Sie **den** Kaffee!
Neuter	**Das** Brot ist frisch.	Nehmen Sie **das** Brot!
Feminine	**Die** Marmelade ist gut.	Nehmen Sie **die** Marmelade!
Plural	**Die** Blumen sind schön.	Nehmen Sie **die** Blumen!

The direct object of a verb is in the accusative case. In the accusative case, the definite article **der** changes to **den**. The articles **das** and **die** do not show case change in the accusative.

I   **Einkaufen gehen**   A friend is shopping for things for her/his room. Ask whether she/he intends to buy the things. The things become direct objects in your questions.

▶   Die Lampe ist lustig.   *Kaufst du die Lampe oder nicht?*

1.   Das Radio ist gut.
2.   Der Stuhl ist billig.
3.   Der Tisch ist schön.
4.   Das Bett ist groß.
5.   Die Uhr ist billig.
6.   Die Blumen sind schön.

6   Word order and case as signals of meaning

Subject	Verb	Direct object
The man	asks	the professor something.
The professor	asks	the man something.

English usually uses word order to signal the difference between a subject and a direct object. The usual word-order pattern in statements is *subject, verb,* and *direct object.* The two sentences above have very different meanings.

Subject (nom.)	Verb	Direct object (acc.)
Der Mann	fragt	den Professor etwas.

Direct object (acc.)	Verb	Subject (nom.)
Den Professor	fragt	der Mann etwas.

German generally uses case to signal the difference between a subject and a direct object. The different case forms of the definite article (e.g., **der, den**) signal the grammatical function of the noun. **Der,** in the example above, indicates that the noun **Mann** is in the nominative case and functions as the subject. **Den** indicates that the noun **Professor** is in the accusative case and functions as the direct object. The word-order pattern in statements may be *subject, verb, direct object,* or *direct object, verb, subject.* The two sentences above have the same meaning.

Since German uses case to signal grammatical function, it can use word order for another purpose: to present information from different perspectives. A speaker may use "normal" word order (*subject, verb, direct object*) or inverted word order (*direct object, verb, subject*). The English equivalents vary, depending on context and the meaning the speaker wishes to convey. The sentence **Der Mann fragt den Professor etwas** is equivalent to *The man asks the professor something.* The sentence **Den Professor fragt der Mann etwas** is equivalent to saying something like *It's **the professor** the man is asking something.*

Der Professor fragt **die** Studentin etwas.	The professor asks the student something.

When only one noun or noun phrase shows case, it may be difficult at first to distinguish meaning. In the example above, **der Professor** has to be the subject, since the definite article **der** clearly shows nominative case. By the process of elimination, therefore, **die Studentin** has to be the direct object.

Die Frau fragt **das** Mädchen etwas.

Sometimes neither noun contains a signal for case. In an example like the one above, one would usually assume normal word order: *The woman asks the girl something.* Depending on context, however, it is possible to interpret it as inverted word order: *It's **the woman** the girl is asking something.*

J   Das Subjekt?   Identify the subject of the sentences below; then give their English equivalents.

▶   Das Mädchen findet der Junge nett.   *der Junge* / It's *the girl* the boy finds nice.

1. Den Kuchen kauft die Frau morgen.
2. Der Mann kocht den Kaffee.
3. Den Mann hört die Frau aber nicht.
4. Der Junge fragt das Mädchen etwas.
5. Den Kuchen essen die Kinder gern.
6. Die Amerikaner kennt die Frau nicht.
7. Das Mädchen kennt die Frau gut.

7   Demonstrative pronouns in the accusative case

Wie findest du **den** Kaffee?   **Den** finde ich gut.
Wie findest du **das** Fleisch?   **Das** finde ich gut.
Wie findest du **die** Wurst?   **Die** finde ich gut.
Wie findest du **die** Eier?   **Die** finde ich gut.

The accusative forms of the demonstrative pronouns are identical to the accusative forms of the definite articles.

K   Nein, das finde ich nicht.   You and Gabi are shopping in a department store. Disagree with all of her opinions.

▶   Ich finde das Musikheft billig. Du auch?   *Nein, das finde ich nicht billig.*

1. Ich finde das Buch über Schach schlecht. Du auch?
2. Ich finde die Buchhandlung zu klein. Du auch?
3. Ich finde den Kugelschreiber billig. Du auch?
4. Ich finde die Lampe schön. Du auch?
5. Ich finde das Radio gut. Du auch?
6. Ich finde den Tisch richtig fürs Zimmer. Du auch?
7. Ich finde die Stühle furchtbar. Du auch?
8. Ich finde die Uhr zu groß. Du auch?

Sie haben das Wort

You run a small store. A customer has come to you with a shopping list. Unfortunately, your store doesn't carry these items. Send her/him to the appropriate store. You may want to refer to the Supplementary Word Sets on page R-25 for names of specialty shops.

Gesprächspartner/in		*Sie*		
Ich brauche	**Kaffee.**	Kaufe	**den**	**bei Müller!**
die	Butter	Kaufen Sie	die	im Supermarkt!
der	Käse		das	beim Metzger!
die	Wurst			beim Bäcker!
das	Brot			im Kaufhaus!
der	Tee			
das	Papier			

8   Accusative of *wer?*

Nominative	Accusative
Wer fragt?	**Wen** fragt sie?

The accusative case form of the interrogative pronoun **wer?** (*who?*) is **wen?** (*whom?*).

L   **Wen?**   You keep missing the ends of people's statements at a party. Ask whom they are talking about. Replace the direct object with **wen?** to pose your questions.

▶   Ich frage den Professor morgen.   *Wen fragst du morgen?*

1.   Thomas fragt Birgit heute abend.
2.   Detlev hat Martina gern.
3.   Martina findet Detlev doof.
4.   Martina hat Wim gern.
5.   Ich finde Stefan intelligent.
6.   Ich habe Lotte gern.
7.   Ich frage Professor Ulmer morgen.
8.   Ulrike kennt die Amerikaner gut.

M   **Wie sagt man das?**   Give the German equivalents of the sentences below.

▶   Where are you buying the fish?   *Wo kaufst du den Fisch?*

1.   We're cooking the fish this evening.
2.   Do you like [to eat] cake?
3.   How do you find the cheese? Good?

4. Give Mrs. Schneider the coffee, Michael.
5. Who's paying [for] everything?
6. Whom are you asking?
7. Who is buying the wine?
   —That [is what] I'm buying.

9 Accusative of *ein* and *kein*

	Nominative	Accusative
Masculine	Wo ist **ein** Bleistift?	Haben Sie **einen** Bleistift?
	Da ist **kein** Bleistift	Ich habe **keinen** Bleistift.
Neuter	Wo ist **ein** Heft?	Haben Sie **ein** Heft?
	Da ist **kein** Heft.	Ich habe **kein** Heft.
Feminine	Wo ist **eine** Uhr?	Haben Sie **eine** Uhr?
	Da ist **keine** Uhr.	Ich habe **keine** Uhr.
Plural	Sind das **Kulis**?	Haben Sie **Kulis**?
	Da sind keine **Kulis**.	Ich habe keine **Kulis**.

The indefinite article **ein** and the negative **kein** change to **einen** and **keinen** before masculine nouns in the accusative singular. The neuter and feminine indefinite articles and their corresponding negatives do not show case changes in the accusative singular. **Ein** has no plural forms. **Kein**, however, does have a plural form: **keine.**

N   Was brauchst du?   You're moving into an apartment with two other students. Tell your friends what you need in the way of furniture and study supplies. Use **ein** with the direct object.

▶   ein Tisch   *Ich brauche einen Tisch.*

1. ein Stuhl
2. eine Lampe
3. ein Bett
4. eine Uhr
5. ein Radio
6. ein Heft
7. ein Kugelschreiber
8. eine Büchertasche

O   Nein, das brauche ich nicht.   You have changed your mind and decided you don't need what your friends suggest. Repeat Ex. N using **kein** with the direct object.

▶   ein Tisch   *Ich brauche keinen Tisch.*

Sie haben das Wort

Have a partner tell you what her/his room has in it. Then report to the class.

Describing one's room

Gesprächspartner/in	*Sie*
Mein Zimmer hat [einen Tisch und zwei Stühle].	Ihr/Sein Zimmer hat [einen Tisch und zwei Stühle].

10   Accusative of possessive adjectives

	Nominative	Accusative
Masculine	Ist das **mein** Bleistift?	Ja, ich habe **deinen** Bleistift.
Neuter	Ist das **mein** Heft?	Ja, ich habe **dein** Heft.
Feminine	Ist das **meine** Uhr?	Ja, ich habe **deine** Uhr.
Plural	Sind das **meine** Kulis?	Ja, ich habe **deine** Kulis.

The possessive adjectives (**mein, dein, sein, ihr, unser, euer, Ihr**) have the same endings as the indefinite article **ein** in both the nominative and accusative cases.

P   Wie, bitte?   Restate, using the cued possessive adjective. The possessive adjective modifies the direct object.

▶   *Freitags bekomme ich Geld. (mein)*   *Freitags bekomme ich mein Geld.*

1. Brauchst du einen Kuli? (dein)
2. Er findet die Arbeit furchtbar. (sein)
3. Frank gibt Anja ein Radio. (sein)
4. Gabi gibt Andreas ein Buch. (ihr)
5. Die Studenten fragen den Professor viel. (ihr)
6. Wir sehen die Freunde oft und gern. (unser)
7. Habt ihr den Garten gern? (euer)
8. Warum ißt du den Kuchen nicht? (dein)

11   The construction *gern + haben*

Ich **habe** Inge **gern**.	I like Inge.
Ich **habe** Mark **nicht gern**.	I don't like Mark.

A common way of expressing fondness for someone in German is to use **gern + haben. Nicht gern** is used to express dislike.

Q   Wen hast du gern?   Say who likes whom, using the cues given below.

▶   Erik / Gabi   *Erik hat Gabi gern.*

1.   ich / Andrea
2.   Herr Müller / Frau Wagner
3.   wir / die Leute hier

4.   du / Bernd / ?
5.   ihr / euer Professor
6.   wir / unser Bäcker

For many people in the German-speaking countries, shopping is an integrated part of daily life. Going shopping several times a week and walking to a store are very common. Although most food shopping is done in supermarkets, specialty stores (*Fachgeschäfte*) like the bakery, butcher shop, or fruit and vegetable store are still frequently patronized. Some customers enjoy the more personal atmosphere and the convenient location of these neighborhood stores, where they are often known and greeted by name.

By law, stores may be open only from 7:00 A.M. to 6:30 P.M., Monday through Friday. Neighborhood stores often close during the early afternoon, from about 1:00 to 3:00. Stores close no later than 2:00 P.M. on Saturday, except for the first Saturday of each month *(langer Samstag)* and the four Saturdays before Christmas; then they may stay open

until 6:00 P.M. On Sundays, stores are closed. Exceptions are made for flower shops (*Blumenläden*), which may open on Sunday morning, and bakery cafés (*Konditoreien*), which often open for a few hours in the afternoon.

Beim Metzger ist es persönlicher.

12   Impersonal expression *es gibt*

Gibt es hier denn keinen Supermarkt?

Isn't there a supermarket here?

Es gibt heute Butterkuchen.

There's [We're having] butter cake today.

Es gibt is equivalent to English *there is* or *there are*. It is followed by the accusative case.

R   Was gibt's?   Form sentences, using the cues below.

▶   es / geben / heute / kein Kuchen   *Es gibt heute keinen Kuchen.*

1.   es / geben / auch / kein Kaffee
2.   geben / es / noch / Brötchen / ?
3.   nein, es / geben / keine Brötchen
4.   es / geben / heute / bestimmt / Schnee
5.   nein, es / geben / kein Schnee
6.   es / geben / aber / Regen

13   Accusative prepositions

durch	through	Sie geht **durch** die Buchhandlung.
für	for	Sie kauft es **für** das Haus.
gegen	against	Sie hat nichts **gegen** den Mann.
ohne	without	Sie geht **ohne** das Kind.
um	around	Sie geht **um** den Tisch.

The prepositions **durch, für, gegen, ohne,** and **um** are always followed by the accusative case.

Er geht **durchs** Zimmer.	durch das = **durchs**
Er kauft es **fürs** Haus.	für das = **fürs**
Er geht **ums** Haus.	um das = **ums**

The prepositions **durch, für,** and **um** often contract with the definite article **das** to form **durchs, fürs,** and **ums.**

S   Etwas anderes.   Substitute the cued words for the italicized words in the sentences below. Make any other necessary changes.

▶   Ursel geht durch die *Buchhandlung.* (Supermarkt)   *Ursel geht durch den Supermarkt.*

1. Walter geht durch das *Zimmer.* (Stadt)
2. Volker sagt etwas gegen die *Frau.* (Mann)
3. Trudi kauft es für *Frau Hof.* (Kind)
4. Wir gehen um die *Stadt.* (Haus)
5. Susanne geht ohne *Frau Wagner.* (Kinder)

14   Accusative of masculine N-nouns

Nominative	Accusative
Der Herr sagt etwas.	Hören Sie **den** Her**rn**?
Der Student sagt etwas.	Hören Sie **den** Student**en**?

German has a class of masculine nouns that have signals for case. Not only the article, but the noun itself ends in **-n** or **-en** in the accusative. This class of nouns may be referred to as masculine N-nouns or "weak nouns." In the vocabularies of this book, masculine N-nouns will be followed by two endings: **der Herr, -n, -en.** The first ending is the singular accusative and the second is the plural ending. The masculine N-nouns you know so far are **der Herr, der Junge, der Mensch, der Nachbar,** and **der Student.**

T   Wie sagt man das?   Give the German equivalents of the conversational exchanges below.

1. Do you like the gentleman there, Mr. Kluge?
   —Yes. He's a neighbor.
2. Why is the neighbor going around the house?
   —Ask Mr. Heidemann.
3. Why is Mr. Leber coming without the children?
   —He's buying books for the children.
4. I have nothing against Mr. Knecht.
   —Who's Mr. Knecht?
5. The boy is going through the city.
   —Do you know the boy, Mrs. Wagner?
6. The professor knows the student well, doesn't he?
   —Yes, and the student knows the professor well.

15   Accusative of personal pronouns

Nominative		Accusative	
Subject	**Object**	**Subject**	**Object**
Er braucht	**mich.**	**He** needs	**me.**
Ich brauche	**ihn.**	**I** need	**him.**

Pronouns used as direct objects are in the accusative case.

Subject pronouns	I	you	he	she	it	we	you	they
Object pronouns	me	you	him	her	it	us	you	them

Some English pronouns have different forms when used as subject or as object.

Nominative	ich	du	er	es	sie	wir	ihr	sie	Sie
Accusative	mich	dich	ihn	es	sie	uns	euch	sie	Sie

Some German pronouns also have different forms in the nominative and accusative.

U   Nein danke!   Mark wants to lend you all his things. Say you don't need them. Use a pronoun in each answer.

▶   Brauchst du mein Buch über Schach?   *Nein, danke, ich brauche es nicht.*

1.   Brauchst du meinen Fußball?
2.   Brauchst du mein Musikheft?
3.   Brauchst du meinen Kugelschreiber?
4.   Brauchst du meine Lampe?
5.   Brauchst du meine Stühle?
6.   Brauchst du meinen Tisch?

V   Wie sagt man das?   Give the German equivalents of the conversational exchanges below.

1.   Who is working for us?
     —We're working for you.
2.   Are you asking me?
     —Yes, I'm asking you.
3.   What do you have against me?
     —I have nothing against you, Frau Neumann.
4.   Do you know Uwe and Barbara?
     —Yes. I like them.

| Wiederholung

A   Noch einmal (Once more)   Restate the sentences below, beginning with the words in italics. Make the necessary changes in word order.

▶   Andrea und Monika essen   *Zum Frühstück essen Andrea und*
     Brötchen *zum Frühstück.*   *Monika Brötchen.*

1.   Monika geht *heute morgen* einkaufen.
2.   Viele Leute gehen *jetzt* in den Supermarkt.
3.   Es ist aber *im Supermarkt* nicht so persönlich.
4.   Monika kauft *den Kaffee* ungemahlen.
5.   Sie geht *dann* auf den Blumenmarkt.
6.   Sie bekommt *für wenig Geld* einen schönen Strauß Blumen.

B   Machen Sie Sätze!   Form sentences, using the cues below.

▶   heute / es / geben / kein Kuchen   *Heute gibt es keinen Kuchen.*

1.   du / essen / kein Fisch / ?
2.   du / nehmen / der Käse / ?
3.   Frank / geben / Ingrid / der Kaffee
4.   was / du / bekommen / zum Frühstück / ?
5.   wie / du / finden / der Wein / ?
6.   Margot / kaufen / Obst / für / die Kinder
7.   warum / du / bezahlen / alles / für / die Jungen / ?
8.   was / du / haben / gegen / der Junge / ?

C   Wie sagt man das?   Give the German equivalents of the conversational exchanges below.

1.   Who's going shopping today?
     —Ask Mr. Braun, Inge.
2.   Erika, give Thomas the coffee.
     —I don't have any coffee.
3.   I'm not buying the table.
     —Why not?
     —It's too small.
4.   Whom do you know here, Ingrid?
     —I know Mr. Leber.
5.   Are there supermarkets in Germany?
     —Of course. Why do you ask, Michael?

D Doch, Helga. Helga is making a number of incorrect assumptions. Correct her, using **doch** in each of your responses.

▶ Gehst du heute nicht einkaufen? *Doch. Ich gehe heute einkaufen.*

1. Kaufst du kein Obst?
2. Ißt du heute kein Brot zum Frühstück?
3. Arbeitest du heute nicht?
4. Gehst du nicht ins Kino?
5. Du glaubst das nicht.
6. Das ist nicht richtig.

E Nicht oder kein? Answer in the negative, using **nicht** or a form of **kein**.

▶ Kauft Erika heute Kartoffeln? *Nein, sie kauft heute keine Kartoffeln.*

1. Kauft sie das Fleisch im Supermarkt?
2. Geht sie heute zum Bäcker?
3. Kauft sie Kuchen?
4. Kauft Gerd heute Käse?
5. Kauft er das Brot beim Bäcker?
6. Kauft er heute Milch?
7. Gibt es hier einen Supermarkt?

F Ingrid hat viele Fragen. Your German friend Ingrid is visiting you. She has a number of questions. Use one of the responses supplied or provide your own to answer those questions (listed below).

Wirklich? □ Heute morgen. □ Morgen. □ Warum fragst du? □ Kauf es bei Müller! □ Sonst noch etwas? □ Ja, was brauchst du denn? □ Jetzt. □ Ich glaube ja. □ Vielleicht. □ Wir haben keine Butter mehr.

1. Gibt es hier eine Apotheke?
2. Was brauchst du denn?
3. Wann gehst du einkaufen?
4. Machst du morgen Spaghetti?
5. Wir haben kein Brot mehr.
6. Wir brauchen Butter.
7. Was machst du jetzt?

G Wie sagt man das? Give the German equivalents of the conversational exchanges below.

1. What color are the flowers?
    —They're red and white.
2. How are you, Mrs. Driesbach?
    —I'm fine, thanks.
3. What are you doing tonight, Erika?
    —I'm working.
4. Horrible weather today, isn't it?
    —Yes, the wind is cold. It'll certainly rain again.

H   Anregung

1. You've just returned from Germany. A friend asks you about German shopping customs. Prepare a brief dialogue you might have with your friend in German.
2. Your friend Erik prefers to shop in **Supermärkte**, but Inge prefers **Tante-Emma-Läden**. Write a paragraph in German in which you state your personal preference and your reasons for it.

| Grammatik zum Nachschlagen

Verbs with stem-vowel change e > i (A–C)

essen	
ich esse	wir essen
du **ißt**	ihr eßt
er/es/sie **ißt**	sie essen
Sie essen	

geben	
ich gebe	wir geben
du **gibst**	ihr gebt
er/es/sie **gibt**	sie geben
Sie geben	

nehmen	
ich nehme	wir nehmen
du **nimmst**	ihr nehmt
er/es/sie **nimmt**	sie nehmen
Sie nehmen	

Several verbs with the stem vowel **e** (including **essen, geben, nehmen**) change **e > i** in the **du-** and **er/es/sie-**forms of the present tense.

Word order with expressions of time and place (D)

	Time	Place
Monika geht	heute abend	ins Kino.
Robert war	gestern	nicht hier.

In German, place expressions generally follow time expressions.

The imperative forms (E–H)

	Infinitive	Imperative	Present
du	sagen	**Sag(e)** etwas bitte!	Sagst du etwas?
ihr		**Sagt** etwas bitte!	Sagt ihr etwas?
Sie		**Sagen Sie** etwas bitte!	Sagen Sie etwas?
du	nehmen	**Nimm** das Brot bitte!	Nimmst du das Brot?
ihr		**Nehmt** das Brot bitte!	Nehmt ihr das Brot?
Sie		**Nehmen Sie** das Brot bitte!	Nehmen Sie das Brot?

In German there are three imperative forms, corresponding to the **du-, ihr-,** and **Sie**-forms of address.

1. The **du**-imperative consists of the stem of a verb plus **-e,** but the **-e** is often dropped in informal usage. If the stem of the verb ends in **-d** or **-t,** the **-e** may not be omitted in written German: **arbeite!** If the stem vowel of a verb changes from **e** to **i,** the imperative has the same vowel change and never has the final **-e.**
2. The **ihr**-imperative is identical with the **ihr**-form of the present tense.
3. The **Sie**-imperative is identical with the **Sie**-form of the present tense. The pronoun **Sie** is always stated and follows the verb immediately.

- *Imperative of **sein** (H)*

du	**Sei** nicht so doof!
ihr	**Seid** ruhig!
Sie	**Seien Sie** so gut!

Direct object vs. predicate noun

Predicate noun	Der Junge ist [heißt] **Dieter Müller.**	The boy is Dieter Müller.
Direct object	Ich kenne **den Jungen** gut.	I know the boy well.

The predicate noun designates a person, concept, or thing that is equated with the subject. A predicate noun completes the meaning of linking verbs such as **sein** and **heißen** and is in the nominative.

   The direct object is the noun or pronoun that receives or is related to the action of the verb. The direct object noun or pronoun is in the accusative case.

Predicate noun	Das ist **nicht** Gisela Meier.
Direct object	Ich kenne Gisela Meier **nicht.**

Nicht precedes a predicate noun and usually follows a noun or pronoun used as a direct object.

Accusative case of nouns   (I, M)

Nominative	
Subject	**Der Kuchen** ist frisch. **Die Uhr** ist schön.

Accusative	
Direct Object	Er nimmt **den Kuchen.** Sie kauft **die Uhr.**

A noun that is used as a direct object of a verb is in the accusative case.

Accusative case of masculine *N*-nouns   (S)

Nominative	Accusative
Der Junge sagt etwas.	Hören Sie **den** Jung**en?**
Der Student sagt etwas.	Hören Sie **den** Student**en?**

A number of masculine nouns add **-n** or **-en** in the accusative singular. The masculine N-nouns you know so far are: **der Herr, der Junge, der Mensch, der Nachbar,** and **der Student.**

Accusative case of the definite articles *der, das, die* (I–J, M)

Nominative	Accusative
Der Käse ist frisch.	Nehmen Sie **den** Käse!
Das Brot ist frisch.	Nehmen Sie **das** Brot!
Die Butter ist frisch.	Nehmen Sie **die** Butter!
Die Eier sind frisch.	Nehmen Sie **die** Eier!

Accusative case of demonstrative pronouns   (K, M)

Accusative nouns	Accusative pronouns
Ich finde den Käse gut.	**Den** finde ich auch gut.
Ich finde das Brot trocken.	**Das** finde ich auch trocken.
Ich finde die Butter frisch.	**Die** finde ich auch frisch.
Ich finde die Eier schlecht.	**Die** finde ich auch schlecht.

Accusative case of *wer* (L, M)

Nominative	Accusative
Wer fragt?	**Wen** fragt er?

Accusative of *ein, kein,* and possessive adjectives (N, O)

Nominative	Accusative
Wo ist **ein** Bleistift?	Haben Sie **einen** Bleistift?
Da ist **kein** Bleistift.	Ich habe **keinen** Bleistift.
Ist das **dein** Bleistift?	Habe ich **deinen** Bleistift?
Wo ist **ein** Heft?	Haben Sie **ein** Heft?
Da ist **kein** Heft.	Ich habe **kein** Heft.
Ist das **dein** Heft?	Habe ich **dein** Heft?
Wo ist **eine** Uhr?	Haben Sie **eine** Uhr?
Da ist **keine** Uhr.	Ich habe **keine** Uhr.
Ist das **deine** Uhr?	Habe ich **deine** Uhr?
Sind das Kulis?	Haben Sie Kulis?
Das sind **keine** Kulis.	Ich habe **keine** Kulis.
Sind das **deine** Kulis?	Habe ich **deine** Kulis?

The indefinite article **ein** and the negative **kein** change to **einen** and **keinen** before masculine nouns in the accusative case. Possessive adjectives (**mein, dein, sein, ihr, unser, euer, Ihr**) have the same endings as the indefinite article **ein**.

Accusative case of personal pronouns (T, U)

Nominative	ich	du	er	es	sie	wir	ihr	sie	Sie
Accusative	mich	dich	ihn	es	sie	uns	euch	sie	Sie

Note that **es, sie,** and **Sie** are the same in nominative and accusative.

Prepositions with the accusative case   (R, S, U)

durch	through	Sie geht **durch** das Zimmer. [durchs Zimmer]
für	for	Sie kauft die Uhr **für** das Haus. [fürs Haus]
gegen	against	Sie hat nichts **gegen** den Mann.
ohne	without	Sie geht **ohne** Herrn Bauer.
um	around	Sie geht **um** das Haus. [ums Haus]

The prepositions **durch, für, gegen, ohne,** and **um** are always followed by the accusative case. **Durch, für,** and **um** often contract with the definite article **das** to form **durchs, fürs,** and **ums.**

Impersonal expression *es gibt* (Q)

Es gibt keinen Kaffee mehr.   There is no more coffee.
Gibt es auch keine Brötchen?   Aren't there any rolls, either?

Es gibt is equivalent to English *there is* or *there are.* It is followed by the accusative case.

The construction *gern haben* (P)

Hast du Lore **gern?**   Do you like Lore?
Ich **habe** sie nicht **gern.**   I don't like her.

A common way of expressing fondness for someone in German is to use **gern + haben. Nicht gern** is used to express dislike.

Kapitel 4

Lernziele

Sprechakte

Borrowing and lending things
Making excuses
Negotiating with a friend about what to do together
Talking about student life and personal interests
Describing one's family, nationality, and profession
Inquiring about abilities and preferences
Describing possibilities and probabilities
Discussing duties and requirements

Grammatik

werden
Verbs with stem-vowel change **e** > **ie**
wissen and **kennen**
der-words
Modal auxiliaries
Separable-prefix verbs

Vokabeln

The adverbs **erst** and **nur**
Family members
Nationalities and professions
Understanding the flavoring particle **eben**

Landeskunde

The playwright Bertolt Brecht
The university system in German-speaking countries

Studenten arbeiten zusammen ihre Notizen durch.

| Bausteine für Gespräche

Notizen für die Klausur

Andreas: Hallo, Michael. Kannst du mir bitte deine Notizen leihen?

Michael: Ja, gern.

Andreas: Das ist nett. Für die Klausur muß ich noch viel lernen.

Michael: Klar, hier hast du sie. Kannst du die morgen wieder mitbringen?

Notes for the test

Hi, Michael. Can you please lend me your notes?

Yes, glad to.

That's nice [of you]. I still have to learn a lot for this test.

Of course, here they are. Can you bring them back tomorrow?

Ist das dein Hauptfach?

Ursel: Grüß dich. Seit wann gehst du denn in die Brecht-Vorlesung? Ich denke, du studierst Geschichte?

Sabine: Nicht mehr. Ich mache jetzt Germanistik.

Ursel: Als Nebenfach?

Sabine: Nein, als Hauptfach.

Ursel: Möchtest du nachher Kaffee trinken gehen?

Sabine: Ich kann leider nicht. Ich muß einen Artikel über Böll lesen. Ich bereite ein Referat für mein Seminar vor.

Is that your major?

Hi! Since when have you been going to the Brecht course? I thought you were studying history.

Not anymore. I'm taking German now.

As a minor?

No, as my major.

Would you like to go out for coffee afterwards?

Unfortunately I can't. I have to read an article on Böll. I'm preparing an oral report for my seminar.

Fragen

1. Warum will Andreas Michaels Notizen leihen?
2. Warum muß Andreas noch viel lernen?
3. Wann soll Andreas die Notizen wieder mitbringen?
4. Warum geht Sabine jetzt in die Brecht-Vorlesung?
5. Was ist Sabines Hauptfach?
6. Was will Ursel hinterher machen?
7. Warum kann Sabine nicht mitgehen?

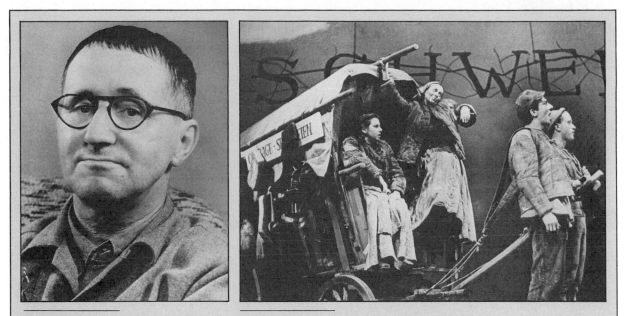

Bertolt Brecht

Eine Szene aus Mutter Courage und ihre Kinder

Bertolt Brecht (1898–1956) is one of the most important figures of the twentieth-century theater. His dramatic theories have influenced many playwrights and theater directors throughout the world. As a young playwright during the twenties, Brecht took the German theater by storm with "The Threepenny Opera" *(Die Dreigroschenoper)*; it shocked and fascinated audiences with its depiction of London's criminal underworld, and the social and political forces underlying it. Brecht's critical focus on society and his dramatic theories revolutionized the German stage and made him a celebrity.

As an outspoken opponent of National Socialism, however, Bertolt Brecht had to flee Germany in 1933. He lived temporarily in several European countries until he settled down in California. Like many other German emigrants, he found refuge in the United States until the end of World War II and the end of the National Socialist regime. Brecht wrote some of his major plays in exile: *Mutter Courage und ihre Kinder* (1941), *Der gute Mensch von Sezuan* (1942), *Leben des Galilei* (1943).

In 1947, after he had been called before the House Committee on Un-American Activities, he moved back to Europe and eventually chose the German Democratic Republic as his home. With his wife Helene Weigel, he founded the *Berliner Ensemble*, a theater in East Berlin that continues to perform Brecht's plays and tries to put his theories into practice.

Sie haben das Wort

A   Leihen   Try to borrow something from a fellow student. She/he responds with *yes* or *no*. Then, out of curiosity, she/he asks why you want the item you requested. You may use the questions and responses provided or make up your own. When you have finished, ask another student.

Borrowing objects/
lending objects

Sie

Kannst du mir	**deine Notizen** leihen?	*Gesprächspartner/in*
	dein Referat	Ja, gern.
	deine Seminararbeit°	Klar.
	deinen Kugelschreiber	Natürlich.
	deinen Bleistift	Ja, ich bringe ihn [es/sie] mit.
		Geht leider nicht. Ich brauche den [das/die] selbst.
		Tut mir leid.

Gesprächspartner/in

Warum brauchst du	**meine Notizen** denn?	*Sie*			
Warum brauchst du	sie	Ich muß	noch	viel	lernen.
	es			etwas	vorbereiten.
	ihn				arbeiten.
				eine Klausur schreiben.	

B   Hauptfach, Nebenfach   Interview four students. Find out their major and minor subjects; then ask what they like to read. You may want to refer to the Supplementary Word Set on page R-26 to find the names of other academic disciplines.

Discussing college
majors and minors

Sie

Was ist dein	Hauptfach?	*Gesprächspartner/in*	
	Nebenfach	Ich studiere	**Germanistik.**
			Anglistik
		Mein **Nebenfach** ist	Psychologie.
		Hauptfach	Philosophie.
			Chemie.
			Physik.
			Mathematik.
			Deutsch.
			Englisch.
Was liest° du gern?		Artikel über	[Sport/Musik/Schach].
		Bücher über	[Psychologie].

The university system in Germany, Switzerland, and Austria is different from that in the United States. Because students are expected to have gained a good general education in high school (*Gymnasium*), they concentrate on one major field at the university. The German university system does not have an equivalent to a Bachelor's degree. In the arts and humanities, students usually take one major and two minor subjects, or two majors, and complete their studies with a Master of Arts (*Magister*). In natural and social sciences, students earn a diploma (*Diplom*), which is equivalent to the M.A. If students intend to become teachers, lawyers, or medical doctors, they finish with state certification after passing a special examination (*Staatsexamen*). The Ph.D. (*Doktor*) is an advanced degree that requires a *Dissertation*. *Professor* is an advanced academic title, which requires writing a postdoctoral thesis (*Habilitationsschrift*).

Students take only a few required courses with exams at the end of each year. They are responsible for their own progress. At the beginning of the semester they choose classes according to type and subject matter. A *Vorlesung* is a lecture with little discussion and no exams. An *Übung* is an exercise class with an extensive test (a *Klausur*) at the end. In a *Seminar*, students write papers and discuss the material. They have to write term papers (*Seminararbeiten* or *Hausarbeiten*) as well.

After the successful completion of a *Seminar* or *Übung*, students receive a certificate (*Schein*), which includes a grade. A minimum number of *Scheine* is necessary before students may take the intermediate qualifying exam *(Zwischenprüfung)* and a comprehensive exam such as the *Staatsexamen*.

Studenten besprechen ein Referat mit ihrem Professor.

C Es tut mir leid You run into a friend in the library who wants to make plans for later. Respond that you are sorry but you can't. Explain why you are busy.

Making excuses

Gesprächspartner/in		*Sie*	
Willst du nachher	**Kaffee trinken** gehen? einkaufen schwimmen ins Kino	Ich kann nicht. Ich	**bereite mein Referat vor.** schreibe meine Seminararbeit. lerne für die Klausur. lese einen Artikel über Böll. mache heute abend Deutsch. muß wieder in die Bibliothek°.
Was [müssen/können/sollen] wir heute abend machen?		Wir müssen Wir sollen Wir können	unser Referat vorbereiten, nicht? **unsere Notizen** durcharbeiten°. die letzte° Vorlesung Deutsch machen.

Vokabeln

— Substantive —

die **Anglistik** English studies (language and literature)
die **Arbeit, -en** work; paper
der **Artikel, -** article
die **Bibliothek, -en** library
die **Chemie** chemistry
(das) **Englisch** English (language)
die **Germanistik** German studies (language and literature)
die **Geschichte, -n** story; history
das **Hauptfach, ¨er** major (subject)
die **Klausur, -en** test; **eine Klausur schreiben** to take a test

die **Mathematik** mathematics
das **Nebenfach, ¨er** minor (subject)
die **Notiz, -en** note
die **Philosophie, -n** philosophy
die **Physik** physics
die **Psychologie** psychology
das **Referat, -e** report
das **Seminar, -e** seminar
die **Seminararbeit, -en** seminar paper
die **Vorlesung, -en** lecture

— Verben —

bringen to bring
durch·arbeiten to work through; to study
dürfen (darf) to be permitted to, to be allowed to; may
können (kann) to be able to; can
leihen to lend; to borrow
lernen to learn; to study
lesen (liest) to read
mit·bringen to bring along

möchten (*subjunctive of* **mögen**) would like
müssen (muß) to have to; must
schreiben to write
sollen (soll) to be supposed to
studieren to study; to go to college
trinken to drink
vor·bereiten to prepare
wollen (will) to want to, intend to

— Andere Wörter ————————————————————————

klar   clear; of course, naturally   **nachher**   afterwards
letzt   last   **seit**   since

— Besondere Ausdrücke ————————————————————

Deutsch machen   to do/study   **seit wann**   since when, how long
   German (*as homework*)

I Studenten in der Bundesrepublik ————————

Vorbereitung auf das Lesen

• *Zum Thema*

A German asks you to give her/him some idea of what life as a student in a college or university in this country is like. List the things that seem to you to be characteristic.

• *Leitfragen*

1. Wenn man studieren will, braucht man Geld. Was kostet viel, wenig, nichts? Wie bekommen Studenten Geld?

2. Es gibt nicht genug Studienplätze in der Bundesrepublik. Wie reguliert man die Studentenzahlen?

    Stichworte: Abitur □ Numerus clausus □ Zensuren □ Regelstudienzeit

3. Der amerikanische Student hat zwei Hauptfächer und macht außerdem Englisch und Mathematik. Warum macht er Englisch und Mathematik?

4. In der Bundesrepublik gibt es fast nur Staatsuniversitäten. Warum findet die deutsche Studentin das gut?

5. Wo gibt es mehr Examen, an deutschen oder amerikanischen Universitäten?

David ist Amerikaner. Er macht eine Reise durch die Bundesrepublik und sieht auch einige Universitätsstädte an. Da sieht er immer° wieder Parolen° wie°

   HER MIT BAFÖG°!

5   WEG MIT DEM N.C.°!

   WIR WOLLEN KEINE REGELSTUDIENZEIT°!

immer wieder: *again and again*

slogans / such as
Give us BAFöG!

Down with N.C.!

limits on time spent at the university

In einer Studentenkneipe kann man sitzen und sich unterhalten.

Er denkt: BAFöG? Was ist denn das? Was ist N.C.? Was ist Regelstudienzeit?

    In einem Café in Hamburg lernt David eine junge Frau kennen. Sie ist
10 Studentin und heißt Nicole. Die fragt er: „Was ist das alles — BAFöG, Regelstudienzeit, N.C.?" Nicole erklärt: „Also mit BAFöG ist das so: Wir bekommen Geld vom° Staat, aber nur ein Darlehen°. Später sollen wir das ganze Geld zurückzahlen°. Das möchten wir natürlich nicht. Viele Studenten glauben, daß wir ein Recht° auf° dieses Geld haben." David
15 kann das nicht verstehen: „Ja arbeitet ihr denn nicht auf dem Campus — im Studentenheim, zum Beispiel?"

Nicole: Nein, an° unseren Unis gibt es wenige Studentenjobs. Und einen anderen Job findet man auch nur schwer.

David: Aber ihr bezahlt doch keine Studiengebühren°.

20 *Nicole:* Natürlich nicht, aber Wohnen° und Essen° sind teuer. Viele Studenten hier haben keine reichen Eltern. Wir brauchen das Geld vom° Staat. Nur so kann jeder studieren. Das ist Chancengleichheit°.

David: Aber will dann nicht jeder studieren?

Nicole: Vielleicht. Wie du weißt, muß man Abitur haben. Aber es gibt
25 immer noch zuviel Studenten. Daher haben viele Fächer N.C., den Numerus clausus°. Das heißt°, nur mit sehr guten Zensuren im Gymnasium bekommt man da einen Studienplatz°. Und Glück muß man auch haben.

    David bestellt noch einen Kaffee. Er sieht Nicole an und sagt: „Es gibt also
30 zuviel Studenten, nicht?"

from the / loan

pay back

right / to

at

tuition

room / board

from the / equal opportunity

closed number (Latin) / **das heißt:** *that is*
bekommt ... Studienplatz: *does one get admitted*

Nicole: Genau. Daher gibt's die Regelstudienzeit. Die meisten Studenten müssen in acht Semestern fertig sein. So wird Platz frei für neue Studenten. Ich muß auch in acht Semestern fertig werden.

David: Was studierst du denn?

35 *Nicole:* Politik° und Geschichte. Und du? political science

David: Wirtschaftswissenschaft° und Deutsch. Aber ich bin erst im economics
zweiten° Semester und muß noch Kurse nehmen in Englisch, Mathe second
und Geschichte, zum Beispiel.

Nicole: Warum das denn?

40 *David:* Na, das muß doch jeder. Du nicht? Machst du denn nur deine
beiden Fächer?

Nicole: Ja, natürlich. Deshalb gehe ich doch auf° die Uni. Fremd- auf ... Uni: to college
sprachen° und Mathe usw.°, das machen wir doch in der Schule. foreign languages / usw. (=
David findet das alles sehr interessant. Er hat noch eine Frage: „Ist und so weiter): etc.

45 Hamburg eigentlich eine Privatuniversität oder eine Staatsuniversität?"

Nicole: Natürlich eine Staatsuniversität. Private Unis gibt es hier eigentlich kaum. Das ist bei euch° anders, nicht? bei euch: in your country

David: Aber klar. Wir haben die ganz großen Namen, die Privatuniversitäten. Und es gibt enorme° Unterschiede. enormous

50 *Nicole:* Aber das ist doch unsozial°! socially unjust

David: Vielleicht. Aber einige Privatuniversitäten sind eben sehr gut.
Einige Privatcolleges auch.

Nicole: Das ist ja interessant. In Amerika kann also jeder Mensch eine
Universität aufmachen, wie einen Supermarkt?

55 *David:* Ja, warum denn nicht?

Nicole steht auf: „Du, es tut mir leid, aber ich muß jetzt gehen. Nächste
Woche habe ich meine Zwischenprüfung°. Die ist nicht leicht, und ich qualifying exam
muß noch sehr viel lernen°." study

David: Ja, das kenne ich. Wir haben auch für jeden Kurs ein Examen, und

60 das jedes Semester.

Nicole: Was? Wir haben nur wenige Kurse mit Examen. Dafür° haben instead
wir aber die Zwischenprüfung nach° vier Semestern und dann DAS EX- after
AMEN am Ende.

David: Dann mußt du wirklich gehen und lernen. Viel Glück!

65 David bleibt noch etwas und trinkt seinen Kaffee aus.° Er überlegt°: trinkt ... aus: finishes / reflects
Möchte er wohl° gern in Deutschland studieren? possibly

Fragen zum Lesestück

1. Was für Städte sieht David auf seiner Reise an?
2. Welche Parolen sieht er immer wieder?
3. Wen lernt David in einem Café kennen?
4. Warum weiß er nicht, was N.C. ist?

5. Wer bekommt ein Darlehen vom Staat?
6. Was haben die Studenten gegen Darlehen?
7. Warum arbeiten wenige deutsche Studenten auf dem Campus?
8. Warum brauchen sie Geld vom Staat?
9. Was muß jeder Student natürlich haben?
10. Warum haben viele Fächer N.C.?
11. Wer bekommt einen Studienplatz?
12. Warum gibt es die Regelstudienzeit?
13. In wieviel Semestern muß Nicole fertig werden?
14. Warum muß David Kurse nehmen wie Englisch und Mathe?
15. Wo macht man diese Kurse in der Bundesrepublik?
16. Welche Fächer studiert Nicole?
17. Warum findet Nicole Privatuniversitäten nicht so gut?
18. Warum muß Nicole gehen?
19. Wieviel Prüfungen muß Nicole machen?

Vokabeln

Substantive

das **Abitur**   diploma from college-track high school [**Gymnasium**]
das **Café, -s**   café
die **Eltern** *(pl.)*   parents
das **Ende, -n**   end, conclusion; **am Ende**   at (in) the end
das **Essen, -**   food; meal
das **Examen**   examination
das **Fach, ̈er**   (academic) subject
der **Film, -e**   film
die **Frage, -n**   question
das **Glück**   luck; **Glück haben**   to be lucky; **viel Glück**   good luck
das **Gymnasium** *(pl.* **Gymnasien***)* college-track high school

der **Job, -s**   job
der **Kurs, -e**   course
der **Name** *(acc.* **-n***),* **-n**   name
das **Picknick, -s**   picnic
der **Platz, ̈e**   space; place; seat
die **Prüfung, -en**   examination, test
die **Reise, -n**   trip
die **Schule, -n**   school
das **Semester, -**   semester
das **Studentenheim, -e**   dormitory
die **Universität, -en**   university; die **Uni, -s** *(abbreviation)*
der **Unterschied, -e**   difference
die **Zensur, -en**   grade, grades

Verben

an·sehen (sieht an)   to look at, watch
auf·machen   to open
auf·stehen   to stand up; to get up (out of bed)
bestellen   to order
erklären   to explain
kennen·lernen   to get to know, make the acquaintance of

sehen (sieht)   to see
verstehen   to understand
werden (wird)   to become
wissen (weiß)   to know (*a fact*)
wohnen   to live: to reside
zahlen   to pay

Andere Wörter

beide both; two
daher therefore, for that reason
deshalb therefore, for that reason
dies (-er, -es, -e) this, these
eben just
eigentlich actually
einige some, several
erst only, just
fertig finished; ready
frei free, available
genau exactly; that's right
interessant interesting
jed (-er, -es, -e) each, every; **jeder** everyone

jung young
kaum hardly, scarcely
leicht easy; light
meist- most; **die meisten (Leute)** most of (the people)
na well *(interjection)*
nächst- next
noch ein another, additional
privat private
reich rich
so [ein] such [a]
teuer expensive
zurück back, in return
zuviel too much, too many

Besondere Ausdrücke

du ... (Sie ...) hey, . . . (*used to get someone's attention*)

immer noch still
viel Glück good luck

More than 1.2 million students are enrolled in the Federal Republic's 75 universities and other institutions of higher education and 118 poly-technical colleges. Admission is limited under a system called *Numerus clausus* (*N.C.*) in about 60 percent of subjects. In these disciplines, among which are medicine, law, pharmacy, and psychology, the limited number of admission "spots" (*Studienplätze*) is distributed mainly on the basis of high school grade point average (*Zensuren*) received during the last years of the *Gymnasium* and grades on the final comprehensive examination (the *Abitur*). There can be a waiting period of up to five years for admission in some disciplines.

The national law to provide financial support for students *(Bundesausbildungsförderungsgesetz*, or *BAFöG)* was passed in 1971 to give everyone an equal chance to study at a university. Today approximately 50 percent of all students are subsidized to some extent. The amount of financial support is dependent on parents' in-

come. Since 1983, students have been required to pay back the full amount of the state loan, but they pay no interest. The *Regelstudienzeit*, in effect in some states, requires that students finish their studies within a prescribed number of semesters.

Im Seminar

Erweiterung des Wortschatzes

1   Die Familie

Willi Clausen — Käthe Clausen — Ernst Hoppe — Johanna Hoppe

Hans Pfeiffer — Kersten Clausen-Pfeiffer — Gabriele Clausen-Hoppe — Volker Hoppe

Angelika Pfeiffer — Jürgen Pfeiffer — Regina Hoppe — Jens Hoppe — Tina Hoppe — Jonas Hoppe

die Mutter, ⸚	der Vater, ⸚
= die Eltern *(pl.)*	
die Tochter, ⸚	der Sohn, ⸚e
die Schwester, -n	der Bruder, ⸚
= Geschwister *(pl.)*	
die Tante, -n	der Onkel, -
die Kusine, -n	der Vetter, -n
die Großmutter, ⸚ (die Oma, -s)	der Großvater, ⸚ (der Opa, -s)
= die Großeltern *(pl.)*	

Refer to the Supplementary Word Set on page R-26 for names of additional family members.

Sie haben das Wort

Erzählen Sie über Ihre Familie.   Give a brief account of your family. You
may include answers to the questions below.

> Describing one's
> family

1. Wie heißt Ihre Mutter? Ihr Vater?
2. Haben Sie Schwestern? Brüder? Wieviel? Wie heißen sie? Wie alt sind
    sie?
3. Wie alt sind Ihre Großeltern? Wo wohnen sie?
4. Haben Sie Tanten und Onkel? Wieviel? Wo wohnen sie?
5. Wieviel Kusinen und Vettern haben Sie? Sind sie noch jung?

Eine junge Familie – Mutter, Vater, Sohn und Tochter

2   Nouns indicating nationalities and professions

David ist Kanadier.	David is (a) Canadian.
Brigitte ist Deutsche.	Brigitte is (a) German.
David ist Student.	David is a student.
Brigitte wird Ingenieurin.	Brigitte is going to be an engineer.

To state a person's nationality, profession, or membership in a group, German uses the noun directly after a form of **sein** or **werden**. The indefinite article is not used, whereas in English these nouns are preceded by an indefinite article.

Herr Becker ist **kein** Ingenieur.	Mr. Becker is not an engineer.
Thomas ist **kein** Österreicher; er ist Deutscher.	Thomas isn't (an) Austrian; he's (a) German.

Kein is used to negate a sentence about someone's nationality, profession, or membership in a group.

Refer to the Supplementary Word Set on page R-25 for names of additional professions.

Approximately seventy thousand foreign students are enrolled at universities in the Federal Republic of Germany. Even in the *Numerus clausus* disciplines, some places are reserved for foreigners, who pay no tuition (*Studiengebühren*). Like a German student, a foreigner pays thirty to eighty marks in semester fees plus about fifty marks a month for health insurance. To be admitted for study in the Federal Republic, an American must usually have had two years of college and must pass a language examination.

To study at a Swiss university an American needs a Bachelor's degree and a working knowledge of the language of instruction, which may be German, French, or Italian. Foreigners may not study medicine in Switzerland unless their parents live there.

In einer Freistunde kann man über die Vorlesungen sprechen.

A   Wie sagt man das?

1. David is a Canadian.
2. He is a student.
3. Brigitte is not a Canadian.
4. She is also not an American; she's a German.
5. She is going to be an engineer.
6. Her brother Helmut lives in Frankfurt; he's a Frankfurter.
7. He is a butcher.

Sie haben das Wort

Persönliche Informationen.   Prepare a brief autobiography. Give: Name, Nationalität, Adresse und Telefonnummer, Hauptfach, Nebenfach. Was wollen Sie werden?

> Describing one's nationality and profession

3   The adverbs *erst* and *nur*

Ich bin **erst** im zweiten Semester.	I'm in only my second semester, freshman year.
Uwe kommt **erst** nächste Woche.	Uwe isn't coming until next week.

The adverb **erst** is used most frequently to refer to a specific point in time and is equivalent to *only, only just,* or *not until.*

Uwe bleibt **nur** eine Woche.	Uwe is staying only a week.

The adverb **nur** is used to refer to a numerical quantity and is equivalent to *only* in the sense of *not more than the quantity indicated.*

B   Was bedeutet das?

1. Erst wenn man Abitur hat, kann man studieren.
2. Nur mit sehr guten Zensuren im Gymnasium bekommt man einen Studienplatz.
3. Man braucht Geld vom Staat. Nur so kann jeder studieren.
4. Einen Studentenjob findet man nur schwer.
5. Wir haben ein großes Examen erst am Ende.
6. Man kann erst nach acht Semestern Examen machen.
7. Erst jetzt verstehe ich, was du sagen willst.
8. Inge kommt erst nächsten Samstag.
9. Sie kann aber nur bis Sonntag bleiben.

4   Flavoring particle *eben*

Einige Privatuniversitäten sind **eben** sehr gut.	Some private universities are after all very good.
Du mußt es **eben** machen.	You'll simply have to do it. [No argument, please.]

Eben may be used by a speaker to support or strengthen a previous statement or idea. It can also be used by a speaker in a discussion in a final or closing statement to imply that she/he has no desire or need to discuss the point further.

C   Was bedeutet das?   Pay special attention to the flavoring particle **eben**.

1. Das ist richtig. Dann nimm eben den teuren Wein.
2. Es regnet, und wir müssen eben zu Hause bleiben.
3. Ich kaufe das Buch doch nicht. Fünfzig Mark sind eben zuviel.
4. Du willst nicht mitkommen? Also gut. Dann bleibst du eben hier.
5. Viele Leute gehen heute in den Supermarkt. Da ist es eben billiger.
6. Es ist eben so. Ich muß heute arbeiten.
7. Ich weiß es eben nicht.
8. Herr Lange arbeitet nicht mehr. Er ist eben zu krank.

Ein Spatz in der Hand ist
besser als eine Taube auf dem Dach.

| Übungen zur Aussprache

Review the pronunciation of long and short **a** in the Reference section at the end of the book. Read aloud the words in each column on this page from top to bottom. Then read each set of word pairs across. Check your pronunciation by listening to your instructor or the tape.

long ā	short *a*	short *a*	short *o*
Bahn	Bann	Bann	Bonn
kam	Kamm	Kamm	komm
Staat	Stadt	Matte	Motte
Schlaf	schlaff	knalle	Knolle
lahm	Lamm	falle	volle

Read the following sentences aloud, paying special attention to the way you pronounce long and short **a** and short **o** in the boldfaced words.

1. **Komm doch** mit in die **Stadt!**
2. **Was soll** ich **noch machen?**
3. Der **Abend war aber interessant.**
4. Wer **sagt das?**
5. Mußt du heute **nachmittag noch** viel **arbeiten?**
6. Ich **habe noch** eine **Frage** für **Professor Bachmann.**

| Grammatik und Übungen

1 Present tense of *werden*

werden: to become	
ich werde	wir werden
du **wirst**	ihr werdet
er/es/sie **wird**	sie werden
Sie werden	
du-*imperative*: werde!	

Werden is irregular in the **du**- and **er/es/sie**-forms in the present tense.

A   Sie werden anders.   People are changing. Say how.

▶   Erik / leider / müde   *Erik wird leider müde.*

1. ich / auch / müde
2. Petra / besser / in Mathe
3. die Kinder / groß
4. du / leider / konservativ

5. wir / nervös
6. ihr / sehr / progressiv
7. Hans und Karin / besser / in Deutsch

2   Verbs with stem-vowel change e>ie

sehen: to see	
ich sehe	wir sehen
du **siehst**	ihr seht
er/es/sie **sieht**	sie sehen
Sie sehen	
du-*imperative:* **sieh!**	

lesen: to read	
ich lese	wir lesen
du **liest**	ihr lest
er/es/sie **liest**	sie lesen
Sie lesen	
du-*imperative:* **lies!**	

Several verbs with the stem-vowel **e** change the **e** to **ie** in the **du**- and **er/es/ sie**-forms of the present tense and in the **du**-imperative. Since the stem of **lesen** ends in a sibilant, the **du**-form ending contracts from **-st** to **-t** (see **Kapitel 1**, page 35).

B   Lesen und sehen   Say what kind of films and reading matter the people mentioned below like.

▶   Erik / ernste Filme   *Erik sieht gern ernste Filme.*

1. Ingrid / lustige Filme
2. Gabi und Jürgen / leichte Filme
3. du / Schwarzweißfilme / ?
4. Christine / Bücher / über Sport

5. Detlev / Bücher / über Musik
6. du / Bücher / über Politik / ?
7. ihr / Bücher / über Geschichte / ?

Sie haben das Wort

Filme und Bücher   Interview three students to find out what kinds of movies they like and what they like to read about. Then report back to the class. Refer to the Supplementary Word Set on page R-26 for additional descriptions of film and literature.

Sie	*Gesprächspartner/in*
Was für Filme siehst du gern?	Ich sehe [lustige] Filme gern.
Über was liest du gern?	Ich lese gern über [Musik].

[Bill] sieht [lustige] Filme gern.
[Judy und Jack] lesen gern über [Geschichte].

Talking about personal interests

3   Present tense of *wissen*

wissen: to know	
ich **weiß**	wir wissen
du **weißt**	ihr wißt
er/es/sie **weiß**	sie wissen
Sie wissen	

Wissen is irregular in the singular forms of the present tense. Note that the **du**-form ending contracts from **-st** to **-t**.

C   Ein Picknick   You and your friends are going to drive in different cars to a picnic spot in the country. Inform Klaus that the people mentioned know where the picnic is. Use pronouns in your responses.

▶   Weiß Jutta, wo das Picknick ist?   *Ja, sie weiß es.*
▶   Und Jürgen?   *Ja, er weiß es.*

1. Und Benno?
2. Und du?
3. Und Christine?

4. Und Ulf und Jochen?
5. Und ihr?

4   *Wissen* and *kennen*

Sie **weiß**, wer Professor Schmidt ist.	She knows who Professor Schmidt is.
Sie **kennt** Professor Schmidt gut.	She knows Professor Schmidt well.

The English equivalent of **wissen** and of **kennen** is *to know*. **Wissen** means *to know something as a fact*. **Kennen** means *to be acquainted with a person, place, or thing*.

    Kennen was used as a verb in Middle English and is still used in Scottish. The noun *ken* means perception or understanding: "That is beyond my ken."

D   Kennen oder wissen?   Complete the sentences below with a form of **kennen** or of **wissen**, as appropriate.

▶   _____ du, wo Bonn liegt?   *Weißt du, wo Bonn liegt?*
▶   Dirk _____ die Stadt gut.   *Dirk kennt die Stadt gut.*

1. _____ ihr den Mann da?
2. Ich _____ , wie er heißt.
3. Petra _____ , wo er arbeitet.
4. _____ Sie Professor Reimanns Buch über Musik?
5. Wir _____ nicht viel über Musik.

6. Aber wir _____ Frau Professor Reimann gut.
7. _____ du Heidelberg gut?
8. _____ du, wo die Bibliothek ist?

5 Der-words

Diese Klausur ist schwer.	This test is hard.
Jede Klausur ist schwer.	Every test is hard.
Welche Klausur hast du?	Which test do you have?
Manche Klausuren sind doch leicht.	Some tests are easy.
Solche Klausuren sind nicht interessant.	Such tests aren't interesting.

	Masculine	Neuter	Feminine	Plural
Nominative	dieser	dieses	diese	diese
Accusative	diesen	dieses	diese	diese

The words **dieser, jeder, welcher?, mancher,** and **solcher** are called **der-**words because they follow the same pattern in the nominative and accusative cases as the definite articles. **Jeder** is used in the singular only. **Welcher?** is an interrogative adjective, used at the beginning of a question. **Solcher** and **mancher** are used almost exclusively in the plural.

E   Welcher? Dieser?   You're shopping with a friend who comments on various items. Ask which things she/he is referring to. Use the nominative of **welcher** and **dieser.**

▶   Der Kuli ist teuer.   *Welcher Kuli ist teuer? Dieser hier?*

1. Das Buch über Sport ist interessant.
2. Die Lampe ist schön.
3. Der Stuhl ist zu schwer.
4. Das Radio ist zu teuer.
5. Der Tisch ist zu klein.
6. Die Bleistifte sind billig.
7. Die Hefte sind teuer.

F   Kannst du mir etwas leihen?   A friend needs to borrow a few things for her/his apartment temporarily. Be generous and tell her/him to take them. Use the accusative of **dieser** in your responses.

▶   Kannst du mir einen Kuli leihen?   *Ja. Nimm diesen!*

1. Kannst du mir auch einen Bleistift leihen?
2. Hast du auch ein Heft?
3. Kannst du mir vielleicht eine Lampe leihen?
4. Hast du ein Buch über Schach?
5. Kannst du mir einen Tisch leihen?
6. Du, kannst du mir eine Wanduhr leihen?
7. Hast du noch ein paar Stühle?
8. Hast du vielleicht drei oder vier Poster für mich?

G   Wie finden Sie diese Bilder?   You are showing pictures of Switzerland and Austria to your friends. Restate the questions and comments, using the cued **der**-word in place of the italicized words.

▶   Finden Sie *die* Städte schön? (dieser)   *Finden Sie diese Städte schön?*

1. Kennen Sie *die* Städte schon? (mancher)
2. *Die* Städte möchten Sie kennenlernen? (welcher?)
3. Im Fenster gibt es immer *diese* Blumen. (solcher)
4. Wie heißt *die* Straße? (dieser)
5. *Die* Universitäten sind alt. (dieser)
6. Wie finden Sie *die* Bilder? (dieser)
7. *Das* Bild ist wirklich schön. (jeder)
8. *Die* Bilder möchten Sie haben? (welcher?)

6   Modal auxiliaries

Ich **muß** jetzt arbeiten.	I *have to* work now.
Erika **kann** es machen.	Erika *can* do it.
Du **darfst** nichts sagen.	You *are not allowed* to say anything.

Both English and German have a group of verbs called *modal auxiliaries*. Modal verbs indicate an attitude about an action; they do not express the action itself. In German, the verb that expresses the action is in the infinitive form and is in last position.

  Modals are irregular in the present-tense singular. They lack endings in the **ich-** and **er/es/sie**-forms, and five of the six modals show stem-vowel change, e.g., **können > kann.**

können: can, to be able to	
ich **kann** es erklären	wir **können** es erklären
du **kannst** es erklären	ihr **könnt** es erklären
er/es/sie **kann** es erklären	sie **können** es erklären
Sie **können** es erklären	

H   Wir können es nicht verstehen.   Your class has been assigned an article on a complicated philosophical problem. Say that the following people can't understand the problem, using the verb **können** in your responses.

▶   Mark   *Mark kann den Artikel nicht verstehen.*

1. Astrid
2. ich
3. Katrin und Peter
4. wir
5. Sie
6. du
7. ihr

Sie haben das Wort

Was kannst du?   Find out from four fellow students whether they can do certain activities. Possible responses are provided.

Inquiring about abilities

Sie		*Gesprächspartner/in*
Kannst du	**Fußball** spielen?	Aber natürlich.
	Schach	Klar.
	Tennis	Ganz bestimmt.
Kannst du gut	**schwimmen?**	Leider nicht.
	tanzen	Nein.
		Nein, nicht mehr.

wollen: to want, wish; to intend to	
ich **will** arbeiten	wir **wollen** arbeiten
du **willst** arbeiten	ihr **wollt** arbeiten
er/es/sie **will** arbeiten	sie **wollen** arbeiten
Sie **wollen** arbeiten	

I   Das will ich auch.   Gisela tells you what Renate is going to do. Ask her to confirm that others plan to do the same things. Use a form of **wollen**.

▶   Renate studiert Geschichte. (Sabine)   *Sabine will auch Geschichte studieren, nicht?*

1.   Renate arbeitet jetzt. (Jens und Katja)
2.   Renate spielt nachher Tennis. (du)
3.   Renate hört heute abend Musik. (ihr)
4.   Renate geht einkaufen. (Nicole)
5.   Renate geht Kaffee trinken. (Erik)
6.   Renate geht später schwimmen. (du)

sollen: to be supposed to /SHOULD	
ich **soll** morgen gehen	wir **sollen** morgen gehen
du **sollst** morgen gehen	ihr **sollt** morgen gehen
er/es/sie **soll** morgen gehen	sie **sollen** morgen gehen
Sie **sollen** morgen gehen	

J   So soll es sein.   Say that what is happening is indeed what is supposed to happen. Restate the following sentences, using **sollen**.

▶   Es regnet heute.   *Es soll heute regnen.*

1.   Es schneit heute abend.
2.   Ich lese einen Artikel über Thomas Mann.

3. Volker leiht mir seine Notizen.
4. Wir arbeiten zusammen für die Klausur.
5. Ihr gebt Volker eure Telefonnummer.

Sie haben das Wort

Wie ist das Wetter?   Write down your weather predictions for three days. At the end of the three days, read your predictions to the class.

Describing possibilities and probabilities

▶ *Es soll morgen regnen. Am Mittwoch soll die Sonne scheinen. Am Donnerstag ...*

müssen: must, to have to	
ich **muß** jetzt arbeiten	wir **müssen** jetzt arbeiten
du **mußt** jetzt arbeiten	ihr **müßt** jetzt arbeiten
er/es/sie **muß** jetzt arbeiten	sie **müssen** jetzt arbeiten
Sie **müssen** jetzt arbeiten	

K   Mußt du schon gehen?   The party is breaking up early. Ask whether the various guests really have to go. Use the appropriate form of **müssen.**

▶ du   *Mußt du wirklich schon gehen?*

1. ihr
2. Michael
3. Paula

4. Sie
5. Sonja und Jens
6. wir

Sie haben das Wort

Was mußt du machen?   Write a schedule for the rest of the week showing what you must do. Then ask a fellow student what she/he must do in the next few days. Use a form of the verb **müssen.**

Discussing duties and requirements

Sie	*Gesprächspartner/in*
Ich muß heute arbeiten. Was machst du?	Ich muß heute auch arbeiten.
Ich muß morgen in die Bibliothek. Was machst du morgen?	morgen ein Buch über Politik lesen.

dürfen: may, to be permitted to	
ich **darf** es sagen	wir **dürfen** es sagen
du **darfst** es sagen	ihr **dürft** es sagen
er/es/sie **darf** es sagen	sie **dürfen** es sagen
Sie **dürfen** es sagen	

L   Das darf man nicht.   Some people are better off avoiding certain things; these people simply are not allowed to have them. Restate the sentences below with the verb **dürfen**.

▶   Frau Hofer soll kein Aspirin nehmen.   *Frau Hofer darf kein Aspirin nehmen.*

1.   Ich soll keinen Kuchen essen.
2.   Das Kind soll keine Milch trinken.
3.   Herr Schmidt soll keine Eier essen.
4.   Wir sollen nicht so viel Bier trinken.
5.   Du sollst keinen Kaffee trinken.
6.   Ihr sollt nicht so viel Fleisch essen.

M   Noch nicht.   It takes a while to recover from the flu. Say that the activities mentioned below are not permitted yet.

▶   Warum spielst du nicht Tennis?   *Ich darf noch nicht Tennis spielen.*

1.   Warum gehst du nicht schwimmen?
2.   Warum arbeitet Frau Sperber nicht?
3.   Warum geht Herr Sperber nicht in die Stadt?
4.   Warum spielen die Kinder nicht Fußball?
5.   Warum spielt ihr nicht Volleyball?
6.   Warum geht ihr nicht einkaufen?

7   *Mögen* and the *möchte*-forms

mögen: to like	
ich **mag** keine Tomaten	wir **mögen** Erik nicht
du **magst** keine Eier	ihr **mögt** Inge nicht
er/es/sie **mag** kein Bier	sie **mögen** Schmidts nicht
Sie **mögen** keinen Kaffee	

Mögen Sie Frau Lenz?   Nein, ich **mag** sie nicht.

The modal **mögen** is often used to express a fondness or dislike for someone or something, much like the construction **gern + haben**. With this meaning it usually does not take a dependent infinitive.

N   Was magst du?   You are raising questions about various people's likes and dislikes. Use a form of **mögen**.

▶   du / Fisch   *Magst du Fisch?*

1.   Mark / deutsches Bier
2.   Ilse und Erik / Rockmusik

3. Frank / Shakespeare
4. du / moderne Musik
5. Professor Schneider / Schwarzbrot
6. ihr / Rotwein
7. Herr und Frau Braun / Österreich

[WOULD LIKE TO]

ich **möchte** gehen	wir **möchten** gehen
du **möchtest** gehen	ihr **möchtet** gehen
er/es/sie **möchte** gehen	sie **möchten** gehen
Sie **möchten** gehen	

The **möchte**-forms are subjunctive forms of **mögen** and are equivalent to *would like to*.

O **Ja, das möchten wir.**   It's going to be a busy evening, and everything sounds good to everyone. Say what the people mentioned below would like to do.

► Dirk / ins Kino gehen / heute abend   *Dirk möchte heute abend ins Kino gehen.*

1. wir / einkaufen gehen / heute nachmittag
2. du / arbeiten / mehr
3. ihr / bleiben / bestimmt / hier
4. Gabi / essen / im Café
5. Lotte und Erik / Musik hören
6. ich / lesen / ein interessantes Buch
7. ich / wandern / am Wochenende

Sie haben das Wort

Was möchtet ihr machen?   Ask three fellow students what they would like to do on the weekend. Use a **möchte**-form in each question.

► Was möchtest du am Wochenende machen?   *Ich möchte [einkaufen gehen].*

Inquiring about future preferences

8   Omission of the dependent infinitive with modals

Ich **kann** das nicht.	= Ich **kann** das nicht **machen.**
Ich **muß** in die Bibliothek.	= Ich **muß** in die Bibliothek **gehen.**
Ich **kann** Deutsch.	= Ich **kann** Deutsch **sprechen**°.
Das **darfst** du nicht.	= Das **darfst** du nicht **tun.**

speak

The dependent infinitive is often omitted in sentences with a modal when the meaning of the infinitive is clear from the context.

P   Was bedeutet das?

1.   Wollen Sie jetzt nach Hause?
2.   Ich muß in die Apotheke.
3.   Peter kann es nicht. Er ist sehr müde.
4.   Was soll ich mit soviel Butter und Brot?
5.   Ich muß noch heute zum Bäcker.
6.   Darf das Kind heute in die Stadt?
7.   Was will Christine denn hier?
8.   Können Sie Deutsch?
9.   Möchten Sie noch etwas Fisch?

Q   Wie sagt man das?

1.   Can you work this afternoon?
     —No, I have to go home.
2.   May I pay (for) the coffee?
     —No, you may not. [Add *das.*]
3.   Dirk wants to go to the movies tonight.
     —What would he like to see?
4.   Barbara intends to study German.
     —Good. She already knows German well.
5.   It's supposed to rain tomorrow.
     —Really? That can't be.

9   Separable-prefix verbs

to get up	I get up early.
to look at	Let's look at a movie tonight.
to throw away	Don't throw away all those papers!

English has a large number of two-word verbs, such as *to get up, to look at, to throw away.* These two-word verbs consist of a verb, such as *get,* and a particle, such as *up.*

aufmachen	Sie **macht** das Fenster **auf.**
mitbringen	**Bringen** Sie bitte Blumen **mit!**

German has a large number of "separable-prefix verbs" that function like certain English two-word verbs. Examples are **ansehen, aufmachen, einkaufen,** and **mitbringen.** In present-tense statements and questions, and in imperative forms, the separable prefix (**an-, auf-, ein-, mit-**) is separated from the base form of the verb and is in the last position.

Sie möchte das Fenster **auf**machen.

In the infinitive form, the prefix is attached to the base form of the verb.

Basic verb	Er **steht** da.	He's standing there.
Separable-prefix verb	Er **steht** um sechs **auf.**	He gets up at six.

The meaning of a separable-prefix verb, such as **aufstehen**, is often different from the sum of the meanings of its parts: **stehen** (stand), **auf** (on).

Er will nicht **auf'**stehen.   Er steht nicht **auf'**.

In spoken German, the stress falls on the prefix of separable-prefix verbs. In vocabulary lists in this textbook, separable prefixes are indicated by a raised dot between the prefix and the verb: **an·sehen, auf·machen, ein·kaufen, mit·bringen.**

R   **Was willst du machen?**   Andreas and Michael are discussing plans for the day.

▶   Wann willst du morgen aufstehen? Spät?   *Ja, ich stehe morgen spät auf.*

1.   Wann mußt du einkaufen? Heute nachmittag?
2.   Was möchtest du Großmutter mitbringen? Blumen?
3.   Wann sollen wir unsere Notizen durcharbeiten? Heute abend?
4.   Wann mußt du dein Referat vorbereiten? Jetzt?
5.   Wann willst du das Geld zurückzahlen? Bald?
6.   Wann willst du Kapitel Fünf ansehen? Heute abend?

Wir laden Sie herzlich ein...

S   **Was ist hier los?**   Describe the activities of the people mentioned below, using the cued modal verbs.

▶   Tanja steht um sechs Uhr auf. (möchte)   *Tanja möchte um sechs Uhr auf-
                                                 stehen.*

1.   Erik macht das Fenster auf. (wollen)
2.   Bringst du Tante Inge Blumen mit? (können)
3.   Wir bereiten unsere Seminararbeit vor. (sollen)
4.   Wir arbeiten unsere Notizen durch. (müssen)
5.   Ich kaufe Samstag ein. (möchten)
6.   Peter zahlt das Geld nicht zurück. (wollen)

| Wiederholung _____

A   Elke muß zu Hause bleiben.   Elke wants to go to the movies but should stay home. Form sentences, using the cues below.

1. Elke / (möchte) / gehen / heute abend / ins Kino
2. sie / müssen / lernen / aber / noch viel
3. sie / können / verstehen / ihre Notizen / nicht mehr
4. sie / müssen / schreiben / morgen / eine Klausur
5. sie / müssen / vorbereiten / auch noch / ein Referat
6. sie / wollen / studieren / später / in Deutschland

B   Was sagen Sie?

1. Möchten Sie in Deutschland studieren?
2. Wissen Sie, wo Sie studieren wollen?
3. Kennen Sie eine deutsche Studentin oder einen deutschen Studenten?
4. Welche Universitäten finden Sie besser, Privatuniversitäten oder Staatsuniversitäten? Warum?
5. Möchten Sie im Sommer eine Reise nach Deutschland machen? Warum oder warum nicht?
6. Können Sie das bezahlen?

C   Mach das!   Tell Thomas what he must do this morning, using **du**-form imperatives.

▶   aufstehen / jetzt   *Steh jetzt auf!*

1. aufmachen / Fenster
2. essen / Ei / zum Frühstück
3. gehen / einkaufen / dann
4. kaufen / alles / bei Meiers
5. kommen / gleich / nach Hause
6. vorbereiten / dein Referat
7. durcharbeiten / deine Notizen

D   Wer arbeitet für wen?   You and your friends work for members of the family. Say who works for whom. Use a possessive adjective.

▶   Annette / Großmutter   *Annette arbeitet für ihre Großmutter.*

1. Felix / Tante
2. ich / Vater
3. du / Mutter / ?
4. Jürgen / Onkel
5. Karin und Sonja / Schwester
6. wir / Eltern
7. ihr / Großvater / ?

E   Wie sagt man das?   Construct a dialogue between Ingrid and Christine, based on the English cues provided below.

Christine: Ingrid, may I ask something?
Ingrid: Yes, what would you like to know?
Christine: What are you reading?
Ingrid: I'm reading a book. It's called *A Trip Through Germany*.
Christine: Do you have to work this evening?
Ingrid: No, I don't believe so.
Christine: Do you want to go to the movies?
Ingrid: Can you lend me money?
Christine: Certainly. But I would like to pay for you.

F   Wo? In Deutschland oder in Amerika?   Indicate whether each statement below is more characteristic of Germany or of the United States.

1. Man kauft Aspirin im Supermarkt.
2. Zum Frühstück gibt es oft Brötchen und Kaffee, vielleicht auch ein Ei.
3. Man ißt zu Mittag (meistens°) warm.   *most of the time*
4. Man ißt zu Abend meistens kalt.
5. Viele Leute kaufen das Brot beim Bäcker und das Fleisch beim Metzger.
6. Andrea nimmt den Kaffee ungemahlen.
7. Fürs Wochenende kauft Barbara Blumen.
8. Mark nimmt viele Vitamintabletten.
9. Viele Studenten bekommen Geld für Wohnen und Essen vom Staat.
10. Anne studiert an einer Privatuniversität.
11. Nach acht Semestern macht Claudia Examen.
12. Die Uni kostet° nichts.   *costs*
13. Hier sind alle Unis Staatsuniversitäten.
14. Cornelia will Ingenieurin werden, aber sie nimmt erst Geschichte und Englisch.
15. Alex hat für jeden Kurs eine Prüfung.

G   Wie sagt man das?

1. Can you lend me your notes?
   —Sorry, I don't have any.
2. What is your major, Thomas? History?
   —No, history is my minor.
3. Veronika works a lot in the summer doesn't she?
   —Naturally. Her parents aren't rich.
4. What are your *(pl.)* friends Rita and Paul studying?
   —German. But they are not our friends.

H   Anregung

1. In 6–8 German sentences give your opinion about the following features of higher education in the Federal Republic of Germany: **BAFöG, keine Studiengebühren, Numerus clausus.**
2. Describe in German a typical Friday at your college or university. You might want to discuss your classes, where you eat, your shopping habits, and your plans for the evening.

Grammatik zum Nachschlagen ⸻

Present tense of *werden*   (A)

werden	
ich werde	wir werden
du **wirst**	ihr werdet
er/es/sie **wird**	sie werden
Sie werden	

Verbs with stem-vowel change e > ie   (B)

sehen	
ich sehe	wir sehen
du **siehst**	ihr seht
er/es/sie **sieht**	sie sehen
Sie sehen	
du-*imperative:* **sieh!**	

lesen	
ich lese	wir lesen
du **liest**	ihr lest
er/es/sie **liest**	sie lesen
Sie lesen	
du-*imperative:* **lies!**	

Present tense of *wissen*   (C)

wissen	
ich **weiß**	wir wissen
du **weißt**	ihr wißt
er/es/sie **weiß**	sie wissen
Sie wissen	

Wissen and kennen (D)

Er **weiß**, wer Frau Braun ist.	He knows who Mrs. Braun is.
Er **kennt** Frau Braun gut.	He knows Mrs. Braun well.

Wissen means *to know something as a fact.* **Kennen** means *to know* (in the sense of *to be acquainted with*) *a person, place, or thing.*

Der-words (E–G)

	Masculine	Neuter	Feminine	Plural
Nom.	dieser Mann	dieses Kind	diese Frau	diese Leute
Acc.	diesen Mann	dieses Kind	diese Frau	diese Leute

Der-words follow the same pattern in the nominative and accusative as the definite articles.

Meanings and uses of der-words (E–G)

dieser	this; these *(pl.)*
jeder	each, every *(used in the singular only)*
mancher	many a, several, some *(used mainly in the plural)*
solcher	such *(used mainly in the plural)*
welcher	which *(interrogative adjective)*

In the singular, **so ein** is usually used instead of **solcher: So eine Uhr ist sehr teuer.**

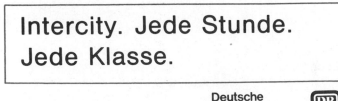

Intercity. Jede Stunde.
Jede Klasse.

Deutsche
Bundesbahn

Modal auxiliaries (H–Q)

Modal verbs indicate an attitude about an action; they do not express the action itself. German modals are irregular in that they lack endings in the **ich-** and **er/es/sie-**forms, and most modals show stem-vowel changes.

	dürfen	können	müssen	sollen	wollen	mögen	(möchte)
ich	darf	kann	muß	soll	will	mag	(möchte)
du	darfst	kannst	mußt	sollst	willst	magst	(möchtest)
er/es/sie	darf	kann	muß	soll	will	mag	(möchte)
wir	dürfen	können	müssen	sollen	wollen	mögen	(möchten)
ihr	dürft	könnt	müßt	sollt	wollt	mögt	(möchtet)
sie	dürfen	können	müssen	sollen	wollen	mögen	(möchten)
Sie	dürfen	können	müssen	sollen	wollen	mögen	(möchten)

Ich **muß** nach Hause.	=	Ich **muß** nach Hause **gehen.**
Ich **kann** es.	=	Ich **kann** es **tun.**
Ich **kann** Deutsch.	=	Ich **kann** Deutsch **sprechen** (= *speak*).

Modal auxiliaries in German are usually used with dependent infinitives. The infinitive is in last position.

The dependent infinitive may be omitted in a sentence containing a modal when the meaning is clear from the context.

Meaning of modals (H–Q)

Infinitive	Meaning	Examples	English equivalents
dürfen	permission	Ich **darf** arbeiten.	I'm allowed to work.
können	ability	Ich **kann** arbeiten.	I can work.
mögen	liking	Ich **mag** es nicht.	I don't like it.
müssen	compulsion	Ich **muß** arbeiten.	I must (have to) work.
sollen	obligation	Ich **soll** arbeiten.	I'm supposed to work.
wollen	wishing, wanting, intention	Ich **will** arbeiten.	I want (intend) to work.

Mögen Sie Fisch?	Do you like fish?
Ich **mag** Paul nicht.	I don't like Paul.
Ich **möchte** jetzt Tennis spielen.	I would like to play tennis now.

Mögen is often used to express a fondness or dislike for someone or something. With this meaning it usually does not have a dependent infinitive.

The **möchte**-forms are subjunctive forms of **mögen** and are equivalent to *would like*. The **möchte**-forms are commonly used with an infinitive.

Separable-prefix verbs   (R, S)

mitbringen	**Bring** Blumen **mit!**	Bring flowers!
aufmachen	Ich **mache** das Fenster **auf.**	I'll open the window.

Many German verbs begin with prefixes such as **mit** or **auf.** Some prefixes are "separable," that is, they are separated from the base form of the verb in the imperative and in the present tense. The prefix generally comes at the end of the sentence. The separable-prefix verbs you have had are **ansehen, aufmachen, aufstehen, durcharbeiten, einkaufen, mitbringen, kennenlernen, vorbereiten, zurückzahlen.** (Kennen, in **kennenlernen**, is a verb and not a separable prefix, but it behaves just like a separable prefix.)

Warum **kauft** er heute **ein?**	Warum möchte er heute **einkaufen?**
Stehst du um sechs **auf?**	Mußt du um sechs **aufstehen?**

The separable prefix is attached to the base form of the verb when the verb is used as an infinitive.

In the vocabularies of this text, separable-prefix verbs are indicated by a raised dot between the prefix and the verb: **an·sehen, auf·stehen.**

Kapitel 5

Lernziele

Sprechakte

Discussing transportation and travel
Making plans for a vacation
Discussing one's daily schedule
Showing connections and relationships
between ideas
Asking whether someone can be believed

Grammatik

Verbs with stem-vowel change **a**>**ä**
Word order with expressions of time
Independent clauses and coordinating
conjunctions
Dependent clauses and subordinating
conjunctions
Dative case
Indirect object

Vokabeln

Means of transportation

Landeskunde

Youth hostels
Austria
Role of public transportation

*Junge Leute wollen in den Ferien andere
Länder kennenlernen.*

| Bausteine für Gespräche

Fährst du morgen zur Uni?

Paul: Fährst du morgen zur Uni?

Birgit: Ja, soll ich dich mitnehmen?
Paul: Bitte, sonst muß ich mit dem Bus fahren. Mein Auto ist wieder kaputt.
Birgit: Schon wieder?
Paul: Hm. Kannst du bei mir vorbeikommen? Ist dir das recht?
Birgit: Ja. Ich fahre um halb neun von zu Hause weg. Fünf Minuten später bin ich dann bei dir. Ist das zu früh?
Paul: Nein. Ich warte dann unten.

In den Ferien

Gerhard: Wohin fährst du in den Ferien?
Rita: Nach Dänemark. Ich möchte Dänemark endlich mal kennenlernen.
Gerhard: Mit wem fährst du?
Rita: Mit meiner Freundin Hanna. Sie spricht gut Dänisch.
Gerhard: Fahrt ihr mit dem Auto?
Rita: Nein, mit der Bahn. Wir wollen dort auch viel wandern.
Gerhard: Wo schlaft ihr?

Rita: In Kopenhagen bei Freunden. Sonst zelten wir. Wenn das Wetter nicht zu schlecht ist.

Are you driving to school tomorrow?

Are you driving to the university tomorrow?
Yes. Should I give you a lift?
Please do, otherwise I'll have to go by bus. My car is out of commission again.
Again, so soon?
Hm. Can you come by my place? Is that all right with you?
Sure. I leave home at eight thirty. I'll be at your place five minutes later. Is that too early?

No. I'll be waiting downstairs.

On vacation

Where are you going on vacation?

To Denmark. I'd finally like to get to know Denmark.

Who are you going with?
With my friend Hanna. She speaks Danish very well.
Are you going by car?
No, by train. And we want to hike a lot there too.
Where are you going to spend the night?
With friends in Copenhagen. Otherwise we'll camp out. If the weather isn't too bad.

Bilder aus Österreich

Oben: **Salzburg**   Mozarts
Geburtshaus. *Unten:* **Wien,
Hauptstadt von Österreich**
Blick auf den Stephansdom.

Ganz links oben: **Handwerk** Ein Holzschnitzer lernt seine Kunst. *Links oben:* **Sezessions-Museum** Wien hat international bekannte Museen. *Links unten:* **Volkskunst in Österreich** Viele alte Bauernhäuser sind bemalt. *Diese Seite:* **St. Christoph am Arlberg** Der Tourismus ist für Österreich eine wichtige Industrie.

Oben: **Am Hochkönig**
Menschen aus vielen Län-
dern machen in den Alpen
Urlaub. *Unten:* **Wien**   Hier
hat das Café seine längste
Tradition.

Fragen

1. Warum kann Paul nicht mit dem Auto zur Uni fahren?
2. Wo wartet Paul?
3. Wohin fährt Rita in den Ferien?
4. Warum fährt sie nach Dänemark?
5. Mit wem fährt Rita?
6. Fährt sie mit dem Auto?
7. Wo schläft Rita in Dänemark?

Sie haben das Wort

A Interview Your car has broken down and you're looking for a ride. Ask three students how they get to school or work, when they leave, and when they return home.

Discussing transportation and travel

Sie	*Gesprächspartner/in*
Fährst du mit dem Auto zur Uni? / Arbeit?	Ja, soll ich dich mitnehmen? Nein, **mein Auto ist kaputt**. ich nehme den Bus°. ich gehe immer zu Fuß°. ich laufe°. ich fahre mit dem Rad°.
Wann **gehst** du zur Uni? / fährst Arbeit?	Um **acht**. halb neun. Ich gehe/fahre um sieben von zu Hause weg.
Wann kommst du wieder nach Hause?	Um vier. Soll ich auf dich warten? Gegen sechs.

B Was machst du in den Ferien? A friend is looking for someone to go on vacation with and asks what you're going to do during the summer vacation. Respond.

Gesprächspartner/in	*Sie*
Hast du schon Pläne° für die Sommerferien?	Ja, ich fahre nach Österreich. ich möchte **wandern**. zelten. viel schwimmen. Tennis spielen. schlafen. Nein, ich habe keine. Ich muß arbeiten. Ich bereite meine Seminararbeit vor.

Away from home, young Germans and foreigners can stay at one of 560 youth hostels (*Jugendherbergen*). They are found not only near vacation spots and national parks, but also in cities and towns.

Traveling to other European countries is very common among German students too, particularly since there are special railway fares for young people under the age of 26. (North Americans within that age group can also obtain reduced fares.) To finance their vacations, many students work for several weeks during the *Semesterferien*.

Die Jugendherberge Stahleck ist eine alte Burg.

Vokabeln

Substantive

das **Auto, -s** automobile, car
die **Bahn, -en** train; railroad
der **Bus, -se** bus
die **Ferien** (*pl.*) vacation

der **Fuß, ⸚e** foot
der **Plan, ⸚e** plan
das **Rad, ⸚er** (*short for* **Fahrrad**) bike, bicycle

Verben

fahren (fährt) to drive; to travel; **mit dem [Auto] fahren** to go by [car]
laufen (läuft) to run; to go on foot
mit·nehmen (nimmt mit) to take along
schlafen (schläft) to sleep

sprechen (spricht) to speak
weg·fahren (fährt weg) to leave; to drive away
vorbei·kommen to come by
warten (auf + *acc.***)** to wait (for)
zelten to camp in a tent

Andere Wörter

dir (*dat.*) to you
dort there
einmal once
früh early
kaputt broken; tired
mal [= einmal] once; sometime

unten downstairs; below
weg away, gone
wem (*dat. of* **wer**) whom
wenn when; if
wohin where to

— Besondere Ausdrücke

in den Ferien   on vacation; during vacation
Ist dir das recht?   Is that all right with you?
bei dir   at your house
bei mir vorbeikommen   to come by my house

mit [dem Auto]   by [car]
zu Fuß   on foot; **Ich gehe immer zu Fuß.**   I always walk.
zu Hause   (at) home

Erweiterung des Wortschatzes

1   *Wo?* and *wohin?*

Wo ist Dieter?
Where is Dieter?

Wohin geht Erika?
Where is Erika going?

English uses the single word *where* for the two meanings *in what place* and *to what place*. German always distinguishes these two meanings: **wo?** for *in what place* (position) and **wohin?** for *to what place* (direction).

Wie bitte?   You don't understand what Nicole is saying. Ask her to repeat her statements.

▶   Cornelia fährt zur Uni.   *Wohin fährt Cornelia?*
▶   Erik arbeitet im Supermarkt.   *Wo arbeitet Erik?*

1.   Dieter fährt in die Schweiz.
2.   Bärbel fährt nach Österreich.
3.   Mark geht nach Hause.
4.   Tanja arbeitet beim Bäcker.
5.   Schmidts wandern in Dänemark.
6.   Fischers kaufen immer im Supermarkt ein.

Austria has a very rich and diverse cultural tradition. In the late eighteenth and early nineteenth centuries, Vienna (*Wien*) was the center of a musical culture associated with such names as Haydn, Mozart, Beethoven, and Schubert. In the second half of the nineteenth century the *Operette* reached its prime with composers like Johann Strauß the Younger and Franz Lehar. At the turn of the century (referred to in French as *Fin de Siècle*), Vienna was a major artistic and intellectual center of Europe. All at about the same time, Sigmund Freud established psychoanalysis; Arthur Schnitzler, Hugo von Hofmannsthal, and Stefan Zweig created important dramas and novels; and Gustav Mahler continued the city's great musical tradition.

Wien – Innenstadt mit Stephansdom

| Österreich

Vorbereitung auf das Lesen

• *Zum Thema*

Was wissen Sie schon über Österreich? Was meinen° Sie?   *think*

1. Wie groß ist Österreich? Größer als New York oder Ontario oder so groß wie Maine oder Neubraunschweig?
2. Wieviel Einwohner hat Österreich? 7,5 Millionen oder 15 Millionen?
3. Wo liegen die Alpen? Im Westen oder im Osten von Österreich?
4. Wo liegt Wien? Im Westen oder im Osten?
5. Wieviel Nachbarn hat Österreich? Drei oder sieben?
6. Wie heißen die Nachbarländer?

Suchen Sie die folgenden Städte und Länder auf der Landkarte!

Länder: Bulgarien □ Italien □ Jugoslawien □ Österreich □ Polen □ Rumänien □ die Sowjetunion □ die Tschechoslowakei □ Ungarn
Städte: Budapest □ Prag □ Triest □ Wien

● *Leitfragen*

1. Warum kommen die Wiener aus vielen verschiedenen Ländern?

   Stichworte: vor 1918 □ Vielvölkerstaat

2. Welche Rolle spielt Österreich im Ost-West-Konflikt?
3. Warum spielt der Ost-West-Handel eine große Rolle?

   Stichworte: Kontakte □ Tradition □ Know-how

4. Warum kommen viele Flüchtlinge nach Österreich?

   Stichworte: neutral □ Konflikt (nicht) mögen □ (nicht) ernst nehmen

---

83.855 qkm°; 7,5 Millionen Einwohner
etwa so groß wie Maine (86.027 qkm)
etwas größer° als Neubraunschweig° (72.000 qkm)
Bundesstaat° mit 9 Bundesländern°
5 Hauptstadt: Wien
parlamentarische Demokratie
7 Nachbarn: I, FL, CH, D, ČS, H, YU*

qkm = Quadratkilometer:
  square kilometers

*larger / New Brunswick,
Canada*
a federation / federal states

Österreich ist vor allem ein Alpenland. Die Berge sind im Westen. Nur der
Osten ist Flach°- und Hügelland°. Daher leben hier die meisten Men-
10 schen. Die Hauptstadt liegt fast am Rande° des° Landes. Das erscheint
wenig praktisch. Wenn man aber das Österreich von vor° 1918 ansieht,
findet man, daß Wien mehr im Westen des° Landes lag°. Zu diesem Land
der Habsburger° gehörten° nämlich° Gebiete°, die° heute in der
Tschechoslowakei, in der Sowjetunion, in Rumänien, Ungarn, Jugo-

low and hilly country
am Rande: *on the edge / of the*
before
of the / was located
*of the Hapsburgs / belonged /
  of course / areas / which*

---

*I = Italien, FL = Fürstentum Liechtenstein, CH = die Schweiz, D = Bundes-
republik Deutschland, ČS = die Tschechoslowakei, H = Ungarn, YU = Jugoslawien

15 slawien und Italien liegen. In diesem Österreich lebten° also viele ver- — *lived*
schiedene Völker zusammen. Es war ein Vielvölkerstaat°. In Wien — *multi-ethnic state*
kamen° Menschen aus allen diesen Völkern zusammen. — *came*

Eine Österreicherin aus Kärnten° sagt dazu°: „Für alle Teile des Landes — *Carinthia (state in Austria) / to that / center*
war Wien das Zentrum°. Das kann man schon an den Namen im
20 Telefonbuch sehen. Da gibt es z.B. mehrere Seiten Dvorak oder Svoboda,
beides tschechische Namen. In vielen Familien ist es ganz normal, daß
der Vater z.B. aus Prag ist, eine Tante in Budapest verheiratet war, daß ein
Onkel aus Triest kommt und daß die Mutter gute Freunde in Jugoslawien
hat.

25 „Auf diese Weise ist Österreich ganz anders als die anderen deutsch-
sprachigen° Länder. Die Geschichte ist ganz anders. Für Österreich ist es — *German-speaking*
eben ganz natürlich, daß wir auch gute Kontakte zu unseren Nachbarn im
Osten haben."

Österreich liegt heute an der Grenze zwischen° Osten und Westen. — *between*
30 Von Wien bis zur ungarischen° Grenze sind es nur etwa fünfzig Kilome- — *Hungarian*
ter. Politisch und wirtschaftlich° gehört Österreich zum Westen. Aber es — *economically*
versucht, in dem Ost-West-Konflikt zu vermitteln°, kulturell, wirtschaft- — *mediate*
lich und politisch.

So überrascht es kaum, daß Österreich nicht nur mit dem Westen, son-
35 dern auch mit dem Osten wirtschaftlich intensiv zusammenarbeitet.
Durch Tradition ist es mit solchen Ländern wie Rumänien, Ungarn und
Bulgarien verbunden°. Die Österreicher haben besonderes Know-how — *connected*
als Ost-Experten. Daher läuft besonders viel Ost-West-Handel über° — *by way of*
Österreich. Der Ost-Handel spielt hier eine größere Rolle als in den mei-
40 sten westeuropäischen Ländern.

Politisch versucht das Land, eine ähnliche Rolle zu spielen, zwischen
Osten und Westen zu vermitteln, neutral zu sein. So ist Wien heute nach
New York und Genf° die dritte° UNO°-Stadt. Auch OPEC sitzt in Wien. — *Geneva / third / United Nations*
Neutral ist das Land auch, wenn es Flüchtlinge aufnimmt°: Es ist egal, — *accepts*
45 aus welchem Land sie kommen. Seit dem Zweiten° Weltkrieg hat dieses — *second*
kleine Land 1,75 Millionen Flüchtlinge aufgenommen°. Viele von ihnen — *accepted*
sind noch heute in Österreich.

In einem von fünf Aufnahmelagern° zählte° man vor kurzem an — *reception camps / counted*
e i n e m Tag 1.500 Neuankömmlinge° aus 34 Nationen. Unter° ihnen ist — *new arrivals / among*
50 z.B. eine Polin°. Ihr Mann und zwei Kinder sind noch in Polen°. Sie — *Polish woman / Poland*
bekommen keinen Paß. Die Frau hat nur einen Paß bekommen°, weil — *received*
man glaubt, daß sie wegen° Mann und Kindern zurückkommt. Sie will — *because of*
aber nicht zurück und bittet um politisches Asyl°. Ein österreichischer — *asylum*
Beamter sagt dazu°: „Wenn sie hier erst einmal° politisches Asyl hat, ist — *to that / **erst einmal:** once*
55 es meistens einfacher° für ihre Familie, nach Österreich zu kommen. Die — *easier*
Aussichten° sind nicht schlecht. Das dauert meist nur einige Jahre." — *prospects*

In der Hofburg residierten früher die Habsburger.

Der österreichische Schriftsteller Gerhard Roth schrieb° über die Österreicher, daß sie den offenen° Konflikt nicht mögen. Diese Einstellung° erklärt ein wenig, warum die Österreicher mit ihrer Neutralität so
60 erfolgreich° sind. Oder vielleicht haben sie in ihrer langen Geschichte gelernt°, die Dinge nicht so ernst zu nehmen wie z.B. die Deutschen. In Deutschland sagt man eher°: „Die Lage° ist ernst, aber nicht hoffnungslos°." In Österreich sagt man dagegen° eher: „Die Lage ist hoffnungslos, aber nicht ernst."

wrote
public
attitude
successful
haben gelernt: *learned*
rather / situation
hopeless / on the other hand

Fragen zum Lesestück

1. Wieviel Nachbarn hat Österreich? Welche liegen im Süden? Im Westen? Im Norden? Im Osten?
2. Wo in Österreich sind die Berge? Wie ist das Land im Osten?
3. Wo in Österreich liegt Wien? Erklären Sie!
4. Bis wann war Österreich ein Vielvölkerstaat?
5. Was für Namen sind Dvorak und Svoboda?
6. Wie kommen z.B. tschechische Namen ins Wiener Telefonbuch?
7. Zu wem haben die Österreicher gute Kontakte?
8. Wie weit ist es von Wien bis zur Grenze zwischen Osten und Westen?
9. Zu wem gehört Österreich politisch und wirtschaftlich — zum Osten oder zum Westen?

10. Welcher Handel spielt in Österreich eine besonders große Rolle?
11. Welche internationalen Organisationen sitzen heute in Wien?
12. Warum nimmt das Land Flüchtlinge aus so vielen Ländern auf?
13. Warum hat die Frau aus Polen einen Paß bekommen?
14. Warum ist es für ihre Familie wichtig, daß sie politisches Asyl bekommt?
15. Warum sind die Österreicher mit ihrer Neutralität so erfolgreich?
16. Warum sagt man in Österreich eher: „Die Lage ist hoffnungslos, aber nicht ernst"?

Erzählen Sie!   Tell something about Austria. You may use some of the cued words below in addition to your own.

> die Hauptstadt Wien im Osten □ Namen aus vielen Ländern □ Grenze zwischen Osten und Westen □ Ost-West-Handel □ dritte UNO-Stadt □ Flüchtlinge □ Dinge nicht ernst nehmen

A very significant period in Austria's history is the era under the rule of the House of Habsburg. In 1273 Rudolf von Habsburg was the first member of the Habsburg family to be elected emperor of the Holy Roman Empire (*Heiliges Römisches Reich*), which existed from 962 until 1806. Under the 400 years of Habsburg rule, the empire expanded greatly. The expansion was due to wars and to a successful *Heiratspolitik*, which deliberately aimed at advantageous marriages with the ruling European houses. The success of Napoleon's wars at the beginning of the nineteenth century led to the end of the empire in 1806. Members of the House of Habsburg continued to rule the Austro-Hungarian empire until 1918, however, when Austria was declared a republic.

Rudolf der Erste von Habsburg, 1218–1291.

Vokabeln

Substantive

die **Alpen** (*pl.*)   Alps
der **Beamte, -n, -n** (ein **Beamter**)/die **Beamtin, -nen**   (government) official
der **Berg, -e**   mountain
das **Ding, -e**   thing
der **Flüchtling, -e**   refugee
die **Grenze, -n**   border
der **Handel**   trade
der **Krieg, -e**   war; der **Weltkrieg, -e**   World War

die **Landkarte, -n**   map
der **Paß**, *pl.* **Pässe**   passport
die **Rolle, -n**   role
der **Schriftsteller, -**/die **Schriftstelle-rin, -nen**   writer, author
die **Seite, -n**   page; side
der **Teil, -e**   part
das **Volk, ̈er**   people, folk
die **Welt, -en**   world
Wien   Vienna

Verben

bitten (+ um)   to request, ask (for)
danken (+ *dat.*) (für)   to thank (for)
dauern   to last
erscheinen   to appear
fliegen   to fly
gehören (+ *dat.*)   to belong to

leben   to live
schenken (*takes indirect object*)   to give (as a gift)
sitzen   sit; to be located
überraschen   to surprise
versuchen   to try, attempt

Andere Wörter

ähnlich   similiar
als (*conj.*)   as
aus (+ *dat.*)   out of; from
beides   both
besonder   particular
bis zu (+ *dat.*)   up to
daß (*conj.*)   that
egal   equal; the same; **Das ist mir egal.**   It's all the same to me.
fast   almost

mehrere   several
meist   most
meistens   mostly, most of the time
ob (*conj.*)   whether, if
österreichisch   Austrian
seit (+ *dat.*)   since [time]
sondern (*conj.*)   but, on the contrary
verheiratet (mit)   married (to)
verschieden   different, various
weil (*conj.*)   because

Besondere Ausdrücke

auf diese Weise   in this way
nicht nur ... sondern auch   not only . . . but also

vor kurzem   recently
eine Rolle spielen   to play a role

Erweiterung des Wortschatzes

2 Wie fährt man? Man fährt ...

das Fahrrad (das Rad)

mit dem Fahrrad/Rad

das Auto, der Wagen

mit dem Auto/dem Wagen

das Motorrad

mit dem Motorrad

der Bus

mit dem Bus

die Straßenbahn

mit der Straßenbahn

die U-Bahn

U1   HAUPTBAHNHOF   17:45

mit der U-Bahn

der Zug

mit dem Zug

das Schiff

mit dem Schiff

das Flugzeug

Man fliegt mit dem Flugzeug.

Sie haben das Wort

Was sagen Sie?   Refer to the Supplementary Word Set on page R-27 for
additional transportation terms.

> Talking about transportation

Haben Sie ein Fahrrad? einen Wagen? ein Motorrad?

Ist es/er neu oder alt?

Wie fahren Sie zur Uni? Mit dem Bus? Mit dem Auto? Mit dem Rad? Mit
der U-Bahn?

Fliegen Sie gern? viel?

| Übungen zur Aussprache

Review the pronunciation of **k, ck, ch,** and **sch** in the Reference section at the
end of the book. Read aloud the words in each pair of columns on this page
from top to bottom. Then read aloud each set of word pairs across. Check
your pronunciation by listening to your instructor or to the tape.

[k]	[x]	[ç]	[š]	[x]	[ç]
Flak	Flach	welche	Welsche	Bach	Bäche
nackt	Nacht	Fächer	fescher	Loch	Löcher
Akt	acht	Wicht	wischt	Bruch	Brüche
buk	Buch	Gicht	Gischt	sprach	spräche
Lack	Lachen	Löcher	Löscher	Buch	Bücher

Wer zuletzt lacht, lacht am besten.

● *The suffix -ig*

In final position, the suffix **-ig** is pronounced [iç] as in **ich**. In all other positions, the **g** in **-ig** has the sound [g] as in English *go*.

[iç]	[ig]
Pfennig	Pfennige
König	Könige
schuldig	schuldige
billig	billiger

Read the sentences aloud, paying special attention to the sounds [k], [x], [ç], and [š] in the boldfaced words.

1. Wir **können noch frischen Kuchen** beim **Bäcker kaufen**.
2. Unsere **Nachbarin** Frau **Gärstig kann wirklich keinen** guten **Kaffee kochen**.
3. **Christl spricht** sehr **wenig**.
4. Oft sagt sie die ganze **Woche nichts**.

| Grammatik und Übungen _____

1   Verbs with stem-vowel change *a > ä*

fahren: to drive	
ich fahre	wir fahren
du **fährst**	ihr fahrt
er/es/sie **fährt**	sie fahren
Sie fahren	

laufen: to run; go on foot	
ich laufe	wir laufen
du **läufst**	ihr lauft
er/es/sie **läuft**	sie laufen
Sie laufen	

Some verbs with stem-vowel **a** or **au** change **a** to **ä** in the **du-** and **er/es/sie-** forms of the present tense.

A   Wohin fährst du?   You are discussing travel plans for the summer with a friend. Tell who is going where. Use a form of **fahren**.

▶   Paula / Italien   *Paula fährt nach Italien.*

1. Frank / auch / Italien
2. meine Großeltern / Spanien

3. ich / Dänemark
4. meine Schwester / Ungarn
5. wir / auch / Schweden
6. du / Österreich / ?
7. ihr / auch / Jugoslawien / ?

B   Wir laufen gern.   You are discussing how and when people you know like to run. Use a form of **laufen**.

▶   Erika / morgens   *Erika läuft morgens.*

1. Gisela / abends
2. ich / zur Uni
3. mein Vater / auch gern
4. wir / gern zusammen
5. du / viel / ?
6. Bärbel / meistens / morgens

2   Word order with expressions of time

	General	Specific
Birgit fährt	morgen	**um acht.**
Birgit is leaving	tomorrow	*at eight.*

When a sentence contains two time expressions, the more specific time element is stressed and comes after the more general time element.

Sie haben das Wort

Was machst du jeden Tag?   You feel you have very busy days and wonder what it's like for others. Ask a fellow student about her/his daily schedule. Use two time expressions in the response.

> Talking about daily routines

Sie	*Gesprächspartner/in*
▶ Wann stehst du morgens auf?	*Ich stehe morgens um [sieben] auf.*

Wann fährst du morgens weg?
Wann gehst du nachmittags zur Vorlesung?
Um wieviel Uhr gehst du nachmittags wieder nach Hause?
Um wieviel Uhr gehst du samstags zu Bett?
Um wieviel Uhr ißt du sonntags zu Mittag?

3   Independent clauses and coordinating conjunctions

Wir wollen am Wochenende zelten. Es soll regnen.
Wir wollen am Wochenende zelten, **aber** es soll regnen.

An independent (or main) clause can stand alone as a complete sentence.
Two or more independent clauses may be connected by coordinating conjunctions. Because coordinating conjunctions are merely connectors and not
part of either clause, they do not affect word order. The coordinating conjunctions you know are **aber, denn, oder, sondern,** and **und**.

Erika kommt morgen, **und** Christel kommt am Montag.
Erika kommt morgen **und** Christel am Montag.
Erik kommt morgen **und** bleibt eine Woche.

In written German, coordinating conjunctions are generally preceded by a
comma. **Oder** and **und** are not preceded by a comma when either the subject
or the verb is identical and omitted in the second clause.

C   **Pläne fürs Wochenende**   Tell what Sabine and Erika are going to do
this week. Combine each pair of sentences below, using the coordinating
conjunctions indicated.

▶   Die Studentin heißt Erika. Ihre   *Die Studentin heißt Erika, und*
     Freundin heißt Sabine. (und)   *ihre Freundin heißt Sabine.*

1.   Erika wohnt bei einer Familie. Sabine wohnt bei ihren Eltern. (aber)
2.   Erika arbeitet zu Hause. Sabine muß in die Bibliothek gehen. (aber)
3.   Erika arbeitet schwer. Am Mittwoch hat sie eine Klausur. (denn)
4.   Sabine hat ihre Klausur nicht am Mittwoch. Sie hat sie am Freitag.
     (sondern)
5.   Was machen die Mädchen in den Ferien? Wissen sie es nicht? (oder)

4   *Sondern* and *aber*

Paul fährt morgen nicht mit dem   Paul isn't going by car tomorrow,
   Auto, **sondern** mit dem Bus.   but (rather) by bus.

Sondern is a coordinating conjunction that expresses a contrast or contradiction. It is equivalent to *but, instead, on the contrary*. It is used after negative
clauses. When the subject is the same in both clauses, it is not repeated.

Er fährt nicht mit dem Auto, **aber**   He isn't going by car, but his father
   sein Vater fährt mit dem Auto.   is.

Aber as a coordinating conjunction is equivalent to *but* or *nevertheless*. It may
be used after either positive or negative clauses.

Public transportation is efficient and much utilized by the people in German-speaking countries. Buses, streetcars, subways, and trains are owned either by the federal or local government and are highly subsidized. In towns, villages, and suburbs there is convenient bus and sometimes streetcar (*Straßenbahn*) service. Cities have a subway (*Untergrundbahn* or *U-Bahn*) and/or a modern commuter rail system (*Schnellbahn/Stadtbahn* or *S-Bahn*). The West German federal post office (*Bundespost*) provides extensive bus service between towns. If useful, even ferries are included in the public transportation network, such as the *Alsterfähre* (ferry on the Alster Lake) in Hamburg. To commute, people often use short-distance trains (*Nahverkehrszüge* and *Personenzüge*). Fast, comfortable *Inter-City* express trains run several times a day between major cities, as do the slower through trains (*D-Züge*), which have more stops on their long-distance trips. A network of trains known as *EuroCity* has replaced most of the *TEE* (*Trans-Europ-Express*) trains. With 56 day trains and 8 night trains, the network connects more than 200 cities, including all of the capitals of 13 countries.

Wer mit der Straßenbahn fährt, kommt gut an.

D   Was macht Annette?   Complete the sentences about Annette's activities with **aber** or **sondern**, as appropriate.

▶   Annette steht nicht früh, _____ spät auf.   *Annette steht nicht früh, sondern spät auf.*

1.   Sie spielt heute nicht Fußball, _____ Tennis.
2.   Sie spielt Tennis nicht gut, _____ sie spielt es sehr gern.
3.   Sie geht nicht zur Vorlesung, _____ in die Bibliothek.
4.   Im Café bestellt sie Bier, _____ sie trinkt Eriks Kaffee.
5.   Sie möchte den Kaffee bezahlen, _____ sie hat kein Geld.
6.   Annette und Erik arbeiten heute abend nicht, _____ sie gehen ins Kino.
7.   Der Film war nicht wirklich gut, _____ doch interessant.

● *Nicht nur ... sondern auch*

| Österreich arbeitet **nicht nur** mit dem Westen, **sondern auch** mit dem Osten. | Austria works not only with the west, but also with the east. |

The German construction **nicht nur ... sondern auch** is equivalent to *not only . . . but also.*

E   Nicht nur dies, sondern auch das.   Restate, using nicht nur ... sondern auch.

| ▶ Die Österreicher kennen den Westen und den Osten auch. | *Die Österreicher kennen nicht nur den Westen, sondern auch den Osten.* |

1. In Österreich gibt es Flachland und Berge.
2. Im Wiener Telefonbuch gibt es österreichische und tschechische Namen.
3. Flüchtlinge kommen aus dem Osten und aus dem Westen.
4. Österreich gehört politisch und wirtschaftlich zum Westen.
5. In Wien gibt es die UNO und OPEC.

5   Dependent clauses and subordinating conjunctions

Independent clause	Conjunction	Dependent clause
Michael glaubt,	**daß**	Inge morgen eine Klausur schreibt.
Erika geht zu Fuß,	**weil**	ihr Auto kaputt ist.

A dependent (or subordinate) clause cannot stand alone as a complete sentence. Two signals distinguish a dependent clause from an independent clause: it is introduced by a subordinating conjunction and the finite verb is at the end. A few common subordinating conjunctions are: **daß**, *that;* **ob**, *whether;* **weil**, *because;* **wenn**, *if, when.*

| Paul fragt Birgit, **ob** sie zur Uni fährt. | Paul asks Birgit *whether* she is driving to the university. |
| Er möchte mitfahren, **wenn** sie zur Uni fährt. | He would like to go along, *if* she is driving to the university. |

Both **wenn** and **ob** are equivalent to English *if.* However, they are not interchangeable. **Ob** can always be translated with *whether* and is used with main clauses such as **er fragt, ob** ... and **ich weiß (nicht), ob** ....

F   Deutsche Studenten   Answer the questions, using **wenn** or **weil**, as appropriate.

▶   Wann bekommen Studenten Geld   *Wenn sie zuwenig Geld haben.*
    vom Staat? (Sie haben zuwenig
    Geld.)

1.   Warum arbeiten die Studenten nicht? (Es gibt wenige Studentenjobs.)
2.   Warum brauchen sie soviel Geld? (Wohnen und Essen sind teuer.)
3.   Wann bekommt man einen Studienplatz? (Man hat gute Zensuren im Gymnasium.)
4.   Warum müssen Studenten in acht Semestern fertig sein? (Es gibt zuviel Studenten.)
5.   Wann ist es billiger zu studieren? (Man wohnt bei den Eltern.)

G   Was weißt du über Birgit?   Practice asking someone for information. Begin your sentences with **weißt du, ob ... ?**

▶   Fährt Birgit morgen zur Uni?   *Weißt du, ob Birgit morgen zur Uni fährt?*

1.   Fährt sie mit dem Bus?
2.   Ist ihr Auto kaputt?
3.   Kommt sie um drei wieder nach Hause?
4.   Wohnt sie noch im Studentenheim?
5.   Arbeitet sie heute abend zu Hause?
6.   Geht sie mit Paul ins Kino?

• *Dependent clauses and separable-prefix verbs*

Statement	Gisela **kauft** im Supermarkt **ein**.
Dependent clause	Gisela sagt, **daß** sie im Supermarkt **einkauft**.

In a dependent clause, the separable prefix is attached to the base form of the verb, which is in final position.

H   Was sagt Gabi?   You want to tell a friend about Gabi's plans. Begin each sentence with **Gabi sagt, daß ...**

▶   Sie steht früh auf.   *Gabi sagt, daß sie früh aufsteht.*

1.   Sie kauft in der Stadt ein.
2.   Renate kommt mit.
3.   Sie fahren um neun von zu Hause weg.
4.   Das Kaufhaus macht um zehn auf.
5.   Sie sehen alles an.
6.   Sie bereitet zu Hause ein Referat vor.

• *Dependent clauses and modal auxiliaries*

Statement	Rita **möchte** in die Schweiz fahren.
Dependent clause	Rita sagt, **daß** sie in die Schweiz fahren **möchte**.

In a dependent clause, the modal auxiliary follows the dependent infinitive and is in final position.

I Weil es so ist. Answer the questions, using **weil**.

▶ Warum möchte Andreas die No-   *Weil er sie durcharbeiten will.*
  tizen von Michael leihen? (Er will
  sie durcharbeiten.)

1. Warum muß er die Notizen heute haben? (Er muß am Mittwoch eine Klausur schreiben.)
2. Warum möchte Michael die Notizen morgen wiederhaben? (Er muß sie auch durcharbeiten.)
3. Warum liest er einen Artikel über Brecht? (Er soll eine Seminararbeit schreiben.)
4. Warum wartet Michael auf ihn? (Sie wollen zusammen Kaffee trinken.)
5. Warum geht er früh nach Hause? (Er will heute abend viel arbeiten.)

• *Dependent clauses beginning a sentence*

	1	2	
	Paul	**fährt**	mit dem Bus.
1		2	
Weil sein Auto kaputt ist,		**fährt**	er mit dem Bus.

In a statement, the finite verb is in second position. If a sentence begins with a dependent clause, the entire clause is considered a single element, and the finite verb of the independent clause is in second position, followed by the subject.

J Wenn es so ist. Combine each pair of sentences with the conjunctions indicated.

▶ (wenn) Das Wetter ist gut. Gerhard   *Wenn das Wetter gut ist, wollen*
  und Paul wollen nach Dänemark.   *Gerhard und Paul nach*
                                          Dänemark.

1. (weil) Sie haben wenig Geld. Sie fahren mit dem Rad.
2. (wenn) Sie fahren mit dem Rad. Sie sehen mehr vom Land.
3. (wenn) Es ist nicht zu kalt. Sie zelten.
4. (wenn) Das Wetter ist sehr schlecht. Sie schlafen bei Freunden.

5. (wenn) Sie lernen interessante Leute kennen. Sie bleiben vier Wochen.
6. (weil) Sie haben nur vier Wochen Ferien. Sie müssen im August wieder zu Hause sein.

● *Question words as subordinating conjunctions*

Direct specific question	**Wann** kommt Birgit heute?
Indirect specific question	Ich weiß nicht, ⎫ Thomas fragt, ⎭ **wann** Birgit heute kommt.

Question words (**wer, was, wann, wie lange, warum**, etc.) function as subordinating conjunctions when they introduce indirect questions.

K   Ich weiß es.   When the discussion at a café turns to Austria, Robert addresses questions to the group. Say you know the answers.

▶   Wie groß ist Österreich?   *Ich weiß, wie groß Österreich ist.*

1. Wieviel Einwohner hat Österreich?
2. Wieviel Nachbarn hat Österreich?
3. Wie heißen die Nachbarländer?
4. Wo liegt Wien?
5. Warum wohnen die meisten Leute im Osten?
6. Wie heißen die drei UNO-Städte?

Pettneu in Tirol

Sie haben das Wort

Ihre Meinung.   Answer the questions below, using **weil**.

1. Warum fliegen Sie in den Ferien (nicht) nach Deutschland?
2. Warum gehen Sie heute (nicht) schwimmen?
3. Warum arbeiten Sie am Wochenende (nicht)?
4. Warum kaufen Sie (k)ein neues Auto?
5. Warum laufen Sie (nicht) zur Uni?
6. Warum leihen Sie Ihren Freunden (kein) Geld?
7. Warum lesen Sie (keine) Bücher über Schach?
8. Warum schlafen Sie so viel/wenig?
9. Warum zelten Sie in den Ferien (nicht)?

6   Dative case

Nominative	**Der** Kaffee ist billig.
Accusative	Kaufst du **den** Kaffee?
Dative	Was hältst du von **dem** Kaffee?

In addition to nominative and accusative, German has a case called *dative*.

Masculine	Neuter	Feminine	Plural
dem Mann	dem Kind	der Frau	den Freunden
diesem Mann	diesem Kind	dieser Frau	diesen Freunden
einem Mann	einem Kind	einer Frau	keinen Freunden
ihrem Mann	unserem Kind	seiner Frau	meinen Freunden

The definite and indefinite articles, **der**-words, and **ein**-words change their form in the dative case. The plural form of a noun in the dative case adds **-n**, unless the plural already ends in **-n** or **-s: meine Freunde > meinen Freunden: but die Frauen > den Frauen; die Autos > den Autos.**

7   Masculine *N*-nouns in the dative

Nom.	der Herr	der Student
Acc.	den Herrn	den Studenten
Dat.	dem Herrn	dem Studenten

Masculine N-nouns, which add **-n** or **-en** in the accusative, also add **-n** or **-en** in the dative singular.

8   Demonstrative pronouns in the dative

Masculine	Neuter	Feminine	Plural
dem	dem	der	denen

The dative forms of the demonstrative pronouns are identical to the dative forms of the definite articles, except that in the dative plural **den** becomes **denen**.

9   Dative of *wer*?

Wer bekommt die Uhr?   Who's getting the clock?
Wem geben Sie die Uhr?   To whom are you giving the clock?

The dative form of the interrogative **wer**? (*who?*) is **wem**? (*[to] whom?*).

10   Dative verbs

Erika **dankt ihrem** Freund für die   Erika thanks her friend for the
    Blumen.   flowers.
Das Haus **gehört meinen** Eltern.   The house belongs to my parents.

Most German verbs take objects in the accusative. However, a few verbs take objects in the dative. The dative object is usually a person. Such verbs can be classified as "dative verbs." The dative verbs in this chapter are **danken, glauben**, and **gehören**. A more complete list of dative verbs is found on page R-12.

Sie **glaubt ihren** Freunden.   She believes her friends.
Erik **glaubt es** nicht.   Erik doesn't believe it.

The verb **glauben** always takes personal objects in the dative case. It can also take impersonal objects in the accusative case.

L   Glauben, danken, gehören   Answer the questions, using the cued words.

▶   Wem glaubst du? (mein Freund)   *Ich glaube meinem Freund.*

1.   Wem glaubt Inge? (ihr Bruder)
2.   Wem glaubt Frank? (seine Freundin)
3.   Wem dankt Gerd für alles? (seine Eltern)
4.   Wem dankt Lore für das Musikheft? (ihr Freund)
5.   Wem gehört das Fahrrad? (der Junge)
6.   Wem gehört das Auto? (der Herr)
7.   Wem gehört der Kugelschreiber? (das Mädchen)
8.   Wem gehört die Tasche? (die Frau)

M   Wem kann man glauben?   Frank has been told some things by various people. He wants to know whether he can believe them. Tell him he can. Use a dative demonstrative pronoun.

▶   Kann man Erik glauben?   *Klar. Dem kann man glauben.*

1. Kann man deinem Bruder glauben?
2. Kann man Tanja glauben?
3. Kann man Dieter und Markus glauben?
4. Kann man deiner Freundin glauben?
5. Kann man unseren Freunden glauben?
6. Kann man deiner Kusine glauben?

11   Indirect object

	Indirect object	Direct object
Inge schenkt	ihrem Freund	ein Radio.
Inge is giving	her friend	a radio.

In both English and German some verbs take two objects, which are traditionally called the direct object (e.g., **Radio** — *radio*) and the indirect object (e.g., **Freund** — *friend*). The indirect object is usually a person and answers the question *to whom* or *for whom* the action of the verb is intended. Some verbs that can take both direct and indirect objects are **bringen, erklären, geben, kaufen, leihen, sagen, schenken,** and **schreiben.**

12   Signals for indirect object and direct object

	Indirect (dative) object	Direct (accusative) object
Inge schenkt	ihren Eltern	ein Radio.
Inge is giving	her parents	a radio.

English signals the indirect object by putting it before the direct object or by using the preposition *to* or *for*. To determine in English whether a noun or pronoun is an indirect object, add *to* or *for* before it: Inge is giving a radio *to* her parents.

German uses case to signal the difference between a direct object and an indirect object. The direct object is in the accusative, and the indirect object is in the dative. Since the case signals are clear, German never uses a preposition to signal the indirect object.

N   Was bedeutet das?   Identify the indirect (dative) object and direct (accusative) object and give the English equivalent of the sentences below.

1. Ich muß meinem Freund meine Notizen leihen.
2. Ich möchte meiner Großmutter diese Blumen schenken.
3. Was kaufst du deiner Freundin zum Geburtstag?
4. Den Plan mußt du meinem Freund genauer erklären.
5. Wem soll ich das schreiben?
6. Ich möchte dem Mädchen etwas sagen.

O   Was macht Dieter?   Answer the questions below about Dieter's activities. Replace **wem?** with the dative possessive adjective and the nouns in parentheses.

▶   Wem kauft Dieter neue Weingläser? (seine Eltern)   *Seinen Eltern.*

1. Wem bringt er Blumen mit? (seine Großmutter)
2. Wem gibt er seinen Fußball? (sein Freund Erik)
3. Wem gibt er sein Radio? (sein Bruder)
4. Wem leiht er etwas Geld? (seine Schwester)
5. Wem leiht er kein Geld? (seine Freunde Gerd und Alex)
6. Wem schenkt er den Fußball? (sein Bruder)
7. Wem schenkt er die Tasche? (seine Tante)
8. Wem erklärt er die Geschichte? (das Kind)
9. Wem schreibt er eine Karte? (der Junge)

P   Wie sagt man das?

1. What are you giving your mother for her birthday?
    —Flowers and a book.
2. Who are you writing the card to?
    —(To) my cousin Achim.
3. Are you lending your girlfriend Lore money?
    —Yes. She's buying her parents flowers.
4. I have to thank my aunt and my uncle for the radio.
    —Bring your aunt flowers.
5. The professor has to explain the story to the students.
    —Why? Don't they understand it?

Sie haben das Wort

You need some ideas for birthday presents for your family. Ask four fellow students what they would like to give members of their families for their birthdays.

Discussing ideas for birthday presents

▶   Was möchtest du [deiner Mutter] zum Geburtstag schenken?

13   Dative prepositions

aus	out of	Er geht früh **aus** dem Haus.
	(*to come*) from [*cities and countries*]	Sie kommt **aus** Deutschland.
außer	besides, except for	Wer ist **außer** den Studenten hier?
bei	with (*at the home of*)	Er wohnt **bei** einer Familie.
	at (*a place of business*)	Sie arbeitet **bei** Siemens.
	near (in the proximity of)	Die Bäckerei ist **bei** der Universität.
mit	with	Sie fährt **mit** ihrem Freund zur Uni.
	by means of (*transportation*)	Fährst du **mit** dem Auto zur Uni?
nach	to (*with cities and countries*)	Sie fährt im Sommer **nach** Österreich.
	after	Er kommt **nach** dem Essen.
seit	since (*time*)	Sie ist **seit** Mittwoch in Wien.
von	from	Was hören Sie **von** Ihrem Freund?
	of	Österreich ist ein Land **von** 7.500.000 Einwohnern.
	by	Die Geschichte ist **von** Böll.
zu	to (*with people and some places*)	Wir gehen gern **zu** unseren Nachbarn.
		Wann fährst du **zur** Uni?

The prepositions **aus, außer, bei, mit, nach, seit, von**, and **zu** are always followed by the dative.

● *bei*

In addition to the meanings listed above, **bei** has many uses that are hard to translate exactly. It is used, in a general way, to indicate a situation: **beim Lesen** (while reading), **bei der Arbeit** (at work), **bei diesem Wetter** (in weather like this).

● *bei/mit*

Sie wohnt **bei** ihren Eltern.	She lives with her parents.
Sie fährt morgen **mit** ihren Eltern.	She's driving with her parents tomorrow.

One meaning of both **bei** and **mit** is *with*. However, they are not interchangeable. **Bei** means *at the home of*. **Mit** expresses the idea of doing something together.

• *nach/zu*

Schmidts fahren morgen **nach** Wien.	The Schmidts are going to Vienna tomorrow.
Ich muß **zum** Bäcker.	I have to go to the bakery.

One meaning of both **zu** and **nach** is *to*. **Zu** is used to show movement toward people and many locations. **Nach** is used with cities and countries.

• *seit*

Tanja ist **seit** Montag in Hamburg.	Tanja has been in Hamburg since Monday.
Jürgen wohnt **seit** drei Wochen in Wien.	Jürgen has been living in Vienna for three weeks.

Seit plus the present tense is used to express an action or condition that started in the past but is still continuing in the present. Note that English uses the present perfect tense (e.g., *has been living*) with *since* or *for* to express the same idea.

Brot kaufen wir nur **beim** Bäcker.	bei dem = **beim**
Er kommt jetzt **vom** Markt.	von dem = **vom**
Sie geht **zum** Supermarkt.	zu dem = **zum**
Sie geht **zur** Schule.	zu der = **zur**

Several dative prepositions contract with **dem** or **der**. The contractions shown above are frequently used.

Q   Nein, das ist nicht richtig.   Correct the information about Ute inquired about below. Replace the object of the preposition with the words in parentheses.

▶   Ute kommt aus Österreich, nicht? (Schweiz)   *Nein, aus der Schweiz.*

1.   Sie kommt doch aus Wien, nicht? (Basel)
2.   Wohnt sie bei ihren Eltern? (eine Familie)
3.   Wohnt sie seit einem Monat da? (zwei Monate)
4.   Sie arbeitet bei einem Bäcker, nicht? (ein Metzger)
5.   Fährt sie mit ihrem Freund Erik nach Dänemark? (ihre Freundin Petra)
6.   Sie fährt mit dem Auto, nicht? (die Bahn)
7.   Hörst du oft von Ute? (ihre Familie)
8.   Hörst du von ihrer Schwester? (ihr Bruder und ihre Eltern)

R Wie sagt man das?

1. Mondays Ilse does not go out of the house.
2. Tuesdays she sleeps at her friend's.
3. Wednesdays she goes to the university early.
4. For breakfast she eats nothing except a roll.
5. She goes [*fahren*] to the university by streetcar.
6. I believe her friend is from Frankfurt.
7. She has been living here for a year.

S Was sagen Sie?

1. Wo wohnen Sie? Im Studentenheim? Bei einer Familie?
2. Aus welcher Stadt kommen Sie?
3. Wie fahren Sie nach Hause? Mit dem Auto? Mit dem Bus?
4. Wohin möchten Sie in den Ferien fahren?
5. Mit wem möchten Sie fahren?
6. Möchten Sie in den Ferien zelten? Warum (nicht)?

| Wiederholung ————————————————

A Eine Reise nach Österreich   Tell about David's trip to Austria by forming sentences, using the cues below.

1. David / sein / Amerikaner
2. er / machen / Reise / durch / Österreich
3. er / ansehen / einige Universitätsstädte
4. er / fahren / mit / Zug / nach / Wien
5. er / kennenlernen / einige Studenten
6. sie / erzählen / von / diese Universität
7. nach / zwei Tage / David / wegfahren

B Noch einmal. (Once again.)   Restate the sentences below, beginning each one with the words in italics.

1. Die Bundesrepublik hat *neun Nachbarländer.*
2. Eins von den Nachbarländern ist *Österreich.*
3. Jedes Land ist anders, *weil es eine eigene Identität hat.*
4. In Österreich spielt *der Ost-Handel* eine große Rolle.
5. Heute liegt *Österreich* an der Grenze zwischen Osten und Westen.
6. Viel Ost-West-Handel läuft *daher* über Österreich.
7. Politisch versucht *das Land* neutral zu sein.

After the end of World War II, it took until 1955 to restore Austria's sovereignty. In the same year, Austria declared its permanent neutrality (*immerwährende Neutralität*)—which it has always interpreted as a commitment to armed neutrality. Austria is a member of neither NATO nor the Warsaw Pact, and it does not belong to either of the two economic alliances: the (West) European Economic Community or the East European COMECON. It is, however, an active member of the United Nations and serves as the site of many international congresses and conferences.

Austria plays an important role in western Europe by serving as a gateway for foreigners who seek political asylum (*politisches Asyl*). Since the end of World War II it has granted temporary and permanent asylum to more than two million people from more than 30 countries. Since 1945 the government's expenditures on refugee welfare have exceeded 7 billion *Schillinge*.

Flüchtlinge kommen aus vielen Ländern nach Österreich.

C   Was macht Monika?   Complete the account of Monika's day by using the cued nouns in the proper case.

1. Monika geht aus _____ . (das Haus)
2. Sie geht zu _____ . (der Bäcker)
3. _____ Andrea arbeitet bei _____ . (ihre Freundin / der Bäcker)
4. Monika arbeitet für _____ . (ihr Onkel)
5. Sie fährt mit _____ zur Arbeit. (das Fahrrad)
6. Nach _____ geht sie zu _____ . (die Arbeit / die Buchhandlung)
7. Sie kauft _____ über Österreich. (ein Buch)
8. _____ bringt sie Blumen mit. (ihre Mutter)
9. Morgen schenkt sie _____ das Buch zum Geburtstag. (ihr Vater)
10. Nächstes Jahr fährt er mit _____ nach Österreich. (die Familie)

D   Wie sagt man das?

1. —Is it O.K. with you if we work together tonight? I have to prepare my report.
    —Of course. Come at seven thirty. We can go to the movies afterwards.
2. —Would you like to go to Austria this summer?
    —Yes. Gladly. Do you want to go by car or by train?
    —By bike. If the weather stays nice.

E   Was bedeutet das?   Form compounds from the words provided below; then give the English equivalent of each compound.

1. der Nachbar + das Land
2. das Jahr + hundert
3. der Student(en) + das Heim
4. das Haupt + die Stadt
5. der Wein + der Markt
6. die Ferien + die Reise
7. die Butter + das Brot
8. das Schiff(s) + die Reise
9. die Welt + der Krieg
10. die Alpen + das Land

F   Jetzt weiß er es.   Dieter Meier sits down at Petra Müller's table in a café and they become acquainted. Read the conversation. Then summarize all the information Dieter learns about Petra. Begin each sentence with **Er weiß, daß ....**

Petra: Ich bin Österreicherin.
Dieter: Kommst du aus Wien?
Petra: Nein, aus Salzburg.
Dieter: Wohnst du in einem Studentenheim?
Petra: Nein, bei einer Familie.
Dieter: Was studierst du denn?
Petra: Wirtschaftswissenschaft ist mein Hauptfach und Englisch mein Nebenfach. Ich möchte in Amerika arbeiten.
Dieter: Warst du schon in Amerika?
Petra: Leider noch nicht.

Überall in Salzburg kann man die Burg sehen.

G   Anregung

1. Your friend Rita wants to study in Europe, but doesn't know whether to go to the Federal Republic of Germany or to Austria. Give her some facts in German about one of the countries. You may wish to include information on the following:

   wie groß das Land ist; wieviel Einwohner es hat; wieviel Nachbarn es hat; ob es viele Berge hat; ob es viel Industrie hat; was die Hauptstadt ist.

2. You are studying in Munich and wish to convince a friend to study there also. Write a short letter in German in which you state the advantages of a German university. Begin the letter with **Liebe** (*Dear*) [Barbara] or **Lieber** [Paul], and end with **Mit herzlichen Grüßen** (*With cordial greetings*), **Deine** or **Dein** [your name]. In a German letter, the words **Du** and **Dein** are always capitalized.

Grammatik zum Nachschlagen ———————

Verbs with stem-vowel change *a* > *ä* (A, B)

fahren	
ich fahre	wir fahren
du **fährst**	ihr fahrt
er/es/sie **fährt**	sie fahren
Sie fahren	

laufen	
ich laufe	wir laufen
du **läufst**	ihr lauft
er/es/sie **läuft**	sie laufen
Sie laufen	

Several verbs with stem-vowel **a** change the **a** to **ä** in the **du-** and **er/es/sie**-forms. Verbs with stem-vowel **au** change **au** to **äu** in the **du-** and **er/es/sie**-forms.

Word order with expressions of time

	General Time	Specific Time	
Ich stehe	morgens	um sieben	auf.

When a sentence contains two time expressions, the more specific time element (e.g., **um sieben**) is stressed and comes after the more general time element (e.g., **morgens**).

Independent clauses and coordinating conjunctions (C)

Erik kommt morgen. Christl kommt am Montag.
Erik kommt morgen, und Christl kommt am Montag.
Erik kommt morgen und Christl am Montag.
Erika kommt morgen und bleibt eine Woche.

An independent (or main) clause can stand alone as a complete sentence. Two or more independent clauses may be connected by coordinating conjunctions. Coordinating conjunctions do not affect the order of subject and verb. Five common coordinating conjunctions are **aber, denn, oder, sondern**, and **und.**

In written German, coordinating conjunctions are generally preceded by a comma. However, **oder** and **und** are not preceded by a comma when either the subject or the verb in both clauses is the same and is not repeated.

Sondern and *aber* (D)

Sylvia geht jetzt nicht in die Bibliothek, **sondern** ins Kino.
Irene geht jetzt in die Bibliothek, **aber** nachher geht sie ins Café.

Sylvia is not going to the library now, but (rather) to the movies.
Irene is going to the library now, but afterwards she's going to the café.

Sondern is a coordinating conjunction that expresses a contrast or contradiction. It is equivalent to *but, instead, rather, on the contrary*. **Sondern** is used only after a negative clause. When the subject is the same in both clauses, it is not repeated.

Aber as a coordinating conjunction is equivalent to *but, however, nevertheless*. It may be used after either a positive or a negative clause.

Nicht nur ... sondern auch (E)

Österreich hat gute Kontakte **nicht nur** mit dem Westen, **sondern auch** mit dem Osten.

Austria has good contacts, not only with the west, but also with the east.

The German construction **nicht nur ... sondern auch** is equivalent to *not only . . . but also.*

Dependent clauses and subordinating conjunctions (F–J)

Independent Clause	Dependent Clause
Sabine sagt,	**daß** Erik diesen Sommer nach Österreich fährt.
Weißt du,	**ob** er mit der Bahn fährt?
Er fährt mit dem Rad,	**wenn** das Wetter nicht zu schlecht ist.
Er zeltet auch,	**weil** es billiger ist.

A dependent (or subordinate) clause cannot stand alone as a complete sentence. Two signals distinguish a dependent clause from an independent clause: (1) it is introduced by a subordinating conjunction such as **daß, ob, weil,** or **wenn**; and (2) the finite verb is in last position.

Question words as subordinating conjunctions (K)

Direct specific question	**Wohin** fährt Tanja diesen Sommer?
Indirect specific question	Ich weiß nicht, **wohin** Tanja diesen Sommer fährt.

Indirect specific questions are introduced by the same question words that are used to introduce direct specific questions. The question words function like subordinating conjunctions.

Word order in dependent clauses (J)

Ich weiß, daß Frank morgen **kommt.**
daß Petra morgen **mitkommt.**
daß Helmut nicht **kommen kann.**

In dependent clauses:

1. The finite verb is in final position.
2. The separable prefix is attached to the base form of the verb in final position.
3. The modal auxiliary follows the infinitive and is in final position.

Weil Erika kein Geld hat, **fährt** sie nicht nach Hause.

When a dependent clause begins a sentence, it is followed directly by the finite verb of the independent clause. In written German, dependent clauses are always set off by commas.

Articles, *der*- and *ein*-words in the dative case　(L–P)

	Masculine	Neuter	Feminine	Plural
Nominative	der Mann	das Kind	die Frau	die Freunde
Accusative	den Mann	das Kind	die Frau	die Freunde
Dative	**dem** Mann	**dem** Kind	**der** Frau	**den** Freunden
	diesem Mann	**diesem** Kind	**dieser** Frau	**diesen** Freunden
	einem Mann	**einem** Kind	**einer** Frau	**keinen** Freunden
	ihrem Mann	**unserem** Kind	**seiner** Frau	**meinen** Freunden

Nouns in the dative plural　(L,O,P)

Nominative	die Männer	die Frauen	die Radios
Dative	den Männer**n**	den Frauen	den Radios

Nouns in the dative plural add **-n** unless the plural already ends in **-n** or **-s**.

Masculine *N*-nouns in the dative case　(L)

Nominative	der Herr	der Mensch
Accusative	den Herr**n**	den Mensch**en**
Dative	**dem** Herr**n**	**dem** Mensch**en**

For the masculine **N**-nouns used in this book, see the Grammatical Tables in the Reference Section.

Dative case of demonstrative pronouns　(M)

Masculine	Neuter	Feminine	Plural
dem	dem	der	denen

Dative case of *wer*

Nominative	**Wer** sagt das?	Who says that?
Dative	**Wem** sagen Sie das?	To whom are you saying that?

Dative verbs   (L–P)

Inge **dankt** ihrer Freundin.
Das Fahrrad **gehört** meinem Bruder.

Most German verbs take objects in the accusative. A few verbs take objects in the dative. The dative object is usually a person. For convenience such verbs can be classified as "dative verbs."

Mark **glaubt** seinem Freund nicht.
Er **glaubt** es nicht.

The verb **glauben** always takes personal objects (e.g. **seinem Freund**) in the dative case. It can also take impersonal objects (**es**) in the accusative case.

For dative verbs used in this book, see the Grammatical Tables in the Reference Section.

Indirect object   (N–P)

Thomas schenkt **seiner Freundin** ein Buch.

Thomas is giving *his friend* a book.
Thomas is giving a book *to his friend*.

In both English and German some verbs take two objects: a primary object (**Buch** — *book*) and a secondary object (**Freundin** — *friend*). Traditionally the primary object is called a direct object and the secondary object is called an indirect object. The indirect object is normally a person and answers the question *to whom* or *for whom* something is done.

Signals for indirect object and direct object (N)

Inge gibt	**ihren Eltern**	die Blumen.
Inge gives	*her parents*	the flowers.

Inge gibt	die Blumen	**ihren Eltern**.
Inge gives	the flowers	*to her parents.*

English signals the indirect object by putting it before the direct object or by using the preposition *to*. German signals the difference between a direct object and an indirect object with case. The direct object is in the accusative; the indirect object is in the dative. Since the case signals are clear, German never uses a preposition to signal the indirect object. Normally an indirect-object noun precedes a direct-object noun.

Dative prepositions (Q–S)

aus	out of; from (= *is a native of*)
außer	except for, besides
bei	with (*at the home of*); at (*a place of business*); near (*in the proximity of*); while or during (*indicates a situation*)
mit	with; by means of (*transportation*)
nach	after; toward; to (*with cities, and with masculine and neuter countries*)
seit	since, for (*referring to time*)
von	from; of; by (*the person doing something*)
zu	to (*with people and some places*)

The above prepositions are always followed by the dative case.

Contractions of dative prepositions

bei dem	=	**beim**
von dem	=	**vom**
zu dem	=	**zum**
zu der	=	**zur**

Kapitel 6

Lernziele

Sprechakte

Talking about food and dining out
Reading and ordering from a menu
Inviting someone to dinner
Accepting and declining invitations
Expressing opinions
Talking about the past
Talking about ecological issues

Grammatik

Perfect tense

Vokabeln

Clothing
Noun suffixes **-heit** and **-keit**
Infinitives used as nouns
Gefallen, gern haben, mögen

Landeskunde

Meals in German-speaking countries and
   bringing gifts when one is a guest
German concern for naturalness
Wine and beer in German-speaking countries
Ecological concerns in the German-speaking
   countries
The alternative movement and **Die Grünen**

Im Café sitzt man gemütlich bei einer Tasse Kaffee.

| Bausteine für Gespräche

Es hat geschmeckt	It tasted great
Christine: Wo warst du gestern abend?	Where were you last night?
Klaus: Warum?	Why?
Christine: Ich habe bei dir angerufen, weil ich meine Notizen bei dir vergessen habe. Aber da war niemand da.	I tried to call you, because I forgot my notes at your house. But there was no one there.
Klaus: Ich bin mit Petra weggewesen. Im Ratskeller. Wir haben ganz toll gegessen.	I was out with Petra. At the Ratskeller. We had a really great meal.
Christine: Du, da ist es ziemlich teuer.	Hey, it's pretty expensive there.
Klaus: Wir haben Petras Geburtstag gefeiert.	We were celebrating Petra's birthday.
Christine: Ah ja?	Oh really?
Klaus: Der Nachtisch war besonders gut — Schokoladencreme. Die hat phantastisch geschmeckt.	Dessert was especially good — chocolate mousse. It tasted fantastic.
Christine: Hör auf, ich kriege gleich Hunger!	Stop it! I'm getting hungry!
Klaus: Weißt du was? Nächstes Mal nehmen wir dich mit.	You know what? Next time we'll take you along.

Fragen

1. Warum hat Christine bei Klaus angerufen?
2. Warum war Klaus nicht zu Hause?
3. Warum haben Klaus und Petra im Ratskeller gegessen?
4. Was hat Klaus zum Nachtisch gegessen?
5. Wie hat der Nachtisch geschmeckt?
6. Was machen Klaus und Petra nächstes Mal?

Sie haben das Wort

In groups of four, practice the questions and responses below. One person
asks the question. Each of the others gives a different response. Then change
roles and practice again.

A   Hast du Hunger?   Ask whether a friend is hungry.

Sie	*Gesprächspartner/in*
Hast du Hunger?	Ja, großen Hunger.
	Ja, ich habe heute noch nichts gegessen.
	Nein, ich habe keinen Hunger.
	Nein, ich habe schon gegessen.

B   Hast du Durst?   Ask whether a friend would like something to drink.

Sie	*Gesprächspartner/in*
Willst du etwas trinken?	Gerne.
	Ja, bitte. Ich möchte **eine Cola°.**
	ein Mineralwasser.
	Nein, danke. Ich habe keinen Durst°.

Filetsteak mit Wacholdersahne

Käse-Tomatenfondue

C   Wie war es im Ratskeller?   Tell a friend you ate in the **Ratskeller.**
She/he will respond.

Sie	*Gesprächspartner/in*
Ich habe gestern im Ratskeller gegessen.	Hast du deinen Geburtstag gefeiert?
	Warst du allein°?
	Was hast du gegessen?
	Hat es geschmeckt?
	Hast du die Schokoladencreme probiert°?

D   Was hast du gegessen?   Ask what your friend(s) had at the **Ratskeller.**

Sie	*Gesprächspartner/in*
Was hast du gegessen?	Steak° und Pommes frites°.
Was habt ihr gegessen?	Spaghetti.
	Wurst und Brot.
	Fisch.

Talking about dining out

E   War das Essen gut?   Ask whether the meal was good.

Sie	*Gesprächspartner/in*
Hat's geschmeckt?	Danke, **gut.**
	sehr gut.
	ganz toll.
	phantastisch.
	Danke, es hat gut geschmeckt.
	Nicht besonders.
	Nein, leider nicht.

F   Kommst du mit?   Tell your friend she/he should come along next time.

Sie	*Gesprächspartner/in*
Nächstes Mal kommst du mit.	Schön. Vergiß° mich aber nicht!
	Schön. Ruf mich dann an!
	Gern. Lädst° du mich ein?
	Hmmmmm. Vielleicht.
	Leider hab' ich kein Geld.
	Hör auf! Soviel Geld hab' ich nicht.

G   Ein Rollenspiel   Use the menu below to create a dialogue between a diner (**Gast**) and a waiter (**Ober**) or waitress (**Fräulein**). You will want to order an appetizer (**Vorspeise**) or soup (**Suppe**), a main course (**Hauptgericht**), and a beverage (**Getränk**). You may want to follow the pattern of the model below. You may also refer to the Supplementary Word Sets for food under *Kapitel 6* in the Reference Section on pages R-27 and R-28.

Ober: Bitte sehr°? Was darf es sein°?	*Yes, please. / May I help you?*
Gast: Was für eine Vorspeise empfehlen° Sie?	*recommend*
Ober: [Der Räucherlachs] ist [sehr gut / besonders gut].	
Gast: Schön. Also, ich nehme zuerst° [den Räucherlachs].	*first*
Dann möchte ich gern [Wiener Schnitzel] mit [Pommes frites and Salat].	
Ober: Und zum Trinken°?	*to drink*
Gast: [Ein Pils° / eine Cola / ein Mineralwasser], bitte.	*Pilsener beer*
Ober: Sonst noch etwas?	
Gast: Nein, danke, das ist alles.	
Ober: Bitte schön°.	*you're welcome*

Ratsweinkeller
HAMBURG

FAMILIE DEHN

HANSESTADT HAMBURG

Vorspeisen　　　　　　　　　　DM

Cocktail von Büsumer Krabben, überzogen
mit pikanter Sauce, Toast und Butter . . . .　15,75
Cocktail of Büsumer shrimps / Cocktail des crevettes de Büsum

Schiffchen von Honigmelone mit gewürfeltem
Katenschinken, Baguette und Butter . . . .　16,—
Chilled melon with smoked ham / Melon glacé, jambon fumé

Norwegischer Räucherlachs mit
Sahnemeerrettich, Toast und Butter . . . .　21,50
Smoked salmon, cream of horseradish / Saumon fumé creme raifort

Suppen

Doppelte Kraftbrühe mit Eigelb
und Rindermark . . . .　5,75
Clear soup with egg and marrow / Consommé double avec œuf et moëlle

Hamburger Krebssuppe mit Weinbrand
und Sahnetupfen . . . .　6,25
Crayfish soup / Bisque d'écrevisses

Gebundene Lachssuppe mit Dillspitzen
und Sahnehäubchen . . . .　6,25
Creamsoup of salmon / Crème de saumon

Klare Fischsuppe „Ratsweinkeller" mit Safran,
Gemüsestreifen und Meeresfrüchten . . . .　7,40
Clear Fish-Soup with seafood / Soupe aux fruites de mer

Fisch-Gerichte frisch von der Auktion　　DM

Kabeljau mit Weißwein pochiert,
überkrustet mit Mornay-Sauce, Blattspinat
und Petersilienkartoffeln . . . .　15,50
Fillet of codfish with cheese-sauce / Filet de cabillaud „florentin"

Goldbarschfilet in brauner Petersilienbutter
gebraten, Salzkartoffeln und
Salatteller . . . .　17,50
Fillet of perch in brown butter / Filet de perche à la meunière

Regenbogenforelle mit Kräutern
und Butterflöckchen gefüllt, in Folie gegart,
Schwenkkartoffeln und Salatteller . . . .　19,90
Trout with herbs in foil / Truite aux herbes en feuille d'aluminium

Schollenfilets „Blankenese" mit
Champignons und Tomatenwürfel, nappiert
mit Sauce Bearnaise, Petersilienkartoffeln
und Salat . . . .　21,90
Fillets of plaice with mushrooms / Filets de plie aux champignons

Nordsee-Seezunge „Müllerin Art"
in schäumender Butter, Petersilienkartoffeln　　Tages-
und Salat . . . .　preis
Sole à la meunière with brown butter / Sole à la meunière

Fleisch-Gerichte　　　　　　　　DM

Kasseler Kotelette mit Burgundersauce,
Ananaskraut und Kartoffelkroketten . . . .　17,40
Smoked pork-cotelette with red wine sauce
Côtelette de pork fumé, sauce bordelaise

Streifen von Putenbrust „Casimir" in
Curryrahmsauce mit Früchten, Butterreis
und Salatteller . . . .　21,30
Flakes of turkey-breast in Currysauce
Eminčé à dé poitrine de dinde au curry

Schweinerückensteak mit Champignons
und Tomatenwürfeln, Berner Salbei-Rösti
und Salatteller . . . .　21,75
Porksteak with mushrooms / Steak de porc avec champignons

Original Wiener Schnitzel vom Kalbfleisch
mit Pommes-frites und Salatteller . . . .　25,50
Veal-Scallops „Vienna style" / Escallope de veau à la viennoise

Kalbsschnitzel „Cordon-bleu" mit Schinken
und Käse gefüllt und in Eihülle gebraten,
feine Erbsen und Pommes frites . . . .　26,85
Veal steak „Cordon bleu" / Escalope de veau „cordon bleu"

Filetsteak vom Rind mit Grilltomate,
Sauce Bearnaise, Pommes-frites
und Salatteller . . . .　34,70
Filetsteak with grilled tomato and Sauce Bearnaise
Filet-steak de bœuf, tomate grillée, Sauce Bearnaise

Biere frisch vom Faß　　　　　　DM

Holsten-Pilsener	0,3 l	3,60
Holsten-Pilsener	0,5 l	5,65
Moravia-Pils	0,3 l	3,65
Moravia-Pils	0,5 l	5,80

Erfrischungen

Coca-Cola	0,2 l	2,95
Fanta oder Sprite	0,2 l	2,95
Alster-Wasser	0,3 l	3,65
Alster-Wasser	0,5 l	5,65
Orangensaft, natur	0,2 l	5,20
Apfelsaft	0,2 l	3,50
Johannisbeermost	0,2 l	4,10

Kaffee und Tee　　　　Tasse/Kännchen

Bohnenkaffee	2,60	5,20
Bohnenmocca	4,10	8,20
Schokolade	2,60	5,20
Engl. Tee	2,60	5,20
Kaffee Hag	2,60	5,20

Im Endpreis sind Bedienungsgeld und gesetzliche Getränke- u. Mehrwertsteuer enthalten

Vokabeln

Substantive

die **Cola, -** cola drink
der **Durst** thirst
der **Hunger** hunger
der **Nachtisch** dessert
das **Mal** time; **nächstes Mal** next time
die **Pommes frites** (*pl.*) French fries
der **Ratskeller** cellar bar/restaurant under the town hall
die **Schokolade** chocolate
die **Schokoladencreme** chocolate mousse
das **Steak, -s** steak
das **Wasser** water; das **Mineralwasser** mineral water

Verben

an•rufen, angerufen to phone
auf•hören to stop (an activity)
ein•laden (lädt ein), eingeladen to invite; to treat (pay for someone)
feiern to celebrate
kriegen to get
mit•kommen, (ist) mitgekommen to come along
probieren to try, taste (something); **probier den Käse** try the cheese
schmecken (+ *dat.***)** to taste; **der Käse schmeckt** the cheese tastes good
vergessen (vergißt), vergessen to forget

Mathäser-Bierstadt
Größter Bierausschank der Welt
am Stachus
Täglich Frühschoppen-Konzerte und Blasmusik
Münchner Spezialitätenküche
Faßbier-Ausschank der weltberühmten
Löwenbräu-Biere
Tiefgarage im Hause Telefon 59 28 96

Andere Wörter

allein alone
gestern abend last night
niemand nobody
phantastisch fantastic
toll great, wild
ziemlich quite; **ziemlich gut** pretty good

Besondere Ausdrücke

bei dir an•rufen to phone you
Durst haben to be thirsty
Hunger haben to be hungry
Hunger kriegen (*or* **bekommen)** to get hungry

Many Germans eat their main meal (*Mittagessen*) at noon. It may consist of two or three courses. Dessert (*Nachtisch* or *Dessert*) is usually fruit, pudding, or ice cream. Cakes and pastries are served at afternoon coffee time (*Kaffeestunde*). It is customary to say *Guten Appetit* or *Mahlzeit* before beginning to eat, and others may wish you the same (*Danke, gleichfalls*).

Even in a restaurant, when sharing a table with a stranger who has asked *Ist hier frei?*, one wishes the stranger *Guten Appetit*. Menus are posted outside most restaurants. One usually pays the waiter (*Ober*) or waitress (*Fräulein*); the service charge (*Bedienung*) or tip is included in the bill, although it is customary to add a little extra by rounding off the bill.

When people are invited to a friend's house for dinner or afternoon coffee (*Kaffeestunde*), it is customary to bring a small gift (*Mitbringsel*). Most often the guest will bring a small bouquet, a box of chocolates, or a bottle of wine.

Zu Mittag ißt man warm.

| Natürlich

Vorbereitung auf das Lesen

- *Zum Thema*

1. Viele Kuchen sind mit künstlichen° Farben dekoriert. Essen Sie solche Kuchen?   *artificial*
2. Sind viele Leute bei Ihnen gegen Konservierungsmittel° in Lebensmitteln?   *preservatives*
3. Gibt es viele Geschäfte, wo man „natürliche" Produkte kaufen kann?
4. Kaufen Sie nur natürliche Produkte: Lebensmittel ohne Insektizide und Konservierungsmittel? natürliche Seife°? chemiefreie Shampoos? Kleidung aus natürlichem Stoff°?   *soap*   *cloth*

• *Leitfragen*

1. Frau Fischer hat einen schönen Kuchen gebacken. Warum mögen ihn die deutschen Gäste nicht?
2. Warum gehen viele Deutsche zur Kur?
3. Warum gibt es in Deutschland viele Bio-Läden?
4. Welches Wort findet man in vielen deutschen Reklamen? Warum?
5. Wer sind „Die Grünen"?

Die Fischers aus Amerika leben erst seit einigen Wochen in der Bundesrepublik. Sie arbeiten bei einer amerikanischen Firma in Hamburg. Die Kinder haben schon Freunde gefunden, und den Eltern gefällt es auch schon besser als zuerst.

5 Eines Tages kommen einige Bekannte zum Kaffee. Frau Fischer hat einen leckeren Kuchen gebacken. Sie hat ihn rot, grün und blau dekoriert, so daß er besonders schön aussieht. Fischers bieten also Kaffee und Kuchen an. Der Kaffee schmeckt allen ausgezeichnet, aber von dem Kuchen probiert jeder nur ein Stück und sagt dann: „Nein, danke; es tut
10 mir furchtbar leid, aber ich kann wirklich nicht mehr." Oder: „Danke, wirklich. Ich muß auf meine schlanke Linie achten.°" Fischers denken: **auf ... achten:** *watch my figure*
Merkwürdig! Was haben wir nur falsch gemacht? Der Kuchen kann es doch wirklich nicht sein. Der hat unseren Gästen zu Hause doch immer gut geschmeckt. Oder haben wir vielleicht etwas Dummes gesagt? Aber
15 das kann es doch auch nicht sein, denn die Gespräche waren lebhaft°   *lively*
und interessant.

Man spricht über Politik, die Kinder und die Schulen. Eine junge Frau erzählt von ihren letzten Ferien: „So ganz richtige Ferien waren es ja nicht. Ich war zur Kur° in Bad Salzuflen*." Herr Fischer fragt: „Zur Kur?   **ich ... Kur:** *I went to a spa*
20 Waren Sie denn krank?" — „Na ja, so richtig krank nicht. Aber ich habe etwas Rheuma°, und da tut das tägliche Baden in den natürlichen Quel-   *rheumatism*
len° doch sehr gut. Außerdem hilft ja auch die Ruhe° sehr — mal ganz   *springs / rest*
weg von der Familie und Arbeit. Es hat wirklich sehr geholfen." Frau
Fischer hat noch eine Frage: „Ist so was° denn nicht sehr teuer?" —   **so was:** *something like that*
25 „Nein, das ist nicht so schlimm. Den größten° Teil hat ja die Kranken-   *largest*
kasse° bezahlt. — Alle finden es ganz richtig, daß die Kasse bezahlt, denn   *health insurance*
„die Kräfte° der Natur sind doch am besten.°"   *powers /* **am besten:** *the best*

Ein junger Mann erzählt, daß er gerade in einem Bio-Laden° eingekauft   *organic food store*
hat. Er fragt Frau Fischer, ob sie schon in so einem Geschäft gewesen ist.
30 „Nein, was ist denn ein Bio-Laden?" Der junge Mann erklärt: „Da gibt es

---

*Towns where spas are located often have names that begin with **Bad** (*bath*). There are 250 registered spas in the **Bundesrepublik** alone.

biologisch angebautes° Gemüse und Obst, überhaupt natürliche Lebens- [biologisch angebaut: *organically grown*]
mittel. Das sind Lebensmittel ohne Insektizide, ohne künstliche Farben,
ohne Kunstdünger°. Sie sind also chemiefrei. Diese Sachen sind auf [*chemical fertilizer*]
natürlichem Mist° gewachsen. Die Bio-Läden gibt es erst seit kurzer Zeit. [*manure*]
35 Sie sind alternativ." Seine Mutter meint aber: „Sie sind fast wie
Reformhäuser.° Und die gibt es ja schon lange. Ich kaufe ziemlich viel da, [*health-food stores*]
Lebensmittel und auch andere Sachen, Seife z.B. und Hautcreme.° Wir [*skin cream*]
kaufen viel Tee, Kamille°, Lindenblüte° und so weiter. Die helfen mir, [*chamomile tea / linden tea*]
wenn es mir mal nicht so gut geht."
40　　Nach diesen Gesprächen fangen Fischers an, ihre Umwelt genauer° [*more carefully*]
anzusehen. Sie haben vorher nie bemerkt, wie wichtig der Begriff° der° [*concept / of (gen.)*]
Natürlichkeit in den Reklamen ist. Aber nun sehen sie:

> **Zeller° Tabletten**　　　　　　　　[*[brand name]*]
> **Pflanzenkräfte° gegen Kopfschmerzen**　　[*plant power*]

Eine andere Firma macht Reklame° für Tee: [macht Reklame: *advertises*]

> **Arzneitees° aus pflanzlichen° Wirkstoffen°**　[*medicinal teas / plant* (adj.) */ ingredients*]

Oder da gibt es die Shampoos von *Viveen°*: [*[brand name]*]

> **Unsere Shampoos sind garantiert aus Pflanzen**

45 Es gibt auch natürliche Hemden und Hosen und Jacken:

> **Sportmoden° von WOHLA°**　　　　　　　　　[*sports fashions / [name of company]*]
> **100% reine Baumwolle° — das natürliche Gewebe°**　[*cotton / material*]
> **für gesundes Leben**

Fischers können nun auch verstehen, warum die Grünen° hier im Parla- [*[environmentalist political party]*]
ment sitzen: Sie sind die Umweltpartei. Sie protestieren gegen
technische Großprojekte, gegen die Zerstörung° der Natur. Sie plädie- [*destruction / plead*]
ren° für mehr Fahrradwege, für reine Luft und reines Wasser, für einen
50 neuen Anfang.
　　Nun wissen Fischers genau, warum der Kuchen ihren Gästen nicht
geschmeckt hat. Die Farben waren nicht natürlich, sie waren künstlich.
Frau Fischer lächelt und sagt zu ihrem Mann: „Da haben wir wieder etwas
gelernt: *Schön* ist eben nicht immer *schön*."

Protection of the environment has become increasingly important for the German-speaking countries. Water and air pollution (*Wasser- und Luftverschmutzung*) have caused serious damage to forests and rivers and have threatened their actual survival. The Europeans speak of the dying forests and rivers (*Wald- und Flußsterben*). About one third of the forests in the *Bundesrepublik* is damaged.

People living in the German-speaking countries have become more aware of the necessity for environmental protection (*Umweltschutz*) in recent years. There is a strong sentiment among some groups against atomic-power plants, and many people use bicycles instead of cars, try to conserve water, and use phosphate-free laundry detergents. In cities, almost every neighborhood provides several containers for recycling glass and paper. Many health-food stores (*Naturkostläden*, or *Bioläden*) sell products that are friendly to the environment (*umweltfreundlich*) — products like organic vegetables and grains grown without insecticides or chemical fertilizers, recycled-paper products and stationery, and even "natural" cosmetic products.

Recycling ist umweltfreundlich.

Fragen zum Lesestück

1. Wie lange leben Fischers schon in der Bundesrepublik?
2. Wo arbeiten sie?
3. Wie gefällt es den Eltern?
4. Wer kommt eines Tages zum Kaffee?
5. Was hat Frau Fischer gebacken?
6. Warum sieht der Kuchen schön aus?
7. Wieviel Stücke ißt jeder von dem Kuchen?
8. Über was spricht man?
9. Von was erzählt die junge Frau?
10. Warum war sie zur Kur?
11. Wer bezahlt die Kur?

12. Warum finden es alle ganz richtig, daß die Krankenkasse den größten Teil bezahlt?
13. Wo hat der junge Mann eingekauft?
14. Was für Sachen kann man da kaufen?
15. Was sehen Fischers oft in den Reklamen?
16. Aus was sind die Shampoos von *Viveen*?
17. Aus was sind die natürlichen Hemden und Hosen?
18. Wer sind die Grünen?
19. Gegen was sind die Grünen? Und für was?
20. Warum hat der Kuchen den Gästen nicht geschmeckt?
21. Was haben Fischers gelernt?

Erzählen Sie!   Select one of the two topics below to talk about the reading selection. Use the cued words.

A Kaffee	B Natürlichkeit
Fischers in Hamburg	Kur: Baden
Bekannte beim Kaffee	Ruhe
Kuchen mit Farben	nicht teuer / Krankenkasse
natürliche und künstliche Farben	Bio-Läden
	natürliche Lebensmittel
	Reklamen: Tabletten gegen
	Kopfschmerzen
	Shampoo
	Kleidung°
	die Grünen

Sie haben das Wort

Interview   Interview a fellow student about her/his views on "naturalness" in her/his life.

> Talking about ecological issues

1. Ißt du (Geburtstags)kuchen mit künstlichen Farben?
2. Kann man in diesem Land „reine" Lebensmittel (ohne Konservierungsmittel) kaufen?
3. Sind solche reinen Lebensmittel teuer?
4. Kaufst du oft in Bio-Läden ein?
5. Über was sprichst du mit Freunden — Politik, Vorlesungen, Umweltprobleme?
6. Wohin kann man in diesem Land zur Kur fahren? Was macht man dort?
7. Gibt es in Amerika oder Kanada eine Umweltpartei?

Man kauft seine natürlichen Lebensmittel im Reformhaus.

Vokabeln

Substantive

der **Anfang, ¨-e** beginning
der **Bekannte, -n, -n (ein Bekannter)/**
  die (eine) **Bekannte, -n** acquaintance
die **Firma**, (*pl.*) **Firmen** company
der **Gast, ¨-e** guest
das **Geschäft, -e** store; business
das **Gespräch, -e** conversation
das **Hemd, -en** shirt
die **Hose, -n** pants
die **Jacke, -n** jacket
der **Laden, ¨-** store, shop

das **Leben** life
die **Luft** air
die **Natur** nature
die **Reklame, -n** advertisement, commercial
die **Sache, -n** thing
die **Seife, -n** soap
das **Shampoo, -s** shampoo
das **Stück, -e** piece
die **Umwelt** environment
die **Zeit, -en** time

Das beste Persil
für Wäsche und Umwelt.

Verben

an·bieten (bietet an), angeboten   to offer

an·fangen (fängt an), angefangen to begin; **mit der Arbeit anfangen** to begin work

aus·sehen (sieht aus), ausgesehen to look like, seem

backen (bäckt), gebacken   to bake

baden   to bathe; swim

bemerken   to notice

dekorieren   to decorate

gefallen (gefällt), gefallen (+ *dat.*) to please, be pleasing to

halten (hält), gehalten   to hold; **halten von**   to think of, have an opinion

helfen (hilft), geholfen (+ *dat.*)   to help; **bei [der Arbeit] helfen**   to help with [work]

kosten   to cost

lächeln (über + *acc.*)   to smile (about)

meinen   to mean; to be of the opinion

tragen (trägt), getragen   to carry; to wear

tun (tut), getan   to do

wachsen (wächst), ist gewachsen   to grow

ICH SCHWÄRME FÜR DIE THERME

Andere Wörter

alle   all

ausgezeichnet   excellent

außerdem   in addition; as well

bekannt   well-known, familiar

falsch   wrong

gerade   just; straight

gesund   healthy

kurz   short

künstlich   artificial

lange   a long time

lecker   delicious

merkwürdig   strange

nie   never

nun   now; well (*interjection*)

rein   clean; pure

schlimm   bad, terrible

täglich   daily

überhaupt   in general; at all

vorher   before

wichtig   important

zuerst   first

Besondere Ausdrücke

eines Tages   one day

etwas Dummes   something dumb

na ja   well now

seit kurzer Zeit   recently

und so weiter (*abbrev.* **usw.**)   and so on, etc.

zum Kaffee   for (afternoon) coffee

Erweiterung des Wortschatzes

1   Kleidungsstücke

1.	der Anzug, ⸚e	7.	der Schuh, -e	13.	die Hose, -n
2.	der Handschuh, -e	8.	der Hut, ⸚e	14.	die Jacke, -n
3.	der Pulli, -s	9.	das Hemd, -en	15.	die Socke, -n
4.	der Regenmantel, ⸚	10.	das Kleid, -er	16.	die Jeans (*pl.*)
5.	der Rock, ⸚e	11.	die Bluse, -n	17.	die Strumpfhose, -n
6.	der Sakko, -s	12.	die (Hand)tasche, -n		

For additional articles of clothing see the Supplementary Word Sets on
clothing for *Kapitel 6* in the Reference Section (R-27).

Sie haben das Wort

A   Was tragen Sie?   Answer the questions below.

1. Was tragen Sie im Winter? Im Sommer?
2. Was tragen Sie, wenn Sie zur Vorlesung gehen?
3. Was tragen Sie, wenn Sie tanzen gehen?
4. Was möchten Sie zum Geburtstag haben?
5. Welche Farben tragen Sie gern?

B   Wie gefällt es Ihnen?   Choose a picture in this text with articles of clothing and ask several fellow students their opinion about some of the items.

Was hältst du von [dem Kleid]?	[Das] muß furchtbar teuer sein. Was kostet [es]?
	[Das] ist schön/phantastisch/praktisch.
	[Das] ist ja interessant/nicht schlecht.
	Das kann ich nicht so genau sagen.
	[Das] sieht billig aus.
	[Das] ist nichts Besonderes.

2   Gefallen

Dein Freund **gefällt** mir.	I like your friend. [I think your friend is O.K.]
Ich habe deinen Freund gern.	I like your friend. [I'm fond of him.]
Deine Freunde **gefallen** mir nicht.	I don't like your friends. [I don't care for them.]
Deine Freunde mag ich nicht.	I don't like your friends. [I dislike them.]

Gefallen, mögen, and **gern haben** are all equivalent to English *like*. However, they express different degrees of liking. **Mögen** and **gern haben** usually express stronger expressions of liking than **gefallen**.

| Das Bild gefällt mir. ⎫
Mir gefällt das Bild. ⎭ | I like the picture. |
| Mir gefällt es nicht, daß Mark so wenig liest. | I don't like (the fact) that Mark reads so little. |

When using the verb **gefallen**, what one likes is the subject and thus in the nominative case. The person who likes something is in the dative. Note that sentences with **gefallen** often begin with the dative.

C   Was bedeutet das?

1. Wie gefällt deinem Freund Mark Hamburg?
2. Dem gefällt es sehr.
3. Diese Vorlesungen gefallen Mark auch.
4. Was gefällt deinem Freund nicht so gut?
5. Dem gefällt es nicht, daß es so viel regnet.
6. Es gefällt Mark auch nicht, daß es soviel Autos gibt.

D   Wie sagt man das?   A friend wants to know how your family is enjoying its stay in Munich. Use the verb gefallen.

1. Does your family like it in Munich?
2. Yes. Very much. My brother likes the fact [es] that there are so many cafés.
3. My sister likes the cafés also.
4. My sister and my brother like the fact [es] that they can speak with students there.
5. My father doesn't like the fact [es] that the stores close so early in the evenings.
6. I don't like that either.

3   Noun suffixes -heit and -keit

die **Gesundheit**   health   die **Natürlichkeit**   naturalness
    gesund   healthy   **natürlich**   natural

Nouns ending in **-heit** or **-keit** are feminine nouns. Many nouns of this type are related to adjectives. The suffix **-keit** is used instead of **-heit** with adjectives ending in **-ig** or **-lich.**

E   Wörter mit -heit   Complete the second sentence in each pair with a noun ending in **-heit** related to the boldfaced adjective.

1. Der Plan ist **einfach**. Eben diese _____ gefällt mir.
2. Das finde ich **dumm** von dir. Da sieht man wieder deine große _____ .
3. Der Garten ist sehr **trocken**. Wie lange dauert diese _____ noch?
4. Baumwolle ist **gesund**. Hosen aus Baumwolle sind gut für die _____ .
5. Ingrid findet die Natur **schön**. Mir gefällt die _____ der Natur auch.
6. Sie liegt **krank** im Bett. Sie hat eine schwere _____ .

F   Wörter mit -keit   Complete the second sentence in each pair with a noun ending in **-keit** related to the boldfaced adjective.

1. Bei vielen Deutschen muß alles **natürlich** sein. Denen gefällt _____ in Essen und Trinken.
2. Die Frage ist **richtig**. Oder glaubst du nicht an ihre _____ ?
3. Das Kind sieht seiner Mutter **ähnlich**. Siehst du nicht die _____ ?
4. Wir machen eine **wichtige** Reise nach Basel. Es ist von großer _____ , daß wir nach Basel fahren.

Wir bauen Vertrauen. *Ford*

4   Infinitives used as nouns

Wandern ist gesund.	Hiking is healthy.
Das Schlafen in frischer Luft ist gesund.	Sleeping in fresh air is healthy.

German infinitives may be used as nouns. An infinitive used as a noun is always neuter. The English equivalent is often a gerund, that is, the *-ing* form of a verb used as a noun.

G   Was bedeutet das?

1. Laufen ist schön.
2. Reinheit und Natürlichkeit in Essen und Trinken gefallen den Deutschen.
3. Es gehört zum Einkaufen am Wochenende, daß man Blumen mitbringt.
4. Schwimmen ist ein schöner Sport.
5. Viele Leute finden Fliegen furchtbar.

Spielen macht Spaß. Klavierspielen.

| Übungen zur Aussprache _____

Review the pronunciation of **s** (before and between vowels), **ß (ss)**, and **z** in the Reference section at the end of the book. Read aloud the words in each column, first from top to bottom and then across. Check your pronunciation by listening to your instructor or the tape.

[s̩]	[ts]		[s̩]	[s]	[ts]
so	Zoo		reisen	reißen	reizen
sehen	zehn		heiser	heißen	heizen
Seile	Zeile		Geisel	Geiß	Geiz
sog	zog		weisen	weißen	Weizen
Sohn	Zone		leise	beißen	beizen

Read the sentences below aloud, paying special attention to the way you pronounce **s**, **ß (ss)**, and **z** in the boldfaced words.

1. Warum haben **Sie zwei Gläser,** und **Sabine** hat nur ein **Glas?**
2. **Sie müssen** doch **wissen, was Sie essen sollen.**
3. Kann man wirklich **zu** viel **lesen?**
4. Wie **heißen diese Sachen?**
5. Wenn ich im **Sommer Zeit** habe, mache ich eine **Reise** in die **Schweiz.**

Wenn die Katze aus dem Haus ist, tanzen die Mäuse.

Grammatik und Übungen

1 The perfect tense

Ich **habe** mit Karin **gesprochen.**   I *have spoken* with Karin.
                                             I *spoke* with Karin.

Sie **ist** nach Hause **gegangen.**   She *has gone* home.
                                             She *went* home.

German has several past tenses. One of them is the perfect tense, which is commonly used in conversation to refer to past actions or states.

The perfect tense is made up of the present tense of the auxiliary **haben** or **sein** and the past participle of the verb. In independent clauses, the past participle is the last element in the sentence.

2 Past participles of regular weak verbs

Infinitive	Past participle	Perfect tense
machen	ge + mach + t	Er **hat** es nicht **gemacht.**
arbeiten	ge + arbeit + et	Sie **hat gearbeitet**.

German verbs may be classified as weak or strong according to the way in which they form their past tenses. A regular weak verb is a verb whose infinitive stem remains unchanged in the past tense forms.

The past participle of a weak verb is formed by adding **-t** to the unchanged stem. The **-t** expands to **-et** in verbs like **arbeiten, baden,** and **regnen.** In the past participle, most weak verbs also have the prefix **ge-.**

3 Auxiliary *haben* with past participles

ich	**habe** etwas **gefragt**	wir	**haben** etwas **gefragt**
du	**hast** etwas **gefragt**	ihr	**habt** etwas **gefragt**
er/es/sie	**hat** etwas **gefragt**	sie	**haben** etwas **gefragt**
	Sie **haben** etwas **gefragt**		

The chart above shows how the perfect tense of a weak verb is formed, using the auxiliary **haben.**

A Wir haben es schon gehört.   Your friend is eager to pass on a bit of gossip to various persons. However, you tell your friend that you and they have already heard it.

▶ Frau Fischer   *Frau Fischer hat es schon gehört.*

1. Klaus
2. ich
3. Professor Weber
4. unsere Freunde
5. wir
6. Karin

B Ich hab's schon gemacht.   Heidi wants you to do all sorts of things. Tell her you've already done what she wants.

▶ Koch jetzt Kaffee!   *Den Kaffee habe ich doch schon gekocht.*

1. Mach die Arbeit!
2. Frag den Professor!
3. Hörst du die Vorlesung?
4. Lern die Vokabeln!
5. Kauf das Buch!
6. Such das Geld!
7. Spiel heute abend Tennis!

4 Past participles of irregular weak verbs

Infinitive	Past participle	Perfect tense
bringen	ge + brach + t	Wer **hat** die Blumen **gebracht?**
denken	ge + dach + t	Jens **hat** an den Wein **gedacht.**
kennen	ge + kann + t	Sie **hat** Thomas gut **gekannt.**
wissen	ge + wuß + t	Wir **haben** es **gewußt.**

A few weak verbs, including **bringen, denken, kennen,** and **wissen,** are irregular. The past participle has the prefix **ge-** and the ending **-t,** but the verb also undergoes a stem change. The past participles of irregular weak verbs are noted in the vocabularies as follows: **denken, gedacht.**

C Alles vorbereiten.   Gerd and his friends are getting ready for a party. Restate each sentence below in the perfect tense.

▶ Gerd denkt an Christine.   *Gerd hat an Christine gedacht.*

1. Christine denkt an den Wein.
2. Gerd weiß den Namen.
3. Klaus weiß den Namen nicht.
4. Gerd kennt das Weingeschäft.
5. Klaus kennt es nicht.
6. Weißt du den Namen?
7. Wer bringt das Essen?
8. Was bringst du?

German wines and beers are famous throughout the world. Most German wines are white wines and they are classified according to quality. Table wine (*Tafelwein*) is considered good; *Qualitätswein* is rated better; the best-quality wine is a *Qualitätswein mit Prädikat*. Depending on the time of vintage and the selection of grapes, one distinguishes between *Kabinett* (picked during general harvest), *Spätlese* (picked after general harvest), *Auslese* (from selected overripe grapes), *Beerenauslese* and *Trockenbeerenauslese* (from selected sun-dried, raisin-like grapes). The most popular kind of grape is the *Riesling*.

Beers in the Federal Republic of Germany are brewed in more than 1,200 breweries. There are many different kinds of beer, of which the *Pils* (a light, slightly bitter beer) is the most popular. Many regions of the Federal Republic have beers that are unique to the area. The Rhineland has its *Alt* (a dark, slightly sweet beer, similar to ale), Dortmund its *Export* (originally brewed to survive long journeys at sea), and Berlin its *Weißbier* (a wheat beer, usually served with raspberry juice). In the southern regions people favor *Weizenbier* (wheat beer, often served with a slice of lemon) and *Bockbier* (a strong, malty, very tasty beer).

Many of the folk festivals in the German-speaking countries are associated with regional beers or wines. The most famous and largest folk festival is the *Oktoberfest* in Munich. It takes place each autumn and offers a great variety of live entertainment, dancing, food and its special brew of *Märzenbier* and *Münchner*. The regions along the Rhine, Moselle, Neckar, and Danube rivers celebrate the new wine every autumn with a local *Weinfest*.

Oktoberfest in München

D　Was wollen Sie sagen?　The verbs listed below are most of the weak verbs you have learned so far. Choose ten of these verbs and use them in the perfect tense.

arbeiten □ brauchen □ danken □ fragen □ glauben □ hören □ kaufen □ kochen □ kosten □ lächeln □ leben □ lernen □ machen □ meinen □ regnen □ sagen □ schenken □ schmecken □ schneien □ spielen □ suchen □ tanzen □ warten □ wohnen □ zahlen □ zelten

5　Use of the perfect tense

Where are you going?
Gerd has invited me to dinner (and we're going this evening).

In English, the present perfect tense and the simple past tense have different meanings. The present perfect tense refers to a period of time that continues into the present and is thus still uncompleted.

What did you do today?
Gerd invited me to dinner (and we went).

The simple past tense, on the other hand, refers to a period of time that is completed at the moment of speaking.

Gerd hat mich zum Essen eingeladen.　$\begin{cases}\text{Gerd has invited me to dinner.}\\\text{Gerd invited me to dinner.}\end{cases}$

In German, the perfect tense refers to all actions or states in the past, whether they are uncompleted (as in the English present perfect) or completed (as in the English past). Context usually makes the meaning clear.

In German, the perfect tense is most frequently used in conversation to refer to past actions or states, and is therefore often referred to as the "conversational past." German also has a simple past tense (see *Kapitel 10*, page 352) that is used to narrate connected events in the past, and which is therefore frequently called the "narrative past."

E　Wie sagt man das?　Give the German equivalents of the conversational exchanges below, using the perfect tense.

▶　What did Erik say?　*Was hat Erik gesagt?*
　　— I didn't hear it.　　— *Ich habe es nicht gehört.*

1.　Christel bought a jacket.
　　— What did it cost?
2.　Why didn't the men work yesterday?
　　— It rained.

3. Why didn't Barbara buy the purse?
   — She didn't have any money.
4. Markus cooked the meal.
   — Really? I didn't know that.
5. Who brought the wine?
   — I don't know. I didn't ask.

6 Past participles of strong verbs

Infinitive	Past participle	Perfect tense
finden	ge + fund + en	Ich **habe** es **gefunden**.
nehmen	ge + nomm + en	Ich **habe** es nicht **genommen**.
sehen	ge + seh + en	Ich **habe** es **gesehen**.

A strong verb is a verb that changes its stem vowel (and occasionally consonants) in the formation of past tenses. The past participle of a strong verb is
formed by adding **-en** to the stem of the past participle. (Note the exception
getan). In the past participle, most strong verbs have the prefix **ge-**. Past
participles of strong verbs are noted in the vocabularies as follows: **nehmen,
genommen**.

For a list of strong verbs, see the grammatical tables in the Reference Section (R-17 and R-18).

Infinitive	Past participle
backen	gebacken
halten	gehalten
schlafen	geschlafen
tragen	getragen
tun	getan

F   Kuchen backen   Tell about Peter's cake-baking experience. Restate in
the perfect tense.

▶ Warum schläft Peter heute so lange?   *Warum hat Peter heute so lange
                                          geschlafen?*

1. Er tut heute nicht viel.
2. Er bäckt nur einen Kuchen.
3. Was halten die Freunde von seinem Plan?
4. Sie backen auch einen Kuchen.
5. Dann tragen sie die Kuchen zu den Nachbarn.
6. Was tun die Nachbarn dann?

Infinitive	Past participle
geben	gegeben
liegen	gelegen
lesen	gelesen
sehen	gesehen
essen	gegessen
sitzen	gesessen

G   Im Café.   You and Klaus start out in the café and end up at the movies. Restate the sentences below in the perfect tense.

▶   Wir sitzen im Café.   *Wir haben im Café gesessen.*

1.   Ein Buch über die Schweiz liegt da.
2.   Ich gebe Klaus das Buch.
3.   Zuerst liest er das Buch.
4.   Dann essen wir ein Wurstbrot.
5.   Ich esse auch ein Ei.
6.   Später sehen wir einen Film.

Infinitive	Past participle
helfen	geholfen
nehmen	genommen
sprechen	gesprochen
finden	gefunden
trinken	getrunken
leihen	geliehen
schreiben	geschrieben

H   Was haben sie getan?   Restate the conversational exchanges below in the perfect tense.

▶   Nehmen Gerd und Serge den Zug?   *Haben Gerd und Serge den Zug*
     — Nein, sie leihen ein Auto.   *genommen?*
                                          — Nein, sie haben ein Auto ge-
                                          liehen.

1.   Trinken Sie Kaffee?
     — Nein, ich nehme Tee.
2.   Schreibst du die Karte?
     — Nein, ich finde sie nicht.
3.   Sprechen Gerd und Susi gut Englisch?
     — Ja, aber David hilft ihnen.

TEEKANNE FÜR TEEKENNER

I   Wie sagt man das?   Give German equivalents of each of the two-line dialogues below.

▶ Have you taken my ballpoint, Gabi?
    — No, I haven't seen it.

Hast du meinen Kuli genommen, Gabi?
    — Nein, den habe ich nicht gesehen.

1. Have you eaten already, Susanne?
    — No, I haven't had time.
2. Did you sleep well, Benno?
    — No, I drank too much coffee last night.
3. Have you spoken with Mrs. Danziger, Tanja?
    — No, but I wrote her daughter.

Sie haben das Wort

Essen und trinken   Find a partner and ask each other questions about yesterday's meals. Use the cued words.

> Talking about meals you ate yesterday

▶ frühstücken:° wann?   *Wann hast du gefrühstückt?*

to eat breakfast

1. essen / trinken: was / zum Frühstück?
2. essen: wann / zu Mittag [zu Abend]?
3. essen / trinken: was / zum Mittagessen [zum Abendessen]?
4. kochen: wer?
5. schmecken?

7   Separable-prefix verbs in the perfect tense

Infinitive	Past participle	Perfect tense
anfangen	an + **ge** + fangen	Kirstin **hat** gestern **angefangen.**
einkaufen	ein + **ge** + kauft	Ingrid **hat** heute **eingekauft**.

The prefix **ge-** of the past participle comes between the separable prefix and the stem of the participle. Both weak and strong verbs may have separable prefixes. Below is a list of some separable-prefix strong verbs you have encountered.

Infinitive	Past participle
anfangen	angefangen
ansehen	angesehen
aussehen	ausgesehen
anbieten	angeboten
einladen	eingeladen
mitnehmen	mitgenommen

J   Studentenleben   Restate the conversational exchanges below in the perfect tense.

▶   Denkst du an dein Referat?   *Hast du an dein Referat gedacht?*
     — Klar. Ich fange heute an.   *— Klar. Ich habe heute*
                                    angefangen.

1.   Hört Gisela mit Geschichte auf?
     — Ja, sie fängt mit Mathematik an.
2.   Lädt Klaus für Samstag einige Freunde ein?
     — Natürlich. Er lädt alle seine Freunde ein.
3.   Kauft er auch Wein ein?
     — Na klar. Er kauft auch Käse, Wurst und Brot ein.
4.   Bringen seine Freunde etwas mit?
     — Natürlich. Sie bringen viel mit.

8   Past participles without the ge- prefix

● *Verbs ending in -ieren*

Infinitive	Past participle	Perfect tense
studieren	studiert	Dirk **hat** in München **studiert**.
probieren	probiert	**Hast** du den Wein **probiert**?

Verbs ending in **-ieren** have no **ge-** prefix in the past participle. They are all weak verbs whose participles end in **-t.**

K   Was hat man diskutiert?   Restate the conversational exchanges below in the perfect tense.

▶   Wo studierst du?   *Wo hast du studiert?*
     — Ich studiere in München.   *— Ich habe in München studiert.*

1.   Buchstabierst du alle Wörter?
     — Nein, ich buchstabiere nur zwei Wörter.

2. Probiert Gerd von dem Kuchen?
   — Nein, er probiert nur den Kaffee.
3. Frau Fischer dekoriert den Kuchen rot und grün.
   — Warum dekoriert sie den Kuchen mit solchen Farben?
4. Die Professoren plädieren für mehr Mathematik.
   — Die Studenten protestieren gegen diesen Plan, nicht?

• *Verbs with inseparable prefixes*

Infinitive	Past participle	Perfect tense
bekommen	bekommen	Ich **habe** nichts **bekommen.**
bemerken	bemerkt	**Hast** du das **bemerkt?**
bestellen	bestellt	Wer **hat** die Wurst **bestellt?**
bezahlen	bezahlt	Wer **hat** das **bezahlt?**
erklären	erklärt	Ich **habe** es schon **erklärt.**
erzählen	erzählt	Erik **hat** es **erzählt.**
gefallen	gefallen	**Hat** es dir **gefallen?**
gehören	gehört	Wem **hat** diese alte Uhr **gehört?**
vergessen	vergessen	Ich **habe** seine Adresse **vergessen.**
verlieren	verloren	Ich **habe** meinen Kuli **verloren.**
verstehen	verstanden	Inge **hat** es nicht **verstanden.**

Some verbs have prefixes that are never separated from the verb stem. An inseparable prefix is not stressed in spoken German. Verbs with inseparable prefixes (**be-, emp-, ent-, er-, ge-, ver-, zer-**) add no **ge-** in the past participle. Both weak and strong verbs may have inseparable prefixes.

L   **Das versteht er nicht.**   Klaus doesn't understand Inge's report. That makes him and her unhappy. Restate the sentences below in the present tense.

▶   Inge hat ein Bier für Klaus bestellt.   *Inge bestellt ein Bier für Klaus.*

1. Sie hat von ihrem Referat erzählt.
2. Klaus hat es nicht verstanden.
3. Inge hat es noch einmal erklärt.
4. Das hat Klaus nicht gefallen.
5. Inge hat das bemerkt.
6. Sie hat daher Klaus' Bier nicht bezahlt.
7. Das hat er auch nicht verstanden.

M Petra erzählt von ihrer Reise.   Petra went to Switzerland. Tell about
her trip. Restate each sentence in the perfect tense.

▶ Petra erzählt von ihren Ferien.   *Petra hat von ihren Ferien erzählt.*

1. Sie bezahlt die Reise selbst.
2. Die Schweiz gefällt Petra sehr.
3. Sie bemerkt viel Interessantes.
4. Sie bekommt da auch leckeren Käse.
5. Sie versteht die Schweizer ziemlich gut.
6. Ein Schweizer erklärt ihr vieles.
7. Er erzählt viel Lustiges.
8. Leider verliert sie ihre Handtasche in Zürich.

9 Auxiliary *sein* with past participles

ich **bin gekommen**	wir **sind gekommen**
du **bist gekommen**	ihr **seid gekommen**
er/es/sie **ist gekommen**	sie **sind gekommen**
Sie **sind gekommen**	

Some verbs use **sein** instead of **haben** as an auxiliary in the perfect.

Warum **ist** Erika so früh **aufge-standen?**	Why did Erika get up so early?
Sie **ist** nach Freiburg **gefahren.**	She drove to Freiburg.

Verbs that require **sein** must meet two conditions. They must:

1. be intransitive verbs (verbs without a direct object) and
2. indicate a change of condition (e.g., **aufstehen**) or location (e.g., **fahren**).

Infinitive	Past participle	Infinitive	Past participle
aufstehen	ist aufgestanden	laufen	ist gelaufen
fahren	ist gefahren	schwimmen	ist geschwommen
fliegen	ist geflogen	wachsen	ist gewachsen
gehen	ist gegangen	wandern	ist gewandert
kommen	ist gekommen	werden	ist geworden

Wer **ist** wieder so lange bei Helmut **geblieben?**	Who stayed so late at Helmut's again?
Ich **bin** es nicht **gewesen.**	It wasn't I.

The verbs **bleiben** and **sein** require **sein** as an auxiliary in the perfect, even
though they do not indicate a change of location or condition.

Wie **war** der Kaffee?   How was the coffee?
Der Kuchen **war** gut.   The cake was good.

The simple past tense of **sein (war)** is used more commonly than the perfect tense of **sein (ist gewesen)**.

N   So war es.   Restate the conversational exchanges below in the perfect tense.

▶   Fahrt ihr mit dem Auto?   *Seid ihr mit dem Auto gefahren?*
     — Nein, wir fliegen.   *— Nein, wir sind geflogen.*

1.   Fahrt ihr nach Österreich?
     — Nein, wir bleiben auch in den Ferien zu Hause.
2.   Gehen Müllers auch schwimmen?
     — Ja, aber sie kommen erst später.
3.   Schwimmt ihr viel?
     — Nein, wir schwimmen nicht. Wir wandern viel.
4.   Warum stehst du heute früh auf?
     — Weil ich zur Uni laufe.

10   Dependent clauses in the perfect tense

Ich möchte wissen, was sie gestern abend gemacht **haben.**
Ich möchte wissen, ob sie ins Kino gegangen **sind.**

In a dependent clause, the auxiliary verb **haben** or **sein** follows the past participle and is the last element in the clause.

O   Ich weiß nicht.   A friend asks about David's and Nicole's college experiences. Say you don't know.

▶   Hat Nicole im Sommer gearbeitet?   *Ich weiß nicht, ob sie im Sommer*
                                          gearbeitet hat.

1.   Hat Nicole einen Studentenjob gefunden?
2.   Hat sie Geld vom Staat bekommen?
3.   Ist alles teuer gewesen?
4.   Ist David auf eine Staatsuni gegangen?
5.   Haben seine Eltern alles bezahlt?
6.   Hat David in Amerika Englisch und Mathematik studiert?

P   Kurze Gespräche   Restate the conversational exchanges below in the perfect tense.

1. Fährst du mit dem Rad zur Uni?
   — Nein, ich laufe.
2. Bestellst du Fisch?
   — Nein, ich esse Fisch am Samstag.
3. Rufst du Erika an?
   — Nein, sie geht einkaufen.
   — Wer sagt denn das?
4. Denkst du an den Wein?
   — Ja, ich kaufe ihn heute.
   Bringst du auch Gläser mit?

Sie haben das Wort

Wer hat was gemacht?   Find six fellow students who have done any one of the activities listed below in the past week.

> Discussing activities in the past

▶   arbeiten   *Hast du letzte Woche gearbeitet?*

einkaufen gehen	mit Freunden wandern
Referat vorbereiten	ins Kino gehen
Notizen durcharbeiten	schwimmen gehen
viel schlafen	Videospiele spielen
Deutsch machen	zu Hause bleiben
[Tennis] spielen	

| Wiederholung

A   Renate hat einen Kuchen gebacken.   Write a paragraph about Renate's experience baking a cake. Use the perfect tense, and the cues provided below.

1. Renate / einladen / am Sonntag / Freunde / zum Kaffee
2. am Samstag / sie / backen / ein Kuchen
3. sie / anfangen / sehr früh
4. sie / haben / keine Butter // und / ihre Schwester Monika / laufen / zu / Lebensmittelgeschäft
5. Kuchen / aussehen / nicht richtig
6. das / gefallen / Renate / natürlich / nicht
7. Monika / helfen / dann / ihre Schwester

B   Der Kuchen hat nicht geschmeckt.   Now tell about Frank's experience with a cake by supplying the missing prepositions.

1. Frank lebt _____ zwei Monaten in Bremen.
2. Er arbeitet _____ einer amerikanischen Firma.
3. _____ Sonntag hat er einige Bekannte _____ Kaffee eingeladen.
4. Die Gäste sind _____ vier gekommen.
5. Frank hat _____ seine Bekannten einen Kuchen gebacken — rot, grün und gelb dekoriert.
6. Der Kaffee hat den Gästen geschmeckt, aber _____ dem Kuchen hat jeder nur ein Stück probiert.
7. „Was können die nur _____ meinen Kuchen haben?" denkt Frank.
8. _____ seinem Freund hört er dann, daß viele Deutsche nur Kuchen _____ künstliche Farben essen.

C   Wann hast du das gemacht?   A friend wants to know — to the hour — how you spent yesterday. Say what time you did the activities mentioned below.

▶   aufstehen   *Gestern bin ich um sieben aufgestanden.*

1. zur Uni gehen
2. eine Cola trinken
3. meine Notizen durcharbeiten
4. Deutsch machen
5. meinem Freund/meiner Freundin helfen
6. zu Bett gehen

Vollkornbrot, Brötchen, Kuchen
und Gebäck aus biologisch
angebautem Getreide.
Für zwischendurch:
Vollkorncrêpes und Kaffee.
Geöffnet von 8.30–18.30
Ffm-Bockenheim
Leipziger Str. 85–87
Tel. 70 02 78

Biobäcker

Sie haben das Wort

Ihre Meinung

1. Kaufen Sie in Bio-Läden ein?
2. Schmecken natürliche Lebensmittel so gut wie andere?
3. Kosten natürliche Lebensmittel in Amerika mehr als andere?
4. Findet man das Wort *natural* oft in amerikanischen Reklamen?
5. Wann gehen Sie zu Bett?
6. Möchten Sie beim Schlafen frische Luft haben? Auch im Winter?
7. Finden Sie es schwer oder leicht, früh aufzustehen?
8. Sind Sie oft müde? Warum (nicht)?

The "alternative movement" (*Alternativbewegung*) has been growing in size and influence in the Federal Republic of Germany and other European industrial countries since the mid 1970s. Its founders and supporters believed that the limits of economic growth had been reached and that existing social, political, and industrial institutions had failed to solve the increasing social and environmental problems of modern society.

The theoretical base of the alternative movement is multifaceted. It integrates many groups with different ideological backgrounds, such as citizens' action groups (*Bürgerinitiativen*), ecologists (*Ökologen*), peace groups (*Friedensgruppen*), women's groups (*Frauengruppen*) and house squatters (*Hausbesetzer*).

The "Green" political party has its roots in the alternative movement and represents its diverse social, political, and ecological concerns. First elected to the *Bundestag* in 1983, the Greens (*Die Grünen*) have created considerable public controversy by rotating representatives, making radical ecological demands, and engaging in nonconformist rhetoric and behavior. *Die Grünen* are increasingly influential in Austria and Switzerland as well.

Die Grünen sind gegen Umweltverschmutzung und für Tempo 100.

D   Was bedeutet das?   The sentences below contain some unfamiliar words that are either compounds of familiar words or related to familiar words. Guess the meaning of the words in boldface, and then give the English equivalent.

1. Das Essen steht auf° dem **Eßtisch** im **Eßzimmer**.
2. Sie trinkt oft **Getränke** wie Bier und Wein.
3. Sie bringt ihren kranken Mann im **Krankenwagen** ins **Krankenhaus**.
4. Bei Regen trägt Herr Roth Regenmantel, Handschuhe und **Überschuhe**.
5. Wagners haben mich für heute abend eingeladen. Was für ein **Mitbringsel** soll ich mitbringen? Blumen oder Schokolade?

on

E   Nicht schwarz, sondern weiß.   Give an antonym for each word listed below.

billig □ immer □ krank □ nachher □ richtig □ schwer □ spät

F   Wie sagt man das?

1.   — Why did you come by bus?
     — My car is broken down.
     — I'm sorry.

2.   — Did you like Denmark?
     — Yes. We hiked a lot.
     — Did you camp (in a tent)?
     — No. It rained too much. We slept at friends' (houses).

3.   — Are you hungry?
     — Yes. Is it OK with you if I try this cake?
     — Of course. How does it taste?
     — It's excellent. Very tasty.

G   Fragen über die Uni   Tell what David discovered about going to a German university; combine the sentences with the conjunction indicated.

1.   David hat viele Fragen. (weil) Er möchte in Deutschland studieren.
2.   Er möchte wissen.... (ob) Ist die Uni sehr teuer?
3.   Nicole sagt ... (daß) Es kostet überhaupt nichts.
4.   Er fragt. (ob) Ist es leicht, einen Studentenjob zu bekommen?
5.   Nicole sagt ... (daß) Es ist nicht leicht. (denn) Es gibt wenige Studentenjobs.

H   Anregung

1.   Two students, Michael and Sabine, are discussing various topics. Select one of the topics below and write the dialogue that takes place between them.

     das Wetter □ einkaufen □ die Vorlesung □ eine Seminararbeit vorbereiten □ das Essen □ das Wochenende □ Ferien

2.   Write a paragraph or conversation on the topic *Natürlich ist natürlich besser.*

3.   Prepare a German commercial for television or radio. Provide a short prose setting for your ad.

| Grammatik zum Nachschlagen _____

The perfect tense

Hast du das Referat endlich **ge-schrieben?**	Have you finally written the report?
Petra **ist** im Bett **geblieben.**	Petra has stayed in bed.

The German perfect tense, like the English present perfect, is a compound tense. It is made up of the present tense of the auxiliary **haben** or **sein** and the past participle. The past participle is in final position, except in a dependent clause.

Use of the perfect tense   (E)

Erik: Was **hast** du denn gestern **gemacht?**	What did you do yesterday?
Jutta: Ich **habe** doch **gearbeitet.**	I worked, of course.

Because the perfect is the tense most frequently used in conversation, it is often referred to as the "conversational past." It is used in many situations that require the simple past tense in English.

Past participles of regular weak verbs   (A, B)

Infinitive	Past participle	Perfect tense
sagen	ge + sag + t	Er **hat** es **gesagt.**
arbeiten	ge + arbeit + et	Sie **hat** schwer **gearbeitet.**
regnen	ge + regn + et	Es **hat** gestern **geregnet.**

German verbs may be classified as weak or strong according to the way in which they form their past tenses. A weak verb is a verb whose infinitive stem remains unchanged in the past tense forms.

The past particle of a weak verb is formed by adding **-t** to the unchanged stem. The **-t** expands to **-et** in verbs whose stem ends in **-d** or **-t (gearbeitet)**, and in some verbs whose stem ends in **-n** or **-m (geregnet)**. Most weak verbs also add the prefix **ge-** in the past participle.

Past participles of irregular weak verbs (C, D)

Infinitive	Past participle	Perfect tense
bringen	ge + brach + t	Wer **hat** das **gebracht**?
denken	ge + dach + t	Sie **hat** nicht an die Zeit **gedacht**.
kennen	ge + kann + t	Sie **hat** deinen Freund gut **gekannt**.
wissen	ge + wuß + t	Sie **hat** es **gewußt**.

A few weak verbs are irregular. The past participle has the prefix **ge-** and the ending **-t;** there is also a change in the stem vowel and occasionally in the consonants.

Past participles of strong verbs (F–I)

Infinitive	Past participle	Perfect tense
nehmen	ge + nomm + en	Ich **habe** das Brot **genommen**.
sitzen	ge + sess + en	Ich **habe** dort **gesessen.**
tun	ge + ta + n	Ich **habe** das nicht **getan.**

A strong verb is a verb that changes its stem vowel (and occasionally consonants) in the formation of the past tenses. The past participle of a strong verb is formed by adding **-en** to the stem. (Note the exception **getan.**) Most strong verbs also add the prefix **ge-** in the past participle.

For a list of the strong verbs used in this book, with their past participles, see the Reference Section (R-17) at the end of the book.

Past participles of separable-prefix verbs (J)

Infinitive	Past participle	Perfect tense
anfangen	an + **ge** + fangen	Gerd **hat** mit der Arbeit **angefangen.**
aufhören	auf + **ge** + hört	Inge **hat** mit der Arbeit **aufgehört.**

The prefix **ge-** of the past participle comes between the separable prefix and the stem of the participle. Some separable-prefix verbs are weak; others are strong.

Past participles without the ge- prefix (K–M)

- *Verbs ending in -ieren*

Present tense	Perfect tense
Jutta **studiert** in Heidelberg.	Jutta **hat** in Heidelberg **studiert**.
Alle **probieren** von dem Kuchen.	Alle **haben** von dem Kuchen **probiert**.

Verbs ending in **-ieren** do not have the prefix **ge-** in the past participle. They are always weak verbs whose participle ends in **-t.** These verbs are generally based on words borrowed from French and Latin; they are often similar to English verbs.

- *Verbs with inseparable prefixes*

Present tense	Perfect tense
Birgit **erklärt** alles.	Sie **hat** alles **erklärt**.
Martin **versteht** uns nicht.	Er **hat** uns nicht **verstanden**.

Some prefixes are never separated from the verb stem. These prefixes are **be-, emp-, ent-, er-, ge-, ver-,** and **zer-.** Inseparable-prefix verbs do not add the prefix **ge-** in the past participle. Some inseparable-prefix verbs are weak; others are strong.

Use of the auxiliary *haben* (A–M)

Christine **hat** heute **gearbeitet.**   Christine worked today.
Gerd **hat** seiner Freundin   Gerd helped his friend.
  geholfen.

Haben is used to form the perfect tense of most verbs.

Use of the auxiliary *sein* (N)

Schmidts **sind** spät nach Hause   The Schmidts came home late.
  gekommen.
Sie **sind** dann spät **aufgestanden.**   Then they got up late.

The auxiliary **sein** is used to form the perfect tense of intransitive verbs (i.e., verbs that do not have a direct object) when these verbs denote a change in location (e.g., **kommen**) or condition (e.g., **aufstehen**).

   Verbs taking **sein** that you already know are **aufstehen, fahren, fliegen, gehen, kommen, laufen, schwimmen, wachsen, wandern,** and **werden**.

Warum **bist** du so lange **geblieben?**	Why did you stay so late?
Es **ist** so schön **gewesen.**	It was so nice.

The intransitive verbs **bleiben** and **sein** require the auxiliary **sein,** even though they do not indicate change of location or condition.

Wie **war** der Kaffee?	How was the coffee?
Der Kuchen **war** gut.	The cake was good.

The simple past tense of **sein** is used more commonly than the perfect tense of **sein,** however.

Use of the perfect tense in dependent clauses (O, P)

Klaus möchte wissen, ob David nach Österreich gefahren **ist.**
Karin möchte wissen, ob er da viel gesehen **hat.**

In a dependent clause, the auxiliary **haben** or **sein** follows the past participle and is the last element in the clause.

Kapitel 7

Lernziele

Sprechakte

Making plans
Expressing likes and dislikes
Expressing agreement and disagreement
Talking about shopping
Giving gifts
Discussing cultural differences

Grammatik

Hin and **her**
Either-or prepositions
Special meanings of prepositions
Time expressions in dative and accusative
Dative personal pronouns
Word order of direct and indirect objects
Da-compounds
Wo-compounds

Vokabeln

Understanding the flavoring particle **mal**
Word families
Noun suffix **-ung**
Verbs **legen/liegen, stellen/stehen, setzen/ sitzen, hängen, stecken**

Landeskunde

TV in the Federal Republic of Germany
German stereotypes
Role of flowers in German-speaking countries
Residence registration
Freund(in) vs. **Bekannte(r)**
Christmas customs

In der Innenstadt von München

233

Bausteine für Gespräche

Was machst du nach dem Seminar?

Alex: Was machst du nach dem Seminar?

Bärbel: Ich treffe Claudia im Café Kranz. Wir wollen dort über unsere Bürgerinitiative reden.

Alex: Was für eine Bürgerinitiative?

Bärbel: Na, die gegen die Mülldeponie.

Wir gehen ins Café

Bärbel: Wir gehen ins Café Kranz. Komm doch mit!

Michael: Dahin? Nein, danke. Bei dem Rauch kriegt man keine Luft.

Bärbel: Wie wär's mit einem Biergarten? Im Waldcafé sitzt man schön draußen.

Michael: Aber du, ich bin pleite.

Bärbel: Macht nichts. Ich lade dich ein.

What are you doing after the seminar?

What are you doing after the seminar?

I'm meeting Claudia at Café Kranz. We want to talk about our citizens' action group there.

What kind of action group?

You know, the one against the garbage dump.

We're going to the café

We're going to Café Kranz. Why don't you come along?

In there? No thanks. With all that smoke you can't get any air.

How about a beer garden then? In the Forest Café we can sit outside.

But hey, I'm broke.

It doesn't matter. I'll treat.

In diesem Café sitzt man schön draußen.

Fragen

1. Wo will Bärbel Claudia nach dem Seminar treffen?
2. Über was wollen sie dort reden?
3. Warum möchte Michael nicht mitkommen?
4. Warum findet Michael einen Biergarten bestimmt besser?
5. Leiht Bärbel Michael Geld? Warum (nicht)?

Sie haben das Wort

A   Was machst du?   A fellow student would like to do something later
and asks what your plans are at various times.

Making plans

Gesprächspartner/in		Sie	
Was machst du	**nach dem Seminar?**	Ich treffe [Alex]	**im Biergarten**.
	nach der Vorlesung?		im Café
	heute nachmittag?		in der Bibliothek
		Ich gehe nach Hause.	
		Ich sehe fern°.	

B   Wohin möchtet ihr?   Form a group of three. One asks where you can go. Another suggests a place, and the third responds.

1.   Wohin möchtet ihr [Samstag] abend?
2.   Wie wär's mit | **dem Ratskeller?**
      | einem Café?
      | einem Biergarten?
3.   Nein, da sind zu viele Leute.
      Nein, da ist es zu laut.
      Nein, da kriegt man keine Luft.
      Gern, das macht immer Spaß°.
      Gern, da kann man schön draußen sitzen.
      Gern, da trifft man viele nette Leute.

C   Interview   Fragen Sie eine Gesprächspartnerin bzw. einen Gesprächspartner:

1.   was sie/er nach der Vorlesung macht
2.   wo sie/er oft Freunde trifft
3.   ob sie/er oft pleite ist
4.   ob sie/er manchmal von Freunden Geld leihen muß
5.   ob sie/er Freunden Geld leihen muß
6.   ob sie/er für oder gegen Mülldeponien ist

Vokabeln

— Substantive

der **Biergarten, ∸** beer garden
der **Bürger, -/die Bürgerin, -nen** citizen
die **Bürgerinitiative, -n** citizens' action group, grassroots movement

die **Mülldeponie, -n** garbage dump
der **Rauch** smoke
der **Spaß** fun; **Späße** (*pl.*) jokes
der **Wald, ∸er** forest

— Verben

fern·sehen (sieht fern), ferngesehen to watch TV

reden to talk
treffen (trifft), getroffen to meet

— Andere Wörter

dahin (to) there
draußen outside

laut loud
pleite broke, out of money

— Besondere Ausdrücke

(Es) macht nichts. (It) doesn't matter.

Das macht Spaß. It's fun.
wie wär's mit ... how about . . .

In the Federal Republic of Germany, there are two national television channels — generally called *Erstes Programm* and *Zweites Programm*. A third channel, *Drittes Programm*, provides regional programming. These channels are run as non-profit public corporations, largely independent of economic and political control. TV is financed primarily by quarterly fees collected from viewers for each TV set they own. Commercials are shown only in ten-minute clusters in the early evening. Although cable television stations now exist in many cities, they have not become strong competitors to the public TV stations.

The regular broadcast-day of the public TV stations begins in the afternoon. In the morning, the *Erstes Programm* or the *Zweites Programm* repeats shows broadcast the night before. Popular programs include news shows, game shows, sports, movies, and situation comedies or detective series—many of which are American. American and other foreign films are usually shown with dubbed-in voices rather than with subtitles. People who live close to a border sometimes receive broadcasts from a neighboring country.

Sender Freies Berlin – im Aufnahmestudio

ARD 1	**ZDF**	**SAT 1**
17.45 Tagesschau *17.55 Regionalprogramme* **20.00 Tagesschau** **20.15 Die letzten Tage von Pompeji (4)** Glaucus wird in den Kerker geworfen **21.15 Vivo quemado** Lebend verbrannt: Carmen Gloria Die Kinder des Diktators Augusto Pinochet. Reportage von Nikolaus Brender über die chilenische Jugend 14 Jahre nach dem Putsch des Generals **22.00 Nur für Busse** Zweischneidiges und Eindeutiges mit Jochen Busse **22.30 Tagesthemen** **23.00 White Star** Deutscher Spielfilm (1982) Mit Terrance Robay und Dennis Hopper. Buch und Regie: Roland Klick **0.30 Tagesschau** **0.35 Nachtgedanken** Voltaire: Über Tugend und Laster	**17.50 Ein Colt für alle Fälle** Bis daß der Tod euch scheide **19.00 heute** **19.30 Verkehrsgericht** Angeklagt: Ein Fahrlehrer **21.00 Ratschläge für Kinogänger** „Angel Heart" von Alan Parker **21.15 WISO** Themen: Vorsitzender-Wechsel bei der DAG. Frühzeitige Rehabilitation alter Menschen. Bundespost: Reform oder Reförmchen? Management: Baumarkt-Experiment mit Umsatzplus. **21.45 heute-journal** **22.10 Bücher im Gespräch** Beate Pinkerneil stellt die Autobiographien von Ingmar Bergmann, Marlene Dietrich und Arthur Miller vor **22.55 ZDF Jazz Club** Das Clark Terry / Red Mitchell-Duo. Moderation: George Gruntz **0.00 heute**	**16.35 Bonanza** Der Goldfinder **17.35 77 Sunset Strip** Zwei und zwei macht sechs **18.30 blick** **18.45 Bezaubernde Jeannie** Sonntags immer **19.09 Glückswirbel** **19.15 blick** **19.20 Raumschiff Enterprise** Die Frauen des Mr. Mudd **20.15 Kampf um Yellow Rose** Die Falle **21.10 Die letzte Ausgabe** Französischer Spielfilm (1978) **23.10 blick** Berichte vom Tage, Sport, Wetter **23.25 Telethema: Umwelt** Bartgeier in Tirol. Rheinauen. Auf Plastik und Papiertüten verzichten? **23.40 Golf International** French Open

Typisch deutsch? Typisch amerikanisch?

Vorbereitung auf das Lesen

• Zum Thema

1. Ein paar Ausländer° wollen etwas über die USA, Kanada oder Deutschland wissen. Beschreiben° Sie Land und Leute für sie.
2. Denken Sie an ein Land — Kanada, Deutschland, die USA. Beschreiben Sie Land und Leute. Was assoziieren Sie mit diesem Land?
3. Was ist für viele Amerikaner typisch deutsch? Was ist für viele Ausländer typisch amerikanisch?

foreigners
describe

• Leitfragen

1. Welche Ähnlichkeiten gibt es zwischen der Bundesrepublik und den USA?
2. In welchen Situationen benutzen die Deutschen Vornamen? Die Amerikaner?
3. Was hat Peter in Deutschland anders gefunden als zu Hause?
4. Welche Schwierigkeiten hat Peter in Deutschland gehabt?
5. Was gefällt Monika an Amerika? Was gefällt ihr weniger?
6. Warum hat jede Nation die Tendenz, das eigene System besser zu finden?

Zwischen den USA und der Bundesrepublik gibt es enge kulturelle, wirtschaftliche° und auch politische Beziehungen°. So überrascht es nicht, daß es zwischen den Ländern viele Ähnlichkeiten gibt. Aber es gibt auch Unterschiede. Viele Deutsche sehen zum Beispiel im Fernsehen jede
5 Woche *Dallas*. Da sehen sie, daß Amerika anders ist als Bayern° oder Niedersachsen°. Viele Amerikaner dagegen° verbinden° Deutschland mit dem Weihnachtsbaum und Weihnachtsliedern und mit klassischer Musik. Die Frage ist nur: Ist *Dallas* typisch für Amerika? Und sind Weihnachten und die Klassiker typisch für Deutschland? Und was ist das
10 überhaupt: „Typisch" für ein Land?

Da kommt zum Beispiel die Austauschstudentin° Monika Berger in ihrer amerikanischen Universitätsstadt an. Der Vater der° Gastfamilie holt sie vom Flughafen ab: „Hallo, Monika! Herzlich° willkommen! Ich heiße Bob." Monika findet diese Begrüßung° merkwürdig. Ihr Vater in
15 Deutschland benutzt den Vornamen nur unter guten Freunden. Und was bedeutet diese Begrüßung nun? Sind die Amerikaner einfach freundlicher°, offener°, kontaktfreudiger°? Oder sind sie unkultiviert°, plump°, ohne Gefühl für feine Unterschiede?

economic / relations

Bavaria
Lower Saxony / on the other hand / associate

exchange student
of the (gen.)
cordially
greeting

friendlier / more open / better mixers / uncultured / unrefined

Nach einiger Zeit sitzt Monika mit einem Freund, Peter, in einer
20 Studentenkneipe. Peter ist ein Jahr in der Bundesrepublik gewesen. Mit
ihm kann man gut über solche Fragen reden. Monika fragt Peter: „Du, sag
mal, was hast du eigentlich so bemerkt, als du in Deutschland warst? Was
hast du beobachtet? Was war anders?"

Peter: Vieles° war ja genauso° wie hier. Aber vieles war doch auch an-   *many things / exactly*
25 ders. Da war zum Beispiel meine erste Fahrt auf der Autobahn.
Fürchtbar, sag' ich dir. Die fahren wie die Wilden, hab' ich gedacht.
Danach° bin ich richtig gern mit dem Zug gefahren. Außerdem macht   *afterwards*
es ja wirklich Spaß, mit dem Zug zu fahren. Es gibt genug Züge. Sie sind
sauber. Und sie fahren pünktlich ab, und sie kommen pünktlich an.
30 Andere Sachen, die° anders waren, ja, was war da noch? Vielleicht die   *that*
Parks in jeder Stadt, die vielen Blumen in den Fenstern, auf den
Märkten, in den Restaurants. Und dann das Essen. Erstens° ist das Essen   *first of all*
selbst anders — mehr Wurst, anderes Bier und so°. Dann wie man ißt —   *and such things*
wie man Messer und Gabel benutzt, meine ich. Und schließlich hab'
35 ich auch gefunden, daß das Essen mehr ein Ereignis° ist. Man sitzt län-   *event*
ger° am Tisch und redet miteinander°.   *for a longer time / with one another*
Monika: Und womit hast du Schwierigkeiten gehabt?
Peter: Da war vor allem die Bürokratie. Man braucht also eine
Aufenthaltserlaubnis°. Die gibt's auf der Polizei. Die bekommt man   *residence permit*
40 aber nur, wenn man vorher beim Ausländerarzt gewesen ist. Dafür
muß man aufs Gesundheitsamt°. Und wenn man endlich eine   *public health office*
Wohnung hat, muß man aufs Einwohnermeldeamt°. Das Formular   *residence registration office*

Man benutzt Messer und Gabel anders.

bekommt man aber nicht hier. Das muß man vorher im Papiergeschäft
kaufen. Aber nun mal was anderes. Was hast du denn hier so be-
45   obachtet?

    Monika: Einige Sachen gefallen mir ausgesprochen° gut. Zum Beispiel   *clearly*
kann ich hier auch abends und am ganzen Wochenende einkaufen
gehen. Das finde ich gut. In Deutschland gibt es nur einmal im Monat
den langen Samstag*.

50   *Peter:* Und was hat dir weniger gefallen?

    Monika: Na ja°, also bitte, sei mir nicht böse. Ich finde die Amerikaner   *well now*
unglaublich freundlich. Das mag ja zunächst° sehr schön sein. Aber   *at first*
diese Freundlichkeit erscheint mir doch sehr oberflächlich°. Sie kann   *superficial*
einfach nicht echt sein.

55   *Peter:* Das sehen wir eben anders. Ein nettes Lächeln im Alltag° macht   *daily life*
das Leben eben einfacher.

    Monika: Das mag wohl sein.

Wer hat nun recht, Monika oder Peter? Beide haben die Tendenz, erst
einmal° die eigene Seite besser zu finden. Und das ist sicher eine   erst einmal: *right away*
60   allgemeine Tendenz. Aber oft sind *andere* Dinge nur neu. Und neue
Dinge machen uns Angst. Daher werten wir sie ab°. Außerdem hat die   abwerten: *discredit*
Gruppenpsychologie vielleicht eine Erklärung: Die Sprecher° einer°   *speakers / of a (gen.)*
Sprache sind eine Gruppe. Damit° die Gruppe zusammenhält, muß sie   *so that*
besser sein als andere Gruppen. Daher hat jede Nation mehr oder weni-
65   ger die Tendenz, das eigene System, die eigene Art besser zu finden als
die anderen.

Fragen zum Lesestück

1. Wie sind die kulturellen, wirtschaftlichen und politischen Beziehungen zwischen den USA und der Bundesrepublik?
2. Was sehen viele Deutsche jede Woche im Fernsehen?
3. Womit verbinden viele Amerikaner Deutschland?
4. Warum findet Monika Bobs Begrüßung am Flughafen merkwürdig?
5. Warum kann man mit Peter gut darüber reden?
6. Wie hat Peter seine erste Fahrt auf der Autobahn gefunden?
7. Warum macht es in Deutschland Spaß, mit dem Zug zu fahren?
8. Was hat Peter sonst noch beobachtet? Was war anders?
9. Was alles ist beim Essen anders?
10. Womit hat Peter vor allem Schwierigkeiten gehabt?

---

*On the first Saturday of each month, stores may stay open until 6 P.M. — thus
the term **langer Samstag**.

11. Wo bekommt man die Aufenthaltserlaubnis?
12. Warum muß ein Ausländer aufs Gesundheitsamt?
13. Wohin muß man, wenn man eine Wohnung hat?
14. Was gefällt Monika gut an Amerika?
15. Was hat Monika gegen die Freundlichkeit in Amerika?
16. Welche Tendenz zeigen Monika und Peter?
17. Warum werten wir neue Dinge oft ab?
18. Warum muß eine Gruppe „besser" sein als andere Gruppen?
19. Welche Tendenz findet man in fast allen Nationen?

Erzählen Sie!   Talk about three or four of the similarities and differences between the Federal Republic of Germany and the United States. Use the cues below.

Fernsehen □ Musik □ Vornamen □ Autofahren □ Züge □ Blumen □ Essen □ Einkaufen □ Freundlichkeit

Adult Germans use first names only with good friends. They do not use the word *Freund* as freely as Americans use *friend*. A *Freund* is a person with whom one is on intimate terms (a person who is often called "a very good friend" by Americans). Germans tend to have fewer *Freunde* and a larger circle of acquaintances (*Bekannte*). Even acquaintances of years' standing do not necessarily become *Freunde*. The change from *Bekannter* to *Freund* has traditionally been accompanied by a change from *Sie* to *du*. It is prudent for an American visitor to let a German-speaking person propose the use of first names and the familiar *du*. Also, in German-speaking countries, friends and acquaintances do not just "drop in," but wait until they receive an invitation for a specific time and date.

Sagt man hier „du" oder „Sie"?

Sie haben das Wort

Ihre Meinung

1. Bei wem benutzen Sie Vornamen — bei den Nachbarn? bei Ihren Professoren? bei Ihren Freunden?
2. Gehen Sie oft in Studentenkneipen?
3. Fahren Sie oft mit dem Zug?
4. Gehen die Amerikaner zu wenig zu Fuß?
5. Sind die Straßen bei Ihnen sauber?
6. Welches Bier schmeckt besser — amerikanisches, kanadisches oder deutsches?
7. Finden Sie die Amerikaner zu freundlich?

Discussing cultural differences

— Substantive

die **Angst, ⸚e**   fear
die **Art, -en**   way, manner
der **Arzt, ⸚e**/die **Ärztin, -nen**   doctor, physician
der **Ausländer, -**/die **Ausländerin, -nen**   foreigner
die **Autobahn, -en**   freeway, expressway
der **Baum, ⸚e**   tree
die **Ecke, -n**   corner
die **Erklärung, -en**   explanation
die **Fahrt, -en**   trip
das **Fernsehen**   television
der **Flughafen, ⸚**   airport
die **Freundlichkeit**   friendliness
die **Gabel, -n**   fork

das **Gefühl, -e**   feeling
die **Kneipe, -n**   pub
das **Lied, -er**   song
das **Messer, -**   knife
der **Park, -s**   park
die **Polizei** (*sing. only*)   the police
das **Restaurant, -s**   restaurant
die **Schwierigkeit, -en**   difficulty
die **Sprache, -n**   language
die **USA** (*pl.*)   U.S.A.
der **Vorname, -n, -n**   first name
das **Weihnachten**   Christmas; (*used often in pl.*) **Fröhliche Weihnachten** Merry Christmas
die **Wohnung, -en**   dwelling; apartment

— Verben

ab·fahren (fährt ab), ist abgefahren to depart, leave
ab·holen   to pick up
an·kommen, ist angekommen (in + *dat.*)   to arrive (in)
bedeuten   to mean, imply; **was bedeutet das?**   what does that mean?
benutzen   to use
beobachten   to observe

hängen   to hang [*something*], put
hängen, gehangen   to be hanging
legen   to lay, put
meinen   to mean; to think, have an opinion; **was meinst du?**   what do you think?
setzen   to set, put
stecken   to stick, put into
stellen   to place
überraschen   to surprise

— Andere Wörter —

allgemein   general
an (+ *acc. or dat.*)   on; at; to
auf (+ *acc. or dat.*)   on, on top of; at; to
böse (**auf** + *acc.*)   angry (at)
echt   genuine; (*slang*) really; **echt toll**   really neat
einfach   simple, simply
eigen   own
einander   one another, each other
eng   close; tight; narrow
erst   first
fein   fine
freundlich   friendly

genug   enough
klassisch   classic; classical
offen   open
pünktlich   punctual(ly), on time
sauber   clean
schließlich   finally; after all
sicher   safe; certain(ly), for sure
typisch   typical
unglaublich   unbelievable
unter (+ *acc. or dat.*)   under; among
wohl   probably, indeed
zwischen (+ *acc. or dat.*)   between; among

— Besondere Ausdrücke —

Angst haben (**vor** + *dat.*)   to be afraid (of)
Angst machen   to frighten
etwas anderes   something different
Das mag wohl sein.   That could be, that may well be.
mehr oder weniger   more or less

recht haben   to be right; **Du hast immer recht.**   You're always right.
vor allem   above all; most important(ly)
sei [mir] nicht böse   don't get mad [at me]

Erweiterung des Wortschatzes

1   Flavoring particle *mal*

Sag **mal,** schreiben wir nächste Woche wieder eine Klausur?
Schreib doch **mal!**

Say, are we having a test again next week?
Do write. Why don't you write sometime?

Mal is frequently used to soften commands. The speaker leaves the time for carrying out the command vague and up to the receiver of the command. **Mal** is short for **einmal** (*once*). **Mal** and **doch** are often used together.

2   Word families

die **Arbeit**	the work
arbeiten	to work
der **Arbeiter**/die **Arbeiterin**	the worker

Like English, German has many words that belong to families and are derived from a common root.

A   Noch ein Wort.   Add a familiar word to each group of related words below, and give the meanings for all of the words.

1.   wohnen, der Einwohner, _____
2.   sprechen, das Gespräch, die Sprecherin, _____
3.   der Koch, die Köchin, das Kochbuch, _____
4.   die Wanderung, der Wanderer, die Wanderlust, der Wanderweg, _____
5.   das Flugzeug, die Flugkarte, der Flughafen, _____
6.   die Bäckerei, backen, _____

3   The suffix -*ung*

wandern	to hike	**die Wanderung**	hike
wohnen	to live	**die Wohnung**	dwelling; apartment

The suffix **-ung** may be added to a verb stem to form a noun. All nouns ending in **-ung** are feminine.

B   Was bedeutet das?   Complete the sentences by forming nouns from the boldfaced verbs. Give the English equivalents of the nouns.

1.   Mark kann es nicht gut **erklären.** Verstehen Sie seine _____ ?
2.   Was **meinen** Sie zu diesem Problem? Was ist Ihre _____ ?

3. Gabi kann gut **erzählen.** Ihre _____ sind immer lustig.
4. Die Autoren **lesen** heute einige von ihren Geschichten. Kommst du zu ihrer _____ ?
5. Brauns haben mich zum Kaffee **eingeladen.** Habt ihr auch eine _____ bekommen?
6. Jans Besuch hat uns alle **überrascht.** Es war eine große _____ , daß er gekommen ist.

4 The verbs _legen/liegen, stellen/stehen, setzen/sitzen, hängen, stecken_

Inge **legt** das Buch auf den Tisch.

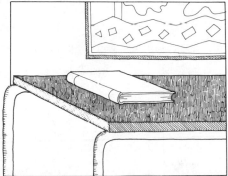

Das Buch **liegt** auf dem Tisch.

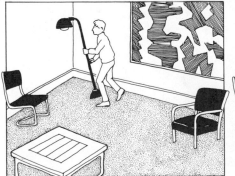

Paul **stellt** die Lampe in die Ecke.

Die Lampe **steht** in der Ecke.

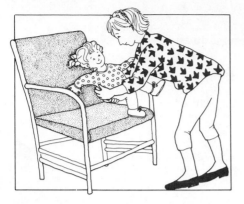

Marta **setzt** das Kind auf den Stuhl.

Das Kind **sitzt** auf dem Stuhl.

Achmed **hängt** die Uhr an die Wand.

Die Uhr **hängt** an der Wand.

Monika **steckt** das Geld in die Tasche.

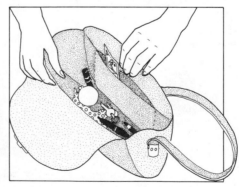

Ihr Geld **steckt** in der Tasche.

In English, the all-purpose verb for movement to a position is *to put,* and the all-purpose verb for the resulting position is *to be.* German uses several verbs to express the meanings *put* and *be.*

Ich **habe** *das Buch* auf den Tisch **gelegt.**

To express *put,* German uses **legen (gelegt),** *to lay;* **stellen (gestellt),** *to stand upright;* **setzen (gesetzt),** *to set;* **hängen (gehängt),** *to hang;* and **stecken (gesteckt),** *to stick.* These verbs all take direct objects and are weak.

Das Buch **hat** auf dem Tisch **gelegen.**

To express position German uses **liegen (gelegen),** *to be lying;* **stehen (gestanden),** *to be standing;* **sitzen (gesessen),** *to be sitting;* **hängen (gehangen),** *to be hanging;* and **stecken (gesteckt),** *to be (inserted).* These verbs do not take direct objects and, except for **stecken,** are strong.

C   Welches Verb?   Indicate which of the following verbs would be used in the German equivalents of the sentences below: **legen, liegen, stellen, stehen, setzen, sitzen, hängen, stecken.**

▶   Put the lamp on the table.   *stellen*

1. The vase of flowers is on the table.
2. My shoes are under the bed.
3. Her books are on the floor again.
4. Put the pot on the stove.
5. He put his hat on his head.
6. The wine glasses are on the table.
7. Mark, put the stamps in the drawer.
8. The car is behind the house.
9. Put your coat in the closet.
10. Why is the umbrella under the chair?
11. Put the newspaper on the chair.
12. The lamp was over the table.
13. The guests are at the table.
14. He put the money in his pocket.

| Übungen zur Aussprache _____

Review the pronunciation of long and short **i** and **e** in the Reference section at the end of the book. Read the word pairs in each set of columns on this page from top to bottom, then across. Check your pronunciation by listening to your instructor or the tape.

long ī	short i	long ē	short e
bieten	bitten	beten	Betten
vieler	Filter	Fehler	Felle
Wiege	Wicke	Weg	weg
stiehlt	stillt	stehlt	stellt
riet	ritt	Reeder	Retter
ihn	in	fehle	Fälle
		gähnt	Gent

Read the sentences below aloud, paying special attention to the way you pronounce long and short **i** and **e** in the boldfaced words.

1. Warum **sind sie nicht hier geblieben?**
2. **Er ist gestern gegen sechs** Uhr **gegangen.**
3. **Wie findest** du **dieses Winterwetter?**
4. **Diese Männer** haben doch **recht.**
5. **Diese** Seite **ist nicht** leicht zu **lesen.**
6. **Jens** hat **mir** einen langen **Brief geschrieben.**
7. **Diese Lieder singt** man **nicht.**

Reden ist Silber,
Schweigen ist Gold.

| Grammatik und Übungen _____

1   *Hin* and *her*

Meine Tante wohnt nicht hier.	My aunt doesn't live here.
Sie wohnt in Hamburg.	She lives in Hamburg.
Wir fahren einmal im Jahr **hin**.	Once a year we go *there*.
Und zweimal im Jahr kommt sie **her**.	And twice a year she comes *here*.

Hin and **her** are used to show direction. **Hin** shows motion away from the speaker, and **her** shows motion toward the speaker. **Hin** and **her** occupy last position in the sentence.

Er war letztes Jahr in Europa. Er möchte wieder **dorthin**.	He was in Europe last year. He wants to go there again.
Kommen Sie mal **herauf**!	Come on up here!

Hin and **her** may be combined with several parts of speech, including adverbs, prepositions, and verbs.

Woher kommen Sie?	**Wo** kommen Sie **her**?
Wohin fahren Sie?	**Wo** fahren Sie **hin**?

In spoken German, **hin** and **her** are often separated from **wo**. **Hin** and **her** occupy last position in the sentence.

A   Ilse und Axel   Ask questions about Ilse and Axel, using **wo, wohin,** or **woher.**

▶   Ilse and Axel wohnen bei München.   *Wo wohnen sie?*
▶   Sie fahren jeden Morgen nach   *Wohin fahren sie? / Wo fahren sie*
     München.   *hin?*

1.   Sie arbeiten in einer Buchhandlung.
2.   Sie gehen am Samstag zum Supermarkt.
3.   Die Blumen kommen vom Markt.
4.   Sie fahren am Sonntag in die Berge.
5.   Sie wandern gern in den Bergen.
6.   Nach der Wanderung gehen sie in ein Restaurant.
7.   Sie essen gern im Restaurant.
8.   Nach dem Essen fahren sie wieder nach Hause.
9.   In den Ferien fahren sie in die Schweiz.
10.   Axel kommt aus der Schweiz.
11.   Da können sie vier Wochen lang in den Bergen wandern.

2   Either-or prepositions

Dative: **wo?**   *Accusative:* **wohin?**

Jürgen sitzt **am** Tisch.   Corinna setzt sich **an den** Tisch.
Jürgen is sitting at the table.   *Corinna sits down at the table.*

German has nine prepositions that take either the dative or the accusative. The dative is used when position (*place where*) is indicated, answering the question **wo?** The accusative is used when a change of location (*place to which*) is indicated, answering the question **wohin?**

   In their basic meanings, the either-or prepositions are "spatial," referring to positions in space (dative) or movements through space (accusative). The either-or prepositions sometimes have special meanings.

an	at (the side of)	Er steht **am** [**an** dem] Fenster.
		Sie geht **ans** [**an** das] Fenster.
auf	on top of	Sein Buch liegt **auf** dem Tisch.
		Sie legt ihr Buch **auf** den Tisch.
hinter	in back of	Sie arbeitet **hinter** dem Haus.
		Er geht **hinter** das Haus.
in	in, inside (of)	Sie arbeitet **im** [**in** dem] Geschäft.
		Er geht **ins** [**in** das] Geschäft.
neben	beside	Ihr Stuhl steht **neben** dem Fenster.
		Er stellt seinen Stuhl **neben** das Fenster.
über	over	Eine Lampe hängt **über** dem Tisch.
		Er hat eine Lampe **über** den Tisch gehängt.
unter	under	Sein Fahrrad steht **unter** dem Balkon.
		Er hat sein Fahrrad **unter** den Balkon gestellt.
vor	in front of	Das Auto steht **vor** dem Haus.
		Sie hat das Auto **vor** das Haus gefahren.
zwischen	between	Eine Blume liegt **zwischen** den Büchern.
		Er legt noch eine Blume **zwischen** die Bücher.

3 Prepositional contractions

Er geht **ans** Fenster.	an das = **ans**
Er steht **am** Fenster.	an dem = **am**
Sie geht **ins** Zimmer.	in das = **ins**
Sie ist **im** Zimmer.	in dem = **im**

The prepositions **an** and **in** often contract with **das** and **dem**. Other possible contractions are **aufs, hinters, hinterm, übers, überm, unters, unterm, vors,** and **vorm.**

4 *An* and *auf* = on

Die Uhr hängt **an der Wand.**   The clock is hanging on the wall.
Mein Buch liegt **auf dem Tisch.**   My book is lying on the table.

An and **auf** can both be equivalent to *on*. **An** = *on (the side of)* is used in reference to vertical surfaces. **Auf** = *on (top of)* is used in reference to horizontal surfaces.

5 *An, auf,* and *in* = to

Veronika geht **an** die Tür.   Veronika goes to the door.
Bernd geht **auf** den Markt.   Bernd goes to the market.
Lore geht **in** die Stadt.   Lore goes to town.

The prepositions **an, auf,** and **in** can be equivalent to the English preposition *to.*

B   *An* oder *auf?*   Answer the questions below, using the cued words and the prepositions **an** or **auf** as appropriate.

▶   Wohin geht Albert? (Tür)   *Er geht an die Tür.*

1. Wo steht er jetzt? (Tür)
2. Wohin geht Astrid? (Fenster)
3. Wo steht sie jetzt? (Fenster)
4. Wohin stellt Anton die Blumen? (Tisch)
5. Wo stehen die Blumen? (Tisch)
6. Wohin legt Elke ihren Pulli? (Bett)
7. Wo liegt der Pulli jetzt? (Bett)
8. Wohin hängt Andreas die Uhr? (Wand)
9. Wo sitzt das Kind? (Stuhl)
10. Wo steht der Stuhl? (Tisch)

C   Ein Jahr in Deutschland   Susan is spending a year in Germany. Form sentences to tell about the things she does during her first days there, using the cues below.

▶   sie / gehen / auf / Polizei   *Sie geht auf die Polizei.*

1.   auf / Polizei / sie / bekommen / eine Aufenthaltserlaubnis
2.   sie / gehen / dann / auf / Markt
3.   auf / Markt / sie / kaufen / Blumen / für / ihr Zimmer
4.   dann / sie / gehen / in / Buchhandlung
5.   Erika / arbeiten / in / Buchhandlung
6.   Susan / müssen / in / Drogerie
7.   in / Drogerie / sie / wollen / kaufen / Vitamintabletten
8.   sie / gehen / dann / in / Café
9.   in / Café / sie / treffen / Erika
10. sie / sitzen / an / Tisch / in / Ecke

D   Ziemlich dumm   Your house guest isn't too bright. Answer her/his questions, using the cued expressions in accusative or dative.

▶   Wohin stell' ich das Radio? (auf / Tisch)   *Auf den Tisch.*

1.   Auf welchen Tisch? (auf / Tisch / zwischen / Fenster, *pl.*)
2.   Wohin leg' ich die Bücher? (neben / Radio)
3.   Wo sind meine Schuhe? (hinter / Bett)
4.   Wohin soll ich sie stellen? (unter / Bett)
5.   Wo hängt meine Jacke? (hinter / Tür)
6.   Wohin stell' ich diesen Stuhl? (an / Tisch)
7.   Wohin stell' ich die Blumen? (auf / Balkon)
8.   Wohin stecke ich die Zeitung? (in / Tasche)
9.   Wir sind jetzt fertig. Wohin fahren wir? (in / Stadt)
10. Wo steht mein Auto? (vor / Haus)

6   Special meanings of prepositions

Ich **denke** oft **an** meine Freunde.	I often *think of* my friends. *acc.*
Uwe **glaubt an** sie.	Uwe *believes in* her. *acc.*
Sie **schreibt an** ihren Freund.	She *writes to* her boyfriend. *acc*
Uwe **studiert an** der Universität.	Uwe *studies at* the university. *dat*
Inge **geht auf** die Universität.	Inge *goes to* college. *acc*
Kannst du mir **bei** meiner Arbeit **helfen?**	Can you *help* me *with* my work? *dat*
Wann **fängt** Inge **mit** der Arbeit **an?**	When is Inge *starting (with)* her work? *dat*
Wann **hört** sie **mit** der Arbeit **auf?**	When is she *stopping (with)* her work? *dat*
Sie **fährt mit** dem Auto.	She's *going by* car. *dat*
Hast du **mit** Frau Meier **gesprochen?**	Did you *speak to* Mrs. Meier? *dat*
Sie **schreibt über** ihre Reise.	She's *writing about* her trip. *acc*
Sie **reden** oft **über** Politik.	They often *talk about* politics. *acc.*
Sie **reden** oft **von** Politik.	They often *talk about* politics. *dat*
Ich **halte** nicht viel **von** dem Plan.	I don't *think* much *of* the plan. *dat*
Inge **erzählt von** ihrer Reise.	Inge *talks about* her trip. *dat*
Hast du Angst **vorm** Fliegen?	*Are* you *afraid of* flying? *dat*

In addition to their basic meanings, prepositions have special meanings when combined with specific verbs. Each verb and preposition combination should be learned as a unit, because it cannot be predicted which preposition is associated with a particular verb. The accusative and dative prepositions take the accusative and dative respectively. The case of the noun following either-or prepositions must be learned. <u>**Über** always takes the accusative case when used idiomatically.</u> (WITH A VERB)

E   Welches Verb?   Make up sentences from the phrases below by adding subjects and verbs. Vary the verbs as much as possible.

▶   in diesem Geschäft   *Er arbeitet in diesem Geschäft.*

1.	ins Geschäft	11.	über Musik
2.	auf dem Markt	12.	über dem Tisch
3.	im Restaurant	13.	zwischen den Büchern
4.	auf die Polizei	14.	an meinen Freund
5.	mit dem Auto	15.	von ihrer Reise
6.	in die Berge	16.	mit der Bahn
7.	im Ratskeller	17.	von dem Plan
8.	auf der Autobahn	18.	mit Professor Schneider
9.	mit der Arbeit	19.	bei der Gartenarbeit
10.	an der Universität	20.	vor Klausuren

F   Eine Reise in die Bundesrepublik   Below are some statements about Peter's visit to the Federal Republic of Germany. Give the German equivalents.

1. Peter lives behind a supermarket.
2. There are parks in every city.
3. In a restaurant there are flowers on every table.
4. Peter goes to the university by bus.
5. He doesn't like to drive on the freeway.
6. One can buy aspirin only in the pharmacy.
7. His friends sit at the table a long time after the meal.
8. They talk about sports, books, and their seminar reports.
9. Monika's father uses first names [*den Vornamen*] only among good friends.

7   Time expressions in the dative

Am Montag bleibt sie immer zu Hause.	On Monday she always stays home.
Er kommt **in** einer Woche.	He's coming in a week.
Ich lese gern **am** Abend.	I like to read in the evening.
Er arbeitet **vor** dem Essen.	He works before dinner.
Sie war **vor** einer Woche hier.	She was here a week ago.

With time expressions, **an, in,** and **vor** take the dative case. The use of **am** + a day may mean *on that one day* or *on all such days*.

sportmagazin
kicker
DEUTSCHLANDS GRÖSSTE SPORTZEITUNG

Holen Sie sich am Donnerstag den kicker bei Ihrem Händler!

G   Wann machst du das?   A friend is making comments about your activities. Correct her/him, using the cues provided in dative time expressions.

▶   Du arbeitest nur am Morgen, nicht? (Abend)   *Nein, nur am Abend.*

1. Frank kommt in fünf Minuten, nicht? (zwanzig Minuten)
2. Sollen wir vor dem Seminar Kaffee trinken gehen? (Vorlesung)

3. Du gehst am Donnerstag schwimmen, nicht? (Wochenende)
4. Du fährst am Samstag nachmittag nach Hause, nicht? (Sonntag abend)
5. Rita kommt in zwei Wochen, nicht? (eine Woche)
6. Du mußt die Arbeit vor dem Wintersemester fertig haben, nicht? (Sommersemester)
7. Im Sommer fahrt ihr in die Berge, nicht? (Herbst)

8 Time expressions in the accusative

| **Definite point** | Er arbeitet **jeden Abend.** | He works every evening. |
| **Duration** | Sie bleibt **einen Tag.** | She's staying one day. |

Nouns expressing a definite point in time or a duration of time are in the accusative.

H Wann und wie lange? Michael wants to know details about the visit of a pianist. Complete the answers, using the English cues.

▶ Wann war die Pianistin in Hamburg? — Sie war *letzten Mittwoch* in Hamburg. (*last Wednesday*)

1. Wann kommt sie zu uns? — Sie kommt _____ zu uns. (*this weekend*)
2. Wie lange bleibt sie? — Sie bleibt _____ . (*a day*)
3. Wie oft übt° sie? — Sie übt _____ . (*every morning*)   practice
4. Wann fährt sie wieder weg? — Sie fährt _____ wieder weg. (*next Monday*)
5. Wann kommt sie wieder? — Sie kommt _____ wieder. (*next year*)
6. Wie lange bleibt sie dann? — Dann bleibt sie _____ . (*a month*)

Sie haben das Wort

Was machen Sie gern?

Expressing likes and dislikes

1. Möchten Sie in einer Großstadt oder in einer Kleinstadt wohnen? Warum?
2. Wandern Sie gern im Wald? Warum (nicht)?
3. Waren Sie schon in den Bergen? Oft? In welchen?
4. Möchten Sie in der Schweiz wohnen? Warum (nicht)?
5. Essen Sie gern im Restaurant? Oft? Warum (nicht)?
6. Welche Kleidung tragen Sie, wenn Sie ins Kino gehen?
7. Gehen Sie oft ins Kino? Warum (nicht)?
8. Kaufen Sie im Supermarkt ein? Warum (nicht)?

9 Dative personal pronouns

	Singular					
Nominative	ich	du	er	es	sie	Sie
Accusative	mich	dich	ihn	es	sie	Sie
Dative	**mir**	**dir**	**ihm**	**ihm**	**ihr**	**Ihnen**

	Plural			
Nominative	wir	ihr	sie	Sie
Accusative	uns	euch	sie	Sie
Dative	**uns**	**euch**	**ihnen**	**Ihnen**

Dative personal pronouns have different forms from the accusative pronouns, except for **uns** and **euch**.

I   *Mir* oder *mich*?   Say that Bärbel is referring to you; use **mir** or **mich**.

▶   Wen hat Bärbel gemeint?   *Sie hat mich gemeint.*
Wem glaubt Bärbel?   *Sie glaubt mir.*

1. Wen hat sie zum Essen eingeladen?
2. Mit wem fährt sie in die Stadt?
3. Wen holt Bärbel später ab?
4. Wem hat sie ihre Notizen geliehen?
5. Wem hat sie geholfen?
6. Mit wem arbeitet sie gern?
7. Für wen hat sie den Pulli gekauft?
8. Von wem hat Bärbel das Buch bekommen?

J   *Dir* oder *dich*?   Jochen asks whether you are referring to him. Say you are, using **dir** or **dich**.

▶   Meinst du mich?   *Ja, ich meine dich.*
Glaubst du mir?   *Ja, ich glaube dir.*

1. Willst du mich etwas fragen?
2. Hast du an mich gedacht?
3. Kannst du mir helfen?
4. Hast du das Hemd für mich gekauft?
5. Kommst du später zu mir?
6. Holst du mich um sieben ab?
7. Bleibst du bei mir?
8. Willst du mit mir Schach spielen?

K   Eine Diskussion   You and your friends are having a discussion. Answer the questions affirmatively, using the pronoun **euch** or **uns.**

▶   Möchtet ihr mit uns Tennis spielen?   *Ja, wir möchten mit euch Tennis spielen.*

1.   Bleibt ihr heute bei uns?
2.   Könnt ihr mit uns arbeiten?
3.   Könnt ihr uns das Referat erklären?
4.   Habt ihr uns verstanden?
5.   Haben wir euch die Bücher geliehen?
6.   Haben wir euch von dem Plan erzählt?
7.   Haben wir euch wirklich geholfen?

L   Viele Fragen   Answer the questions below; use **Ihnen** or **Sie.**

▶   Für wen machen Sie das?   *Ich mache das für Sie, Frau Braun.*
▶   Mit wem sprechen Sie?   *Ich spreche mit Ihnen, Frau Braun.*

1.   Wen meinen Sie?
2.   Wen möchten Sie fragen?
3.   Für wen haben Sie die Uhr gekauft?
4.   Wem schenken Sie diese Blumen?
5.   Wem sagen Sie das?
6.   Von wem sprechen Sie?
7.   Mit wem fahren Sie?

M   Die Bundesrepublik gefällt ihnen.   Say that people like the features of the Federal Republic of Germany mentioned below. Use **ihm, ihr,** or **ihnen,** as appropriate.

▶   Gefallen Robert die vielen Parks?   *Ja, sie gefallen ihm.*

1.   Gefallen Barbara die vielen Blumen?
2.   Gefallen den Ausländern die Märkte?
3.   Gefallen deinem Freund die Bäckereien?
4.   Gefallen den Amerikanern die Autobahnen?
5.   Gefällt deiner Freundin das Essen?
6.   Gefällt den Deutschen das Fernsehen?

N   Was machst du denn?   Answer in the affirmative. Use nominative, accusative, and dative pronouns in your answers.

▶ Hat dir der Wein geschmeckt?   *Ja, er hat mir geschmeckt.*
▶ Kaufst du den Wein?   *Ja, ich kaufe ihn.*

1. Kommst du heute zu uns?
   Fährst du morgen zu Thomas?
2. Hast du deine Freunde im Biergarten getroffen?
   Hast du Erik eingeladen?
3. Hat Michael dich gemeint?
   Geht er morgen mit dir schwimmen?
4. Hast du das für Gabi getan?
   Tust du auch etwas für Erika und Christine?
5. Hast du mit Hans und Erich gesprochen?
   Arbeiten die Jungen zusammen?

10   Word order of direct and indirect objects

	Indirect Object	Direct Noun Object
Inge leiht	*ihrem Freund*	**ihr Radio.**
Inge leiht	*ihm*	**ihr Radio.**

The direct (accusative) object determines the order of objects. If the direct object is a noun, it usually follows the indirect (dative) object.

	Direct Pronoun Object	Indirect Object
Inge leiht	**es**	*ihrem Freund.*
Inge leiht	**es**	*ihm.*

If the direct (accusative) object is a personal pronoun, it always precedes the indirect (dative) object.

O   Beim Einkaufen   You're shopping with a friend who wants to know for whom you're buying various things and when you're going to give people their presents. Answer the questions, using accusative and dative pronouns as in the model.

▶ Wem kaufst du den Pulli? Deiner   *Ja, ich kaufe ihn meiner Schwester.*
  Schwester?
▶ Wann schenkst du ihn deiner   *Ja, ich schenke ihn ihr zum*
  Schwester? Zum Geburtstag?   *Geburtstag.*

1. Wem kaufst du das Messer? Deinem Bruder?
2. Wann schenkst du es deinem Bruder? Zu Weihnachten?

3. Wem kaufst du die Blumen? Deiner Tante?
4. Wann schenkst du sie deiner Tante? Morgen?
5. Wem kaufst du das Radio? Deinen Eltern?
6. Wann schenkst du es deinen Eltern? Zu Weihnachten?

Christmas (*Weihnachten*) in the German-speaking countries is celebrated on Christmas Eve (*Heiliger Abend*) and on the two following days. The season starts with the first day of Advent, the fourth Sunday before Christmas. In many homes, an advent wreath (*Adventskranz*) and advent calendar (*Adventskalender*) are displayed until Christmas. In many town squares, special markets create a festive Christmas atmosphere. On December 6, Santa Claus (*Sankt Nikolaus*) brings small gifts such as candies, nuts, and fruit to good children, and sometimes a switch (*Rute*) to naughty ones. Christmas Eve is usually celebrated with the immediate family. Only then is a Christmas tree set up and decorated in the living room, and presents are opened. The Christmas tree was introduced to the United States in the 18th century by German immigrants; their *Weihnachtsmann* was transformed into Santa Claus by Thomas Nast, a German cartoonist who had come to the United States in 1846.

Die Familie feiert Weihnachten mit richtigen Kerzen.

Sie haben das Wort

Zum Geburtstag   Say what you would like to give six people — members of your family, relatives, and friends — for their birthdays or other holidays.

▶   *[Zum Geburtstag] möchte ich [meinem Bruder] [ein Hemd] schenken.*

11   *Da*-compounds

Erzählt sie von ihrer Reise?   Ja, sie erzählt viel **davon.**
Erzählt sie von ihrem Freund?   Ja, sie erzählt viel **von ihm.**

In German, pronouns used after prepositions normally refer only to persons. To refer to things and ideas, a **da**-compound consisting of **da** + a preposition is generally used: **dadurch, dafür, damit. Da-** expands to **dar-** when the preposition begins with a vowel: **darauf, darin, darüber.**

P   Was hält Monika von Amerika?   Assure Gerd that Monika's activities and reactions in the United States are as he thinks. Use a **da**-compound or a preposition + a pronoun.

▶   Gefällt es Monika bei den ame-   *Ja, es gefällt Monika bei ihnen.*
      rikanischen Freunden?
▶   Hat sie Spaß an ihren Vorlesungen?   *Ja, sie hat Spaß daran.*

1.   Hat sie Hunger auf deutsches Brot?
2.   Redet sie gern mit Peter?
3.   Reden sie oft über kulturelle Unterschiede?
4.   Hilft sie Peter oft mit seinem Deutsch?
5.   Geht sie gern mit ihren Freunden essen?
6.   Denkt Monika oft an zu Hause?
7.   Erzählt sie gern von ihrem Leben in Deutschland?
8.   Fährt sie oft mit dem Fahrrad?
9.   Erzählt sie oft von ihren Freunden?

12   Wo-compounds

Wovon sprechen sie?   Sie sprechen **von** ihrer Reise.
Von wem sprechen sie?   Sie sprechen **von** ihrem Freund.

The interrogative pronouns **wen** and **wem** are used with a preposition to refer only to persons. The interrogative pronoun **was** refers to things and ideas. As an object of a preposition, **was** is generally replaced by a **wo**-compound consisting of **wo** + a preposition: **wofür, wodurch, womit. Wo-** expands to **wor-** when the preposition begins with a vowel: **worauf, worin, worüber.**

Karl wohnt seit September in   **Seit wann** wohnt er in München?
   München.

Wo-compounds are not used to inquire about time. To inquire about time, **wann, seit wann,** or **wie lange** is used.

Q   Wie, bitte?   Rolf mumbles because he's tired, so you don't hear about what or whom he is speaking. Ask what he said, using a **wo-**compound or a preposition + a pronoun to replace the boldfaced words, as appropriate.

▶   Klaus hat die Arbeit **mit dem**   *Womit hat er sie geschrieben?*
     Kugelschreiber geschrieben.

▶   Er hat sie **mit Annette** geschrieben.   *Mit wem hat er sie geschrieben?*

1.   Susanne hat **von ihrer Vorlesung** erzählt.
2.   Sie hat auch **von Professor Weiß** erzählt.
3.   Udo arbeitet **für Frau Schneider.**
4.   Sabine ist **mit Gerd** essen gegangen.
5.   Beim Essen hat sie **von ihrer Arbeit** erzählt.
6.   Nachher hat sie **mit Udo** Tennis gespielt.
7.   Sie hat nur **über das Tennisspiel** geredet.
8.   Sie denkt nur **an Tennis.**
9.   Sie wohnt jetzt wieder **bei ihren Eltern.**
10. Sie denkt nicht mehr **an eine eigene Wohnung.**

Sie haben das Wort

Was meinen Sie?   An Austrian friend comments on some things that strike her/him in the United States. Agree or express some doubts about her/his views, using some of the words and phrases below.

> Expressing agreement and disagreement

Richtig. □ Genau. □ Natürlich. □ Eben. □ Du hast recht. □ Wirklich? □ Meinst du? □ Ja, vielleicht. □ Vielleicht hast du recht. □ Das finde ich gar nicht. □ Was hast du gegen [Freundlichkeit]? □ Ich sehe das ganz anders. □ Das siehst du ganz falsch.

Amerikaner sind zu freundlich. Das kann nicht echt sein.
Das amerikanische Fernsehen ist prima.
Rock ist besser als klassische Musik.
Kuchen mit Farben wie rot, grün und blau sehen furchtbar aus.

| Wiederholung

A   Das hat Monika beobachtet.   Form sentences in the perfect tense. Tell about Monika's experiences in the United States, using the cues below.

1. der Vater der Gastfamilie / abholen / sie / von / Flughafen
2. er / benutzen / gleich / den Vornamen
3. sie / verstehen / das / nicht
4. das Einkaufen / gefallen / sie
5. sie / finden / Amerikaner / sehr freundlich
6. viele Leute / nehmen / Vitamintabletten
7. man / dekorieren / Kuchen / mit / Farben
8. man / essen / zuwenig / biologisch angebautes Gemüse
9. die Leute / gehen / wenig / zu Fuß

B   Das hat Peter in Deutschland beobachtet.   Now tell about Peter's experiences in the Federal Republic of Germany, using the cued words in the perfect tense.

1. Peter / fahren / nicht gern / auf / Autobahn
2. Leute / fahren / wie die Wilden
3. viele Leute / sehen / *Dallas* / im Fernsehen
4. die vielen Blumen und Parks / gefallen / er
5. viele Leute / trinken / an / Sonntag / um vier / Kaffee
6. man / benutzen / Messer und Gabel / anders
7. man / sitzen / nach / Essen / lange / an / Tisch
8. er / sehen / viel Reklame / mit / Wort / natürlich

C   Ferien   Complete the sentences about vacations in the Federal Republic of Germany and Switzerland, using one of the cued prepositions.

1. Im Sommer kommen viele Ausländer _____ Deutschland. (an, nach, zu)
2. Viele kommen _____ ihre Kinder. (mit, ohne, von)
3. Sie fahren natürlich _____ der Autobahn. (an, über, auf)
4. Junge Leute wandern gern _____ Freunden. (bei, ohne, mit)
5. Einige fahren _____ dem Fahrrad. (bei, an, mit)
6. Engländer fahren gern _____ die Schweiz. (an, in, nach)
7. _____ den Märkten kann man schöne Sachen kaufen. (auf, an, in)
8. Zu Hause erzählen die Engländer dann _____ ihrer Reise. (über, von, um)

D   Etwas über Musik   Answer the questions according to the cues. Use pronouns — alone or with prepositions — or **da**-compounds, as appropriate.

▶   Hast du gestern mit deiner   *Ja, ich habe gestern mit ihr gegessen.*
Freundin gegessen? (Ja)

1.   Habt ihr viel über Musik geredet? (Ja)
2.   Kennst du viel von Schönberg? (Ja)
3.   Hältst du viel von seiner Musik? (Nein)
4.   Möchtest du Frau Professor Koepke kennenlernen? (Ja)
5.   Sie weiß viel über Schönberg, nicht? (Ja)
6.   Liest°sie dieses Semester über seine Musik? (Ja)   *Is she lecturing*
7.   Meinst du, ich kann die Vorlesung verstehen? (Nein)

E   Welches Land?   Indicate whether the following statements describe something most likely in the United States, a German-speaking country, or both.

1.   Herr Meier hat einen Kuchen gebacken und ihn schön mit roten und blauen Farben dekoriert.
2.   Seit einigen Wochen wird Frau Lange leicht müde. Sie fährt zur Kur.
3.   Inge gebraucht das Shampoo *Viva*, weil es aus Pflanzen ist.
4.   Da Richard viel Aspirin nimmt, kauft er es im Supermarkt, denn da ist es sehr billig.
5.   Erik trägt nur Hemden aus Baumwolle.
6.   Barbara trinkt kein Bier mit Chemikalien.
7.   In den Ferien fahren Schmidts immer mit dem Zug.
8.   In ihrer Vorlesung über Brecht hat Nicole dieses Semester schon drei Klausuren geschrieben.
9.   Man benutzt oft den Vornamen auch bei neuen Bekannten.
10.   David hat gestern seine Aufenthaltserlaubnis bei der Polizei abgeholt.
11.   Die Züge sind fast immer pünktlich.
12.   Viele Leute sehen im Fernsehen jede Woche *Dallas*.

F   Wie sagt man das?   Erik Schulz goes to the University of Zürich. Tell a little about his experiences there.

1.   Erik Schulz goes to the University of Zürich°.   *Universität Zürich*
2.   In the summer he works for his neighbor.
3.   On the weekend he goes with his girlfriend Karin to the mountains.
4.   They drive her car.
5.   They like to hike.
6.   Afterwards they are hungry and thirsty.
7.   They go to a café, where they have coffee and cake.

G   Anregung

1. Write three sentences in German about **die Bundesrepublik** and **Österreich.**
2. Choose one of the following topics and write several sentences in German, relating them to the Federal Republic and to your country.

   Musik □ Weihnachten □ Blumen □ Wetter □ Autofahren □
   Bürokratie □ Fernsehen

Grammatik zum Nachschlagen

Hin and *her* (A)

Wohin fährst du? }
Wo fährst du **hin**? }   Where are you going?

Woher kommen Sie? }
Wo kommen Sie **her**? }   Where do you come from?

Komm mal **herunter**!   Come on down.
Wir müssen morgen **hinfahren.**   We have to drive there tomorrow.

The adverbs **hin** and **her** are used to show direction. **Hin** indicates motion in a direction away from the speaker, and **her** shows motion toward the speaker. **Hin** and **her** occupy last position in a sentence. They may also be combined with various parts of speech such as adverbs (**dorthin**), prepositions (**herunter**), and verbs (**hinfahren**).

Either-or prepositions (B–D)

Irmgard arbeitet **in der Stadt.**   Irmgard works in town.
Michael fährt **in die Stadt.**   Michael drives to town.

Nine prepositions take either the dative or the accusative. The dative is used for the meaning *place where*, in answer to the question **wo?** The accusative is used for the meaning *place to which*, in answer to the question **wohin?** To distinguish *place where* from *place to which*, German uses different cases; English sometimes uses different prepositions (e.g., *in* vs. *into*).

English equivalents of the either-or prepositions (F)

an	at; on; to
auf	on, on top of; to
hinter	behind, in back of

in	in, into; to
neben	beside, next to
über	above, over; across; about
unter	under, beneath; among
vor	in front of; before; ago
zwischen	between

The English equivalents of these prepositions may vary, depending on the object with which they are used. For example, English equivalents of **an der Ecke** and **an der Wand** are *at the corner* and *on the wall.*

Prepositional contractions (B–D)

am = an dem	**im** = in dem
ans = an das	**ins** = in das

The prepositions **an** and **in** may contract with **das** and **dem.** Other possible contractions are **aufs, hinters, hinterm, übers, überm, unters, unterm, vors,** and **vorm.**

Special meaning of prepositions

denken an (+ *acc.*)	to think about
glauben an (+ *acc.*)	to believe in
schreiben an (+ *acc.*)	to write to
studieren an *or* **auf** (+ *dat.*)	to study at
helfen bei	help with (activity)
anfangen mit	to start with, on
aufhören mit	to stop
fahren mit	to go by (means of)
sprechen mit	to speak to
reden / sprechen über (+ *acc.*)	to speak about
reden / sprechen von	to talk about
schreiben über (+ *acc.*)	to write about
erzählen / sprechen von	to tell about
halten von	to think of, think about
Angst haben vor (+ *dat.*)	to be afraid of

Prepositions have special meanings when combined with specific verbs. Each verb and preposition combination should be learned as a unit, because it cannot be predicted which preposition is associated with a particular verb. The accusative and dative prepositions take the accusative and dative respectively. The case of the noun following either-or prepositions must be learned. **Über** always takes the accusative case when used idiomatically.

Der undressierte Mann

Time expressions in the dative (G)

am Montag	on Monday, Mondays
am Abend	in the evening, evenings
in der Woche	during the week
in einem Jahr	in a year
vor dem Essen	before dinner
vor einem Jahr	a year ago

In expressions of time, the prepositions **an, in,** and **vor** are followed by the dative case.

Time expressions in the accusative (H)

Definite point	Er arbeitet **jeden Abend.**	He works every evening.
Duration	Sie bleibt **einen Tag.**	She's staying one day.

Nouns expressing a definite point in time or a duration of time are in the accusative. Note that words such as **nächst** and **letzt** have endings like the endings for **dies: diesen / nächsten / letzten Monat; dieses / nächstes / letztes** Jahr.

Dative personal pronouns (I–N)

	Singular					Plural			
Nominative	ich	du	er	es	sie	wir	ihr	sie	Sie
Accusative	mich	dich	ihn	es	sie	uns	euch	sie	Sie
Dative	**mir**	**dir**	**ihm**	**ihm**	**ihr**	**uns**	**euch**	**ihnen**	**Ihnen**

Dative pronouns have different forms from the accusative pronouns, except for **uns** and **euch**.

Word order of direct and indirect objects (O)

	Indirect Object	Direct Object Noun
Inge schenkt	*ihrer Schwester*	**den Kugelschreiber.**
Inge schenkt	*ihr*	**den Kugelschreiber.**

The direct (accusative) object determines the order of objects. If the direct object is a noun, it follows the indirect (dative) object.

	Direct Object Pronoun	Indirect Object
Inge schenkt	**ihn**	*ihrer Schwester.*
Inge schenkt	**ihn**	*ihr.*

If the direct (accusative) object is a personal pronoun, it precedes the indirect (dative) object.

Da-compounds (P)

Spricht sie oft von der Reise?   Ja, sie spricht oft **davon**.
Spricht sie gern von ihrem Freund?   Ja, sie spricht gern **von ihm**.

In German, pronouns after prepositions normally refer only to persons. German uses a **da**-compound, consisting of **da** + preposition, to refer to things or ideas. **Da-** expands to **dar-** when used with a preposition beginning with a vowel: **darüber.**

Wo-compounds (Q)

Wovon spricht sie?   Sie spricht von der Reise.
Von wem spricht sie?   Sie spricht von ihrem Freund.

The interrogative pronoun **wen** or **wem** is used with a preposition to refer to persons. German uses a **wo**-compound, consisting of **wo** + preposition, to ask questions referring to things or ideas. **Wo-** expands to **wor-** when used with a preposition beginning with a vowel: **worüber.**

Karl wohnt seit September in   **Seit wann** wohnt er in München?
  München.

Wo-compounds are not used to inquire about time. To inquire about time, **wann, seit wann,** or **wie lange** is used.

Kapitel 8

Lernziele

Sprechakte

Talking about household chores
Making plans
Expressing happiness or enthusiasm
Describing objects
Expressing disappointment
Expressing doubt or perplexity
Discussing personal issues

Grammatik

Genitive case
Attributive adjectives
Ordinal numbers
Dates

Vokabeln

Rooms in a house or apartment
The prefix **un-**
The suffix **-los**

Landeskunde

German vs. American sense of privacy
Pedestrian zones in cities of German-speaking
   countries
German love of hiking and swimming
Homes and apartments in German-speaking
   countries

Vorbereitungen zum Sonntags-Brunch

Bausteine für Gespräche

Vorbereitung auf eine Geburtstagsfete

Klaus: O je, wie es hier aussieht!

Mark: Ja, und in zwei Stunden kommen die Gäste.

Klaus: Komm, ich wasche schnell ab.

Mark: Schön. Ich trockne ab, und dann mache ich die Küche sauber.

Klaus: Dann räume ich das Wohnzimmer auf.

Preparations for a birthday party

Oh gosh, what a mess!

Yes, and in two hours the guests are coming.

Come on, I'll do the dishes quickly.

Great. I'll dry, and then I'll clean up the kitchen.

Then I'll straighten up the living room.

Wer kommt zur Fete?

Mark: Wieviel Leute hast du denn eingeladen?

Klaus: Ach, ungefähr zwanzig. Ein paar bringen was zu essen mit, und Wolfgang bringt Kassetten mit.

Mark: Ah gut. Wolf hat gute Musik. Ist dein Kassettenrecorder schon wieder repariert?

Klaus: Nein, der alte ist kaputt. Ich habe einen neuen. Geburtstagsgeschenk meiner Eltern.

Mark: He, nicht schlecht!

Who's coming to the party?

How many people did you invite?

Oh, around twenty. A few are bringing along something to eat and Wolfgang's bringing his cassettes.

Oh, good. Wolf has [some] good music. Is your tape deck fixed yet?

No, the old one is wrecked. I've got a new one. Birthday present from my parents.

Hey, not bad!

Fragen

1. Warum machen Klaus und Mark die Wohnung sauber?
2. Wann kommen die Gäste?
3. Welche Arbeiten machen Mark und Klaus?
4. Wieviel Gäste sind bei Klaus eingeladen?
5. Was bringen die Gäste mit?
6. Warum bringt Wolfgang Kassetten mit?
7. Was hat Klaus von seinen Eltern zum Geburtstag bekommen?
8. Wie findet Mark das Geschenk?

Eine Studentenparty für gute Freunde

Sie haben das Wort

A   **Geburtstage**   Ask a fellow student all about her/his birthday. You may wish to refer to the Supplementary Word Sets on clothing for *Kapitel 6* and audio/stereo equipment for *Kapitel 8,* in the Reference Section.

> Talking about birthdays

Sie	*Gesprächspartner/in*
Wann hast du Geburtstag?	Im [Mai].
Was hast du letztes Jahr zum Geburtstag bekommen?	[Eine Stereoanlage°.]
Was möchtest du dieses Jahr zum Geburtstag haben?	[Ein Buch über Schach.]
Das ist ja | **toll.**	
| phantastisch.	

B   Eine Fete   A friend has invited you to a party. Ask about the plans and what you should bring.

Making plans

Sie	*Gesprächspartner/in*
Was macht ihr auf der Party°?	Wir **tanzen.**
	hören Musik
	essen viel
	trinken etwas
	reden viel
Was soll ich zur Fete mitbringen?	Bring doch **die Bilder von deiner Ferienreise** mit.
	etwas zu essen
	trinken
	ein paar Flaschen° Cola
	Platten°
	Kassetten
	einen Plattenspieler°
	einen Kassettenrecorder

C   Hausarbeit   Find out from several fellow students which chores they do or don't do at home. You may wish to refer to the Supplementary Word Sets in the Reference Section for additional chores.

Talking about household chores

Sie	*Gesprächspartner/in*
Welche Arbeiten machst du zu Hause?	Ich **wasche ab.**
Welche Arbeiten machst du nicht?	trockne ab
	mache [die Küche] sauber
	räume nicht auf
	koche nicht

D   Was sagen Sie?   Respond to questions and comments from your partner, using responses from the list below and adding a few of your own.

Gesprächspartner/in	*Sie*
Was für eine tolle **Platte!**	Möchtest du sie hören?
Kassette!	Ich hab' keine Zeit.
Kannst du jetzt **abwaschen?**	Gratuliere.
abtrocknen?	Ich habe sie gestern gekauft.
aufräumen?	Muß ich?
Ich habe heute Geburtstag.	Wie alt wirst du denn?
	Ein Geschenk meiner Eltern.
	Gern. Willst du abtrocknen?

Vokabeln

— Substantive

die **Fete, -n** party
die **Flasche, -n** bottle
das **Geschenk, -e** present
die **Kassette, -n** cassette
der **Kassettenrecorder, -** cassette deck
die **Küche, -n** kitchen
die **Musikstunde, -n** music lesson

die **Party, -s** party
die **Platte, -n** (*abbrev. of* **Schallplatte**) record
der **Plattenspieler, -** record player
die **Stereoanlage, -n** stereo system
die **Stunde, -n** hour; lesson
das **Wohnzimmer, -** living room

— Verben

ab·trocknen to dry dishes
ab·waschen (wäscht ab), abge-waschen to wash (dishes)

auf·räumen to straighten up
reparieren to repair

— Andere Wörter

he! hey!
schnell fast

ungefähr approximately
was (*abbrev. of* **etwas**) something

— Besondere Ausdrücke

O je! Oh gosh!

| Türen

Vorbereitung auf das Lesen

• *Zum Thema*

1. Welche Türen schließt man bei Ihnen —
   a. Schlafzimmertüren, wenn Sie im Schlafzimmer arbeiten oder schlafen? Wenn Sie nicht im Zimmer sind?
   b. Bürotüren, wenn man im Büro arbeitet?
2. Stört es Sie, wenn eine Schlafzimmertür oder eine Bürotür offen ist? Wenn sie geschlossen ist?
3. Kann man von der Haustür in Ihr Wohnzimmer oder Eßzimmer sehen? Stört Sie das?
4. Haben die Einfamilienhäuser bei Ihnen einen Zaun oder eine Hecke?

- *Leitfragen*

1. Was macht die Österreicherin nach Meinung der Amerikanerin „falsch"?
2. Was ist der Unterschied zwischen vielen amerikanischen Türen und österreichischen Türen?
3. Warum sind die Türen in Österreich, in Deutschland und in der Schweiz meistens geschlossen?
4. Warum haben die Einfamilienhäuser in deutschsprachigen Ländern oft eine Hecke oder einen Zaun?
5. Was halten die Österreicher von offenen Türen?
6. Was halten die Amerikaner von geschlossenen Türen?

Jutta Gruber, eine Österreicherin, studiert zwei Jahre an einer amerikanischen Universität. Während ihres ersten Jahres hat sie ein Zimmer bei einer Familie. Sie spricht gut Englisch. Das Zimmer gefällt ihr. Die Familie ist nett. Da fragt die Mutter der Familie sie eines Tages:

5 „Haben Sie etwas gegen uns?" Die Österreicherin ist erstaunt:

„Nein, natürlich nicht. Aber bitte, warum fragen Sie?"

„Wegen der Tür, wegen der geschlossenen Tür! Ich meine, weil Ihre Tür immer geschlossen ist, wenn Sie in Ihrem Zimmer sind."

Die Österreicherin ist sprachlos. Sie kann nur sagen: „Aber ... aber das
10 bedeutet doch nichts. Ich tue das ganz automatisch. In Österreich tun wir das immer."

„Wirklich?" antwortet die Amerikanerin und denkt: Das muß ja ein eigenartiges° Land sein, wo die Türen immer geschlossen sind!   *strange*

Die Österreicherin geht langsam in ihr Zimmer und schließt trotz des
15 Gesprächs wieder die Tür. Sie muß an einen Satz denken, den° sie oft von   *that*
ihrer Mutter gehört hat: „Jeder Mensch braucht ein Plätzchen°, wo er die   *little place*
Tür hinter sich° zumachen kann."   *oneself*

Was für eine Zimmertür hält unsere Studentin denn immer geschlossen? Nun, sie ist leicht, nicht so schwer wie eine Zimmertür in Österreich,
20 in Deutschland oder in der Schweiz.* Auch muß man wissen, daß die
österreichischen Türen ein Schloß mit einem Schlüssel haben. Sie passen
auch besser in den Türrahmen°. Und unten° haben sie anstatt eines   *door frame / below*
kleinen freien Zwischenraumes° auch heute noch oft eine Schwelle°.   *space / door sill*

In Amerika sind die Türen nicht nur in einer Privatwohnung meistens
25 offen, sondern auch in Büros. Manchmal haben sie eine klare Glas-
scheibe°. Wenn eine österreichische Bürotür eine Glasscheibe hat, dann   *glass pane*
ist sie meistens aus Milchglas, d.h. sie ist nicht durchsichtig°.   *transparent*

---

*Doors in Austria, Germany, and Switzerland generally have door handles
(**Klinken**) rather than knobs.

Vom Flur führen die Türen in die einzelnen Zimmer.

Jutta Gruber ist die Häuser in Österreich gewohnt.° Da hat das Grund-   *accustomed to*
stück° eines Einfamilienhauses z.B. fast immer einen Zaun, oft auch eine   *property*
30 undurchsichtige Hecke. Wenn man die Haustür öffnet, kommt man in
größeren° Häusern zuerst in einen Flur. Von da geht man durch die   *larger*
eigentliche Wohnungstür in einen zweiten Flur, den Flur der Wohnung.
Von diesem Flur führen die Türen ins Wohnzimmer und Eßzimmer, in die
Schlafzimmer, in die Küche und ins Badezimmer. Da diese Türen fast im-
35 mer geschlossen sind, kann der Besucher von hier nicht in die Zimmer
sehen. Auch kleine Mietwohnungen° haben immer einen solchen Flur.   *rental apartments*
Während ihres zweiten° Jahres hat Jutta Gruber eine kleine moderne   *second*
Wohnung. Es stört sie, daß sie hier keinen Flur hat. Nach einigen Wochen
hat sie eine Idee: Sie baut einen Flur aus Bücherregalen. Jetzt kann man
40 von der Wohnungstür nicht mehr direkt ins Wohnzimmer sehen.

Die Österreicher nehmen ihre private Sphäre also° sehr ernst. Ihre pri-   *thus*
vate Sphäre ist schon verletzt, wenn man sie sehen kann. Daher sind auch
ihre Balkons und Terrassen anders gebaut als in Amerika. Man kann die
Menschen darauf nicht oder nicht leicht sehen.

45   E.T. Hall (*The Hidden Dimension*) zeigt, wie „die Tür" zu ernsten
Schwierigkeiten führen kann, wenn amerikanische Firmen Büros in
Österreich haben. Wenn die Türen offen sind, stört das die Österreicher
der Firma. Auch bedeuten offene Türen für sie Unordnung°. Und wer will   *disorder*
schon in einer unordentlichen Firma arbeiten? Die Türen müssen also
50 geschlossen bleiben. Das stört aber die Amerikaner dieser Firma. Sie
glauben nun, daß sie ausgeschlossen° sind, daß man vor ihnen etwas   *excluded*
verheimlichen° will. Beide Seiten müssen also lernen, daß eine offene   *keep secret*
Tür und eine geschlossene Tür etwas bedeuten. Und sie müssen lernen,
daß sie in Österreich etwas anderes bedeuten als in Amerika.

Fragen zum Lesestück

1. Wo wohnt Jutta Gruber?
2. Kann sie gut Englisch?
3. Wie gefällt ihr ihr Zimmer?
4. Wie gefällt ihr ihre amerikanische Familie?
5. Was fragt die Mutter der Familie Jutta eines Tages?
6. Warum glaubt die Mutter, daß Jutta etwas gegen die Familie hat?
7. Warum ist Jutta erstaunt?
8. Warum schließt sie immer ihre Tür?
9. Wer hat gesagt, daß jeder Mensch ein Plätzchen braucht, wo er die Tür
   hinter sich zumachen kann?
10. Wie ist eine österreichische Tür? Eine amerikanische Tür?
11. Welche Tür hat manchmal eine durchsichtige Glasscheibe, die öster-
    reichische oder die amerikanische?
12. Wohin kommt man, wenn man durch die Wohnungstür eines öster-
    reichischen Hauses geht?
13. Warum kann man nicht in die Zimmer sehen?
14. Was hat Jutta aus Bücherregalen gebaut? Warum?
15. In welchem Land arbeitet man hinter geschlossenen Bürotüren?
16. Wer glaubt, daß man vor ihnen etwas verheimlichen will, wenn die
    Bürotüren geschlossen sind?

Erzählen Sie!   Tell about single-family homes in Austria. Use the cues below in addition to your own sentences.

Einfamilienhäuser in Österreich □ Zaun und Hecke □ Balkon und
Terrasse □ Flur □ Zimmer mit geschlossenen Türen □ offene Türen

Sie haben das Wort

Discussing one's home

Interview   Fragen Sie eine(n) Bekannte(n):

1. ob sie/er in einem Studentenheim wohnt.
2. ob sie/er ein Zimmer bei einer Familie hat.
3. ob sie/er die Tür schließt, wenn sie/er arbeitet.
4. was für eine Zimmertür es ist — eine leichte oder eine schwere.
5. ob ihre/seine Familie in einem Einfamilienhaus wohnt.
6. ob die Zimmertüren in ihrem/seinem Haus meistens geschlossen oder offen sind.
7. ob viele Häuser bei ihr/ihm einen Balkon haben.
8. ob sie/er die Nachbarn sehen kann, wenn sie auf der Terrasse sitzen.

Vokabeln

— Substantive

das **Badezimmer, -**   bathroom
der **Balkon, -s**   balcony
der **Besucher, -/die Besucherin, -nen** visitor, guest
das **Bücherregal, -e**   bookcase
das **Büro, -s**   office
das **Einfamilienhaus, ˝er**   single-family home
das **Eßzimmer, -**   dining room
der **Flur, -e**   (entrance) hall

die **Hecke, -n**   hedge
die **Idee, -n**   idea
der **Satz, ˝e**   sentence
das **Schlafzimmer, -**   bedroom
das **Schloß**, *pl.* **Schlösser**   lock; castle
der **Schlüssel, -**   key
der **Stock**, *pl.* **Stockwerke**   floor (story) of building
die **Terrasse, -n**   terrace, patio
der **Zaun, ˝e**   fence

— Verben

antworten (+ *dat.*)   to answer (*as in* **ich antworte der Frau**)
antworten auf (+ *acc.*)   to answer (*as in* **ich antworte auf die Frage**)
bauen   to build
führen   to lead

öffnen   to open
passen (+ *dat.*)   to fit; to suit
stören   to disturb
verletzen   to injure
zeigen   to show
zu•machen   to close

— Andere Wörter

(an)statt (+ *gen.*)   instead of
da (*conj.*)   since, because
dunkel   dark
erstaunt   astonished
hell   bright
langsam   slow(ly)

modern   modern
sprachlos   speechless
trotz (+ *gen.*)   in spite of
während (+ *gen.*)   during
wegen (+ *gen..*)   on account of

Erweiterung der Wortschatzes

1   Das Haus

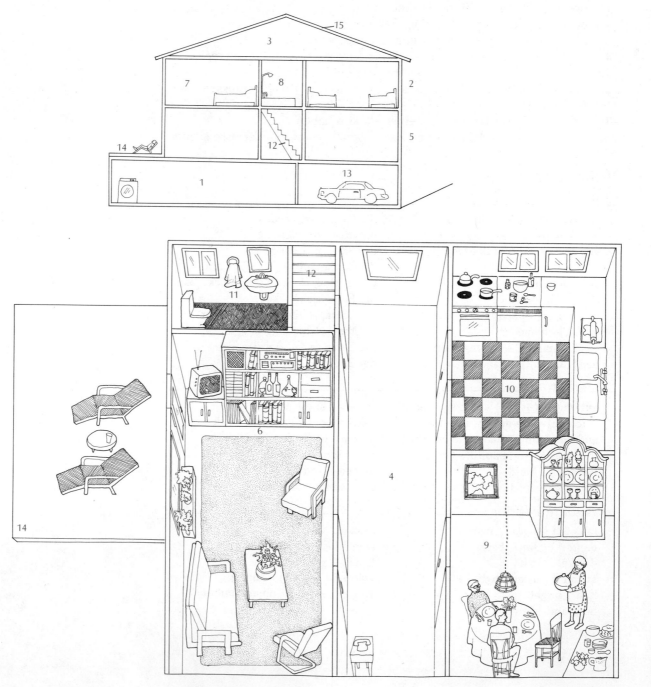

1. der Keller, -	9. das Eßzimmer, -
2. der erste Stock	10. die Küche, -n
3. der Dachboden, ⸚	11. die Toilette, -n
4. der Flur, -e	12. die Treppe, -n
5. das Erdgeschoß	13. die Garage, -n
6. das Wohnzimmer, -	14. die Terrasse, -n
7. das Schlafzimmer, -	15. das Dach, ⸚er
8. das Badezimmer, -	

The second floor is called **der erste Stock,** the third floor **der zweite Stock,** and so on, because the first floor is called **das Erdgeschoß.**

A   Antworten Sie!

1. Wo kocht man?
2. In welchem Zimmer schläft man?
3. Wo badet man?
4. In welchem Zimmer sitzt man abends und liest?
5. In welchem Zimmer hört man Musik oder sieht fern?
6. In welchem Zimmer ißt man, wenn Gäste da sind?

Sie haben das Wort

Interview   Answer the questions below. Then find students whose answers correspond to yours.

1. Wohnen Sie zu Hause, bei einer Familie oder im Studentenheim?
2. Wo wohnt Ihre Familie? In einem Einfamilienhaus? In einer Mietwohnung?
3. Wieviel Stockwerke hat Ihr Haus?
4. Hat Ihr Haus einen Keller? Einen Balkon? Eine Terrasse? Eine Hecke oder einen Zaun?
5. Wo schlafen Sie? Im Erdgeschoß? Im ersten Stock?
6. Was für eine Farbe haben Ihre Schlafzimmerwände — eine helle° oder eine dunkle°?
7. In welchem Zimmer essen Sie?
8. In welchem Zimmer sehen Sie fern?

2   The prefix *un-*

Viele Deutsche glauben, daß Kuchen mit künstlichen Farben **ungesund** ist.	Many Germans believe that cake with artificial colors is *unhealthy.*

As in English, the prefix **un-** causes a word to have a negative or an opposite meaning. The prefix **un-** is stressed: **un'gesund.**

Although many people in German-speaking countries live in apartments, either rented (*Mietwohnung*) or owned (*Eigentumswohnung*), many others live in single- and two-family homes. A typical dwelling has stucco-coated walls and a tile or slate roof. Normally there is a full basement that is used primarily for storage or as a work area, although the "family room" (*Unterhaltungsraum*) or shop (*Hobbykeller*) is becoming popular. The first floor (*erster Stock*) is what is considered the second story in American homes. Privacy is assured not only by closed doors but also by window curtains (*Gardinen*) and drapes (*Vorhänge*). Many homes and apartments are equipped with attractive shutters (*Rollläden*) that unfold vertically over the windows.

Dieses Haus hat Fensterläden statt Rolläden.

B   Wörter mit *un-* Give each sentence an opposite meaning by adding the prefix **un-** to the boldfaced word.

1. Ich finde diese Lampe sehr **praktisch.**
2. Unsere Nachbarn sind sehr **freundlich.**
3. Ich glaube, daß Regina sehr **gern** kommt.
4. Diese Kurzgeschichte ist **interessant.**
5. Professor Müller ist meistens **pünktlich.**
6. Ich glaube, Mark hat **recht.**

3   The suffix *-los*

Jutta war **sprachlos,** als sie das gehört hat.

Jutta was *speechless* when she heard that.

The German suffix **-los** is used to form adjectives and adverbs from nouns. The suffix **-los** is often equivalent to the English suffix *-less*, denoting *a lack of.*

C   Was bedeutet das? Give the German noun related to the boldfaced adjective or adverb. Then give the English equivalent of each sentence.

1. Jutta antwortet nicht, sondern geht **wortlos** aus dem Zimmer.
2. Die Kurzgeschichte ist so uninteressant, weil sie so **farblos** ist.
3. Nicoles Antwort ist **fraglos** die beste.
4. Herbert ist schon ein Jahr **arbeitslos.**
5. Erik ist wirklich ein **gefühlloser** Mensch.

¡Übungen zur Aussprache

Review the pronunciation of **r** and **l** in the Reference section at the end of the book. Read aloud the words in each column on this page from top to bottom. Then read each set of columns across. Check your pronunciation by listening to your instructor or the tape.

[r]	[l]	full [r]	full [r]	full [r]
wird	wild	fragt	ragt	warum
Schmerzen	schmelzen	kriechen	riechen	gierig
Karte	kalte	trugen	rufen	führen
Schurz	Schulz	Preis	Reis	Tiere
Worte	wollte	grünen	rühmen	schnüren

Read the following sentences aloud, paying special attention to the way you pronounce **l** and **r** in the boldfaced words.

1. Wer hat **Frau Kugel** das **gefragt?**
2. Es hat **Cornelia** nicht **gefallen,** daß wir so **schnell gefahren** sind.
3. Im **Juli wollen** wir im **Schwarzwald** wandern und **zelten.**
4. Im **Frühling fahre** ich mit **Freunden** nach **Österreich.**

Wer anderen eine Grube gräbt,
fällt selbst hinein.

| Grammatik und Übungen

1   Genitive case

Das ist die Frage **eines Kindes.**   That is a child's question.
Ich habe mit dem Sohn **des**   I talked to the baker's son.
   Bäckers gesprochen.
Der Flur **der Wohnung** ist nicht   The entrance hall of the apart-
   sehr groß.   ment is not very large.

English shows possession or other close relationships by adding '*s* to a noun or by using a phrase with *of*. English generally uses the '*s* form only for persons. For things and ideas, English uses the *of*-construction.

   German uses the genitive case to show possession or other close relation-ships. The genitive is used for things and ideas as well as for persons. The genitive generally follows the noun it modifies.

Das ist ein Freund **eines Freundes.**
Das ist ein Freund **von einem Freund.**

Von with the dative case often replaces the genitive construction, especially in colloquial German.

• *Masculine and neuter nouns*

Hast du den Namen **des Kindes**   Did you understand the child's
   verstanden?   name?
Das ist die Meinung **eines Profes-**   That is a professor's opinion.
   sors.

Masculine and neuter nouns of one syllable generally add **-es** in the genitive; nouns of two or more syllables add **-s.** The corresponding articles, **der-**words, and **ein**-words end in **-s** or **-es** in the genitive.

A   Kommen die wirklich?   Barbara wants to know whether various friends are really coming to visit you. Say that they are — but later than you had thought.

▶   Kommt Mark wirklich dieses Jahr?   *Ja, aber erst gegen Ende des Jahres.*

   1.   Kommt Ingrid wirklich noch in diesem Monat?
   2.   Kommt Gisela im Winter?
   3.   Kommen Christel und Dieter im Sommer?
   4.   Kommt Sigrid dieses Semester?
   5.   Kommt Uwe im Herbst?

The physical layout of cities in the German-speaking countries is generally different from that of cities in the United States. The concept of building large suburbs and shopping malls around a city is uncommon in most of Europe. A city (*Großstadt*) or town (*Stadt*) in German-speaking countries has a center containing office buildings as well as apartment houses, stores, and places for cultural events. Many downtown areas have been converted to traffic-free pedestrian zones (*Fußgängerzonen*). A typical pedestrian zone has many stores, restaurants, and outdoor cafés. The streets are often lined with plants and trees and sometimes lead into small squares, where people can rest on benches. The downtown shopping areas are used not only by people who live in the city, but also by people who live in the outskirts or in nearby villages.

Fußgängerzone im Zentrum von Frankfurt am Main

• *Feminine and plural nouns*

Die Farbe **der Bluse** gefällt mir.	I like the color of the blouse.
Frau Genscher ist eine Bekannte **der Eltern**.	Mrs. Genscher is an acquaintance of the parents.

Feminine and plural nouns do not add a genitive ending. The corresponding articles, **der**-words, and **ein**-words end in **-er** in the genitive.

B   Hast du die Adresse?   Your friend is getting settled near where you live and needs the addresses of various places. Help her/him.

▶ Kennst du eine Apotheke?   *Hier ist die Adresse einer Apotheke.*

1. Kennst du eine Bäckerei?
2. Und eine Metzgerei?
3. Wo ist eine Drogerie?
4. Gibt es hier eine Buchhandlung?
5. Wo ist die Bibliothek?
6. Wo ist die Polizei?

• *Possessive adjectives*

Gerda ist die Freundin **meines Bruders.**	Gerda is my brother's girlfriend.
Frau Genscher ist eine Bekannte **seiner Eltern**.	Mrs. Genscher is an acquaintance of his parents.

Possessive adjectives take the case of the noun they modify. Even though a possessive adjective already shows possession (**mein** = my, **sein** = his), it must itself be in the genitive case when the noun it goes with is in the genitive (**meines Bruders** = of my brother). Thus a phrase like **die Freundin meines Bruders** shows *two* possessive relationships.

C   Die richtige Telefonnummer?   You're conducting an opinion poll about a proposed garbage dump on behalf of your **Bürgerinitiative.** Ask your friend to confirm the telephone numbers of various people you want to call.

▶   deine Eltern   *Ist das die Telefonnummer deiner Eltern?*

1.	deine Tante	4.	deine Schwester
2.	dein Bruder	5.	deine Großeltern
3.	dein Freund Mark	6.	dein Vetter

• *Masculine N-nouns*

Die Frau **des Herrn** da kommt aus Österreich.	The wife of the man there is from Austria.
Haben Sie die Frage **des Jungen** verstanden?	Did you understand the boy's question?

Masculine nouns that add **-n** or **-en** in the accusative and dative singular also add **-n** or **-en** in the genitive. A few masculine nouns add **-ns: des Namens.**

D   Verloren — Gefunden   Ask Mrs. Wagner whether she has found the lost articles.

▶   Dieser Herr hat seine Jacke verloren.   *Haben Sie die Jacke dieses Herrn gefunden?*

1. Dieser Junge hat seinen Schlüssel verloren.
2. Dieser Student hat seine Büchertasche verloren.
3. Mein Nachbar hat seinen Kugelschreiber verloren.
4. Der Herr da hat sein Taschenmesser verloren.
5. Der Junge da hat seine Uhr verloren.
6. Der Student da hat sein Geld verloren.

E   **Neue Sätze**   Restate the sentences below, replacing the genitive expressions with the genitive form of the cued words.

▶   Das Referat dieser Studentin war   *Das Referat dieses Studenten war*   sehr interessant. (dieser Student)   *sehr interessant.*

1. Das ist die Telefonnummer meiner Frau. (mein Mann)
2. Der Flur unseres Hauses ist klein. (diese Wohnung)
3. Haben Sie die Antwort seiner Freundin gehört? (unser Nachbar)
4. Das ist die Sprache eines Kindes. (ein Student)
5. Kennen Sie den Namen dieser Firma? (dieses Geschäft)
6. Haben Sie die Adresse des Biergartens? (der Ratskeller)
7. Wie heißen die Bekannten ihrer Tante? (ihre Eltern)

F   **Wie sagt man das?**

1. the man's plan
2. the woman's story
3. the entrance hall of this apartment
4. your friend's explanation
5. Heike's bicycle
6. Mr. Schmidt's car
7. the names of the countries

**Willkommen
im Kreis
des Kronprinzen**

Am oberen Kurfürstendamm
Zentral. Im Grünen. Messe-nah.
EZ ab DM 90,–; DZ ab DM 120,–

HOTEL KRONPRINZ BERLIN
Kronprinzendamm 1, 1000 Berlin 31
Telefon (030) 89 60 30

●   *The interrogative pronoun* **wessen?**

Wessen Plattenspieler ist das?   Whose record player is that?
Wessen Platten sind das?   Whose records are those?

Wessen? is the genitive form of **wer?** and is equivalent to English *whose.*

G   **Wem gehört das?**   Everyone seems to be borrowing things. Ask whose things they are.

▶   Uschi hat gestern eine tolle Ste-   *Wessen Stereoanlage war das*   reoanlage gehabt.   *denn?*

1. Stefan hat eine schöne Jacke getragen.
2. Andrea hat eine tolle Kassette gespielt.
3. Ursel hat die Notizen genommen.
4. Michael hat einen schönen Pulli getragen.
5. Frau Lange hat ein interessantes Buch gelesen.
6. Christel hat eine schöne Uhr getragen.
7. Herr Weiß hat ein tolles Auto gefahren.

Sie haben das Wort

Familie und Freunde   How much do you know about your family, relatives, and friends?

> Discussing friends
> and family

1. Wo wohnt der Freund Ihrer Schwester?
2. Wo wohnt die Freundin Ihres Bruders?
3. Wie ist die Telefonnummer Ihres Freundes? Ihrer Freundin?
4. Wissen Sie die Adresse Ihrer Tante? Ihres Onkels? Ihrer Großeltern?
5. Was für ein Auto hat der Freund Ihrer Schwester? die Freundin Ihres Bruders?
6. Wie heißen die Bekannten Ihrer Eltern?

2   Genitive of time

Indefinite past	**Eines Tages** hat mir Jutta alles erklärt.	*One day* Jutta explained everything to me.
Indefinite future	**Eines Tages** mache ich das vielleicht.	*Someday* maybe I'll do that.

Nouns expressing an indefinite point in time are in the genitive.

3   Prepositions with the genitive

(an)statt	instead of	Kommt Inge **(an)statt** ihrer Schwester?
trotz	in spite of	**Trotz** des Wetters fahren wir in die Berge.
während	during	**Während** des Sommers bleiben wir nicht in Hamburg.
wegen	on account of *because of*	**Wegen** des Wetters gehen wir nicht schwimmen.

The prepositions **anstatt** or **statt, trotz, während,** and **wegen** require the genitive case.

H   Gegen die Mülldeponie   Answer the questions below regarding a demonstration against improper disposal of waste materials. Use the cues.

▶   Warum ist Cornelia gestern in die   *Wegen der Demonstration.*
     Stadt gefahren? (wegen/die De-
     monstration)

1. Bist du auch mitgefahren? (ja, trotz / das Wetter)
2. Warum ist Paul zu Hause geblieben? (wegen / seine Arbeit)
3. Ist deine Schwester mitgegangen? (ja, statt / mein Bruder)

4. Sind die Leute lange auf der Straße geblieben? (nein, nur / während / der Nachmittag)
5. Warum sind so wenige Leute gekommen? (wegen / das Wetter)
6. Machen wir noch eine Demonstration? (ja, wegen / die Mülldeponie)
7. Wann machen wir Pläne für die nächste Demonstration? (während / die Weihnachtsferien)

Many people in the German-speaking countries love to go hiking (*wandern*) and walking. There are well-maintained trails everywhere. Some are no more than paths through local scenic spots or city parks, while others are part of a vast complex of trails. Some parks in the Federal Republic, for instance, feature *Trimm-dich-Pfade* (*jogging/exercise paths*).

Swimming is also a popular activity. In addition to seashore and lakeside beaches, town pools—both indoors and outdoors—provide ample opportunity for bathing. An outdoor pool (*Freibad*), with a nominal admission fee, is generally located on the outskirts of a city. It is often large and surrounded by lawns. People come with food and blankets to spend the day picnicking, swimming, and playing volleyball or badminton. Indoor pools (*Hallenbäder*) are becoming more and more elaborate. Cities are building them with cafés, movies, and shopping areas, as well as sometimes with a solarium (*Solarium*), bodybuilding room (*Bodybuildingraum*), and hot tubs (*Hot-Whirl-Pools*).

Am Wochenende wandert man gern im Taunus.

4 Adjectives

• *Predicate adjectives*

Die Schallplatte ist **toll**.
Der Wein wird sicher **gut**.

Predicate adjectives are adjectives that follow the verbs **sein** or **werden** and modify the subject. Predicate adjectives do not take endings.

- *Attributive adjectives*

Das ist eine **tolle** Schallplatte.
Das ist ein **guter** Wein.

Attributive adjectives are adjectives that precede the nouns they modify.
Attributive adjectives have endings.

5 Preceded adjectives

- *Adjectives preceded by definite articles or **der**-words*

	Masculine	Neuter	Feminine	Plural
Nom.	der alt**e** Mann	das klein**e** Kind	die jung**e** Frau	die gut**en** Freunde
Acc.	den alt**en** Mann	das klein**e** Kind	die jung**e** Frau	die gut**en** Freunde
Dat.	dem alt**en** Mann	dem klein**en** Kind	der jung**en** Frau	den gut**en** Freunden
Gen.	des alt**en** Mannes	des klein**en** Kindes	der jung**en** Frau	der gut**en** Freunde

An adjective preceded by a definite article or by a **der**-word ends in **-en** or **-e**, as follows: **-en** in the dative, the genitive, the accusative masculine, and all plurals; **-e** in the nominative singular and in the accusative singular neuter and feminine.

	M.	N.	F.	Pl.
Nom.	e	e	e	en
Acc.	en	e	e	en
Dat.	en	en	en	en
Gen.	en	en	en	en

Das Zimmer ist zu **dunkel.**   Wer kann in diesem **dunklen** Zimmer lesen?

Diese Handschuhe sind **teuer.**   Willst du diese **teuren** Handschuhe wirklich kaufen?

Adjectives ending in **-el** omit the **-e** when the adjective takes an ending. Adjectives ending in **-er** may follow the same pattern.

I   **Noch einmal.**   Restate the model sentences, using the cued adjectives in the nominative singular.

▶   Ist dieser Pulli noch gut? (alt)   *Ist dieser alte Pulli noch gut?*

1. rot
2. grün

3. schwer
4. leicht

▶ Wem gehört dieses Radio? (klein)　*Wem gehört dieses kleine Radio?*

5. toll
6. neu

7. kaputt
8. teuer

▶ Hoffentlich war die Platte nicht sehr teuer. (neu)　*Hoffentlich war die neue Platte nicht sehr teuer.*

9. furchtbar
10. schlecht

11. amerikanisch
12. kaputt

J　Welche meinst du?　In a department store Ingrid comments on a number of items; ask which she is referring to. Use adjectives in the accusative singular.

▶ Der rote Pulli ist toll, nicht?　*Meinst du diesen roten Pulli?*

1. Der leichte Regenmantel ist praktisch, nicht?
2. Der helle Rock ist schön, nicht?
3. Das grüne Kleid ist sehr kurz, nicht?
4. Das gelbe Hemd ist toll, nicht?
5. Die kleine Handtasche ist praktisch, nicht?
6. Die weiße Bluse ist wirklich schön, nicht?
7. Die schwarzen Schuhe sind furchtbar, nicht?
8. Die kurzen Handschuhe sind billig, nicht?

Sie haben das Wort

Was hast du verloren?　You have lost something. When a friend asks you what you have lost, answer by mentioning some of the objects listed below. When the friend asks *which* object, describe the article by using adjectives from the second list.

Describing objects

Gesprächspartner/in　　*Sie*

▶ Was hast du verloren?　*Meinen Kugelschreiber.*

Buch □ Radio □ Kassettenrecorder □ Uhr □ Handschuhe □ Pulli □ Hut □ Jacke

Gesprächspartner/in　　*Sie*

▶ Welchen?　　*Den tollen, kleinen.*

alt	klein	hell	grün
groß	kurz	toll	braun
lang	modern	leicht	blau
neu	schwer	dunkel	

K   Ich bin gern da.   A friend makes favorable comments about various places you occasionally go. Agree and say you enjoy being there. Use adjectives in the dative singular.

▶   Die alte Stadt ist interessant, nicht?   *Ja, ich bin gern in der alten Stadt.*

1.   Der neue Park hat viele Blumen, nicht?
2.   Diese dunkle Kneipe ist toll, nicht?
3.   Diese kleine Buchhandlung ist interessant, nicht?
4.   Das große Musikgeschäft ist phantastisch, nicht?
5.   Das kleine Café ist ruhig, nicht?
6.   Der alte Biergarten ist billig, nicht?
7.   Die frühe Vorlesung ist interessant, nicht?

L   Wir fahren.   You and a friend are having a disagreement about whether to visit some friends. He brings up reasons not to go, but you insist on going in spite of the problems. Use adjectives in the genitive.

▶   Das Wetter ist so schlecht.   *Wir fahren. Trotz des schlechten Wetters.*

1.   Du, die Straßen sind so schlecht.
2.   Die Zeit ist so kurz.
3.   Der Weg ist sehr lang.
4.   Das Auto ist aber kaputt.
5.   Weißt du, der Zug ist teuer.
6.   Aber die Wohnung ist so klein.
7.   Wir haben nur diese schlechte Landkarte.

M   Viele Fragen   Peter has lots of questions. Rephrase them by combining the sentences in each pair below. Use the boldfaced adjectives with the plural nouns.

▶   Warum trägst du immer noch diese   *Warum trägst du immer noch*
Schuhe? Sie sind schon **alt.**   *diese alten Schuhe?*

1.   Wer hat diese Handschuhe gekauft? Sie sind schön **warm.**
2.   Was hast du mit den Jeans gemacht? Sie sind zu **eng.**
3.   Wann hast du diese Hemden bekommen? Sie sind wirklich **toll.**
4.   Warum hast du diese Schuhe gekauft? Sie sind wirklich **furchtbar.**
5.   Was hältst du von diesen Kassetten? Sie sind **neu.**
6.   Wohin hängst du diese Poster? Sie sind **lustig.**
7.   Wer hat dir diese Bücher geliehen? Sie sind sehr **interessant.**

N So lebt man in Amerika. Restate some of Jutta Gruber's experiences in America by combining the sentences in each pair below. Use preceded adjectives in your sentences.

▶ Jutta studiert an der Universität.   *Jutta studiert an der großen*
Die Universität ist groß.   *Universität.*

1. Die Amerikaner gefallen ihr. Die Amerikaner sind freundlich.
2. Sie wohnt bei dieser Familie. Die Familie ist nett.
3. Das Zimmer gefällt ihr. Das Zimmer ist schön.
4. Jutta spricht mit der Tochter der Familie. Die Tochter ist klein.
5. Sie gehen auf die Terrasse. Die Terrasse ist klein.
6. Die Mutter möchte mit Jutta wegen der Tür sprechen. Die Tür ist geschlossen.
7. Die Türen in amerikanischen Häusern stören Jutta. Sie sind offen.
8. Auch stört sie das Bier. Das Bier ist immer so kalt.
9. Zu Weihnachten hört Jutta gern die deutschen Weihnachtslieder. Die Lieder sind schön.

• *Adjectives preceded by indefinite articles or **ein**-words*

	Masculine	Neuter	Feminine	Plural
Nom.	ein alt**er** Mann	ein klein**es** Kind	eine jung**e** Frau	meine gut**en** Freunde
Acc.	einen alt**en** Mann	ein klein**es** Kind	eine jung**e** Frau	meine gut**en** Freunde
Dat.	einem alt**en** Mann	einem klein**en** Kind	einer jung**en** Frau	meinen gut**en** Freunden
Gen.	eines alt**en** Mannes	eines klein**en** Kindes	einer jung**en** Frau	meiner gut**en** Freunde

Adjectives preceded by **ein**-words have the same endings as those preceded by **der**-words except when the **ein**-word itself has no ending (i.e., masculine and neuter nominative, and neuter accusative).

Nom.	ein alt**er** Mann	ein klein**es** Kind
Acc.	—	ein klein**es** Kind

When the **ein**-word has no ending, the adjective that follows has the ending of **dies*er*/dies*es***.

O   Du hast recht.   Regina comments on class work. Agree with her. Use adjectives in the nominative case.

▶   Professor Schmidts Musikvorle-   *Ja, das war wirklich eine trockene*
     sung war trocken, nicht?   *Vorlesung.*

1. Das Buch ist auch trocken, nicht?
2. Aber das Bier nachher war gut, nicht?
3. Die Klausur in Deutsch war lang und schwer, nicht?
4. Professor Langes Seminar ist interessant, nicht?
5. Eriks Referat war ziemlich kurz, nicht?
6. Das Referat war auch ziemlich schlecht, nicht?
7. Professor Memmels Kurs ist leicht, nicht?

P   Ein neues Zimmer   Your friend Robert, who is a student at a Swiss university, has moved to a new room. Describe his new surroundings. Use the cued adjectives in the accusative case.

▶   Robert hat ein Zimmer. (groß, hell)   *Robert hat ein großes helles Zimmer.*

1. Das Zimmer hat einen Balkon. (schön, privat)
2. Es hat eine Tür. (schwer)
3. Robert hat eine Lampe. (modern, lustig)
4. Er hat ein Bücherregal. (klein, praktisch)
5. Er hat einen Stuhl. (teuer, unpraktisch)
6. Er hat ein Bild. (groß, furchtbar)

Sie haben das Wort

Was ist los?   You have lost something again. Tell your friend what kind of item it was.

Describing objects

▶   Was ist denn los?   *Ich habe mein Heft verloren.*

Kugelschreiber	Jacke
Buch	Pulli
Radio	Fahrrad
Kassettenrecorder	Messer

▶   Was für ein Heft war das denn?   *Ein kleines, blaues.*

alt	neu	dunkel	hell
klein	groß	rot	gelb
modern	schön	schwarz	weiß
teuer	billig	warm	toll

Q   Erzähl mal!   Andrea tells you about her activities last week. Ask for more details. Use adjectives in the dative.

▶   Am Montag habe ich eine tolle   *Erzähl mal von deiner tollen*
    Vorlesung gehört.   *Vorlesung!*

1. Im Seminar habe ich ein ausgezeichnetes Referat gehört.
2. Am Dienstag habe ich eine sehr schwere Klausur geschrieben.
3. Am Mittwoch haben wir über eine neue Bürgerinitiative gesprochen.
4. Am Freitag habe ich ein schlechtes Buch gelesen.
5. Am Samstag habe ich im Ratskeller ein ausgezeichnetes Essen gegessen.
6. Am Sonntag bin ich zu einer lustigen Geburtstagsfete gegangen.

R   Moderne Bilder   You and Martina are in an art gallery looking at some modern paintings. Martina seems to see things you don't. Express doubt about what she sees. Use adjectives in the genitive.

▶   Das ist ein Bild eines Mannes. Er   *Das ist ein Bild eines alten Man-*
    ist alt.   *nes? Ich bitte dich!*

1. Das ist ein Bild einer Frau. Sie ist schön.
2. Das ist ein Bild eines Mädchens. Sie ist jung.
3. Das ist ein Bild eines Gartens. Er ist klein.
4. Das ist ein Bild eines Autos. Es ist kaputt.
5. Das ist ein Bild eines Hauses. Es ist modern.
6. Das ist ein Bild eines Berges. Er ist klein.
7. Das ist ein Bild einer Marktfrau. Sie ist lustig.

. . .Ausklang eines
schönen Tages.

6   Unpreceded adjectives

	Masculine	Neuter	Feminine	Plural
Nom.	guter Wein	gutes Brot	gute Wurst	gute Brötchen
Acc.	guten Wein	gutes Brot	gute Wurst	gute Brötchen
Dat.	gutem Wein	gutem Brot	guter Wurst	guten Brötchen
Gen.	guten Weines	guten Brotes	guter Wurst	guter Brötchen

Adjectives not preceded by a definite article, a **der**-word, an indefinite article, or an **ein**-word have the same endings as **der**-words, except the masculine and neuter genitive, which have the ending **-en**.

S Peter ißt gern.   Make each of Peter's comments more descriptive by using the appropriate unpreceded form of the cued adjective.

▶   Brötchen schmecken gut. (frisch)   *Frische Brötchen schmecken gut.*

1.   Bier schmeckt auch gut. (deutsch)
2.   Ich trinke gern Wein. (trocken)
3.   Blumen auf dem Tisch gefallen mir. (frisch)
4.   In vielen Städten kann man Fisch kaufen. (frisch)
5.   Ich koche gern mit Wein. (deutsch)
6.   Ich habe Hunger. (groß)
7.   Zum Mittagessen esse ich gern Steak. (amerikanisch)
8.   Zum Abendessen esse ich gern Wurst. (deutsch)

7   Ordinal numbers

1.	erst-	**6.**	sechst-	**21.**	einundzwanzigst-
2.	zweit-	**7.**	siebt-	**32.**	zweiunddreißigst-
3.	dritt-	**8.**	acht-	**100.**	hundertst-
				1000.	tausendst-

An ordinal number is a number indicating the position of something in a sequence (e.g., the first, the second). In German the ordinal numbers are formed by adding **-t** to numbers 1–19 and **-st** to numbers beyond 19. Exceptions are **erst-, dritt-, siebt-,** and **acht-.**

Die neue Wohnung ist im **dritten** Stock.
Am **siebten** Mai habe ich Geburtstag.

The ordinals take adjective endings.

8   Dates

Den wievielten haben wir heute?   What is the date today?
Heute haben wir **den 1.** März.   ⎫
Heute haben wir **den ersten** März.   ⎬   Today is March first.

In German, dates are expressed with ordinal numbers preceded by the masculine form of the definite article referring to the noun **Tag.** A period after a number indicates that it is an ordinal. The day always precedes the month: **5. 2. 88. = den fünften Februar 1988.**

Hamburg, **den 2. März 1990.**

Dates in letter headings or news releases are in the accusative.

T   Zwei Tage später   Frank has forgotten the exact date of his friends' birthdays. The birthdays are two days later than he thinks. Correct him.

▶   Hat Inge am neunten Mai Geburtstag?   *Nein, am elften.*

1.   Hat Gisela am dreizehnten Juli Geburtstag?
2.   Hat Willi am ersten Januar Geburtstag?
3.   Hat Uwe am zweiten März Geburtstag?
4.   Hat Elke am sechsten November Geburtstag?
5.   Hat Claudia am achtundzwanzigsten April Geburtstag?
6.   Hat Gerd am fünfundzwanzigsten Dezember Geburtstag?

Sie haben das Wort

Zwei Fragen   Find out from four fellow students when their birthdays are and in what year or semester they are.

Asking for personal information

Sie	*Gesprächspartner/in*
Wann hast du Geburtstag?	Am [siebten Juni].
In welchem Semester/Jahr bist du?	[Im zweiten.]

| Wiederholung ———————————

A   Ein Amerikaner in Deutschland   Complete the paragraph by supplying the correct adjective ending where necessary.

Ein amerikanisch _____ Student studiert an einer deutsch _____ Universität. Er wohnt in einem klein _____ , modern _____ Zimmer bei einer nett _____ Familie. In der erst _____ Woche ist er sehr erstaunt. Etwas versteht er nicht. Wenn er von seinen Vorlesungen nach Hause kommt, sieht er immer eine geschlossen _____ Zimmertür, aber ein offen _____ Fenster. Endlich erklärt ihm die Mutter der Familie, wie das ist. „Das Fenster ist wegen der frisch _____ Luft offen. Die geschlossen _____ Tür bedeutet, daß es Ihr privat _____ Zimmer ist."

B Eine Schweizerin in Deutschland Tell where Susanne studies and what she does during the summer vacation by completing the sentences. Use the cued words.

1. Susanne studiert an _____ . (die Universität Göttingen)
2. Sie wohnt in _____ . (ein großes Studentenheim)
3. Sie denkt oft an _____ . (ihre Freunde zu Hause)
4. Sie kommt aus _____ . (die Schweiz)
5. In _____ fährt sie nach Hause. (die Sommerferien)
6. Sie arbeitet bei _____ . (ihre Tante)
7. Sie fährt mit _____ zur Arbeit. (der Bus)
8. Am Sonntag macht sie mit _____ eine kleine Wanderung. (ihr Freund)
9. Nach _____ gehen sie in ein Café. (die Wanderung)
10. Leider vergißt sie oft zu Hause _____ . (ihr Geld)
11. Ihr Freund muß _____ etwas Geld leihen. (sie)
12. Nachher gehen sie zu _____ . (eine Fete)

Sie haben das Wort

Was sagen Sie?

Discussing personal issues

1. Den wievielten haben wir heute?
2. Wann haben Sie Geburtstag?
3. Wann hat Ihr Vater Geburtstag? Ihre Mutter?
4. Was für eine Familie haben Sie? Eine große oder eine kleine?
5. Wo wohnen Sie? Bei einer Familie? Oder wo?
6. In was für einem Haus (oder einer Wohnung) wohnen Sie?
7. In welchem Stock ist Ihr Schlafzimmer?
8. In welchen Fächern haben Sie dieses Semester Kurse?
9. Haben Sie dieses Semester eine Seminararbeit geschrieben?
10. Was machen Sie während der Sommerferien?
11. Möchten Sie eines Tages bei einer amerikanischen Firma in Deutschland, Österreich oder in der Schweiz arbeiten? Warum (nicht)?

C Vorbereitungen Form sentences to tell about the arrangements for getting the house in shape before guests arrive, using the cues below.

1. du / wollen / abwaschen / jetzt / ?
2. ich / können / abtrocknen / dann
3. ich / müssen / saubermachen / Küche / nachher
4. du / möchten / aufräumen / Wohnzimmer / ?
5. wer / sollen / saubermachen / Badezimmer / ?

D   Wie sagt man das?

1. —My friend Karin is studying at the University of Göttingen.
    —Does she live with a family?
    —Yes. The family is nice, and she likes her large room.
2. —What's the date today?
    —It's February 28.
    —Oh oh. Karin's birthday was yesterday.
3. —Are you going swimming in spite of the cold weather?
    —Yes, the cold weather doesn't bother me.
4. —What time is it?
    —It's 11:30.
    —Then I'll have to go.
    —OK. So long.

E   Letzte Woche   Tell what various people did last week.

▶   Ute macht Hausarbeit.   *Ute hat Hausarbeit gemacht.*

1. Sie räumt ihr Schlafzimmer auf.
2. Gerd wäscht jeden Tag ab.
3. Ute trocknet manchmal ab.
4. Ich kaufe immer ein.
5. Ich fahre mit dem Fahrrad auf den Markt.
6. Gerd kocht am Wochenende.
7. Ute bäckt für das Wochenende zwei Kuchen.

F   Was bedeutet das?   Context alone will often tell you the meaning of a new word. Try to guess the meanings of the boldfaced words in the sentences below.

1. Wieviel Familien wohnen in einem **Zweifamilienhaus?**
2. Zehn Wohnungen sind in diesem **Wohnhaus** frei.
3. Jede Uhr hat einen **Stundenzeiger** und einen **Minutenzeiger.** Der Stundenzeiger zeigt die Stunden an; der Minutenzeiger zeigt die Minuten an.
4. Ich komme immer zu spät. Meine Uhr **geht nach.** Gerd kommt immer zu früh. Seine Uhr **geht vor.**
5. War deine **Geburtstagsfeier** schön? Ja, wir haben auch den Geburtstag meiner Freunde gefeiert.
6. Die **Reparatur** meines Plattenspielers war letztes Mal zu teuer. Hoffentlich kannst du ihn diesmal reparieren.
7. Ich muß zum Arzt. Weißt du, wann Dr. Ortner **Sprechstunde** hat?

G   Anregung

1. Hans-Jürgen, a student in Munich, plans to study for a year at an American university. Write him a letter in German telling him what to expect in the way of housing and courses at the university as well as American customs that differ from German customs. Draw on your knowledge about the sense of privacy, eating habits, cars and public transportation, natural foods, or the lack of a requirement for an *Aufenthaltserlaubnis*.

2. Rewrite the episode in lines 1-17 of the reading selection on page 274 from the point of view of an American visiting her/his relatives in a German-speaking country. She/he always leaves the door to her/his bedroom open.

| Grammatik zum Nachschlagen _____

Forms of the genitive

● *Forms of nouns*

Masculine		Neuter		Feminine		Plural	
des		des		der		der	
eines	Mannes	eines	Mädchens	einer	Frau	meiner	Eltern
dieses		dieses		dieser		dieser	

In the genitive case, masculine and neuter nouns of one syllable generally add **-es**; masculine and neuter nouns of two or more syllables add **-s**; the corresponding articles, **der**-words, and **ein**-words end in **-es**.

   Feminine and plural nouns do not add a genitive ending. The corresponding articles, **der**-words, and **ein**-words end in **-er**.

● *Forms of masculine N-nouns*

Nom.	der Herr	der Student
Acc.	den Herrn	den Studenten
Dat.	dem Herrn	dem Studenten
Gen.	des Herrn	des Studenten

Masculine nouns that add **-n** or **-en** in the accusative and dative singular also add **-n** or **-en** in the genitive. A few masculine nouns add **-ns: des Namens**.

- *The interrogative pronoun **wessen**?*

Nom.	wer?
Acc.	wen?
Dat.	wem?
Gen.	**wessen?**

Wessen? is the genitive form of the interrogative **wer?**; it is equivalent to *whose*.

Uses of the genitive

- *Possession and other relationships*

das Buch **meines Freundes**	my friend's book
die Mutter **meines Freundes**	my friend's mother
die Farbe **der Blumen**	the color of the flowers

The genitive case is used to show possession and other close relationships.

der Name **der Frau**	the woman's name
der Name **der Stadt**	the name of the city

In English, a possessive structure with *'s* is used mainly for persons. A phrase with *of* is often used to refer to things and ideas. In German, the genitive is used regularly with things and ideas as well as with persons. The genitive noun-phrase generally follows the noun it modifies.

- *Prepositions*

(an)statt	instead of	Kommt Erika **(an)statt** ihrer Freundin?
trotz	in spite of	**Trotz** des Wetters wandern wir.
während	during	**Während** der Ferien wandern wir.
wegen	on account of	**Wegen** des Wetters bleiben sie zu Hause.

A number of prepositions take the genitive. Four of the most common ones are **anstatt** or **statt, trotz, während**, and **wegen.**

trotz **dem Regen**	
wegen **dem Wetter**	

In colloquial usage many people use the dative instead of the genitive with the prepositions **statt, trotz**, and **wegen** and sometimes **während.**

- *Genitive of time*

Indefinite past	**Eines Tages** hat mir Jutta alles erklärt.	*One day* Jutta explained everything to me.
Indefinite future	**Eines Tages** mache ich das vielleicht.	*Someday* maybe I'll do that.

Nouns expressing an indefinite point in time are in the genitive.

Adjectives

- *Adjectives preceded by a definite article or* **der**-*word*

	Masculine	Neuter	Feminine	Plural
Nom.	der alt**e** Mann	das klein**e** Kind	die jung**e** Frau	die gut**en** Freunde
Acc.	den alt**en** Mann	das klein**e** Kind	die jung**e** Frau	die gut**en** Freunde
Dat.	dem alt**en** Mann	dem klein**en** Kind	der jung**en** Frau	den gut**en** Freunden
Gen.	des alt**en** Mannes	des klein**en** Kindes	der jung**en** Frau	der gut**en** Freunde

	M.	N.	F.	Pl.
Nom.	e	e	e	en
Acc.	en	e	e	en
Dat.	en	en	en	en
Gen.	en	en	en	en

- *Adjectives preceded by an indefinite article or* **ein**-*word*

	Masculine	Neuter	Feminine	Plural
Nom.	ein alt**er** Mann	ein klein**es** Kind	eine jung**e** Frau	meine gut**en** Freunde
Acc.	einen alt**en** Mann	ein klein**es** Kind	eine jung**e** Frau	meine gut**en** Freunde
Dat.	einem alt**en** Mann	einem klein**en** Kind	einer jung**en** Frau	meinen gut**en** Freunden
Gen.	eines alt**en** Mannes	eines klein**en** Kindes	einer jung**en** Frau	meiner gut**en** Freunde

	M.	N.	F.	Pl.
Nom.	er	es	e	en
Acc.	en	es	e	en
Dat.	en	en	en	en
Gen.	en	en	en	en

• *Unpreceded adjectives*

	Masculine	Neuter	Feminine	Plural
Nom.	gut**er** Wein	gut**es** Brot	gut**e** Wurst	gut**e** Brötchen
Acc.	gut**en** Wein	gut**es** Brot	gut**e** Wurst	gut**e** Brötchen
Dat.	gut**em** Wein	gut**em** Brot	gut**er** Wurst	gut**en** Brötchen
Gen.	gut**en** Weines	gut**en** Brotes	gut**er** Wurst	gut**er** Brötchen

	M.	N.	F.	Pl.
Nom.	er	es	e	e
Acc.	en	es	e	e
Dat.	em	em	er	en
Gen.	en	en	er	er

Ordinal numbers

1.	erst-
2.	zweit-
3.	dritt-
6.	sechst-
7.	siebt-
8.	acht-

21.	einundzwanzigst-
32.	zweiunddreißigst-
100.	hundertst-
1000.	tausendst-

Dies ist die 367. von 6000 Fragen aus dem neuen Spiel

Trivial Pursuit

WER WEISS – GEWINNT

"Was fährt im Jahr mehr als 50mal
in das Empire State Building?"

PARKER

The ordinals (numbers indicating position in
a sequence) are formed by adding -**t** to the
numbers 1–19 and -**st** to numbers beyond 19.
Exceptions are **erst-, dritt-, siebt-,** and **acht-.**

Dies ist mein **drittes** Semester.   This is my third semester.

The ordinals take adjective endings.

Dates

Den wievielten haben wir heute?   What is the date today?
Heute haben wir **den ersten** März.   Today is March first.
Am siebten Mai habe ich Ge-   My birthday is on the seventh of
burtstag.   May.

In German, dates are expressed with ordinal numbers preceded by the masculine form of the definite article. The day precedes the month. Dates in
letter headings or news releases are in the accusative.

Kapitel 9

Lernziele

Sprechakte

Discussing someone's health
Describing morning rituals
Making comparisons and contrasts
Stating preferences
Talking about household chores

Grammatik

Comparison of adjectives and adverbs
Reflexive constructions
Reflexive verbs
Definite article with parts of the body
Infinitives with **zu**
The construction **um ... zu** + infinitive

Vokabeln

Parts of the body
Hygiene
Adjectives used as nouns
Viel and **wenig**

Landeskunde

Switzerland
Standard of living

*Die Straßenbahnen sind pünktlich
(Bahnhofstraße in Zürich).*

Bausteine für Gespräche

Hast du dich erkältet?

Elisabeth: Du hustest ja fürchterlich.
Rainer: Ja, ich habe mich erkältet. Der Hals tut mir furchtbar weh.
Elisabeth: Hast du Fieber?
Rainer: Ein bißchen — 38.
Elisabeth: Du siehst ganz schön blaß aus.
Rainer: Ich fühle mich auch krank. Vielleicht ist es besser, wenn ich zum Arzt gehe.
Elisabeth: Ja, wir wollen doch am Sonntag zusammen Ski laufen.

Have you caught a cold?

You're coughing terribly.

Yes, I've caught a cold. My throat's hurting me a lot.
Do you have a fever?
A little — 38 [= 100.4°F].
You look pretty pale.

I do feel pretty sick. Maybe I'd better go to the doctor.

Yes, after all we do want to go skiing together on Sunday.

Fragen

1. Beschreiben° Sie Rainers Krankheit°!
2. Warum ist es besser, daß er zum Arzt geht?

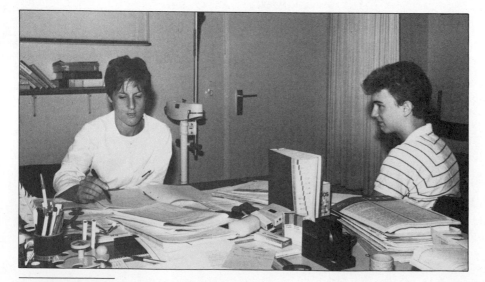

Bei einer Ärztin in der Sprechstunde

Sie haben das Wort

A   Was hast du?   A fellow student looks pale. Ask what the matter is.

Sie	*Gesprächspartner/in*
Du siehst blaß aus. Was hast du°?	Mir geht es nicht gut.
	Ich fühle mich nicht wohl°.
	Mir ist schlecht°.
	Ich habe | **Kopfschmerzen**°.
	Zahnschmerzen°
	Magenschmerzen°
	Ich bin erkältet.
	Ich habe etwas Fieber.
	Mir tut der Hals° weh.

B   Geht es dir besser?   Ask a friend about her/his cold.

Sie	*Gesprächspartner/in*
Was macht deine Erkältung?	Es geht mir | **besser.**
	schon besser
	schlechter
	Ich fühle mich | **krank.**
	schwach°
	schwächer als gestern
	elend°

C   Das tut mir leid.   You can't join in various plans because of a cold. Your friend expresses regret.

Sie	*Gesprächspartner/in*
Ich bin furchtbar erkältet.	Ach, wie dumm!
Ich kann heute nicht | **Ski laufen.**	Schade°.
zur Fete kommen	Das tut mir leid.
ins Kino gehen	Hoffentlich fühlst du dich morgen besser.

D   Wie fühlst du dich?   Ask a fellow student about health matters.

Fragen Sie eine(n) Bekannte(n),

1. ob sie/er sich wohl fühlt.
2. ob sie/er sich erkältet hat.
3. ob sie/er Fieber hat.
4. was sie/er macht, wenn sie/er Fieber hat.
5. ob sie/er zum Arzt geht, wenn sie/er sich erkältet hat.
6. wie oft sie/er zum Zahnarzt geht.

Vokabeln

— Substantive

die **Erkältung, -en**   cold (*illness*)
das **Fieber**   fever
der **Hals, ⸚e**   throat, neck
der **Kopf, ⸚e**   head
die **Krankheit, -en**   illness

der **Magen**   stomach
der **Schmerz, -en**   pain
der **Ski, -er (Ski** *is pronounced and
sometimes spelled* **Schi)**   ski
der **Zahn, ⸚e**   tooth

— Verben

beschreiben, beschrieben   to describe
sich erkälten   to catch a cold
sich fühlen   to feel [ill; well]

husten   to cough
Ski laufen (läuft Ski), ist Ski gelaufen   to ski

Wer in diesen Wochen in deutschen Landen unterwegs ist, sollte sich vorsehen: Erkältungskrankheiten drohen an verschiedenen Plätzen.

— Andere Wörter

bißchen: ein bißchen   a little bit
blaß   pale
elend   miserable
fürchterlich   horrible, horribly

schade   that's too bad, a pity
schwach   weak; **schwächer**   weaker
wohl   well

— Besondere Ausdrücke

ganz schön   really quite . . . , pretty
. . . ; **ganz schön blaß**   pretty pale
Mir ist schlecht.   I feel nauseated.

Was hast du?   What is wrong with
you?
weh tun (+ *dat.*)   to hurt

Erweiterung des Wortschatzes

1   Körperteile

1. der Arm, -e
2. der Finger, -
3. der Fuß, ⸚e
4. der Kopf, ⸚e
5. der Mund, ⸚er
6. der Hals, ⸚e
7. der Magen
8. das Auge, -n
9. das Bein, -e
10. das Gesicht, -er
11. das Haar, -e
12. das Ohr, -en
13. die Nase, -n
14. die Hand, ⸚e

A   Was tut dir weh?   Your hypochondriac friend asks whether something hurts. Respond.

Gesprächspartner/in	*Sie*
Tut dir | **der Kopf** weh? ⎮ der Hals Tun dir die | **Füße** weh? ⎮ Augen ⎮ Ohren	Ja, mir tut [der Kopf] furchtbar weh. Nein, [der Kopf] tut mir (gar) nicht weh.

B   Warum fragst du?   This time respond to your friend's questions with a puzzled response.

Gesprächspartner/in	*Sie*
Hast du **Magenschmerzen?** Zahnschmerzen Kopfschmerzen	Warum fragst du? Sehe ich denn schlecht aus?

C   Beschreiben Sie!   Describe a friend. Include answers to the questions below.

1.   Ist Ihr Freund/Ihre Freundin groß oder klein?
2.   Hat sie/er blonde/schwarze/braune/rote Haare?
3.   Was hat sie/er für Augen? Blaue, grüne oder braune?
4.   Und die Nase? Ist sie klein oder groß?
5.   Und die Beine? Sind sie lang oder kurz?

| Die Schweiz

Vorbereitung auf das Lesen

● *Zum Thema*

Was wissen Sie über die Schweiz? Was meinen Sie?

1.   Wie groß ist die Schweiz? Größer als Österreich oder nur halb so groß?
2.   Wieviel Einwohner hat die Schweiz? 6,5 Millionen oder 12 Millionen?
3.   Was ist die Hauptstadt der Schweiz?
4.   Wieviel Nachbarländer hat die Schweiz? Acht oder fünf?
5.   Wie heißen die Nachbarländer?

Suchen Sie die folgenden Städte auf der Landkarte!

Basel □ Bern □ Chur □ Genf □ Lugano □ Luzern □ St. Moritz □ Zermatt □ Zürich

● *Leitfragen*

1.   CH bedeutet „Confoederatio Helvetica". Was hat das mit der Autonomie der Kantone zu tun?
2.   Wie wird man Schweizer Bürger(in)?

Stichworte: Gemeinde □ **ein** Ort □ kosten □ Bern □ politische Einstellung

3. Warum ist die Qualität der Produkte aus der Schweiz so wichtig?

    Stichworte: Rohstoffe ☐ bezahlen ☐ Lebensstandard ☐ Neutralität

4. Wie kann es in einem so kleinen Land 26 verschiedene Kantone geben?

    Stichworte: Geschichte ☐ 13. bis 19. Jahrhundert ☐ besondere Mischung ☐ Schweizerdeutsch

5. Was sind die Unterschiede zwischen der Schweiz und den anderen deutschsprachigen Ländern?

    Stichworte: Mentalität ☐ Geschichte ☐ Sprache

Eine Schlittenbahn für die Skiläufer bei Grindelwald im Berner Oberland

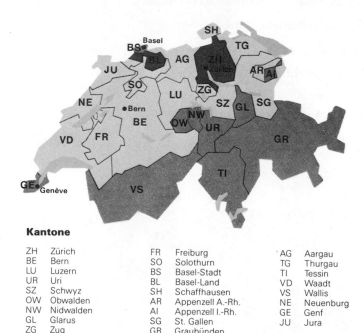

Kantone

ZH	Zürich	FR	Freiburg	AG	Aargau
BE	Bern	SO	Solothurn	TG	Thurgau
LU	Luzern	BS	Basel-Stadt	TI	Tessin
UR	Uri	BL	Basel-Land	VD	Waadt
SZ	Schwyz	SH	Schaffhausen	VS	Wallis
OW	Obwalden	AR	Appenzell A.-Rh.	NE	Neuenburg
NW	Nidwalden	AI	Appenzell I.-Rh.	GE	Genf
GL	Glarus	SG	St. Gallen	JU	Jura
ZG	Zug	GR	Graubünden		

41.228 qkm
6,4 Millionen Einwohner
etwa halb so groß wie Österreich oder Maine
etwas kleiner als Neuschottland° (52.841 qkm)   *Nova Scotia*
5 Bundesstaat° mit 26 Kantonen°   *Federal State / cantons*
parlamentarische Demokratie
Hauptstadt: Bern
5 Nachbarn: F, D, A, FL, I*

Der offizielle Name für die Schweiz ist „Schweizerische Eidgenossen-
10 schaft°", auf lateinisch „Confoederatio Helvetica". Daher das internatio-   *confederation*
nale Autokennzeichen° CH. Dieser Name deutet an°, daß die Schweiz   *abbr. for country of registry /*
weniger *ein* Land ist als eine Sammlung° von autonomen Kantonen.   *deutet an: indicates*
                                                                             collection
Die 26 Kantone nehmen ihre Autonomie sehr ernst. Zum Beispiel wird
ein Ausländer nicht in der Hauptstadt Schweizer Bürger, sondern der
15 Prozeß beginnt in der Gemeinde°. Eine junge Schweizerin — sie ist ge-   *community*
rade Bürgerin geworden — erzählt: „Um Bürger zu werden, muß man erst
einmal lange, 12 Jahre, an *einem* Ort wohnen. Diese Gemeinde muß

---

*Autokennzeichen: F = Frankreich, D = Bundesrepublik Deutschland, A =
Österreich, FL = Fürstentum Liechtenstein, I = Italien

mich also als Bürgerin akzeptieren. Das Ganze hat zweitausend Franken
gekostet. Das kann auch viel mehr sein. Wenn eine Gemeinde Leute und
20 Steuerzahler° braucht, ist es billiger. Wenn nicht, ist es teurer. Nach *taxpayers*
diesem ersten Schritt gehen die Papiere zum Bund°, also nach Bern. *Federal Government*
Danach geht's weiter an den Kanton. Irgendwann° überprüft° man auch *at some point / test*
die politische Einstellung°. Da gibt's Fragen wie: ‚Welche Zeitungen *orientation*
lesen Sie? Welche Fernsehsendungen sehen Sie?' So kompliziert ist der
25 ganze Prozeß.''

Bei einem Gespräch in einer amerikanischen Deutschklasse fragten die
Studenten zwei Besucherinnen, Helena aus Chur und Marta aus Luzern:
„Wenn ihr an die Schweiz denkt, welche Stichwörter fallen euch ein?''

Marta: Also zuerst einmal Qualität, Präzision, Zuverlässigkeit° und *dependability*
30   Pünktlichkeit. Dann eine starke Wirtschaft.

Helena: Und ganz bestimmt Neutralität. Vielleicht dann noch
    Fremdenverkehr°, also Tourismus. *tourism*

Marta: Mir fallen auch noch die Unterschiede zwischen den Kantonen
    ein.

35 *Studentin:* Könnt ihr mal erklären, was ihr mit Qualität meint?

Helena: Wir sind ein kleines Land, fast ohne Rohstoffe. Wir müssen Roh-
    stoffe und Lebensmittel importieren. Um die bezahlen zu können,
    müssen wir auf den Weltmärkten° konkurrieren können. Das können *world markets*

*Die Schweizer machen Qualitätsprodukte – z.B.
Uhren, Instrumente und Apparate.*

wir nur mit Qualität. Wir machen also Qualitätsprodukte, Maschinen
40 z.B., chemische Produkte, Instrumente und Apparate. Die sind die Basis für unseren hohen Lebensstandard.

Student: Was meinst du damit genau?

Helena: Na ja, z.B. steht bei den meisten Leuten heute ein Auto vor der Tür. Auch eine Waschmaschine, ein Kühlschrank und ein Farbfern-
45 seher gehören heute zum ‚normalen' Haushalt°. Und ein Telefon. **household**
Stereoanlage und Geschirrspüler sind keine Luxusgegenstände° mehr. *luxury items*
Über die Hälfte der Haushalte hat einen Gefrierschrank. Die
Wohnungen sind besser eingerichtet°, d.h. die Leute haben sich *furnished*
moderne Möbel gekauft. Und die alten haben sie weggeworfen, auch
50 wenn sie noch gut waren.

Marta: Die starke Wirtschaft ist auch die Basis für unsere Neutralität. Nur
wenn wir wirtschaftlich stark sind, können wir unabhängig° sein. Und *independent*
nur wenn man unabhängig ist, kann man neutral sein. Neutralität ist für
die Schweiz ein zentraler Wert°. *value*

55 *Student:* Warum eigentlich?

Marta: Wir haben in zwei Weltkriegen die Erfahrung gemacht°, daß **Erfahrung gemacht:** *learned*
Neutralität gute Politik ist.

Student: Ich möchte noch wissen, warum ihr die Unterschiede zwischen
den Kantonen erwähnt habt. Schließlich ist die Schweiz doch nur ein
60 sehr kleines Land. Und in diesem Land soll es 26 verschiedene Kantone
geben?

Helena: Ja, das hängt wieder mit der Geschichte zusammen. Das Land
hat sich eben langsam entwickelt. Mit drei Kantonen hat es im dreizehnten Jahrhundert angefangen. Erst im neunzehnten Jahrhundert
65 war die Schweiz komplett, sozusagen°. Man muß sich klar machen, *so to speak*
daß jeder Kanton zu° einer bestimmten Zeit, unter bestimmten Um- *at*
ständen° und mit ganz bestimmten Menschen Teil der Schweiz *circumstances*
geworden ist. So hat jeder Kanton seine besondere Mischung aus Menschenart, Religion, Geschichte und Sprache. Zum Beispiel gibt es im
70 Schweizerdeutsch noch Unterschiede. Die sind zum Teil so stark, daß
die Leute manchmal Schwierigkeiten haben, einander zu verstehen.

Studentin: Nun noch einmal eine ganz andere Frage: Wo oder wie seht
ihr eigentlich die Unterschiede zu den anderen deutschsprachigen
Ländern?

75 *Marta:* Gegenüber Deutschland sehe ich eigentlich nicht so große Unterschiede. In beiden Ländern ist die Wirtschaft gleich stark. Und ich
sehe oft eine ähnliche Mentalität°. Dagegen° scheint mir die Menta- *mentality / in contrast*
lität in Österreich anders zu sein. Da sehe ich mehr Nonchalance.

Helena: Zu der Frage muß man vielleicht auch noch sagen, daß die
80 Schweizer sich durch ihre Geschichte von den Deutschen unterscheiden und vor allem durch ihre Sprache. Die Umgangssprache°, die *colloquial language*
Alltagssprache° ist eben Schweizerdeutsch. Und das unterscheidet *everyday language*
sich doch ganz enorm vom Hochdeutschen. Mir fällt da gerade ein

berndeutsches Chanson° von Mani Matter ein. Es heißt „Heidi" und   *song*
85   beginnt so:

        Är wont a dr glyche gass
        und i bin mit dir i d'klass
        so ischs cho, das mir grad beidi
        ds härz a di verlore hei.
90   Heidi, mir wei di beidi,
          beidi, Heidi, hei di gärn.

Die hochdeutsche Übersetzung ist:
        Er wohnt in der gleichen Gasse°,   *street*
        und ich bin mit dir in der Klasse.
95   So ist es, daß wir gerade beide
        das Herz an dich verloren haben.
          Heidi, wir wollen dich beide,
          beide, Heidi, haben dich gern.

Switzerland's roots reach back more than 2,000 years, when a Celtic people called the Helvetians lived in the area that is now Switzerland. Over the course of several hundred years, the Alemanni, the Burgundians, and the Franks settled there as well. When the Holy Roman Empire came into existence in A.D. 962, most of this area became part of it. Soon after the Habsburg family, as the rulers of the Empire, had gained control over these regions, the cantons (*Kantone*) Schwyz, Uri, and Unterwalden started the Swiss Confederation (1291) and fought together for their independence. Between 1315 and 1388 Switzerland defeated Austria in three different wars and finally gained independence from the Holy Roman Empire in 1499. A period of expansion and integration of more cantons followed.

Today Switzerland is composed of 23 cantons, three of which are divided into half-cantons. It does not have a strong central government. The cantons function with a large degree of political autonomy.

Auf dieser Wiese, dem Rütli im Kanton Uri, begann die Schweizer Eidgenossenschaft 1291.

Fragen zum Lesestück

1. Was deutet der Name „Confoederatio Helvetica" an?
2. Wie lange muß man an *einem* Ort wohnen, wenn man Bürger werden will?
3. Was hat es für die junge Schweizerin gekostet, Bürgerin zu werden?
4. Was will man wissen, wenn man die politische Einstellung überprüft?
5. Nennen Sie fünf Stichwörter zum Thema Schweiz!
6. Warum müssen die Schweizer Qualitätsprodukte exportieren?
7. Was gehört heute zu einem „normalen" Haushalt? Nennen Sie fünf Sachen!
8. Warum ist die starke Wirtschaft für die Neutralität wichtig?
9. Warum ist Neutralität für die Schweiz so zentral?
10. Wieviel Kantone gibt es in der Schweiz?
11. Wieviel Kantone hat es im 13. Jahrhundert gegeben?
12. Warum ist jeder Kanton anders?
13. Warum haben Schweizer manchmal Schwierigkeiten, einander zu verstehen?
14. Warum sieht Marta keine großen Unterschiede zwischen der Schweiz und Deutschland?
15. Was sieht sie in der österreichischen Mentalität?
16. Was unterscheidet die Deutschen von den Schweizern?
17. In welchem Dialekt ist Matters Chanson?

Vokabeln

— Substantive

der **Apparat, -e** apparatus, appliance
der **Fernseher, -** television set; der **Farbfernseher, -** color television set
die **Fernsehsendung, -en** TV program
der **Gefrierschrank, ⁻e** freezer
das **Geschirr** dishes; der **Geschirrspüler, -** dish washer
die **Gruppe, -n** group
die **Hälfte, -n** half
das **Herz, -ens, -en** heart
das **Hochdeutsch** High German
das **Jahrhundert, -e** century
die **Klasse, -n** class; die **Deutschklasse** German class

der **Kühlschrank, ⁻e** refrigerator
die **Möbel** (*pl.*) furniture; das **Möbelstück, -e** piece of furniture
der **Ort, -e** place
das **Produkt, -e** product
die **Regierung, -en** government
der **Rohstoff, -e** raw material
der **Schritt, -e** step
die **Steuer, -n** tax
die **Übersetzung, -en** translation
die **Waschmaschine, -n** washing machine
die **Wirtschaft** economy

__ Verben __

akzeptieren to accept
(sich) an·ziehen (+ *acc.*), **angezogen**
  to get dressed; **ich ziehe mich an**
  I get dressed
(sich) an·ziehen (+ *dat.*), **angezogen**
  to put on; **ich ziehe mir die
  Schuhe an** I put on my shoes
(sich) aus·ziehen (+ *acc.*), **ausgezogen** to get undressed; **ich
  ziehe mich aus** I get undressed
(sich) aus·ziehen (+ *dat.*), **ausgezogen** to take off; **ich ziehe mir
  die Schuhe aus** I take off my
  shoes
beginnen, begonnen to begin

(sich) duschen to shower
ein·fallen (fällt ein), ist eingefallen
  to occur (to one's mind)
(sich) entwickeln to develop
(sich) kämmen to comb
putzen to clean
(sich) rasieren to shave
scheinen, geschienen to appear,
  seem
(sich) unterscheiden, unterschieden
  to distinguish
(sich) waschen (wäscht), gewaschen
  to wash
werfen (wirft), geworfen to throw

__ Andere Wörter __

auch wenn even if
gegenüber (+ *dat.*) opposed to; in
  relation to
hoch (höher, höchst) high; **(hoh-**
  before nouns, as in **ein hoher Preis**)

irgendwann at some time
stark (ä) strong
unabhängig independent

__ Besondere Ausdrücke __

erst einmal first of all
um ... zu (+ *infinitive*) (in order) to

zum Teil in part

Erweiterung des Wortschatzes

1   Wann macht man was?

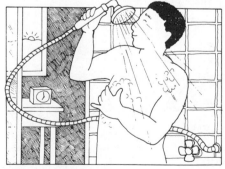

Wann duschst du dich?
Ich dusche mich morgens.

Wann putzt du dir die Zähne?
Ich putze mir morgens die Zähne.

Wann rasierst du dich?
Ich rasiere mich morgens.

Wann ziehst du dich an?
Ich ziehe mich morgens an.

Wann kämmst du dich?
Ich kämme mich morgens.

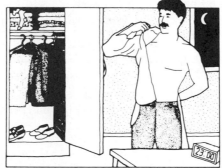

Wann ziehst du dich aus?
Ich ziehe mich abends aus.

Wann wäschst du dir Gesicht und
    Hände?
Ich wasche mir abends Gesicht und
    Hände.

Wann putzt du dir wieder die Zähne?

Ich putze mir abends wieder die
    Zähne.

Sie haben das Wort

A friend asks you when you shower, get dressed, and so on. Respond.

Describing morning rituals

Ziehst du dich vor dem Frühstück an?
Wie oft kämmst du dich?
Putzt du dir vor oder nach dem Frühstück die Zähne?
Duschst du dich morgens oder abends?

Jakob kann beim Zähneputzen
seine Paste nicht benutzen;

aus der Tube kommt nichts raus.
Doch dafür gibt's ja im Haus

einen Schraubstock – immerhin
zeigt der bald: noch ist was drin!

Aber löst man ein Problem,
ist das oft nicht angenehm.

2   Adjectives used as nouns

Herr Schmidt ist **ein Bekannter** von mir.

Mr. Schmidt is an acquaintance of mine.

Frau Schneider ist **eine Bekannte** von mir.

Ms. Schneider is an acquaintance of mine.

So ein Auto ist nur für **die Reichen**.

Such a car is only for the rich.

Many adjectives can be used as nouns. They retain the adjective endings as though a noun were still there: **ein Deutscher (Mann), eine Deutsche (Frau).** In writing, adjectives used as nouns are capitalized.

A   Was bedeutet das?

1. Kennen Sie den Alten da?
2. Das ist Herr Wolf, ein guter Bekannter von mir.
3. Meine Eltern haben gute Bekannte in der Schweiz.
4. Mein Vater erzählt oft von einem Bekannten in Luzern.
5. Meine Mutter erzählt von ihrer Bekannten in Bern.
6. Zwei Bekannte wohnen in Basel.
7. Die Deutschen arbeiten nicht gern bei offener Tür.
8. Ein freundlicher junger Deutscher hat mir das gesagt.
9. Einige Leute, vor allem Alte, haben es heute schwer, weil das Leben sehr teuer ist.

Das Gute daran ist, daß es billig ist.	The good thing about it is that it is cheap.
Hast du **etwas Neues** gehört?	Have you heard anything new?
Ja, aber **nichts Gutes.**	Yes, but nothing good.

Adjectives expressing abstractions (**das Gute,** the good; **das Schöne,** the beautiful) are considered neuter nouns. They frequently follow words such as **etwas, nichts, viel,** and **wenig,** and take the ending **-es (etwas Schönes).** Note **etwas anderes,** where **anderes** is not capitalized.

B   Was bedeutet das?

1. In den Ferien haben wir viel Schönes gesehen.
2. Christl hat etwas Tolles zu erzählen.
3. Gestern haben wir nichts Besonderes gemacht.
4. Jetzt verstehe ich dich. Das ist etwas anderes.
5. Oliver hat etwas Merkwürdiges gesagt.
6. Es gibt hier wenig Interessantes zu lesen.

3   The adjectives *viel* and *wenig*

Wir haben **wenig** Geld, aber **viel** Zeit.	We have little money but lots of time.

When used as adjectives, **viel** and **wenig** usually have no endings in the singular.

Dieter hat **viele** Freunde.	Dieter has lots of friends.
Das kann man von **vielen** Menschen sagen.	You can say that about many people.

In the plural, **viel** and **wenig** take regular adjective endings.

Sie haben das Wort

Say whether you have little (or few) or lots of the items listed below.

Geld □ Zeit □ Bücher □ Ideen □ Schuhe

Using viel and wenig

Bilder aus der Schweiz

Oben: **Die Fahne der Schweiz** Ein weißes Kreuz auf rotem Grund. *Unten:* **Bern, Hauptstadt der Schweiz** Blick auf die Altstadt.

Ganz links: **Thuner See**
Berge und Wasser, Wandern
und Segeln — hier macht Ur-
laub Spaß. *Diese Seite oben:*
Matterhorn bei Zermatt
Der Tourismus ist für die
Wirtschaft der Schweiz
wichtig. *Diese Seite unten:*
Montreux Das Jazz-Festival
ist in ganz Europa und
Nordamerika bekannt.

Oben links: **Käserei** Die Schweizer exportieren ihren Käse in viele Länder. *Oben rechts:* **Kanton Appenzell** Volkskunst an einem alten Gasthaus. *Unten:* **Schweizer Uhren** Nur mit Qualität kann die Schweiz auf dem Weltmarkt konkurrieren.

Übungen zur Aussprache

Review the pronunciation of final **-en, -e,** and **-er** in the Reference section at the end of the book. Read aloud the words in each column on this page first from top to bottom, then across. Check your pronunciation by listening to your instructor or the tape.

[ən]	[ə]	[ər]
bitten	bitte	bitter
fahren	fahre	Fahrer
denken	denke	Denker
fehlen	fehle	Fehler
besten	beste	bester

Read the sentences below aloud, paying special attention to your pronunciation of final **-en, -e,** or **-er** in the boldfaced words.

1. **Fahren** Sie **bitte** etwas **langsamer!**
2. **Viele Amerikaner fliegen** im **Sommer** nach Europa.
3. **Manche Länder brauchen** mehr **Schulen.**
4. Die **Tage werden kürzer** und **kälter.**
5. **Diese Männer arbeiten** wirklich schwer.
6. **Viele Wörter** sind relativ, zum Beispiel **länger, größer** oder **jünger.**

Morgen, morgen, nur nicht heute, sagen alle faulen Leute.

Grammatik und Übungen

1   Comparison of adjectives and adverbs

• *Comparison of equality*

Ute ist **so** groß **wie** Christel.
Erik schwimmt nicht **so** gut **wie** Klaus.
Diese Reise ist genau **so** schön **wie** die letzte.

Ute is as tall as Christel.
Erik doesn't swim as well as Klaus.
This trip is just as nice as the last one.

The construction **so ... wie** is used to express the equality of a person, thing, or activity to another. It is equivalent to English *as . . . as.*

A   Alle sind gleich.   Someone wants to know something about your friends. Say in each case that they are equal. Use the construction **so ... wie.**

▶   Beate ist intelligent. Ist Dieter auch intelligent?   *Ja, Dieter ist genauso intelligent wie Beate.*

1.   Barbara spricht gut Deutsch. Spricht Mark auch gut?
2.   Birgit ist freundlich. Ist Regina auch freundlich?
3.   Du, Frank fährt schnell. Fährt Franks Bruder auch so schnell?
4.   Rita ist nervös. Ist Ritas Schwester auch so nervös?
5.   Martina arbeitet schwer. Arbeitet Martinas Mutter auch so schwer?

• *Comparative forms*

Base form	**klein**	Österreich ist **klein.**	Austria is small.
Comparative	**kleiner**	Die Schweiz ist noch **kleiner.**	Switzerland is even smaller.

The comparative of an adjective or adverb is formed by adding **-er** to the base form.

Lore arbeitet **schwerer als** Kai.   Lore works harder than Kai.
Lore ist **fleißiger als** Kai.   Lore is more industrious than Kai.

The comparative form plus **als** is used to compare people, things, or activities. **Als** is equivalent to English *than.*

Base form	dunkel	teuer
Comparative	**dunkler**	**teurer (teuerer)**

Adjectives ending in **-el** drop the final **-e** of the base form before adding **-er.**
Adjectives ending in **-er** may follow the same pattern.

B   Meine neue Wohnung   Describe your new apartment to a friend by comparing it to the old one that she/he knew. Use the comparative form of the predicate adjective.

▶   Deine alte Wohnung war schön.   *Meine neue ist noch schöner.*

1.   Deine alte war schön hell.
2.   Die alte war sehr praktisch.
3.   Deine alte Wohnung war aber klein.
4.   Die war aber modern.
5.   Deine alte war wirklich toll.
6.   Die alte war auch teuer.

Base form	groß	Hamburg ist **groß**.
Comparative	größer	Hamburg ist **größer** als Bremen.

Many common one-syllable words with stem vowel **a, o,** or **u** add an umlaut in the comparative form, including **alt, dumm, jung, kalt, kurz, lang, oft, rot,** and **warm**. Adjectives and adverbs of this type are indicated in the vocabularies of this book as follows: **kalt (ä).**

C   Erik ist anders.   Your parents have met your new friend Andreas, but not your friend Erik. Tell them Erik is just the opposite of what they think.

▶   Ist Erik kleiner als Andreas?   *Nein, er ist größer.*

1.   Ist er älter?
2.   Sind seine Haare kürzer?
3.   Ist er nervöser?
4.   Ist er intelligenter?
5.   Ist er fleißiger?
6.   Ist er lustiger?
7.   Ist er konservativer?

Base form	gern	gut	hoch	viel
Comparative	lieber	besser	höher	mehr

A few adjectives and adverbs have irregular comparative forms.

Jörg sieht **gern** fern.	Jörg likes to watch TV.
Karin liest **lieber**.	Karin prefers [likes more] to read.

The English equivalent of **lieber** is *to prefer*, or *preferably* , or *rather* with a verb.

D   Die Bundesrepublik heute   In a **Studentenkneipe** you are discussing present-day aspects of the Federal Republic of Germany. Agree with the observations made below. Use the comparative of each adjective or adverb.

▶   Man baut gern große Häuser.   *Ja, man baut lieber größere Häuser.*

1.   Man fährt gern mit dem Auto.
2.   Man kauft gern im Supermarkt ein.
3.   Man kauft gern einen großen Kühlschrank.
4.   Man hört gern Stereo.
5.   Man hat viel Freizeit.
6.   Man hat viel Geld.
7.   Der Export läuft gut.
8.   Der Lebensstandard ist hoch.
9.   Die Preise sind jetzt hoch.

Man wird schneller älter als man denkt

Allgemeine Rentenanstalt
Lebens- und Rentenversicherungs-AG Stuttgart

| Das ist ein besser**er** Plan. | That's a better plan. |
| Hast du eine besser**e** Idee? | Do you have a better idea? |

Preceded comparative adjectives take the same adjective endings as those in the base form.

E   Es ist heute besser.   Agree with the statements made below about life in Switzerland. Restate each sentence, using a comparative form of the adjective with the proper ending.

▶   Die Schweizer führen ein gutes Leben.   *Ja, sie führen jetzt ein besseres Leben.*

1.   Sie tragen gute Kleidung.
2.   Sie wohnen in großen Wohnungen.
3.   Sie kaufen teure Autos.
4.   Sie haben lange Ferien.
5.   Sie fahren mit schnellen Wagen.
6.   Sie haben einen hohen Lebensstandard.

Sie haben das Wort

Was machen Sie lieber? Tell which chores and leisure activities you prefer.

> Stating preferences

Gesprächspartner/in   *Sie*

Was machen Sie lieber? | **Laufen oder radfahren?**   Ich [laufe] lieber.
                       | Zeitungen lesen oder
                       | Bücher?
                       | Klassische Musik hören
                       | oder Rock?
                       | Das Badezimmer sauber-
                       | machen oder das
                       | Wohnzimmer auf-
                       | räumen?
                       | Abwaschen oder ab-
                       | trocknen?
                       | Gartenarbeit oder
                       | Hausarbeit?
                       | Ins Kino gehen oder zu
                       | einer Party gehen?

- *Superlative forms*

| **Base form** | **alt** | Trier ist sehr **alt.** |
| **Superlative** | **ältest-** | Es ist die **älteste** Stadt in Deutschland. |

The superlative of an adjective or adverb is formed by adding **-st** to the base form. The **-st** is expanded to **-est** if the adjective stem ends in **-d, -t,** or a sibilant. The superlative of **groß** is an exception: **größt-.** The words that add umlaut in the comparative also add umlaut in the superlative. Preceded superlative adjectives take the same endings as those of the base form.

F   Was weißt du über Deutschland?   You friend is checking on her/his facts about the Federal Republic. Tell your friend that the places she/he asks about are actually the oldest, largest, and so on.

▶   Trier ist eine alte Stadt, nicht?   *Ja, Trier ist die älteste Stadt der Bundesrepublik.*

1.   Heidelberg ist eine alte Universität, nicht?
2.   Herdecke in Nordrhein-Westfalen ist eine junge Universität, nicht?
3.   Bayern ist ein großes Land, nicht?
4.   Bremen ist ein kleines Land, nicht?
5.   Berlin ist sicher eine sehr große Stadt.
6.   Der Rhein ist bestimmt ein langer Fluß°.   *river*

Im Winter arbeitet Frau Greif **am schwersten.**	In the winter Mrs. Greif works *(the) hardest.*
Im Winter sind die Tage **am kürzesten.**	In the winter the days are *(the) shortest.*

The superlative of adverbs is formed by inserting the word **am** in front of the adverb and adding the ending **-(e)sten** to the adverb. The superlative of predicate adjectives is formed according to the same pattern.

G   Alles ist am größten.   Claudia speaks in superlatives. When someone says something, she repeats it and makes it the greatest, coldest, slowest, etc. Take her role.

▶   Im Sommer sind die Tage lang.   *Im Sommer sind die Tage am längsten.*

1.   Im Herbst sind die Bäume interessant.
2.   Im Frühling sind die Blumen schön.
3.   Im Winter sind die Tage kalt.
4.   Regina fährt langsam.
5.   Hans-Jürgen arbeitet schwer.
6.   Ingrid und Thomas tanzen schön.

Erich ist der jüngste Sohn und Hans ist **der älteste (Sohn).**	Erich is the youngest son and Hans is *the oldest (son).*

The superlative of attributive adjectives (with a following noun expressed or understood) is formed by inserting **der/das/die** in front of the adjective and adding an ending to the superlative form of the adjective.

Adverb or predicative adjective		Attributive adjective	
lang	long	**der lange** Weg	the long way
länger	longer	**der längere** Weg	the longer way
am längsten	(the) longest	**der längste** Weg	the longest way

The chart above summarizes the comparison of adverbs and adjectives. Preceded comparative and superlative adjectives have regular adjective endings.

H   Die schönsten, neuesten Sachen   Like Claudia, Peter finds everything the greatest. Take his role.

▶   Diese Schuhe sind sehr billig.   *Diese Schuhe sind die billigsten.*

1.   Diese Blumen sind sehr schön.
2.   Dieses Auto ist sehr teuer.

3. Diese Waschmaschine ist sehr praktisch.
4. Dieser Fernseher ist ganz neu.
5. Dieser Gefrierschrank ist groß.
6. Diese Stereoanlage ist ziemlich teuer.

Base form	gern	gut	hoch	viel
Comparative	**lieber**	**besser**	**höher**	**mehr**
Superlative	**liebst-**	**best-**	**höchst-**	**meist-**

The adjectives and adverbs that are irregular in the comparative are also irregular in the superlative. Irregular forms are indicated in the vocabularies of this book as follows: **gern (lieber, liebst-).**

I **Viele Fragen** Answer the questions below, using the superlative.

▶ Heike trinkt lieber Bier als Kaffee. Und Wein? *Wein trinkt sie am lieb- sten.*

1. Frank spielt lieber Tennis als Basketball. Und Fußball?
2. Peter schreibt besser als Erik. Und Heidi?
3. Inge kocht besser als Erik. Und Mark?
4. Ein großer Opel kostet mehr als ein kleiner Volkswagen. Und ein Mercedes?
5. Klaus spricht mehr als seine Schwester. Und sein Bruder?
6. Heidi arbeitet lieber nachmittags als abends. Und morgens?
7. Am Nachmittag ist das Fieber höher als am Morgen. Und am Abend?

Kabelanschluß
Mehr Programme, bestes Bild, bester Ton.

Ihr Anschluß an die Zukunft.

J **Wie sagt man das?**
1. Dietmar is taller than his brother.
   —Yes, but still shorter than his father.
2. I work best in the mornings.
   —Really? I prefer to work evenings.
3. Today is the coldest day of the year.
   —Yes. It simply won't get warmer.
4. Do you like to work with younger people?
   —Yes. But I like to work with older people best of all.

K   Ihre Meinung

1. Was trinken Sie am liebsten?
2. Was essen Sie am liebsten?
3. An welchem Tag gehen Sie am spätesten ins Bett?
4. Welche Sprache sprechen Sie am besten?
5. Was studieren Sie am liebsten?
6. Wer arbeitet in Ihrer Familie am schwersten?
7. Welchen Sport treiben Sie am liebsten?
8. Welchen Teil Amerikas finden Sie am schönsten?
9. Welcher amerikanische Politiker spricht am besten?
10. Welche amerikanische Stadt ist die schönste?

2   Reflexive constructions

Ich habe **mich** gewaschen.	I washed (*myself*).

Kaufst du **dir** einen neuen Farb-
    fernseher?
	Are you going to buy (*yourself*) a
	    new color TV?

A reflexive pronoun indicates the same person or thing as the subject. A reflexive pronoun may be in either the accusative or the dative case.

3   Forms of reflexive pronouns

	ich	du	er/es/sie	wir	ihr	sie	Sie
Acc.	mich	dich	**sich**	uns	euch	**sich**	**sich**
Dat.	mir	dir	**sich**	uns	euch	**sich**	**sich**

Reflexive pronouns differ from personal pronouns only in the **er/es/sie, sie** (*pl.*), and **Sie** forms, which are all **sich.**

• *Accusative reflexive pronouns*

Ich habe **mich** schnell gewaschen.	I washed myself in a hurry.
Frag **dich** mal warum!	Ask yourself why sometime.

A reflexive pronoun is in the accusative case when it functions as a direct object.

L   Sie duschen sich abends.   Say that the people mentioned below shower at night. Use the appropriate accusative reflexive pronoun in each instance.

▶   Veronika duscht sich abends. (Andreas)   *Andreas duscht sich abends.*

1. Gabi und Rolf		3. ich		5. ihr	
2. du		4. wir		6. Uwe	

Although political life in Switzerland is essentially based in the cantons, federal affairs are represented by several constitutional bodies.

Swiss citizens who are more than twenty years old have the right to vote for the National Council (*Nationalrat*). Each citizen can vote for a party and a candidate. Elections for the Council of States (*Ständerat*) vary according to cantonal law. The National Council and the Council of States form the Federal Assembly (*Bundesversammlung*), which elects a cabinet of Federal Ministers (*Bundesrat*) and the Federal President (*Bundespräsident*). Although the President is the head of state, his duties are largely ceremonial and he does not hold special power within the government.

Usually several times a year the Swiss voters take part in binding referenda on initiatives that propose new federal or cantonal laws.

In einer direkten Demokratie stimmen die Bürger selbst ab – Landesgemeinde in Glarus.

• *Dative reflexive pronouns*

Ich kann **mir** nicht helfen.	I can't help myself.
Kaufst du **dir** einen neuen Kassettenrecorder?	Are you going to buy yourself a new cassette deck?

A reflexive pronoun that follows a dative verb or functions as an indirect object is in the dative case.

M Was kaufen sie sich?   Say what the people mentioned below would like to buy for themselves on their next shopping spree. Use the dative reflexive pronoun.

▶   Margot / ein neues Fahrrad   *Margot möchte sich ein neues Fahrrad kaufen.*

1. Schmidts / neue Möbel
2. ich / eine gute Stereoanlage
3. wir / ein kleiner Farbfernseher
4. Paul / ein neuer Kassettenrecorder
5. Brauns / ein besserer Geschirrspüler
6. ich / ein teurer Plattenspieler
7. du / ein amerikanisches Auto
8. ihr / eine neue Waschmaschine
9. du / ein lustiges Poster

Sie haben das Wort

Was möchtest du dir kaufen?   You would like to buy something new for your room. What will it be? Ask four other persons what they would like to buy.

Ich möchte mir [einen Farbfernseher] kaufen. Was möchtest du dir kaufen?

Discussing wants

4   Reflexive verbs

Setz dich!	Sit down.
Fühlst du **dich** nicht wohl?	Don't you feel well?
Hast du **dich** gestern **erkältet?**	Did you catch a cold yesterday?
Hast du **dich** zu leicht **angezogen?**	Did you dress too lightly?

In German, some verbs regularly have a reflexive pronoun as part of the verb pattern. The English equivalents of these verbs do not have reflexive pronouns. In general, the reflexive construction is used more frequently in German than in English. In the vocabularies of this book, reflexive verbs are listed with the pronoun **sich: sich fühlen.**

N   Noch einmal   Restate the sentences below with the cued subjects.

▶ Ich fühle mich nicht wohl. (Heike)   *Heike fühlt sich nicht wohl.*

1. Fühlt Heike sich heute besser? (du)
2. Inge hat sich gestern erkältet. (ich)
3. Wie hast du dich erkältet? (Dieter)
4. Paul zieht sich später an. (wir)
5. Wann ziehst du dich an? (ihr)
6. Wir haben uns an den Tisch gesetzt. (die Gäste)
7. Warum setzt Sonja sich nicht zu uns? (du)

O   Wie sagt man das?

1. Do you feel better today, Mr. Meier? *Fühlen Sie sich besser heute, Herr Meier?*
   —No, I don't feel well. *Nein, ich fühle mich nicht wohl.*
2. How did Astrid catch cold? *Wie hat Astrid sich erkältet?*
   —I don't know. Did she catch cold again? *Ich weiß nicht. Hat sie sich wieder erkältet?*
3. Lotte, why haven't you dressed yet? *Lotte, warum hast du dich noch nicht angezogen?*
   —It's still early. I'll get dressed later. *Es ist noch schon Früh. Ich ziehe mich später an.*
4. Please sit down, Erna. *Bitte, setz dich, Erna!*
   —Thanks, I'll sit on this chair. *Danke, ich setze mich auf den Stuhl.*
5. Why haven't you bathed yet? *Warum hast du dich noch nicht gebadet?*
   —I'll shower later. *Ich dusche mich später.*

5   Definite article with parts of the body

Ich habe **mir die** Hände gewaschen.	I washed *my* hands.
Hast du **dir die** Zähne geputzt?	Did you brush *your* teeth?

The reflexive pronoun in the dative often indicates that the accusative object belongs to the subject of the sentence. This is especially common with parts of the body. German uses a definite article and a dative pronoun where English uses a possessive adjective.

P   Schon fertig.   Say that you have washed and dressed and are ready to go out.

▶ Gesicht waschen   *Ich habe mir das Gesicht gewaschen.*

1. Hände waschen
2. Haare waschen
3. Haare kämmen
4. Zähne putzen
5. saubere Jeans anziehen
6. ein sauberes Hemd anziehen

Q   Was sagen Sie?

1. Wann duschen oder baden Sie sich?
2. Waschen Sie sich abends oder morgens die Haare?
3. Mit was für einem Shampoo waschen Sie sich die Haare?
4. Wann putzen Sie sich die Zähne?
5. Mit welcher Zahnpasta° putzen Sie sich die Zähne?   *toothpaste*
6. Ziehen Sie sich die Schuhe aus, wenn Sie arbeiten?
7. Ziehen Sie sich alte Sachen an, wenn Sie abends nach Hause kommen?

6   Infinitives with *zu*

Infinitives with zu	Ich brauche heute nicht **zu** arbeiten.	I don't have to [need to] work today.
Modal and infinitive	Mußt du morgen arbeiten?	Do you have to work tomorrow?

In English, dependent infinitives used with most verbs are preceded by *to*. In German, dependent infinitives used with most verbs are preceded by **zu.** Dependent infinitives used with modals are not preceded by **zu**.

Das Kind versucht auf**zu**stehen.	The child tries to get up.
Vergiß nicht, Kuchen mit**zu**bringen.	Don't forget to bring cake.

When a separable-prefix verb is in the infinitive form, the **zu** comes between the prefix and the base form of the verb.

If an infinitive phrase contains **zu** + an infinitive and modifiers, it is set off by commas in writing. Note that an infinitive phrase after **brauchen** (e.g., **Ich brauche heute nicht zu arbeiten**) is not set off by commas.

Some verbs you know that can be followed by **zu** + an infinitive are **aufhören, brauchen, scheinen, vergessen,** and **versuchen.**

R   Das macht man in Österreich.   Tell about some of David's experiences in Austria and what he has learned or not learned.

▶   Er gibt jedem die Hand. (Er hat gelernt ...)   *Er hat gelernt, jedem die Hand*
zu geben.

1. Er macht die Tür zu. (Er vergißt oft ...)
2. Er ißt mit Messer und Gabel. (Er versucht ...)
3. Er bringt Blumen mit. (Er vergißt nicht ...)
4. Er läuft mehr. (Er versucht ...)
5. David geht am Sonntag spazieren. (Er kann ...)
6. Er kauft im Bio-Laden ein. (Er hat angefangen ...)
7. Er fährt eines Tages zur Kur. (Er möchte ...)

Sie haben das Wort

Ich brauche das nicht zu tun.   You have moved into a dormitory or apartment with friends. List the chores you no longer have to do now that you don't live at home. Talk to the other students about the chores they no longer need to do.

Talking about household chores

Sie	*Gesprächspartner/in*
Mußt du [abwaschen]?	Ja, ich muß [abwaschen].
	Nein, ich brauche nicht [abzuwaschen].

abtrocknen ☐ [im Garten] arbeiten ☐ aufräumen ☐ früh aufstehen ☐ kochen ☐ einkaufen ☐ [bei der Hausarbeit] helfen ☐ [das Auto] reparieren ☐ Wäsche° waschen

laundry

Es macht Spaß, mit dem Zug zu fahren.	It's fun to go by train.
Es ist schwer, früh aufzustehen.	It's hard to get up early.

Infinitives with **zu** are used after a number of expressions, such as **es ist Zeit, es ist schön, es ist schwer,** and **es macht Spaß.**

Ihre Wünsche zu erfüllen,
ist bei uns ein leichtes Spiel.

Zürich, Strehlgasse 29, Tel. 01 221 31 04

S   Nicole studiert in Hamburg.   Tell about some of Nicole's experiences at the University of Hamburg.

▶   Sie steht früh auf. Es ist schwer.   *Es ist schwer, früh aufzustehen.*

1.   Sie fährt mit dem Zug. Es macht Spaß.
2.   Sie versteht die Vorlesungen. Es ist nicht leicht.
3.   Sie sitzt mit Freunden im Biergarten. Es ist gut.
4.   Sie findet einen Studentenjob. Es ist schwer.
5.   Sie wandert am Wochenende mit Freunden. Es ist schön.
6.   Sie bereitet ihr Referat vor. Sie hat wenig Zeit.

7   The construction *um ... zu* + infinitive

Um Bürger **zu** werden, muß man   *(In order) to* become a citizen one
   12 Jahre an einem Ort wohnen.   must live 12 years in one place.

The German construction **um ... zu** + infinitive is equivalent to the English
construction *(in order) to* + infinitive.

"Die neue was? Sinco Cola? Nicht doch, Kind.
Das kann man doch bestenfalls zu der neuen
deutschen Da-da-da-Musik trinken - zu Wiener Walzer
ist das doch taktlos."

Neu. Sinco Cola - zu erfrischend, um taktvoll zu sein.

T   Es geht ihnen gut.   The Kohls are a product of the affluent society.
Tell why they do some of the things they do.

▶   Sie kaufen einen Geschirrspüler,   *Sie kaufen einen Geschirrspüler,*
    denn sie wollen weniger Arbeit   *um weniger Arbeit zu haben.*
    haben.

1. Herr Kohl kauft nur *New Sport*, denn er möchte schön angezogen sein.
2. Sie kaufen sich eine teure Stereoanlage, denn sie möchten gute Musik
    hören.
3. Sie putzen sich die Zähne mit *Forte 2000*, denn sie möchten weißere
    Zähne haben.
4. Sie waschen sich die Haare mit *Viveen*, denn sie möchten gesundes
    Haar haben.
5. Sie fahren oft Rad, denn sie wollen gesund bleiben.

| Wiederholung

A   Was machen Sie lieber?   Answer each of the questions below.

1. Schlafen Sie lieber bei offenem oder geschlossenem Fenster?
2. Stehen Sie lieber früh oder spät auf?
3. Duschen Sie sich lieber morgens oder abends?
4. Was trinken Sie am liebsten, Milch, Kaffee, Wein oder Bier?
5. Wo kaufen Sie lieber ein, im Supermarkt oder in kleinen Geschäften?
6. Fahren Sie lieber mit dem Auto, oder gehen Sie lieber zu Fuß?
7. Wo arbeiten Sie lieber, in der Bibliothek oder zu Hause?
8. Was lesen Sie lieber, Bücher oder Zeitungen?
9. Was machen Sie am liebsten, fernsehen, lesen oder Musik hören?

B   Wie sagt man das?

Inge: Why did you get up so late?
Erik: I don't feel well.
Inge: Do you have a fever?
Erik: No. I caught a cold. My throat hurts.
Inge: You look pale. Maybe it's better if you go to the doctor.
Erik: You're right. I do feel weak.

C   So beginnt mein Tag.   Describe the beginning of your day. You may use the expressions provided below and add some of your own.

aufstehen ☐ sich baden oder duschen ☐ sich anziehen ☐ tragen ☐ etwas trinken und essen ☐ sich die Zähne putzen ☐ sich die Haare kämmen

D   Zeit und Ort   Answer the questions below in complete sentences that contain both time expressions and place expressions.

1. Wann gehen Sie in Ihre erste Vorlesung? Um 8? Um 9?
2. Wann gehen Sie nach Hause? Um 3? Um 5?
3. Wann arbeiten Sie in der Bibliothek? Am Mittwoch? Jeden Tag?
4. Wie oft gehen Sie ins Kino? Einmal in der Woche? Einmal im Monat?
5. Wann möchten Sie in die Ferien gehen? Im Juli? Im August?

E   In Deutschland ist es anders.   Join the sentences below, using a conjunction from the list.

aber □ da □ daß □ denn □ ob □ oder □ und □ weil □ wenn

▶   Diane Müller studiert in Deutsch-   *Dianne Müller studiert in*
     land. Sie möchte mehr Deutsch   *Deutschland, denn sie möchte mehr*
     lernen.   *Deutsch lernen.*

1.   Sie geht mit ihrer Freundin Nicole. Ihre Freundin geht einkaufen.
2.   Diane ist erstaunt. Nicole geht jede Woche zweimal einkaufen.
3.   Nicole kauft fast alles im Supermarkt. Die Sachen sind da oft billiger.
4.   Sie kauft Tabletten in der Apotheke. Sie kauft Brot beim Bäcker.
5.   Sie kauft frischen Kuchen. Sie kauft Brot von gestern.
6.   Diane ist erstaunt. Nicole geht in so viele Geschäfte.

CIRCUS KNIE

ZOO

Fr. 4.—

Erwachsene 54256 **Adultes**

Gültig für 1 Besuch   Valable pour 1 visite

Bitte aufbewahren und auf Verlangen   A conserver et à présenter sur toute
vorweisen.   Ohne Coupon ungültig   demande. Non valable sans le coupon

Guhl + Scheibler AG, Aesch/BL

F   Bei Beckers in Zürich   Robert is an American student staying with the Becker family in Zürich. The following dialogue reflects some of his experiences. Complete each sentence with an appropriate possessive adjective.

Anja: Du, Robert, _____ Mutter sieht das nicht gern, daß _____ Zimmertür immer offen steht.

Robert: Ich soll _____ Zimmertür schließen?

Anja: Ja, bitte. Es sieht besser aus.

Robert: Ach, jetzt verstehe ich. Ich hab' bemerkt, wie deine Mutter _____ Tür immer zumacht. Ihr macht alle _____ Türen zu.

Anja: Klar. Deshalb hat man Türen! Aber genug von Türen. Wir machen _____ Ferienpläne. Wir fahren nach Österreich zu _____ Freunden. Du kommst doch mit, nicht?

Robert: Gern. Wie lange bleibt ihr denn bei _____ Freunden?

Anja: Eine Woche. Du kannst _____ Arbeit mitnehmen.

Robert: Ja, das muß ich. Ich muß _____ Referat vorbereiten.

G   Was bedeutet das?   The sentences below contain new words that are related to words you already know. Give the English equivalents of the sentences.

1. Ich danke Ihnen für Ihre *Hilfe*. Sie haben mir wirklich sehr geholfen.
2. Wenn man in Deutschland fahren will, muß man eine *Fahrschule* besuchen. Der *Fahrschulkurs* ist natürlich sehr teuer.
3. Es gefällt dem *Arbeitgeber*, wenn seine Arbeitnehmer gut arbeiten.
4. Auf dem Land fährt Susanne mit dem Motorrad; auf dem Wasser fährt sie im *Motorboot*.
5. Mein Freund Richard *reist* im Sommer nach Deutschland. So eine Reise ist sehr schön.
6. Wir haben uns ein neues *Zelt* gekauft. Im August machen wir Camping.
7. Läufst du gern *Wasserski*?
8. Die *Übersetzung* dieses Artikels über Brecht ist ausgezeichnet. Wer hat ihn übersetzt?

H   Anregung

1. Prepare a short paragraph in German that contains answers to some or all of the questions below.
   a. Baut man in Amerika mehr Wohnungen oder mehr Einfamilienhäuser?
   b. Wohnen Sie lieber in einer Wohnung oder in einem Einfamilienhaus?
   c. Gibt es genug Häuser und Wohnungen in Amerika?
   d. Haben alle Amerikaner eine Waschmaschine und einen Kühlschrank?
   e. Haben alle Amerikaner einen Fernseher? Ein Auto?
   f. Haben alle Amerikaner genug zu essen?
   g. Gibt es in Amerika genug Schulen und Krankenhäuser?
   h. Geht es den Amerikanern heute besser als vor zwanzig Jahren? Vor zehn Jahren?
   i. Wie finden Sie den amerikanischen Lebensstandard? Hoch genug? Zu hoch?
2. Write a short paragraph in German on one of the following topics: *Mein Lebensstandard* or *Lebensstandard in Amerika.*
3. The Federal Republic has a national *Trimm dich!*° campaign, urging its citizens "*Halt dich fit!*"° Write one or two public-service ads for TV or radio that could be used in this campaign. For example: urge people to walk or ride bikes rather than using their cars; encourage people to get out and enjoy sports such as hiking, camping, swimming. You may wish to incorporate ideas on *Umweltprobleme,* such as pollution from traffic.

fitness
keep in shape

dsb Deutscher Sportbund

| Grammatik zum Nachschlagen _____

Comparison of adjectives and adverbs (A–K)

- *Forms of the comparative and superlative*

Base form	**laut**	loud	**schön**	beautiful
Comparative	**lauter**	louder	**schöner**	more beautiful
Superlative	**lautest-**	loudest	**schönst-**	most beautiful

English forms the comparative of adjectives and adverbs by adding the suffix *-er* to the base form or by using the modifier *more*. It forms the superlative by adding the suffix *-est* or by using the modifier *most*.

German has one way to compare both adjectives and adverbs. German forms the comparative by adding the suffix **-er** to the base form. It forms the superlative by adding the suffix **-st** to the base form. The ending **-est** is added to words ending in **-d (gesündest-)**, **-t (leichtest-)**, or a sibilant **(kürzest-)**. An exception is **größt-**.

Base form	alt	groß	jung
Comparative	**älter**	**größer**	**jünger**
Superlative	**ältest-**	**größt-**	**jüngst-**

Many one-syllable adjectives and adverbs with stem vowel **a, o,** or **u** add an umlaut in the comparative and the superlative.

Base form	gern	gut	hoch	viel
Comparative	**lieber**	**besser**	**höher**	**mehr**
Superlative	**liebst-**	**best-**	**höchst-**	**meist-**

A few adjectives and adverbs are irregular in the comparative and superlative forms.

- *Special constructions and uses*

Bernd ist nicht **so groß wie** Jens.
Es ist heute **so kalt wie** gestern.

Bernd is not *as tall as* Jens.
Today it is just *as cold as* yesterday.

In German the construction **so ... wie** is used to make comparisons of equality. It is equivalent to English *as . . . as*.

| Erika ist **größer als** ihre Mutter. | Erika is *taller than* her mother. |
| Es ist **kälter als** gestern. | It is *colder than* yesterday. |

The comparative form of an adjective or adverb is used to make comparisons of inequality. **Als** is equivalent to English **than**.

Sie singt **am schönsten**.	She sings the best.
Im Frühling ist das Wetter hier **am schönsten**.	The weather here is nicest in the spring.
Die kleinsten Blumen sind **die schönsten**.	The smallest flowers are the prettiest (flowers).

The pattern **am** + superlative + **-en** is used for adverbs (as in the first example above), and for predicate adjectives (as in the second example). The superlative of attributive adjectives, with a following noun that is expressed or understood, is preceded by the article **der/das/die** (as in the third example). The superlative form of the adjective has an ending.

Sprachen lernen– auf dem kürzesten Weg

- Englisch
- Französisch • Italienisch
- Spanisch • Latein
- Deutsch

AKAD

Reflexive constructions   (L–M)

- *Forms of reflexive pronouns*

| Ich habe **mich** gewaschen. | I washed (myself). |
| Ich habe **mir** neue Jeans gekauft. | I bought (myself) new jeans. |

A reflexive pronoun is a pronoun that indicates the same person or thing as the subject. A reflexive pronoun may be either in the accusative or dative case.

	ich	du	er/es/sie	wir	ihr	sie	Sie
Accusative reflexive	mich	dich	sich	uns	euch	sich	sich
Dative reflexive	mir	dir	sich	uns	euch	sich	sich

- *Use of reflexive constructions*

Ich habe **mich** gewaschen.	I washed (myself).
Hast du **dich** geduscht?	Did you shower?

A reflexive pronoun is in the accusative case when it functions as a direct object.

Ich kann **mir** nicht helfen.	I can't help myself.
Hast du **dir** ein neues Auto gekauft?	Did you buy yourself a new car?
Wir möchten **uns** die Stadt ansehen.	We'd like to look at the city.

A reflexive pronoun is in the dative case if the verb takes a dative object, or if there is some other direct object in the sentence.

Reflexive verbs (N–O)

Ich habe **mich angezogen**.	I got dressed.
Er hat **sich erkältet**.	He has caught a cold.
Fühlst du **dich** nicht wohl?	Don't you feel well?
Setzen Sie **sich!**	Sit down!

Some German verbs regularly have a reflexive pronoun as part of the verb pattern. The English equivalents of these verbs do not have reflexive pronouns.

Definite articles with parts of the body (P–Q)

Ich habe **mir die** Hände gewaschen.	I washed *my* hands.
Sie hat **sich die** Haare gekämmt.	She combed *her* hair.

In referring to parts of the body, German often uses a definite article and a dative pronoun. English uses a possessive adjective.

Infinitives with *zu* (R–S)

Er versucht, alles **zu** verstehen.	He tries to understand everything.
Er kann alles verstehen.	He can understand everything.

Dependent infinitives used with most verbs are preceded by **zu**. Dependent infinitives used with modals are not preceded by **zu**.

Sie hat keine Zeit, die Arbeit **zu** machen.	She has no time to do the work.
Es war schwer, die Vorlesung **zu** verstehen.	The lecture was difficult to understand.

Infinitives with **zu** are also used after a large number of expressions like **es ist Zeit** and **es ist schwer**. If an infinitive phrase contains **zu** + infinitive and modifiers, it is set off by commas in writing.

Das brauchst du nicht **zu** machen.	You don't need to do that.
Es scheint mir anders **zu** sein.	That seems to me to be different.

Infinitive phrases after **brauchen** and **scheinen** are not set off by commas.

Es ist schwer, so früh auf**zu**stehen.
Es ist Zeit, jetzt auf**zu**hören.

When a separable prefix is in the infinitive form, the **zu** comes between the prefix and the base form of the verb.

The construction *um ... zu* + infinitive   (T)

Amerikaner kommen öfter nach Deutschland, **um** dort **zu** studieren	Americans often come to Germany *in order to* study there.

The German construction **um ... zu** + infinitive is equivalent to the English construction *(in order) to* + infinitive.

Kapitel 10

Lernziele

Sprechakte

Telling about one's qualifications for a job
Expressing agreement and disagreement
Expressing annoyance
Expressing regret
Expressing resignation
Narrating events in the past

Grammatik

Simple past tense
Past perfect tense
Conjunctions **als, wenn,** and **wann**

Vokabeln

Professions

Landeskunde

Women in the workforce of the Federal
   Republic of Germany
Social legislation contributing to women's
   rights in the Federal Republic of Germany
Women at the university

*In der Bundesrepublik gibt es etwa 25
Prozent Ärztinnen.*

| Bausteine für Gespräche

Die alte Stelle

Personalchefin: ... Also, Frau Halbach, erzählen Sie mal von sich selbst.

Frau Halbach: Ich habe an der Universität Informatik studiert. Seit drei Jahren arbeite ich als Informatikerin bei einer kleineren Bank.

Personalchefin: Warum wollen Sie die Stelle wechseln?

Frau Halbach: Als ich vor drei Jahren dort anfing, fand ich die Arbeit interessant. Aber jetzt möchte ich neue Erfahrungen sammeln.

Die neue Stelle

Personalchefin: Warum wollen Sie bei uns arbeiten?

Frau Halbach: Ihre Firma ist jung. Ich hoffe, daß ich hier mehr Verantwortung bekomme.

Personalchefin: Wie Sie wissen, sind wir eine Exportfirma. Können Sie Englisch und Französisch?

Frau Halbach: Ja, ich hatte acht Jahre Englisch. Mein Französisch ist nicht ganz so gut, aber es geht.

...

Personalchefin: Also, vielen Dank, daß Sie gekommen sind. Sie hören dann von uns.

The old job

. . . Well, Ms. Halbach, tell me a little bit about yourself.

I studied computer science in college. For the last three years I've been working as a computer specialist at a small bank.

Why do you want to change jobs?

When I started there three years ago I found the work interesting. But now I'd like to get some new experience.

The new job

Why do you want to work for us?

Your company is new. I hope that I'll get more responsibility here.

As you know, we're exporters. Do you know English and French?

Yes, I had eight years of English. My French isn't quite so good, but it'll do.

Well, thanks for coming. You'll be hearing from us.

Fragen

1. Was hat Frau Halbach studiert?
2. Wo hat sie drei Jahre gearbeitet?
3. Warum will sie die Stelle wechseln?
4. Warum will die bei der neuen Firma arbeiten?
5. Welche Sprachen kann sie?

Sie haben das Wort

A   Eine neue Stelle   Take the part of one of the participants in a job interview. Before the interview decide what you know.

Applying for a job

Sie

Sprechen Sie | **Englisch?**
                Französisch
                Deutsch
                Spanisch

Können Sie | **Schreibmaschine schreiben°?**
               mit Wortprozessoren° arbeiten?
               mit dem Computer arbeiten?

Warum wollen Sie die Stelle wechseln?

Gesprächspartner/in

Ja, | **fließend°.**
     | ziemlich gut

Nur | **gebrochen°.**
     | ein bißchen

Ich verstehe es.
Ich lese es nur.
Es geht.
Nein, ich spreche keine Fremdsprache°.

Ja. Sehr gut.
Ich kenne BASIC und ein bißchen Pascal.
Nein, tut mir leid.

Ich möchte | **neue Erfahrungen sammeln.**
              mehr Verantwortung bekommen
              mehr verdienen°
              bei einer Exportfirma arbeiten
              bei einer größeren Firma arbeiten

Bei einer Exportfirma kann ich mein [Deutsch] gebrauchen°.
Ich finde die Arbeit nicht mehr interessant.
Am Anfang war die Arbeit interessanter.

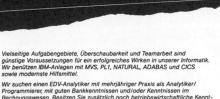

EDV-Analytiker

Vielseitige Aufgabengebiete, Überschaubarkeit und Teamarbeit sind günstige Voraussetzungen für ein erfolgreiches Wirken in unserer Informatik. Wir benützen IBM-Anlagen mit MVS, PL1, NATURAL, ADABAS und CICS sowie modernste Hilfsmittel.

Wir suchen einen EDV-Analytiker mit mehrjähriger Praxis als Analytiker/ Programmierer, mit guten Bankkenntnissen und/oder Kenntnissen im Rechnungswesen. Besitzen Sie zusätzlich noch betriebswirtschaftliche Kenntnisse und suchen Sie eine neue Herausforderung, dann sind Sie unser Mann oder unsere Frau.

Wählen Sie 01 219 32 56. Herr R. Stöckli, Personaldienst, stellt die Verbindung zur Informatik her.

Bank Leu

Bank Leu AG Personaldienst
Postfach 8022 Zürich
sox63517oc

Stadt Winterthur

Unsere Verwaltung mit über 3000 Mitarbeitern erweitert ihre Informatikdienste, um den gesteigerten Anforderungen an eine effiziente Verwaltung zu genügen. In diesem langfristigen Konzept wird einem einwandfreien und zuverlässigen Daten-Design in der Informatik grösste Bedeutung zugemessen. Für diese Aufgabe suchen wir einen

Daten-Administrator

Der Stelleninhaber ist verantwortlich für das konzeptionelle und physische Design der Daten im Rahmen von Informatik-Projekten sowie für die Analyse und Dokumentation der Datenelemente. Er hat eine Daten-Design-Methode und einen Data-Dictionary aufzubauen sowie eine Datenbank-Software mit modernen Computersystemen einzuführen.

Sie sollten als Bewerber Erfahrung in der Datenadministration und mit Datenbanken aufweisen. Gute Kontaktfreudigkeit und Verhandlungsgeschick wird vorausgesetzt.

Wir bieten einem initiativen Bewerber eine interessante und herausfordernde Aufgabe mit zeigemässen Arbeitsbedingungen im Rahmen eines kleinen Teams.

Bitte senden Sie uns Ihre Bewerbung mit den üblichen Unterlagen an untenstehende Adresse. Ergänzende Auskünfte erteilt Ihnen gerne P. Brunner, Organisator, Tel. (052) 84 51 91.

Stadt Winterthur
Organisationsabteilung
8402 Winterthur

SOX633433E

More than half of the population in Germany is female. Women make up 38% of the German work force, and 57% of these women are married. The wages and salaries of female employees are on the average one third lower than those of their male colleagues. The number of girls being trained in traditionally male occupations rose by 259% between the years 1977 and 1982, from 11,500 to 41,300. Still, traditional male and female roles tend to persist, as seen in a recent study of career choices of boys and girls. The most popular careers among boys have long been engineering, business, and auto mechanics. Girls have chosen jobs in the medical services, teaching, office work, and sales clerking.

Since the founding of the *Bundesrepublik* in 1949 the number of women with academic degrees has risen substantially. However, women still face obstacles when faced with employment.

Women make up 43% of degree-holding job hunters, but among those hired only 29% are women. It is hard for women to climb to the top. In large companies only 4% of those in top management are women. At universities women comprise only 6% of the faculty, and only 2.4% of the faculty in the highest salary group are women.

Eine Werkzeugmacherin im ersten Lehrjahr bei Ford in Köln

B   Eine neue Stelle: Gespräch   With four partners, decide which skills and qualifications are important for a particular job. Interview several students who are applying for the job. Use the questions in A and develop your own questions as well. Report on whom you will hire and why.

C   Berufspläne°   Ask four fellow students what profession they would like to pursue.

Sie	*Gesprächspartner/in*	
Was möchten Sie werden?	Ich möchte	**Lehrer/in°** werden.
		Professor/in
		Jurist/in°
		Geschäftsmann°/Geschäftsfrau°
		Musiker/in°
		Programmierer/in°
		Arzt/Ärztin
		Zahnarzt/Zahnärztin°
		Ingenieur/in

D   Wenn es sein muß.   You have just returned home from a long, tiring day at work. You are greeted by some unexpected news. Respond to your conversational partner in three different registers of emotion: calmly, with resignation, and with annoyance.

Expressing emotions

Gesprächspartner/in

Du mußt am Samstag arbeiten.
Du mußt das Badezimmer saubermachen.
Wir müssen am Wochenende zu Hause bleiben.

Sie

Das habe ich mir gedacht.
Das macht nichts.
Na, wenn schon.

Da kann man nichts machen.
Wenn es sein muß.

Muß ich das?
O je.
Warum denn immer ich?
Das gefällt mir nun wirklich nicht.

Vokabeln

Substantive

die **Bank, -en**   bank
der **Chef, -s**/die **Chefin, -nen**   boss
der **Computer, -**   computer; **mit dem ~ arbeiten**   to work on a computer
der **Dank**   thanks ; **vielen Dank**   many thanks, thanks a lot
die **Erfahrung, -en**   experience
die **Fremdsprache, -n**   foreign language
(das) **Französisch**   French [language]
der **Ingenieur, -e**/die **Ingenieurin, -nen**   engineer
die **Informatik**   computer science
der **Informatiker, -**/die **Informatikerin, -nen**   computer specialist
der **Jurist, -en**/die **Juristin, -nen**   lawyer
der **Geschäftsmann, -leute**/die **Geschäftsfrau, -en**   businessman, businesswoman

der **Lehrer, -**/die **Lehrerin, -nen** teacher
der **Musiker, -**/die **Musikerin, -nen** musician
der **Programmierer, -**/die **Programmiererin, -nen**   programmer
die **Schreibmaschine, -n**   typewriter; **~ schreiben können**   to be able to type
(das) **Spanisch**   Spanish [language]
die **Stelle, -n**   position, job; place
die **Verantwortung**   responsibility
der **Wortprozessor, -en**   word processor; **mit dem ~ arbeiten**   to do word processing
der **Zahnarzt, -̈e**/die **Zahnärztin, -nen**   dentist

— Verben

brechen (bricht), brach, gebrochen   **sammeln**   to collect
    to break   **verdienen**   to earn
gebrauchen   to use   **wechseln**   to change
hoffen   to hope

— Andere Wörter

fließend   fluently

— Besondere Ausdrücke

es geht   it's OK, it'll do

A few milestones in the progress of women toward equality:

1901   German universities begin to admit women.

1919   German women receive the right to vote.

1949   The Basic Law of the Federal Republic (*Grundgesetz*) guarantees the right of a person to decide on her or his role in society.

1955   The Federal Labor Court (*Bundesarbeitsgericht*) states that there should be no discrimination on the basis of sex in compensation for work performed.

1977   Women and men are judged by law to be equal in a marriage. Either can take the surname of the other, or a combination of both names.

1979   Professional women gain the right to a six-month leave to care for a newly born child.

1986   Child-raising years are included in the calculation of retirement pensions; long-term, financially supported child-rearing leaves are introduced for women and men.

Viele Frauen arbeiten doppelt: als Mutter und im Beruf.

| Frauen in der Bundesrepublik _____

Vorbereitung auf das Lesen

• *Zum Thema*

Was sind einige Ziele° der berufstätigen° Frauen in diesem Land?   *goals / working*

> Stichworte (in der Wirtschaft): Arbeit ☐ Geld verdienen ☐ typische
> Männer- und typische Frauenarbeit
> (in der Politik): Senat ☐ Politikerinnen ☐ Präsidentin ☐ Regierung
> (Hausarbeit): Kinder ☐ Küche

• *Leitfragen*

1. Peters Ideen über die Frauen und Mädchen sind ziemlich traditionell. Was für Ideen sind das? Woher kommen sie?
2. Was garantiert das Grundgesetz?
3. Was paßt in Frau Wielands Geschichte zum Grundgesetz? Was paßt in Frau Wielands Geschichte nicht zum Grundgesetz?

> Stichworte: Rabenmutter ☐ Nachbar ☐ meine Familie

4. Warum ist es bis zur wirklichen Gleichberechtigung noch ein weiter Weg?

> Stichworte: Reserve des Arbeitsmarktes ☐ Berufe wie Elektriker ☐ Vorurteile

---

Eine Frau ist für die Hausarbeit da. Sie muß einkaufen gehen und gut kochen können. Sie muß für den Mann und die Kinder sorgen. Auch soll sie gut aussehen und freundlich sein. Nachdem eine Frau den ganzen Tag gearbeitet hat, ist sie abends müde.

5   Peter Kraft, 11 Jahre

Solche und ähnliche Briefe schrieben Kinder an eine deutsche Zeitung auf die Frage: „Was ist eine Frau? Was tut sie? Wie sieht sie aus? Schreibt uns eure Meinung!" Paßt Peters Meinung zur Wirklichkeit von heute? Schließlich arbeiten doch heute viele Frauen außerhalb des Hauses.
10 Warum oder woher haben Kinder diese Vorstellungen von der Frau?

Vielleicht haben die Kindermeinungen etwas mit den Büchern zu tun, die° die Kinder lesen. Wenn man sich die vielgekauften Kinderbücher   *that*
ansieht, findet man nämlich° darin auch heute noch oft Peters   *namely, to be sure*
Frauenbild. Das Mädchenbild paßt dazu und ist anders als das Jungen-
15 bild. Die Mädchen sehen° meistens zu, wenn die Jungen etwas bauen   **zusehen:** *to watch*

Die Frauen von heute suchen sich aus,
welche Karriere sie machen wollen.
freundin

freundin
freundin

Die Frauen von heute lassen sich
nicht über einen Kamm scheren.
freundin

Die Frauen von heute gefallen den Männern,
weil sie sich weniger gefallen lassen.
freundin

Die Frauen von heute bauen weniger Unfälle,
weil sie den Männern nicht alles nachmachen.
freundin

Die Frauen von heute machen
lieber Karriere als Betten.
freundin

oder Fußball spielen. Sie sind passiv, machen nie etwas Gefährliches. Sie
helfen im Haus oder spielen mit Puppen. Es ist auch interessant, daß es in
den meisten Kinderbüchern mehr Jungen als Mädchen gibt. In den Titeln
der Bücher erscheinen öfter männliche° als weibliche° Personen. Bei   *male / female*
20 solcher Kinderliteratur überrascht es nicht, daß viele Kinder solche Vorstellungen wie Peter Kraft haben.

 Aber nicht nur viele Kinder denken so. Viele Erwachsene° haben die   *adults*
gleichen Vorstellungen. Das Grundgesetz° garantiert zwar° schon seit   *constitution of the FRG / in-*
1949 die Gleichberechtigung° von Mann und Frau. Es garantiert auch die   *deed*
                                                                           equal rights
25 freie Entfaltung° der Persönlichkeit°. Aber in den Köpfen der Menschen   *development / personality*
und in der deutschen Wirklichkeit sieht es zum Teil noch immer anders
aus.

 Frau Wieland ist eine voll berufstätige Elektroingenieurin. Sie erinnert
sich z.B. gut an die Kritik ihrer Nachbarn und Bekannten, als sie mit der
30 Arbeit anfing. Als Ingenieurin war sie jede Woche vier Tage und vier
Nächte von zu Hause weg. Sie sagt: „Kaum jemand fand das toll, was wir
da versuchten. Man nannte mich eine Rabenmutter° und eine Karriere-   *unfit mother*
macherin°. Plötzlich tat allen möglichen Leuten° mein Mann leid. Das   *interested only in a career /*
Interessante war, daß unser Nachbar etwa zur gleichen Zeit auch vier   *allen … Leuten: all sorts of*
                                                                          people
35 Tage pro Woche weg war. Der war kein Rabenvater, und seine Frau tat
niemandem leid. Da konnte man schon den Mut und die Geduld° ver-   *patience*
lieren. Aber meine Familie hat mir sehr geholfen." Klaus, ihr sechzehn-

jähriger° Sohn, sagt: „Als Mutter zu arbeiten anfing, mußten wir alle viel   *16-year-old*
lernen. Ich hatte z.B. vorher noch nie die Wäsche gewaschen. Zum
40 Einkaufen war ich auch noch nicht oft gegangen. Aber man lernt ja alles."
Frau Wieland sagt: „Ich höre immer wieder von Kolleginnen, daß sie die
ganze Hausarbeit neben ihrem Beruf auch noch machen. Das ist bei uns
nicht so. Meine Familie hilft mir sehr."

Bei der Berufstätigkeit von Frauen° spielen persönliche Entscheidung°   **Bei ... Frauen:** *regarding the*
45 und natürlich auch wirtschaftliche Fragen eine Rolle. Einige Frauen wol-   *work of women / decision*
len arbeiten. Andere müssen arbeiten. Wieder andere wollen und müs-
sen arbeiten. Alle haben es jedoch° in Zeiten hoher Arbeitslosigkeit sehr   *nonetheless*
schwer, denn die Arbeitslosigkeit ist bei Frauen immer viel höher als bei
Männern. Deshalb fühlen sich viele Frauen zur *Reserve des Arbeits-*
50 *marktes* degradiert. Sie kritisieren, daß sie nur dann eine Stelle finden
können, wenn die Wirtschaft blüht°. Sie kämpfen gegen den Reserve-   *thrives (blooms)*
status, der° nichts mit Gleichberechtigung zu tun hat.   *that*

Wenn Frauen Berufe wie Elektrikerin und Kraftfahrzeugmechanikerin°   *auto mechanic*
gelernt haben, haben sie es besonders schwer, nun auch eine Stelle in
55 diesem Beruf zu finden. Monika Beerman, eine Kfz°-Mechanikerin, sagt: **Kfz = Kraftfahrzeug**
„Wir konkurrieren° mit den Männern um° die Stellen. Und es ist genauso   *compete / for*
wie vor dreieinhalb° Jahren, als ich mit der Lehre anfing. Ich höre die   *three and a half*
gleichen Vorurteile wie damals."

Bis zur wirklichen Gleichberechtigung ist es noch ein weiter Weg. Aber
60 viele Deutsche glauben, daß Emanzipation und Gleichberechtigung
wichtige und gute Ziele sind.

Fragen zum Lesestück

1. Was ist Peters Vorstellung von der Frau?
2. Was machen die Mädchen nach dem Bild der Kinderbücher?
3. Und die Jungen?
4. Was garantiert das Grundgesetz? Seit wann?
5. Wann haben die Nachbarn und Bekannten Frau Wieland kritisiert?
6. Warum kritisierten sie den Nachbarn nicht?
7. Was hat Klaus gelernt, als seine Mutter zu arbeiten anfing?
8. Was müssen viele Kolleginnen neben ihrer Arbeit machen?
9. Warum gehen viele Frauen in den Beruf?
10. Warum haben Frauen es in Zeiten hoher Arbeitslosigkeit sehr schwer?
11. Was kritisieren viele Frauen?
12. Warum können Frauen in Berufen wie Elektriker nur schwer eine Stelle finden?

Sie haben das Wort

Ihre Meinung

1. Welches Mädchenbild geben Kinderbücher bei Ihnen?
2. Welches Jungenbild geben Kinderbücher bei Ihnen?
3. Soll eine Mutter mit kleinen Kindern in den Beruf gehen?
4. Wer macht in den Familien bei Ihnen die Hausarbeit?
5. Ist die Arbeitslosigkeit für Frauen bei Ihnen höher als für Männer?
6. Gibt es in Berufen wie Mechaniker Vorurteile gegen Frauen?
7. Verdienen bei Ihnen Frauen und Männer für die gleiche Arbeit gleich viel?
8. Finden Sie einen Mann als Chef akzeptabel?
9. Finden Sie eine Frau als Chefin akzeptabel?

Vokabeln

Substantive

der **Beruf, -e** occupation; profession
der **Brief, -e** letter
die **Hausarbeit** housework
der **Kollege, -n, -n**/die **Kollegin, -nen** colleague
die **Lehre, -n** apprenticeship
die **Literatur** literature
die **Meinung, -en** opinion
der **Mut** courage

die **Nacht, ⸚e** night
die **Person, -en** person
die **Puppe, -n** doll
die **Vorstellung, -en** idea, concept; performance (play)
das **Vorurteil, -e** prejudice
die **Wäsche** wash, laundry
die **Wirklichkeit** reality
das **Ziel, -e** goal

Verben

(sich) erinnern (an + *acc.***)** to remember (someone or something)
kämpfen to fight
kritisieren to criticize

nennen, nannte, genannt to call; to name
sorgen (für) to care (for)

Andere Wörter

außerhalb (+ *gen.***)** outside of, beside
berufstätig employed
damals at that time
gefährlich dangerous
jemand someone, anyone
möglich possible

nachdem (*conj.*) after
persönlich personal
plötzlich suddenly
pro per
voll full; complete(ly)
weit far

Besondere Ausdrücke

noch immer still

zur gleichen Zeit at the same time

| Übungen zur Aussprache

Review the pronunciation of **sp** and **st** in the Reference section at the end of the book. Read the words in the columns from top to bottom. Then read the words in each pair of columns across. Check your pronunciation by listening to your instructor or the tape.

[sp]	[šp]	[st]	[št]
lispeln	spielen	Listen	stehlen
knuspern	springen	Hengst	streng
Espen	spenden	Küste	Stucke
Knospe	Sprossen	kosten	stocken
Haspe	Spatz	Last	Stall

Read the sentences aloud, paying special attention to your pronunciation of **sp** and **st** in the boldfaced words.

1. Die **Studentin spricht** die deutsche **Sprache** sehr schön.
2. Woher hat **Stefan** diese **Vorstellung?**
3. In der **Stadt** müssen Kinder oft auf den **Straßen spielen.**
4. **Sport** treiben macht **Spaß.**
5. Es hat **gestern** am **späten** Nachmittag **stark** geregnet.

Stille Wasser sind tief.

The women's policy (*Frauenpolitik*) of the Federal Republic's government covers a number of areas in women's lives. One aim is to help both women and men reconcile their professional and personal lives. In recent years opportunities to arrange flexible work hours, to work part time, or to share a job have improved. Many single mothers receive financial aid and every woman has the right to a maternity leave of six weeks preceding and eight weeks after the birth of the child (*Mutterschutz*), while receiving her full salary. Another benefit is the child-rearing leave (*Erziehungsurlaub*), which allows either parent to stay home with a baby for up to twelve months. During that time the parent on leave receives her/his salary and an additional DM 600 monthly (*Erziehungsgeld*) for a total of six months. Housewives with no outside job are also entitled to receive this stipend.

Im Bundestag haben Frauen bei den Grünen führende Positionen.

| Grammatik und Übungen _____

1   Simple past tense

Als Frau Wieland **anfing** zu arbeiten, **mußte** Klaus zu Hause mehr helfen. Er **wusch** die Wäsche, **räumte auf** und **ging** oft einkaufen.	When Mrs. Wieland started to work, Klaus had to help more at home. He did the laundry, straightened up the house, and often went shopping.

The simple past tense, like the perfect (see *Kapitel 6*, page 213) is used to refer to events in the past. However, the simple past and the perfect are used in different circumstances. The simple past tense is often called the narrative past because it is used to narrate a series of connected events in the past.

Monika: Was hast du gestern abend gemacht?
Dieter: Ich habe ein paar Briefe geschrieben.

The perfect tense is often called the conversational past because it is used in a two-way exchange to talk about events in the past.

Monika: Jürgen konnte nicht zur Fete kommen.
Dieter: War er krank, oder hatte er keine Zeit?

The simple past tense forms of the modals, **sein**, and **haben**, are used more frequently than the perfect tense, even in conversation.

2   Weak verbs in the simple past

Infinitive	Stem	Tense marker	Simple past
machen	mach-	-te	machte
sagen	sag-	-te	sagte

ich mach**te**	wir mach**ten**
du mach**test**	ihr mach**tet**
er/es/sie mach**te**	sie mach**ten**
Sie mach**ten**	

In the simple past tense, weak verbs add the past tense marker **-te** to the infinitive stem. All forms except the **ich**- and **er/es/sie**-forms add endings to the **-te** tense marker.

A   So war es früher.   Tell how it used to be in a woman's life. Use the simple past.

▶   Die Frau kocht das Essen.   *Die Frau kochte das Essen.*

1.   Schon die kleinen Mädchen lernen kochen.
2.   Nur sie spielen mit Puppen.
3.   Nur die Jungen spielen Fußball.
4.   Die Frauen machen die Hausarbeit nach der Arbeit.
5.   Frauen gehören nicht in Männerberufe.
6.   Man hört viele Vorurteile.
7.   Frauen verdienen weniger als Männer.

Früher als Krankenschwester arbeitete ich im St. Franziskus.
Heute fliege ich nach San Francisco.

Kommen Sie als Flugbegleiter zur Lufthansa.
Ⓢ **Lufthansa**

3   Weak verbs with tense marker *-ete*

Infinitive	Stem	Tense marker	Simple past
reden	red-	-ete	redete
arbeiten	arbeit-	-ete	arbeitete
regnen	regn-	-ete	regnete

The tense marker **-te** expands to **-ete** when added to verbs with a stem ending in **-d** or **-t**, or to verbs like **regnen** and **öffnen**. The addition of the **-e** ensures that the **-t**, as signal of the past, is audible.

B Wir fahren zelten. Tell about an outing some friends made. Use the simple past.

▶ Am Samstag regnet es nicht. *Am Samstag regnete es nicht.*

1. Gerd arbeitet nur bis 12 Uhr.
2. Gerd und Klaus zelten in den Bergen.
3. Alle baden im See°.   *lake*
4. Susi und Alex warten auf ihre Freunde.
5. Am Abend öffnen sie eine Flasche Bier.
6. Sie reden über dies und das.

4 Modals in the simple past

Infinitive	Simple past	English equivalent
dürfen	**durfte**	was allowed to
können	**konnte**	was able to
mögen	**mochte**	liked
müssen	**mußte**	had to
sollen	**sollte**	was supposed to
wollen	**wollte**	wanted to

In the simple past, the modals add the tense marker **-te** to the infinitive stem. **Dürfen, können, mögen**, and **müssen** lose the umlaut. **Mögen** also has a consonant change.

Though most English modals have past-tense forms, they are confusing because they are commonly used with conditional meanings. For example, the past of *may* is *might*. But since that form is used in conditional sentences (*I might go*), *was allowed to* is generally used to express the simple past of *may* (*I was allowed to go*). Similarly, the past of *can* is *could*. But since *could* is used in conditional sentences (*I could go*), *was able to* (*I was able to go*) is often substituted to distinguish it from the conditional use.

C Schade Say it's too bad that Klaus's attitude and lack of abilities kept him from getting the job he applied for. Use a **daß**-clause with the modal in last position.

▶ Klaus konnte keine Fremdsprachen. *Schade, daß er keine Fremdsprachen konnte.*

1. Er sollte sonntags arbeiten.
2. Er konnte auch nicht mit dem Computer arbeiten.
3. Er wollte es auch nicht lernen.
4. Er mochte den Chef nicht.
5. Klaus durfte also nicht dort arbeiten.
6. Er mußte sich einen anderen Job suchen.

In addition to the official *Frauenpolitik*, there exists an independent women's movement (*Frauenbewegung*), which encourages women to deal with their problems on a self-help basis. Many of the projects the *Frauenbewegung* inaugurated in the 1970s are now subsidized by the government: shelters for battered women (*Frauenhäuser*) and many of the day-care centers and individual day care in people's homes (*Kinderkrippen* and *Tagesmütter*). In some cities the influence of the *Frauenbewegung* can be seen in women's art centers, businesses, book stores (*Frauenbuchläden*) or cafés (*Frauencafés*), and in occupational training facilities for women.

D   Auf einer Geburtstagsfete   You and your friends planned a birthday party. Recall what happened, using the simple past of the modals.

▶   Ich will meine Freunde einladen.   *Ich wollte meine Freunde einladen.*

1.   Klaus kann die Platten nicht mitbringen.
2.   Katja muß noch abwaschen.
3.   Frank will abtrocknen.
4.   Michael soll das Wohnzimmer saubermachen.
5.   Die Gäste sollen in zwei Stunden kommen.
6.   Wir müssen daher schnell aufräumen.
7.   Jens kann leider nicht lange bleiben.

5   Irregular weak verbs + *haben* in the simple past

Infinitive	Simple past	Examples
bringen	brachte	Peter **brachte** die Blumen nach Hause.
denken	dachte	Jutta **dachte** an ihre Arbeit.
kennen	kannte	Wir **kannten** ihre Chefin.
nennen	nannte	Sie **nannten** das Kind nach dem Vater.
wissen	wußte	Du **wußtest** das schon, nicht?
haben	hatte	Ihr **hattet** wieder kein Geld?

Irregular weak verbs have a stem-vowel change in the simple past. **Haben** has a consonant change. The verbs **bringen** and **denken** also each have a consonant change.

E Vor Jahren Tell how people regarded the role of women a few years ago.

▶ Viele Leute haben wenig über die Emanzipation gewußt.

Viele Leute wußten wenig über die Emanzipation.

1. Sie haben nur typische Rollen von Mann und Frau gekannt.
2. Viele Frauen haben aber anders gedacht.
3. Sie haben neue Ideen gehabt.
4. Wir haben auch die Probleme gekannt.
5. Die Frau hat oft nur die Hausarbeit gekannt.
6. Die Kinder haben natürlich wie die Eltern gedacht.
7. Viele Männer, aber auch viele Frauen, haben Vorurteile gehabt.
8. Sie haben berufstätige Frauen „Rabenmütter" genannt.

F Eine Reise in die USA Tell about Monika's experiences. Use the simple past.

1. Last summer Monika made a trip to the U.S.A.
2. She traveled to Boston.
3. She thought Boston was [use *ist*] fantastic.
4. She could speak English well.
5. She wanted to study at a university there.
6. The semester cost a lot of money.

7. At a party, she talked with a German student.
8. They talked about life in America.
9. He knew a lot about Boston.
10. Monika had many questions.

6 Strong verbs in the simple past

Infinitive	Simple past stem
sprechen	sprach
gehen	ging

ich sprach	wir sprach**en**
du sprach**st**	ihr sprach**t**
er/es/sie sprach	sie sprach**en**
Sie sprach**en**	

A strong verb undergoes a stem change in the simple past. The tense marker **-te** is not added to strong verbs in the simple past. The **ich-** and **er/es/sie-** forms have no verb endings.

You must memorize the simple-past forms of strong verbs, because the stem change cannot always be predicted. Fortunately, the number of strong verbs in German is relatively small. Fewer than 125 of them are commonly used, and only about 60 of those are used in this book. Most of the remaining thousands of verbs are weak verbs.

A list of strong verbs used in this book is found in the Reference Section. In the vocabularies of this book, the simple past is printed after the infinitive, followed by the past participle: **liegen, lag, gelegen.**

G Ein Gespräch mit der Nachbarin Say that the people mentioned below spoke with a neighbor. Use the cued subjects and the simple past.

▶ Frau Berger spricht oft mit der Nachbarin.   *Frau Berger sprach oft mit der Nachbarin.*

1. Herr Wagner
2. Katja
3. ich
4. du
5. unsere Großeltern
6. Michael und Anja

Infinitive	Simple past stem
essen	aß
geben	gab
lesen	las
nehmen	nahm
sehen	sah
sprechen	sprach
treffen	traf

Infinitive	Simple past stem
liegen	lag
sitzen	saß
kommen	kam
tun	tat

H   Klaus' Geburtstagsparty   Tell a friend about Klaus's birthday party. Use the simple past.

▶   Wir kommen auch zu Klaus' Geburtstag.   *Wir kamen auch zu Klaus' Geburtstag.*

1. Karin and Ute sprechen natürlich über die Bürgerinitiative.
2. Alle essen Spaghetti.
3. Es gibt auch viel zu trinken.
4. Die Geschenke liegen auf dem Tisch.
5. Gerd sieht Monika auf der Party nicht.
6. Karin und Peter sitzen in der Küche.
7. Sie lesen die Zeitung.
8. Ihre Freunde tun nichts Besonderes.

Infinitive	Simple past stem
brechen	brach
helfen	half
stehen	stand
vergessen	vergaß
werfen	warf

Infinitive	Simple past stem
finden	fand
schwimmen	schwamm
trinken	trank

I   Letzten Sommer   Tell about the job you had last summer. Use the simple past.

▶   Ich stehe früh auf.   *Ich stand früh auf.*

1. Zuerst verstehe ich nichts.
2. Herr Schmidt hilft mir.
3. Frau Schneider und ich finden die Arbeit dann leicht.
4. Wir helfen der Chefin.
5. Um 10 Uhr trinken alle Kaffee.
6. Wir vergessen, wieder an die Arbeit zu gehen.
7. Nach der Arbeit schwimmen wir oft.

Infinitive	Simple past stem
bleiben	blieb
heißen	hieß
leihen	lieh
scheinen	schien
schreiben	schrieb
treiben	trieb

Infinitive	Simple past stem
gefallen	gefiel
halten	hielt
schlafen	schlief
laufen	lief

J   Ferien in den USA   Tell about Bärbel's vacation in the United States. Use the simple past.

▶ Sie bleibt nur zwei Wochen in den USA.   *Sie blieb nur zwei Wochen in den USA.*

1. Da scheint die Sonne auch nicht immer.
2. Kaum jemand läuft zu Fuß zum Supermarkt.
3. Sie schreibt viele Karten an ihre Freunde.
4. Die Kinder der Gastfamilie heißen Jennifer und Pamela.
5. Sie treibt viel Sport.
6. Sie leiht sich ein Auto.
7. Sie bleibt zwei Tage in Washington.
8. Das heiße Wetter gefällt ihr nicht.

Infinitive	Simple past stem
fahren	fuhr
tragen	trug
wachsen	wuchs
waschen	wusch

Infinitive	Simple past stem
fliegen	flog
schließen	schloß
verlieren	verlor
gehen	ging

K   Die Reise nach Frankfurt   Stefan and Elke meet at a street corner. Stefan talks about Jürgen's trip to Frankfurt. Restate in the simple past.

▶ Jürgen fährt mit dem Zug nach Frankfurt.   *Jürgen fuhr mit dem Zug nach Frankfurt.*

1. Seine Freundin fährt mit.
2. Sie gehen in viele Geschäfte.
3. Aber leider schließen die Geschäfte um 6 Uhr.
4. Dann gehen sie ins Kino.
5. Sie tragen einfach ihre Jeans.
6. Dann gehen sie ein Glas Wein trinken.
7. Sie fahren dann am Abend wieder nach Hause.

Infinitive	Simple past stem
sein	war
werden	wurde *To BECoME*

L   Noch einmal   Restate the conversational exchanges below in the simple past.

▶   Wie ist deine Erkältung?   *Wie war deine Erkältung?*
    — Ach, die ist nicht so schlimm.   *— Ach, die war nicht so schlimm.*

1.   Bist du in den Ferien zu Hause?
     — Nein, ich bin bei meinem Onkel.
2.   Seid ihr heute in der Bibliothek?
     — Ja, wir sind den ganzen Tag da.

M   Berufe   State the occupation of various people. Use the simple past.

▶   Erika wird Ingenieurin.   *Erika wurde Ingenieurin.*

1.   Du wirst Lehrer.
2.   Wir werden Programmierer.
3.   Inge wird Mathematiklehrerin.
4.   Klaus wird Sportlehrer.
5.   Marion und Monika werden Ärztinnen.
6.   Gerd wird Jurist.
7.   Karen wird Informatikerin.

7   Separable-prefix verbs in the simple past

Present	Simple past
Schmidts **laden** Ruth zum Kaffee **ein**.	Schmidts **luden** Ruth zum Kaffee **ein**.
Sie **zieht** sich früh **an**.	Sie **zog** sich früh **an**.
Sie **kommt** pünktlich **an**.	Sie **kam** pünktlich **an**.

In the simple past, as in the present, the separable prefix is separated from the base form of the verb and is in final position.

N   Sie hatte viel vor.   Tell what Karin did yesterday. Use the simple past.

▶   Karin steht früh auf.   *Karin stand früh auf.*

1.   Sie zieht sich an.
2.   Sie kauft schnell noch etwas ein.
3.   Sie lädt Hans zum Frühstück ein.

4. Peter kommt auch noch mit.
5. Sie haben vor, in die Stadt zu fahren.
6. Der Zug kommt pünktlich an.
7. In der Stadt sehen sie sich die Geschäfte an.

O Gestern Tell what you did yesterday, using the simple past.

▶ Ich stehe spät auf. *Ich stand spät auf.*

1. Ich ziehe mich schnell an.
2. Ich lade Peter ins Café ein.
3. Karin kommt mit.
4. Wir sehen uns die Universität an.
5. Es fängt an zu regnen.
6. Karin sieht müde aus.
7. Ich lade sie zu einem Bier ein.

Sie haben das Wort 5 (+ Remark)

Alles an einem Tag. Write what you did on a particular day last week. Put all of your sentences in chronological order except one. Read your sentences to a partner and see whether she/he can tell which one is out of place.

Telling about activities

8 Past perfect tense

Ich **hatte** vorher noch nie die Wäsche **gewaschen**.	I *had* never *washed* clothes before.
Zum Einkaufen **war** ich auch nicht oft **gegangen**.	I *had* also not *gone* shopping often.

The English past perfect tense consists of the auxiliary *had* and the past participle of the verb. The German past perfect tense consists of the simple past of **haben** or **sein** and the past participle of the verb.

Sie hat die Stelle bekommen, weil sie **gelernt hatte**, Programme zu schreiben.	She got the job because she had learned to write programs.
Sie konnte am Montag nicht anfangen, weil sie am Sonntag krank **geworden war**.	She couldn't begin on Monday, because she had gotten sick on Sunday.

The past perfect tense is used to report an event or action that took place before another event or action that was itself in the past.

P Ferien in den USA Thomas made a trip last year, but he tells about the one before that. Give the English equivalents.

▶ Ich war schon einmal in den USA gewesen.　　*I had already been in the USA once.*

1. Meine Freunde hatten mich eingeladen.
2. Sie waren alle zum Flughafen gekommen.
3. Ich hatte sie seit mehreren Jahren nicht gesehen.
4. Am ersten Tag hatten wir in einem guten Restaurant gegessen.
5. Die Freundlichkeit in Amerika hatte mir gefallen.
6. Wir hatten über die Unterschiede zwischen Deutschland und den USA geredet.
7. Ich hatte zum ersten Mal im Leben Weihnachtslieder im November gehört.

Q Es war niemand mehr da. Paul tells about the party that was over when he arrived at 1:30 A.M. Restate in the past perfect tense.

▶ Die Party hat schon aufgehört.　　*Die Party hatte schon aufgehört.*

1. Karin hat 30 Leute eingeladen.
2. Sie haben getanzt und Musik gehört.
3. Jeder hat etwas mitgebracht.
4. Alle haben Spaghetti gegessen.
5. Die ganze Küche war voll Spaghetti.
6. Alle haben die Party toll gefunden.
7. Erst um 1 Uhr morgens sind alle Gäste gegangen.
8. Wegen seiner Erkältung ist Wolfgang nicht gekommen.

R Jetzt hilft die Familie. Restate the sentences below. Put the main clause in the simple past or the perfect, and the dependent clause in the past perfect.

▶ Die Kinder haben alte Vorstel-　　*Die Kinder hatten alte Vorstel-*
lungen, weil sie alte Kinderbücher　　*lungen, weil sie alte Kinderbücher*
gelesen haben.　　*gelesen hatten.*

1. Die Bekannten kritisieren Frau Wieland, nachdem sie wieder mit der Arbeit angefangen hat.
2. Immer wenn sie abends nach Hause kommt, hat Herr Wieland schon das Essen vorbereitet.
3. Viele Frauen müssen die Hausarbeit machen, nachdem sie den ganzen Tag im Beruf gearbeitet haben.
4. Die Kinder können die Wäsche waschen, weil die Eltern es ihnen gezeigt haben.
5. Frau Wieland hat es leichter, nachdem die Familie angefangen hat zu helfen.

9   Uses of *als, wenn, wann*

Als Paula gestern in Hamburg war, ging sie ins Theater.	*When* Paula was in Hamburg yesterday, she went to the theater.
Wenn Erik in Hamburg war, ging er jeden Tag ins Theater.	*When [whenever, if]* Erik was in Hamburg, he went to the theater every day.
Wenn Renate in Hamburg ist, geht sie viel ins Kino.	*When [whenever, if]* Renate is in Hamburg, she goes to the movies a lot.
Wann gehen wir ins Kino?	*When* are we going to the movies?
Ich weiß nicht, **wann** wir ins Kino gehen.	I don't know *when* we're going to the movies.

Als, wenn, and **wann** are all equivalent to English *when*, but they are not interchangeable. **Als** is used to introduce a clause concerned with a single event in the past. **Wenn** is used to introduce a clause concerned with repeated events (*whenever*) or possibilities (*if*) in past time. **Wenn** is used also for single or repeated events in present or future time. **Wann** is used to introduce direct and indirect questions.

gegenüber dem Schauspielhaus

Espresso- und Cocktailbar · Biertheke · Restaurant

von morgens um 8 Uhr bis tief in die Nacht.

Kirchenallee 9
2000 Hamburg 1
Tel. 280 35 60

S   Eine berufstätige Mutter   Working both outside and inside the home is not easy for Frau Wieland. Tell about her situation by joining the sentences with **als, wenn,** or **wann** as appropriate.

▶ Frauen fangen mit der Arbeit an. Sie müssen oft noch die ganze Hausarbeit machen.

Wenn Frauen mit der Arbeit anfangen, müssen sie oft noch die ganze Hausarbeit machen.

1. Frau Wieland fing zu arbeiten an. Klaus lernte die Wäsche zu waschen.
2. Sie war oft müde. Sie kam nach Hause.
3. Klaus wollte essen. Er mußte erst einkaufen gehen.
4. Sie war letzten Sommer jede Woche vier Tage weg. Ihre Nachbarn kritisierten sie.
5. Ein Mann ist vier Tage weg. Niemand kritisiert ihn.
6. Ihre Nachbarn fragten sie. Will sie zu arbeiten aufhören?

Sie haben das Wort

Erzähle von dir.   Complete the following statements and share them with a partner. She/he may ask questions.

Recounting events

1. Als ich sieben Jahre alt war, ...
2. Als ich in die Schule ging, ...
3. Wenn ich müde bin, ...
4. Wenn ich Hausarbeit machen muß, ...
5. Wenn ich ...
6. Als ich ...

| Wiederholung

A   Neue Erfahrungen   The Fischers have learned something about German ideas. Tell about their experiences. Use the simple past.

1. Fischers leben erst seit einigen Wochen in Deutschland.
2. Viele Sachen sind noch neu für sie.
3. Da kommen an einem Sonntag deutsche Bekannte zum Kaffee.
4. Frau Fischer backt den Kuchen selbst.
5. Man sitzt am Kaffeetisch und spricht über Kinder, Schulen und Geschäfte.
6. Die Gäste trinken den Kaffee, aber sie essen nur wenig Kuchen.
7. Die Deutschen finden den Kuchen etwas merkwürdig.
8. Die Fischers lernen etwas Neues.

B   Ergänzen Sie!   Be sure to use the correct form of a verb from the list in each sentence.

     ansehen □ aussehen □ sehen

1. Der Kuchen _____ gut _____ .
2. _____ Sie mal das moderne Bild _____ . Furchtbar, nicht?
3. Karl _____ das Problem nicht.

     aufstehen □ stehen □ verstehen

4. Wir _____ sonntags spät _____ .
5. Klaus hat das Referat nicht _____ .
6. Warum _____ die Leute auf der Fete?

ankommen □ bekommen □ hereinkommen □ kommen

7. Kannst du morgen zu mir _____ ?
8. Haben Sie den Brief _____ ?
9. Karin und Udo _____ heute in München _____ .
10. Die Gäste sollen doch _____ .

C   **Was bedeutet das?**   The following sentences contain new words that are cognates or are related to German words you already know. Give the English equivalents of the sentences.

1. Ich kann mir nicht *vorstellen*, daß viele Kinder solche Vorstellungen von Frauen haben wie Peter Kraft.
2. Die Bilder sind eine schöne *Erinnerung* an meine Ferien in Deutschland. Ich erinnere mich besonders gern an die vielen schönen Blumen.
3. Vor der Vorlesung muß ich mich noch mit einem starken Kaffee *stärken*.
4. Berufstätige Frauen haben heute noch oft einen schweren *Kampf* zu kämpfen.
5. Haben Sie Herrn Schmidts Flaschen*sammlung* schon gesehen? Er sammelt Flaschen seit 20 Jahren.
6. Frag den *Franzosen* auf Französisch, wo das Restaurant ist!
7. Diesen Sommer bekommen wir Besuch aus der Schweiz. Meine Tante und mein Onkel *besuchen* uns eine Woche.

D   **Erzählen Sie von gestern!**   Use the simple past to tell what you did yesterday morning. Use appropriate expressions from the list; add other expressions, if you wish.

aufstehen □ sich baden □ sich die Haare kämmen □ sich anziehen □ Kaffee kochen □ ein Stück Toast essen □ Kaffee trinken □ Zeitung lesen □ sich die Zähne putzen □ zur Vorlesung gehen

E   **Was bedeutet das?**   Form compounds using the following words. Give the English equivalents of the compounds.

1. die Bilder + das Buch
2. die Farb(e) + der Fernseher
3. die Blumen + das Geschäft
4. die Kinder + der Garten
5. die Geschicht(e) + s + der Lehrer
6. die Weihnacht + s + das Geschenk
7. das Hotel + der Gast

F　Ihre Meinung

1. Wer macht die Hausarbeit bei Ihnen zu Hause?
2. Hat Ihre Mutter einen Beruf?
3. Sollen auch Jungen mit Puppen spielen?
4. Sind Frauen und Männer in Amerika gleichberechtigt?
5. Finden Sie, daß eine Frau berufstätig sein kann, auch wenn die Kinder noch klein sind?
6. Möchten Sie in einem Flugzeug sitzen, das eine Frau fliegt?

G　Wie sagt man das?

1. Helga Nolte is a doctor. Her husband is a lawyer.
2. Christa is an engineer. Her brother is a student.
3. Christine is a programmer. Her father is a butcher.
4. Mrs. Brown is a professor. Her son is a teacher.

H　Anregung

1. In German, list five points that describe how the situation for women was twenty years ago (*vor zwanzig Jahren*) and how it is today.
2. In German, compare the different status of men and women either as it was or as it is now. Are there still areas of inequality today? What are they?

Grammatik zum Nachschlagen ────────

Simple past of weak verbs　(A)

Infinitive	Stem	Tense marker	Simple past
glauben	glaub-	-te	glaubte
spielen	spiel-	-te	spielte

ich glaub**te**	wir glaub**ten**
du glaub**test**	ihr glaub**tet**
er/es/sie glaub**te**	sie glaub**ten**
Sie glaub**ten**	

In the simple past tense, weak verbs add the past tense marker **-te**. All forms except the **ich-** and **er/es/sie-** forms add endings to the tense marker **-te**.

Weak verbs with tense marker -*ete* (B)

Infinitive	Stem	Tense marker	Simple past
baden	bad-	-ete	badete
arbeiten	arbeit-	-ete	arbeitete
regnen	regn-	-ete	regnete

In verbs with a stem ending in **-d** or **-t**, and in some verbs ending in **-n** or **-m**, the tense marker **-te** expands to **-ete**.

Irregular weak verbs + *haben* in the simple past (E–F)

Infinitive	Simple past
bringen	brachte
denken	dachte
kennen	kannte
nennen	nannte
wissen	wußte
haben	hatte

Irregular weak verbs + **haben** undergo a stem change in the simple past.

Modals in the simple past (C–D)

Infinitive	Simple past
dürfen	durfte
können	konnte
mögen	mochte
müssen	mußte
sollen	sollte
wollen	wollte

In the simple past, the modals add the tense marker **-te** to the infinitive stem. **Dürfen, können, mögen,** and **müssen** lose the umlaut in the past tense. **Mögen** also has a consonant change.

Schubert kannte keine Musik-Box.

Er trug seine Musik im Kopf und in seinem Herzen.

Eltern, die auch ihr Kind zu aktivem Musizieren führen und es gegen die vielen Tagesreize schützen wollen, investieren frühzeitig in ein eigenes Instrument.

Beratung und Unterrichtsvermittlung in Ihrem Piano-Fachgeschäft.

Musizieren bringt ein Leben lang Freude!
Herzlich willkommen in Ihrem Piano-Fachgeschäft!

Simple past of strong verbs (G–M)

Infinitive	Simple past
gehen	ging
sehen	sah
schreiben	schrieb

ich ging	wir ging**en**
du ging**st**	ihr gingt
er/es/sie ging	sie ging**en**
Sie ging**en**	

Strong verbs undergo a stem change in the simple past. They do not take the past tense marker **-te**. The **ich-** and **er/es/sie-**forms have no verb endings.

Separable-prefix verbs in the simple past (N–Q)

Present tense	Simple past
Sie **kauft** immer im Supermarkt **ein**.	Sie **kaufte** immer im Supermarkt **ein**.
Er **kommt** immer **mit**.	Er **kam** immer **mit**.

In the simple past tense, as in the present tense, the separable prefix is separated from the base form of the verb and is in final position.

Past perfect tense (P–R)

Ich **hatte** vor zwei Tagen **angefangen** zu arbeiten.	I had started working two days before.
Er **war** am Montag **angekommen**.	He had arrived on Monday.

The German past perfect is a compound tense that consists of the simple past of either **haben** or **sein** plus the past participle of the main verb.

Sie ging am Samstag nicht mit, weil sie den Film schon am Freitag **gesehen hatte**.	She didn't go along (with us) on Saturday because she had already seen the film on Friday.

The past perfect tense is used to report an event or action that took place before another event or action that was itself in the past.

Uses of *als, wenn, wann* (S)

Als Inge Dieter gestern sah, sprachen sie über Politik.	*When* Inge saw Dieter yesterday, they talked about politics.
Wenn sie ihn sah, redete sie immer über Politik.	*When [whenever, if]* she saw him, she always spoke about politics.
Wenn wir in München sind, gehen wir ins Theater.	*When [whenever, if]* we are in Munich, we go to the theater.
Wann beginnt die Vorstellung?	*When* does the performance begin?
Ich weiß nicht, **wann** die Vorstellung beginnt.	I don't know *when* the performance begins.

Als, wenn, wann are equivalent to English *when,* but they are not interchangeable. Each word has a specific use. **Als** is used to introduce a clause concerned with a single event in past time. **Wenn** is used to introduce a clause concerned with repeated events (*whenever*) or possibilities (*if*) in past time. **Wenn** is used also for single or repeated events in present or future time. **Wann** introduces direct and indirect questions.

Kapitel 11

Lernziele

Sprechakte

Discussing leisure-time activities
Talking about potential, uncertain, or
  hypothetical situations in the present and
  the past
Making polite requests
Expressing wishes

Grammatik

Subjunctive
Conditional sentences

Vokabeln

Hobbies
Diminutive endings **-chen** and **-lein**
Immer + comparative

Landeskunde

Leisure time in the Federal Republic of
  Germany
Holidays in the Federal Republic of Germany
Three composers: Mozart, Beethoven, and
  Bach
Theater and film in the Federal Republic of
  Germany

Das alte Opernhaus in Frankfurt

Bausteine für Gespräche

Was hast du vor?

Beate: Sag mal, was machst du am Wochenende?

Stefanie: Unsere WG° macht eine Radtour an den Bodensee. Da fahre ich mit. Was hast du denn vor?

Beate: Unsere Band spielt bei einer Wahlveranstaltung.

Das würde ich lieber machen

Stefanie: Du, so was würde ich viel lieber machen als eine Radtour.

Beate: Wirklich? Wir könnten noch jemand für die Gitarre gebrauchen.

Stefanie: Ist das dein Ernst?

Beate: Klar. Der Achim kann nicht. Wegen Examen. Könntest du heute abend zur Probe kommen? Wir treffen uns um acht bei mir.

Stefanie: Ja, das ginge.

Beate: Also, bis dann!

What are your plans?

Say, what are you doing on the weekend?

My roommates are taking a bike trip down to Lake Constance. And I'm going along. What are your plans?

Our band is playing at a campaign rally.

I'd rather do that

Hey, I'd much rather do something like that than a bike trip.

Really? We could use another person on guitar.

Are you serious?

Sure. Achim can't make it. Because of his comprehensives. Could you come to rehearsal this evening? We'll meet at eight at my place.

Yes, that would be fine.

OK, till then!

WG = Wohngemeinschaft

Fragen

1. Was macht Stefanies Wohngemeinschaft?
2. Was hat Stefanie vor?
3. Warum kann Beate nicht mitfahren?
4. Was spielt Stefanie?
5. Warum braucht die Band jemand für die Gitarre?
6. Warum trifft sich die Band um acht?

Sie haben das Wort

A   Was machst du in der Freizeit?   Find out what a fellow student likes to do for fun. You may wish to refer to the Supplementary Word Set for *Kapitel 11* in the Reference Section for additional leisure-time activities.

Sie

Was sind deine Hobbys?

Gesprächspartner/in

Radfahren
Fußball
Musik
Science Fiction
Skilaufen
Spazierengehen°
Fotografieren°
Jogging°
Malen°
Sprachen lernen
ins Kino gehen
Computer-Programme schreiben

Was hast du am
   Wochenende vor?

Ich gehe | segeln°.
         | schwimmen
         | Ski laufen
         | windsurfen°
         | tanzen
Ich mache eine Wanderung°.
Ich will | Musik machen.
         | viel lesen
         | faulenzen°
         | arbeiten

Was würdest du gern in
   den Sommerferien machen?

Ich würde gern | nach Europa fliegen.
               | eine Radtour machen
               | jobben°
               | durch Europa trampen
               | faulenzen
Ich würde mich gern vom Streß° des
Semesters erholen°.

B   Was machst du gern?   Choose three answers for each of the questions in A. Then find fellow students who share your interests.

C   Was sagen Sie?

1. Was haben Sie am Wochenende gemacht?
2. Was haben Sie dieses Wochenende vor?
3. Möchten Sie eine Radtour machen? Wohin?
4. Spielen Sie ein Musikinstrument?
5. Möchten Sie in einer Band spielen?
6. Möchten Sie bei einer Wahlveranstaltung mitmachen°?

Vokabeln

— Substantive

die **Band, -s**   band
der **Bodensee**   Lake Constance
das **Examen, -**   (comprehensive) examination
das **Hobby, -s**   hobby
das **Jogging**   jogging, running
das **Musikinstrument, -e**   musical instrument
die **Probe, -n**   rehearsal

das **Programm, -e**   program
der **See, -n**   lake
der **Streß**   stress
die **Tour, -en**   tour, trip
die **Wanderung, -en**   hike
die **WG, -s** (*abbrev. for* die **Wohngemeinschaft, -en**)   group of people sharing an apartment

— Verben

sich erholen (von)   to recuperate (from) [an illness, fatigue, etc.]
faulenzen   to lounge around, be idle
fotografieren   to photograph
jobben (*colloq.*)   to have a job
malen   to paint
mit•machen (bei + *a group*)   to join in, participate; **Ich mache bei einem Spiel mit.**   I participate in a game.
segeln   to sail

spazieren•gehen, ging spazieren, ist spazierengegangen   to go for a walk
trampen   to hitch-hike
sich treffen (trifft), traf, getroffen (mit)   to meet; **Ich treffe mich mit Freunden.**   I'm meeting friends.
vor•haben   to intend, have in mind
windsurfen gehen   to go windsurfing; **surfen**   to surf
würde (*subjunctive of* **werden**)   would

— Andere Wörter

so was   something (like that)

— Besondere Ausdrücke

bis dann   till later
das ginge (nicht)   that would (not) be possible; that would (not) work

Ist das dein Ernst?   Are you serious?

The Federal Republic of Germany celebrates three secular holidays: New Year's Eve (*Silvester*), New Year's day (*Neujahr*) and *Tag der Arbeit* on May 1; and *Tag der deutschen Einheit* on June 17. May 1 is celebrated in honor of the workers, and June 17 commemorates an uprising of East Berlin workers in 1953.

The following Christian holidays are observed throughout the country: Good Friday (*Karfreitag*); Easter (*Ostern* — both *Ostersonntag* and *Ostermontag*); Ascension Day (*Christi Himmelfahrt*), the sixth Thursday after Easter; Pentecost (*Pfingsten*), the seventh Sunday and Monday after Easter; and December 25 and 26 (*erster Weihnachtstag* and *zweiter Weihnachtstag*). Five other Christian holidays are observed in some states, but not in all.

Der Deutsche Gewerkschaftsbund feiert den Ersten Mai (Marienplatz, München).

Freizeit

Vorbereitung auf das Lesen

• Zum Thema

1. Was ist Ihnen am wichtigsten: Arbeit, Freizeit, Freunde oder Familie?
2. Was meinen Sie? Was ist den typischen Amerikanern am wichtigsten: Arbeit oder Freizeit? Was ist den typischen Deutschen am wichtigsten?
3. Was machen Studenten an Ihrer Uni in der Freizeit?
4. Und was machen andere junge Leute?

• Leitfragen

1. Manche Leute glauben, daß für die Deutschen die Arbeit zuerst kommt. Wie ist es in Wirklichkeit?
2. Die Deutschen haben viel Freizeit. Wer hat wann frei: Arbeitnehmer, Jugendliche, Studenten?
3. Was machen junge Leute in ihrer Freizeit: Klaus, Susanne, eine Musikgruppe, Susannes Freunde, Susannes Bruder?

DIE DEUTSCHEN ARBEITEN IMMER. SIE SIND SEHR FLEISSIG.
UND SIE HABEN NIE ZEIT.

Dieses Bild von den Deutschen war lange Zeit sehr verbreitet°. Der *widespread*
Fleiß° der Deutschen war ebenso sprichwörtlich° wie ihre Ordnung. *diligence / proverbial*
In einer Umfrage° des Instituts für Freizeitforschung° in Hamburg *opinion poll / research on*
zeigten sich die Deutschen aber von einer ganz anderen Seite. Man fragte *leisure time*
5 sie: „Was ist Ihnen von diesen vier Dingen am wichtigsten: Arbeit,
Familie und Partnerschaft, Freizeit oder Freunde?" Die Antworten
zeigten dieses Bild: Am wichtigsten waren Familie und Partnerschaft. An
zweiter Stelle schon stand Freizeit, an dritter Freunde, und erst ganz am
Ende folgte Arbeit.
10 Die Freizeit wird schon aus dem Grund immer wichtiger, weil die
Deutschen immer mehr davon haben. Sonnabends haben die meisten
Arbeitnehmer frei. Die Arbeitswoche hat sich in den letzten 10 Jahren
von 45 auf 40 Stunden verkürzt°. In einigen Industrien arbeitet man schon *shortened*
38,5 Stunden. Das Ziel ist die 35-Stunden-Woche. Jugendliche gehen im
15 Durchschnitt° sechs Stunden am Tag zur Schule, den ganzen Nachmittag *on the average*
und Abend haben sie frei. Auch Studenten haben relativ viel Zeit, die° sie *which*
sich selbst einteilen° können. Sie sind unabhängiger° in ihrem Studium *arrange / more independent*
und nicht so gebunden durch den Stundenplan wie amerikanische
Studenten.
20 Klaus geht zum Beispiel morgens für eine Stunde zu einer Vorlesung,
dann noch einmal am späten Nachmittag. Dazwischen° sitzt er fast im- *in between*
mer in der Bibliothek und arbeitet, damit er den Abend frei hat. Dann
trifft er sich oft mit Freunden, und sie gehen in eine der Studenten-
kneipen, um ein Bierchen° zu trinken. Er geht am liebsten in Kneipen mit *small glass of beer*
25 live Musik. Man findet viele solche Gaststätten im Univiertel. Manchmal
spielen dort sogar klassische Gruppen, aber meistens gibt es Rock. Klaus
mag die Atmosphäre da. Gute Musik, gute Gespräche und gutes Bier —
was braucht man mehr?
Er geht auch sehr gern ins Kino, meistens in eines der Programmkinos° *art theaters*
30 in der Nähe der Uni. Neulich gab es eine Serie von französischen Filmen.
Die hat ihm gut gefallen. Und die Faßbinder-°Retrospektive fand er auch *[a German movie director]*
sehr gut.
Susanne würde auch gern öfter ins Kino gehen, wenn sie mehr Zeit
hätte. Aber sie studiert Musik und verbringt den größten Teil ihrer Freizeit
35 mit Musik. So spielt sie in einem Orchester und in einem Streich-
quartett°. Mit beiden hat sie viele Proben. *string quartet*
Angefangen hat sie in einem Jugendorchester, wo sie vor allem das
klassische Repertoire von Komponisten wie Mozart, Bach und Beethoven
kennenlernte. Seit etwa drei Monaten macht sie bei einer Musikgruppe
40 mit, die° vor allem politische und kritische Lieder singt. Die Gruppenmit- *that*

glieder schreiben ihre Texte und Lieder selbst, was° Susanne besonderen
Spaß macht. Überhaupt ist diese Gruppe eine ganz neue Erfahrung für sie,
weil sie bisher immer nur klassische bzw.° „ernste" Musik gemacht hat.
Ein paar Mal haben sie schon auf der Straße gespielt. Und im Moment
45 bereiten sie sich gerade auf ein Hinterhoffest° in ihrem Stadtviertel vor.
Die lokale Bürgerinitiative hat sie gefragt, ob sie Lust hätten, da
mitzumachen, und sie haben natürlich ja gesagt.

    Wenn sie mehr Zeit hätte, würde Susanne gern öfter ein paar Freunde
auf dem Lande besuchen. Die haben sich vor kurzem ein Bauernhaus
50 gemietet. Sie basteln dauernd° an dem Haus herum°. Den Freunden
macht das Renovieren soviel Spaß, daß sie ihre ganze Freizeit damit verbringen.

    Vor kurzem hat Susannes Bruder sie mit dem Motorrad hingefahren.
Für den ist das natürlich nur eine Entschuldigung, wieder eine Tour zu
55 machen, denn er ist begeisterter° Motorradfahrer. Und Susanne fährt
gern mit. Peter, einer der Freunde, hat ihr ganz stolz den Garten gezeigt.
Sie haben Tomaten, Mohren°, Gurken° und Zwiebeln° gepflanzt, und
alles sah sehr gut aus. Peter meinte: „Am liebsten würden wir nämlich nur
frisches, ungespritztes° Gemüse aus unserem eigenen Garten essen.
60 Wenn wir ein paar Jahre früher mit diesem Projekt hier angefangen hätten, könnten wir das heute schon. Na ja, vielleicht können wir das dann
im nächsten Jahr."

which

*bzw. = beziehungsweise: or,
rather*

courtyard party

continually / here and there

enthusiastic

carrots / cucumbers / onions

unsprayed

Fragen zum Lesestück

1. Welches Bild der Deutschen war lange sehr bekannt?
2. Was zeigte sich in der Umfrage?
   a. Was ist den Deutschen am wichtigsten?
   b. Was steht an zweiter (dritter, vierter) Stelle?
3. Warum wird die Freizeit immer wichtiger?
4. Wieviel Stunden am Tag gehen Jugendliche zur Schule?
5. Wann haben sie frei?
6. Wann geht Klaus zur Vorlesung?
7. Was machen er und seine Freunde abends oft?
8. Was gehört zu einem netten Abend für Klaus?
9. In was für Kinos geht Klaus gern?
10. Warum hat Susanne wenig Freizeit?
11. Wo hat Susanne Komponisten wie Bach, Beethoven und Mozart ken-
   nengelernt?
12. Was macht die Gruppe, bei der° sie seit drei Monaten mitspielt?
13. Was ist für Susanne bei dieser Gruppe neu?
14. Worauf bereiten sie sich gerade vor?

whom

15. Wen würde Susanne gern besuchen?
16. Was machen ihre Freunde mit dem Bauernhaus?
17. Was macht Susannes Bruder gern in seiner Freizeit?
18. Was würden die Freunde gern essen?
19. Warum können sie noch nicht viel Gemüse aus dem eigenen Garten essen?

Erzählen Sie!   Select one of the three topics below, A, B or C, to talk about this reading selection. Use the cued words.

A. Klaus in der Freizeit

   Stichworte: Vorlesung □ Bibliothek □ Kneipen □ Kino

B. Susanne in der Freizeit

   Stichworte: klassische Musik □ Jugendorchester □ Liedergruppe

C. Susannes Fahrt aufs Land

   Stichworte: mit dem Motorrad □ Bauernhaus renovieren □ Garten

Sie haben das Wort

A   In der Freizeit   Ask a fellow student about her/his leisure-time activities.

Fragen Sie eine(n) Bekannte(n),

1. was ihr/ihm am wichtigsten ist — Arbeit, Freizeit, Freunde oder Familie
2. wieviel Stunden sie/er in der Woche arbeitet
3. wo sie/er meistens arbeitet — in der Bibliothek oder zu Hause
4. ob sie/er viel Zeit in einer Kneipe verbringt
5. ob sie/er gern ausländische Filme sieht
6. welchen Film sie/er vor kurzem gesehen hat
7. welche klassische Musik sie/er gern hört — Mozart, Beethoven, Bach
8. ob sie/er gern moderne Musik hört
9. ob sie/er oft live Musik hört
10. welche Gruppe sie/er besonders gern hört
11. ob sie/er gern in einem Orchester oder in einer Rockgruppe spielen würde
12. ob sie/er gern ein Bauernhaus renovieren würde
13. was sie/er gern machen würde und warum sie/er das nicht macht

B   Ein Gespräch   With a partner, develop a conversation using one or two of the questions in A as a starting point.

> Discussing leisure-time activities

Johann Sebastian Bach.
Geb. d. 21. März 1685 zu Eisenach, gest. d. 28. Juli 1750 zu Leipzig.

Joh. Chrysost. Wolfgang Amadeus Mozart.
Geb. d. 27. Jan. 1756 zu Salzburg, gest. d. 5. Dez. 1791 zu Wien.

Ludwig van Beethoven.
Geb. d. 17. Dez. 1770 zu Bonn, gest. d. 26. März 1827 zu Wien.

Johann Sebastian Bach (1685–1750) is now considered the great musical genius of the baroque period. During his lifetime, however, he was acknowledged only as an organist. From 1723 on, Bach was the director of music at St. Thomas Church in Leipzig. Bach's reputation as a composer was established as late as 1829, when Felix Mendelssohn revived his "Passion according to St. Matthew" (*Matthäuspassion*). Other famous works by Bach include many of his 300 cantatas (*Kantaten*), his fugues (*Fugen*), the "Mass in B minor" (*Messe in h-moll*), and the "Brandenburg Concertos" (*Brandenburgische Konzerte*).

Wolfgang Amadeus Mozart (1756–1791) was born in Salzburg, Austria. He spent his last ten years in Vienna, where he died in poverty. During his short life Mozart wrote more than 600 works, including 40 symphonies. Among his best-known operas are "The Marriage of Figaro" (*Le Nozze Di Figaro*), *Don Giovanni*, *Cosi fan tutte*, and "The Magic Flute" (*Die Zauberflöte*).

Ludwig van Beethoven (1770–1827) was born in Bonn, Germany, but moved in 1792 to Vienna. He began to lose his hearing at the age of twenty and was unable to hear his own last compositions. The composer of nine symphonies, concerti, quartets and trios, sonatas, and an opera (*Fidelio*), Beethoven is regarded as one of the founders of musical romanticism.

Vokabeln

Substantive

die **Antwort, -en**   answer; **die Antwort auf eine Frage**   the answer to a question

der **Arbeitnehmer, - / die Arbeitnehmerin, -nen**   worker, employee

der **Bauer, -n, -n / die Bäuerin, -nen** farmer; peasant; das **Bauernhaus, -̈er**   farmhouse

die **Entschuldigung, -en**   excuse; apology; **Entschuldigung!**   Excuse me.

der **Fahrer, -** / die **Fahrerin, -nen**
  driver
das **Fest, -e**   celebration; feast; party
die **Freizeit**   leisure time
die **Gaststätte, -n**   restaurant, pub,
  bar
der **Grund, ⸚e**   reason; **aus diesem**
  Grund   for this reason
der **Hof, ⸚e**   courtyard
die **Industrie, -n**   industry
die **Jugend**   youth
der/die **Jugendliche, -n** (*noun decl. like*
  adj.)   young person

der **Komponist, -en, -en** / die
  Komponistin, -nen   composer
das **Mitglied, -er**   member (*of group*)
der **Moment, -e**   moment; **im Mo-**
  ment   at the moment; **Einen Mo-**
  ment, bitte!   Just a minute, please.
das **Orchester, -**   orchestra
die **Ordnung**   order
das **Studium**   studies
der **Stundenplan, ⸚e**   schedule
das **Viertel, -**   district; das
  Stadtviertel   city district

— Verben

basteln   to tinker (with), to work at a
  hobby
besuchen   to visit
binden, band, gebunden   to tie
mieten   to rent
pflanzen   to plant

singen, sang, gesungen   to sing
verbringen, verbrachte, verbracht
  to spend (*time*)
sich vor·bereiten (auf + *acc.*)   to
  prepare (for)

— Andere Wörter

bisher   until now
damit (*conj.*)   so that
ebenso   just as
französisch   French (*adj.*)

neulich   recently
sogar   even
stolz   proud(ly)

— Besondere Ausdrücke

auf dem Lande   in the country; **aufs**
  Land   to the country
immer mehr   more and more
in der Nähe   nearby, in the vicinity
Lust haben   to feel like; **Ich habe**

keine Lust zu arbeiten.   I don't
  feel like working; **Dazu habe ich**
  keine Lust.   I don't feel like it.
na ja   oh well
noch einmal   again, once more

Erweiterung des Wortschatzes

1   Dative -e

Susanne würde gern ein paar Freunde **auf dem Land(e)** besuchen. Wann
  fährt sie wieder **nach Haus(e)?**

An optional **-e** may be added to one-syllable masculine and neuter nouns in
the dative singular.

2   *Immer* + comparative

Die Freizeit wird **immer wichtiger**, weil die Deutschen **immer mehr** davon haben.	Leisure time becomes more and more important because the Germans have more and more of it.

The construction **immer** + comparative indicates an increase in the quantity, quality, or degree expressed by the adjective or adverb. English equivalents of this type of construction repeat the adjective or adverb.

A   Was bedeutet das?

1. Der Lebensstandard der Deutschen wird immer höher.
2. Die Wohnungen werden immer größer.
3. Sie tragen immer bessere Kleidung.
4. Die Arbeitszeit wird immer kürzer.
5. Die Ferien werden immer länger.
6. Immer weniger Leute bleiben während der Ferien zu Hause.
7. Das Leben wird immer schöner.

3   Diminutives *-chen* and *-lein*

die Stadt	city	**das Städtchen**	small town
das Buch	book	**das Büchlein**	little book
das Brot	bread	**das Brötchen**	roll

The diminutive form of nouns is made by adding the suffix **-chen** or **-lein**. The vowels **a, au, o,** and **u** take umlaut. Nouns ending in the suffix **-chen** or **-lein** are neuter, regardless of the gender of the original noun.

B   Hänschen klein   Form diminutives by adding **-chen** to the words listed below.

1. die Tochter
2. das Glas
3. die Hand
4. das Haus
5. die Karte
6. Hans
7. der Schlaf
8. der Sohn
9. Katrin

C   Brüderlein und Schwesterlein   Form diminutives by adding **-lein** to the words listed below.

1. das Auge
2. die Blume
3. der Brief
4. das Kind
5. der Vogel
6. der Tisch

| Übungen zur Aussprache

Review the pronunciation of **ei, eu (äu), au,** and **ie** in the Reference section at the end of the book. Read the words in each set of columns on this page first down, then across. Check your pronunciation by listening to your instructor or the tape.

[ai]	[oi]	[au]	[oi]	[ī]	[ai]
nein	neun	Maus	Mäuse	Miene	meine
heiser	Häuser	Haus	Häuser	Biene	Beine
Seile	Säule	Bauch	Bäuche	viele	Feile
Eile	Eule	Haufen	häufen	diene	deine
leite	Leute	Laute	Leute	Liebe	Leibe

Read the following sentences aloud, paying special attention to the way you pronounce the **eu (äu), au, ei,** and **ie** in the boldfaced words.

1. Herr **Neumann** ist **heute** nicht **einkaufen** gegangen.
2. Hat **Paula** schon **einen Brief** an **euch geschrieben?**
3. **Eugen** hat **Deutsch studiert.**
4. Abends geht **Klaus** mit **seinen Freunden** in **eine Kneipe.**
5. **Heike läuft** jeden Tag zur **Arbeit.**
6. **Dieter** hat **seit** Anfang **Mai sein eigenes Auto.**

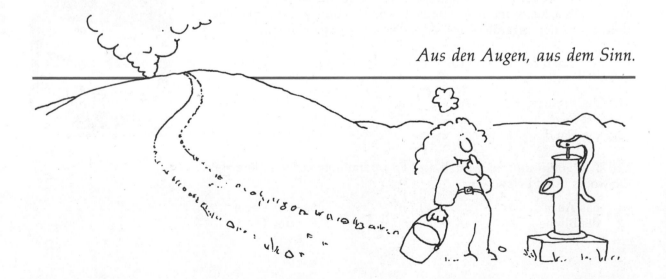

Aus den Augen, aus dem Sinn.

Bilder aus dem Alltag

Einkaufen Blumen spielen eine wichtige Rolle (Markt in Freiburg).

Oben links: **Ausbildung** Das Leibniz-Denkmal vor dem Hochhaus der Universität in Leipzig. *Oben rechts:* **Wohnen** Dorfstraße in den Schweizer Alpen. *Unten:* **Feste** Man feiert bei Kaffee und Kuchen. *Nächste Seite:* **Arbeit** Eine Bergbäuerin treibt im Frühjahr die Schafe auf die Weide (Tirol).

Oben links: **Freizeit** Zum Fußballspielen braucht man nur etwas Platz und einen Ball. *Unten ganz links:* **Einkaufen** Ein türkischer Imbißstand in München. *Unten links:* **Wohnen** Wohnblocks in Hamburg — viele Menschen wohnen auf engem Raum zusammen. *Diese Seite oben:* **Ausbildung** Diese Azubis lernen im Ausbildungszentrum bei Ford in Köln. *Diese Seite unten:* **Verkehr** Die Straßenbahn ist ein bequemes und sicheres Verkehrsmittel (Innsbruck).

Oben: **Freizeit** Türkische Gastarbeiter in Berlin-Kreuzberg spielen in ihrer freien Zeit. *Unten:* **Urlaub** Strandkörbe schützen gegen Wind und Sonne (an der Nordsee). *Nächste Seite:* **Freizeit** Man geht zusammen in die Stadt — Studenten in Berlin (Ost).

Oben links: **Freizeit** Der Schrebergarten — ein kleines Stück Land für den Großstädter. *Oben rechts:* **Einkaufen** Diese Verkaufsstelle bekommt ihre Backwaren aus einer zentralen Bäckerei (DDR). *Unten:* **Einkaufen** Auf dem Markt in Mainz.

| Grammatik und Übungen

1   General subjunctive

Indicative	Trudi kommt heute nicht.	Trudi is not coming today.
	Vielleicht kommt sie morgen.	Perhaps she'll come tomorrow.

In *Kapitel 1–10* you have been using verbs in sentences that make statements and ask questions dealing with "real" situations. Verbs of this type are said to be in the *indicative mood*. The indicative mood is used to make factual statements: *Trudi is not coming*, or statements that may possibly be or become true: *Perhaps she will come tomorrow.*

Subjunctive	Ich täte das nicht.	I would not do that.
	Hätte Stefan das getan?	Would Stefan have done that?

It is possible to talk about "unreal" situations by using verbs in the *subjunctive mood*. The subjunctive mood indicates a speaker's attitude toward a situation, a feeling that the situation is hypothetical, uncertain, potential, or contrary to fact. When a speaker says "I wouldn't do that," she/he means "if I were you [or he, she, or someone else]." When the speaker asks "Would Stefan have done that?" she/he is postulating a hypothetical situation.

Present time	Wenn ich heute nur Zeit hätte.	If I only had time today.
Past-time	Wenn ich gestern nur Zeit gehabt hätte.	If I only had had time yesterday.

Subjunctive forms express two time categories: present time (which can refer to the future as well) and past time.

2   The *würde*-construction

Würdest du mir **helfen**?   *Would* you *help* me?
Ich **würde** das nicht **machen**.   I *wouldn't do* that.

To talk about "unreal" situations in the present German often uses a **würde**-construction. English uses a *would*-construction. The **würde**-construction is used to express a speaker's attitude showing she/he thinks that a situation is potential or unlikely.

ich **würde** es **machen**	wir **würden** es **machen**
du **würdest** es **machen**	ihr **würdet** es **machen**
er/es/sie **würde** es **machen**	sie **würden** es **machen**
Sie **würden** es **machen**	

The **würde-**construction consists of a form of **würde** plus an infinitive. **Würde** is the subjunctive form of **werden**. It is formed by adding an umlaut to **wurde**, the simple past of **werden**.

A   Würden Sie mitfahren?   Schmidts are not having much luck in planning an outing. Tell who would not go along. Restate, using each of the cued subjects and the **würde-**construction.

▶   Ich würde nicht mitfahren. (Andrea)   *Andrea würde nicht mitfahren.*

1. Christoph
2. ihr
3. Eva und Hilde
4. du

5. mein Großvater
6. deine Tante
7. Christiane
8. wir

Theater in the German-speaking countries has a long tradition. The present system, of theater buildings with resident staffs, goes back to the eighteenth century. Some theaters started to operate regularly then, under the auspices of feudal courts. Today there are more than 200 theaters in the Federal Republic, 70 in the GDR, 20 in Austria, and 12 in Switzerland. In the Federal Republic, most of the theaters are repertory theaters under the jurisdiction of city governments *(Stadttheater)*, some are repertory theaters under the jurisdiction of an individual state *(Staatstheater)*, and some are private theaters *(Privattheater)*. In addition to the institutionalized theaters there are also many independent theaters *(Freie Theatergruppen)*. Because of the large government subsidies they receive every year, most theaters are able to keep ticket prices low, especially for students. Their repertory *(Spielplan)* usually includes a variety of German and foreign classics and modern plays.

Die Schaubühne am Lehniner Platz (Kurfürstendamm), West-Berlin.

3   Uses of the *würde*-construction

Hypothetical conclusions	Ich **würde** ihm **helfen**.	I *would help* him.
Wishes	Wenn er mir nur **helfen würde**!	If only he *would help* me!
Polite requests	**Würden** Sie mir bitte **helfen**?	*Would* you please *help* me?

The **würde**-construction is used in hypothetical conclusions, in wishes, and in polite requests.

B   Sabine würde das auch gern machen.   Say that Sabine would like to do things Susanne does. Use the **würde**-construction.

▶   Susanne spielt Gitarre.   *Sabine würde auch gern Gitarre spielen.*

1.   Susanne studiert Musik.
2.   Sie lernt neue Lieder.
3.   Susanne macht Musik auf der Straße.
4.   Sie besucht Freunde auf dem Land.
5.   Sie hilft im Garten.
6.   Abends gehen sie in eine Kneipe.

C   Beim Renovieren   Susanne's friends are renovating a farm. Restate their wishes, using the **würde**-construction.

▶   Hoffentlich helfen unsere Freunde bei der Arbeit.   *Wenn unsere Freunde nur bei der Arbeit helfen würden!*

1.   Hoffentlich hilft Christian beim Kochen.
2.   Hoffentlich bringt Susanne ihre Gitarre mit.
3.   Hoffentlich scheint bald die Sonne.
4.   Hoffentlich pflanzt Inge bald die Tomaten.
5.   Hoffentlich regnet es nicht.
6.   Hoffentlich kommt Christoph.

D   Beim Kaffee   The Bergers have invited their neighbors for coffee. Restate the sentences below, as polite requests, using the **würde**-construction.

▶   Kommen Sie bitte herein!   *Würden Sie bitte hereinkommen?*

1.   Gehen Sie bitte ins Wohnzimmer!
2.   Setzen Sie sich bitte!
3.   Nehmen Sie bitte von dem Kuchen!
4.   Erzählen Sie bitte von Ihrer Reise!
5.   Bleiben Sie bitte noch ein wenig!

4 Present-time subjunctive

Wenn du sie heute **sähest**, was würdest du sagen?	If you saw her today, what would you say?
Wenn ich morgen Zeit **hätte**, würde ich hingehen.	If I had time tomorrow, I would go there.
Wenn du viel Geld **hättest**, was würdest du tun?	If you had a lot of money, what would you do?

English sometimes uses a past tense (*saw, had*) to express the subjunctive in present or future time because it does not have a special subjunctive form. German uses the present-time subjunctive (**sähe, hätte**) to express the subjunctive in present or future time. For weak verbs, the present-time subjunctive is identical to the simple-past tense; for strong verbs, it is based on the simple-past tense.

5 Present-time subjunctive vs. the *würde*-construction

Present-time subjunctive	Würde-construction
Wenn er nur besser **spielte**!	Wenn er nur besser **spielen würde**!
Wenn sie nur etwas **täte**!	Wenn sie nur etwas **tun würde**!
Wenn er nur **ginge**!	Wenn er nur **gehen würde**!
Wenn sie nur **bliebe**!	Wenn sie nur **bleiben würde**!

In present-time the general subjunctive of the main verb may be used in place of the **würde**-construction to express hypothetical conclusions, wishes, and polite requests.

6 Subjunctive verb endings

ich	käm **e**	wir	käm **en**
du	käm **est**	ihr	käm **et**
er/es/sie	käm **e**	sie	käm **en**
	Sie	käm **en**	

The subjunctive endings above are used for all verbs. The endings **-est** and **-et** often contract to **-st** and **-t: kämest > kämst, kämet > kämt**.

E Wer möchte mitkommen? Beate and Mark are going to the museum on Saturday morning. Say that the people mentioned below would like to come along also.

▶   Christel käme gern mit. (Michael)   *Michael käme auch gern mit.*

1.	meine Eltern	3.	Julia	5.	er
2.	du	4.	Frau Berger	6.	Kai und Monika

7   Subjunctive of strong verbs

	Simple past	Present-time subjunctive
er/es/sie	blieb war zog sich an fuhr	blieb**e** w**ä**re z**ög**e sich an f**üh**re

The present-time subjunctive of a strong verb is formed by adding subjunctive endings to the simple-past stem of the verb. An umlaut is added to the stem vowels **a, o,** or **u**.

F   Wenn das nur ginge!   The Webers are going on a short trip to Berlin. Restate their wishes, using present-time subjunctive.

▶   Wenn Christian nur mitkommen würde!   *Wenn Christian nur mitkäme!*

1.   Wenn wir nur länger bleiben würden!
2.   Wenn wir nur öfter ins Kino gehen würden!
3.   Wenn wir nur den Dörrie-Film sehen würden!
4.   Wenn Stephanie nur ein schönes Kleid finden würde!
5.   Wenn Sascha sich nur schneller anziehen würde!
6.   Wenn wir nur bald etwas essen würden!
7.   Wenn wir nur nach Ost-Berlin fahren würden!
8.   Wenn die Berliner nur nicht so schnell sprechen würden!
9.   Wenn wir nur bald nach Berlin zurückkommen würden!

8   Subjunctive of weak verbs

	Simple past	Present-time subjunctive
er/es/sie	spielte kaufte arbeitete badete	**spielte** **kaufte** **arbeitete** **badete**

The present-time subjunctive forms of weak verbs are identical to the simple-past forms.

G   Wenn Susanne das nur machte!   Susanne's friends at the farm hope she'll come and play for them. Restate their wishes, using present-time subjunctive of the weak verbs.

▶   Vielleicht besucht Susanne uns.   *Wenn Susanne uns nur besuchte!*

1. Vielleicht arbeitet sie morgen nicht.
2. Vielleicht spielt sie etwas für uns.
3. Vielleicht machen ihre Freunde mit.
4. Vielleicht hören wir die neuen Lieder.
5. Vielleicht lernen wir sie morgen.
6. Vielleicht kauft Dieter auch eine Gitarre.
7. Vielleicht kostet sie nicht viel.

9   Subjunctive of irregular weak verbs and of *haben*

	Simple past	Present-time subjunctive
er/es/sie	brachte	brächte
	dachte	dächte
	kannte	kennte
	nannte	nennte
	wußte	wüßte
	hatte	hätte

The present-time subjunctive forms of irregular weak verbs and of **haben** are like the simple-past forms, but with an umlaut added. Note that **kennte** and **nennte** are written with an **e** instead of an **ä**.

H   Ein gebrauchtes Motorrad   Adrian is talking to friends about going to buy a used motorcycle. Stefanie has the newspaper with the ad. Restate Adrian's wishes, using the present-time subjunctive of the irregular weak verbs.

▶   Hoffentlich bringt Stefanie die   *Wenn Stefanie nur die Zeitung*
Zeitung mit.   *mitbrächte!*

1. Hoffentlich denkt sie daran.
2. Hoffentlich hast du Zeit, das Motorrad anzusehen.
3. Hoffentlich weiß Stefanie, wo die Straße ist.
4. Hoffentlich weiß sie, wie spät es ist.
5. Hoffentlich bringt sie genug Geld mit.

The German movie industry flourished during the era of silent films and early "talkies" (1919–1932). Directors like Fritz Lang, F. W. Murnau, and F. W. Pabst were considered among the finest in the world, and the German use of the "moving camera" influenced many directors.

During the Nazi era (1933–1945), many great German and Austrian filmmakers emigrated to the United States and other countries. Some of them never returned; this loss led to a period of mediocrity in German filmmaking that lasted until the mid-sixties. At that point a generation of young filmmakers began to introduce the New German Cinema (*Neuer deutscher Film*). Many of those directors are now famous, including the late Rainer Werner Fassbinder, Werner Herzog, Wim Wenders, and Wolfgang Petersen. Since then other directors such as Margarethe von Trotta, Volker Schlondorff, and Doris Dörrie have gained international recognition.

---

oben links: *Rainer Werner Fassbinder.* unten links: *Margarethe von Trotta.* rechts: *Günter Grass bei den Dreharbeiten zu dem Film* **Die Blechtrommel.**

Sie haben das Wort

A   Hättest du Lust?   A friend asks whether you feel like doing something. Respond.

Expressing wishes

Gesprächspartner/in

Hättest du Lust,
| **schwimmen zu gehen?** |
| ins Kino zu gehen |
| eine Party zu geben |
| eine Radtour zu machen |
| Musik zu hören |
| fernzusehen |
| Russisch zu lernen |

Sie

Das wäre schön.
Wenn es nur wärmer wäre.
Das würde ich gern machen.
Das würde Spaß machen.
Wenn ich nur Zeit hätte.
Dazu hätte ich keine Lust.

B   Das ist ja merkwürdig!   Think of several unusual activities and try to find people who would like to do them. You may wish to refer to the Supplementary Word Sets for *Kapitel 11* in the Reference Section.

▶   Hättest du Lust, Insekten zu sammeln?

10   Modals in present-time subjunctive

er/es/sie	Simple past	Present-time subjunctive	Infinitive
	durfte	**dürfte**	dürfen
	konnte	**könnte**	können
	mochte	**möchte**	mögen
	mußte	**müßte**	müssen
	sollte	**sollte**	sollen
	wollte	**wollte**	wollen

Modals with an umlaut in the infinitive also have an umlaut in the present-time subjunctive.

Müßtest du die Arbeit allein machen?	Would you have to do the work alone?

The modals are generally used in their subjunctive form rather than as infinitives with the **würde-**construction.

Dürfte ich auch mitkommen?	Might I come along, too?
Könntest du noch etwas bleiben?	Could you stay a while?
Müßte sie vor allen Leuten sprechen?	Would she have to speak in front of all the people?
Möchten Sie in einer Stunde essen?	Would you like to eat in an hour?
Solltet ihr jetzt nicht gehen?	Shouldn't you be going now?

The subjunctive forms of the modals are frequently used to express polite requests or wishes.

Ich wollte, ich hätte Zeit.	I wish I had time.
Ich wollte, sie käme bald.	I wish she would come soon.

The expression **ich wollte** is used frequently to introduce wishes. Note that the verb **wollte** is subjunctive. Thus, strictly, **ich wollte** is equivalent to *I would wish*.

I   Etwas höflicher, bitte!   You and some friends are getting ready to go out for the evening. You express some concerns and some orders. Soften the tone of the statements and questions by using the present-time subjunctive of the modals.

▶   Können wir die Gaststätte allein finden?   *Könnten wir die Gaststätte allein finden?*

1. Können wir nicht bald gehen?
2. Du mußt noch abwaschen.
3. Kann ich dir helfen?
4. Kann die Musik etwas lauter sein?
5. Dürfen Susi und Christiane mitkommen?

6. Sollen wir Gerd nicht auch einladen?
7. Darf ich für euch alle etwas zu trinken kaufen?

J   Wenn es nur anders wäre.   Espress wishes to a friend about many things in your dormitory you would like to be different.

▶   Klaus kocht immer Spaghetti.   *Ich wollte, Klaus kochte nicht immer Spaghetti.*

▶   Michael macht das Zimmer nicht sauber.   *Ich wollte, Michael machte das Zimmer sauber.*

1. Martin lernt nicht für das Examen.
2. Christoph hört immer Musik.
3. Bernd redet so viel.
4. Wolfgang kommt immer zu spät.

5. Stefan macht die Tür nicht zu.
6. Dieters Sachen liegen hier herum.

Sie haben das Wort

Schön wär's!   Think of several "wishes" related to your own living situation. Share these with a partner.

> Expressing wishes

▶   Ich wollte, ich müßte nicht im Garten arbeiten.

11   Conditional sentences

A conditional sentence contains two clauses: the condition (**wenn**-clause) and the conclusion. The **wenn**-clause states the conditions under which some event mentioned in the conclusion may or may not take place.

• *Conditions of fact*

Wenn ich Zeit **habe, komme** ich **mit.**

If I *have* time (maybe I will, maybe I won't), I'll *come* along.

Conditions of fact are conditions that are capable of fulfillment. Indicative verb forms are used in conditions of fact.

• *Conditions contrary to fact*

Wenn ich Zeit **hätte, würde** ich **mitkommen**.	If I *had* time [but I don't], I *would* come along.
Wenn ich Zeit **hätte, käme** ich mit.	

A sentence with a condition contrary to fact indicates a situation that will not take place. The speaker only speculates on how some things could or would be under certain conditions (if the speaker had time, for example).

In present time, the condition (**wenn**-clause) contains the subjunctive form of the main verb, and the conclusion usually contains a **würde**-construction. In formal usage the conclusion may contain a subjunctive form of the main verb instead.

K   In den Ferien   Take the role of Frank. Tell what you would do during your vacation if certain conditions were fulfilled. Use the general subjunctive for the condition and the **würde**-construction for the conclusion.

▶   Wenn ich ein Auto habe, fahre ich   *Wenn ich ein Auto hätte, würde*
    in die Schweiz.   *ich in die Schweiz fahren.*

1.   Wenn es dort schneit, laufe ich Ski.
2.   Wenn es Sommer ist, zelte ich.
3.   Wenn ich nicht müde bin, wandere ich in den Bergen.
4.   Wenn ich Zeit habe, schreibe ich viele Karten.
5.   Wenn ich zu Hause bleibe, lese ich viel.
6.   Wenn ich aber viel Geld habe, fliege ich nach Australien.

• *Modals,* haben, *and* sein *in conditions contrary to fact*

Ich **könnte** eine Reise machen, wenn ich Geld hätte.	I *could take* a trip, if I *had* money.
Es **wäre** schön, wenn ich Geld hätte.	It *would be* nice, if I *had* money.
Ich **hätte** ein neues Auto, wenn ich Geld hätte.	I'd *have* a new car, if I *had* money.

The modals and the verbs **haben** and **sein** are generally used in their subjunctive form rather than as infinitives with the **würde**-construction.

L   Nach dem Examen   Tell Ruth what she could do if her comprehensive exams were over — depending on certain conditions, of course.

▶   Wenn du dein Examen hinter dir hast, mußt du nicht mehr lernen.   *Wenn du dein Examen hinter dir hättest, müßtest du nicht mehr lernen.*

1.   Wenn das Wetter schön ist, kannst du zelten gehen.
2.   Wenn du eine Reise machen willst, sollst du nach Dänemark fahren.
3.   Wenn du müde bist, kannst du schlafen.
4.   Wenn du Geld hast, kannst du dir viele Platten kaufen.
5.   Wenn du willst, kannst du auch zu einer Party gehen.
6.   Wenn du Hunger hast, kannst du Steak essen.

Sie haben das Wort

Was ich gern machen würde, wenn ...   Think of five things you would do if conditions were different. Share your thoughts about your hypothetical situations with a partner who may ask you for more details.

Sie	*Gesprächspartner/in*
Wenn ich Geld hätte, würde ich ein neues Auto kaufen.	Warum würdest du ein neues Auto kaufen?

> Talking about hypo-thetical situations

12   Past-time subjunctive

Wenn sie das **gewußt hätte, hätte** sie mir **geholfen**.	If she *had known* that, she *would have helped* me.
Wenn sie das **gewußt hätte, wäre** sie nicht **mitgekommen**.	If she *had known* that, she *would* not *have come* along.

The past-time subjunctive consists of the subjunctive forms **hätte** or **wäre** + past participle. The past-time subjunctive is used to express hypothetical conclusions, wishes, and contrary-to-fact conditions in past time.

M   Sie hätten es anders gemacht.   Several of your friends are not satisfied with yesterday's activities. Restate the sentences below, using the past-time subjunctive.

▶   Karin ginge lieber schwimmen.   *Karin wäre lieber schwimmen gegangen.*

1.   Du hättest doch keine Zeit, schwimmen zu gehen.
2.   Es wäre phantastisch, schwimmen zu gehen.
3.   Ich täte das auch gern.
4.   Ich ginge gern mit.
5.   Ich brächte ein Picknickessen mit.
6.   Ihr kämt sicher auch.
7.   Heike und Horst wanderten lieber.

N Wenn sie das gewußt hätte ... Restate the sentences below, telling what Ursel would or would not have done if only she had known that the weather was going to be nice over the weekend.

▶ Sie ist übers Wochenende nicht weggefahren.

Wenn sie das gewußt hätte, wäre sie übers Wochenende weggefahren.

▶ Sie ist zu Hause geblieben.

Wenn sie das gewußt hätte, wäre sie nicht zu Hause geblieben.

1. Sie ist nicht an den See gefahren.
2. Sie hat ihre Freunde nicht zum Picknick eingeladen.
3. Sie hat nicht gezeltet.
4. Sie ist nicht schwimmen gegangen.
5. Sie ist ins Kino gegangen.
6. Sie hat soviel geschlafen.

13 Modals in past-time subjunctive

Das hättest du wissen sollen.   You *should have known* that.
Ich hätte dir helfen können.   I *could have helped* you.

When a modal is used in the past subjunctive with another verb, an alternative past participle of the modal, identical with the infinitive, is used. This is called the "double infinitive" construction. The modal always occurs at the very end of the clause.

O Was wäre passiert, wenn ... ? Dieter's company is expecting a foreign visitor. He speculates what they will do once the visitor arrives. However, the visit does not take place. Take Dieter's role and say what would have happened if the visit had taken place. Use the past-time subjunctive of the modal.

▶ Ich müßte Englisch sprechen.   *Ich hätte Englisch sprechen müssen.*

1. Die Besucherin könnte mein Englisch nicht verstehen.
2. Ich könnte ihr Deutsch nicht verstehen.
3. Wir könnten einander kaum verstehen.
4. Ich müßte ihr die Firma zeigen.
5. Wir könnten uns auch die Stadt ansehen.
6. Wir dürften in einem teueren Restaurant essen.
7. Wir dürften mit dem Taxi fahren.
8. Ich müßte sie zum Bahnhof bringen.

| Wiederholung

A   Was hat er gemacht?   Tell what Klaus did yesterday. Restate the sentences below in the simple past tense.

1. Er geht morgens für eine Stunde zu einer Vorlesung.
2. Nachmittags sitzt er in der Bibliothek und arbeitet.
3. Den Abend hat er frei.
4. Er trifft sich in einer Kneipe mit Freunden.
5. Es gibt da live Musik.
6. Es ist eine Volksliedgruppe.
7. Alle Studenten singen mit.

B   Meine Freundin Susanne   Complete each sentence below with an appropriate preposition.

1. Erinnerst du dich _____ meine Freundin Susanne?
2. Mit sechs Jahren hat sie _____ Klarinette angefangen.
3. Sie macht _____ einer Volksliedgruppe mit.
4. Sie bereiten sich _____ das Hinterhoffest vor.
5. Susanne erzählt ihrem Freund Dieter _____ ihrer Musik.
6. Er arbeitet _____ Siemens.
7. In seiner Freizeit renoviert er ein Bauernhaus, und er spricht gern _____ Susanne _____ seine Pläne.

C   Was möchten Sie?   Tell what you would like by using one or more of the adjectives in parentheses — or by supplying your own — to modify the boldfaced nouns.

1. Wenn ich Geld hätte, würde ich mir ein _____ **Auto** kaufen. (klein, groß, billig, teuer)
2. Ich wollte, man würde mich zu einer _____ **Fete** einladen. (nett, toll, klein, laut, interessant)
3. Ich möchte einen _____ **Pulli** kaufen. (warm, blau, leicht, toll)
4. Ich würde gern mal einen _____ **Film** sehen. (toll, interessant, schön, modern, klassisch, gut)
5. Ich möchte eine _____ **Reise** nach Deutschland machen. (lang, kurz, billig)
6. Ich möchte einen Computer haben, aber es müßte ein _____ **Computer** sein. (billig, teuer, klein, einfach, groß, schnell, bedienungsfreundlich°)

user-friendly

D   Was sagen Sie?   Say what you would do under certain conditions.

Was würden Sie tun, ...

1.   wenn Sie plötzlich viel Geld bekämen?
2.   wenn heute Sonntag wäre?
3.   wenn Sie heute Geburtstag hätten?
4.   wenn Sie jetzt zwei Wochen Ferien hätten?
5.   wenn Sie das teure Essen im Restaurant nicht bezahlen könnten?
6.   wenn Freunde eine Party gäben und Sie nicht einlüden?

E   Der Lebensstandard in der Bundesrepublik   Bärbel makes a few comments about the standard of living in the Federal Republic of Germany. Restate her comments by completing the second sentence in each pair below. Supply **zu** where necessary.

▶   Die Deutschen haben einen hohen   *Die Deutschen scheinen einen*
Lebensstandard   *hohen Lebensstandard zu haben.*
Die Deutschen scheinen _____ .

1.   Natürlich arbeiten sie schwer.   4.   (Man) versteht das.
Sie müssen _____ .   Das ist leicht _____ .
2.   Einige fahren in den Ferien ins Ausland.   5.   Energie wird teurer.
Einige haben genug Geld _____ .   Energie fängt an _____ .
3.   Viele kaufen immer mehr.   6.   Viele verstehen die Umweltprobleme besser.
Viele wollen _____ .   Viele scheinen _____ .

F   Wie sagt man das?

1.   I have nothing planned on the weekend.   4.   Would you like to take a walk?
(*use* **vorhaben**)   —Sure. How would it be this afternoon?
—Would you like to take a bike trip?   5.   Could you help me, please?
2.   Our group could still use someone for   —I wish I had (the) time.
the guitar on Saturday night.   6.   Would you like to watch TV?
Could you play?   —No. I don't feel like it.
—Yes, that would be fine.
3.   Could it be that Erik is ill?
—I don't know. You could ask him.

G   Anregung

1.   Keep a diary (**Tagebuch**) in German for a week, making entries concerning leisure-time activities.
2.   Imagine you are attending a German university for a year. Write a letter in German to a friend, telling what you and your German friends do in your free time.

| Grammatik zum Nachschlagen ———————

General subjunctive

Indicative	Ich **komme** nicht zur Party. Was **hast** du gemacht?	I*'m* not *coming* to the party. What *did* you *do*?
Subjunctive	Ich **käme** nicht zur Party. Was **hättest** du gemacht?	I *wouldn*'t *come* to the party. What *would* you *have done*?

In both English and German, the indicative mood is used to talk about real conditions or factual situations. The subjunctive mood is used to talk about unreal, hypothetical, uncertain, or unlikely events.

For example, the first subjunctive sentence above, *I wouldn't come to the party [even if I had been asked]*, refers to a hypothetical situation; it makes clear the person hasn't been asked.

Present-time subjunctive	Wenn er nur heute nach Hause **ginge!**	If he *would* only *go* home today!
Past-time subjunctive	Wenn er nur gestern nach Hause gegangen **wäre!**	If he *had* only *gone* home yesterday!

Subjunctive forms express two time categories: present time (which can refer to the future as well) and past time.

The würde-construction (A–D)

• *Uses*

Ich **würde** das nicht **machen.**   I *would* not *do* that.
Würden Sie dieses Buch **kaufen?**   *Would* you *buy* this book?

To talk about "unreal" situations in the present, German may use a **würde**-construction. The **würde**-construction consists of a form of **würde** + infinitive (e.g., **machen, kaufen**) and is equivalent to the English construction *would* + infinitive (e.g., *do, buy*). The **würde**-construction is often called the *conditional*.

• *Forms*

ich **würde** es **machen**	wir **würden** es **machen**
du **würdest** es **machen**	ihr **würdet** es **machen**
er/es/sie **würde** es **machen**	sie **würden** es **machen**
	Sie **würden** es **machen**

The **würde**-construction consists of a form of **würde** + infinitive. **Würde** is the subjunctive form of **werden**. It is formed by adding an umlaut to **wurde**, the simple past of **werden**.

Present-time subjunctive

Wenn ich morgen nur Zeit **hätte**.   If I only *had* time tomorrow.

English sometimes uses a past-tense form (e.g., *had*) to express present- or future-time subjunctive. English does not have a special subjunctive form for most verbs.

Ich **täte** das nicht.
Ich **würde** das nicht **tun**. }   I *wouldn't do* that.

German does have subjunctive forms of main verbs (e.g., **täte**) that may be used in place of the **würde**-construction.

Subjunctive verb endings (E)

ich käm **e**	wir käm **en**
du käm **est**	ihr käm **et**
er/es/sie käm **e**	sie käm **en**
	Sie käm **en**

The subjunctive endings above are used for all verbs. The subjunctive verb endings **-est** and **-et** often contract to **-st** and **-t: kämest** > **kämst, kämet** > **kämt**.

Subjunctive of strong verbs (F)

Infinitive	Simple past	Present-time subjunctive
gehen	ging	**ginge**
sein	war	**wäre**
anziehen	zog an	**zöge an**
fahren	fuhr	**führe**

The present-time subjunctive of strong verbs is formed by adding subjunctive endings to the simple-past stem. An umlaut is added to the stem vowels **a, o,** and **u.**

Subjunctive of weak verbs (G)

Infinitive	Simple past	Present-time subjunctive
kaufen	kaufte	**kaufte**
arbeiten	arbeitete	**arbeitete**

The present-time subjunctive forms of weak verbs are identical to the simple-past forms.

Subjunctive of irregular weak verbs and of *haben* (H)

Infinitive	Simple past	Present-time subjunctive
bringen	brachte	**brächte**
denken	dachte	**dächte**
kennen	kannte	**kennte**
nennen	nannte	**nennte**
wissen	wußte	**wüßte**
haben	hatte	**hätte**

The present-time subjunctive forms of irregular weak verbs and of **haben** are like the simple-past forms, but with an umlaut added. Note that **kennte** and **nennte** are written with an **e** instead of an **ä**.

Modals in present-time subjunctive (I, J)

Infinitive	Simple past	Present-time subjunctive
dürfen	durfte	**dürfte**
können	konnte	**könnte**
mögen	mochte	**möchte**
müssen	mußte	**müßte**
sollen	sollte	**sollte**
wollen	wollte	**wollte**

A modal that has an umlaut in the infinitive also has an umlaut in the present-time subjunctive.

Past-time subjunctive (M, N)

Wenn ich Zeit **gehabt hätte, wäre** ich **gekommen**.

If I *had had* time, I *would have come*.

Wenn sie hier **gewesen wäre, hätte** ich sie **gesehen**.

If she *had* been here, I *would have seen* her.

The past-time subjunctive consists of the subjunctive forms **hätte** or **wäre** + a past participle. A **würde**-construction exists in past-time, but it is not commonly used: **Ich würde es nicht getan haben.**

Modals in past-time subjunctive (O)

Das **hättest** du **wissen sollen**.

You *should have known* that.

Ich **hätte** dir **helfen können**.

I *could have helped* you.

When a modal is used in the past subjunctive with another verb, an alternative past participle of the modal, identical with the infinitive, is used. This construction is called the "double infinitive" construction. The modal always occurs at the very end of the clause.

Uses of the *würde*-construction and the subjunctive of the main verb

- *Hypothetical conclusions*

Ich **würde** das nicht **tun.** }
Ich **täte** das nicht.

I *would*n't *do* that [if I were you].

Ich **hätte** das auch **getan**.

I *would have done* that too.

- *Wishes*

Wenn Inge das nur **tun würde!** }
Wenn Inge das nur **täte!**

If only Inge *would do* that!

Wenn Gabi das nur **getan hätte!**

If only Gabi *had done* that!

- *Polite requests*

Würden Sie das für mich **tun?** }
Täten Sie das für mich?

Would you *do* that for me?

Könnten Sie das für mich **tun?**

Could you *do* that for me?

- *Conditions contrary to fact*   (K, L)

Present time	
Wenn ich Zeit **hätte, käme** ich. Wenn ich Zeit **hätte, würde** ich **kommen.**	If I *had* time [but I don't], I *would come.*

Past time	
Wenn ich Zeit **gehabt hätte, wäre** ich **gekommen.**	If I *had had* time [but I didn't], I *would have come.*

Contrary-to-fact sentences consist of two clauses: the condition (**wenn**-clause) and the conclusion. Conditions contrary to fact are not capable of fulfillment. Subjunctive verb forms are used to express conditions contrary to fact. To speculate about how the condition could be in the present or future, the present-time subjunctive is used in the **wenn**-clause, and the present-time subjunctive or a **würde**-construction is used in the conclusion. To speculate about how conditions might have been in the past, the past-time subjunctive is used.

The *würde*-construction vs. present-time subjunctive

Wenn Petra hier wäre, **würde** sie es mir **erklären.**
Wenn ich Geld hätte, **würde** ich die Tasche **kaufen.**

The **würde**-construction is regularly used in colloquial German in the conclusion of contrary-to-fact conditions in present time.

Wenn Frank arbeitete, **verdiente** er gut.	When Frank *was working*, he *earned* well.
Wenn Frank arbeitete, **würde** er gut **verdienen.**	If Frank *were working*, he *would earn* well.

The **würde**-construction is used in place of the subjunctive form of the weak verbs when the sentence could be otherwise interpreted as indicative past.

Wenn Jutta hier **wäre** und Zeit **hätte, könnte** sie es mir er-klären.	If Jutta *were* here and *had* time, she *could* explain it to me.

The general subjunctive of the main verb is preferred to the **würde**-construction for the modals, **sein**, and **haben**.

Ich würde die Arbeit machen, wenn Sie mir **helfen würden.**

The subjunctive of the main verb is generally preferred in the **wenn**-clause. In colloquial German, however, the **würde**-construction is sometimes used in the **wenn**-clause.

Anton Steinhart, *Gartentor im Winter*, Ölgemälde, 1937

Schlittenfahren

Helga M. Novak

Helga Novak was born in 1935 in Berlin. She studied philosophy and journalism in Leipzig and worked in various types of places: factories, a laboratory, and a bookstore. In 1961 she moved to Iceland and returned to Germany in 1967 to live in Frankfurt as a writer. In 1980, the New Literary Society in Hamburg gave her an award for her novel *Die Eisheiligen*, as the best first novel by a German speaker.

   In her stories, Helga Novak deals with ordinary people in everyday situations. Through the use of simple sentences and a dry, unemotional style, she suggests much more about human relationships than she actually says. In "Schlittenfahren," taken from her work *Geselliges Beisammensein* (1968), the father does not communicate with his children but simply leaves his retreat long enough to shout the same sentences in their direction, sentences devoid of meaning for them and him. However, the repetition of "kommt rein" at the end of the story takes on a new and possibly serious dimension and reveals the problem of using language just to be saying something.

   In what sense do the private home *(Eigenheim)* and the garden represent two separate and unrelated scenes of activity? What do the father's actions say about his relationship with the children?

Schlittenfahren

Das Eigenheim° steht in einem Garten. Der Garten ist groß. Durch den
Garten fließt° ein Bach°. Im Garten stehen zwei Kinder. Das eine der
Kinder kann noch nicht sprechen. Das andere Kind ist größer. Sie sitzen
auf einem Schlitten°. Das kleinere Kind weint. Das größere sagt, gib den
5   Schlitten her. Das kleinere weint. Es schreit°.

    Aus dem Haus tritt° ein Mann. Er sagt, wer brüllt°, kommt rein°. Er geht
in das Haus zurück. Die Tür fällt hinter ihm zu.

    Das kleinere Kind schreit.

    Der Mann erscheint wieder in der Haustür. Er sagt, komm rein. Na
10   wirds bald°. Du kommst rein. Nix°. Wer brüllt, kommt rein. Komm rein.

    Der Mann geht hinein. Die Tür klappt°.

    Das kleinere Kind hält die Schnur° des Schlittens fest°. Es schluchzt°.

    Der Mann öffnet die Haustür. Er sagt, du darfst Schlitten fahren, aber
nicht brüllen. Wer brüllt, kommt rein. Ja. Ja. Jaaa. Schluß jetzt°.

15   Das größere Kind sagt, Andreas will immer allein fahren.

    Der Mann sagt, wer brüllt, kommt rein. Ob er nun Andreas heißt oder
sonstwie°.

    Er macht die Tür zu.

    Das größere Kind nimmt dem kleineren den Schlitten weg. Das
20   kleinere Kind schluchzt, quietscht°, jault°, quengelt°.

    Der Mann tritt aus dem Haus. Das größere Kind gibt dem kleineren den
Schlitten zurück. Das kleinere Kind setzt sich auf den Schlitten. Es
rodelt°.

    Der Mann sieht in den Himmel°. Der Himmel ist blau. Die Sonne ist
25   groß und rot. Es ist kalt.

    Der Mann pfeift° laut. Er geht wieder ins Haus zurück. Er macht die Tür
hinter sich zu.

    Das größere Kind ruft°, Vati°, Vati, Vati, Andreas gibt den Schlitten
nicht mehr her.

30   Die Haustür geht auf. Der Mann steckt° den Kopf heraus. Er sagt, wer
brüllt, kommt rein. Die Tür geht zu.

    Das größere Kind ruft, Vati, Vativativati, Vaaatiii, jetzt ist Andreas in
den Bach gefallen.

    Die Haustür öffnet sich einen Spalt° breit°. Eine Männerstimme° ruft,
35   wie oft soll ich das noch sagen, wer brüllt, kommt rein.

Glossary (right margin):

- *private home*
- *flows / brook*
- *sled*
- *screams*
- *steps / bawls / rein = herein: in*
- **Na ... bald:** *hurry up /* **Nix =** *nichts*
- *slams*
- *rope /* **hält fest:** *holds tight / sobs*
- **Schluß jetzt:** *that's enough*
- *otherwise*
- *squeals / howls / whines*
- *sleds*
- *sky*
- *whistles*
- *calls / daddy*
- *sticks*
- *crack / wide / man's voice*

Fragen

1. In was für einem Haus wohnt die Familie?
2. Was wissen Sie über den Garten?
3. Was wissen Sie über die Kinder?
4. Warum weint das kleinere Kind?
5. Warum kommt der Mann aus dem Haus? Was sagt er?
6. Wie ist das Wetter?
7. Wer fährt am Ende mit dem Schlitten?
8. Warum ruft das ältere Kind am Ende den Vater?
9. Was antwortet der Vater?

Fragen zur Diskussion

1. Der Mann kommt mehrere Male zur Tür. Welche Sätze beschreiben das? Was sagen diese Sätze über den Mann?
2. Der Mann geht mehrere Mal ins Haus. Welche Sätze beschreiben das? Was ist damit gesagt?
3. Welchen Satz sagt der Mann immer wieder? Welchen Effekt hat das auf die Kinder? Auf den Leser?
4. Was wird über Jahreszeit und Wetter gesagt? Welche Rolle spielt das?
5. Warum benutzt die Autorin immer wieder das Wort „der Mann"? Welches andere Wort könnte sie benutzen?
6. Wie meint der Mann den letzten Satz? Wie verstehen Sie ihn?

Kapitel 12

Lernziele

Sprechakte

Conducting business negotiations
Expressing degrees of certainty
Making comparisons
Comparing future plans
Expressing assumptions and probability
Suggesting things to do together
Talking about personal preferences
Asking for and giving permission

Grammatik

Future tense
The verb **lassen**
Relative clauses and pronouns

Vokabeln

Fractions
Suffix **-lich**

Landeskunde

The economy of the Federal Republic of
Germany: major businesses, labor relations
and co-determination
Social legislation in the Federal Republic of
Germany
The effects of inflation on the German
economy
The apprenticeship system in the Federal Re-
public of Germany, Austria and
Switzerland

An der Börse in Düsseldorf

| Bausteine für Gespräche

Ein Termin

Im Vorzimmer

Herr Wieland: Guten Tag. Wieland ist mein Name. Ist Frau Dr. Schulze zu sprechen? Ich habe einen Termin bei ihr.

Sekretärin: Guten Tag, Herr Wieland. Ja bitte, gehen Sie doch gleich hinein. Sie erwartet Sie schon.

Im Chefbüro

Herr Wieland: ... Also, Frau Dr. Schulze, hier habe ich die Preisliste, die ich Ihnen versprochen habe. Bitte sehr.

Frau Schulze: Danke. Hm, ja ... Ich werde ein wenig Zeit brauchen, um sie mir etwas näher anzusehen. Am Montag in acht Tagen lasse ich Sie wissen, ob wir interessiert sind.

An appointment

In the outer office

Hello. My name is Wieland. May I speak to Dr. Schulze? I have an appointment with her.

Hello, Mr. Wieland. Yes, please, go right in. She's expecting you.

In the executive office

... Well, Dr. Schulze. I've got the price list here that I promised you. Here you are.

Thank you. Hm, yes ... I'll need a little time to look it over more closely. I'll let you know a week from Monday whether we're interested.

Fragen

1. Wen möchte Herr Wieland sprechen?
2. Warum soll Herr Wieland gleich hineingehen?
3. Weiß Frau Dr. Schulze, daß Herr Wieland eine Preisliste mitbringt?
4. Wann wird Herr Wieland wissen, ob Frau Dr. Schulze interessiert ist?

Sie haben das Wort

A   Interview   Fragen Sie eine(n) Bekannte(n):
1. ob sie/er mit dem Computer arbeiten kann
2. welche Programmiersprachen sie/er kennt
3. ob sie/er selbst Programme geschrieben hat

4. ob sie/er mit dem Wortprozessor arbeiten kann
5. ob sie/er glaubt, daß jeder Student Informatik studieren sollte
6. ob sie/er Schreibmaschine schreiben kann

B   Im Büro   Take the role of one of the people involved in a business conversation.

Frau/Herr Wieland	*Sekretärin*
Ist Frau/Herr Dr. Schulze zu sprechen?	Es tut mir leid. Sie/Er ist im Moment beschäftigt°.
	Sie/Er telefoniert gerade, und um drei hat sie/er einen Termin.
	Haben Sie einen Termin?
	Gehen Sie bitte gleich hinein! Sie/Er erwartet Sie.

Frau/Herr Wieland	*Frau/Herr Dr. Schulze*
Was halten Sie von unseren Preisen?	Sie sehen sehr interessant aus.
	Ich fürchte°, **Ihre Sachen sind zu teuer.**
	Ihre Preise sind zu hoch
	Sie müssen mir alles genauer erklären.
	Ich weiß es noch nicht. Ich habe einige Fragen.
	Ich kann es Sie erst am Montag wissen lassen.
	Ich rufe Sie morgen an.

C   Ich bin nicht sicher.   Answer your friend's questions with responses that imply that you are only partly sure of your answer.

Gesprächspartner/in	*Sie*
Mußt du am Wochenende viel arbeiten?	Ich glaube ja.
Hast du Zeit, [Tennis] zu spielen?	Ich nehme an°.
Hat [Andrea] eine neue Stelle bekommen?	Soviel ich weiß.
Verdient ein/e Programmierer/in gut?	Hoffentlich.
	Ich fürchte nein.

Vokabeln

Substantive

die **Liste, -n** list
der **Preis, -e** price

der **Termin, -e** appointment

Verben

an·nehmen (nimmt an), nahm an, angenommen to assume; to accept

beschäftigen to occupy, keep busy; **beschäftigt sein** to be busy; **sich beschäftigen (mit)** to be occupied (with)

erwarten to expect

(sich) fürchten (vor + *dat.*) to fear, be afraid (of)

(sich) interessieren (für) to be interested (in)

lassen (läßt), ließ, gelassen to leave; to let, permit; to have something done

telefonieren (mit jemandem) to telephone (someone)

versprechen (verspricht), versprach, versprochen (+ *dat. of persons*) to promise

Andere Wörter

interessiert sein (an + *dat.*) to be interested (in)

nahe (näher, nächst) near, close

Besondere Ausdrücke

Bitte sehr. Here you are. (*said when handing someone something*)

hinein in (*as in* **hineingehen** to go in)

[Montag] in acht Tagen a week from [Monday]

| Zur Wirtschaft der Bundesrepublik

Vorbereitung auf das Lesen

• *Zum Thema*

Was wissen Sie über die amerikanische oder kanadische Wirtschaft?

1. Ist der Export oder der Import größer?
2. Was sind wichtige Exportgüter — Maschinen, Autos, Chemikalien, Elektrotechnik, Schuhe, Textilien, anderes?
3. Gibt es viele oder wenige Rohstoffe?
4. Gibt es viele Streiks?
5. Sind die Preise stabil? Wie hoch ist die Inflationsrate?
6. Wie ist das soziale Klima? Hilft der Staat den Leuten bei finanziellen Problemen, z.B. im Alter, bei Krankheit und Arbeitslosigkeit?

• *Leitfragen*

1. Import und Export sind für die Bundesrepublik sehr wichtig. Was sind die Gründe dafür?

   Stichworte: Einwohner □ Rohstoffe □ verdienen

2. Der deutsche Export ist bisher ziemlich erfolgreich gewesen. Was sind die Gründe für diesen Erfolg?

   Stichworte: Qualität □ Organisation □ Preise □ pünktlich liefern

3. Die deutsche Wirtschaft ist eine „soziale Marktwirtschaft". Was bedeutet hier „sozial"? Was bedeutet „Markt"?
4. Was haben die Gewerkschaften erreicht?
5. Die Deutschen halten die Stabilität der Preise für sehr wichtig. Warum?

   Stichworte: Ersparnisse verloren □ verdienen □ kosten □ Mark — 10 Pfennig

6. Wie sieht die Zukunft für die deutsche Wirtschaft aus?

   Stichworte: zwei Märkte □ z.B. Schuhe — billiger □ z.B. Computer — U.S.A. und Japan □ konkurrieren

---

„Bundeskanzler° warnt vor Protektionismus" — „Bundeswirtschafts-   *prime minister*
minister: Wir brauchen einen freien Welthandel" — Solche Über-
schriften° erscheinen oft in deutschen Zeitungen. Und das ist nicht sehr   *headlines*
überraschend°, denn in der Bundesrepublik spielen Import und Export   *surprising*
5 eine besonders große Rolle. Die wichtigsten Exportgüter° sind Ma-   *export goods*
schinen, Kraftfahrzeuge°, chemische Produkte und Elektrotechnik°.   *automobiles / electrical engi-*
Diese Industrien hängen etwa zur Hälfte vom Export ab.   *neering products*
    Gründe für die relativ wichtige Rolle des Außenhandels° gibt es sicher   *foreign trade*
viele. Aber einer der wichtigsten ist wohl, daß das Land viele Einwohner
10 hat, aber nur wenige Rohstoffe. Wenn die Menschen essen, wohnen und
arbeiten wollen, muß das Land Rohstoffe und Lebensmittel einführen°,   *import*
die es sich durch seine Exporte verdienen muß.
    Mit seinen Exporten ist das Land im Lauf der Jahre° ziemlich erfolg-   *im ... Jahre: over the years*
reich° gewesen. Ein Außenhandelskaufmann sagt dazu: „Qualitäts-   *successful*
15 produkte ,Made in Germany' verkaufen sich immer noch recht gut. Aber
sie verkaufen sich natürlich auch nicht von selbst. Man muß einen langen
Atem° haben, d.h. man muß über lange Jahre planen und eine Organisa-   *einen ... haben: to take the*
tion aufbauen°. Man muß den Markt systematisch pflegen°. Außerdem   *long view*
hat es mir natürlich geholfen, daß die Bundesrepublik immer eine relativ   *build up / foster*
20 niedrige Inflationsrate° gehabt hat. So können meine Kunden mit ziem-   *rate of inflation*
lich stabilen Preisen rechnen°. Schließlich ist es wichtig, daß ich meine   *count on*

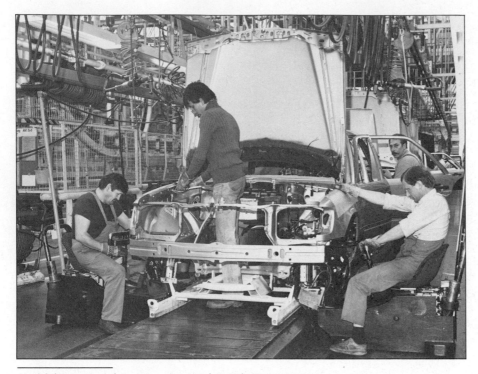

Kraftfahrzeuge gehören zu den wichtigsten Exportgütern.
(Fließband bei Mercedes)

Waren pünktlich liefern° kann. Das kann ich meistens, denn Streiks sind   *deliver*
in der Bundesrepublik recht selten."

    Dieser Export basiert° auf einer ganz allgemein gut entwickelten Wirt-   *is based*
25 schaft. Die Wirtschaftsform ist die° der „sozialen Marktwirtschaft°". Das   *that / socially oriented free*
heißt, man läßt den Markt entscheiden, was und wieviel die Wirtschaft   *market*
produziert. Zugleich° ist das soziale Netz° gut entwickelt, das den   *at the same time / das ...*
einzelnen bei ihren finanziellen Problemen im Alter°, bei Krankheit, Un-   *Netz: social security / old age*
fall und Arbeitslosigkeit hilft. Darüber hinaus° zahlt der Staat z.B.   *beyond that*
30 Kindergeld° für jedes Kind, Wohngeld° für wirtschaftlich schwache Bür-   *child support / rent supple-*
ger und Sozialhilfe° für Bedürftige°.   *ment*
                                                      welfare / needy
    Für das soziale Klima der Bundesrepublik ist es auch sehr positiv, daß
Gewerkschaften und Arbeitgeber einander mehr als Partner und weniger
als Gegner° sehen. Streiks sind daher relativ selten. Trotzdem sind die   *opponents*
35 Gewerkschaften erfolgreich gewesen. Ernst Bruch, Mitglied der IG-
Metall°, kommentiert: „Wir haben Lohnfortzahlung° bei Krankheit er-   *metal workers' union / con-*
reicht, sechs Wochen bezahlten Urlaub und die Mitbestimmung°." Zur   *tinued payment of wages*
Frage, was er sich noch wünscht, sagt er: „Da ist vor allem die Arbeits-   *codetermination*
losigkeit. Es macht mir große Sorgen, wann und wie wir dieses Problem
40 lösen werden."

Schließlich gibt es wohl noch einen Grund für das relativ gute Klima, das auf dem deutschen Arbeitsmarkt herrscht°: Eine große Mehrheit° des Volkes sieht die Stabilität der Preise als eine der wichtigsten, wenn nicht d i e wichtigste wirtschaftliche Aufgabe an. „Daß wir die Stabilität der
45 Preise so ernst nehmen, ist ja kein Wunder°", sagt eine Ärztin von etwa 50 aus Hannover. „Meine Eltern haben schließlich zweimal ihre Ersparnisse° durch die Inflation verloren, nach dem Ersten und nach dem Zweiten Weltkrieg. Und meine Familie war keine Ausnahme°. Ich selbst erinnere mich noch gut an die Zeit nach dem Zweiten Weltkrieg, als mein
50 Vater gut° fünfhundert Mark im Monat verdiente. Damals hat ein Pfund Butter auf dem schwarzen Markt zweihundert gekostet. Oder eine amerikanische Zigarette sechs bis acht Mark. Auf dem normalen Markt war alles rationiert. Dann kam 1948 die Währungsreform°. Da war die Mark nur noch zehn Pfennig wert. Für zehn Reichsmark° bekam man e i n e D-
55 Mark. Es ist also nicht so überraschend, daß wir die Inflationsrate so niedrig wie möglich halten wollen."

Einige Stichworte zur deutschen Wirtschaft sind also Außenhandel, soziale Marktwirtschaft, Partnerschaft und Stabilität. Wie gut die Bundesrepublik damit in Zukunft fahren wird, ist eine andere Sache. E i n e Frage ist, was die Bundesrepublik exportiert und wie die Zukunft für diese
60 Güter° auf dem Weltmarkt aussehen wird. Es gibt heute immer mehr Länder, die Waren wie Schuhe und Textilien billiger herstellen°. Mit ihnen wird die Bundesrepublik immer weniger konkurrieren können. Neue Jobs wird es dagegen° in den Industrien geben, die Güter wie Computer und Maschinen produzieren. Hier wird die Bundesrepublik mit Ja-
65 pan und den USA konkurrieren müssen. Wie die Resultate aussehen werden, wird die Zukunft zeigen.

prevails / majority

wonder

savings

exception

as much as

currency reform
*(currency of Germany intro-
duced in 1923–1924)*

goods

produce

on the other hand

Fragen zum Lesestück

1. Warum warnt der Bundeskanzler oft vor Protektionismus?
2. Wieviel Arbeitsplätze hängen in einigen Industrien vom Export ab?
3. Was für Produkte exportiert die Bundesrepublik vor allem?
4. Warum ist der Außenhandel so wichtig?
5. Was muß das Land einführen?
6. Warum ist das Land bisher mit seinem Export erfolgreich gewesen? Geben Sie drei Gründe.
7. Was heißt „Marktwirtschaft"?
8. Geben Sie Beispiele für soziale Hilfen des Staates!
9. Warum heißt die Wirtschaftsform „soziale Marktwirtschaft"?
10. Wie sehen die Gewerkschaften und Arbeitgeber einander vor allem?
11. Worin sind die Gewerkschaften erfolgreich gewesen?
12. Welches Problem ist nicht gelöst?

13. Warum halten viele Deutsche die Stabilität der Preise für so wichtig?
14. Wieviel hat ein Pfund Butter nach dem Krieg auf dem schwarzen Markt gekostet?
15. Was hat der Vater der Ärztin verdient?
16. Nennen Sie einige Stichworte zur deutschen Wirtschaft! Erklären Sie jedes in einem Satz.
17. Welche großen Gruppen von Exportgütern gibt es für die Bundesrepublik? Nennen Sie Beispiele für jede Gruppe!
18. Auf welchem Markt wird es neue Arbeitsplätze geben?
19. Warum wird es auf dem anderen Markt immer schwieriger für die Bundesrepublik werden?
20. Mit wem wird die Bundesrepublik konkurrieren müssen?

Sie haben das Wort

A   Was sagen Sie?

	Discussing the economy

1. Wie heißen zwei große Gewerkschaften in Ihrem Land?
2. Welche Ziele haben die Gewerkschaften bei Ihnen?
3. Wie hoch ist die Inflationsrate bei Ihnen (wieviel Prozent pro Jahr)?
4. Mit wem muß die Industrie bei Ihnen konkurrieren?
5. Sind Sie für größeren Protektionismus in der Industrie?

Democratic codetermination (*Mitbestimmung*) is a right guaranteed by law in the Federal Republic of Germany. It allows employees to participate in the industrial decision-making process by sending representatives to special committees and/or supervisory boards.

The employees' councils (*Betriebsrat* or *Personalrat*) perform mainly monitoring functions on behalf of workers and employees. These councils try to ensure that laws, wage agreements, and other regulations are carried out.

For companies with more than 2,000 employees, the law requires that an equal number of representatives of shareholders and of employees sit on the supervisory board (*Aufsichtsrat*). In Austria, the ratio of workers to shareholders on the supervisory board is 1:3. Switzerland does not require codetermination on boards.

Ein Ziel der Gewerkschaften ist die Fünfunddreißigstundenwoche.

B   Ein Vergleich zwischen Ihrem Land und der Bundesrepublik   Was meinen Sie?

1. Welches Land lebt mehr vom Außenhandel?
2. Welches Land hat mehr Rohstoffe?
3. In welchem Land gibt es mehr Streiks?
4. Welches Land zahlt Kindergeld?
5. In welchem Land spielt Mitbestimmung eine größere Rolle?
6. Welches Land hat höhere Arbeitslosigkeit?
7. In welchem Land ist die Angst vor Inflation größer?

Vokabeln

Substantive

der **Arbeitgeber, -** / die **Arbeitgeberin, -nen**   employer

die **Arbeitslosigkeit**   unemployment

die **Aufgabe, -n**   assignment, task

die **D-Mark** (*abbrev. for* **Deutsche Mark**)   *basic unit of German currency*

die **Gewerkschaft, -en**   trade union

der **Kunde, -n, -n** / die **Kundin, -nen**   customer, client

der **Kaufmann, -leute** / die **Kauffrau, -en**   merchant, businessman/woman

der **Pfennig, -e**   *unit of German currency,* = *1/100th of a* **Mark**

die **Sorge, -n**   care, worry

der **Streik, -s**   strike

der **Unfall, ⸚e**   accident

der **Urlaub**   vacation; **in Urlaub fahren**   to go on vacation; **im Urlaub sein**   to be on vacation

die **Ware, -n**   wares, merchandise, goods

die **Zigarette, -n**   cigarette

die **Zukunft**   future

— Verben

ab·hängen, hing ab, abgehangen (von) to depend on

entscheiden, entschied, entschieden to decide; **sich entscheiden** to make a decision after reflecting on it

erreichen to reach; to attain

konkurrieren to compete

lösen to solve

planen to plan

warnen (vor + *dat.*) to warn (against)

verkaufen to sell

(sich) wünschen to wish; **Was wünschst du dir zum Geburtstag?** What do you want for your birthday?

— Andere Wörter

also thus

einzeln single, individual

niedrig low

selten seldom, rare(ly)

trotzdem nevertheless

wert worth; worthwhile; **das ist viel wert** that is worth a lot

Erweiterung des Wortschatzes

1 Brüche

1/3	**ein Drittel**	one third
3/4	**drei Viertel**	three fourths
1/20	**ein Zwanzigstel**	one twentieth

A German fraction is called **der Bruch** (*pl.* **Brüche**). The numerator consists of a cardinal number such as **ein** or **drei**. The denominator is a neuter noun consisting of an ordinal number such as **dritt-, viert-,** or **zwanzigst-** plus the suffix **-el** (from the noun **Teil**).

Ich habe eine **halbe** Stunde gewartet.	I waited for half an hour.
Die chemische Industrie exportiert fast **die Hälfte** ihrer Produkte.	The chemical industry exports almost half of its products.

When used as an adjective, the fraction *1/2* is expressed as **halb**. When used as a noun, *1/2* is expressed as **die Hälfte**. Note that German uses the definite article and English does not: **die Hälfte** = *half*.

A Wie sagt man das? Give the fractions listed below, in German.

1. 1/5	3. 7/8	5. 3/20
2. 5/6	4. 9/15	6. 1/2

The foundations of German social legislation were laid during the time that Otto von Bismarck (1815–1898) was chancellor. Statutory health insurance (*Krankenversicherung*), worker's compensation (*Unfall- und Invalidenversicherung*), and retirement pension (*Rentenversicherung*) were introduced at this time. The costs were to be shared by the employer, the employee, and the state. Retirement age was set at 65. Since 1949, the Federal Republic of Germany has passed additional social legislation concerning child allowances, rent subsidies, savings bonuses, and compensation for the victims of war.

Social welfare (*Sozialhilfe*) is provided by the state for those in dire need. The majority of the recipients are in health-care facilities such as nursing homes, rehabilitation centers, or hospitals. Besides providing low-income housing, the government also subsidizes rent payments with *Wohngeld*.

Pensionäre haben Zeit und Mittel, sich Sehenswürdigkeiten anzusehen.

2   The suffix *-lich*

der Freund	friend	**freundlich**	friendly
fragen	to ask	**fraglich**	questionable
krank	ill, sick	**kränklich**	sickly

German adjectives and adverbs may be formed from some nouns or verbs by adding the suffix **-lich**. The suffix **-lich** may also be added to other adjectives. Some stem vowels are umlauted: **ä, ö,** and **ü.** The English equivalent is often an adjective or adverb ending in *-ly.*

B   Neue Wörter   Form adjectives or adverbs from the nouns listed below by adding **-lich**. (Words with an * add umlaut.) Then give the English equivalents of the adjectives and adverbs you have formed.

1. die Angst*
2. das Geschäft
3. das Kind
4. der Mann*
5. der Mensch
6. der Monat
7. die Mutter*
8. die Natur*
9. der Staat
10. der Tag*
11. der Vater*
12. das Wort*

C   Was bedeutet das?   Give English equivalents of the sentences below. Then identify the verbs, nouns, or adjectives that are related to the bold-faced words.

1. Es ist **fraglich**, ob wir morgen kommen können.
2. Er weiß heute nicht mehr, was er gestern gesagt hat. Er ist sehr **vergeß-lich**.
3. Ich kann seinen Brief kaum lesen. Er schreibt immer so **unleserlich**.
4. Daß Eva das gesagt hat, ist wirklich **unglaublich**.
5. Hat Präsident Löwe das wirklich **öffentlich** gesagt?
6. Hans-Jürgen ist gestern abend **schließlich** doch noch gekommen.
7. Die Geschichte ist **sprachlich** sehr schön, aber was bedeutet sie?
8. Ich kann soviel Deutsch, daß ich mich **verständlich** machen kann.

During the years after World War I (1914–1918), Germany went through a period of rapid inflation. Particularly affected were the people of the middle class, many of whom lost their savings and the money they had put in investments. In 1914, 4.2 *Papiermark* equaled $1.00. In January 1923, it was 17,972 M to $1.00, and in November of that year 4.2 trillion M to $1.00. Inflation was at its peak in 1923. The national bank — even though it was using 135 print shops — could not keep pace with the rapidly increasing need for money, and communities began to print "emergency money" (*Notgeld*). With the introduction of the new *Reichsmark* in 1923–4, inflation came to a halt, but socio-economic problems continued to exist throughout the twenties.

As a result of World War II (1939–1945), the *Reichsmark* lost value on both world and home markets. The population was in dire need of material goods, most of which were available only on the illegal black market (*Schwarzmarkt*). There people exchanged foods and goods, or they paid high prices for essentials. The Allies introduced a new currency, the *Deutsche Mark*, in June 1948. Every inhabitant of what is now the Federal Republic of Germany received the same amount, DM 60 (*Kopfgeld*). Savings accounts were devalued at the rate of 10 to 1, and the *Reichsmark* was declared invalid.

Inflation Anfang der Zwanziger Jahre: Die Zeitungsverkäuferin braucht einen Wäschekorb für die Millionen von Mark.

Übungen zur Aussprache

Review the pronunciation of **d** and **t** in the Reference section at the end of the book. Read the words in the columns first down, then across. Check your pronunciation by listening to your instructor or the tape.

[d]	[t]
hindern	hintern
Sonde	sonnte
Seide	Seite
hieder	Bieter
Mieder	Mieter

Read the sentences aloud, paying special attention to the way you pronounce **d** and **t** in the boldfaced words.

1. **Die Kinder trugen** ihre **beste Kleidung** zur **Fete.**
2. Im **Winter arbeitet Walter** in einem **Hotel.**
3. Sein **Vater hat** viele **Freunde eingeladen.**
4. **Dieters Bruder hat** einen **tollen Kassettenrecorder.**
5. **Der Bundeskanzler redete** über **die Ost-West-Politik.**

Ende gut, alles gut.

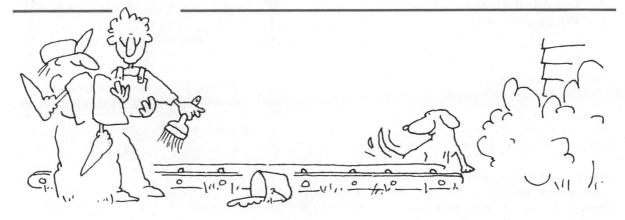

| Grammatik und Übungen

1   Future tense

Jutta **wird** uns **besuchen**.   Jutta is going to visit us.
Wir **werden** unsere Freunde   We're going to invite our friends.
   einladen.

In both English and German, the future is a compound tense. In English, the future is a verb phrase consisting of *will* or *shall* plus the main verb. In German, the future is also a verb phrase and consists of a form of **werden** plus an infinitive in final position.

ich **werde** es **finden**	wir **werden** es **finden**
du **wirst** es **finden**	ihr **werdet** es **finden**
er/es/sie **wird** es **finden**	sie **werden** es **finden**
Sie **werden** es **finden**	

A   Kein Streik   The union leader is reporting the results of a meeting with management. Restate the sentences below in the future tense.

▶   Wir verdienen mehr.   *Wir werden mehr verdienen.*

1.   Wir arbeiten 38 Stunden die Woche.
2.   Bei Krankheit zahlt die Firma weiter.
3.   Wir bekommen sechs Wochen bezahlten Urlaub.
4.   Der Arbeitstag fängt um halb acht an.
5.   Das Arbeitsklima wird besser.
6.   Wir streiken nicht.

HOLLAND-HOTEL   BADEN-BADEN

IDYLLE IM HERZEN
DER STADT
WIEDERERÖFFNUNG
1. März 1987
Alles wird in neuem
Glanz erscheinen.
111 Betten, Hotelpark, Grill +
Bar, Tagungsmöglichkeiten
für 9–99 Personen.

SOFIENSTRASSE 14, 7570 BADEN-BADEN, TELEFON (07221) 25596

Michael weiß nicht, ob Ursel ihn   Michael doesn't know whether
   besuchen wird.   Ursel will visit him.
Hans sagt, daß sie sicher **kommen**   Hans says she'll come for sure.
   wird.

The auxiliary **werden** is in final position in a dependent clause. It follows the infinitive.

B　Ein tolles Wochenende　Inge and Wolf are planning their weekend. Erik asks them about their plans. Restate the sentences below, beginning as shown in the second sentence of each pair.

▶　Inge und Wolf werden zusammen　　*Erik fragt sie, ob sie zusammen*
　　arbeiten.　　　　　　　　　　　*arbeiten werden.*
　　Erik fragt sie, ob ＿＿＿ .

1.　Inge wird ihre Notizen durcharbeiten.
　　Inge sagt, daß ＿＿＿ .
2.　Wolf wird sein Referat vorbereiten.
　　Wolf sagt, daß ＿＿＿ .
3.　Sie werden auch zum Hinterhoffest gehen.
　　Erik möchte wissen, ob ＿＿＿ .
4.　Susannes Gruppe wird beim Fest spielen.
　　Erik fragt, ob ＿＿＿ .
5.　Sie werden hinterher in eine Gaststätte gehen.
　　Inge nimmt an, daß ＿＿＿ .
6.　Sie werden sich in der Gaststätte treffen.
　　Erik glaubt, daß ＿＿＿ .

2　Future tense of modals

Du **wirst** mir sicher **helfen können.**	You'll surely be able to help me.
Das **wird** Silke wohl nicht **machen wollen**.	Silke probably won't want to do that.

In the future tense, modals are in infinitive form. They are in last position and follow the dependent infinitive. Some English modals have no infinitive form. For example, one must use *to be able* as an infinitive for the verb *can*.

C　Das Leben wird anders.　When Regina announces she has a job with a brokerage firm, her roommates discuss the changes in her life. Regina agrees that things will probably be the way they state. Take the part of Regina; use the future tense in your responses.

▶　Du mußt früher aufstehen.　　*Ja, ich werde früher aufstehen müssen.*

1.　Du mußt dich schön anziehen.
2.　Du kannst mit Christel in die Stadt fahren.
3.　Du mußt oft abends arbeiten.
4.　Martina kann nicht so oft ins Kino gehen.
5.　Beate muß öfter das Abendessen machen.
6.　Ihr müßt nach der Arbeit einkaufen gehen.
7.　Wir müssen einen Geschirrspüler kaufen.
8.　Du kannst weniger fernsehen.

Sie haben das Wort

Was hast du vor? Make up a list of five things you fully intend to accomplish in the future; organize them according to categories. Find two partners. Explain your goals, then ask them for their goals in the same categories. Record the data and report the results to the class.

Comparing future plans

Ausbildung □ Beruf □ Einkommen □ Familie □ Reisen □ Freizeit □ Wohnen

Sie	*Gesprächspartner/in*
Wohnen: In fünf Jahren werde ich eine Fünf-Zimmer-Wohnung haben; in zehn Jahren werde ich ein eigenes Haus kaufen. Und du?	In fünf Jahren werde ich in Europa leben.

3   Present tense to express future time

Ich **komme** morgen bestimmt.	I'll come tomorrow for sure.
Gehen Sie heute abend ins Kino?	Are you going to the movies this evening?

The future tense is used less frequently in German than in English. German generally uses the present tense to express future time if it is clear from context that the events will take place in the future.

D   Wie sagt man das? Give the German equivalents of the sentences below. Use the present tense to express future time.

1. Are you going to watch TV tonight?
2. No, I'm going to the movies.
3. What are you going to do tomorrow?
4. My vacation starts tomorrow.
5. Tonight I shall have to do my laundry. (*use* **waschen**)
6. Are you going to Lake Constance again?
7. No, we'll go there next summer.

4   Uses of the future tense

Present probability	Inge **wird** wohl zu Hause **sein**.	Inge is probably at home.
Supposition	Das **wird** sicher falsch **sein**.	That's probably wrong.
Determination	Ich **werde** die Arbeit allein **machen**.	I'm going to do the work alone.

The future tense may express probability in present time when it is used with adverbs such as **wohl, sicher**, or **schon**. The future tense is also regularly used to express a supposition or a determination to do something.

E   Was ist mit Jürgen los?   Sabine is wondering about Jürgen's problems. Say that you assume her statements are probably correct.

▶   Jürgen ist zu Hause, nicht?   *Ja, Jürgen wird wohl zu Hause sein.*

1. Er ist krank, nicht?
2. Er hat Fieber, nicht?
3. Er liegt im Bett, nicht?
4. Er hat großen Durst. Oder?
5. Er hat keinen Hunger. Oder?
6. Er kann nichts essen. Oder?
7. Er bleibt die ganze Woche zu Hause. Oder?

Sie haben das Wort

So wird es wohl sein.   Form a group of three. One student makes a comment; the other two react, each with a different assumption.

[Andrea] gibt am Samstag eine Party.	Das wird sicher lustig/toll/ uninteressant sein/werden.
Ich schreibe nächste Woche eine Klausur [in Informatik].	Das wird sicher schwer/leicht sein/werden.
Professor Schmidt hält eine Vorlesung über [die französische Kurzgeschichte].	Das wird wohl phantastisch/aus- gezeichnet/interessant/ furchtbar sein/werden.
Wir machen eine Radtour um den Bodensee.	Das wird wohl teuer/billig sein/ werden.
Wir machen eine Bürgerinitiative gegen die neue Mülldeponie.	

> Expressing assumptions

5   Constructions with *lassen*

• *Forms of* lassen

Present tense	
ich lasse	wir lassen
du läßt	ihr laßt
er/es/sie läßt	sie lassen
Sie lassen	

Simple past stem:	ließ
Past participle:	gelassen

- *Uses of* lassen

Laß den Schlüssel nicht im Auto!	Don't leave the key in the car.
Laß mich dir helfen!	Let me help you.

Lassen is a commonly used verb that occurs in a variety of constructions. Like the modals, **lassen** can stand alone or take a dependent infinitive without **zu**.

Wirst du deinen Bruder **fahren lassen?**	Are you going to let your brother drive?

In the future tense, **lassen** is in last position and comes after its dependent infinitive.

Hast du deinen Bruder zu Hause **gelassen?**	Did you leave your brother at home?
Hast du ihn fahren **lassen?**	Did you let him drive?

Lassen has two past participles: **gelassen** and **lassen**. The participle **gelassen** is used when the verb occurs without a dependent infinitive. The alternate participle **lassen** is used when the verb occurs with a dependent infinitive. The alternate participle **lassen** is identical with the infinitive; this construction is called the "double infinitive" construction.

- *Meanings of* lassen

Lassen has four basic meanings.

1. **lassen** = *to leave*

Laß das Buch hier!	Leave the book here.
Ich habe meine Tasche zu Hause **gelassen**.	I've left my bag at home.

2. **lassen** = *to let* or *to permit*

Lassen Sie mich die Arbeit machen!	Let me do the work.
Wie lange **läßt** du ihn arbeiten?	How long are you going to let him work?

3. **lassen** = *let's*

Gerd, **laß** uns jetzt gehen!	Gerd, let's go now.
Freunde, **laßt** uns essen!	Let's eat, folks.

The imperative form of **lassen** plus the pronoun **uns** is often used in place of the first-person plural imperative: **Gehen wir! Essen wir!** In talking to a person you address with **du**, use **laß**; with **ihr** use **laßt**.

4. **lassen** = *to have someone come* or *to have something done*

Frau Lange **läßt** den Elektriker kommen.	Mrs. Lange is sending for the electrician.
Wir **lassen** unser Auto reparieren.	We're having our car repaired.

Sie haben das Wort

A   Wo lasse ich das?   Discuss your plans for your trip to Europe with a friend. Tell her/him what you will leave with family or friends.

▶ *Ich lasse meine Schallplatten bei meinem Freund.*

> Giving things to people to keep

B   Was machen wir dann?   Find a partner to do things with. You suggest an activity; your partner will suggest what to do afterward. Then take turns suggesting other activities to each other.

> Suggesting things to do together

Sie	Gesprächspartner/in
Laß uns schwimmen gehen!	Gut. Dann laß uns Kaffee trinken gehen.

F   Was bedeutet das?   The verb **lassen** can be translated in several different ways. Give all the possible English equivalents for each sentence below.

▶ Er ließ seinen Freund fahren.   { *He let his friend drive.*
                                    He had his friend drive.

1. Sie läßt uns allein arbeiten.
2. Ich lasse meinen Chef den Brief schreiben.
3. Sie ließen das Auto reparieren.
4. Weil unser Auto nicht lief, ließen wir ein Taxi kommen.
5. Hast du den Schlüssel im Hotelzimmer gelassen?
6. Laß mich nicht zu lange auf eine Antwort warten!
7. Laßt uns aufs Land fahren!
8. Laßt uns das Wohnzimmer aufräumen!
9. Laß bitte das Fenster offen! Es ist hier sehr heiß.
10. Laßt mich wissen, was ihr für das Wochenende vorhabt.
11. Ich werde morgen die Waschmaschine reparieren lassen.
12. Ich lasse dich entscheiden, ob wir morgen fahren oder nicht.
13. Darf ich mein Auto über Nacht auf der Straße stehen lassen?
14. Wir wissen nicht, was Dieter vorhat. Wir lassen uns überraschen.
15. Wo hast du das Fahrrad stehen lassen?
16. Ich habe es in der Garage gelassen.
17. Warum hast du mich so lange schlafen lassen?
18. Hast du deinen Kassettenrecorder reparieren lassen?

G Noch einmal Restate the sentences below, using the cued subjects with the verb **lassen**.

▶ Wie lange lassen Sie die Leute da   *Wie lange läßt du die Leute da*
   stehen? (du)   *stehen?*

1. Wann lassen Sie uns wissen, wann Sie kommen? (du)
2. Wo habt ihr euer Auto gelassen? (Sabine)
3. Wen läßt du den Brief schreiben? (ihr)
4. Andrea läßt dich warnen. (deine Eltern)
5. Ich lasse meinen Fernseher reparieren. (wir)
6. Wann lassen Sie Tanja mit der Arbeit anfangen? (du)
7. Warum hat er uns so lange arbeiten lassen? (du)
8. Ich muß das Auto reparieren lassen. (Sie)

6 Relative clauses

Wer ist **die Frau, die** gerade her-   Who is the woman (who is) just
   einkommt?   coming in?

Ist das **der Mann, den** Sie mei-   Is that the man (whom) you
   nen?   mean?

A relative clause is introduced by a relative pronoun, which refers back to a noun or pronoun in the preceding clause. Since a relative clause is a dependent clause, the finite verb stands in last position.

Das ist das Auto, **das** ich kaufen   That's the car (that) I'd like to
   möchte.   buy.
Ist das die Frau, **die** Sie meinen?   Is that the woman (whom) you
                                           mean?

In English, the relative pronoun may or may not be stated. In German, the relative pronoun is always stated. In written German, relative clauses are set off from main clauses by commas.

7 Relative pronouns

	Masculine	Neuter	Feminine	Plural
Nom.	der	das	die	die
Acc.	den	das	die	die
Dat.	dem	dem	der	**denen**
Gen.	**dessen**	**dessen**	**deren**	**deren**

The forms of the relative pronoun are the same as the forms of the definite articles, except for the dative plural and all genitive forms.

Masculine	Das ist der Mann, **der** uns gefragt hat.
Neuter	Das ist das Kind, **das** uns gefragt hat.
Feminine	Das ist die Frau, **die** uns gefragt hat.
Plural	Das sind die Leute, **die** uns gefragt haben.

The *gender* of the relative pronoun depends on the gender of the noun to which it refers. In the examples above, **der** is masculine because it refers to **der Mann** and **die** is feminine because it refers to **die Frau**. Whether a pronoun is singular or plural also depends on the noun to which it refers. The pronoun **die** that refers to **die Leute** is plural and therefore requires the plural verb **haben**.

Nominative	Ist das der Mann, **der** hier war?
Accusative	Ist das der Mann, **den** Sie meinen?
Dative	Ist das der Mann, **dem** Sie es gesagt haben?
Genitive	Ist das der Mann, **dessen** Auto Sie gekauft haben?

The *case* of a relative pronoun depends on its grammatical function in the relative clause. In the examples above, **der** is nominative because it is the subject of its clause; **den** is accusative because it is the direct object of the verb **meinen** in that clause; **dem** is dative because it is an indirect object in the clause; and **dessen** is genitive because it shows possession.

Ist das die Frau, **für die** Sie arbeiten?	Is that the woman for whom you work?
Ist das die Firma, **bei der** Sie arbeiten?	Is that the firm (that) you work for?

A preposition followed by a relative pronoun may introduce a relative clause. The case of the relative pronoun then depends on what case the preposition takes. In **für die, die** is accusative because of **für**; in **bei der, der** is dative because of **bei**.

In German, whenever a relative pronoun is the object of a preposition, the preposition precedes the pronoun. In colloquial English the preposition is usually in last position.

H   Die deutsche Wirtschaft   Below are sentences on the German economy. Identify the relative pronouns. Indicate the case and function of each relative pronoun, and name its antecedent.

▶ Der Bundeskanzler arbeitet für   *der = nominative, subject,*
    einen Welthandel, der wirklich frei   *Welthandel*
    ist.

1. Ein Land wie die Bundesrepublik, das wenig Rohstoffe hat, lebt vom Handel.

2. Die Produkte, die man produziert, müssen von bester Qualität sein.
3. Denn es gibt mehrere Länder, mit denen die Bundesrepublik konkurrieren muß.
4. In der Zukunft ändert sich der Markt, für den die Bundesrepublik produzieren muß.
5. Einige Firmen, die Sachen produzieren, die man nicht mehr kauft, werden pleite machen.
6. Das bedeutet, daß die Arbeitnehmer, deren Firmen pleite sind, arbeitslos werden.
7. Die Arbeitslosigkeit ist ein Problem, das nur schwer zu lösen ist.
8. Die Gewerkschaften, die sich vor allem als Partner der Arbeitgeber sehen, werden auch im neuen Markt eine große Rolle spielen.

I   **Die sind doch gar nicht kaputt.**   Your friend is good at fixing electrical things and audio equipment, only he can't seem to find the right ones. Tell him the things he wants to fix for you aren't the broken ones. Use the nominative of the relative pronoun.

▶   Jetzt werde ich diese Schreibmaschine reparieren, ja?   *Das ist doch nicht die Schreibmaschine, die kaputt ist.*

1. Jetzt werde ich diesen Fernseher reparieren, ja?
2. Jetzt werde ich diesen Kassettenrecorder reparieren, ja?
3. Jetzt werde ich diese Stereoanlage reparieren, ja?
4. Jetzt werde ich diesen Plattenspieler reparieren, ja?
5. Jetzt werde ich dieses Radio reparieren, ja?
6. Jetzt werde ich diese Lampen reparieren, ja?
7. Jetzt werde ich diese Uhren reparieren, ja?

J   **Die Sachen sind toll.**   Gabi shows you various articles of clothing. Show your interest by asking whether they are the ones she got for her birthday. Use the accusative of the relative pronoun.

▶   Wie gefällt dir diese Jacke?   *Toll. Ist das die Jacke, die du zum Geburtstag bekommen hast?*

1. Wie gefällt dir diese Hose?
2. Wie gefällt dir dieses Hemd?
3. Wie gefällt dir dieser Rock?
4. Wie gefällt dir diese Bluse?
5. Wie gefällt dir dieser Pulli?
6. Wie gefallen dir diese Jeans?
7. Wie gefallen dir diese Schuhe?

The Federal Republic of Germany is a federal country, where the individual states (*die Bundesländer*) each maintain a constitution. However, the central government holds a strong position.

National elections of the House of Representatives (*der Bundestag*) take place every four years. All German citizens over 18 have a "first vote" (*Erststimme*) and a "second vote" (*Zweitstimme*), which permits them to vote for a particular candidate as well as for a political party. The representative one votes for need not belong to the party one votes for. The constitution (*Grundgesetz*) of the Federal Republic stipulates that a political party has to have a minimum of 5% of all the votes cast to be represented in the *Bundestag*. In 1983 the Greens (*Die Grünen*) gained seats in the *Bundestag* for the first time.

The *Bundestag* is the only federal body elected directly by the people. The Federal Council (*Bundesrat*) consists of delegates of the states. The Federal President (*Bundespräsident*) is elected by the Federal Convention, a constitutional body that convenes only for this purpose. The President's tasks are mainly ceremonial in nature.

The head of the government in the Federal Republic of Germany is the Federal Chancellor (*Bundeskanzler*), who is nominated by the President and elected by the *Bundestag*. The Chancellor nominates a head for each Federal Ministry (*Bundesministerium*). They are then formally appointed by the President. The Federal Ministers and the Chancellor together form the Federal Government (*Bundesregierung*) until new elections are called.

Bundestag in Bonn

K   Nichts paßt ihnen.   Andreas is complaining about the negative attitude of several people. Say that you also know people whom nothing suits. Use the dative of the relative pronoun.

▶   Mein Bruder findet alles schlecht.   *Ich habe auch einen Bruder, dem nichts paßt.*

1. Mein Onkel ist immer böse.
2. Mein Professor findet alles uninteressant.
3. Meine Schwester findet alles dumm.
4. Meine Tante findet alles furchtbar.
5. Mein Chef ist sehr unfreundlich.
6. Mein Freund Erik findet immer alles doof.
7. Unsere Nachbarn sind sehr unfreundlich.
8. Meine Großeltern finden alles falsch.

L   Informationen für Touristen   Combine each pair of sentences, using a preposition and a relative pronoun.

▶   Meyers ist ein Lebensmittelge-   *Meyers ist ein Lebensmittelge-*
     schäft. Man kann alles in dem   *schäft, in dem man alles finden*
     Lebensmittelgeschäft finden.   *kann.*

1.   Die „Krone" ist ein gutes Restaurant. Man kann billig in diesem Restaurant essen.
2.   Dinkelsbühl ist ein interessantes Städtchen. Man hört oft von diesem Städtchen.
3.   Frankfurt ist eine wichtige Stadt. Man hört oft von dieser Stadt.
4.   Der „Peterhof" ist ein großer Biergarten. Man hört gute Musik in diesem Biergarten.
5.   Heidelberg ist eine alte und gute Universität. Jeder möchte auf diese Universität gehen.
6.   München ist eine attraktive Stadt. Jeder möchte in dieser Stadt leben.

M   Wer sind diese Leute?   Veronika is a guest at a party where she knows no one. Your friend tells her something about the people. But since she knows no German you must translate.

▶   Das ist die Frau, deren Sohn in   *That is the woman whose son is*
     Marburg studiert.   *studying in Marburg.*

1.   Das ist der Mann, dessen Tochter bei Siemens arbeitet.
2.   Das sind die Leute, deren Kinder fließend Englisch sprechen.
3.   Das ist der Mann, dessen Sohn arbeitslos ist.
4.   Das ist der Mann, dessen Frau Chefärztin ist.
5.   Das ist die junge Frau, deren Vater ein bekannter Jurist ist.
6.   Das ist der junge Mann, dessen Eltern sehr reich sind.

N   Wie sagt man das?

1.   Here's the letter (that) Uwe wrote [*perfect tense*].
2.   He wrote [*perfect tense*] about the company for which he works.
3.   He has a boss (whom) he likes. (*use* **mögen**)
4.   He's doing (a) work (which) he finds very interesting.
5.   Recently, he bought [*perfect tense*] a new bicycle (with) which he rides to work.
6.   He also has a large apartment, which he likes very much. (*use* **gefallen**)

Sie haben das Wort

Erzähl mal! Tell fellow students to make two or three comments about
some activity. You may use activities from the list below, or come up with
some of your own. Report orally or in writing.

Describing personal
activities

Stadt besuchen □ Ferien machen □ Radtour machen □ Job haben
□ Buch lesen □ Auto kaufen □ Vorlesung hören □ Reise machen

Sie	*Gesprächspartner/in*
Erzähl mal über eine Reise, die du gern machen würdest!	Ich möchte eine Reise nach China machen.

Wiederholung ——————————————

A   Eine bekannte Autorin   Tell about Kirsten Elsner's start as an author.
Restate in the simple past.

1. Herr Elsner bekommt eine neue Stelle in einer anderen Stadt.
2. Weil Frau Elsner keine Arbeit findet, bleibt sie zu Hause und sorgt für
   die Kinder.
3. Am Anfang macht sie alles gern.
4. Sie kocht, putzt, geht einkaufen und hilft den Kindern bei den Schul-
   aufgaben.
5. Um etwas für die Kinder zu tun, fängt sie an, Kurzgeschichten zu
   schreiben.
6. Sie wird durch die Kurzgeschichten bald bekannt.
7. Man nennt sie nicht mehr Kirsten Elsner, die Frau von Herrn Elsner.
8. Sie heißt Kirsten Wiener, und Herr Elsner ist der Mann von der
   bekannten Autorin.

B   Gabi weiß jetzt mehr.   Tanja wants to know whether you helped Gabi
understand some facts about the economic situation in the Federal Republic
of Germany. Answer the questions below. Replace the boldfaced words
with a pronoun or use a **da**-compound.

▶ Wollte Gabi etwas über **die**   *Ja, sie wollte etwas darüber wis-*
  deutsche Wirtschaft wissen?   *sen.*
  Ja, sie _____ .

1. Hast du ihr von **der Rolle des Außenhandels** erzählt?
   Ja, ich _____ .
2. Hat sie **die Rolle** verstanden?
   Ja, sie _____ .

3. Ein Land wie die Bundesrepublik lebt **vom Handel**, nicht?
   Ja, es _____ .
4. Interessiert sich Gabi auch für **die Rolle der Gewerkschaften**?
   Ja, sie _____ .
5. Weiß sie etwas über **die Ziele der Gewerkschaften**?
   Ja, sie _____ .
6. Haben die Deutschen große Angst vor **Inflation**?
   Ja, sie _____ .
7. Findet Gabi **den Lebensstandard der Deutschen** hoch?
   Ja, sie _____ .

C   Ein Student an der Uni   Bernd wonders how Peter is getting along at the university. Tell him things are not going well, but that Peter doesn't seem to mind. Complete the sentences below with adjective endings, where necessary. Then answer the questions in the negative, using adjectives from the list as antonyms for the adjectives in the questions.

alt □ dumm □ dunkel □ interessant □ faul □ groß □ lustig □ leicht □ schlecht □ teuer

▶   Geht Peter auf eine klein___   *Geht Peter auf eine kleine Univer-*
    Universität?   *sität? Nein, auf eine große.*

1. Ist er ein fleißig___ Student?
2. Ist er intelligent___ ?
3. Liest er gern ernst___ Geschichten?
4. Wohnt er in einer modern___ Wohnung?
5. Wohnt er in einem hell___ Zimmer?
6. Führt er ein schwer___ Leben?
7. Hat er einen gut bezahlt___ Studentenjob?
8. Findet er Wohnen und Essen billig___ ?

D   Markus schreibt über Frauen.   Markus has written some brief comments about *Frauen in der Bundesrepublik*. Complete his work by supplying appropriate relative pronouns.

1. Peter hat ein Frauenbild, _____ in vielen Lesebüchern noch zu finden ist.
2. In diesen Büchern ist es immer ein Junge, _____ etwas baut oder Fußball spielt.
3. Und es ist immer ein Mädchen, _____ im Hause hilft oder mit Puppen spielt.
4. Viele Leute haben leider oft die gleichen Vorstellungen, _____ Kinder haben.
5. Die Frauen, _____ Berufe wie Elektrikerin und Mechanikerin gelernt haben, haben es besonders schwer.
6. Ein Vorurteil, gegen _____ man kämpfen muß, ist, daß Elektriker und Mechaniker „Männerberufe" sind.
7. Es gibt also noch traditionelle Rollen, von _____ Männer und Frauen sich emanzipieren müssen.

Young people who want a career that requires special skills in business or industry serve an apprenticeship (*Lehre*) after graduating at the 9th- or 10th-grade level from a secondary school called the *Hauptschule*. They are generally called *Lehrlinge*, although the official term is *Auszubildender* for a boy, *Auszubildende* for a girl. They work 3 to 4 days a week while taking related courses at a specialized continuation school. After 2½ to 3½ years as apprentices, upon passing an examination they become journeymen or journeywomen (*Gesellen*) in the trades and assistants (*Gehilfen*) in office jobs. The master's examination (*Meisterprüfung*) may be taken after five more years of work and additional schooling. With a diploma (*Meisterbrief*), which is displayed much as a doctor's or lawyer's license, the successful candidate is qualified to train *Auszubildende (Azubis)* and/or to open her or his own business in the chosen occupation.

Azubis zeigen, was sie gelernt haben.

E   **Was sagen Sie?**

1. Arbeiten Sie während der Ferien oder während des Semesters bei einer Firma?
2. Wo arbeiten Sie?
3. Wie gefällt Ihnen Ihre Arbeit?
4. Wie ist das Arbeitsklima, wo Sie arbeiten?
5. Gehören Sie zu einer Gewerkschaft?
6. Wofür interessieren Sie sich? (Möchten Sie mehr verdienen? Möchten Sie längere Ferien haben?)
7. Wie könnten die Gewerkschaften mehr gegen die Arbeitslosigkeit tun?

Sie haben das Wort

Erzählen Sie mal!

> Talking about personal preferences

1. Erzählen Sie mal über ein Buch, das Sie gern kaufen würden!
2. Erzählen Sie mal über eine Reise, die Sie gern machen würden!
3. Erzählen Sie mal über Ferien, die Sie gern machen würden!
4. Erzählen Sie mal über einen Politiker, den Sie gern reden hören würden!
5. Erzählen Sie mal über einen Film, den Sie gern sehen würden!

F   Wie sagt man das?

Mrs. Böhme: I would like to speak with Mr. Schultz.
Secretary: Do you have an appointment?
Mrs. Böhme: No. I just wanted to ask him whether he received our price list.
Secretary: I'll see whether he's free. . . . I'm sorry. He's busy at the moment.
   He'll call you tomorrow, if that is all right with you.

G   Anregung

Write a paragraph in German about some of the differences between
the economies of the USA or Canada and the Federal Republic of Germany. Use the questions below as a guideline.

In welchem Land spielt der Außenhandel eine größere Rolle? Warum?
Welches Land hat mehr Rohstoffe?
Welche Produkte exportieren die Länder vor allem?
In welchem Land sehen die Chancen für eine gesunde Wirtschaft
   besser aus? Warum?

| Grammatik zum Nachschlagen

The future tense (A, B)

ich **werde** es **machen**	wir **werden** es **machen**
du **wirst** es **machen**	ihr **werdet** es **machen**
er/es/sie **wird** es **machen**	sie **werden** es **machen**
Sie **werden** es **machen**	

The German future tense consists of the auxiliary **werden** plus an infinitive
in final position.

Erika sagt, daß sie es **machen wird**.

In a dependent clause, the auxiliary **werden** is in final position. It follows the
infinitive.

Future tense of modals (C)

Er **wird** es bestimmt nicht
   machen wollen.

He will certainly not want to do it.

Sie **wird** es **machen müssen**.

She will have to do it.

In the future, a modal is in its infinitive form and is in last position. The
modal follows the dependent infinitive.

Uses of the future tense   (D, E)

Supposition	Es **wird** sicher **regnen**.	It'll rain for sure.
Determination	Ich **werde** Deutsch **lernen**.	I will learn German.

Present probability	Er **wird** wohl krank **sein**.	He is probably sick.
	Du **wirst** sicher müde **sein**.	You must be tired.
	Du **wirst** schon recht **haben**.	You are undoubtedly right.

The future tense expresses the probability of something happening in present time when used with adverbs like **wohl, sicher**, and **schon**.

Ich **komme** morgen bestimmt.	I'll come tomorrow for sure.
Fahren Sie nächstes Jahr nach Deutschland?	Are you going to Germany next year?

German uses the future tense less frequently than English. German generally uses the present tense to express future time if the time reference is clearly future.

Constructions with *lassen*   (F, G)

Present tense	
ich lasse	wir lassen
du läßt	ihr laßt
er/es/sie läßt	sie lassen
Sie lassen	

Simple past stem:	ließ
Past participle:	gelassen

• *Uses of* lassen

Inge **ließ** ihren Bruder zu Hause.	Inge left her brother at home.
Inge **ließ** ihre Schwester fahren.	Inge let her sister drive.

Lassen behaves like the modals, in that it can stand alone or take a dependent infinitive without **zu**.

Wirst du deinen Bruder **fahren lassen?**	Will you let your brother drive?

In the future tense, **lassen** is in last position and comes after its dependent infinitive.

Hast du deinen Bruder zu Hause **gelassen**?	Did you leave your brother at home?
Hast du ihn fahren **lassen**?	Did you let him drive?

Lassen has two past participles: **gelassen** and **lassen**. The participle **gelassen** is used when the verb occurs without a dependent infinitive. The alternate participle **lassen** is used when the verb occurs with a dependent infinitive. The participle **lassen** is identical with the infinitive; this construction is called the "double infinitive" construction.

• *Meanings of* lassen

Lassen is one of the most commonly used verbs in German. **Lassen** has four basic meanings.

1. **lassen** = *to leave*

Uwe **hat** seinen Freund allein **gelassen**.	Uwe left his friend alone.
Hast du deine Jacke zu Hause **gelassen**?	Did you leave your jacket at home?

2. **lassen** = *to let* or *to permit*

Wir **lassen** euch arbeiten.	We'll let you work.
Lassen Sie mich Ihnen helfen!	Let me help you.

3. **lassen** = *let's*

Inge, **laß** uns jetzt lesen!	Inge, let's read now.
Kinder, **laßt** uns singen!	Children, let's sing.

In talking to a person you address with **du**, use **laß**; with **ihr**, use **laßt**.

4. **lassen** = *to cause something to be done* or *to have something done*

Uschi **läßt** ihr Radio reparieren.	Uschi is having her radio repaired.
Haben Sie den Elektriker kommen **lassen**?	Did you send for the electrician?

Relative clauses   (H)

Ist das **die Schallplatte, die** du gestern gekauft hast?	Is that the record (that) you bought yesterday?
Wie alt ist **das Auto, das** du verkaufen möchtest?	How old is the car (that) you want to sell?

A relative clause provides additional information about a previously mentioned noun or pronoun. The clause is introduced by a relative pronoun, which refers back to the noun or pronoun (called an antecedent). A relative clause is a dependent clause, and the verb is in final position. In German the relative pronoun is always stated. In English the relative pronoun may or may not be stated. In written German, relative clauses are set off from main clauses by commas.

Relative pronouns (I–N)

	Singular			**Plural**
Nom.	der	das	die	die
Acc.	den	das	die	die
Dat.	dem	dem	der	denen
Gen.	**dessen**	**dessen**	**deren**	**deren**

The forms of the relative pronouns are the same as the forms of the definite articles, except for the dative plural and all genitive forms, as shown in the chart above.

Nominative	Ist das der Mann, **der** immer so viel fragt?
Accusative	Ist das der Mann, **den** Sie meinen?
	für den Sie arbeiten?
Dative	Ist das der Mann, **dem** Sie oft helfen?
	von dem Sie erzählt haben?
Genitive	Ist das der Mann, **dessen** Auto Sie gekauft haben?

The *gender* (masculine, neuter, or feminine) and *number* (singular or plural) of the relative pronoun are determined by its antecedent, i.e., the noun to which it refers. The *case* of the relative pronoun is determined by its function within its clause (subject, direct object, object of a preposition, etc.).

Theodor Rosenhauer, *Bildnis des Vaters*, Ölgemälde, 1931

| Als ich noch jung war

Werner Schmidli

Werner Schmidli was born in 1939 in Basel, Switzerland. He has been publishing short stories, novels, and poetry since 1966.

In his writings, Werner Schmidli explores the relationship of language to the reality it represents. He writes in a clear, matter-of-fact prose style. Through language he tries to help the reader see the familiar in a new light. The narrator of "Als ich noch jung war," taken from the collection of prose *Sagen Sie nicht: beim Geld hört der Spaß auf* (1971), contrasts the time of his/her youth with the present day. The narrator's judgments consist of statements commonly heard among the "older" generation. By piling comment upon comment and mixing judgments with observations the narrator lets readers see the exaggeration of the claims and forces them to think carefully about all the statements. Upon close examination many of them turn out to say nothing.

Which statements have some concrete substance to them? Which statements imply judgments that are hard to prove? Which statements say nothing at all?

Als ich noch jung war

Als ich noch jung war, da hatten wir Respekt vor den Alten. Als ich jung war, da waren die Kinder noch Kinder und haben zugehört°, wenn man ihnen etwas sagte. Man hat gehorcht° und den Mund gehalten°, wenn die Erwachsenen redeten. Als ich jung war, hat man nicht soviel Wert°
5 aufs Äußere° gelegt, die Mädchen waren noch Mädchen und die Frauen wußten, wo ihr Platz ist. Die jungen Männer waren noch Männer und wußten, was sie wollten. Da hat man die Nachbarn gekannt. Da war nicht alles so hygienisch, und wir leben immer noch.

Als ich jung war, mußte man nicht Angst haben, überfahren° zu wer-
10 den, wenn man auf die Straße ging. Die Luft war nicht verpestet°, die Flüsse° waren noch sauber, der Sommer war noch ein richtiger Sommer, im Winter hatten wir Schnee und das Holz° verfaulte° nicht in den Wäl-dern.

Als ich jung war, hatten wir noch Anstand°. In der Straßenbahn
15 standen wir auf, am Sonntagmorgen ging die Familie in die Kirche°, am Nachmittag spazieren und wenn einer krank war, dann war er wirklich krank.

Als ich jung war, da war der Franken° noch ein Franken und wenn wir etwas wollten, haben wir zuerst gefragt. Als ich jung war, da waren wir
20 nicht so verweichlicht°. Wir hatten gute Zähne. Das Obst war gesund und die Milch fetter°. Wir lebten gesünder. Da hat man noch Kartoffeln gegessen und Huhn° gab es nur am Sonntag.

Als ich jung war, war alles anders!
Die Bauern waren noch Bauern.
25 Die Leute hatten Zeit.
Eine Familie war eine Familie.
Handarbeit° wurde geschätzt°.
An Weihnachten hatten wir immer Schnee.
In den Städten konnte man wohnen.
30 Kinder waren ein Segen°.
Die Zimmer waren größer.
Man wußte, was man den Eltern schuldig° ist.

listened
obeyed / den ... gehalten: kept one's mouth shut
value
appearances

überfahren ... werden: to be run over / polluted
rivers
wood / rotted

good manners
church

(Swiss unit of currency)

pampered
thicker
chicken

manual work / appreciated

blessing

schuldig ist: owes

Fragen

Früher war alles anders.

1. Geben Sie Beispiele für die Kinder! Wie waren sie früher? Wie sind sie heute?
2. Und die Mädchen, Frauen und Männer?
3. Was hat „man" früher alles anders gemacht?
4. Und die Umwelt? Wie war die früher, und wie ist sie heute?
5. Und die Jahreszeiten?
6. Und das Geld?

Fragen zur Diskussion

Hier spricht ein anonymes Ich. Dieses Ich findet viele Unterschiede zwischen früher und heute.

1. Finden Sie, daß das Ich einige Unterschiede ganz richtig sieht? Welche?
2. Welche Unterschiede finden Sie weniger richtig gesehen?
3. In welchen Unterschieden zeigt sich der Sprecher als reaktionär?
4. Warum verfaulte früher das Holz nicht in den Wäldern?
5. Wie war es früher mit Hygiene und Krankheiten? Und heute? Was ist besser?
6. Ist aus dem jungen Ich wirklich ein Erwachsener geworden? Warum (nicht)?
7. Kennen Sie Menschen, die so reden wie dieses Ich? Was sagen sie?

Kapitel 13

Lernziele

Sprechakte

Discussing leisure activities
Talking about cultural events
Comparing lifestyles

Grammatik

Passive voice
Summary of uses of **werden**
Substitutes for the passive voice

Landeskunde

The special status of Berlin
The German Democratic Republic: history,
economics, and social system

Wohnhäuser und Geschäfte im Zentrum von Berlin (Ost), mit Blick auf Rathaus und Fernsehturm

Bausteine für Gespräche

Was wird gespielt?

Adrian: Hättest du Lust, heute abend ins Theater zu gehen?

Bettina: In welches?

Adrian: Ins Berliner Ensemble.

Bettina: Vielleicht ja. Was wird gespielt?

Adrian: Ein Brecht-Stück. „Leben des Galilei".

Bettina: O gut! Das würde ich mir gern ansehen.

What's playing?

Would you feel like going to the theater tonight?

Which one?

The Berliner Ensemble.

Maybe. What's playing?

A play by Brecht. "Galileo."

Oh good! I'd love to see that.

WILLKOMMEN BEIM

BERLINER ENSEMBLE

AM BERTOLT-BRECHT PLATZ

Hast du Karten?

Bettina: Hast du denn schon Karten für heute abend?

Adrian: Ja, ganz gute sogar. Von meinen Eltern. Die können nicht.

Bettina: So ein Glück! Weißt du, wer den Galilei spielt?

Adrian: Der Klaus Martens.

Bettina: O, der ist bestimmt spitze.

Adrian: Na, das wird sich zeigen ...

Have you got tickets?

Have you already got tickets for tonight?

Yes, very good ones as a matter of fact. From my parents. They can't go.

What luck! Do you know who's playing Galileo?

Klaus Martens.

Oh, he'll be top notch for sure.

Well, that remains to be seen.

Fragen

1. Wohin gehen Bettina und Adrian heute abend?
2. Was wird gespielt?
3. Warum geht Bettina mit?
4. Woher bekommen sie die Karten?
5. Wer erwartet viel von der Vorstellung?

Sie haben das Wort

A   Kommst du mit? Find out from a fellow student what kind of entertainment she/he likes and then invite her/him to join you in attending an event.

Sie

Gehst du gern	ins	**Theater?**
		Konzert°
		Kino
	in die	**Oper°**

Gehst du mit	**ins**	**Theater** heute abend?
		Kino
		Konzert
		Pop-Konzert
		Open-Air-Konzert
	in die	Oper

Gesprächspartner/in

Natürlich.
Wenn ich Zeit habe.
Wenn etwas Gutes gespielt wird.
Ja, sehr gern.
Nein, das interessiert mich nicht.
Nicht besonders.

Ja, gern.
In welche(s)?
Oh ja, das interessiert mich sehr.
Gute Idee.
Wenn du mich einlädst, schon.
Hast du Karten?

| Wer | **spielt?** |
| | singt |

Nein, ich habe leider keine Zeit.

Nein, ich habe keine	**Lust.**
	große Lust
	besondere Lust

Gesprächspartner/in	*Sie*
Was wird gespielt?	*Die Dreigroschenoper [The Threepenny Opera].*
	Goethes *Faust.*
	Ende gut, alles gut.
	Die Zauberflöte [The Magic Flute].
	Fidelio.
	Lohengrin.
	Beethovens *Neunte.*
	Schumanns *Klavierkonzert°.*

Nach dem Theater kann man bei einer Tasse Kaffee über das Stück diskutieren.

B   Interview   Interview a fellow student about her/his taste in entertainment. Keep track of your findings and report them.

Fragen Sie eine(n) Bekannte(n),

1. ob er/sie oft ins Theater geht
2. was für Theaterstücke er/sie gern sieht
3. ob er/sie lieber ins Kino geht
4. wie oft er/sie ins Kino geht — einmal in der Woche, zweimal im Monat
5. welche neuen Filme er/sie gut findet
6. ob er/sie manchmal in die Oper geht
7. welche Opern er/sie kennt
8. ob er/sie oft ins Konzert geht
9. was für Musik er/sie gern hört
10. welche Rockbands er/sie gut findet
11. welche Fernsehsendung er/sie gut findet

Bilder aus der Deutschen Demokratischen Republik

Oben: **Die Fahne der DDR** Schwarz, Rot, Gold mit Hammer und Zirkel. *Unten:* **Berlin (Ost), Hauptstadt der DDR** Unter den Linden.

Oben: **Großveranstaltung in Potsdam** Die FDJ (Freie Deutsche Jugend) organisiert die Jugendlichen der DDR. *Rechts:* **Eiskunstlauf-Weltmeisterin Katarina Witt** Die DDR ist besonders stark im Sport. *Ganz rechts oben:* **Der Thomanerchor in Leipzig** Einer der großen Chöre Europas. *Ganz rechts unten:* **Leipzig** Geschäftsleute aus Ost und West kommen nach Leipzig zur Messe.

Oben: **Gräfenhainichen, Bezirk Halle** Hier baut man ein neues Konsum-Lebensmittelgeschäft für die Stadt. *Unten:* **Die Sächsische Schweiz** Hier kann man gut Urlaub machen.

Vokabeln

Substantive

die **Karte, -n**   ticket
das **Klavier, -e**   piano
das **Konzert, -e**   concert; concerto
die **Oper, -n**   opera

das **Stück, -e** (das **Theaterstück**)
   play (*live theater*)
das **Theater, -**   theater

Andere Wörter

spitze (*colloq.*)   first-rate, top notch

Berlin has special status under international law. After World War II, the four Allies divided Germany into four zones of occupation, and its capital Berlin into four sectors: American, British, French, and Soviet. Currency reforms in the three Western zones and then the Soviet zone in 1948, the blockade of Berlin by the Soviets, and the establishment of the *Bundesrepublik* and the *Deutsche Demokratische Republik (DDR)* in 1949 together led to the separation of Berlin into two parts: a Western and an Eastern part. However, since there was an open border between the two, Berlin provided an escape route for East Germans seeking refuge in the West. By 1961, between 2 and 3.5 million East Germans (an estimated 15% of the work force) had left the *DDR* for the West. To prevent the loss of workers, the *DDR* had gradually sealed its border with the *Bundesrepublik*. In 1961, the *DDR* permanently halted emigration with the construction of the Berlin Wall *(die Mauer)*, thus completing the division of Berlin.

Berlin's special status — meaning that it belongs to neither the *Bundesrepublik* nor the *DDR* — was confirmed by all four Allies in 1971. Theoretically, Berlin is a remnant of prewar Germany, still waiting for a definite status. In practice, both parts of Berlin are closely connected to their respective systems. Many countries recognize *Berlin–Hauptstadt der DDR* as the capital of the *DDR*.

Der Kurfürstendamm zwischen Café Kranzler und Gedächtniskirche (West-Berlin)

| Eindrücke aus der DDR

Vorbereitung auf das Lesen

● *Zum Thema*

Was wissen Sie schon über die Deutsche Demokratische Republik?

1. Sind die Wirtschaftsformen in der DDR und der Bundesrepublik gleich oder verschieden?
2. Ist Arbeitslosigkeit in der DDR ein Problem? Warum (nicht)?
3. Was wissen Sie über den Lebensstandard in der DDR?
4. Wie leicht oder wie schwer ist es für DDR-Bürger, in den Westen zu reisen?
5. Es hat nach dem Zweiten Weltkrieg eine Ost-West-Wanderung gegeben. Von wann bis wann hat sie gedauert? Woher sind die Menschen gekommen? Wohin sind sie gegangen?

● *Leitfragen*

1. In Halle sprach die Journalistin mit einem Industriearbeiter. Was waren die Haupteindrücke?

   Stichworte: modernisieren □ Umschulung □ Staat □ Recht auf Arbeit □ Plan

2. In Dresden sprach sie mit einer jungen Frau. Was waren die Haupteindrücke?

   Stichworte: für Kinder sorgen □ Staat □ etwas extra □ Auto — Lieferfrist □ Verdienst □ Freiraum

3. Die Journalistin ging durch Kaufhäuser und Läden. Was hat sie bemerkt?

   Stichworte: Reklame □ Charakter der Waren □ Schwierigkeiten □ Lebensstandard

4. In Jena sprach sie mit einem Rentner. Wovon sprach er?

   Stichworte: gleich viel verdienen □ ein Drittel des Lohnes □ zuviel alte Menschen

5. Sie sprach auch mit jüngeren Menschen. Was hörte sie von ihnen?

   Stichworte: Leistung □ hier bleiben □ London - Paris - Rom

Bezirke der DDR
mit Bezirksstädten

Eine Journalistin aus den USA ist gerade von einer Informationsreise
durch die Deutsche Demokratische Republik zurückgekommen. Sie hat
dort viele größere und kleinere Städte besucht und überall mit DDR-Bürgern gesprochen. Nun hat sie eine große Zahl von Interviews vor sich
5 liegen, die geordnet° werden müssen.
    Sie begann ihre Reise im Industriegebiet° von Halle. In Halle sprach sie
mit einem Arbeiter, der zur Zeit noch in einem volkseigenen°
Chemiekombinat° beschäftigt ist. Während des Interviews sagte er: „In
zwei Wochen werde ich eine Umschulung° anfangen. Denn unser Be-
10 trieb° wird so modernisiert, daß nicht mehr alle Arbeitskräfte° dort
gebraucht werden. Viele Arbeiter werden jetzt durch Computer ersetzt.
Darum bezahlt der Staat uns die Umschulung und bringt uns an einen
neuen Arbeitsplatz, an dem man uns braucht. Bei uns hat ja jeder das
Recht auf Arbeit. Der Plan sieht für die nächsten fünf Jahre eine bedeu-
15 tende° Erhöhung° der Arbeitsproduktivität in der Industrie vor°. Und da
muß natürlich so effektiv wie möglich gearbeitet werden.''

put in order

industrial area

state-owned

chemical concern

retraining program

company / workers

significant / increase / **sieht**
vor: *calls for*

Jazzabend in einer Gaststätte in Halle

In Dresden sprach die Journalistin mit einer jungen Frau — verheiratet, zwei Kinder, voll berufstätig. Auf die Frage, wer für die Kinder sorgt, sagte sie: „Der Staat. Es gibt hier in unserem Neubaugebiet° einen Kindergar-
20 ten und eine Kinderkrippe°. Dort kostet der Platz nur etwa eine Mark am Tag pro Kind. Und ich bin froh, daß ich mitverdienen° kann. Mieten° und alle lebensnotwendigen° Dinge sind ja nicht teuer, und die Preise sind stabil, aber man will ja auch mal etwas extra haben. Wir haben seit zwei Jahren einen Farbfernseher! Und im nächsten Jahr soll auch unser Tra-
25 bant° geliefert° werden. Endlich! Vor zehn Jahren haben wir ihn bestellt. So lang ist die Lieferfrist°. Von einer Freundin weiß ich, daß das kein billiges Vergnügen wird. Wenn im Sommer schönes Wetter ist und sie Freunde auf dem Lande besucht, dann kommt sie auf° über 250 Mark Benzingeld im Monat. Versicherung° und Kfz-Steuer° sind auch nicht bil-
30 lig, so daß sie fast die Hälfte ihres Gehalts für das Auto ausgibt. Bei unseren zwei Gehältern läßt es sich etwas leichter machen. Ich finde auch, daß es das wert ist. Denn mit dem Auto sind wir ein bißchen unabhängiger und können einfach mal rausfahren°, wenn wir wollen. Wir freuen uns schon sehr auf diese Unabhängigkeit°, gerade weil es in
35 diesem Land soviel Bevormundung° gibt. Das Auto vergrößert° unseren Freiraum° ein wenig.

Interessant war für die Journalistin auch, durch verschiedene Kauf-

new-housing development
day-care center
also earn money / rents
essential

(brand name of car) / delivered / delivery time

up to
insurance / automobile tax

drive into the country
independence
(government) controls / increases / freedom of movement

häuser und Läden zu bummeln°. Hier und da sah sie Leute Schlange   *stroll*
stehen. Es gab kein Reklamegeklingel° und keine Musik. Alles diente nur   *din of advertising*
40 der Bedarfsdeckung°. Daher hatten die Waren einen ganz anderen   *satisfaction of needs*
Charakter als in den USA, denn sie sollten ja nicht zum Kauf° verführen°,   *purchase / seduce*
sondern nur ihren Zweck erfüllen°. Auswahl° gab es z.B. bei Kleidung   *fulfill / selection*
kaum. Von verschiedenen Leuten hörte sie, daß sie immer wieder
Schwierigkeiten beim Einkaufen haben: „Heute gibt es dieses nicht, mor-
45 gen jenes nicht. Man weiß nie, wann es was gibt oder nicht gibt. Und
bestimmte Sachen gibt es überhaupt nicht." Aber in den Zeitungen war
zu lesen, daß der Lebensstandard, verglichen mit den anderen sozialisti-
schen Ostblockstaaten, in der DDR am höchsten ist.

In Jena sprach sie mit einem Rentner°, der früher bei Zeiß° gearbeitet   *pensioner / (name of optical*
50 hatte. Er erklärte ihr: „Bei uns wird überall etwa gleich viel verdient.   *instrument company)*
Dadurch gibt es hier nicht die großen sozialen Unterschiede wie in der
BRD° zum Beispiel. Und das finde ich wirklich gut. Aber wenn man mal   BRD = Bundesrepublik
Rentner ist, so wie ich jetzt, dann muß man sich ganz schön umstellen°.   Deutschland / *adjust*
Jetzt muß ich mit etwa einem Drittel meines früheren Arbeitslohnes aus-
55 kommen°. Und einen Platz im Altersheim°, den bekommen nur wenige.   *get by / retirement home*
Es gibt eben zuviel alte Menschen hier. Wenn nicht so viele in den We-
sten gegangen wären,* ginge es uns heute sicher auch besser. Manchmal
hat man das Gefühl, daß der Staat nur darauf wartet, daß wir Alten auch in
den Westen gehen. Aber schließlich haben wir das alles hier aufgebaut°.   *built up*
60 Das kann man doch nicht einfach so stehen und liegen lassen."

Als sie mit jüngeren Menschen darüber sprach, wie sie mit ihrem Leben
hier zufrieden wären, hörte sie: „Hier sind wir zu Hause. Man muß auch
nicht unbedingt° Genosse° sein, um stolz auf unsere Leistung° zu sein.   *necessarily / party member /*
Wir haben den Aufbau° hier unter ziemlich schwierigen Bedingungen°   *achievement / (re)con-*
65 gemacht. Nein, wir wollen hier bleiben — wenn wir nur hoffen dürften,   *struction / conditions*
bald auch einmal nach London, Paris und Rom fahren zu können."

Fragen zum Lesestück

1. Woher ist die Journalistin gerade gekommen?
2. Wo begann sie ihre Reise?
3. Warum wird der Chemiearbeiter eine Umschulung anfangen?
4. Wer bezahlt die Umschulung?
5. Wer hat ein Recht auf Arbeit?
6. Wer sorgt für ihre Kinder, wenn die Frau in Dresden arbeitet?
7. Was kostet ein Platz in einem Kindergarten am Tag?
8. Welche besonderen Sachen kann sich ihre Familie kaufen?
9. Wieviel Geld gibt die Freundin im Monat für ihr Auto aus?

*See cultural note on Berlin, p.447.

10. Wieviel verdient die Freundin etwa?
11. Warum will die Frau trotzdem ein Auto?
12. Was gab es in den Kaufhäusern nicht?
13. Warum hatten die Waren einen anderen Charakter?
14. Warum glaubt der Rentner, daß es in der DDR keine großen sozialen Unterschiede gibt?
15. Wieviel bekommt der Rentner jetzt, verglichen mit früher?
16. Warum gibt es so viele alte Menschen?
17. Worauf sind viele Leute stolz?
18. Worauf hoffen viele?

Erzählen Sie! Interview aus der DDR   Choose one of the people interviewed by the journalist to talk about. Use the cued words in addition to your own.

1. der Arbeiter aus Halle

   Stichwörter: Umschulung □ durch Computer ersetzt

2. die berufstätige Mutter aus Dresden

   Stichwörter: zwei Kinder □ voll berufstätig □ Kindergarten □ Farbfernseher und Auto □ unabhängig

3. der Rentner aus Jena

   Stichwörter: keine großen sozialen Unterschiede □ ein Drittel seines früheren Arbeitslohnes □ Altersheim □ zuviel alte Menschen

Sie haben das Wort

Was sagen Sie?

1. Werden Arbeiter in Ihrem Land durch Computer ersetzt? In welchen Berufen?
2. Sind die Preise stabil?
3. Wieviel muß man pro Monat für Benzin, Versicherung und Kfz-Steuer bezahlen?
4. Man hört oft Musik und laute Reklamen in den Kaufhäusern. Stört Sie das?
5. Gibt es in Ihrem Land zuviel alte Menschen?

Vokabeln

_ Substantive

der **Arbeiter, -** / die **Arbeiterin, -nen** worker

das **Benzin** gasoline, fuel

der **Eindruck, ¨e** impression

das **Gehalt, ¨er** salary

der **Journalist, -en, -en** / die **Journalistin, -nen** journalist, reporter

der **Kindergarten, ¨** kindergarten

der **Lohn, ¨e** wage; reward

das **Recht, -e** right; **Recht auf Arbeit** right to work

das **Vergnügen** enjoyment, fun; **Viel Vergnügen!** Have a good time!

der **Zweck, -e** purpose

_ Verben

aus·geben (gibt aus), gab aus, ausgegeben to spend (money)

dienen (+ _dat._) to serve

ersetzen to replace

sich freuen (auf + _acc._) to look forward to; **sich freuen (über** + _acc._) to be pleased about

vergleichen, verglich, verglichen (mit) to compare (to, with)

_ Andere Wörter

dadurch thereby, by this means

darum therefore, for that reason

froh glad, happy

früher former(ly), earlier

jen(er, -es, -e) that; the former

schwierig difficult

überall everywhere

zufrieden satisfied

_ Besondere Ausdrücke

Schlange stehen to stand in line

zur Zeit (_abbrev._ **z.Z.**) at the time; currently

| Übungen zur Aussprache _____

Review the pronunciation of the letters **b**, **d**, and **g** in the Reference section at the end of the book. Read the words in each pair of columns across, then down. Check your pronunciation by listening to your instructor or the tape.

[b]	[p]	[d]	[t]	[g]	[k]
graben	Grab	finden	Fund	Tage	Tag
gaben	gab	Hunde	Hund	Wege	Weg
Staube	Staub	senden	Sand	trugen	trug
hoben	hob	Bäder	Bad	Kriege	Krieg

Read the sentences aloud, paying special attention to the way you pronounce the letters **b**, **d**, and **g** in the boldfaced words.

1. **Haben** Sie das **Bild** meines **Bruders** und seiner **Freundin** gesehen?
2. Ich **habe über** ein **halbes** Jahr in **Freiburg gelebt**.
3. Es ist **gesund**, mit dem **Rad** aufs **Land** zu fahren.
4. Am **Montag habt** ihr **Probe** fürs Konzert, nicht?
5. Wieviel **Tage bleibt** ihr in **Hamburg**?

Glücklich ist, wer vergißt, was
nicht mehr zu ändern ist.

| Grammatik und Übungen

1   The passive voice

Active voice	
Helga Klein schreibt das Buch.	Helga Klein is writing the book.
Hoffentlich lesen **viele** das Buch.	Let's hope that many read the book.

Passive voice	
Das Buch wird von Helga Klein geschrieben.	The book is being written by Helga Klein.
Hoffentlich wird **es** gelesen.	Let's hope it will be read.

In the active voice, the subject is "active": the subject is the agent that performs the action expressed by the verb. Active voice focuses attention on the agent. The attention in the active sentences above is focused on Helga Klein, who is writing a book, and on the many people who will read it.

In the passive voice, the subject is "passive": the subject is acted upon by an expressed or unexpressed agent. Passive voice focuses attention on the receiver of the action. The attention in the passive sentences above is focused on the book, which is being written by Helga Klein or read by the public.

The subject (e.g., **Buch**) of a passive sentence corresponds to the accusative object of an active sentence. The agent (e.g., **Helga Klein**) of a passive sentence corresponds to the subject of an active sentence. The agent is often omitted in a passive sentence, as if the corresponding active sentence had no subject.

In everyday conversation, speakers of German use the active voice much more often than the passive voice. The passive is very often used in technical and scientific writing, however, where an impersonal style is frequently preferred.

2   Tenses in the passive voice

Present	Das Buch **wird geschrieben.**	The book is being written.
Simple past	Das Buch **wurde geschrieben.**	The book was being written.
Perfect	Das Buch **ist geschrieben worden.**	The book has been written.
Past perfect	Das Buch **war geschrieben worden.**	The book had been written.
Future	Das Buch **wird geschrieben werden.**	The book will be written.

In English, a passive verb phrase consists of a form of the auxiliary verb *to be* and the past participle of the verb. In German, the passive verb phrase consists of a form of the auxiliary **werden** and the past participle of the main verb. The passive voice can occur in all tenses. In the perfect and past perfect tenses, the participle **worden** is used in place of **geworden.**

3   *Von* + agent

Die Bürger wurden **von der Journalistin** interviewt.

The citizens were interviewed *by the journalist.*

Umschulung wird **vom Staat** bezahlt.

Retraining is being paid *by the state.*

In the passive voice, the role of the agent is secondary in importance to the receiver of the action. In German, the agent is in the dative case and is the object of the preposition **von.**

4   *Durch* + means

Das Geld wurde **durch schwere Arbeit** verdient.

The money was earned *through hard work.*

In den Kaufhäusern werden die Kunden nicht **durch Musik** gestört.

In the department stores the customers are not bothered *by music.*

The means by which something is brought about is in the accusative case and is the object of the preposition **durch.**

A   Ein Theaterabend   Bettina has written a letter to a friend about her evening at the theater with Adrian. Give the English equivalent.

Ich wurde von Adrian wieder ins Theater eingeladen. Wir haben *Leben des Galilei* gesehen. Du weißt, das Stück ist von Brecht und wurde 1938 geschrieben. Ich wurde ziemlich früh von Adrian abgeholt, und wir konnten vorher ein bißchen spazierengehen. Da Galilei von Klaus Martens gespielt wurde, war das Theater voll. Der war spitze.

B   Von wem wird das gemacht?   State by whom the following things are done in your family. Use the passive voice.

▶   Von wem wird das Essen gekocht?   *Das Essen wird von [meinem Vater] gekocht.*

1.   Von wem wird das Auto gewaschen?
2.   Von wem wird das Brot gekauft?
3.   Von wem wird das Haus saubergemacht?
4.   Von wem wird das Geschirr abgewaschen?
5.   Von wem wird die Wäsche gewaschen?
6.   Von wem wird Kuchen oder Brot gebacken?
7.   Von wem wird die Gartenarbeit gemacht?

In 1949 the Soviet Zone of Occupation became the *Deutsche Demokratische Republik (DDR)*. The economic and social structures of the Third Reich and capitalism were gradually replaced by a centralized, socialized state with a planned economy (*Planwirtschaft*). As part of prewar Germany, the region's economy was based on agriculture and light industry. After the war a build-up of heavy industry was stressed. Over the years many farm cooperatives have been established, resulting in a decrease of more than half of the total number of farms.

In 1963 *das neue ökonomische System (NöS)* was introduced, which brought about some decentralization and some orientation toward profit. With *NöS*, more consumer goods became available. The system also allowed the rise of young, well-educated specialists, whose style is determined more by technical professionalism than by ideology. Today the *DDR* has a high per capita production ratio.

Containerschiffe im Bau (Warnow-Werft in Rostock-Warnemünde)

Sie haben das Wort

Wer war das?   Think of five trivia questions to ask a partner. Use the passive voice.

Von wem wurde der Film _____ gedreht°?   *made a movie*
Von wem wurde _____ erfunden°?   *invented*
Von wem wurde _____ entdeckt°?   *discovered*
Von wem wurde _____ gebaut?
Von wem wurde _____ komponiert°?   *composed*

C   Gleichberechtigung gab es damals nicht.   Mark listened to a discussion about the former position of women in society. Give the English equivalents of his notes.

1. Warum wurde Frau Meier denn eigentlich immer schlechter bezahlt als ihr Mann?
   — Na ja, eine Erklärung ist, daß die besseren Stellen immer den Männern gegeben wurden.
2. Die Kinder von Speemanns sind durch die Vorurteile der Kinderbücher beeinflußt worden, nicht?
   — Ja, in ihren Büchern ist eben immer nur das traditionelle Frauenbild gezeigt worden.
3. Von wem wurde denn bei Gardes das Geld verdient?
   — Von Herrn Garde. Und die Hausarbeit wurde natürlich von Frau Garde gemacht.
   — Ja, für sie war das immer ein langer Tag. Nachdem abends die Kinder ins Bett gebracht worden waren, war ihr Tag immer noch nicht zu Ende.
4. Und bei den jungen Kortes, von wem wird da die Wäsche gewaschen und das Haus geputzt?
   — Oft von der ganzen Familie. Schließlich wird ja ein Teil des Geldes auch von Frau Korte verdient.
5. Ganz allgemein kann man sagen, daß früher die Probleme der Gleichberechtigung anders gesehen wurden als heute.
   — Schon die Kinder wurden auf eine traditionelle Rolle als Mann oder Frau vorbereitet.

Since its establishment in 1949, the German Democratic Republic has developed into a highly industrialized nation. Industry accounts for 70% of the national income, providing jobs for 40% of the work force. Since 1950, national income has increased by more than 800% and living conditions have improved steadily. A recent study showed that 46% of all households have a car, 92% a TV set, 100% a refrigerator, and 97% a washing machine. Health and retirement insurance is inexpensive, and an average of only 5% of a family's income is spent on rent.

Education is free at all levels, and mandatory in public schools for ten years. Work experience for older children one day a week is intended to combine theoretical and practical education. Students may then take two years of college preparatory work or of job training.

Women in the *DDR* enjoy a high rate of promotion. A good percentage of union officials, work arbitrators, and mayors are women.

92% aller Kinder gehen in den Kindergarten. Berlin (Ost)

5   Modals plus passive infinitive

Einige Interviews von DDR-Bürgern **müssen** noch **gemacht werden**.

Some interviews of DDR-citizens still *have to be conducted.*

Der Artikel **konnte** nur von einer Journalistin **geschrieben werden**.

The article *could* only *be written* by a journalist.

The passive infinitive consists of the past participle of a verb plus **werden** (e.g., **gemacht werden**). Modals are often used with a passive infinitive.

D   Die deutsche Wirtschaft   Give the English equivalents of the observations below about the German economy.

1. Rohstoffe müssen importiert werden.
2. Von den Firmen sollen Qualitätsprodukte produziert werden.
3. Qualitätsprodukte können meistens gut verkauft werden.
4. Die Inflationsrate soll niedrig gehalten werden.
5. Das Problem der Arbeitslosigkeit darf nicht vergessen werden.
6. Arbeit soll für alle Leute gefunden werden.

E   Eindrücke aus der DDR   In a discussion about aspects of life in the *DDR*, a journalist makes the following points. Restate the sentences with the cued modals.

▶   In der Industrie muß so effektiv   *In der Industrie soll so effektiv wie*
     wie möglich gearbeitet werden.   *möglich gearbeitet werden.*
     (sollen)

1.   Viele Firmen sollen modernisiert werden. (müssen)
2.   Nur Waren für das tägliche Leben dürfen produziert werden. (sollen)
3.   Die Preise können ziemlich stabil gehalten werden. (müssen)
4.   Für viele Kinder muß im Kindergarten gesorgt werden. (können)
5.   Mehr Plätze in Altersheimen müssen gefunden werden. (sollen)
6.   Die Rentner sollen nicht vergessen werden. (dürfen)

6   Dative verbs in the passive voice

| Active voice | Wir haben **ihm** nicht geholfen. | We didn't help him. |
| Passive voice | **Ihm** wurde nicht geholfen. | He wasn't helped. |

In German, a dative object in an active sentence (e.g., **ihm**) remains unchanged in the corresponding passive sentence. The resulting passive sentence has no subject. Since English makes no distinction between the dative and accusative, the object of the active sentence (e.g., *him*) corresponds to the subject of the passive sentence (e.g., *he*).

7   Impersonal passive constructions

| Active voice | Jeder arbeitet jetzt. | Everyone is working now. |
| Passive voice | Jetzt **wird gearbeitet.** | (There is work going on now.) |

An English active sentence without a direct object does not have a corresponding passive sentence. A German active sentence without a direct object can have a corresponding passive sentence. A passive construction without a subject or agent is called an impersonal passive construction. An English equivalent of the impersonal passive often uses an introductory phrase such as *there is* or *there are*.

Es wird hier viel gearbeitet. }
Hier wird viel gearbeitet.   } There's a lot of work going on here.

The pronoun **es** begins an impersonal passive construction if no other words precede the verb. The pronoun **es** is a "dummy" or "apparent" subject.

F   Gleichberechtigung   In a discussion about equal rights, Monika makes a number of general observations. Restate the sentences, beginning with **es**, and give the English equivalents.

▶ Den Frauen wurde weniger bezahlt
  als den Männern.
  { *Es wurde den Frauen weniger*
  bezahlt als den Männern.
  Women were paid less than men. }

1. Von allen sollte gleich viel verdient werden.
2. Manchen Frauen ist bei der Hausarbeit nicht geholfen worden.
3. Den Kindern ist alles erklärt worden.
4. Jedem muß eine Chance gegeben werden.
5. In vielen Familien wird samstags geputzt.
6. Sonntags wird nicht gearbeitet.

G   Das Leben in der DDR   Give the English equivalents of the statements below about the *DDR*.

1. Die Leute wurden nach dem Leben in der DDR gefragt.
2. Der Rentner war dafür, daß etwa gleich viel verdient wird.
3. Viele Firmen sollen modernisiert werden.
4. Es muß noch viel getan werden.
5. Die Kinder werden in den Kindergarten geschickt.
6. In diesem Land muß viel gearbeitet werden.
7. Für die alten Leute muß auch gesorgt werden.

8   Participle in passive vs. participle as predicate adjective

Passive	Das Fenster **wird geschlossen.**	The window is being closed.
Predicate adjective	Das Fenster **ist geschlossen.**	The window is closed.

The passive expresses the act of doing something to the subject (e.g., **Fenster**); it uses **werden** and the past participle (e.g., **geschlossen**). The past participle can also be used with the verb **sein** to express the state or condition of the subject that results from the action. The participle then functions like a predicate adjective. Because of its similarity to the passive, the construction **sein** + participle is often referred to as an "apparent passive" or "statal passive." In English the verb *to be* is used both for the passive and for predicate adjectives. For this reason the difference between the passive and predicate adjectives is sometimes not clear. No confusion is possible in German. The agent with **von** and the means with **durch** can be used only with the passive.

H   Viel Hausarbeit   Talk about past and future chores. Give the German equivalents of the following sentences.

1.   The house was cleaned by my brother.   *Das Hause wurde von meinem Bruder (CLEANED)*   *saubergemacht*
2.   The dishes were done by my sister.   *Das Geshir wurde von meiner Schwester abgewaschen.*
3.   The car is already washed.   *Das Auto ist schon gewaschen.*
4.   The yardwork is already done.
5.   Are the clothes already washed?
6.   Are the windows done [cleaned]?
7.   Does the bathroom still have to be cleaned?   *Muß das Badenzimmer jetzt saubergemacht werden*
8.   Does the living room still have to be straightened up?

9   Summary of the uses of *werden*

• *Main verb*

Herr Heller **wird** alt.	Mr. Heller is growing old.
Die Kinder **wurden** müde.	The children were getting tired.
Frau Ullmann **ist** Chefin der Firma **geworden**.	Mrs. Ullmann has become head of the company.

Werden as a main verb is equivalent to English *to grow, get,* or *become.*

• *Auxiliary verb in future tense*

Er **wird** hoffentlich mehr **arbeiten**.	I hope he will work more.
Du **wirst** das wohl **wissen**.	You probably know that.

Werden is used with a dependent infinitive to form the future tense. The future tense also expresses present probability.

• *Auxiliary verb in the passive voice*

Die Wirtschaft der DDR **wird** vom Staat **geplant**.	The economy of the *DDR* is planned by the state.
Die Industrie **wurde modernisiert**.	Industry was modernized.
In einigen Firmen **sind** viele Arbeiter durch Computer **ersetzt worden**.	In some firms many workers have been replaced by computers.

Werden is used with a past participle to form the passive voice. The passive voice can occur in any tense. The participle **worden** is used in place of **geworden** in the perfect and past perfect tenses.

I   Was bedeutet das?   Identify the verb phrase with **werden** in each sentence below. Tell whether **werden** is being used (a) as a main verb in the active voice (give the tense), (b) to express future or present probability, or

(c) as a tense of the passive voice (give the tense). Then give English equivalents for the sentences.

▶   Das Problem ist gelöst worden.   *perfect passive / The problem has been solved.*

1.   Hier muß noch viel gemacht werden.
2.   Die Situation wird im nächsten Jahr sicher besser.
3.   Der Export wird langsam weniger.
4.   Wer wird dem Land helfen?
5.   Werden die Waren auf dem Weltmarkt eine Zukunft haben?
6.   Es ist bekannt, daß das Land immer weniger Rohstoffe haben wird.
7.   Das Leben ist in letzter Zeit teurer geworden.
8.   Allen armen Menschen muß geholfen werden.
9.   Die Industrie wird sich wohl neue Markte suchen müssen.
10.   Das Wetter wird hoffentlich in den nächsten Tagen besser.
11.   Es wird schon so sein, wie du sagst.
12.   Erik will einfach nicht arbeiten. Was soll aus ihm werden?
13.   Die Arbeit muß noch gemacht werden.
14.   Jörg ist krank, aber er wird wohl bald wieder gesund.

Besser informiert ist, wer besser informiert wird.
Süddeutsche Zeitung
Das Weltblatt aus München

10   Substitutes for the passive voice

The passive voice is used less frequently in German than in English. In German, other constructions are frequently substituted for the passive voice.

• man *as subject*

Man sagt das oft.	One often says that.
(Das wird oft gesagt.)	That's often said.
Wie kann **man** das machen?	How can people do that?
(Wie kann das gemacht werden?)	How can that be done?

In German, the pronoun **man** is used frequently instead of the passive voice, whenever there is no expressed agent. English has several possible equivalents of **man:** *one, you, we, they,* or *people.*

J   Die Universität in der Schweiz   Diane has many questions about universities in Switzerland. Give the English equivalents of the sentences below.

Universität
Zürich

1. Wie lange geht man auf die Universität?
2. Wieviel bezahlt man dafür?
3. Muß man viel lernen?
4. Wie lange darf man studieren?
5. Was kann man später machen?
6. Wieviel Klausuren muß man im Semester schreiben?
7. Soll man mehrere Fächer auf einmal studieren?
8. Hatte man früher an der Universität mehr Freiheit?

K   Noch einmal   Restate the sentences below, using **man**.

▶   Wie wird das gemacht?   *Wie macht man das?*

1. Hier wird gearbeitet.
2. Wann wird Kaffee getrunken?
3. Es darf nicht geredet werden.
4. Die Schreibmaschine soll benutzt werden.
5. Wie wird das Wort geschrieben?
6. Wann wird mit der Arbeit aufgehört?

● **sein ... zu** + *infinitive*

Das **ist** leicht **zu verstehen**.	That's easy to understand.
(Das kann leicht verstanden werden.)	That can be understood easily.
Die Arbeit **ist** noch **zu machen**.	The work is still to be done.
(Die Arbeit muß noch gemacht werden.)	The work must still be done.

A form of **sein ... zu** + infinitive is often used in German instead of a passive verb phrase. The **sein ... zu** + infinitive construction expresses the possibility or necessity of doing something.

L   Dieter geht ins Theater.   Dieter asks questions about the play you want to see. Respond as suggested, using **sein ... zu** + infinitive.

▶   Kann man das Theater leicht finden? (Ja)   *Ja, das Theater ist leicht zu finden.*

1. Kann man das Theater mit dem Bus erreichen? (Ja)
2. Muß man die Karten vorher kaufen? (Ja)

3. Kann man noch gute Plätze haben? (Ja)
4. Kann man noch billige Karten bekommen? (Ja)
5. Kann man das Stück leicht verstehen? (Nein)

M Berufstätige Frauen Various students contribute to a seminar discussion about women and the economic situation. Give the English equivalents of the sentences below.

1. Es ist kaum zu glauben, wie wenige Frauen in „Männerberufen" arbeiten.
2. Wirkliche Gleichberechtigung ist nur zu erreichen, wenn die Männer sich auch emanzipieren.
3. Manche Probleme sind durch die wirtschaftliche Situation zu erklären.
4. Antworten sind schwer zu finden.
5. Viele Vorurteile sind auch heute noch zu hören.
6. Gute Kindergärten sind nicht leicht zu finden.

- *Reflexive constructions*

Diese Sache **erklärt sich** sehr einfach.	This matter can be explained very easily.
(Diese Sache kann sehr einfach erklärt werden.)	
Die Tür **öffnete sich**.	The door opened.
(Die Tür wurde geöffnet.)	The door was opened.

A reflexive construction may sometimes be used in place of a passive verb phrase.

N Natürlich Inge is going to write a report on Germans' interest in health and "natural" living. Give the English equivalents.

1. In Deutschland verkaufen sich Sachen leichter, wenn sie „natürlich" sind.
2. Das zeigt sich an den vielen Reklamen mit den Wörtern „Natur" und „natürlich".
3. Es versteht sich daher, daß es in Deutschland viele Reformhäuser und Bio-Läden gibt.
4. Viele Leute glauben, daß es sich besser lebt, wenn man natürliche Sachen benutzt.
5. Die Frage ist nicht, ob natürliche Kleidung sich länger trägt, sondern ob sie gesünder ist.
6. Bei geöffnetem Fenster schläft es sich gut.
7. In Wald und frischer Luft läuft es sich gut.
8. So erklären sich die vielen deutschen Wanderlieder.

O   In Dänemark   The Hubers are worried about their move to Denmark. Their relatives are reassuring them it will all work out. Restate the sentences below, using a reflexive construction.

▶   Die alte Wohnung ist leicht zu verkaufen.   *Die alte Wohnung verkauft*
                                                sich leicht.

1.   Eine neue Wohnung ist schon zu finden.
2.   Die Fremdsprache ist schon zu lernen.
3.   Eine gute Schule ist leicht zu finden.
4.   Einige Probleme sind nur schwer zu lösen.
5.   Aber die meisten Probleme sind leicht zu lösen.
6.   Neue Freunde sind wohl auch zu finden.

• sich lassen + *infinitive*

Das **läßt sich** machen.   That can be done.
(Das kann gemacht werden.)

Läßt sich dieses Auto überhaupt   Can this car be paid for at all?
   bezahlen?
(Kann dieses Auto überhaupt
   bezahlt werden?)

A form of **sich lassen** + infinitive can be used in place of a passive verb phrase. This construction expresses the possibility of something being done.

P   Die Wirtschaft heute   Dieter Meier has taken notes on a report about modern industrial society. Give the English equivalents.

1.   Hoffentlich läßt sich ein Weg finden, die Arbeitslosen wieder zu beschäftigen.
2.   Das läßt sich aber nicht von heute auf morgen machen.
3.   Ältere Arbeiter lassen sich oft nur schwer in moderne Industriefirmen integrieren.
4.   Einige Probleme lassen sich nicht leicht lösen.
5.   Bei diesen Problemen läßt sich nicht sagen, was die Zukunft bringen wird.
6.   Es läßt sich auch nicht sagen, ob der Staat all das bezahlen kann.

Q   Alles läßt sich machen!   In a business conference, Ms. Hohner asks whether most matters are taken care of. Answer her questions, using a form of **sich lassen** + infinitive.

▶   Kann man das machen?   *O ja! Das läßt sich machen.*

1.   Kann man die Ware billig produzieren?   5.   Kann man das bezahlen?
2.   Kann man das Problem lösen?   6.   Kann man das leicht erklären?
3.   Kann man darüber reden?   7.   Kann man die Ware gut verkaufen?
4.   Kann man einen Weg finden?

| Wiederholung

A   Der Theaterabend   Tell about Stefanie's and Christian's night at the theater. Restate the sentences below in the perfect tense.

▶   Stefanies Eltern bieten ihr zwei   *Stefanies Eltern haben ihr zwei*
Theaterkarten an.   *Theaterkarten angeboten.*

1.   Sie lädt Christian ein mitzugehen.
2.   Christian nimmt die Einladung gern an.
3.   Er holt Stefanie um sieben Uhr ab.
4.   Sie sehen ein Stück von Bertolt Brecht.
5.   Nach dem Theater gehen sie etwas trinken.
6.   Sie entscheiden sich für eine Studenten-kneipe.
7.   Da treffen sie einige Freunde.
8.   Sie hören eine Jazzgruppe.
9.   Sie reden über die letzten Sommerferien.

B   Ein Wochenende am Bodensee   Silke can't accept Sabine's invitation for the weekend at Lake Constance. Restate the conversation between them in the future tense.

▶   *Silke:* Was machst du am Wochenende?   *Was wirst du am Wochenende machen?*

Sabine: Wir fahren an den Bodensee. Kannst du mitkommen?
Silke: Es geht leider nicht. Meine Freunde und ich spielen bei einem Fest.
Sabine: Kannst du das nächste Mal mitkommen?
Silke: Sicher. Das macht bestimmt Spaß.

C   Interviews in der DDR   A journalist tells about several interviews in the German Democratic Republic. Complete the sentences by adding appropriate word endings where needed.

1.   Die Journalistin erzählt von ihr__ Reise durch d__ Deutsche Demokratische Republik.
2.   In Halle sprach sie mit ein__ älter__ Arbeiter.
3.   Er sprach über sein__ Arbeit in d__ Chemieindustrie.
4.   Er ist zufrieden mit sein__ Leben.
5.   Er kann jed__ Sommer ein__ schön__ Urlaub machen.
6.   Die Journalistin sprach auch mit ein__ jung__ verheiratet__ Frau, d__ voll berufstätig__ war.
7.   D__ Frau erzählt, daß d__ Staat viel für d__ Familie tut.
8.   D__ Wohnung und d__ Kindergarten sind sehr billig.
9.   Aber für ein__ neu__ Auto muß man sehr viel__ Geld bezahlen.
10.   Sie müssen auch einig__ Jahre darauf warten.
11.   Aber dies__ Jahr werden sie d__ Auto bekommen.
12.   Trotz d__ hoh__ Preis__ freuen sie sich da__ .
13.   Mit d__ Auto besuchen sie dann ihr__ Freunde auf d__ Land.

D   Ergänzen Sie!   Complete each sentence below with the correct form of the appropriate verb from the lists given.

aufhören □ gehören □ hören

1. _____ du gern Musik?
2. Wem _____ die Kassetten?
3. Wenn ich mit der Arbeit _____ , _____ ich oft klassische Musik.
4. Hast du schon meine neueste Platte _____ ?

einkaufen □ kaufen □ verkaufen

5. Ich muß noch schnell _____ gehen.
6. Was _____ du denn heute?
7. Ich weiß noch nicht, manchmal _____ sie das Gemüse abends billiger.

besuchen □ suchen □ versuchen

8. Christoph _____ seine Freunde in München.
9. Er _____ die Adresse.
10. Ein Mann _____ , ihm den Weg zu erklären.

E   Wie sagt man das?

Ingrid: What would you like to do this evening?
Thomas: I'd go to the theater if I had money.
Ingrid: Could I invite you?
Thomas: That would be nice.
Ingrid: Could you drive?
Thomas: I'd drive if I had my car. My brother has it.
Ingrid: We could go by streetcar.
Thomas: For that I have enough money.
Ingrid: Good.

F   Ihre Meinung

1. Sollte der Staat die Preise kontrollieren? Für Lebensmittel? Für Miete? Für was? Warum (nicht)?
2. Sollte der Staat Kindergartenplätze für Kinder berufstätiger Eltern bezahlen oder subventionieren°?   *subsidize*
3. Sollte es in Amerika ein Recht auf Arbeit geben? Warum (nicht)?
4. Sollte die Firma oder der Arbeiter oder der Staat eine Umschulung bezahlen?
5. Sind Sie dafür, daß Frauen in „Männerberufen" arbeiten?
6. Sollten amerikanische Frauen eine größere Rolle in der Politik spielen?
7. Tut der Staat genug für alte Leute in Amerika?

G   Anregung

1. In a short paragraph in German, compare the role of women in the **Bundesrepublik** and in the **DDR**. You may wish to refer back to *Kapitel 10*, pages 347–349.
2. Write a short paragraph in German in which you compare some major feature of life in the **DDR** with life in the United States. Indicate what your preferences are and why.
3. Write a short paragraph in German in which you make a few comparisons between the **Bundesrepublik** and the **DDR**. You may wish to discuss size, standard of living, population, and physical characteristics of the two countries.

| Grammatik zum Nachschlagen ──────────

The passive voice   (A, C)

Active voice	
Inge singt das Lied.	Inge is singing the song.

Passive voice	
Das Lied wird von Inge gesungen.	The song is being sung by Inge.
Es wird zweimal gesungen.	It is being sung twice.

In the active voice, the subject is active. The subject is the agent that performs the action expressed by the verb. In the passive voice, the subject is passive. The subject is acted upon.

The subject of a passive sentence corresponds to the accusative object of an active sentence (e.g., **das Lied**). The agent of a passive sentence corresponds to the subject of an active sentence (e.g., **Inge**). The agent is often omitted in a passive sentence, as if the corresponding active sentence had no subject.

Passive voice occurs more frequently in written German than in spoken German.

Tenses in the passive voice (A, C)

Present	Der Brief **wird geschrieben.**	The letter is being written.
Simple past	Der Brief **wurde geschrieben.**	The letter was being written.
Perfect	Der Brief **ist geschrieben worden.**	The letter has been written.
Past perfect	Der Brief **war geschrieben worden.**	The letter had been written.
Future	Der Brief **wird geschrieben werden.**	The letter will be written.

The passive voice consists of the auxiliary **werden** and the past participle of the main verb. Passive voice can occur in any tense.
NOTE: In the perfect and past-perfect tenses the participle **worden** is used in place of **geworden**.

Agent or means expressed (B)

von + agent	
Das Geld wurde **von den Arbeitern** verdient.	The money was earned *by the workers.*

durch + means	
Das Geld wurde **durch schwere Arbeit** verdient.	The money was earned *through hard work.*

The passive voice focuses attention away from the agent or means onto the receiver of an action. The agent is in the dative case and is the object of the preposition **von**. The means is in the accusative case and is the object of the preposition **durch**. The agent or means may be omitted.

Modals + passive infinitive (D, E)

Der Brief muß **geschrieben werden**.	The letter must be written.
Kann diese Arbeit schnell **gemacht werden?**	Can this work be done quickly?

The passive infinitive consists of the past participle of a verb plus **werden**. Modals are often used with a passive infinitive.

Dative verbs in the passive voice (F, G)

Active voice	Man hat **ihr** geholfen.	They helped her.
Passive voice	**Ihr** wurde nicht geholfen.	She was not helped.

In German, a dative object in an active sentence (e.g., **ihr**) remains unchanged in the corresponding passive sentence. The resulting passive sentence has no subject. In English, the object of the active sentence (e.g., *her*) corresponds to the subject of the passive sentence (e.g., *she*).

Impersonal passive constructions (F, G)

Active voice	Jeder arbeitet jetzt.	Everyone is working now.
Passive voice	Jetzt **wird gearbeitet.** **Es wird** jetzt **gearbeitet.** }	(There's work going on now.)

An English active sentence without a direct object does not have a corresponding passive sentence. A German active sentence without a direct object can have a corresponding passive sentence. A passive construction without a subject or agent is called an impersonal passive construction.

   The pronoun **es** begins an impersonal passive construction if no other words precede the verb. **Es** is a "dummy" or "apparent" subject.

Participle in passive vs. participle as predicate adjective (H)

Passive	Der Brief **wird** jetzt **geschrieben.**	The letter is being written now.
Predicate adjective	Der Brief **ist** schon **geschrieben.**	The letter is already written.

The passive expresses the act of doing something to the subject; it uses **werden** and the past participle. The past participle can also be used with the verb **sein** to give the state or condition of the subject that results from the action. Because the verb *to be* is used both for the passive and for predicate adjectives in English, it is sometimes hard to tell the difference between them. No confusion is possible in German. The agent with **von** and the means with **durch** can only be used with the passive:

Der Brief wird (von Inge) jetzt geschrieben.

Substitutes for the passive voice (J–Q)

The passive voice is used less frequently in German than in English. In German, other constructions are frequently substituted for the passive voice.

Passive Voice		
1. **man**	Deutsch **kann** leicht **gelernt werden.**	German can be learned easily.
2. **sein ... zu** + *infinitive*	Deutsch kann **man** leicht lernen.	One can learn German easily.
3. ***reflexive construction***	Deutsch **ist** leicht **zu lernen.**	German is easy to learn.
4. **sich lassen** + *infinitive*	Deutsch **lernt sich** leicht.	German is easy to learn.
	Deutsch **läßt sich** leicht **lernen.**	German can be learned easily.

Otto Dix, *Kleine Verkündigung*, 1950

Ich geh' da nicht mehr hin! ─────────────

Christa Wolf

Christa Wolf was born in 1929 in Landsberg. She studied German literature in Leipzig and Jena and worked as an editor. Since 1962 she has devoted herself entirely to writing. She lives in Kleinmachnow near East-Berlin.

Christa Wolf's belief in humanistic socialism is reflected in her work. In her numerous novels, novellas, and short stories, she explores the extent to which society allows people to develop and tries to indicate ways in which individuals can determine their own destiny and at the same time bring about changes in society itself. In "Ich geh' da nicht mehr hin" from *Kindheitsmuster* (1977), the young girl Nelly is invited to her classmate Lori's birthday party. Lori's parents try to use their superior social position to manipulate Nelly. How Nelly reacts to this assault on her human dignity is the theme of the story.

What situation and events cause Nelly to feel uncomfortable at Lori's party? How does Lori's mother make her attitude toward her daughter's classmates clear? Why does Nelly say to her mother "Ich geh' da nicht mehr hin"?

Ich geh' da nicht mehr hin!

Nelly merkte° es ja doch, daß der Mutter an der Geburtstagsfeier bei | noticed
Tietzens mehr lag° als an jeder anderen Einladung, und sie wußte auch, | daß ... lag: *meant more to mother* / *factory owner*
warum: Loris Vater war der einzige Fabrikbesitzer° in der Klasse. |
— Benimm° dich, wie du es gewöhnt bist, und red, wie dir der Schnabel | behave
5 gewachsen ist°! | red ... ist: *don't mince your words* / *drizzle*

Dann regnete es auch noch, Nieselregen°. Nudelfabriken sind un-
schön, das freute Nelly. Die Villa lag hinter der roten Backsteinfabrik°, | brick factory
man ging durch einen gewölbten° Mauerbogen°. Nelly hätte gerne | vaulted / stone archway
gewußt, was eine Villa von einem Haus unterscheidet. Der rote Trep-
10 penläufer° ist mit blitzblanken° Messingstangen° festgemacht°, viel- | carpet runner / shiny / brass rods / fastened
leicht war es das. Und es öffnete ein Mädchen in schwarzem Kleidchen,
mit weißem Häubchen° und weißem Schürzchen°, wie die Kellnerin- | cap / apron
nen° im Café Staege. Loris Mutter erschien. Du bist also die kleine Nelly. | waitresses
Ich habe ja soviel Gutes von dir gehört... Lori selbst mit aufgedrehten° | curled
15 Löckchen°, in kariertem° Taftkleid° mit großer Schleife°. Nun, Lori, küm- | curls / plaid / taffeta dress / sash
mere dich um deinen Gast. Papa — sie betonte das Wort auf der letzten
Silbe° — hat angerufen; er wird später zu uns hereinschaun. — Ach, die | syllable
armen Männer. Arbeitet dein armer Vater auch soviel? — Ziemlich viel,
sagte Nelly. Aber meine Mutter arbeitet vielleicht noch mehr.
20 — Köstlich°, das Kind. | charming

Beim warmen Kakao fängt Nellys Nase zu laufen an. Ihre Freundin Hel-
la, die mit schwierigen Lagen° leichter fertig wird° als sie, bittet höflich°, | situations / fertig wird: *masters* / *politely* / *get*
ihr Taschentuch aus dem Mantel holen° zu dürfen, und wird beschwo-
ren°, sich doch um Himmels willen keinen Zwang anzutun°. Reizend°! | implored / keinen ... anzutun: *feel free* / *charming*
25 sagt Frau Tietz zu ihren Freundinnen, als Hella draußen ist. Jetzt kann
Nelly doch nicht auch noch aufstehn. Sie zweifelt° auch stark, ob sie das | doubts
Taschentuch eingesteckt° hat, das ihr die Mutter zurechtgelegt° hatte. | took along / put out
Sie trinkt fünf Tassen Kakao, damit sie ihre Nase immer in die Tasse stek-
ken kann. Das freut uns aber wirklich, wie wir deinen Geschmack° ge- | taste
30 troffen haben...

Bei der „stillen Post", die Frau Tietz mit dem schönen Satz: Alle Kinder
feiern gerne Geburtstag angefangen hat, gibt Nelly an die Offiziers-
tochter Ursel die Botschaft° weiter: Britta und Sylvia sind doof. Ursel, ein | message
Mädchen wie aus Semmelteig°, wagt° nicht zu verstehen. Hella | dough / dares
35 verkündet° am Ende: Komm mit mir auf den Schwof°. | announces / public dance (colloq.) / uninhibited

Reizend, sagt Frau Tietz. So ungezwungen°, die Kinder heute! Und nun
könnt ihr gerne „Hänschen, piepe° mal" spielen oder „Mein rechter Platz | chirp
ist leer..." Herr Direktor Tietz, der dann wirklich erscheint, ist ein kleiner,
fast rundlicher° Mann mit dünnem, fadem°, zurückgekämmtem Haar | plump / dull

40 und einer gewaltigen° dunklen Hornbrille°. Nelly hat noch nie einen Mann gesehen, der einen Ring mit einem schwarzen Stein° am kleinen Finger trägt, den er abspreizt°, während er im Stehen aus einem winzigen° Täßchen° Kaffee trinkt, den Frau Tietz „Mokka" nennt. Herr Tietz fragt Nelly nach ihren Zensuren und vergleicht sie mit denen seiner

45 Tochter Lori. Er seufzt° vorwurfsvoll° und kann sich den Unterschied nicht erklären, obwohl die Erklärung kinderleicht ist und Nelly auf der Zunge° liegt: Lori ist dumm und faul.

Die Erkenntnis° schlägt° ein wie ein Blitz°. Tatsächlich°: Lori ist einfach dumm, und Herr Warsinski, der es längst gemerkt hat, kann es nur

50 hin und wieder° durch einen Blick° zu verstehen geben und durch den süßlichen° Ausdruck° seiner Stimme°, wenn er freundlich mit ihr spricht. Aber Dumme verstehen ja Blicke nicht, das ist es eben. Sie aber, Nelly, begreift° genau, was der Blick bedeutet, den Herr Direktor Tietz mit seiner Frau wechselt, ehe er Nelly vorschlägt°, Lori doch ab und an zu

55 besuchen und bei der Gelegenheit gleich ein paar Schularbeiten mit ihr zu machen. Herr und Frau Tietz stellen sich das reizend vor, Kakao gibt es natürlich jedesmal, und anschließend° würde man in Loris schönem Kinderzimmer spielen, das Nelly doch gut gefallen hat, nicht wahr? Frau Tietz hat es genau gesehen.

60 Da widerfährt° Nelly — nicht zum erstenmal, aber selten vorher so deutlich° —, daß sie sich in zwei Personen spaltet°; die eine der beiden spielt harmlos mit allen zusammen „Jule hat ein Schwein° geschlacht'°, was willste° davon haben!", die andere aber beobachtet sie alle und sich selbst von der Zimmerecke her und durchschaut alles. Die andere sieht:

65 Hier will man etwas von ihr. Man ist berechnend°. Man hat sie eingeladen, um ihr etwas zu stehlen°, was man auf keine andere Weise bekommen kann. Nelly, zu einer Person vereinigt°, steht plötzlich im Flur und zieht ihren Mantel an. Ein Griff°, mechanisch: Na also. Taschentuch in der linken° Tasche. Frau Tietz hat ihre Augen überall. Aber Nellychen,

70 was ist denn? Es gibt ja noch Götterspeise° mit Sahne°, und meine Freundin kann dich dann mit ihrem Auto nach Hause fahren.

O nein. Nelly ist entschlossen° zu gehen, und wenn sie, um wegzukommen, ein bißchen unverschämt° werden, ein bißchen schwindeln° muß, so mag das bedauerlich° sein, ist aber nicht zu ändern. Götter-

75 speise, behauptet° sie, kriegt sie partout nicht runter°, und von Schlagsahne° wird ihr regelmäßig schlecht. Leider, leider. Und was das Autofahren betrifft°: Mit einer Frau am Steuer° fährt sie nun mal nicht, da ist nichts zu machen. Seltsam°, seltsam. Also geh schon, wenn du nicht zu halten bist.

Margin glossary:

enormous / horn-rimmed glasses / stone

raises

tiny / cup

sighs / reproachfully

tongue

realization / strikes / lightning / really

hin ... wieder: now and again / glance / sweet / expression / voice

understands

suggests

afterwards

happens to

clearly / splits

pig / slaughtered

willste = willst du

calculating

steal

unified

reach

left

gelatin dessert / whipped cream

determined

impertinent / fib

regrettable

declares / kriegt ... runter: can't swallow at all / whipped cream

concerns / wheel

strange

80   Das tut Nelly. Die Mutter, telefonisch unterrichtet°, sieht sie prüfend   *informed*
an, faßt° ihr sogar an die Stirn°. Fieber hast du nicht etwa? Nein, sagt   *touches / forehead*
Nelly. Ich geh' da nicht mehr hin. Die Mutter schmiert° ihr ein   *spreads*
Leberwurstbrot°. Auf einmal treffen sich ihre Blicke, und sie müssen   *liver sausage sandwich*
beide lachen°, erst verstohlen°, dann platzt° es heraus, am Ende schreien   *laugh / furtively / bursts*
85   sie vor Gelächter°, schlagen° sich auf die Schenkel°, wischen° sich mit   *laughter / slap / thighs / wipe*
dem Handrücken° die Lachtränen° vom Gesicht. Ach du Schwin-   *back of hand / tears of laugh-*
delmeier°, sagt Charlotte Jordan. Na warte, du!   *ter / swindler*

Fragen

1.   Warum findet Nellys Mutter es so wichtig, daß Nelly zu Loris Geburts-
     tag geht?
2.   Was ist in der Villa von Tietz anders als bei Nelly zu Hause?
3.   Wer ist in der Familie Tietz berufstätig? Wer arbeitet in der Familie
     Jordan?
4.   Warum trinkt Nelly soviel Kakao?
5.   Warum gibt Nelly bei der „stillen Post" nicht den Satz von Frau Tietz
     weiter, sondern einen anderen?
6.   Was wissen Sie über Herrn Tietz?
7.   Wer ist in der Schule besser, Lori oder Nelly?
8.   Wie erklärt Nelly sich den Unterschied?
9.   Welchen Plan haben Herr and Frau Tietz, um Lori zu helfen?
10. Wie sieht Nelly den Plan?
11. Warum will sie so plötzlich nach Hause?
12. Wie erklärt sie Frau Tietz, daß sie so plötzlich nach Hause will?
13. Warum faßt die Mutter Nelly an die Stirn?
14. Warum lachen beide am Ende ganz furchtbar?

Fragen zur Diskussion

1. Welche Unterschiede bemerkt Nelly zwischen ihrer Familie und der Familie Tietz? Sehen Sie weitere Unterschiede?
2. Gibt es in der Geschichte eine mögliche Erklärung für diese Unterschiede?
3. Warum geht Nelly nicht mehr zu Lori?
4. Warum sagt Frau Tietz mehrere Male „köstlich" und „reizend"? Findet sie wirklich alles köstlich und reizend?
5. Wer sind die „besseren" Menschen, Familie Tietz oder Familie Jordan? Was sagt der Text? Was sagen Sie?

Kapitel 14

Lernziele

Sprechakte

Giving factual information
Stating opinions
Restating what someone else has said or written
Paraphrasing information
Mediating decisions

Grammatik

Indirect discourse
Special subjunctive

Vokabeln

City names used as adjectives

Landeskunde

Foreign workers in the Federal Republic of Germany
Political problems facing foreign workers
Political asylum for foreigners in the Federal Republic of Germany

Türkisches Geschäft in Düsseldorf

| Bausteine für Gespräche _____

Was steht in der Zeitung?

Holger: Hast du die Zeitung von heute schon gelesen?

Cornelia: Nein, warum?

Holger: Ich finde den Artikel über das Buch des Monats sehr interessant.

Cornelia: Wovon handelt es denn?

Holger: Von den Gastarbeitern. In dem Artikel steht: „Die Autorin hält dieses Buch für ihr wichtigstes. Sie glaubt, Deutsche und Gastarbeiter sollten es lesen. Es zeige besonders klar die Probleme der Gastarbeiter".

Cornelia: Das würde mich interessieren. Ob es das wohl schon als Taschenbuch gibt?

Holger: Keine Ahnung.

What's in the newspaper?

Have you read today's paper already?

No, why?

I think the article about the Book of the Month is very interesting.

What's it about?

It's about guest workers. It says in the article: "The author regards this as her most important book. She thinks that Germans and guest workers should read it. It shows especially clearly the problems of guest workers."

That interests me. Do you think it's available in paperback yet?

No idea.

DIESE WOCHE

9/10   Wenn Kolonialvölker Engländer werden
Rudolf Walter Leonhardt: Die Polizei als Sündenbock für die Wut der jungen Schwarzen

17/18   Wieder gesellschaftsfähig
Heinz Blüthmann über die Versöhnung der Deutschen mit dem Automobil

57   Ein Macho fürs Vaterland
Siegfried Schober: Der fragwürdige US-Filmhit „Rambo" läuft jetzt in Deutschland

71/72   Psychoanalyse in Aktion
Edith Zundel über Virginia Satir, die Begründerin der Familientherapie

magazin

CAPA
Er fotografierte fünf Kriege, er war ein Charmeur und Hasardeur, ein Abenteurer mit der Kamera, Legende schon zu Lebzeiten. Peter Sager beschreibt die Geschichte von Liebe und Tod des Kriegsphotographen Robert Capa.

Fragen

1. Worüber hat Holger in der Zeitung etwas gelesen?
2. Wovon handelt das Buch?
3. Warum sollte jeder das Buch lesen?

Sie haben das Wort

Die Zeitung   Ask three fellow students about their newspaper reading habits. Take notes and report on your findings.

> Giving factual information

Sie	*Gesprächspartner/in*
Welche Zeitung liest du?	Ich lese [*Die Zeit*].
Warum liest du Zeitung—wofür interessierst du dich?	Für | **Politik.** Wirtschaft Sport Musik Theater Literatur Comics
Berichte° über die wirtschaftliche oder politische Situation° von heute!	Wir haben | **hohe Arbeitslosigkeit.** | wenig Arbeitslosigkeit Wir haben immer noch [sieben] Prozent | **Arbeitslose.** | Inflation | Wachstum° Die Regierung hat Importbeschränkungen° beschlossen°. Man spricht von einer | **Steuersenkung°.** | Steuererhöhung° Bei [Siemens] wird gestreikt°. In [Münster] gab es eine Demonstration° gegen ein Atomkraftwerk°.

Bonner Rundschau

UNABHÄNGIGE ZEITUNG FÜR BONN

Samstag, 25. Januar 1986
Nummer 21 — Jahrgang 41

Z 1842 A

1.— DM
Ruf: Bonn 72 11

Seite 3
Platte mit Lili Marleen war längst ausrangiert

At present, about 4.5 million foreigners (*Ausländer*) live in the *Bundesrepublik* and make up 7% of the total population. Turks form the largest group, with 37%; Yugoslavs, Italians, and Greeks are also represented in large numbers. Most of the 1.6 million foreign workers (*Gastarbeiter*) live in urban, industrial areas, and perform unskilled labor in assembly plants, in mines, and at construction sites. About 100,000 foreigners are self-employed owners of restaurants and small businesses. When unemployment rises, statistics show that the unemployment rate for foreign workers is about 5% above the national average. Foreigners from other member nations of the European Community (*Europäische Gemeinschaft*, or *EG*) are more likely to find a job than workers from nonmember nations, such as Turkey and Yugoslavia. Citizens of *EG* member nations have full freedom of movement among those countries and can live and work in them without having to apply for a visa or a work permit.

Since the early 1980s, the *Bundesregierung* has instituted a number of laws and initiatives to reduce the number of foreign workers, including financial compensation for those who wish to return to their homeland.

Italienische und jugoslawische Gastarbeiter in München

Vokabeln

Substantive

die **Ahnung, -en**   idea; **keine Ahnung**   no idea

das **Atomkraftwerk, -e**   nuclear power plant

der **Autor, -en/Autorin, -nen**   author

die **Demonstration, -en**   demonstration

der **Gastarbeiter, -/**die **Gastarbeiterin, -nen**   guest (foreign) worker

die **Importbeschränkung, -en**   import restriction

die **Inflation**   inflation

das **Prozent, -e**   percent

die **Situation, -en**   situation

die **Steuererhöhung, -en**   raising of taxes

die **Steuersenkung, -en**   lowering of taxes

das **Taschenbuch, ̈er**   paperback

der **Wachstum**   growth

Verben

berichten (über + *acc.*) to report (on, about)

beschließen, beschloß, beschlossen to decide

handeln von to be about, be concerned with

streiken to strike

| Ausländische Arbeitnehmer

Vorbereitung auf das Lesen

• *Zum Thema*

Einige Millionen Ausländer leben und arbeiten in Deutschland. Diese Situation bringt einige Probleme mit sich.

1. Welche möglichen Schwierigkeiten sehen Sie?
2. Was sind mögliche Gründe für diese Schwierigkeiten?

• *Leitfragen*

1. In Berlin-Kreuzberg gibt es viele Ausländer. Wie zeigt es sich, daß da viele Ausländer wohnen?
2. Die ausländischen Arbeiter arbeiten in den deutschen Firmen. Die ausländischen Kinder gehen in die deutschen Schulen. Warum ist es für die Kinder besonders schwer?

   Stichworte: Sprache □ Kultur □ Eltern □ Schule

3. Ein Theaterstück handelt von einem türkischen Mädchen: Was möchte sie? Was möchte ihr Vater?
4. Was wird über die Probleme von anderen Kindern gesagt? Wie hängen Sprache, Schule und später der Beruf zusammen?
5. Wie reagieren die Deutschen: Wie reagiert der Staat? Wie reagieren viele Bürger?

In der Bundesrepublik leben seit mehreren Jahren mehr als vier Millionen Ausländer. Sie sind aus der Türkei, aus Jugoslawien, Italien, Griechenland, Spanien und einigen anderen Ländern in die Bundesrepublik gekommen, weil es hier Arbeit für sie gab. Sie werden „Gastarbeiter"
5 genannt. Offiziell heißen sie „ausländische Arbeitnehmer".

In vielen Ländern Europas gibt es solche ausländischen Arbeitnehmer. In der Bundesrepublik findet man diese Arbeiter mehr oder weniger in allen Teilen des Landes. Am sichtbarsten° sind sie natürlich in einigen

most visible

Türkische Frauen in Berlin-Kreuzberg

Vierteln der großen Industriestädte. Berlin-Kreuzberg ist ein solches

10 Viertel, das im ganzen Land als Klein-Istanbul° bekannt ist. Es gibt   (Turkey's chief commercial
türkische Läden mit türkischen Schildern und Namen und Waren. Auf   center and seaport)
den Straßen spielen türkische Kinder. Türkische Frauen mit Babys und
Kleinkindern gehen spazieren und kaufen ein.

    In einem solchen Viertel wie Kreuzberg leben° die ausländischen   leben für sich: *keep to them-*

15 Arbeitnehmer für sich. Aber natürlich müssen sie auch an der deutschen   *selves*
Welt teilnehmen. Die Eltern müssen mit Deutschen zusammen arbeiten.
Die Kinder müssen mit deutschen Kindern zusammen in die Schule
gehen. Für die Kinder ist das Leben besonders schwer. In der Schule
gelten° die deutsche Sprache und Kultur. Zu Hause gelten die Sprache   *prevail*

20 und Kultur der Eltern. Keine der beiden Sprachen können sie richtig. Mit
keiner der beiden Kulturen identifizieren sie sich wirklich. Sie sind
sozusagen° kulturell heimatlos°.   *so to speak / homeless*

    Über das Thema der Jugendlichen zwischen den Kulturen berichtete
vor kurzem eine Kölner° Zeitung. In dem Artikel stand, eine Gruppe   *Cologne*

25 deutscher und türkischer Teenager bereite unter professioneller
Anleitung° ein Theaterstück vor, das die türkische Hauptdarstellerin°   *guidance / female lead*
selbst geschrieben habe. Auf diese Weise höre man wenigstens die Aus-
länder auch mal selbst. Es handele von einem türkischen Mädchen, 15

Jahre alt, das in eine deutsche Schule gehe, fließend Deutsch spreche und
30 so leben möchte wie die deutschen Mädchen in ihrem Alter°. Aber als   *age*
Türkin könne sie keinen Schritt tun, der nicht ihrem Vater berichtet
würde. Der Artikel fuhr fort°: „Eines Tages erzählen die Nachbarn und   **fuhr fort:** *continued*
ihre Brüder ihrem Vater, daß sie sie mit einem deutschen Jungen hätten
flirten sehen°. Das ist aber das Schlimmste, was° ein türkisches Mädchen   **hätten... sehen:** *had seen*
35 tun kann. Sie müßte eigentlich zu Hause sitzen, dürfte überhaupt keinen   *[her] flirting / that*
Kontakt zu Jungen haben und müßte warten, bis sie vom Vater an einen
Türken verheiratet würde.“

Das Mädchen in dem Theaterstück ist im Vergleich zu anderen Türkin-
nen noch gut dran°, denn sie kann fließend Deutsch. Viele der ausländi-   **ist ... dran:** *is well off*
40 schen Kinder und Jugendlichen können aber nicht richtig Deutsch und
haben keinen Schulabschluß°. Daher können sie keine Berufsaus-   **haben ... Schulabschluß:** *do*
bildung° anfangen, so daß sie eine Zukunft als ungelernte° Arbeiter oder   *not finish school*
Arbeitslose vor sich haben. Daß viele Eltern ihre Kinder nicht gern in die   *job training / unskilled*
deutsche Schule schicken, ist auch wieder verständlich. Sie müssen Angst
45 haben, ihre Kinder durch die deutsche Schule und die deutsche Sprache
zu verlieren.

Die andere Seite des Problems sind nun die Bürger der Bundesrepublik.
Sie stehen in Kreuzberg und anderswo° auch vor einer Welt, die sie nicht   *elsewhere*

*Ausländische Kinder bekommen Nachhilfeunterricht, weil sie die Sprache nicht
richtig können.*

verstehen. Die Regierung versucht, den Zuzug° zu stoppen, so daß — *immigration*
50 wenigstens nicht noch mehr Ausländer ins Land kommen. Gleichzeitig° — *at the same time*
diktieren humanitäre° Gründe, daß man Familien zusammenkommen — *humanitarian*
läßt. Wenn z.B. eine Türkin in Deutschland einen Bekannten in der
Türkei heiratet, dann will er als ihr Mann wahrscheinlich auch herkom-
men. Was kann man da machen?
55   Bei den Deutschen wächst mittlerweile° die Ausländerfeindlichkeit°. — *in the meantime / hostility*
Manche Bürger glauben, daß die Ausländer den Deutschen die — *toward foreigners*
Arbeitsplätze wegnähmen. Oder sie meinen, daß die Ausländer für das
niedrige Niveau° in den Schulen verantwortlich seien. — *level of performance*
      Die ganze Geschichte hat ganz plausibel und unschuldig begonnen. In
60 der Bundesrepublik gab es eine blühende° Industrie und zu wenig — *flourishing*
Arbeitskräfte°. In den mediterranen Ländern gab es viele Arbeitslose. Die — *workers*
kamen als billige Arbeitskräfte. Kaum jemand hat aber damals gesehen,
daß eine Massenzuwanderung° von Ausländern problematisch ist. Die — *mass immigration*
Probleme sind enorm. Überzeugende° und praktische Lösungen scheint — *convincing*
65 das Land bisher noch nicht entwickelt zu haben.

Fragen zum Lesestück

1. Aus welchen Ländern kommen die Gastarbeiter?
2. Warum sind sie gekommen?
3. Wo in der Bundesrepublik findet man diese Arbeiter?
4. Wo sind sie am sichtbarsten?
5. Warum nennt man Kreuzberg „Klein-Istanbul"?
6. Was für Läden gibt es dort?
7. Was machen die Frauen?
8. Warum ist das Leben für die Kinder besonders schwer?
9. Womit identifizieren sich die Eltern? Und die Kinder?
10. Welche Sprache können die Eltern gut? Welche kaum oder nicht?
11. Und die Jugendlichen?
12. Von wem handelt das Theaterstück?
13. Was hat die Türkin eines Tages getan?
14. Von wem wird sie verheiratet? An wen?
15. Warum können viele ausländische Jugendliche keine Berufsaus-
    bildung anfangen?
16. Was versucht der Staat zu tun?
17. Warum kann man den Zuzug von Ausländern nicht wirklich stoppen?
18. Was wächst in der Bundesrepublik?
19. Was glauben manche Bürger?
20. Warum sind die Arbeiter am Anfang gekommen? Was gab es in der
    Bundesrepublik? Was gab es in den mediterranen Ländern?

Sie haben das Wort

Ihre Meinung

1. Warum ist die Integration der türkischen Gastarbeiter schwierig?
2. Warum haben die Gastarbeiterkinder es besonders schwer?
3. Soll man die Gastarbeiter nach Hause schicken? Warum (nicht)?
4. Sehen Sie eine Lösung des Gastarbeiterproblems?

Vokabeln

— Substantive

das **Baby, -s** baby
die **Heimat** homeland
die **Kultur, -en** culture

die **Lösung, -en** solution
das **Schild, -er** sign

— Verben

heiraten to marry
schicken to send
**teil·nehmen (nimmt teil), nahm teil,
teilgenommen (an + *dat.*)** to take

part in, participate in; **Ich habe an
dem Gespräch teilgenommen.** I
took part in the conversation.

— Andere Wörter

ausländisch foreign
arbeitslos unemployed
fremd foreign
unschuldig innocent(ly); not guilty

wahrscheinlich probable, probably
wenigstens at least
verantwortlich (für) responsible
(for)

Erweiterung des Wortschatzes

City names used as adjectives

Haben Sie eine **Kölner** Zeitung?

Do you have a Cologne
newpaper?

Waren Sie je auf der **Leipziger**
Messe?

Have you ever been to the Leipzig
Trade Fair?

Names of cities used as adjectives end in **-er**. The **-er** ending is never declined and no additional adjective endings are used to indicate gender or
case.

AN WEN WENDE ICH MICH?
Ein Ratgeber für unsere Berliner Postkunden

Übungen zur Aussprache

Review the pronunciation of **ng, pf,** and **kn** in the Reference section at the end of the book. Read the words in each pair of columns, first down, then across. Check your pronunciation by listening to your instructor or the tape.

[ŋ]	[f]	[pf]	[n]	[kn]
Fi**ng**er	**f**and	**Pf**and	**N**abe	**Kn**abe
lä**ng**er	**f**eil	**Pf**eil	**N**arren	**Kn**arren
Vorstellu**ng**	**f**logen	**pf**logen	**n**icken	**kn**icken
Hu**ng**er	**F**lug.	**Pf**lug	**n**ie	**Kn**ie
si**ng**en	**F**und	**Pf**und	**N**oten	**Kn**oten
Di**ng**e				

Read the sentences aloud, paying special attention to the way you pronounce **ng, pf,** and **kn** in the boldfaced words.

1. Im **Frühling** werden die Tage **länger**.
2. Während der **Vorstellung sang** die große **Sängerin** Ilse **Lange**.
3. **Nach** der **Vorstellung** gehen wir in eine **neue Kneipe.**
4. Zum Geburtstag hat **Inge fünf Pflanzen** bekommen.
5. Ein **Pfund Kartoffeln** kostet **fünfzig Pfennig.**
6. **Inge** und ihr **Junge** hatten großen **Hunger.**

Aller guten Dinge sind drei.

| Grammatik und Übungen ──────

1   Indirect discourse

| **Direct discourse** | Mark said, "I don't know." |
| **Indirect discourse** | He said that he didn't know. |

Direct discourse (also called direct quotation) is used to report another person's exact words. In writing, the direct quotation is set off by quotation marks.

Indirect discourse (also called indirect quotation) is used to give the substance of the message, not the exact words. When someone else's statement is being reported, the pronouns are changed to correspond to the perspective of the speaker.

2   Indirect discourse in English

In English, indirect discourse often shows a tense shift.

Present time	
Direct discourse	Erika said, "I*'m writing* a letter."
Indirect discourse (Formal)	She said (that) she *was writing* a letter.
(Colloquial)	She said (that) she*'s writing* a letter.

If the present tense is used in a direct quotation, the past tense is often used in the corresponding indirect quotation. In colloquial English the change in verb tense is sometimes not made, and present tense is used.

Past time	
Direct discourse	She said, "I *wrote* the letter yesterday."
Indirect discourse (Formal)	She said (that) she *had written* the letter yesterday.
(Colloquial)	She said (that) she *wrote* the letter yesterday.

If any past tense is used in a direct quotation, the past perfect tense is used in the corresponding indirect quotation. In colloquial English the change in verb tense is sometimes not made. The same tense is then used in both direct and indirect discourse.

3 Indirect discourse in German: statements

Direct discourse	Sie sagte: „**Ich schreibe** einen Brief."
Indirect discourse	Sie sagte, daß **sie** einen Brief **schriebe**.
	Sie sagte, **sie schriebe** einen Brief.

The pronouns change in indirect discourse to correspond to the perspective of the speaker.

The verbs in indirect discourse are in the subjunctive. By using the subjunctive in indirect discourse, the speaker indicates that she/he does not take responsibility for the accuracy of the original statement. Although subjunctive is required for indirect discourse in formal writing, indicative is used more and more in colloquial German.

Indirect discourse occurs in three time categories: present, past, and future. The time used depends on the tense used in the direct quotation. The verb expresses a time relationship to the introductory statement.

The conjunction **daß** may or may not be stated. When **daß** is used, the finite verb is in last position.

- *Present time*

Direct discourse	Erika sagte: „Ich **schreibe** einen Brief."	Erika said, "I'm writing a letter."
Indirect discourse	Erika sagte, sie **schriebe** einen Brief.	Erika said she was writing [she's writing] a letter.

In German, when the present tense is used in a direct quotation, the present-time subjunctive is used in the corresponding indirect quotation. The verb in the introductory statement can be in any tense and does not affect the time category of the indirect quotation. The present-time subjunctive shows that the action or event was happening at the same time the speaker was telling about it. In the examples above, Erika was writing the letter at the time she was talking about it.

A Ja, das hat sie gesagt.   Confirm that Gabi really said the things mentioned below about Christiane, a new student she met in Bonn. Begin the indirect quotation with **daß.**

▶ Hat Gabi gesagt, Christiane wäre nett?   *Ja, Gabi hat gesagt, daß Christiane nett wäre.*

1. Hat sie gesagt, Christiane wohnte im Studentenheim?
2. Hat sie gesagt, Christiane studierte Informatik?
3. Hat sie gesagt, Christiane käme aus der Schweiz?

4. Hat sie gesagt, Christiane hätte schwarzes Haar?
5. Hat sie gesagt, Christiane spielte gut Gitarre?
6. Hat sie gesagt, Christiane arbeitete viel?

B   Gastarbeiter: Herrn Brehmers Meinung   Tell what Mr. Brehmer said about the foreign workers in Germany. Begin with **Er sagte**, and use present-time subjunctive in the indirect quotation.

▶   Ich versuche das Problem zu verstehen.   *Er sagte, er versuchte das Problem zu verstehen.*

1. In diesem Viertel leben nur Türken.
2. Die Kinder müssen in deutsche Schulen gehen.
3. Die Kinder haben es besonders schwer.
4. Die Gastarbeiter leben oft in zwei Welten.
5. Sie bringen ihre Familie in die Bundesrepublik.
6. Sie nehmen den Deutschen die Arbeitsplätze weg.
7. Ich spreche ihre Sprache nicht.
8. Sie können nur wenig Deutsch.

Sie haben das Wort

Echo   Form a group of three. One person speaks on a topic, a second listens and asks questions, and the third paraphrases every few sentences. Possible topics are:

| Paraphrasing information |

> ein Fach, das man gern studiert □ Familie □ was man gern oder nicht gern tut

• Past time

Direct discourse	Erika sagte: „Ich **habe** den Brief gestern **geschrieben**."	Erika said, "I wrote the letter yesterday."
Indirect discourse	Erika sagte, sie **hätte** den Brief gestern **geschrieben**.	Erika said she had written [she wrote] the letter yesterday.

In German, when a past tense (simple past, perfect, past perfect) is used in a direct quotation, the past-time subjunctive is used in the corresponding indirect quotation. The verb in the introductory statement can be in any tense and does not affect the time category of the indirect quotation. The past-time subjunctive shows that the action or event happened at a time prior to the moment when the statement was being made. In the examples above, Erika wrote the letter the day before she talked about it.

C   Die neue Stelle   Tell what Christoph said about his new job. Begin with **Christoph sagte**, and use past-time subjunctive in the indirect quotation.

▶   Ich habe Schreibmaschine   *Christoph sagte, er hätte*
    schreiben gelernt.   *Schreibmaschine schreiben gelernt.*

1.   Ich habe um 8 Uhr morgens angefangen.
2.   Ich habe 20 DM in der Stunde verdient.
3.   Ich habe Briefe auf englisch geschrieben.
4.   Die Kollegen waren nett.
5.   Die Chefin war mit der Arbeit zufrieden.
6.   Ich freute mich trotzdem auf das Wochenende.

• *Future time*

Direct discourse	Erika sagte: „Ich **werde** den Brief später **schreiben.**"	Erika said, "I'll write the letter later."
Indirect discourse	Erika sagte, sie **würde** den Brief später **schreiben**.	Erika said she would [she will] write the letter later.

In German, when the future tense is used in a direct quotation, the **würde**-construction is used in the corresponding indirect quotation. The verb in the introductory statement can be in any tense and does not affect the time category of the indirect quotation. The **würde**-construction shows that the action or event was to happen at a time that had not yet occurred when the statement was made. In the examples above, Erika said that she had not yet written the letter but would do so later.

D   Die Familie wird helfen.   Gisela Wieland has gone back to work. Tell what her husband said about how the family would help. Begin with **Herr Wieland sagte**, and use the **würde**-construction in the indirect quotation.

▶   Ich werde meiner Frau helfen.   *Herr Wieland sagte, er würde seiner Frau*
                                      helfen.

1.   Ich werde auch einkaufen gehen.
2.   Stefan wird manchmal das Essen kochen.
3.   Barbara wird das Geschirr abwaschen.
4.   Wir alle werden die Wohnung sauber machen.
5.   Sonntags werden wir in einem Restaurant essen.
6.   Vielleicht werde ich nächstes Jahr nur noch halbtags arbeiten.
7.   Die Kinder werden die Wäsche waschen.

Sie haben das Wort

Eine Einladung für Samstagabend   Work in groups of three. One person wishes to invite a second person to do something on Saturday night. The third person acts as a courier and goes between the two, trying to get the invitation asked, and all the details planned.

Mediating decisions

4   Indirect discourse in German: questions

Questions in indirect discourse follow the same pattern as statements, and they may occur in present, past, or future time. Indirect questions are dependent clauses, with the verb in last position.

- *Specific questions*

Direct discourse	Hans fragte Erika: „**Wann** hast du den Brief geschrieben?"	Hans asked Erika, "When did you write the letter?"
Indirect discourse	Hans fragte Erika, **wann** sie den Brief geschrieben hätte.	Hans asked Erika when she had written [she wrote] the letter.

An indirect specific question begins with an interrogative, which functions like a subordinating conjunction.

- *General questions*

Direct discourse	Hans fragte Erika: „Hast du den Brief geschrieben?"	Hans asked Erika, "Did you write the letter?
Indirect discourse	Hans fragte Erika, **ob** sie den Brief geschrieben hätte.	Hans asked Erika whether she had written [she wrote] the letter.

An indirect general question begins with the conjunction **ob** (*whether if*).

E   Wie war es in der Schweiz?   You and several friends were on vacation. Report what Michael asked about your vacation, using the past-time subjunctive.

▶   Wohin seid ihr gefahren?   *Er fragte, wohin wir gefahren wären.*

1. Wart ihr in der Schweiz?
2. Habt ihr von dem guten Käse probiert?
3. Seid ihr viel gewandert?
4. Habt ihr schönes Wetter gehabt?
5. Warum habt ihr nicht gezeltet?
6. Waren die Leute nett?
7. Wie lange seid ihr geblieben?

5 Indirect discourse in German: commands

Direct discourse	Hans sagte zu Erika: „Schreib den Brief!"	Hans said to Erika, "Write the letter."
Indirect discourse	Hans sagte Erika, sie **sollte** den Brief schreiben.	{ Hans told Erika she *should write* the letter. { Hans told Erika *to write* the letter.

In German, an indirect command uses the subjunctive form of the modal **sollen** + infinitive. The English equivalents can be expressed in two ways: with *should* plus the main verb, or with an infinitive (e.g., *to write*).

The phrase **sagen zu** is used to introduce direct quotations. **Sagen** may be used without **zu** to introduce indirect quotations.

F Was soll ich machen? Report what Ingrid has told you to do to prepare for a picnic. Begin with **Ingrid sagte mir**, and use the subjunctive of **sollen** plus an infinitive.

▶ Geh einkaufen! *Ingrid sagte mir, ich sollte einkaufen gehen.*

1. Kauf Wurst und Käse!
2. Denk an den Wein!
3. Vergiß die Messer und Gabeln nicht!
4. Back das Brot!
5. Nimm den Regenmantel mit!
6. Komm nicht zu spät!

G Giselas Einladung Express the following narrative in German. Tell a friend about your plans to go to the theater with Gisela next Saturday.

1. Gisela asked whether I wanted to go to the theater next Saturday. *Gisela fragte, ob ich nächsten Samstag ins Kino gehen wollte.*
2. She asked whether I had time. *Sie fragte, ob ich Zeit hätte.*
3. She said she had not seen the play yet. *Sie sagte, sie ~~sah das Theat~~ hatte das Theaterstück noch nicht gesehe*
4. She said she would read it tomorrow. *Sie sagte, daß sie es morgen lesen würde.*
5. She said she had bought the tickets. *Sie sagte, daß sie die Karten gekauft hätte.*
6. She said I should come at seven o'clock. *Sie sagte, daß ich um sieben Uhr kommen sollten*
7. She said she would wait in front of the theater for me.
    Sie sagte, das sie vor dem Theater auf mich wartete.

6 Special subjunctive

Special subjunctive	Uwe sagte, er **habe** eine gute Stelle.
General subjunctive	Uwe sagte, er **hätte** eine gute Stelle.

German has a special subjunctive that is usually used in formal writing, such as newspapers and literature. The meaning of special and general subjunctive is the same.

7   Present-time special subjunctive

schreiben	
ich schreibe	wir schreib**en**
du schreib**est**	ihr schreib**et**
er/es/sie schreib**e**	sie schreib**en**
Sie schreib**en**	

The present-time special subjunctive is composed of the infinitive stem plus the subjunctive endings. Most of the forms of the special subjunctive are basically the same as the indicative forms. Use of the special subjunctive is generally limited to the **er/es/sie**-form, since it is the only form that is clearly different from the indicative.

Infinitive	Special subjunctive: *er/es/sie*-form	Indicative: *er/es/sie*-form
fahren	**fahre**	fährt
lesen	**lese**	liest
werden	**werde**	wird
können	**könne**	kann
haben	**habe**	hat
sein	**sei**	ist

Verbs that have a vowel change in the **du**- and **er/es/sie**-forms of the indicative do not undergo a vowel change in the special subjunctive.

8   Special subjunctive of *sein*

ich **sei**	wir **seien**
du **seiest**	ihr **seiet**
er/es/sie **sei**	sie **seien**
Sie **seien**	

Sein is the only verb that occurs with some frequency in the special subjunctive form in indirect discourse, since the forms are clearly different from the indicative. Note that **sei** does not have the **-e** ending characteristic of the **er/es/sie**-form in the special subjunctive.

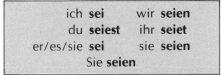

**Und fast alle dachten,
die Braun Rasur
sei nicht zu verbessern**

Foreign workers have many problems to face. Depending on which country and region they are from, moving to a modern industrial nation like the Federal Republic of Germany, Austria, or Switzerland can often mean moving from a pre-industrial to a post-industrial, highly technological society. The urban lifestyle in these German-speaking countries is very different from that of the rural areas many *Gastarbeiter* come from. Such foreigners often feel isolated, especially if they do not speak German or do not work outside the home. Many foreign women find themselves at odds with the role of women in the contemporary German-speaking family and society. Traditional families have to deal with educational values, family structures, and sometimes religious beliefs that are unfamiliar and that may be in conflict with their own. Children of foreign workers (*Gastarbeiterkinder*) often have no social contact with their German-speaking peers outside of school. Straddling two languages and cultures, they may have difficulties establishing their own identities.

Kinder aus elf Ländern gehen in die Zille-Schule in Berlin-Kreuzberg.

9   Past-time special subjunctive

Heike sagte, sie **habe** einen Job **gefunden**.
Uwe sagte, er **sei** allein **gefahren**.

Past-time special subjunctive is composed of the special subjunctive forms of the auxiliaries **haben** or **sein** plus the past participle of the main verb.

10   Future-time special subjunctive

Christl sagte, sie **werde** die Arbeit machen.

The future-time special subjunctive is composed of the special subjunctive forms of **werden** plus the infinitive of the main verb.

11   Special vs. general subjunctive

There are no specific rules that govern the use of the special vs. the general subjunctive, but the guidelines below will help you.

1. The special subjunctive is used mainly in indirect discourse in formal German. The general subjunctive is more common in colloquial German.

2. The special subjunctive is generally used only in the **er/es/sie**-form, which is clearly different from the indicative. The special subjunctive is replaced by general subjunctive when the special subjunctive forms are identical to the indicative forms.

Indicative and special subjunctive	Sie sagte, die Kinder **haben** es **gemacht**.
General subjunctive	Sie sagte, die Kinder **hätten** es **gemacht**.

3. General and special subjunctive are often mixed in the same paragraph or even in the same sentence.

    Eine Lehrerin erzählte von einem Schulexperiment mit Kindern. Die Kinder **hätten** berichtet, daß die Mutter berufstätig **wäre**, den ganzen Tag **arbeite**, und dann noch zu Hause das Essen **koche, einkaufe, putze** und die Wäsche **wasche**. Vater dagegen **läse** Bücher und Zeitungen, **sähe** fern, **tränke** Bier und **spiele** Fußball. Es **habe** sich also gezeigt, daß die Frauen in vielen Familien zwei Berufe **hätten**. Vielleicht **wäre** das einer der Gründe, warum es seit einigen Jahren in vielen Familien weniger Kinder **gebe**.

    The paragraph above also illustrates one of the great advantages of having distinct forms for indirect discourse. The use of the subjunctive makes it clear that the writer or speaker is not speaking for herself/himself.

H   Wie muß es heißen?   Give the special and general subjunctive forms of the verbs listed below.

▶   er geht   *er gehe (special); er ginge (general)*

1. sie findet	5. sie spricht	9. sie ist gelaufen
2. er ist	6. er liest	10. er hat gearbeitet
3. sie wird	7. sie hat gesehen	11. er wird bleiben
4. er kann	8. er ist gefahren	12. sie wird helfen

I   Ferienpläne   It is the end of the semester. Frank tells about his friends' conversations regarding their vacation plans. Restate in the general subjunctive.

▶   Kirstin fragte, ob Andreas nach   *Kirstin fragte, ob Andreas nach*
Amerika fliegen werde.   *Amerika fliegen würde.*

▶   Andreas meinte, er wisse es noch   *Andreas meinte, er wüßte es noch*
nicht genau.   *nicht genau.*

1. Beate fragte Bärbel, warum sie jetzt so wenig Zeit habe.
   Bärbel antwortete, sie habe ihr Referat noch fertig zu machen.
2. Christian fragte Beate, ob sie schon einen Ferienjob gefunden habe.
   Beate sagte, sie habe einen guten Job gefunden.
3. Kirstin meinte, sie werde in einem Geschäft arbeiten.
   Bärbel erzählte, sie werde für drei Wochen in die Schweiz fahren.
4. Martin meinte, er könne dieses Jahr nicht wegfahren.
   Christian sagte, er finde das schade.

J   Die Gastarbeitersituation   Give the English equivalents of the following comments by a German journalist on the situation of the foreign workers.

Der Journalist schrieb:

1. Man finde ausländische Arbeitnehmer vor allem in den großen Industriestädten.
2. Dort lebten sie aber ziemlich für sich.
3. Vor allem für die Kinder sei es oft besonders schwer.
4. Das Kind gehe zwar in eine deutsche Schule, aber seine Eltern fürchteten diese andere Welt.
5. Der Arbeiter lasse sich nur langsam in die fremde Umwelt integrieren.
6. Aber oft könne er auch nicht mehr in seine alte Heimat zurück.
7. So lebe er mehr oder weniger in zwei Welten.
8. Auf der anderen Seite wachse bei den Deutschen die Ausländerfeindlichkeit.
9. Sie hätten Angst um° die wenigen Arbeitsplätze.   *for*
10. Der Staat versuche, zu einer humanitären Lösung des Problems zu kommen.

In diesem Viertel leben viele Türken.

| Wiederholung

A   Eine Fete wird vorbereitet.   Tell about the party Christiane and Stefan are preparing. Form sentences in the present tense, using the cues below.

1. Stefan / abwaschen / Geschirr
2. Christiane / einkaufen / noch / für / Fete
3. wann / Gäste / sollen / kommen / ?
4. Dann / Volker / müssen / saubermachen / Wohnzimmer / schnell
5. Gerd / mitbringen / sein Plattenspieler / ?
6. Michael / können / mitbringen / neu / Platten / ?
7. hoffentlich / Monika / finden / Haus
8. Fete / machen / alle / Spaß

B   Rainer schreibt über die Gastarbeiter.   Rainer writes about some of the problems of foreign workers. Complete the sentences below with appropriate relative pronouns.

1. In dem Brief, _den_ Rainer an Thomas schrieb, berichtet er über die Gastarbeiter.
2. Es gibt viele Gastarbeiter, _die_ in den großen Industriestädten leben.
3. In manchen Vierteln, in _denen_ Ausländer wohnen, leben fast keine Deutschen mehr.
4. Dort gibt es Läden, in _denen_ die Gastarbeiter die Lebensmittel kaufen können, _die_ sie aus ihrer Heimat kennen.
5. Es sind vor allem die Kinder, _die_ es schwer haben, weil sie in zwei Welten groß werden.
6. Die Kinder lernen Deutsch, _das_ sie dann oft besser sprechen als die Eltern.
7. Die Kinder haben Probleme, _die_ schwer zu lösen sind.

C   Einiges über die Rolle der Frau   Hans-Jürgen asks you questions about the role of women today. Answer the questions. Use pronouns and prepositions or **da**-compounds to replace the boldfaced words, as appropriate.

▶ Hat **Peter Kraft** über **die Rolle der   *Ja, er hat darüber geschrieben.*
Frau** geschrieben?

1. Haben **die Kinder** oft traditionelle Vorstellungen von **der Rolle der Frau?**
2. Haben **die Kindermeinungen** etwas mit **den Kinderbüchern** zu tun?
3. Findet man **das traditionelle Frauenbild** auch heute noch in **Kinderbüchern?**
4. Sollen auch **Jungen** mit **Puppen** spielen?
5. Müssen **berufstätige Frauen die Hausarbeit** oft allein machen?
6. Reden **die Nachbarn** über **den Vater, der jede Woche zwei Tage von zu Hause weg ist?**
7. Reden **die Nachbarn** über **die Mutter, die jede Woche zwei Tage von zu Hause weg ist?**

D   Wandern und Zelten   Andreas and Tanja discuss plans to go hiking and camping. Complete the sentences below with the cued infinitives. Use **zu** where appropriate.

1. Wann hört es endlich auf _____ ? (regnen)
2. Wir können dann _____ . (wandern)
3. Hättest du Lust _____ ? (mitkommen)

4. Es ist schön, im Wald _____ . (spazierengehen)
5. Hast du auch vor _____ ? (zelten)
6. Wir können uns um neun Uhr _____ . (treffen)
7. Es ist leider schwer, so früh bei dir _____ . (sein)
8. Kannst du dann um zehn bei mir _____ ? (sein)
9. Wir brauchen nicht gleich _____ . (wegfahren)
10. Ich muß mir noch neue Schuhe kaufen. Meine alten sind nicht mehr _____ . (tragen)

E   Lösungen sind schwer zu finden.   Give the English equivalents of the sentences below about the situation of the foreign workers in the Federal Republic of Germany. The sentences have verbs in the passive voice or substitutes for the passive.

1. Die Ausländer kamen nach Deutschland, weil es hier Arbeit für sie gab.
2. Sie werden von den Deutschen Gastarbeiter genannt.
3. Sie meinten, daß sich in Deutschland leicht Geld verdienen ließe.
4. Diese Arbeiter sind heute in allen Teilen des Landes zu finden.
5. In einigen Vierteln der großen Industriestädte sind nur Ausländer zu sehen.
6. Die Ausländer sind von vielen Deutschen nicht akzeptiert worden.
7. Die Kinder der Gastarbeiter werden in die deutschen Schulen geschickt.
8. In diesen Schulen muß eine neue Sprache gelernt werden.
9. Wenn man jung ist, läßt sich eine neue Sprache leicht lernen.
10. Wenn man älter ist, ist Deutsch nicht mehr so leicht zu lernen.
11. Die Kinder leben dann in zwei Welten und werden von den Eltern nicht mehr richtig verstanden.
12. Die Probleme der Gastarbeiter sind leider nicht so leicht zu lösen.

F   Ein Journalist schreibt über die DDR.   Restate in indirect discourse the comments below on the *DDR*. Use subjunctive forms for indirect discourse. Begin with: *Der Journalist schrieb, daß er ...*

Ich bin gerade aus der DDR zurückgekommen. Dort habe ich mit vielen Menschen gesprochen. Einige von ihnen sind stolz auf den Lebensstandard. Man kann nicht erwarten, daß man alle Sachen immer kaufen kann. Aber dafür sind die Preise für einige Sachen niedrig und stabil. So garantiert der Staat jedem Bürger einen bestimmten Lebensstandard. Ich fand aber auch mehrere Rentner, die meinen, daß der Staat für sie nicht sorgt. Sie haben mir erzählt, daß sie daher auch in den Westen reisen dürfen. Kein Mensch interessiert sich wirklich dafür, ob sie wiederkommen oder nicht.

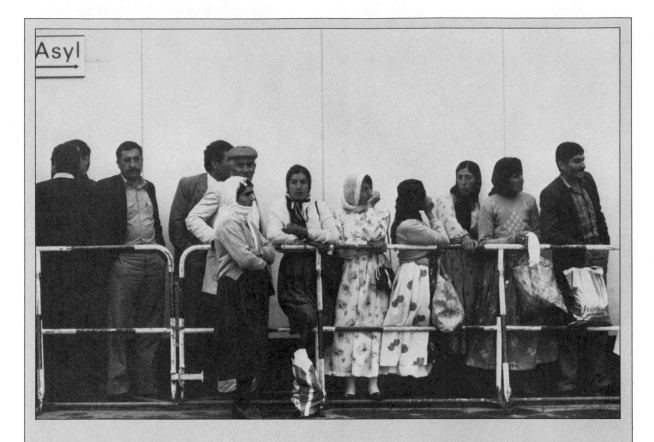

In recent years, a new dimension to the problem of cultural integration of foreigners has surfaced in the Federal Republic of Germany. Because of the persecution of opposition groups by National Socialists during the Third Reich, the framers of the Constitution (*Grundgesetz*) of the Federal Republic of Germany included an article that guaranteed the right to asylum to all persons persecuted on political grounds. Since 1979 political refugees have also received financial aid from the Federal Government (*Bundesregierung*).

In recent years the number of requests for political asylum has increased substantially. How to deal with the great number of refugees and how to integrate them into society have become hotly debated issues in the Federal Republic of Germany, as well as in Austria and to some extent Switzerland. In the Federal Republic of Germany, some politicians advocate changing the policy governing political asylum.

Asylbewerber

G   Ihre Meinung   Express your opinion by answering the questions below.

1.   Möchten Sie in einem anderen Land studieren? Warum (nicht)?
2.   Möchten Sie während des Sommers in einem anderen Land arbeiten? Warum (nicht)?
3.   Möchten Sie in einem anderen Land leben? In welchem Land?
4.   Möchten Sie in einem Land leben, dessen Sprache Sie nicht können? Warum (nicht)?
5.   Würden Sie in einem anderen Land für weniger Geld als in Amerika arbeiten? Warum (nicht)?

H   Anregung

1.   In German, list some difficulties or problems that the **Gastarbeiter** or any minority group face in a country. Then in groups of four discuss your lists. Try to make one list that all agree upon, ranking the problems. Share your list with the class.
2.   In German, write a paragraph to support or refute the following statement: **Es ist für Kinder gut, in zwei Sprachen und zwei Kulturen aufzuwachsen.**

ǀ Grammatik zum Nachschlagen

Indirect discourse: statements   (A–D)

Direct discourse	Uwe sagte: „**Ich habe** keine Zeit."	Uwe said, "I *have* no time."
Indirect discourse	Uwe sagte, daß **er** keine Zeit **hätte.**	Uwe said that *he had [has]* no time.
	Uwe sagte, **er hätte** keine Zeit.	Uwe said *he had [has]* no time.

Direct discourse is used to state the exact words of another person. *Indirect discourse* is used to give the substance of the message. When someone else's statement is being reported, the pronouns are changed to correspond to the speaker's point of view.

The conjunction **daß** may or may not be stated. When the conjunction is stated, the finite verb is in last position. When the conjunction is not stated, the finite verb is in second position.

In German, indirect discourse is quite often in the subjunctive. The subjunctive of indirect discourse can occur in three time categories: present, past, and future.

● *Present time*

Direct	Erika sagte: „Ich **schreibe** einen Brief."
Indirect	Erika sagte, sie **schriebe** einen Brief.

If the present tense is used in the direct quotation, the present-time subjunctive is used in the indirect quotation. The verb in the introductory statement can be in any tense.

● *Past time*

Direct	Erika sagte: „Ich **habe** den Brief gestern **geschrieben**."
Indirect	Erika sagte, sie **hätte** den Brief gestern **geschrieben**.

If a past tense (simple past, perfect, past perfect) is used in the direct quotation, the past-time subjunctive is used in indirect discourse. The verb in the introductory statement can be in any tense.

● *Future time*

Direct	Erika sagt: „Ich **werde** den Brief später **schreiben**."
Indirect	Erika sagte, sie **würde** den Brief später **schreiben**.

If the future tense is used in the direct quotation, the **würde**-construction is used in the indirect quotation. The verb in the introductory statement can be in any tense.

Time relationship between direct and indirect statements

Introductory statement	Direct statement	Indirect statement	Time relationship to introductory statement
Any tense	Present tense	Present-time subjunctive	Occurring at same time
Any tense	Simple past, perfect, past perfect	Past-time subjunctive	Has already occurred
Any tense	Future	**würde** + infinitive	Has not yet occurred, but will occur

Indirect discourse: questions (E)

Indirect questions follow the same pattern as indirect statements and may be in present, past, or future time. Since indirect questions are dependent clauses, the verb is in last position.

- *Specific questions*

Direct	Hans fragte Erika: „**Wann** hast du den Brief geschrieben?"
Indirect	Hans fragte Erika, **wann** sie den Brief geschrieben hätte.

An indirect specific question begins with an interrogative, which functions like a subordinating conjunction.

- *General questions*

Direct	Hans fragte Erika: „Hast du den Brief geschrieben?"
Indirect	Hans fragte Erika, **ob** sie den Brief geschrieben hätte.

An indirect general question begins with the conjunction **ob** (*whether*).

Indirect discourse: commands   (F, G)

Direct	Hans sagte zu Erika: „Schreib den Brief!"	Hans said to Erika, "Write the letter."
Indirect	Hans sagte Erika, sie **sollte** den Brief schreiben.	Hans told Erika she *should write* the letter. Hans told Erika *to write* the letter.

In German, an indirect command uses the subjunctive form of the modal **sollen** + infinitive of the main verb. The English equivalents can be expressed in two ways: with *should* plus the main verb, or with the infinitive of the main verb.

Special subjunctive

German has a special subjunctive that is sometimes used in place of the general subjunctive in indirect discourse, especially in formal writing, such as newspapers or literature. The meaning of the two subjunctive forms is the same.

Present time of special subjunctive   (H–J)

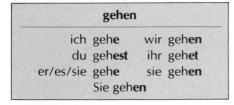

gehen		
ich gehe	wir gehen
du gehest	ihr gehet
er/es/sie gehe	sie gehen
Sie gehen	

The present-time special subjunctive is composed of the infinitive stem plus subjunctive endings.

Usually only the **er/es/sie**-form of the special subjunctive is used, since it is the only form that is clearly different from the indicative.

Infinitive	Special subjunctive: er/es/sie-form	Indicative: er/es/sie-form
schlafen	**schlafe**	schläft
essen	**esse**	ißt
sehen	**sehe**	sieht
werden	**werde**	wird
müssen	**müsse**	muß
haben	**habe**	hat
sein	**sei**	ist

Verbs that have vowel change in the **du-** and **er/es/sie**-forms of the indicative do not undergo a vowel change in the special subjunctive.

Special subjunctive of *sein*

ich	**sei**	wir	**seien**
du	**seiest**	ihr	**seiet**
er/es/sie	**sei**	sie	**seien**
	Sie	**seien**	

Sein is the only verb that occurs with some frequency in the special subjunctive form in indirect discourse. Note that **sei** does not have the **-e** ending characteristic of the **er/es/sie**-form in the special subjunctive.

Past-time special subjunctive

Erika sagte, sie **habe** den Brief gestern geschrieben.
Hans sagte, er **sei** allein gefahren.

Past-time special subjunctive is composed of the special subjunctive form of the auxiliary **haben** or **sein** plus the past participle of the main verb.

Future-time special subjunctive

Erika sagt, sie **werde** den Brief schreiben.

Future-time special subjunctive is composed of the special subjunctive form of **werden** plus the main verb.

Reference Section

Contents

❘ Pronunciation and Writing Guide ⎯⎯⎯⎯⎯⎯

Stress

Nearly all native German words are stressed on the "stem syllable," that is, the first syllable of the word, or the first syllable that follows an unstressed prefix.

Without prefix

den'ken   to think
kom'men   to come

With unstressed prefix

beden'ken   to think over
entkom'men   to escape

In the end vocabulary of this book, words that are not stressed on the first syllable are marked. A stress mark follows the stressed syllable.

German vowels

German has short vowels, long vowels, and diphthongs. The short vowels are clipped, and are never "drawled" as they often are in English. The long vowels are monophthongs ("steady-state" vowels) and not diphthongs (vowels that "glide" from one vowel sound toward another). The diphthongs are similar to English diphthongs except that they, like the short vowels, are never drawled. Compare the English and German vowels in the words below.

English (with off-glide)

bait
vein
tone
boat

German (without off-glide)

Beet
wen
Ton
Boot

Spelling as a reminder of vowel length

By and large, the German spelling system clearly indicates the difference between long and short vowels. German uses the following types of signals:

1. A vowel is long if it is followed by an **h** (unpronounced): **ihn, stahlen, Wahn.**
2. A vowel is long if it is double: **Beet, Saat, Boot.**
3. A vowel is generally long if it is followed by one consonant: **den, kam, Ofen, Hut.**
4. A vowel is generally short if it is followed by two or more consonants: **denn, Sack, offen, Busch, dick.**

Pronunciation of vowels

*Long and short **a***

Long [ā] = aa, ah, a (Saat, Bahn, kam, Haken): like English *a* in *spa*, but with wide-open mouth and no off-glide.
Short [a] = a (satt, Bann, Kamm, Hacken): between English *o* in *hot* and *u* in *hut*.

*Long and short **e***

Long [ē] = e, ee, eh, ä, äh (wen, Beet, fehlen, gähnt): like *ay* in English *say*, but with exaggeratedly spread lips and no off-glide.
Short [e] = e, ä (wenn, Bett, fällen, Gent): Like *e* in English *bet*, but more clipped.

Unstressed [ə] and [ər]

Unstressed [ə] = e (bitte, endet, gegessen): like English *e* in *begin, pocket*.
Unstressed [ər] = er (bitter, ändert, vergessen): When the sequence [ər] stands at the end of a word, before a consonant, or in an unstressed prefix, it sounds much like the final *-a* in English *sofa*; the **-r** is not pronounced.

*Long and short **i***

Long [ī] = ih, ie (ihn, Miete, liest): like *ee* in *see*, but with exaggeratedly spread lips and no off-glide.
Short [i] = i (in, Mitte, List): like *i* in *mitt*, but more clipped.

*Long and short **o***

Long [ō] = oh, o, oo (Moos, Tone, Ofen, Sohne): like English *o* in *so*, but with exaggeratedly rounded lips and no off-glide.
Short [o] = o (Most, Tonne, offen, Sonne): like English *o* often heard in the word *gonna*.

*Long and short **u***

Long [ū] = uh, u (Huhne, schuf, Buße, Mus): like English *oo* in *too*, but with more lip rounding and no off-glide.
Short [u] = u (Hunne, Schuft, Busse, muß): like English *u* in *bush*, but more clipped.

Diphthongs

[ai] = ei, ai, ey, ay (nein, Kaiser, Meyer, Bayern): like English *ai* in *aisle*, but clipped and not drawled.
[oi] = eu, äu (neun, Häuser): like English *oi* in *coin*, but clipped and not drawled.
[au] = au (laut, Bauer): like English *ou* in *house*, but clipped and not drawled.

*Long and short **ü***

Long [ǖ]= üh, ü (Bühne, kühl, lügen): To pronounce long [ǖ], keep your tongue in the same position as for long [ī], but round your lips as for long [ū].
Short [ü] = ü (Küste, müssen, Bünde): To pronounce short [ü], keep your tongue in the same position as for short [i], but round your lips as for short [u].

Long and short ö

Long [ȫ] = **ö, öh (Höfe, Löhne, Flöhe)**: To pronounce long [ȫ], keep your tongue in the same position as for long [ē], but round your lips as for long [ō].

Short [ö] = **ö (gönnt, Hölle, Knöpfe)**: To pronounce short [ö], keep your tongue in the same position as for short [e], but round your lips as for short [o].

Consonants

Most of the German consonant sounds are similar to English consonant sounds. There are four major differences.

1. German has two consonant sounds without an English equivalent: [x] and [ç]. Both are spelled **ch**.
2. The German pronunciation of [l] and [r] differs from the English pronunciation.
3. German uses sounds familiar to English speakers in unfamiliar combinations, such as [ts] in an initial position: **zu**.
4. German uses unfamiliar spellings of familiar sounds.

*The letters **b**, **d**, and **g***

The letters **b, d,** and **g** generally represent the same consonant sounds as in English. German **g** is usually pronounced like English *g* in *go*. When the letters **b, d,** and **g** occur at the end of a syllable, or before an **s** or **t**, they are pronounced like [p], [t], and [k] respectively.

b = [b] **(Diebe, gaben)**	**b** = [p] **(Dieb, Diebs, gab, gabt)**
d = [d] **(Lieder, laden)**	**d** = [t] **(Lied, Lieds, lud, lädt)**
g = [g] **(Tage, sagen)**	**g** = [k] **(Tag, Tags, sag, sagt)**

*The letter **j***

The letter **j (ja, jung)** represents the sound *y* as in English *yes*.

*The letter **l***

English [l] typically has a "hollow" sound to it. When an American pronounces [l], the tongue is usually "spoon-shaped": It is high at the front (with the tongue tip pressed against the gum ridge above the upper teeth), hollowed out in the middle, and high again at the back. German [l] **(viel, Bild, laut)** never has the "hollow" quality. It is pronounced with the tongue tip against the gum ridge, as in English, but with the tongue kept flat from front to back. Many Americans use this "flat" [l] in such words as *million, billion,* and *William.*

*The letter **r***

German [r] can be pronounced in two different ways. Some German speakers use a "tongue-trilled [r]," in which the tip of the tongue vibrates against the gum ridge above the upper teeth — like the *rrr* that children often use in imitation of a telephone bell or police whistle. Most German speakers, however, use a "uvular [r]," in which the back of the tongue is raised toward the uvula, the little droplet of skin hanging down in the back of the mouth.

You will probably find it easiest to pronounce the uvular [r] if you make a gargling sound before the sound [a]: ra. Keep the tip of your tongue down and out of the way; the tip of the tongue plays no role in the pronunciation of the gargled German [r].

r = [r] + vowel **(Preis, Jahre, Rose)**: When German [r] is followed by a vowel, it has the full "gargled" sound.

r = vocalized [r] **(Tier, Uhr, Tür)**: When German [r] is not followed by a vowel, it tends to become "vocalized," that is, pronounced like the vowel-like glide found in the final syllable of British English *hee-uh* (here), *thay-uh* (there).

The letters *s, ss, ß*

s = [ş] **(sehen, lesen, Gänse)**: Before a vowel, the letter **s** represents the sound [ş], like English *z* in *zoo*.

s = [s] **(das, Hals, fast)**: In most other positions, the letter **s** represents the sound [s], like English [s] in *so*.

[s] = **ss, ß (wissen, Flüsse, weiß, beißen, Füße)**: The letters **ss** and **ß** (called **ess-tsett**) are both pronounced [s]. When they are written between vowels, the double letters **ss** signal the fact that the preceding vowel is short, and the single letter **ß** signals the fact that the preceding vowel is long (or a diphthong). The letter **ß** is also used before a consonant and at the end of a word.

The letter *v*

v = [f] **(Vater, viel)**: The letter **v** is generally pronounced like English [f] as in *father*.

v = [v] **(Vase, November)**: In words of foreign origin, the letter **v** is pronounced [v].

The letter *w*

w = [v] **(Wein, Wagen, wann)**: Many centuries ago, German **w** (as in **Wein**) represented the sound [w], like English *w* in *wine*. Over the centuries, German **w** gradually changed from [w] to [v], so that today the **w** of German **Wein** represents the sound [v], like the *v* of English *vine*. German no longer has the sound [w]. The letter **w** always represents the sound [v].

The letter *z*

z = final and initial [ts] **(Kranz, Salz, Zahn, zu)**: The letter **z** is pronounced [ts], as in English *rats*. In English, the [ts] sound occurs only at the end of a syllable; in German, [ts] occurs at the beginning as well as at the end of a syllable.

The consonant clusters *gn, kn, pf, qu*

To pronounce the consonant clusters **gn, kn, pf, qu** correctly, you need to use familiar sounds in unfamiliar ways.

gn: pronunciation is [gn]   **pf:** pronunciation is [pf]
kn: pronunciation is [knl   **qu:** pronunciation is [kv]

gn = [gn-] **(Gnade, Gnom)**
kn = [kn-] **(Knie, Knoten)**
pf = [pf-] **(Pfanne, Pflanze)**
qu = [kv-] **(quälen, Quarz, quitt)**

The combination ng

ng = [ŋ] (**Finger, Sänger, Ding**): The combination **ng** is pronounced [ŋ], as in English *singer*. It does not contain the sound [g] that is used in English *finger*.

The combinations sch, sp, and st

sch = [š] (**Schiff, waschen, Fisch**)
sp = [šp] (**Spaten, spinnen, Sport**)
st = [št] (**Stein, Start, stehlen**)

Many centuries ago, both German and English had the combinations **sp, st, sk**, pronounced [sp], [st], [sk]. Then two changes took place. First, in both languages, [sk] changed to [š], as in English *ship, fish*, and German **Schiff, Fisch**. Second, in German only, word-initial [sp-] and [st-] changed to [šp-] and [št-]. The *sp* in English *spin* is pronounced [sp-], but in German **spinnen** it is pronounced [šp-]. The *st* in English *still* is pronounced [st-], but in German **still** it is pronounced [št-]. Today, German **sch** always represents [š] (like English *sh*, but with more rounded lips); **sp-** and **st-** at the beginning of German words or word stems represent [šp-] and [št-].

The letters ch

The letters **ch** are usually pronounced either [x] or [ç]. The [x] sound is made in the back of the mouth where [k] is produced.

If you have ever heard a Scotsman talk about "Lo*ch* Lomond," you have heard the sound [x]. The sound [x] is produced by forcing air through a narrow opening between the back of the tongue and the back of the roof of the mouth (the soft palate). Notice the difference between [k], where the breath stream is stopped in this position and [x], where the breath stream is forced through a narrow opening in this position.

To practice the [x] sound, keep the tongue below the lower front teeth and produce a gentle gargling sound, without moving the tongue or lips. Be careful not to substitute the [k] sound for the [x] sound.

ck, k = [k] (**Sack, pauken, Pocken, buk**)
ch = [x] (**Sache, hauchen, pochen, Buch**)

The [ç] sound is similar to that used by many Americans for the *h* in such words as *hue, huge, human*. It is produced by forcing air through a narrow opening between the front of the tongue and the front of the roof of the mouth (the hard palate). Notice the difference between [š], where the breath stream is forced through a wide opening in this position and the lips are rounded, and [ç], where the breath stream is forced through a narrow opening in this position and the lips are spread.

To practice the [ç] sound, round your lips for [š], then use a slit-shaped opening and spread your lips. Be careful not to substitute the [š] sound for [ç].

sch = [š] (**misch, fischt, Kirsche, Welsch, Menschen**)
ch = [ç] (**mich, ficht, Kirche, welch, München**)

Note two additional points about the pronunciation of **ch:**

1. **ch** = [x] occurs only after the vowels **a, o, u, au.**
2. **ch** = [ç] occurs only after the other vowels and **n, l,** and **r.**

*The combination **chs***

chs = **[ks] (sechs, Fuchs, Weichsel)**
chs = **[xsl or [çs] (des Brauchs, du rauchst, des Teichs)**

The fixed combination **chs** is pronounced [ks] in words such as **sechs, Fuchs,** and **Ochse.** Today, **chs** is pronounced [xs] or [çs] only when the **s** is an ending or part of an ending **(ich rauche, du rauchst; der Teich, des Teichs).**

*The suffix **-ig***

-ig = **[iç] (Pfennig, König, schuldig):** In final position, the suffix **-ig** is pronounced [iç] as in German **ich.**
-ig = **[ig] (Pfennige, Könige, schuldige):** In all other positions, the **g** in **-ig** has the sound [g] as in English *go.*

The glottal stop

English uses the glottal stop as a device to avoid running together words and parts of words; it occurs only before vowels. Compare the pairs of words below. The glottal stop is indicated with an *.

an *ice man	a nice man
not *at *all	not a tall
an *ape	a nape

German also uses the glottal stop before vowels to avoid running together words and parts of words.

Wie *alt *ist *er?
be*antworten

The glottal stop is produced by closing the glottis (the space between the vocal cords), letting air pressure build up from below, and then suddenly opening the glottis, resulting in a slight explosion of air. Say the word *uh-uh,* and you will notice a glottal stop between the first and second *uh.*

The Writing System

German punctuation

Punctuation marks in German are generally used as in English. Note the following major differences.

1. In German, dependent clauses are set off by commas.
   German   Der Mann, der hier wohnt, ist alt.
   English   The man who lives here is old.

2. In German, independent clauses joined by **und** (*and*) or **oder** (*or*) are set off by commas if the second clause contains both a different subject and a different verb.
    German   Robert singt, und Karin tanzt.
    English   Robert is singing and Karin is dancing.

3. In German, a comma is not used in front of **und** in a series as is often done in English.
    German   Robert, Ilse und Karin singen.
    English   Robert, Ilse, and Karin are singing.

4. In German, opening quotation marks are placed below the line.
    German   Er fragte: „Wie heißen Sie?"
    English   He asked, "What is your name?"
    Note that a colon is used in German before a direct quotation.

5. In German, commas stand outside of quotation marks.
    German   „Meyer", antwortete sie.
    English   "Meyer," she answered.

German capitalization

1. In German, all nouns are capitalized.
    German   Wie alt ist der Mann?
    English   How old is the man?

2. Adjectives are not capitalized, even if they denote nationality.
    German   Ist das ein amerikanisches Auto?
    English   Is that an American car?

3. The pronoun **ich** is not capitalized, unlike its English counterpart *I*.
    German   Morgen spiele ich um zwei Uhr Tennis.
    English   Tomorrow I am playing tennis at two o'clock.

Grammatical Tables

1. Personal pronouns

Nominative	ich	du	er	es	sie	wir	ihr	sie	Sie
Nominative	ich	du	er	es	sie	wir	ihr	sie	Sie
Accusative	mich	dich	ihn	es	sie	uns	euch	sie	Sie
Dative	mir	dir	ihm	ihm	ihr	uns	euch	ihnen	Ihnen

2. Reflexive pronouns

	ich	du	er/es/sie	wir	ihr	sie	Sie
Accusative	mich	dich	sich	uns	euch	sich	sich
Dative	mir	dir	sich	uns	euch	sich	sich

3. Interrogative pronouns

Nominative	wer	was
Accusative	wen	was
Dative	wem	
Genitive	wessen	

4. Relative and demonstrative pronouns

	Masculine	**Neuter**	**Feminine**	**Plural**
Nominative	der	das	die	die
Accusative	den	das	die	die
Dative	dem	dem	der	denen
Genitive	dessen	dessen	deren	deren

5. Definite articles

	Masculine	**Neuter**	**Feminine**	**Plural**
Nominative	der	das	die	die
Accusative	den	das	die	die
Dative	dem	dem	der	den
Genitive	des	des	der	der

6. *Der*-words

	Masculine	Neuter	Feminine	Plural
Nominative	dieser	dieses	diese	diese
Accusative	diesen	dieses	diese	diese
Dative	diesem	diesem	dieser	diesen
Genitive	dieses	dieses	dieser	dieser

The **der**-words are **dieser, jeder, mancher, solcher**, and **welcher**.

7. Indefinite articles and *ein*-words

	Masculine	Neuter	Feminine	Plural
Nominative	ein	ein	eine	keine
Accusative	einen	ein	eine	keine
Dative	einem	einem	einer	keinen
Genitive	eines	eines	einer	keiner

The **ein**-words include **kein** and the possessive adjectives: **mein, dein, sein, ihr, unser, euer, ihr,** and **Ihr.**

8. Plural of nouns

Type	Plural signal	Singular	Plural	Notes
1	Ø (no change)	das Zimmer	**die Zimmer**	Masculine and neuter nouns
	¨ (umlaut)	der Garten	**die Gärten**	ending in **el, -en, -er**
2	-e	der Tisch	**die Tische**	
	¨e	der Stuhl	**die Stühle**	
3	-er	das Bild	**die Bilder**	Stem vowel **e** or **i** cannot take umlaut
	¨er	das Buch	**die Bücher**	Stem vowel **a, o, u** takes umlaut
4	-en	die Uhr	**die Uhren**	
	-n	die Lampe	**die Lampen**	
	-nen	die Freundin	**die Freundinnen**	
5	-s	das Radio	**die Radios**	Mostly foreign words

9. Masculine *N*-nouns

	Singular	Plural
Nominative	der Herr	die Herren
Accusative	den Herrn	die Herren
Dative	dem Herrn	den Herren
Genitive	des Herrn	der Herren

Some other masculine N-nouns are **der Bauer, der Journalist, der Junge, der Jurist, der Kollege, der Mensch, der Nachbar, der Student.**

A few masculine N-nouns add **-ns** in the genitive: **der Name > des Namens.**

10. Preceded adjectives

	Singular			*Plural*
	Masculine	Neuter	Feminine	
Nom.	der **alte** Tisch ein **alter** Tisch	das **alte** Buch ein **altes** Buch	die **alte** Uhr eine **alte** Uhr	die **alten** Bilder keine **alten** Bilder
Acc.	den **alten** Tisch einen **alten** Tisch	das **alte** Buch ein **altes** Buch	die **alte** Uhr eine **alte** Uhr	die **alten** Bilder keine **alten** Bilder
Dat.	dem **alten** Tisch einem **alten** Tisch	dem **alten** Buch einem **alten** Buch	der **alten** Uhr einer **alten** Uhr	den **alten** Bildern keinen **alten** Bildern
Gen.	des **alten** Tisches eines **alten** Tisches	des **alten** Buches eines **alten** Buches	der **alten** Uhr einer **alten** Uhr	der **alten** Bilder keiner **alten** Bilder

11. Unpreceded adjectives

	Masculine	Neuter	Feminine	Plural
Nominative	kalt**er** Wein	kalt**es** Bier	kalt**e** Milch	alt**e** Leute
Accusative	kalt**en** Wein	kalt**es** Bier	kalt**e** Milch	alt**e** Leute
Dative	kalt**em** Wein	kalt**em** Bier	kalt**er** Milch	alt**en** Leuten
Genitive	kalt**en** Weines	kalt**en** Bieres	kalt**er** Milch	alt**er** Leute

12. Nouns declined like adjectives

● *Nouns preceded by definite articles or **der**-words*

	Masculine	Neuter	Feminine	Plural
Nominative	der Deutsche	das Gute	die Deutsche	die Deutschen
Accusative	den Deutschen	das Gute	die Deutsche	die Deutschen
Dative	dem Deutschen	dem Guten	der Deutschen	den Deutschen
Genitive	des Deutschen	des Guten	der Deutschen	der Deutschen

● *Nouns preceded by indefinite article or **ein**-words*

	Masculine	Neuter	Feminine	Plural
Nominative	ein Deutscher	ein Gutes	eine Deutsche	keine Deutschen
Accusative	einen Deutschen	ein Gutes	eine Deutsche	keine Deutschen
Dative	einem Deutschen	einem Guten	einer Deutschen	keinen Deutschen
Genitive	eines Deutschen	—	einer Deutschen	keiner Deutschen

Other nouns declined like adjectives are **der/die Bekannte, Erwachsene, Fremde, Jugendliche, Verwandte.**

13. Comparison of irregular adjectives and adverbs

Base form	bald	gern	gut	hoch	nah	viel
Comparative	eher	lieber	besser	höher	näher	mehr
Superlative	ehest-	liebst-	best-	höchst-	nächst-	meist-

14. Comparison of adjectives and adverbs taking umlaut

alt	jung	oft
arm	kalt	rot
blaß (blasser *or* blässer)	krank	schwach
dumm	kurz	schwarz
gesund (gesünder *or* gesunder)	lang	stark
groß	naß (nässer *or* nasser)	warm

15. Prepositions

With accusative	With dative	With either accusative or dative	With genitive
bis	aus	an	(an)statt
durch	außer	auf	trotz
für	bei	hinter	während
gegen	mit	in	wegen
ohne	nach	neben	
um	seit	über	
	von	unter	
	zu	vor	
		zwischen	

16. Verbs and prepositions with special meanings

abhängen von

anfangen mit

anrufen bei

antworten auf (+ *acc.*)

arbeiten bei (*a company*)

aufhören mit

beginnen mit

sich beschäftigen mit

danken für

denken an (+ *acc.*)

sich erinnern an (+ *acc.*)

erzählen über (+ *acc.*) *or* von

fahren mit (*vehicle*)

sich freuen auf (+ *acc.*)

sich freuen über (+ *acc.*)

sich fürchten vor (+ *dat.*)

halten von

helfen bei

hoffen auf (+ *acc.*)

sich interessieren für

sich kümmern um

lächeln über (+ *acc.*)

mitmachen bei (*a group*)

reden über (+ *acc.*)

riechen nach

schicken nach

schreiben an (+ *acc.*)

schreiben über (+ *acc.*)

sorgen für

sprechen über (+ *acc.*), von *or* mit

suchen nach

teilnehmen an (+ *dat.*)

vergleichen mit

sich vorbereiten auf (+ *acc.*)

warnen vor (+ *dat.*)

warten auf (+ *acc.*)

wissen über (+ *acc.*) *or* von

wohnen bei

zeigen auf (+ *acc.*)

17. Dative verbs

The number indicates the chapter in which each verb is introduced.

antworten 8   gefallen 6   helfen 6   schmecken 6

danken 5   gehören 5   leid tun 1   weh tun 9

dienen 13   glauben 1   passen 8

The verbs **glauben, erlauben**, and **schmecken** may take an impersonal accusative object: **ich glaube es; ich erlaube es.**

18. Present tense

	lernen[1]	arbeiten[2]	tanzen[3]	geben[4]	lesen[5]	fahren[6]	laufen[7]	auf·stehen[8]
ich	lerne	arbeite	tanze	gebe	lese	fahre	laufe	stehe … auf
du	lernst	arbeitest	tanzt	gibst	liest	fährst	läufst	stehst … auf
er/es/sie	lernt	arbeitet	tanzt	gibt	liest	fährt	läuft	steht … auf
wir	lernen	arbeiten	tanzen	geben	lesen	fahren	laufen	stehen … auf
ihr	lernt	arbeitet	tanzt	gebt	lest	fahrt	lauft	steht … auf
sie	lernen	arbeiten	tanzen	geben	lesen	fahren	laufen	stehen … auf
Sie	lernen	arbeiten	tanzen	geben	lesen	fahren	laufen	stehen … auf
Imper. sg.	lern(e)	arbeite	tanz(e)	gib	lies	fahr(e)	lauf(e)	steh(e) … auf

1. The endings are used for all verbs except the modals, **wissen, werden**, and **sein**.
2. A verb with stem ending in **-d, -t, Cm**, or **Cn** (where **C** = any consonant other than l or **r**) has an **e** before the **-st** and **-t** endings.
3. The **-st** ending of the **du**-form contracts to **-t** when the verb stem ends in a sibilant (**-s, -ss, -ß, -z**, or **-tz**). Thus the **du-** and **er/es/sie**-forms are identical.
4. Some strong verb have a stem-vowel change **e > i** in the **du-** and **er/es/sie**-forms and the imperative singular.
5. Some strong verbs have a stem-vowel change **e > ie** in the **du-** and **er/es/sie**-forms and the imperative singular. The strong verbs **gehen** and **stehen** do not change their stem vowel.
6. Some strong verbs have a stem-vowel change **a > ä** in the **du-** and **er/es/sie**-forms.
7. Some strong verbs have a stem-vowel change **au > äu** in the **du-** and **er/es/sie**-forms.
8. In the present tense, separable prefixes are separated from the verbs and are in last position.

19. Simple past tense

	Weak verbs		Strong verbs
	lernen[1]	arbeiten[2]	geben[3]
ich	lernte	arbeitete	gab
du	lerntest	arbeitetest	gabst
er/es/sie	lernte	arbeitete	gab
wir	lernten	arbeiteten	gaben
ihr	lerntet	arbeitetet	gabt
sie	lernten	arbeiteten	gaben
Sie	lernten	arbeiteten	gaben

1. Weak verbs have the past-tense marker **-te** + endings.
2. A weak verb with stem endings in **-d, -t, Cm**, or **Cn** (where **C** = any consonant other than l or **r**) has a past-tense marker **-ete** + endings.
3. Strong verbs have a stem-vowel change + endings.

20.　Auxiliaries *haben, sein, werden*

ich	habe	bin	werde
du	hast	bist	wirst
er/es/sie	hat	ist	wird
wir	haben	sind	werden
ihr	habt	seid	werdet
sie	haben	sind	werden
Sie	haben	sind	werden

21.　Modal auxiliaries: present, simple past, and past participle

	dürfen	**können**	**müssen**	**sollen**	**wollen**	**mögen**	**(möchte)**
ich	darf	kann	muß	soll	will	mag	(möchte)
du	darfst	kannst	mußt	sollst	willst	magst	(möchtest)
er/es/sie	darf	kann	muß	soll	will	mag	(möchte)
wir	dürfen	können	müssen	sollen	wollen	mögen	(möchten)
ihr	dürft	könnt	müßt	sollt	wollt	mögt	(möchtet)
sie	dürfen	können	müssen	sollen	wollen	mögen	(möchten)
Sie	dürfen	können	müssen	sollen	wollen	mögen	(möchten)
Simple past	durfte	konnte	mußte	sollte	wollte	mochte	
Past participle	gedurft	gekonnt	gemußt	gesollt	gewollt	gemocht	
Past part. with dependent inf.	dürfen	können	müssen	sollen	wollen	mögen	

22.　Verb conjugations: strong verbs *sehen* and *gehen*

● *Indicative*

	Present		**Simple past**	
ich	sehe	gehe	sah	ging
du	siehst	gehst	sahst	gingst
er/es/sie	sieht	geht	sah	ging
wir	sehen	gehen	sahen	gingen
ihr	seht	geht	saht	gingt
sie	sehen	gehen	sahen	gingen
Sie	sehen	gehen	sahen	gingen

	Present perfect						Past perfect				
ich	habe			bin			hatte			war	
du	hast			bist			hattest			warst	
er/es/sie	hat			ist			hatte			war	
wir	haben		gesehen	sind		gegangen	hatten		gesehen	waren		gegangen
ihr	habt			seid			hattet			wart	
sie	haben			sind			hatten			waren	
Sie	haben			sind			hatten			waren	

	Future				
ich	werde			werde	
du	wirst			wirst	
er/es/sie	wird			wird	
wir	werden		sehen	werden	gehen
ihr	werdet			werdet	
sie	werden			werden	
Sie	werden			werden	

- *Imperative*

	Imperative	
Familiar singular	Sieh!	Geh(e)!
Familiar plural	Seht!	Geht!
Formal	Sehen Sie!	Gehen Sie!

- *Subjunctive*

	Present-time subjunctive			
	General subjunctive		Special subjunctive	
ich	sähe	ginge	sehe	gehe
du	sähest	gingest	sehest	gehest
er/es/sie	sähe	ginge	sehe	gehe
wir	sähen	gingen	sehen	gehen
ihr	sähet	ginget	sehet	gehet
sie	sähen	gingen	sehen	gehen
Sie	sähen	gingen	sehen	gehen

Past-time subjunctive							
General subjunctive				Special subjunctive			
ich	hätte		wäre		habe		sei
du	hättest		wärest		habest		seiest
er/es/sie	hätte		wäre		habe		sei
wir	hätten	gesehen	wären	gegangen	haben	gesehen	seien	gegangen
ihr	hättet		wäret		habet		seiet
sie	hätten		wären		haben		seien
Sie	hätten		wären		haben		seien

Future-time subjunctive							
General subjunctive				Special subjunctive			
ich	würde		würde		werde		werde
du	würdest		würdest		werdest		werdest
er/es/sie	würde		würde		werde		werde
wir	würden	sehen	würden	gehen	werden	sehen	werden	gehen
ihr	würdet		würdet		werdet		werdet
sie	würden		würden		werden		werden
Sie	würden		würden		werden		werden

- *Passive voice*

	Present passive		Past passive	
ich	werde		wurde	
du	wirst		wurdest	
er/es/sie	wird		wurde	
wir	werden	gesehen	wurden	gesehen
ihr	werdet		wurdet	
sie	werden		wurden	
Sie	werden		wurden	

	Present perfect passive		Past perfect passive	
ich	bin		war	
du	bist		warst	
er/es/sie	ist		war	
wir	sind	gesehen worden	waren	gesehen worden
ihr	seid		wart	
sie	sind		waren	
Sie	sind		waren	

23. Principal parts of strong and irregular weak verbs

The following list includes all the strong and irregular verbs used in this book. Compound verbs like **hereinkommen** and **hinausgehen** are not included, since the principal parts of compound verbs are identical to the basic forms: **kommen** and **gehen**. Separable-prefix verbs like **einladen** are included only when the basic verb (**laden**) is not listed elsewhere in the table. Basic English meanings are given for all verbs in this list. For additional meanings, consult the German-English vocabulary on pages R-36–R-58. The number indicates the chapter in which the verb was introduced.

Infinitive	Present-tense vowel change	Simple past	Past participle	General subjunctive	Meaning
anbieten		bot an	angeboten	böte an	to offer 6
anfangen	fängt an	fing an	angefangen	finge an	to begin 6
backen	bäckt	backte	gebacken	backte	to bake 6
beginnen		begann	begonnen	begönne or begänne	to begin 9
binden		band	gebunden	bände	to bind, tie 11
bitten		bat	gebeten	bäte	to ask, beg 5
bleiben		blieb	ist geblieben	bliebe	to stay 2
brechen	bricht	brach	gebrochen	bräche	to break 10
bringen		brachte	gebracht	brächte	to bring 4
denken		dachte	gedacht	dächte	to think 2
einladen	lädt ein	lud ein	eingeladen	lüde ein	to invite 6
entscheiden		entschied	entschieden	entschiede	to decide 12
essen	ißt	aß	gegessen	äße	to eat 3
fahren	fährt	fuhr	ist gefahren	führe	to drive, travel 5
finden		fand	gefunden	fände	to find 3
fliegen		flog	ist geflogen	flöge	to fly 5
geben	gibt	gab	gegeben	gäbe	to give 3
gefallen	gefällt	gefiel	gefallen	gefiele	to please 6
gehen		ging	ist gegangen	ginge	to go 1
haben	hat	hatte	gehabt	hätte	to have 2
halten	hält	hielt	gehalten	hielte	to hold; to stop 6
hängen		hing	gehangen	hinge	to hang 7
heißen		hieß	geheißen	hieße	to be called, named E
helfen	hilft	half	geholfen	hülfe or hälfe	to help 6
kennen		kannte	gekannt	kennte	to know 3
kommen		kam	ist gekommen	käme	to come 3
lassen	läßt	ließ	gelassen	ließe	to let, allow 12
laufen	läuft	lief	ist gelaufen	liefe	to run 5
leihen		lieh	geliehen	liehe	to borrow 4
lesen	liest	las	gelesen	läse	to read 4
liegen		lag	gelegen	läge	to lie 2
nehmen	nimmt	nahm	genommen	nähme	to take 3
nennen		nannte	genannt	nennte	to name 10
riechen		roch	gerochen	röche	to smell 3

Infinitive	Present-tense vowel change	Simple past	Past participle	General subjunctive	Meaning
scheinen		schien	geschienen	schiene	*to shine* 2; *to seem* 9
schlafen	schläft	schlief	geschlafen	schliefe	*to sleep* 5
schließen		schloß	geschlossen	schlösse	*to close* 3
schreiben		schrieb	geschrieben	schriebe	*to write* 4
schwimmen		schwamm	ist geschwommen	schwömme *or* schwämme	*to swim* 1
sehen	sieht	sah	gesehen	sähe	*to see* 4
sein	ist	war	ist gewesen	wäre	*to be* 1
singen		sang	gesungen	sänge	*to sing* 11
sitzen		saß	gesessen	säße	*to sit* 5
sprechen	spricht	sprach	gesprochen	spräche	*to speak* 5
stehen		stand	gestanden	stände *or* stünde	*to stand* 3
tragen	trägt	trug	getragen	trüge	*to wear; to carry* 6
treffen	trifft	traf	getroffen	träfe	*to meet; to hit* 7
treiben		trieb	getrieben	triebe	*to engage in* 1
trinken		trank	getrunken	tränke	*to drink* 4
tun		tat	getan	täte	*to do* 6
unterscheiden		unterschied	unterschieden	unterschiede	*to distinguish* 9
vergessen	vergißt	vergaß	vergessen	vergäße	*to forget* 6
vergleichen		verglich	verglichen	vergliche –	*to compare* 13
verlieren		verlor	verloren	verlöre	*to lose* 3
wachsen	wächst	wuchs	ist gewachsen	wüchse	*to grow* 6
waschen	wäscht	wusch	gewaschen	wüsche	*to wash* 9
werden	wird	wurde	ist geworden	würde	*to become* 4
werfen	wirft	warf	geworfen	würfe	*to throw* 9
wissen	weiß	wußte	gewußt	wüßte	*to know* 4

Supplementary Expressions

1.   Expressing skepticism

Red' keinen Unsinn/Stuß.   Don't talk nonsense.

Ist das dein Ernst?   Are you serious?

Hier ist was faul.   There's something fishy here.

Meinst du? Wirklich? Meinst du das wirklich?
Do you think so? Really? Do you really mean
that?

Das ist ja komisch/eigenartig/merkwürdig.
That's funny/strange.

Irgendetwas stimmt hier nicht.   Something's
wrong here.

Ist das wahr?   Is that true?

Wer sagt das? Wer hat das gesagt?   Who says
that? Who said that?

**Woher weißt du das? Wo/Von wem hast du das
gehört?**   How do you know that? Where/
From whom did you hear that?

2.   Expressing insecurity or doubt

Das ist unwahrscheinlich.   That's unlikely.

Das glaub' ich nicht.   I don't believe that.

**Es ist unwahrscheinlich, daß [sie das gesagt
hat].**   It's unlikely [that she said that].

Das ist zweifelhaft.   That's doubtful.

**Ich glaube nicht/ich bezweifle, daß [er das
gesagt hat].**   I don't believe [he said that].

Ich glaube das nicht.   I don't believe that.

Das kann nicht sein.   That can't be.

3.   Expressing annoyance

Quatsch! / Unsinn! / Blödsinn!   Nonsense!

Blödmann! / Dussel! / Idiot!   Idiot!

Der hat wohl nicht alle Tassen im Schrank.   He
doesn't have all his marbles.

Bei der ist wohl eine Schraube los/locker.
She's got a screw loose.

Hör mal.   Listen.

Geh.   Go on.

Also, wissen Sie. / Wirklich. / Tsk, tsk, tsk.
Well, you know. / Really. / Tsk,tsk,tsk.

(Das ist doch) nicht zu glauben.   (That is) not to
be believed.

(Das ist) unerhört/unglaublich.   (That is) un-
heard of/unbelievable.

(Das ist eine) Schweinerei.   That's a mess, a
dirty trick.

Das tut/sagt man nicht.   One doesn't do/say
such a thing.

Das kannst du doch nicht machen/sagen.   You
can't do/say that.

So eine Gemeinheit.   That's mean.

Frechheit!   The nerve!; She's/He's/You've got
some nerve!

Also komm.   Come on.

4.   Stalling for time

Also. / Na ja. / Ja nun.   Well. / Well, of course.
/ Well, now.

hmmmmmmmmmm   hmmmmmmmmmm

Laß mich mal nachdenken.   Let me think about
it.

Darüber muß ich (erst mal) nachdenken.   I
have to think about that (first).

Das kann ich so (auch) nicht sagen.   I can't say
that (either).

Das muß ich mir erst mal überlegen.   I have to
think about it.

Da muß ich erst mal überlegen.   Let me think.

5.   Being noncommittal

(Das ist ja) interessant.   (That is) interesting.

hmmmmmmmmmm   hmmmmmmmmmm

Wirklich?   Really?

Ach ja?   Oh really?

So so.   Oh yes, I see.

6. Expressing good wishes

Ich halte/drücke [dir] die Daumen. I'll cross my fingers [for you].

Gesundheit! Bless you!

(Ich wünsche) guten Appetit/gesegnete Mahlzeit. (I hope you) enjoy your meal.

Prost! / Auf Ihr Wohl! / Zum Wohl! Cheers! / To your health!

Herzlichen Glückwunsch! Congratulations!

Herzlichen Glückwunsch zum Geburtstag! Happy birthday!

Ich wünsche Ihnen gute Reise! / Gute Reise! Bon voyage!

Gute Besserung. Get well soon.

Viel Glück! Good luck!

Viel Vergnügen/Spaß! Have fun!

Alles Gute! All the best!

Hals- und Beinbruch! Good luck! Break a leg!

7. Courtesy expressions

Bitte (sehr/schön). Please.

Danke (sehr/schön). Thanks (very much).

8. Saying "you're welcome"

Bitte (sehr/schön). You're (very) welcome.

Gern geschehen. Glad to do it.

Nichts zu danken. Don't mention it.

9. Expressing surprise

Ach nein! Oh no!

(Wie) ist das (nur) möglich? (How) is that possible?

Das hätte ich nicht gedacht. I wouldn't have thought that.

Das ist ja prima/toll/klasse/stark/Wahnsinn! That's great/fantastic/terrific, etc.!

Ich werd' verrückt. I must be crazy.

(Das ist ja) nicht zu glauben! (That's) unbelievable!

Kaum zu glauben. Hard to believe.

Ich bin von den Socken/sprachlos. I'm bowled over/speechless.

Um Himmels willen! For heaven's sake!

Sag' bloß. You don't say.

Was für 'ne Überraschung! What a surprise!

Das haut/wirft mich um. That bowls me over/knocks me out/blows me away.; *(neg.)* That's a bummer.

10. Expressing agreement (and disagreement)

Natürlich (nicht)! / Selbstverständlich (nicht)! Naturally, of course (not)!

Klar. Sure.

Warum denn nicht? Why not?

Das kann (nicht) sein. That can(not) be.

(Das) stimmt (nicht). (That's) (not) right.

Richtig. / Falsch. Right. / Wrong.

Das finde ich auch/nicht. I think so, too./I don't think so either.

Genau. / Eben. Exactly. / That's right.

Du hast recht. You're right.

11. Responding to requests

Bitte. / Selbstverständlich. / Natürlich. / Klar. Glad to. / Of course. / Naturally.

Gern. / Machen wir. / Mit Vergnügen. Glad to. / Let's do it. / With pleasure.

(Es tut mir leid, aber) das geht nicht. (I'm sorry but) that won't work.

Das kann ich nicht [reparieren]. I can't [repair that].

Das habe ich nicht. I don't have it.

Das ist zu schwer/groß/teuer. That's too difficult/big/expensive.

12. Expressing regret

(Das) tut mir leid. I'm sorry.

(Es) tut mir leid, daß [ich nicht kommen kann]. I'm sorry [I can't come].

Leider [kann ich morgen nicht]. Unfortunately [I can't tomorrow].

(Es) geht leider nicht. That won't work, unfortunately.

Schade. That's a shame. / Too bad.

(So ein) Pech. That's tough luck.

13. Excusing oneself

Bitte entschuldigen Sie mich. Please excuse me. / I beg your pardon.

Bitte verzeihen Sie mir [die Verspätung]. Please pardon [my delay].

Entschuldigung. / Verzeihung. / Entschuldigen Sie. Excuse (pardon) me.

Entschuldigen Sie bitte, daß [ich erst jetzt komme]. Please excuse me [for arriving so late].

Das ist keine Entschuldigung. That's no excuse.

14. Expressing indifference

(Das) ist mir egal. That's all the same to me.

Es ist mir egal, ob [er kommt]. I don't care whether [he comes].

Das macht mir nichts aus. It doesn't matter to me.

Das ist nicht meine Sorge. That's not my problem.

Es macht mir nichts aus, daß [sie mehr verdient]. I don't care that [she earns more].

Macht nichts. Doesn't matter.

Das ist mir wurscht. I couldn't care less.

Das kannst du machen, wie du willst. You can do as you please.

Das kannst du halten wie der Dachdecker. You can do/take that as you wish.

Ich habe nichts dagegen. / Meinetwegen. I have nothing against it.

15. Expressing admiration

Ach, wie schön! / Klasse! Oh, how nice! / Great! / Terrific!

Phantastisch! / Toll! / Super! / Stark! / Irre! / Einsame spitze! Fantastic! / Great! / Super! / Incredible!, Really great!, etc.

Erstklassig! / Ausgezeichnet! First-rate! / Excellent!

Das ist aber nett [von Ihnen/dir]. That's really nice [of you].

Der/Die ist nett. He/She is nice.

Das sind nette Leute. Those are nice people.

16. Expressing rejection

(So ein) Mist! (What) rubbish!

(Das ist) schrecklich! (That is) awful!

Das ärgert mich. That annoys me.

Der/Das/Die gefällt mir (gar) nicht. I don't like him/that/her (at all).

Ich mag ihn/sie nicht. I don't like him/her.

Ich kann ihn/sie nicht leiden. I don't like him/her.

Ich finde, er/sie ist langweilig/doof/uninteressant. I think he/she is boring/stupid/uninteresting.

Ich finde das schlecht/langweilig. I think that is bad/boring.

Ich finde ihn/sie nicht sympathisch/nett. I don't find him/her likeable/nice.

17. Expressing joy and pleasure

Wir freuen uns. We're pleased.

Wir freuen uns auf [seinen Besuch/die Ferien]. We're looking forward to [his visit/our vacation].

Wir sind begeistert. We are enthusiastic.

Wir sind froh (darüber), daß [er wieder arbeitet]. We're happy (about the fact) that [he's working again].

Es freut mich, daß [sie gekommen ist]. I'm happy that [she has come].

Das tun/kochen/essen wir gern. We like to do/cook/eat that.

Das macht mir/uns Spaß. I/We enjoy that. / That's fun.

Das machen wir zum Vergnügen. We do that for fun.

18. Expressing sadness

Ach (nein)! Oh (no)!

Wie schrecklich! How awful/horrible!

Mein Gott/O je! My God!

Ich bin traurig, weil [er/sie nicht hier ist]. I am unhappy, because [he/she isn't here].

Ich bin sehr traurig darüber. I am very unhappy about that.

Ich bin deprimiert/frustriert. I am depressed/frustrated.

19. *Making requests*

Hätten Sie Lust [mitzukommen]? Would you like [to come along]?

Hätten Sie Zeit, [uns zu besuchen]? Would you have time [to come see us]?

Hätten Sie etwas [Zeit] für mich? Would you have some [time] for me?

Ich hätte gern [ein Pfund Äpfel]. I'd like [a pound of apples].

Könnten Sie [mein Auto reparieren]? Could you [repair my car]?

Würden Sie mir bitte helfen? Would you please help me?

Hätten Sie etwas dagegen? Would you mind?

Hätten Sie/Hast du etwas dagegen, wenn [ich mitkomme]? Would you mind if [I come along]?

Dürfte ich [ein Stück Kuchen haben]? May I/ Is it OK if I [have a piece of cake]?

Macht es Ihnen etwas aus? Do you mind?

Sei so gut. Be so kind.

Ich möchte fragen, ob ich [mitkommen] darf/ kann. I'd like to ask if I may/can [come along].

Könnte ich [um neun Uhr zu Ihnen kommen]? Could I [come see you at nine o'clock]?

Ist es dir/Ihnen recht? Is it OK with you?

20. *Asking for favors*

Könntest du mir einen Gefallen tun und [mich mitnehmen]? Could you do me a favor and [take me along]?

Ich hätte eine Bitte: könntest/würdest du [mich mitnehmen]? I have a request: could/would you [take me along]?

21. *Making surmises*

Ich glaube schon. / Ich denke ja. I think so.

Ich glaube (schon), daß [sie das gesagt hat]. I do believe [she said that].

Das dürfte/könnte wahr/richtig sein. That might/could be true/right.

Wahrscheinlich [stimmt das]. Probably [that's right].

Sicher. / Ich bin sicher. / Ich bin ziemlich sicher, daß [er das gesagt hat]. Sure / I'm sure. / I'm quite sure that [he said that].

Ich vermute. / Ich nehme das an. I assume so.

Ich nehme an, daß [das stimmt]. I assume that [that's right].

Das scheint [nicht zu stimmen]. That appears [not to be right].

22. *Expressing expectation*

Hoffentlich. / Hoffentlich [kommt sie]. I hope. / I hope [she comes].

Ich hoffe (es) (sehr). I hope (so) (very much).

Ich hoffe, daß [er das Paket bekommen hat]. I hope [he received the package].

Ich freue mich auf [die Ferien]. I'm looking forward to [my vacation].

Ich kann es kaum erwarten. I can hardly wait.

23. *Expressing fears*

Ich befürchte/ich fürchte, daß [sie nicht kommt]. I'm afraid [she's not coming].

Ich habe Angst, [nach Hause zu gehen]. I'm afraid [to go home].

Davor habe ich Angst. I'm afraid of that.

Ich habe Angst vor [dem Hund]. I'm afraid of [the dog].

[Der Hund] jagt mir Angst ein. [The dog] scares me.

Das ist mir unheimlich. It scares me.

24. *Giving advice*

Ich schlage vor, daß [wir um acht anfangen]. I suggest that [we begin at eight].

Ich rate dir, [zu Hause zu bleiben]. I advise you [to stay home].

Das würde ich dir (nicht) raten. I would (not) advise that.

Das würde ich (nicht) machen/sagen. I would (not) do/say that.

Das würde ich anders/so machen. I would do that differently/this way.

Das mußt du so machen. You have to do it this way.

Ich zeige dir, [wie man das macht]. I'll show you [how one does that].

An [deiner/seiner/ihrer] Stelle würde ich [zu Hause bleiben]. If I were [you/him/her], I'd [stay home].

25. *Correcting misunderstandings*

Das habe ich nicht so gemeint. I didn't mean it that way.

Das habe ich nur aus Spaß gesagt. I only said that in fun/jest.

Das war doch nicht so gemeint. It wasn't meant that way.

Das war nicht mein Ernst. I wasn't serious.

Nimm doch nicht alles so ernst. Don't take everything so seriously.

Supplementary Word Sets

The following word lists will help you to increase the number of things you can say and write.

Einführung

Classroom objects

der **Filzstift** felt-tip pen
das **Klassenzimmer** classroom
die **Kreide** chalk
der **Kurs** course
die **Landkarte; die Wandkarte** map; wall map
der **Papierkorb** wastebasket
das **Ringbuch** loose-leaf binder
der **Schwamm** sponge
das **Sprachlabor** language lab
die **(Wand)tafel** chalkboard

Colors

dunkel[blau] dark [blue]
hell[blau] light [blue]
lila purple
orange orange
rosa pink

Chapter 1

Adjectives for mood or personality

ausgezeichnet excellent
elend miserable
erstklassig first-rate
furchtbar horrible
kaputt worn out, tired
klasse terrific
miserabel miserable
phantastisch fantastic
prima excellent
schrecklich dreadful
toll great

Adjectives for personality

clever clever
fies disgusting; unfair
freundlich friendly
klug smart

lahm slow, sluggish
langsam slow
praktisch practical
verrückt crazy

Physical description of people

blond blond
dick fat
dunkel brunette
fett fat
gut aussehend handsome
häßlich ugly
hübsch pretty
mager thin
normal normal
schön beautiful
schwach weak
stark strong
vollschlank full-figured

Sports and Games

Billard billiards
Dame checkers
Eishockey hockey
Flipper; ich flippere pinball machine; I play the pinball machine
Federball badminton
Handball, Hallenhandball handball
Hockey field hockey
Wasserball water polo

Farewells (and Greetings)

Auf Wiederhören! Good-by! *(on the telephone)*
Bis bald! See you soon!
Bis dann! See you later!
Tschüß! 'Bye!
Mach's gut! Take it easy!
Tschau! So long!
Grüß Gott! Good-by! Hello! *(used in southern Germany and Austria)*

Servus! Good-by! Hello! *(used in southern Germany and Austria)*
Adé! 'Bye! *(used in southern Germany and Austria)*
Grüetzi! Hello! *(used in Switzerland)*

Chapter 2

Weather expressions

der **Wetterbericht** weather report
die **Wettervorhersage** weather prediction
die **Warmfront** warm front
die **Kaltfront** cold front
der **Niederschlag** precipitation
der **Tau** dew
der **Schneefall** snowfall
der **Hagel** hail
der **Landregen** all-day rain
das **Schauer** shower
der **Nieselregen (der Sprühregen)** drizzle
der **Luftdruck** air pressure
das **Gewitter** thunderstorm
der **Blitz/der Donner** lightning/thunder
die **Windrichtung** wind direction
Es gießt (in Strömen). It's pouring.
Es regnet Bindfäden. It's raining cats and dogs.
Es ist naßkalt. It's damp and cold.
neblig; der Nebel foggy; fog
sonnig sunny
schwül humid
eisig icy cold
klar/wolkenlos cloudless
heiter fair
bedeckt overcast
bewölkt cloudy
stürmisch stormy
das **Tief** low-pressure system
das **Hoch** high-pressure system

Chapter 3

Small specialty shops

die **Apotheke** pharmacy
das **Blumengeschäft** florist shop
die **Buchhandlung** bookstore
die **chemische Reinigung** dry cleaning shop
die **Drogerie** drugstore
das **Eisenwarengeschäft** hardware store

das **Elektrogeschäft** appliance store
das **Feinkostgeschäft** delicatessen
das **Fotogeschäft** camera store
der **Juwelier** jeweler's; jewelry store
das **Kaffeegeschäft** store selling coffee
der **Kiosk** kiosk, stand
der **Klempner** plumber
die **Konditorei** coffee and pastry shop
das **Möbelgeschäft** furniture store
der **Optiker** optician's shop
das **Schreibwarengeschäft** stationery store
das **Schuhgeschäft** shoe store
der **Schuhmacher; der Schuster** shoe repair (shop)
das **Sportgeschäft; die Sportausrüstungen** sporting goods store; sporting goods

Chapter 4

Professions

ein **Angestellter**/eine **Angestellte** employee
der **Apotheker**/die **Apothekerin** pharmacist
der **Arzt**/die **Ärztin** physician
der **Betriebswirt**/die **Betriebswirtin** manager
der **Dolmetscher**/die **Dolmetscherin** translator
der **Elektriker**/die **Elektrikerin** electrician
der **Ingenieur**/die **Ingenieurin** engineer
der **Journalist**/die **Journalistin** journalist
der **Krankenpfleger**/die **Krankenschwester** nurse
der **Lehrer**/die **Lehrerin** teacher
der **Mechaniker**/die **Mechanikerin** mechanic
der **Pfarrer**/die **Pfarrerin** clergyperson
der **Rechtsanwalt**/die **Rechtsanwältin** lawyer
der **Sekretär**/die **Sekretärin** secretary
der **Sozialarbeiter**/die **Sozialarbeiterin** social worker
der **Sozialpädagoge**/die **Sozialpädagogin** social worker (with college degree)
der **Steward**/die **Stewardeß; der Flugbegleiter**/die **Flugbegleiterin** flight attendant
der **Verkäufer**/die **Verkäuferin** salesperson
der **Volkswirt**/die **Volkswirtin** economist
der **Wissenschaftler**/die **Wissenschaftlerin** scientist

Film and literature

der **Abenteuerfilm** adventure movie
der **Action-Film** action movie
der **Horrorfilm** horror film
der **Liebesfilm** romance
der **Science-Fiction-Film** science fiction movie

die **Außenaufnahme** location shot
das **Drehbuch** (film) script
die **Filmfestspiele** *(pl.)* film festival
die **Filmkomödie** comedy film
die **Filmkritik** movie criticism
die **(Film)leinwand** (movie) screen
der **(Film)schauspieler**/die **(Film)schauspielerin**
  movie actor/actress
die **(Film)szene** (movie) scene
das **(Film)studio** (movie) studio
der **Kameramann** cameraman
der **Regisseur**/die **Regisseurin** director

die **Anthologie** anthology
das **Drama** drama, play
das **Gedicht** poem
die **Kurzgeschichte** short story
der **Roman** novel
die **Zeitschrift** magazine
die **Illustrierte** illustrated magazine

der **Autor**/die **Autorin** author
der **Dichter**/die **Dichterin** poet
der **Dramatiker**/die **Dramatikerin** dramatist
der **Schriftsteller**/die **Schriftstellerin** writer

Family members

der **Neffe** nephew
die **Nichte** niece
die **Oma** grandma
der **Opa** grandpa
die **Stiefmutter** stepmother
der **Stiefvater** stepfather
die **Schwiegermutter** mother-in-law
der **Schwiegervater** father-in-law
die **Schwägerin** sister-in-law
der **Schwager** brother-in-law

College majors

Amerikanistik American studies
Anglistik English language and literature
Betriebswirtschaft business administration
Biologie biology

Chemie chemistry
Englisch English
Französisch French
Gemeinschaftskunde social studies
Germanistik German language and literature
Informatik computer science
Ingenieurwesen engineering
Italienisch Italian
Jura law
Kommunikationswissenschaft communications
Kunstgeschichte art history
Medizin medicine
Philosophie philosophy
Physik physics
Politik political science
Psychologie psychology
Publizistik journalism
Religionswissenschaft/**Theologie** religion
Rechnungswesen accounting
Romanistik Romance languages and literature
Soziologie sociology
Spanisch Spanish
Sprachwissenschaft/**Linguistik** linguistics
Theaterwissenschaft theater studies
Volkswirtschaft economics

Chapter 5

Geographic terms

die **Anhöhe;** der **Hügel** hill
der **Atlantik** Atlantic (Ocean)
der **Bach** brook
der **Berg** mountain
das **(Bundes)land** (federal) state in the FRG
der **(Bundes)staat** (federal) state in the U.S.A.
die **Ebbe**/die **Flut** low tide/high tide
der **Fluß** river
das **Gebirge** mountain range
die **Gezeiten** *(pl.)* tide
der **Gipfel** peak
der **Gletscher** glacier
die **Hauptstadt** capital
die **Insel** island
der **Kanal** canal; channel
die **Küste** coast
das **Meer** sea
der **Pazifik** Pacific (Ocean)

der **See**   lake
die **See**   sea
der **Strand**   beach
das **Tal**   valley
der **Teich**   pond
das **Ufer**   shore
der **Wald**   woods
die **Wiese**   meadow
die **Wüste**   desert

Modes of transportation

die **Kutsche**   carriage
der **Pferdewagen**   horse-drawn wagon

der **LKW (= Lastkraftwagen)**/der **Laster**   truck
der **PKW (= Personenkraftwagen)**   passenger car
der **Anhänger**   trailer
der **Campingwagen, der Wohnwagen**   camper (pulled by a car)
der **Caravan**   camper (recreational vehicle)
der **Combi**   station wagon

die **Bergbahn**   mountain railway; cable car
die **Eisenbahn**   train, railway
der **Güterzug**   freight train

das **Boot**   boat
das **Containerschiff**   container ship
die **Fähre**   ferry
der **Frachter**   freighter
das **Kanu**   canoe
das **Motorboot**   motorboat
der **Passagierdampfer**   passenger ship
das **Ruderboot**   rowboat
der **Schleppkahn**   barge
das **Segelboot**   sailboat
das **Segelschiff**   sailing ship
der **Tanker**   tanker

der **Hubschrauber**   helicopter
der **Jet**   jet
der **Jumbojet**   jumbo jet
das **(Propeller)flugzeug**   propeller plane
das **Raumschiff**   spaceship
das **Segelflugzeug**   glider; sailplane

Chapter 6

Clothing for men and women

der **Anorak**   jacket with hood, parka
der **Blazer**   blazer
die **Daunenjacke**   down jacket
der **Hosenrock**   culottes
der **Hut**   hat
die **Kniestrümpfe** *(pl.)*   knee socks
die **Latzhose**   bib overalls
der **Mantel**   coat
die **Mütze**   cap
der **Overall**   jumpsuit
der **Parka**   parka
das **Polohemd**   polo shirt
der **Regenmantel**   raincoat
der **Rollkragenpullover**   turtleneck
die **Sandalen** *(pl.)*   sandals
der **Schlafanzug**   pajamas
die **Shorts** *(pl.)*   shorts
die **Sportschuhe** *(pl.)*   sneakers
die **Strickjacke**   (cardigan) sweater
das **T-Shirt**   t-shirt
der **Trainingsanzug**   sweat suit
die **Turnschuhe** *(pl.)*   fitness/workout shoes
die **Weste**   vest
der **Wintermantel**   winter coat

Clothing for women

das **Abendkleid**   evening dress/gown
der **Badeanzug**   bathing suit
das **Kostüm**   suit
das **Trägerkleid**   jumper

Clothing for men

der **Anzug**   suit
die **Badehose**   bathing trunks
das **Freizeithemd**   casual shirt

Breakfast foods

das **Ei (weich gekocht)**   egg (soft-boiled)
der **Honig**   honey
der **Joghurt**   yogurt
der **Kakao**   cocoa
die **Marmelade**   jam, marmalade
der **Orangensaft**   orange juice
die **Schokolade**   hot chocolate
der **Tee**   tea
der **Tomatensaft**   tomato juice

das **Graubrot**   light rye bread
der **Pumpernickel**   pumpernickel bread
das **Schwarzbrot**   dark rye bread
das **Vollkornbrot**   coarse, whole-grain bread
das **Weißbrot**   white bread

Noon meal foods

die **Suppe**   soup
der **gemischte Salat**   vegetable salad plate
der **grüne Salat**   tossed (green) salad

der **Fisch**   fish
der **Braten**   roast
das **Kalbfleisch**   veal
das **Kotelett**   chop
das **Rindfleisch**   beef
die **Roulade**   roulade
der **Schinken**   ham
das **Schnitzel**   cutlet
das **Schweinefleisch**   pork
der **Speck**   bacon

die **Bohnen** *(pl.)*   beans
die **Erbsen** *(pl.)*   peas
die **Karotten, gelbe Rüben** *(pl.)*   carrots
die **Kartoffeln** *(pl.)*   potatoes
der **Kohl**   cabbage
die **(gefüllte) Paprikaschote**   (stuffed) pepper
die **Pilze** *(pl.)*   mushrooms
der **Reis**   rice
das **Sauerkraut**   sauerkraut
der **Spargel**   asparagus
die **Tomate**   tomato
die **Zwiebel**   onion

die **Nudeln** *(pl.)*   noodles

das **Salz**   salt
der **Pfeffer**   pepper
der **Zucker**   sugar

Evening meal foods

der **Käse**   cheese
die **saure Gurke**   half-sour pickle
die **Wurst**/der **Aufschnitt**   sausage/cold cuts
das **Würstchen**   frankfurter

Desserts and fruit

das **Eis**   ice cream
der **Karamelpudding**   custard
das **Kompott**   stewed fruit
die **Schokoladencreme**   chocolate mousse
der **Vanillepudding**   vanilla pudding

die **Ananas**   pineapple
der **Apfel**   apple
die **Banane**   banana
die **Erdbeeren** *(pl.)*   strawberries
die **Himbeeren** *(pl.)*   raspberries
die **Orange, Apfelsine**   orange
der **Pfirsich**   peach
die **Pflaume**   plum
der **Rhabarber**   rhubarb
die **Zitrone**   lemon
die **Zwetsch(g)e**   plum

Table setting

das **Besteck**   flatware
die **Butterdose**   butter dish
der **Eierbecher**   egg cup
der **Eßlöffel**   tablespoon
das **Gedeck**   table setting
die **Kaffeekanne**/die **Teekanne**   coffeepot/tea-pot
das **Milchkännchen**   creamer (small pitcher for cream or milk)
die **Schüssel**   bowl
die **Serviette**   napkin
der **Teelöffel**   teaspoon
der **Teller**   plate
die **Untertasse**   saucer
die **Zuckerdose**   sugar bowl

Chapter 7

TV Programs

das **Familiendrama**, die **Seifenoper**   soap opera
die **Fernsehserie**   serial
die **Fernsehkömodie**   sitcom (situation comedy)
die **Fernsehshow**, die **Unterhaltungsshow**   game show
der **Krimi**   detective or crime drama
die **Nachrichten**   news
die **Quizsendung**, das **Fernsehquiz**   quiz show
die **Sportschau**   sports program

Chapter 8

Stereo and audio-visual equipment

die **Compact Disk**   compact disc
der **CD-Spieler**   compact disc player
der **Farbfernseher**   color television
der **Kassettenrecorder**   cassette deck
der **Kopfhörer**   headphone
der **Lautsprecher**   loudspeaker
das **Mikrophon**   microphone
der **Radiorecorder**   cassette radio
der **Schwarzweißfernseher**   black-and-white
   television
das **Tonband,** das **Band**   tape
das **Tonbandgerät**   (reel-to-reel) tape recorder
der **Tuner**   tuner
der **Verstärker**   amplifier
der **Videorecorder**   video recorder
der **Walkman**   personal stereo

Chores

abstauben   to dust
Fenster putzen   to clean windows
(das) **Abendessen vorbereiten, machen**   to prepare supper
(das) **Mittagessen kochen**   to cook dinner
(die) **Wäsche bügeln**   to iron the wash, laundry
Wäsche, Kleider flicken   to mend clothes

(die) **Bäume beschneiden/pflanzen/fällen**   to
   prune/to plant/to cut down trees
das **Haus**/den **Zaun**/das **Boot streichen**   to
   paint the house/the fence/the boat
die **Hecke schneiden**   to trim the hedge
(das) **Holz sägen/spalten/hacken**   to saw/to
   split/to chop wood
(den) **Rasen mähen**   to mow the lawn
(den) **Schnee fegen, kehren/schippen**   to
   sweep/to shovel snow
(das) **Unkraut jäten**   to pull out weeds

Chapter 9

Body care and hygiene

der **Haartrockner,** der **Föhn**   hair dryer
die **Haarbürste**   hair brush
das **Handtuch**   hand towel
der **Kamm**   comb

das **Make-up**   makeup
der **Rasierapparat**   razor
die **Schere**   scissors
die **Seife**   soap
die **Sonnenbrille**   sun glasses
der **Spiegel**   mirror
das **Taschentuch**   handkerchief
die **Zahnbürste**   toothbrush
die **Zahnpasta**   toothpaste

Chapter 10

Computer terminology

der **Anwender**   program user
anzeigen   to display
mit dem Computer arbeiten   to work on the
   computer
auswählen   to select a program
der **Bildschirm**   screen
der **Computer**   computer
der **Personalcomputer**   personal computer
die **Diskette**   diskette
das **Diskette-Laufwerk**   diskette drive
der **Drucker**   printer
der **Matrixdrucker**   matrix printer
der **Typendrucker**   letter-quality printer
das **Typenrad**   daisy wheel
laden   to load
ein **Programm laufen lassen**   to run a program
der **Monitor**   monitor
der **Positionsanzeiger**   cursor
programmieren   to program
die **Programmiersprache**   computer language
die **Software;** das **Softwarepacket**   software;
   software package
speichern   to store
auf Diskette speichern   to store on diskette
ein **30 MB Speicher**   a 30 megabyte memory
die **Tastatur**   keyboard
die **Taste;** die **Funktionstaste**   key; function key
der **Textverarbeiter,** der **Wortprozessor**   word
   processor

Chapter 11

Musical instruments

das **Akkordeon**   accordion
die **Blockflöte**   recorder

die **Bratsche** viola
das **Cello** cello
das **Fagott** bassoon
die **Flöte** flute
die **Geige, Violine** violin
die **Gitarre** guitar
die **Harfe** harp
die **Klarinette** clarinet
das **Klavier** piano
der **Kontrabaß** double bass
die **Oboe** oboe
die **Orgel** organ
die **Posaune (+ blasen)** trombone (to play)
die **Pauke** kettle drum
das **Saxophon** saxophone
das **Schlagzeug** percussion (instrument)
die **Trommel** drum
die **Trompete (+ blasen)** trumpet (to play)
die **Tuba (+ blasen)** tuba (to play)
das **(Wald)horn (+ blasen)** French horn (to play)

Hobbies

angeln to fish
Blumen (z.B. Rosen, Dahlien, Lilien, Nelken) flowers (*e.g.*, roses, dahlias, lilies, carnations)
die **Gartenarbeit** gardening
malen to paint
schreiben [Gedichte, Geschichten, Romane, Dramen] to write [poems, stories, novels, plays]
zeichnen to draw

Collectibles

sammeln to collect
alte Flaschen old bottles
Briefmarken stamps
Glas glass
Münzen coins
Pflanzen (getrocknet) plants (dried)
Puppen dolls
Silber silver
Streichholzschachteln matchboxes
Zinn pewter

Sports

das **Ballonfahren** ballooning
boxen to box
das **Fallschirmspringen** parachute jumping
fechten to fence
Turnen, Gymnastik gymnastics
das **Gewichtheben** weightlifting
jagen to hunt
das **Jogging; joggen** jogging; to jog
kegeln to bowl
die **Leichtathletik** track and field
der **Radsport,** das **Radfahren** bicycling
ringen to wrestle
rudern to row
schießen to shoot
das **Segelfliegen** glider flying
das **Windsurfen** wind surfing
das **Drachenfliegen** hang gliding

Chapter 13

Music and theater

das **Theaterstück;** die **Tragödie;** die **Komödie;** der **Einakter** play; tragedy; comedy; one-act play
das **Musical** musical comedy
die **Oper** opera
die **Operette** operetta

der **Dirigent**/die **Dirigentin** conductor
der **Regisseur**/die **Regisseurin** director
der **Sänger**/die **Sängerin** singer
der **Schauspieler**/die **Schauspielerin** actor/actress
der **Zuschauer**/der **Zuschauerin** spectator

der **Beifall,** der **Applaus** applause
die **Bühne** stage
die **Inszenierung** mounting of a production
das **Orchester** orchestra
die **Pause;** das **Foyer** intermission; hallway, lobby
das **Programmheft** program
die **Vorstellung** performance

Chapter 14

Buildings and other landmarks

die **Autobahnauffahrt (-ausfahrt)** expressway
   on-ramp (off-ramp)
der **Bahnhof** train station
die **Bahnlinie** railroad line
der **Bauernhof** farm
die **Brücke** bridge
die **Bundesstraße** federal highway
die **Burg** fortress
das **Denkmal** monument
die **Fabrik** factory
der **Fernsehturm** TV tower
der **Flughafen** airport
der **Friedhof** cemetery
der **Funkturm** radio and TV tower
der **Fußweg** footpath
die **Kapelle** chapel
die **Kirche**/die **Kathedrale** church/cathedral
das **Kloster** monastery
die **Mühle** mill
das **Museum** museum
das **Parkhaus** parking garage
die **Polizei** police
die **Post** post office
die **Ruine** ruin
das **Schloß** castle
die **Tiefgarage** underground garage
der **Tunnel** tunnel

Asking directions

Wo ist [der Bahnhof]? Where is the [train station]?
Wie weit ist es [zum Bahnhof]? How far is it [to the train station]?
Wie komme ich am schnellsten [zum Bahnhof]? What is the quickest way [to the train station]?
Wo ist hier in der Nähe [ein Café]? Is there [a café] around here?
Wissen Sie den Weg nach [Obersdorf]? Do you know the way to [Obersdorf]?
Wir wollen nach [Stuttgart]. Wie fahren wir am besten? We're going to [Stuttgart]. What is the best route?

Giving directions

Da fahren Sie am besten mit [der U-Bahn]. It's best if you go by [subway].
Fahren Sie mit der [Drei]; Nehmen Sie die [Drei]. Take number [3].
[Dort/An der Ecke/An der Kreuzung] ist die Haltestelle. [Over there/on the corner/at the intersection] is the [bus] stop.
An der [ersten] Kreuzung gehen Sie [rechts]. At the [first] intersection turn [right].
Gehen Sie die [erste] Straße [links]! Take the [first] street [to the left].
Gehen Sie geradeaus! Go straight ahead.
Bei der Ampel biegen Sie [rechts] ab! At the traffic light turn [right].

Supplementary Dialogues

The following dialogues contain phrases that may be particularly useful to you if you ever have the opportunity to travel or live in a German-speaking country.

Was steht in der Zeitung?

Thomas: Was steht Neues in der Zeitung?
Ulf: Keine Ahnung. Mich interessieren nur die Anzeigen.
Thomas: Was suchst du denn?
Ulf: Einen Job und eine Wohnung.

Auf einer Party

Frau Schwarz: Frau Schiller, darf ich bekannt machen? Herr Busch.
Frau Schiller: Guten Tag, Herr Busch.
Herr Busch: Guten Tag, Frau Schiller.

Auf Wohnungssuche

Volker: *(nimmt Hörer ab)* Volker Hornung.
Martin: Ja, guten Tag. Ich rufe wegen der Anzeige im Tagesblatt an. Ist das Zimmer in eurer Wohngemeinschaft noch frei?
Volker: Nein, tut mir leid. Wir haben es gestern abend vermietet. Aber die WG in der Wohnung unter uns hat auch ein Zimmer zu vermieten.
Martin: Weißt du, wie hoch die Miete ist?
Volker: Nein, da sprichst du besser mit den Leuten selbst. Ihre Telefonnummer ist 781 66 54. Am Besten fragst du nach Beate und Bärbel. Das Zimmer ist auf jeden Fall groß, und es hat einen Balkon.
Martin: Das hört sich ja toll an. Also danke, Volker. Ich rufe die WG jetzt gleich an. Tschüß.

In der Tankstelle

Kunde: Volltanken, bitte.
Tankwart: Super oder Normal?
Kunde: Normal. Und kontrollieren Sie bitte Öl- stand und Reifendruck!

What's in the newspaper?

What's new in the newspaper?
No idea. I'm only interested in the classifieds.

What are you looking for?
A job and an apartment.

At a party

Ms. Schiller, I'd like you to meet Mr. Busch.

How do you do, Mr. Busch.
How are you, Mrs. Schiller?

Apartment hunting

(lifts the receiver) Volker Hornung.
Yes, hello. I'm calling about the advertisement in the daily newspaper. Is the room in your apart- ment still available?
No, I'm afraid not. We rented it out yesterday evening. But there's a room for rent in the apartment downstairs too.

Do you know how much the rent is?
No, you'd better speak to them about that. Their telephone number is 781 66 54. The best thing would be to ask to speak to Beate and Bärbel. In any case the room is large, and it has a bal- cony.
That sounds great. Well thanks, Volker. I'll call the people in the apartment right away. Bye.

At the service station

Fill it up, please.
Super or regular?
Regular. And please check the oil and tires.

Auf der Post

Kundin: Ich möchte diesen Brief per Luftpost schicken.

Beamter: Nach Amerika? Bis 5 Gramm kostet er DM 1,40.

Kundin: Geben Sie mir bitte 5 Briefmarken zu DM 1,40. Kann ich dieses Paket hier aufgeben?

Beamter: Nein, die Paketannahme ist am Schalter nebenan.

Auf der Bank

Kunde: Ich möchte gern Reiseschecks einlösen, Dollarschecks.

Angestellte: Bitte schön. Wieviel möchten Sie wechseln?

Kunde: Fünfzig. Wie steht der Dollar heute?

Angestellte: Der Kurs für Reiseschecks ist 1,80 (eins achtzig). Das sind also 90 Mark minus 1 Mark Gebühren.

Im Kaufhaus

Kundin: Darf ich bitte diese Jacke anprobieren?

Verkäuferin: Selbstverständlich ... Das Blau steht Ihnen gut, wirklich.

Kundin: Leider ist sie etwas zu eng.

Verkäuferin: Hier habe ich die gleiche Jacke eine Nummer größer. Die müßte Ihnen passen.

Im Café

1. Dame: Sind diese zwei Plätze noch frei?

Gast: Ja, bitte.

Ober: Was wünschen die Damen?

2. Dame: Was können Sie uns denn empfehlen?

Ober: Der Apfelstrudel ist ausgezeichnet.

1. Dame: Zwei Stück bitte. Mit Sahne. Und zwei Kännchen Kaffee.

Ober: Aber gern.

At the post office

I'd like to send this letter air mail.

To America? The cost is 1 mark 40 for up to 5 grams.

Please give me five 1-mark-40 stamps. Can I mail this package here?

No, the package window is the next one over.

At the bank

I'd like to cash some traveler's checks, dollar checks.

Fine. How much would you like to change?

Fifty dollars' worth. What's the exchange rate to-day?

The rate for traveler's checks is 1,80 (one eighty). So that comes to 90 marks, minus 1 mark fee.

In the department store

May I please try on this jacket?

Of course . . . Blue looks good on you, really.

I'm afraid it's somewhat too tight.

Here, I have the same jacket a size larger. It should fit you.

In the Café

Are these two seats taken [unoccupied]?

Yes, please sit down.

What would you like, ladies?

What would you recommend?

The apple strudel is excellent.

Two pieces, please. With whipped cream. And two pots of coffee.

Certainly.

Bei der Ärztin

Patient: Frau Doktor, ich habe immer solche Rückenschmerzen.
Ärztin: Wie lange haben Sie die Schmerzen denn schon?
Patient: Seit zwei Wochen.
Ärztin: Zeigen Sie mir mal genau, wo es weh tut!

Im Hotel

Touristin: Haben Sie noch ein Einzelzimmer frei?
Empfangschefin: Ja. Wir haben eins mit Dusche (im sechsten Stock).
Touristin: Wieviel kostet es?
Empfangschefin: Vierzig Mark. Mit Frühstück, natürlich.
Touristin: Schön. Ich nehme es für eine Nacht.
Empfangschefin: Bitte sehr. Tragen Sie sich hier ein, bitte! Hier ist der Schlüssel.

An der Theaterkasse

Student: Ich möchte gern zwei Karten für den ersten Rang, für heute abend.
Angestellte: Tut mir leid. Ich habe nur noch Karten fürs Parkett.
Student: Wie teuer sind die Karten? Ich habe einen Studentenausweis.
Angestellte: Dann bekommen Sie Ihre Karte fünfzig Prozent billiger.

Am Flughafen

Fluggast: Fliegt die Maschine direkt nach Istanbul?
Angestellter: Nein, sie macht eine Zwischenlandung in Athen. Möchten Sie Raucher oder Nichtraucher?
Fluggast: Nichtraucher, bitte.
Angestellter: Gang- oder Fensterplatz?
Fluggast: Ich hätte gern einen Fensterplatz.

Im Flugzeug

Flugbegleiter: Wir bitten Sie, sich jetzt anzuschnallen und die Rückenlehnen senkrecht zu stellen.

At the doctor's

Doctor, my back aches all the time.

How long have you had the pain?

Two weeks.
Show me exactly where it hurts.

In the hotel

Do you still have a single room available?
Yes. We have one with a shower (on the seventh floor).
How much is it?
Forty marks. Breakfast is included, of course.

Fine. I'll take it for one night.
Fine. Please register here. Here's the key.

At the theater box office

I'd like two tickets in the first balcony for this evening.
I'm sorry. I only have orchestra tickets left.

How much are the tickets? I have a student I.D.

Then you get a fifty percent discount.

At the airport

Does the plane go directly to Istanbul?

No, it makes a stop in Athens. Would you like smoking or non-smoking?

Non-smoking, please.
Aisle or window seat?
I would like a window seat.

In the airplane

Please fasten your seat belts and place your seat backs in the upright position.

Bei der Zugauskunft

Tourist: Können Sie mir sagen, wann der nächste Zug nach München fährt?
Beamtin: Um 14 Uhr 20 fährt ein Intercity ab.

Am Fahrkartenschalter

Reisender: Einmal erster Klasse München, bitte.
Beamter: Hin und zurück oder einfach?
Reisender: Einfach, bitte. Von welchem Bahnsteig fährt mein Zug ab?
Beamter: Gleis elf.

Im Zug

Reisende: Warten Sie! Ich hebe den Koffer ins Gepäcknetz. *(Schaffnerin macht die Tür auf.)*
Schaffnerin: (Ist) hier noch jemand zugestiegen? *(Reisende reicht ihr die Fahrkarte.)*
Schaffnerin: Sie müssen in München umsteigen. Der Anschlußzug wartet auf Gleis 7.
Reisende: Können Sie mir sagen, wo der Speisewagen ist?
Schaffnerin: Ja, in der Mitte des Zuges.

At the railway station information desk

Can you tell me when the next train leaves for Munich?
An Intercity-train leaves at 2:20 p.m.

At the ticket window

One ticket to Munich, please. First class.
Round trip or one-way?
One-way, please. From which platform does my train leave?
Track eleven.

In the train

Just a minute, I'll put the suitcase up on the rack. *(The conductor opens the door.)*
Has anyone here just gotten on? *(Passenger hands her the ticket.)*
You have to change trains in Munich. The connecting train will be waiting on Track 7.
Can you tell me where the dining car is?

Yes, in the middle of the train.

German-English vocabulary

This vocabulary includes all the words used in *Deutsch heute* except numbers. The definitions given are limited to the context in which the words are used in this book. Chapter numbers (and E for *Einführung*) are given for all words and expressions occurring in the chapter vocabularies and in the *Erweiterung des Wortschatzes* sections to indicate where a word or expression is first used. Passive vocabulary does not have a chapter reference. The symbol ~ indicates repetition of the key word (minus the definite article, if any).

Nouns are listed with their plural forms: **der Abend, -e.** No plural entry is given if the plural is rarely used or nonexistent. If two entries follow a noun, the first one indicates the genitive and the second one indicates the plural: **der Herr, -n, -en.**

Strong and irregular weak verbs are listed with their principal parts. Vowel changes in the present tense are noted in parentheses, followed by simple-past and past-participle forms. All verbs take **haben** with the past participle unless indicated with **sein.** For example: **fahren (ä), fuhr, ist gefahren.** Separable-prefix verbs are indicated with a raised dot: **auf•stehen.**

Adjectives and adverbs that require an umlaut in the comparative and superlative forms are noted as follows: **warm (ä).**

Stress marks are given for all words that are not accented on the first syllable. The stress mark follows the accented syllable: **Amerika'ner.** In some words, either of two syllables may be stressed.

The following abbreviations are used:

abbr.	abbreviation	*fam.*	familiar
acc.	accusative	*gen.*	genitive
adj.	adjective	*m.*	masculine
adv.	adverb	*n.*	neuter
colloq.	colloquial	*p.p.*	past participle
comp.	comparative	*part.*	participle
conj.	conjunction	*pl.*	plural
dat.	dative	*sg.*	singular
decl.	declined	*subj.*	subjunctive
f.	feminine	*sup.*	superlative

A automobile symbol for Austria

der **Abend, -e** evening; **Guten ~!** Good evening! 1; **zu ~ essen** to have supper 3

abend: gestern ~ last night 6; **heute ~** this evening 1

das **Abendessen** dinner, supper 3; **zum ~** for supper 3

abends evenings, in the evening 3

aber *(conj.)* but, however 1; *(flavoring particle)* really, certainly 2

ab•fahren (ä), fuhr ab, ist abgefahren to depart 7

ab•hängen, hing ab, abgehangen (+ von) to depend on 12

ab•holen to pick up 7

das **Abitur'** *Gymnasium* diploma 4

absolut' absolute(ly)

ab•spreizen to raise

ab•trocknen to dry dishes 8

ab•waschen (ä), wusch ab, abgewaschen to wash (dishes) 8

ab•werten to discredit

Ach so.' Oh, I see.

achten (auf + acc.) to watch

der **Adler, -** eagle

die **Adres'se, -n** address E; **Wie ist Ihre ~?** What is your address? E

ähnlich (+ dat.) similar 5

die **Ähnlichkeit, -en** similarity

die **Ahnung, -en** idea; **keine ~** no idea 14

akzepta'bel acceptable

akzeptie'ren to accept 9

alle all 6

allein' alone 6

alles everything 3

allgemein general 7

die Alltagssprache colloquial speech

die Alpen (pl.) Alps 5

das Alpenland alpine country

das Alphabet' alphabet E

als (conj.) when 10; as 5; (after a comp.) than 2

also therefore 2; thus 12

alt (ä) old E; Wie ~ sind Sie? How old are you? E; Ich bin 19 Jahre ~. I am 19 years old. E

das Alter (old) age

alternativ' alternative (adj.)

die Alternati've, -n alternative (noun)

das Altersheim, -e retirement home, rest home

die Altstadt old part of city or town

(das) Ame'rika America 2

der Amerika'ner, -/die Amerika'nerin, -nen American (person) 2

amerika'nisch American (adj.) 2

an (+ acc./dat.) on; at; to 7

an•bieten, bot an, angeboten to offer 6

andere other 2

anderes something else, anything else

(sich) ändern to change

anders different 2

anderswo elsewhere

an•deuten to indicate

der Anfang, ⁓e beginning 6

an•fangen (ä), fing an, angefangen to begin 6; mit [der Arbeit] ~ to begin [(the) work] 6

an•fassen to touch

angebaut (p.p. of an•bauen) grown

angenehm pleasant

die Angli'stik English studies (language and literature) 4

die Angst, ⁓e fear 7; ~ haben to be afraid 7; ~ machen to cause fear; ~ um fear for 7

an•kommen, kam an, ist angekommen to arrive 7

die Anleitung guidance

an•nehmen (i), nahm an, angenommen to assume; to accept 12

an•rufen, rief an, angerufen to call, telephone; bei [dir] ~ to call [your] home 6

an•sehen (ie), sah an, angesehen to look at, to watch; ich sehe es mir an I look it over 4

der Anstand good manners

(an)statt' (+ gen.) instead of 8

die Antwort, -en answer; die ~ auf eine Frage the answer to a question 11

antworten [auf eine Frage] to answer [a question] (as in ich antworte auf die Frage) 8; (+ dat. of person) to answer (as in ich antworte der Frau) 8

an•zeigen to indicate, show

(sich [acc.]) an•ziehen, zog an, angezogen to dress 9; ich ziehe mich an I get dressed 9

(sich [dat.]) an•ziehen, zog an, angezogen to put on; ich ziehe mir [die Schuhe] an I put on [my shoes]

der Anzug, ⁓e man's suit 6

die Apothe'ke,-n pharmacy; in die ~ to the pharmacy 3

der Apparat', -e apparatus 9

der April' April 2

die Arbeit, -en work; (school or academic) paper 4

arbeiten to work; to study 1; bei [einer Firma] ~ to work at [a company] 1

der Arbeiter, -/die Arbeiterin, -nen worker 13

der Arbeitgeber, -/die Arbeitgeberin, -nen employer 12

der Arbeitnehmer, -/die Arbeitnehmerin, -nen worker 11

die Arbeitskräfte (pl.) workers

der Arbeitslohn, ⁓e wage

arbeitslos unemployed 14

die Arbeitslosigkeit unemployment 12

der Arbeitsmarkt, ⁓e job market

der Arbeitsplatz, ⁓e job, position

die Arbeitsproduktivität worker productivity

die Arbeitswelt work world

die Arbeitswoche, -n work week

das Argument' argument

arm (ä) poor

der Arm, -e arm 9

die Armut poverty, scarcity

das Aro'ma aroma

arrangie'ren to arrange

die Art, -en way, manner 7

der Arti'kel, - article 4

der Arznei'tee medicinal tea

der Arzt, ⁓e/die Ärztin, -nen doctor, physician 7

der Aspekt', -e aspect

das Aspirin' aspirin 3

der Atem breath

der Atlan'tische Ozean Atlantic Ocean

atmen to breathe 7

die Atmosphä're atmosphere

atmungsaktiv conducive to breathing

das Atom'kraftwerk, -e nuclear power plant 14

attraktiv' attractive

auch also 1; ich ~ me, too 1; ~ wenn even if 9

auf (+ acc./dat.) on; at; to 7; ~ Wiedersehen! Good-by! 1; ~ [englisch] in [English]

der Aufbau (re)construction

auf•bauen to build (up)

auf•drehen to curl

die Aufenthaltserlaubnis residence permit

die Aufführung, -en performance

die Aufgabe, -n assignment, task 12

auf•hören (mit) to stop 6; **mit [der Arbeit]** ~ to stop [work]

auf•machen to open 4

das **Aufnahmestudio, -s** recording studio

auf•nehmen (i), nahm auf, aufgenommen to accept, to take in

auf•räumen to straighten up, clean 8

auf•stehen, stand auf, ist aufgestanden to stand up 4; to get up

auf•wachsen (wächst auf), wuchs auf, ist aufgewachsen to grow up

das **Auge, -n** eye 9

der **August'** August 2

aus (+ dat.) out of; from 5

die **Ausbildung** training, development

der **Ausdruck, ⁻e** expression

aus•geben (i), gab aus, ausgegeben to spend 13

ausgesprochen definitely, clearly

ausgezeich'net excellent(ly) 6

aus•kommen, kam aus, ist ausgekommen to get by (manage)

das **Ausland** foreign country; **ins** ~ **gehen** to go abroad

der **Ausländer, -/die Ausländerin, -nen** foreigner 7

die **Ausländerfeindlichkeit** hostility towards foreigners

ausländisch foreign 14

die **Ausnahme, -n** exception

aus•schließen, schloß aus, ausgeschlossen to exclude

aus•sehen (ie), sah aus, ausgesehen to look like, seem 6

der **Außenhandel** foreign trade

die **Außenpolitik** foreign policy

außer (+ dat.) besides, except for 5

außerdem besides 6

das **Äußere** external appearance

außerhalb (+ gen.) outside of, beyond 10

die **Äußerlichkeit, -en** superficiality

die **Aussprache** pronunciation

aus•steigen, stieg aus, ist ausgestiegen to get off (a vehicle); to drop out

der **Austauschstudent, -en, -en/die Austauschstudentin, -nen** exchange student

(das) **Austra'lien** Australia

aus•trinken, trank aus, ausgetrunken to drink up

ausverkauft sold out

die **Auswahl** choice

(sich [+ acc.]) **aus•ziehen, zog aus, ausgezogen** to get undressed; **ich ziehe mich aus** I get undressed 9

(sich [+ dat.]) **aus•ziehen, zog aus, ausgezogen** to take off; **ich ziehe mir [die Schuhe] aus** I take off [my shoes] 9

das **Auto, -s** automobile, car 5

die **Autobahn, -en** freeway, expressway 7

das **Autokennzeichen, -** abbreviation for country of registry for automobiles

automa'tisch automatic(ally)

autonom' autonomous

die **Autonomie'** autonomy

der **Autor, -en/die Autorin, -nen** author 14

der/die **Azubi, -s** (abbr. of **Auszubildende**) apprentice

das **Baby, -s** baby 14

der **Bach, ⁻e** brook

backen (ä), backte, gebacken to bake 6

der **Bäcker, -/die Bäckerin, -nen** baker 3; **beim Bäcker** at the bakery 3; **zum Bäcker** to the bakery 3

die **Bäckerei', -en** bakery 3

der **Backstein** brick

das **Bad, ⁻er** bath; bathroom

baden to bathe 6

das **Baden** bathing

die **Badewanne, -n** bathtub

das **Badezimmer, -** bathroom 8

das **BAFöG = das Bundesausbildungsförderungsgesetz** national law to support education in the FRG

die **Bahn, -en** train, railroad 5

der **Bahnhof, ⁻e** train station

bald (eher, ehest-) soon 2

der **Balkon', -s** balcony 8

der **Ball, ⁻e** ball

die **Bana'ne, -n** banana

die **Band, -s** (music) band 11

die **Bank, -en** bank 10

basie'ren (auf + dat.) to be based (on)

die **Basis, Basen** basis

der **Basketball** basketball 1

basteln to tinker (with), to work at a hobby 11

bauen to build 8

der **Bauer, -n, -n/die Bäuerin, -nen** farmer, peasant 11

das **Bauernhaus, ⁻er** farmhouse 11

der **Baum, ⁻e** tree 7

die **Baumwolle** cotton

der **Baustein, -e** building block

(das) **Bayern** Bavaria

der **Beam'te** (noun decl. like adj.) (government) official (m.)

die **Beam'tin, -nen** (government) official (f.)

die **Bedarfs'deckung** satisfaction of needs

bedau'erlich regrettable

bedeu'ten to mean, imply; **Was bedeutet das?** What does that mean? 7; to indicate

bedeu'tend significant

die **Bedin'gung, -en** condition

der/die **Bedürf'tige** (adj. used as noun) needy person

beein'flussen to influence 2

begei'stert enthusiastic

begin'nen, begann, begonnen to begin 9; **mit [der Arbeit]** ~ to begin [(the) work]

begrei'fen, begriff, begriffen to grasp, understand

die **Begrü'ßung, -en** greeting

behaup'ten to declare

bei (+ *dat.*) at (a place of business); at (the home of) 3; ~ **uns** in our country; ~ **[dir]** at [your] house 5; near 5; while, during; **beim Fernsehen** while watching TV

beide both 4

beides both 5

das **Bein, -e** leg 9

das **Beispiel, -e** example 2; **zum** ~ (**z.B.**) for example 2

bekannt' familiar; well known 6

der/die **Bekann'te** (*noun declined like adj.*) acquaintance 6

(das) **Belgien** Belgium

bekom'men, bekam, bekommen to receive 3

bema'len to paint, decorate

bemer'ken to notice 6

sich **beneh'men (i), benahm, benommen** to behave oneself

benut'zen to use 7

das **Benzin'** gasoline, fuel 13

beob'achten to observe 7

bequem' comfortable

berech'nend calculating

der **Berg, -e** mountain 5

berich'ten to report 14

der **Beruf', -e** job, profession 10

die **Berufs'ausbildung** job training

berufs'tätig employed (in a profession) 10

(sich) **beschäf'tigen (mit)** to occupy (oneself) (with), to keep busy 12

beschäf'tigt sein to be busy 12

beschlie'ßen, beschloß, beschlossen to decide 14

beschrei'ben, beschrieb, beschrieben to describe 9

die **Beschrei'bung, -en** description

beschwö'ren, beschwor, beschworen to implore

besie'delt populated

der **Besitz'** property

beson'der- particular 5; **nichts Besonderes** nothing special 1

beson'ders especially 3

bespre'chen (i), besprach, besprochen to discuss, talk about

besser (*comp. of* **gut**) better 3

(die) **Besserung: gute** ~! Get well soon!

beste'hen, bestand, bestanden to exist

bestel'len to order 4

bestimmt' certain(ly) 2

die **Bestimmt'heit** certainty

der **Besuch',-e** visit 3; ~ **haben** to have company 3

besu'chen to visit 11

der **Besu'cher, -/die Besu'cherin, -nen** visitor, guest 8

beto'nen to reinforce, emphasize

betref'fen (i), betraf, betroffen to concern

der **Betrieb', -e** company

das **Bett, -en** bed E; **zu** ~ **gehen** to go to bed

die **Bevöl'kerung** population

bevor' (*conj.*) before

die **Bevor'mundung** paternalism, control

sich **bewe'gen** to move

die **Bewe'gung, -en** movement

bewußt' aware of, conscious

bezah'len to pay for 3

die **Bezie'hung, -en** relation(ship)

bezie'hungsweise (*abbr.* **bzw.**) that is to say; respectively

der **Bezirk, -e** district

die **Bibliothek', -en** library 4

das **Bier** beer 3

das **Bierchen** small glass of beer

der **Biergarten, -̈** beer garden 7

das **Bild, -er** picture; photograph; image E

das **Bilderbuch, -̈er** picture book

billig cheap 3

binden, band, gebunden to tie 11

der **Bio-Laden, -̈** health food store

die **Biologie'** biology

biolo'gisch biological(ly)

bis (+ *acc.*) until 3; ~ **zu** up to 5; ~ **dann** till later

bisher' until now 11

bißchen: ein ~ a little 10

bitte please; you're welcome E; ~ **sehr** (*said when handing someone something*) Here you are. 12

bitten, bat, gebeten (+ um) to request, ask (for) 5

Bitteschön. You're welcome.

blaß pale 9

blau blue E

bleiben, blieb, ist geblieben to remain 2

der **Bleistift, -e** pencil E

der **Blick, -e** glance, look; view

der **Blitz** lightning

blitzblank shiny

blond blond

blühen to bloom; to flourish; **blühend** flourishing

die **Blume,-n** flower 3

das **Blumengeschäft, -e** flower shop

der **Blumenmarkt** flower market

die **Bluse,-n** blouse 6

der **Boden, -̈** floor

der **Bodensee** Lake Constance 11

bombardie'ren to bombard

böse angry 7; **Sei mir nicht** ~. Don't be angry with me. 7

die **Botschaft, -en** message

brauchen to need 3

braun brown E

die **BRD (= Bundesrepublik Deutschland)** Federal Republic of Germany

brechen (i), brach, gebrochen to break 10

der **Brei** porridge; stew

breit wide

der **Brief, -e** letter 10

der **Briefträger, -/die Briefträgerin, -nen** mail carrier

bringen, brachte, gebracht to bring 4

das **Brot, -e** bread; sandwich 3

das **Brötchen, -** hard-crusted (breakfast) roll 3

der **Bruder, -̈** brother 4

brüllen to bawl

das Buch, "er book E

das Bücherregal, -e bookcase 8

die Büchertasche, -n book bag E

die Buchhandlung, -en bookstore 3

buchstabie'ren to spell E

bummeln to stroll

der Bund federation

der Bundeskanzler, - prime minister

(das) Bundesland federal state in the FRG

die Bundespost German Federal Post Office

die Bundesrepublik Deutschland Federal Republic of Germany (West Germany [FRG]) 2

der Bundesstaat, -en federal state (in the U.S.A.)

der Bundestag lower house of Parliament in the FRG

bunt colorful

die Burg, -en castle

der Bürger, -/die Bürgerin, -nen citizen 7

die Bürgerinitiative, -n citizens' action group, grassroots movement 7

das Büro', -s office 8

die Bürokratie' bureaucracy

der Bus, -se bus 5

die Butter butter 3

das Butterbrot bread-and-butter sandwich

bzw. (= bezie'hungsweise) that is to say; respectively

das Café', -s café 4

das Camping camping

der Campus campus

CH (= Confoederatio Helvetica) automobile symbol for Switzerland

die Chance, -n opportunity, chance

die Chancengleichheit equal opportunity

der Charakter character

der Chef, -s/die Chefin, -nen boss 10

der Chefarzt, "e/die Chefärztin, -nen chief [doctor] of staff

die Chemie' chemistry 4

chemie'frei free of chemicals

das Chemie'kombinat chemical works

die Chemika'lien (pl.) chemicals

chemisch chemical

der Chor, "e choir

circa (abbr. ca.) approximately

die Cola cola drink 6

das College, -s college

der Compu'ter, - computer 10

ČS automobile symbol for Czechoslovakia

D automobile symbol for FRG

da there E; then 9; (conj.) since, because 8

das Dach, "er roof 8

dadurch thereby, by this means 13

dafür for that; instead

dage'gen against it; on the other hand

daher therefore, for that reason 4

dahin there (to that place) 7

damals at that time 10

damit' so that 11

danach after that

(das) Dänemark Denmark

der Dank thanks 10; vielen ~ many thanks, thanks a lot 10

danke thanks E; Danke sehr. Thank you very much.

danken (+ dat. of person) to thank 5

dann then 3

darauf on (it)

darf (dürfen): Was darf es sein? What would you like?

darin in (it)

das Darlehen, - loan

dar•stellen to present

darü'ber over, above

darü'ber hinaus' beyond that

darum therefore, for that reason 13

das that; the (n.) E

daß (conj.) that 5

das Datum, Daten date

dauern to last 5; dauernd continuously

da'zu for that, to that

dazu' in addition, with it

dazwi'schen in between

die DDR (= Deutsche Demokra'tische Republik') German Democratic Republic 2

degradie'ren to degrade

dein your (fam. sg.) 2

dekorie'ren to decorate 6

die Demokratie', -n democracy

die Demonstration', -en demonstration 14

denken, dachte, gedacht (an + acc.) to think (of) 2

das Denkmal, "er monument, memorial

denn (conj.) because, for 2; (flavoring particle adding emphasis to questions) 3

der that; the (m.) E

deshalb therefore 4

deutlich clear(ly)

deutsch German (adj.) 2

(das) Deutsch German (language) 1; ~ machen to do German (homework) 4; auf ~ in German; ich mache ~ I'm doing German homework 1

die Deutsche Demokra'tische Republik' (DDR) German Democratic Republic (East Germany [GDR]) 2

der/die Deutsche (noun decl. like adj.) German person 2

(das) Deutschland Germany 2

deutschsprachig German-language

der Dezem'ber December 2

d.h. = das heißt i.e., that is

der Dialekt', -e dialect

dicht dense(ly)

die that; the (f.) E

dienen (+ dat.) to serve 13

der Dienstag Tuesday E

dies (-er, -es, -e) this, these 4; the latter

diesmal this time

diktie'ren to dictate

die Dimension', -en dimension

das Ding, -e thing 5

dir (dat. of du) (to) you 5

direkt' direct(ly)

die Diskussion', -en discussion

(dividiert') durch divided by E

DM (= Deutsche Mark) unit of currency used in FRG

D-Mark (= Deutsche Mark) German mark (coin) 12

doch (flavoring particle) after all, indeed 3; Yes, of course; on the contrary (positive response to negative statement or question) 3

der Dom, -e cathedral

der Donnerstag Thursday E

doof silly, stupid 1

doppelt double

das Dorf, ̈-er village

dort there 5

dran: ist gut ~ is well off

drängen to crowd in

drastisch drastic(ally)

draußen outside 7

drin (= darin) in it

das Drittel, - third 12

die Drogerie', -n drugstore 3

du you (fam. sg.) 1; Du! Hey! (used to get someone's attention) 4

duftig light

dumm (ü) dumb, stupid 1; etwas Dummes something dumb 6

die Dummheit, -en stupidity

dunkel (dunkler, dunkelst-) dark 8

durch (+ acc.) divided by E; through 3

durch·arbeiten to work through, to study 4

der Durchschnitt average; im ~ on the average

durchsichtig transparent

dürfen (darf), durfte, gedurft to be permitted or allowed 4

der Durst thirst 6; ~ haben to be thirsty 6

sich duschen to shower 9

eben just 4; (flavoring particle denoting finality) 4

ebenso just as 11; likewise, the same 14

echt real, genuine; (slang) really; ~ toll really neat 7

die Ecke, -n corner 7

effektiv' effective(ly)

die EG (abbr. for Europä'ische Gemein'schaft) European Community

egal' equal; the same 5; Das ist mir ~. It's all the same to me. 5

der Ehemann, ̈-er husband

eher (comp. of bald) rather, sooner

das Ei, -er egg 3

die Eidgenossenschaft confederation

eigen own 7

eigenartig strange

das Eigenheim, -e private home

eigentlich actually 4

ein a, an 1; ~ paar a few 3

einan'der one another 7

der Eindruck, ̈-e impression 13

einfach simple; simply 7

die Einfachheit simplicity

ein·fallen (fällt ein), fiel ein, ist eingefallen (+ dat.) to occur (to one's mind) 9

das Einfamilienhaus, ̈-er single-family home 8

ein·führen to import

die Einführung introduction

einheitlich unified

einige some, several 4

einiges something

ein·kaufen to shop 3

die Einkaufstasche,-n shopping bag 3

ein·laden (ä), lud ein, eingeladen to invite 6

die Einladung, -en invitation

einmal once 5; noch ~ again, once more 11

ein·richten to furnish

ein·schlagen (ä), schlug ein, eingeschlagen to strike

ein·schließen, schloß ein, eingeschlossen to include

ein·stecken to pack, to take along

die Einstellung, -en attitude

ein·teilen to arrange

einverstanden agreed

der Einwohner, -/die Einwohnerin, -nen inhabitant 2

das Einwohnermeldeamt residence registration office

einzeln single, individual 12

einzig only, sole

der Eiskunstlauf figure skating

elegant' elegant

der Elek'triker, -/die Elek'trikerin, -nen electrician

elek'trisch electrical

der Elek'troingenieur, -e/die Elek'troingenieurin, -nen electrical engineer

die Elek'trotechnik electrical engineering products

elend miserable 9

die Eltern (pl.) parents 4

die Emanzipation' emancipation

emanzipie'ren to emancipate

empfeh'len (ie), empfahl, empfohlen to recommend

das Ende, -n end; am ~ in/at the end 4

endlich finally 3

die Energie' energy

eng close; tight, narrow 7

(das) England England 10

(das) Englisch English (language) 4; auf englisch in English

englisch English (adj.)

der Enkel, -/die Enkelin, -nen grandson/granddaughter

enorm' enormous(ly)

entde'cken to discover

die Entfal'tung development

entle'gen out of the way

entschei′den, entschied, entschieden to decide 12; **sich entscheiden** to make a decision (after reflecting on it) 12

die Entschei′dung, -en decision

entschlos′sen (*p.p. of* **entschließen**) determined

die Entschul′digung, -en excuse; apology 11

Entschul′digung! Excuse me! 11

entste′hen, entstand, ist entstanden to arise, to come about

(sich) entwi′ckeln to develop 9

er he; it E

die Erbse, -n pea

die Erde earth

das Erdgeschoß ground floor 8

das Ereig′nis,-se event

die Erfah′rung, -en experience 10

der Erfolg′ success

erfolg′reich successful

erfül′len to fulfill

die Erhö′hung, -en increase

sich erho′len (von) to recover (from), recuperate (from) 11

(sich) erin′nern (an + *acc.*) to remember [someone or something] 10

die Erin′nerung, -en remembrance

sich erkäl′ten to catch a cold 9

die Erkäl′tung, -en cold 9

die Erkennt′nis, -se realization

erklä′ren to explain 4

die Erklä′rung, -en explanation 7

erlau′ben to allow

ernst serious 1; **Ist das dein Ernst?** Are you serious? 11

errei′chen to reach 12

erschei′nen, erschien, ist erschienen to appear 5

erset′zen to replace 13

die Erspar′nisse (*pl.*) savings

erst only, just 4; first 7; **~ einmal** first, sometime; first of all 9; once

erstaunt′ astonished 8

der Erste Weltkrieg World War I

erstens first of all

der/die Erwach′sene (*noun decl. like adj.*) adult

erwäh′nen to mention

erwar′ten to expect 12

die Erwei′terung expansion

erzäh′len (von/über + *acc.*) to tell (about) 2

die Erzäh′lung, -en story, narrative

es it 1; **~ gibt (+** *acc.*) there is, there are 3

das Essen meal; food; eating 4; **~ und Wohnen** board and room

essen (ißt), aß, gegessen to eat 3

der Eßtisch dining table

das Eßzimmer, - dining room 8

etwa about, approximately 2

etwas some, somewhat 3; **~ anderes** something different 7

euch: bei ~ in your country

euer (*fam. pl.*) your 2

(das) Euro′pa Europe 2

der Europä′er, -/die Europä′erin, -nen European (person)

eventuell′ possibly

das Exa′men, - comprehensive examination 4

experimentie′ren to experiment

der Export′ export

die Export′güter (*pl.*) export goods

exportie′ren to export

der Extrakt′, -e extract

F automobile symbol for France

die Fabrik′, -en factory

der Fabrik′besitzer, - factory owner

das Fach, ¨er (academic) subject 4

das Fachgeschäft, -e specialty store

fad dull

die Fahne, -n flag

fahren (ä), fuhr, ist gefahren to drive; to travel; **mit [dem Auto] ~** to go by [car] 5

der Fahrer, -/die Fahrerin, -nen driver 11

das Fahrrad, ¨er bicycle 5

die Fahrschule driving school

der Fahrschulkurs driving-school course

die Fahrt, -en trip 7

die Fakten (*pl.*) facts

falsch wrong 6

die Fami′lie, -n family 4

die Farbe, -n color; **Welche ~ hat ... ?** What color is . . . ? E

der Farbfernseher, - color television (set) 9

die Faser, -n fiber

fast almost 5

(die) Fastnacht carnival, Mardi Gras

faszinie′rend fascinating

faul lazy 1

faulenzen to lounge around, be idle 11

der Februar February 2

die Feier, -n party, celebration

feiern to celebrate 6

der Feiertag, -e holiday

fein fine 7

das Fenster, - window E

der Fensterladen, ¨ shutter

die Ferien (*pl.*) vacation 5; **in den ~** on vacation, during vacation 5

die Ferienreise vacation trip

das Fernsehen television 7

fern•sehen (ie), sah fern, ferngesehen to watch TV 7

der Fernseher, - TV (set) 9

die Fernsehsendung, -en TV program 9

fertig finished; ready 4; **mit etwas ~ werden** to deal with, master something

das Fest, -e celebration; feast; party 11

fest•halten (ä), hielt fest, festgehalten to hold tight

fest•machen to fasten

die Fete, -n party 8

fett thick, fat

fettig greasy

das Fieber fever 9

die Figur′, -en figure; illustration

der Film, -e film, movie 4

finanziell′ financial(ly)

finden, fand, gefunden to find 3

der **Finger, -** finger 9
finster dark
die **Firma, Firmen** company 6
der **Fisch, -e** fish 3
der **Fischmann, -̈er** fish seller
fit fit, trim
FL automobile symbol for Liechtenstein
das **Flachland** lowland
die **Flasche,-n** bottle 8
das **Fleisch** meat 3
der **Fleiß** diligence
fleißig industrious, hard-working 1
fliegen, flog, ist geflogen to fly 5
fließen, floß, ist geflossen to flow
fließend fluent(ly) 10
flirten to flirt
der **Flüchtling, -e** refugee 5
der **Flughafen, -̈** airport 7
das **Flugzeug, -e** airplane 5
der **Flur, -e** entrance hall 8
der **Fluß, Flüsse** river
der **Föderalis'mus** federalism
folgen, ist gefolgt (+ dat.) to follow
folgend following
die **Form, -en** form
das **Formular', -e** form
die **Forschung** research
fort·fahren (ä), fuhr fort, ist fortgefahren to continue
fotografie'ren to photograph 11
die **Frage, -n** question 4
fragen to ask 3
fraglich questionable 12
der **Franken** Swiss unit of currency
(das) **Frankreich** France
der **Franzose, -n, -n**/die **Französin, -nen** Frenchman/Frenchwoman
franzö'sisch French (adj.) 11
(das) **Franzö'sisch** French (language) 10
die **Frau, -en** woman; **Frau** (term of address for married women and officially for all adult women) Mrs.; Ms. E

die **Frauenbewegung** women's movement
das **Frauenbild** image of women
das **Fräulein, -** young lady; Miss E; **Fräulein!** term used to call a waitress
frei free 4
die **Freiheit, -en** freedom
der **Freiraum** freedom of movement
die **Freistunde, -n** free period
der **Freitag** Friday E
die **Freizeit** leisure time 11
fremd foreign 14
der **Fremdenverkehr** tourism
die **Fremdsprache, -n** foreign language 10
sich **freuen (über** + acc.**)** to be pleased (about) 13; **~ auf (** + acc.**)** to look forward to 13
der **Freund, -e**/die **Freundin, -nen** friend 3
freundlich friendly 7
die **Freundlichkeit** friendliness 7
frisch fresh 3
froh glad, happy 13
früh early 5
früher formerly 13
das **Frühjahr** spring
der **Frühling** spring 2
das **Frühstück, -e** breakfast 3; **zum ~** for breakfast 3
frühstücken to eat breakfast
sich **fühlen** to feel [ill, well, etc.] 9
führen to lead 8; **führend** leading, prominent
für (+ acc.) for 2
furchtbar horrible, horribly 2
(sich) **fürchten (vor** + dat.**)** to fear, be afraid (of) 12
fürchterlich horrible, horribly 9
der **Fuß, -̈e** foot 5; **zu ~** on foot 5
der **Fußball** soccer 1
die **Fußgängerzone, -n** pedestrian precinct

die **Gabel, -n** fork 7
ganz complete, whole; very; **~ gut** not bad, O.K. 1; **~ schön** really quite pretty; **~ schön blaß** pretty pale 9
gar: ~ nicht not at all
die **Gara'ge, -n** garage 8
garantie'ren to guarantee
garantiert' guaranteed
der **Garten, -̈** garden E
die **Gasse, -n** small, narrow street
der **Gast, -̈e** guest 6
der **Gastarbeiter, -/**die **Gastarbeiterin, -nen** foreign worker 14
das **Gasthaus, -̈er** restaurant, pub, bar
die **Gaststätte, -n** restaurant, pub, bar 11
geben (i), gab, gegeben to give 3; **es gibt** (+ acc.) there is, there are 3
das **Gebiet', -e** area, field
gebrau'chen to use 10
gebraucht' used, second-hand
gebraut' (p.p. of **brauen**) brewed
der **Geburts'tag, -e** birthday 2; **zum ~** for one's birthday 2
die **Geburts'tagsfeier** birthday celebration
die **Geduld'** patience
geeig'net suited
gefähr'lich dangerous 10
gefal'len (ä), gefiel, gefallen (+ dat.) to please; to be pleasing (to) 6
der **Gefrier'schrank, -̈e** freezer 9
das **Gefühl', -e** feeling 7
gegen (+ acc.) against 3; **~ Ende des Jahres** around the end of the year
gegenü'ber (+ dat.) opposite; on the opposite side; opposed to; in relation to 9
der **Gegner, -/**die **Gegnerin, -nen** opponent
das **Gehalt', -̈er** salary 13

gehen, ging, ist gegangen to go 1; **es geht (nicht)** it will (it won't) do, it's (not) O.K. 10; it's (not) possible 2; **mir geht's schlecht** I'm not well; **Wie geht es Ihnen?** How are you? *(formal)* 1; **Wie geht's?** How are you? *(informal)* 1

gehö'ren (+ *dat.*) to belong to 5

das **Geklin'gel** din, noise

das **Geläch'ter** laughter

die **Gelas'senheit** casualness

gelb yellow E

das **Geld** money 3

die **Gele'genheit, -en** opportunity

gelten (gilt), galt, gegolten to be worth, valid; prevail

die **Gemein'de, -n** community

das **Gemü'se** vegetable 3·

gemüt'lich comfortable, informal

genau' exactly, that's right 4

genau'so exactly (as)

Genf Geneva

der **Genos'se, -n, -n** party member

genug' enough 7

die **Geographie'** geography

gera'de just; straight 6

die **Gera'nien** *(pl.)* geraniums

geräu'chert smoked

die **Germani'stik** German studies (language and literature) 4

gern (lieber, liebst-) gladly, willingly; *used with verbs to indicate liking for, as in* **ich spiele gern Tennis** I like to play tennis 1; ~ **haben** to like, *as in* **ich habe sie ~** I like her

der **Geruch', ÷e** odor

das **Geschäft', -e** store; business 6

die **Geschäfts'frau, -en** businesswoman 10

der **Geschäfts'mann, Geschäfts'leute** businessman 10

das **Geschenk', -e** present, gift 8

die **Geschich'te, -n** story; history 4

geschicht'lich historic(al)

der **Geschichts'lehrer, -/**die **Geschichts'lehrerin, -nen** history teacher

das **Geschirr'** dishes 9

der **Geschirr'spüler, -** dishwasher 9

der **Geschmack'** taste

die **Geschwi'ster** *(pl.)* brothers and sisters 4

die **Gesell'schaft, -en** society; company

das **Gesetz', -e** law

das **Gesicht', -er** face 9

das **Gespräch', -e** conversation 6

gestern yesterday 2; ~ **abend** last night 6

gesund' healthy 6

die **Gesund'heit** health

das **Gesund'heitsamt** public health office

das **Getränk', -e** drink, beverage

gewal'tig enormous

das **Gewe'be** material, weave

die **Gewerk'schaft, -en** trade union 12

gewin'nen, gewann, gewonnen to win; to acquire

sich **gewöh'nen (an +** *acc.*) to become accustomed (to)

gewohnt' accustomed to

gewölbt' vaulted

ginge (*subj. of* **gehen**): **das ~ (nicht)** that would (not) be possible, that would (not) work 4

die **Gitar're, -n** guitar E

das **Glas, ÷er** glass 3

glauben (*dat. of person*) to believe 1

gleich same; ~ (+ *dat.*) similar (to) 3; immediately 6

gleichberechtigt having equal rights

die **Gleichberechtigung** equal rights

gleichzeitig simultaneously

die **Glocke, -n** bell

das **Glück** luck 4; **viel ~** good luck 4; ~ **haben** to be lucky 4; **zum ~** luckily

glücklich happy

der **Glückwunsch, ÷e** congratulations; **Herzlichen ~ zum Geburtstag!** Happy Birthday!

die **Götterspeise** gelatin dessert

graben (ä), grub, gegraben to dig

das **Gramm** (*abbr.* **g**) gram 3

die **Gramma'tik** grammar

gramma'tisch grammatical

das **Gras** grass

gratulie'ren (+ *dat.*) to congratulate

grau gray E

die **Grenze, -n** border 5

(das) **Griechenland** Greece

der **Griff, -e** reach; handle; **in den ~ bekommen** to get a handle on

groß (ö) large, big; tall (of people) E

die **Großeltern** *(pl.)* grandparents 4

die **Großmutter, ÷** grandmother 4

die **Großstadt, ÷e** city

der **Großvater, ÷** grandfather 4

die **Großveranstaltung** big event

die **Grube, -n** hole, ditch

grün green E; **ins Grüne** out into the country

der **Grund, ÷e** reason; basis, background; **aus diesem ~** for this reason 11

das **Grundgesetz** constitution of the FRG

gründlich thorough

das **Grundstück, -e** property (real estate)

die **Grünen** *(pl.)* environmentalist political party in the FRG

die **Gruppe, -n** group 9

die **Grup'penpsychologie'** group psychology

der **Gruß, ÷e** greeting

grüßen: Grüß dich! Hello! *(informal)* 1

die **Gurke, -n** cucumber

gut (besser, best-) good, well; fine 1; **sei so ~** be so kind 4; **ist ~ dran** is well off

die **Güter** *(pl.)* goods

das **Gymna'sium, Gymnasien** German secondary school 4

H automobile symbol for Hungary

das **Haar, -e** hair 9

haben (hat), hatte, gehabt to have 2; **Was hast du?** What is wrong with you? 9

der **Hafen, ⁻** harbor, port

halb half 1; **halb [zwei]** half past [one], [one-thirty]

halbtags half-days

die **Hälfte** half 9; **zur ~** half

hallo hello; hey 1

der **Hals, ⁻e** throat, neck 9

halten (ä), hielt, gehalten hold; **~ von** (+ dat.) to think of, have an opinion of 6; **sich fit ~** to keep fit

die **Hand, ⁻e** hand 9

die **Handarbeit** manual work

der **Handel** trade 5

handeln von to be about 14

der **Handrücken** back of the hand

der **Handschuh, -e** glove 6

die **Handtasche, -n** handbag 6

hängen, hing, gehangen to be suspended, hanging 7; **hängen, gehängt** to hang, put 7

das **Häubchen** cap

die **Hauptdarstellerin, -nen** actress playing the lead

das **Hauptfach, ⁻er** major (subject) 4

das **Hauptgericht** main course of a meal

die **Hauptstadt, ⁻e** capital (city) 2

das **Haus, ⁻er** house 3; **nach Hause** [to go] home 3; **zu Hause** [to be] at home 5

die **Hausarbeit** housework 10; homework

der **Haushalt** household; housekeeping

die **Haut** skin

die **Hautcreme, -s** skin cream

He! Hey! 8

die **Hecke, -n** hedge 8

die **Hefe** yeast

das **Heft, -e** notebook E

die **Heimat** native land 14

heimatlos displaced, without a home country, homeless

heiraten to marry 14

heiratsfähig marriageable

die **Heiratspolitik** arrangement of marriages for political reasons

heiß hot 2

heißen, hieß, geheißen to be named E; **Wie heißen Sie?** What is your name? E; **Sie heißen [Mark], nicht?** Your name is [Mark], isn't it? E; **das heißt (d.h.)** that is to say (i.e.); **es heißt** it says

helfen (i), half, geholfen (+ dat.) to help 6; **bei [der Arbeit] ~** to help with [work] 6

hell bright; light (color) 8

das **Hemd, -en** shirt 6

das **Henna** henna

her (to) here 7

der **Herbst** autumn, fall 2

herein' in

herein'·schauen to look in

der **Herr, -n, -en** gentleman; **Herr** Mr. 1

herrschen to prevail; to rule

herum' around; **sie basteln an dem Haus ~** they're tinkering around on the house

das **Herz, -ens, -en** heart

herzlich warm(ly), cordial(ly); **~ willkommen** welcome

heute today E; **~ abend** this evening 1; **~ morgen** this morning 1; **~ nachmittag** this afternoon 1

hier here 2

die **Hilfe** help

der **Himmel** sky; heaven; **um Himmels willen** for heaven's sake

hin (to) there 7; **~ und wieder** now and again

hinein' in(to) 12

hin·fahren (fährt hin), fuhr hin, ist hingefahren to drive there

hinter (+ acc./dat.) behind, in back of 7

hinterher afterwards

das **Hinterhoffest** block party

der **Hinweis, -e** allusion

histo'risch historic

das **Hobby, -s** hobby 11

hoch (höher, höchst-) high 9; **hoh-** before nouns, as in **ein hoher Preis** a high price

das **Hochdeutsch** High German, standard German 9

das **Hochgebirge** high mountains

das **Hochhaus, ⁻er** high-rise building, skyscraper

der **Hof, ⁻e** courtyard 11

die **Hofburg** residence, palace of reigning monarch

hoffen (auf + acc.) to hope (for) 10

hoffentlich I hope 2

hoffnungslos hopeless

höflich polite(ly)

holen to get

das **Holz** wood; der **Holzschnitzer** woodcarver

horchen to listen

hören to hear 1

die **Hornbrille** horn-rimmed glasses

die **Hose, -n** pants 6

das **Hotel, -s** hotel

das **Huhn, ⁻er** chicken

humanitär' humanitarian

der **Hund, -e** dog

der **Hunger** hunger 6; **~ bekommen/kriegen** to get hungry 6; **~ haben** to be hungry 6

husten to cough 9

der **Hut, ⁻e** hat 6

das **Hügelland** hilly country

I automobile symbol for Italy

ich I E; **~ auch** me, too

die **Idee', -n** idea 8

identifizie'ren to identify

die **Identität'** identity

IG-Metall' (IG = Industriegewerk-schaft) metal workers' union

ihr you (fam. pl.); her; their

Ihr your (formal) E

die **Illustrier'te, -n** magazine

der **Imbißstand, ⸚e** snack bar, hot dog stand

immer always 3; ~ **mehr** more and more 11; ~ **noch** still 4; **noch** ~ still 10; ~ **wieder** again and again; **wie** ~ as always 3

der **Import'** import

die **Import'beschränkung, -en** import restriction 14

importie'ren to import

in (+ *acc./dat.*) in 2; into; to 3

die **Industrie', -n** industry 11; die **Industrie'stadt, ⸚e** industrial city

die **Inflation'** inflation 14

die **Inflations'rate** rate of inflation

die **Informa'tik** computer science 10

der **Informa'tiker, -/die Informa'tikerin, -nen** computer scientist

die **Information'** information

der **Ingenieur', -e/die Ingenieu'rin, -nen** engineer 10

die **Innenstadt** town or city center

das **Insektizid', -e** insecticide

das **Institut', -e** institute

das **Instrument', -e** instrument

integrie'ren to integrate

intelligent' smart, intelligent 1

interessant' interesting 4

das **Interes'se, -n** interest

(sich) **interessie'ren (für)** to be interested (in) 12

interessiert' sein (an + dat.) to be interested (in) 12

international' international

das **Interview', -s** interview

intervie'wen to interview

irgendwann sometime, at some point 9

(das) **Ita'lien** Italy

italie'nisch Italian (adj.)

ja yes E; indeed, of course 3

die **Jacke, -n** jacket 6

das **Jahr, -e** year E; **ich bin [19] Jahre alt** I'm [19] years old E; **vor [10] Jahren** [10] years ago 9

das **Jahrhun'dert, -e** century 9

-jährig -year-old

der **Januar** January 2

(das) **Japan** Japan

jaulen to howl

der **Jazz** jazz

je: O ~! Oh my! 8

die **Jeans** (pl.) jeans 6

jed- (er, es, e) each; every; everyone 4

jedoch' nonetheless, however

jemand someone, anyone 10

jen- (er, es, e) that; the former 13

jetzt now 2

der **Job, -s** job 4

jobben (colloq.) to have a job 11

das **Jogging** jogging, running 11

der **Journalist', -en, -en/die Journali'stin, -nen** journalist, reporter 13

die **Jugend** youth 11

die **Jugendherberge, -n** youth hostel

der/die **Jugendliche** (noun decl. like adj.) young person 11

(das) **Jugosla'wien** Yugoslavia

der **Juli** July 2

jung (ü) young 4

der **Junge, -n, -n** boy E

der **Juni** June 2

der **Jurist', -en, -en/die Juri'stin, -nen** lawyer 10

der **Kaffee** coffee 3; **zum** ~ for (afternoon) coffee 6

das **Kaffeehaus, ⸚er** coffee house

die **Kaffeemaschine, -n** coffee machine

kalt (ä) cold 2

die **Kamil'le** camomile

der **Kamm, ⸚e** comb

(sich) **kämmen** to comb 9

der **Kampf, ⸚e** fight, battle

kämpfen to fight 10

der **Kanton', -e** canton

das **Kapitel, -** chapter

kaputt' broken; tired 5

kariert' plaid

die **Karies** (pronounced **Ka-ri-es**) tooth decay

der **Karrie'remacher/die Karrie'remacherin** (pronounced **Ka-ri-e'-re**) person interested only in a career

die **Karte, -n** card; post card 1; die **Karten** (pl.) playing cards 1; ticket 13; **Karten spielen** to play cards

die **Kartof'fel, -n** potato 3

der **Käse** cheese 3

die **Käserei'** cheese dairy

die **Kasset'te, -n** (tape) cassette 8

der **Kasset'tenrecorder** cassette deck 8

kasta'nienbraun chestnut brown

die **Katze, -n** cat

der **Kauf, ⸚e** purchase

kaufen to buy 3

das **Kaufhaus, ⸚er** department store 3

der **Kaufmann, -leute/die Kauffrau, -en** merchant 12

kaum hardly 4

kein not a, not any 2; ~ **... mehr** no . . . more 3

der **Keller, -** basement 8

der **Kellner, -/die Kellnerin, -nen** waiter/waitress

kennen, kannte, gekannt to know [people, places, or things] 3

kennen•lernen to get to know, make the acquaintance of 4

die **Kerze, -n** candle

die **Kfz-Steuer, -n** automobile tax

das **Kilo(gramm)'** (abbrev. **kg**) kilo(gram) 3

der **Kilome'ter, -** kilometer 2

das **Kind, -er** child E

das **Kinderbuch, ⸚er** children's book

der **Kindergarten, ⸚** kindergarten, nursery school 13

das **Kindergeld** government subsidy for children

die **Kinderkrippe** day nursery

das **Kino, -s** movie theater; **ins ~** to the movies 1

die **Kirche, -n** church

das **Kissen, -** pillow

klappen to slam

klar clear; of course; naturally 4

die **Klarinet'te, -n** clarinet

die **Klasse, -n** class 9; die **Deutschklasse** German class 9

klasse! first-rate, great

der **Klassiker, -** author of a standard or classic work

klassisch classic(al) 7

die **Klausur', -en** test 4; **eine ~ schreiben** to take a test

das **Klavier', -e** piano 13

das **Kleid, -er** dress; *(pl.)* clothing 6

die **Kleidung** clothing 6

klein small; short (of people) E

die **Kleinigkeit, -en** detail, trifle

die **Kleinkinder** *(pl.)* small children, toddlers

die **Kleinstadt, ̈e** small town

das **Klima** climate 2

die **Kneipe, -n** pub, bar 7

der **Koch, ̈e**/die **Köchin, -nen** cook

kochen to cook 3

die **Kohle, -n** coal

Köln Cologne

der **Kolle'ge, -n, -n**/die **Kolle'gin, -nen** colleague 10

kommen, kam, ist gekommen to come 3; **~ auf** to come up to

der **Kommentar', -e** commentary

kommentie'ren to comment

komplett' complete

kompliziert' complicated

die **Komponen'te, -n** component

der **Komponist', -en, -en**/die **Komponi'stin, -nen** composer 11

die **Konfession', -en** creed, confession

konkurrie'ren to compete 12

können (kann), konnte, gekonnt can, to be able to 4

konservativ' conservative 1

das **Konservie'rungsmittel** preservative

konspirie'ren to conspire

der **Konsum'** consumption

der **Kontakt', -e** contact

kontakt'freudig able to make friends easily

kontrollie'ren to control

das **Konzept', -e** concept; rough copy

das **Konzert', -e** concert; concerto 13

der **Kopf, ̈e** head 9

die **Kopfschmerzen** *(pl.)* headache 3

die **Kornblume, -n** cornflower

kosten to cost 6

die **Kraft, ̈e** strength; power

das **Kraftfahrzeug** *(abbr. Kfz)* automobile

der **Kraftfahrzeugmechaniker, -**/die **Kraftfahrzeugmechanikerin, -nen** auto mechanic

krank (ä) ill, sick 1

das **Krankenhaus, ̈er** hospital

die **Krankenkasse** health insurance

der **Krankenwagen** ambulance

die **Krankheit, -en** illness 9

das **Kreuz, -e** cross

der **Krieg, -e** war 5

kriegen to get, obtain 6

die **Kriminalität'** criminality

die **Krise** crisis

die **Kritik', -en** criticism; review

kritisch critical

kritisie'ren to criticize 10

die **Küche, -n** kitchen 8

der **Kuchen, -** cake 3

der **Kugelschreiber, - (der Kuli, -s** *colloq.)* ballpoint pen E

kühl cool 2

der **Kühlschrank, ̈e** refrigerator 9

der **Kuli, -s** *(colloq. for* **Kugelschreiber)** ballpoint pen E

die **Kultur'** culture 14

kulturell' cultural

sich **kümmern um** to take care of 14

der **Kunde, -n, -n**/die **Kundin, -nen** customer, client 12

die **Kunst** art; skill

der **Kunstdünger, -** chemical fertilizer

künstlich artificial 6

die **Kur** cure (at a spa)

der **Kurs, -e** course 4

kurz (ü) short 6; **vor kurzem** recently 5

die **Kürze** brevity

die **Kurzgeschichte, -n** short story

kürzlich recent(ly)

die **Kusine, -n** cousin *(f.)* 4

lächeln (über + *acc.)* to smile (about) 6

lachen to laugh

der **Laden, ̈** store, shop 6

die **Lage, -n** situation

die **Lampe, -n** lamp E

das **Land, ̈er** country; land 2; **auf dem Lande** in the country; **auf das Land** to the country 11

die **Landkarte, -n** map 5

die **Landsgemeinde** country community

lang (ä) *(adj.)* long

lange (ä) *(adv.)* for a long time 6

langsam slow(ly) 8

längst long ago

langweilig boring

der **Lärm** noise

lassen (läßt), ließ, gelassen to leave; to let, permit; to have something done 12

(das) **Latein** Latin

latei'nisch Latin *(adj.)*

der **Lauf** course; **im ~ (+** *gen.)* during the course (of)

laufen (ä), lief, ist gelaufen to run; to go on foot 5

laut loud(ly) 7

leben to live 5; **für sich ~** to keep to oneself

das **Leben, -** life 6

leben'dig lively

der **Lebenslauf** résumé

die **Lebensmittel** (*pl.*) groceries 3
lebensnotwendig essential
der **Lebensstandard** standard of living 11
das **Leberwurstbrot** liverwurst sandwich
lebhaft lively
lecker tasty 6
legen to lay 7
die **Lehre, -n** apprenticeship 10
der **Lehrer, -/**die **Lehrerin, -nen** teacher 10
das **Lehrjahr, -e** year as an apprentice
leicht easy; light 4
das **Leichtmetall** light metal
leid: (es) tut mir ~ I'm sorry 1
leider unfortunately 2
leihen, lieh, geliehen to lend; to borrow 4
die **Leistung, -en** achievement
lernen to learn; to study 4
das **Lernziel, -e** learning objective
das **Lesebuch, ̈er** primer, reader
lesen (ie), las, gelesen to read 4
der **Leserbrief, -e** letter from a reader
das **Lesestück, -e** reading selection
die **Lesung, -en** reading
letzt last 4
die **Leute** (*pl.*) people 3
das **Licht, -er** light
lieb (*adj.*) dear; **Liebe [Barbara], Lieber [Paul]...** Dear [Barbara, Paul] (*used at the beginning of a letter*)
lieber (*comp. of* **gern**) preferably, rather 9
das **Lied, -er** song 7
liefern to deliver
liegen, lag, gelegen to lie; to be situated 2
die **Linde, -n** linden or lime tree
links left
der **Lippenstift, -e** lipstick
die **Liste, -n** list 12
der **Liter, -** (*abbr.* l) liter 3
die **Literatur'** literature 10
live live, *as in* **live Musik**

locker fluffy, loose
der **Lohn, ̈e** wage; reward 13
die **Lohnfortzahlung** continued payment of wages
lokal' local
los: Was ist ~ ? What's wrong? 1
lösen to solve 12; to loosen
die **Lösung, -en** solution 14
die **Luft** air 6
die **Lust** pleasure, enjoyment 11; ~ **haben** to feel like 11; **Ich habe keine Lust zu arbeiten** I don't feel like working.; **Dazu habe ich keine Lust.** I don't feel like it. 11
lustig funny; merry, cheerful 1
der **Luxusgegenstand, ̈e** luxury item

machen to do; to make 1; **(es) macht nichts** (it) doesn't matter 7; **Deutsch** ~ to do/study German homework
die **Macht** power
mag (*present tense of* **mögen**) to like; **das** ~ **wohl sein** that may be
das **Mädchen, -** girl E
der **Magen, ̈** stomach 9
mahlen, mahlte, gemahlen to grind
der **Mai** May 2
mal time; times (in multiplication) E; **dreimal** three times; **mal (= einmal)** once, sometime 5; (*flavoring particle that softens a command and leaves the time indefinite*) 7
das **Mal, -e** time 6
malen to paint 11
man one, people 3
manch (-er, -es, -e) many a (*sg.*); some (*pl.*)
manchmal sometimes 3
der **Mann, ̈er** man E
die **Männerstimme, -n** man's voice
männlich masculine
der **Mantel, ̈** coat
die **Mark** mark (*basic monetary unit in both the FRG and the GDR*)

der **Markt, ̈e** market 3; **der schwarze** ~ black market
die **Marktwirtschaft** market economy
die **Marmela'de** marmalade, jam 3
der **März** March 2
die **Maschi'ne, -n** machine
die **Massa'ge, -n** massage
die **Massenzuwanderung** mass immigration
die **Mathe** math
die **Mathematik'** mathematics 4
die **Maus, ̈e** mouse
der **Mecha'niker, -/**die **Mecha'nikerin, -nen** mechanic
mediterran' Mediterranean
die **Medizin'** medicine
das **Meer, -e** ocean
mehr (*comp. of* **viel**) more 2; ~ **oder weniger** more or less 7; **kein** ~ no more; **nicht** ~ no longer
mehrere several 5
die **Mehrheit** majority
die **Meile, -n** mile
mein my E
meinen to mean; to think, have an opinion 6; **Was meinst du?** What do you think? 7
die **Meinung, -en** opinion 10; **[ihrer]** ~ **nach** in [their] opinion
meist mostly 5
meist(en) (*sup. of* **viel**) most 4; **die meisten** most of 4
meistens mostly, most of the time 5
Mensch! Man! Wow!
der **Mensch, -en, -en** person, human being 1
die **Menschenart** (kind of) people, folk
die **Mentalität', -en** mentality
merken to notice
merkwürdig strange 6
die **Messe, -n** trade fair
das **Messer, -** knife 7
die **Messingstange, -n** brass rod
der **Meter, -** (*abbr.* m) meter

der **Metzger, -** butcher 3; **beim ~** at the butcher shop 3; **zum ~** to the butcher shop 3

die **Metzgerei', -en** butcher shop, meat market 3

die **Miete, -n** rent

mieten to rent 11

die **Mietwohnung, -en** rental apartment

die **Milch** milk 3

das **Milchglas** frosted glass

mild mild

die **Million', -en** million 2

das **Mineral'wasser** mineral water 6

der **Mini'ster, -** minister

die **Minu'te, -n** minute 1

der **Minu'tenzeiger, -** the minute hand (on a clock or watch)

mischen to mix

die **Mischung, -en** mixture

der **Mist** manure

mit (+ *dat.*) with 1; **~ [dem Auto]** by [car] 5; **~ mir** with me 1; **Ich mache bei dem Spiel ~.** I participate in the game. 11

die **Mitbestimmung** codetermination

mit•bringen, brachte mit, mitgebracht to bring along 4

das **Mitbringsel** small gift for the host(ess)

miteinan'der with one another

mit•fahren (fährt mit), fuhr mit, ist mitgefahren to drive/ride along/with

das **Mitglied, -er** member 11

mit•kommen, kam mit, ist mitgekommen to come along/with 6

mit•machen (bei + *a group*) to participate in, join in 11

mit•nehmen (nimmt mit), nahm mit, mitgenommen to take along 5

der **Mittag, -e** noon; **zu ~ essen** to have lunch 3

das **Mittagessen** lunch 3; **zum ~** for lunch 3

die **Mittel** (*pl.*) means

mittlerweile in the meantime

der **Mittwoch** Wednesday E

mit•verdienen to earn money (second income)

die **Möbel** (*pl.*) furniture 9; **das Möbelstück** piece of furniture 9

möchte (*subj. of* **mögen**) would like 4

die **Mode, -n** fashion

moderie'ren to moderate

modern' modern 8

modernisie'ren to modernize

mögen (mag), mochte, gemocht to like 4; **Das mag wohl sein.** That may well be. 7

möglich possible 10

die **Möhre, -n** carrot

der **Moment', -e** moment 11; **im ~** at the moment 11; **Einen Moment, bitte!** Just a minute, please! 11

der **Monat, -e** month 2

der **Montag** Monday E; **~ in acht Tagen** a week from Monday 12

morgen tomorrow 2

der **Morgen** morning; **Guten ~!** Good morning! 1; **heute morgen** this morning 1

morgens mornings 3

das **Motor'boot, -e** motor boat

das **Motor'rad, ¨er** motorcycle 5

müde tired 1

die **Mühle, -n** mill

die **Mülldeponie, -n** garbage dump 7

der **Mund, ¨er** mouth 9; **den ~ halten** to keep one's mouth shut

die **Musik'** music 1

der **Musiker, -/die Musikerin, -nen** musician 10

das **Musik'instrument, -e** musical instrument 11

die **Musik'stunde, -n** music lesson 8

müssen (muß), mußte, gemußt must, to have to 4

der **Mut** courage 10

die **Mutter, ¨** mother 4

na well (*interjection*) 4; **~ ja** well now 6; oh well 11

nach (+ *dat.*) after 1; to (*with cities and countries, e.g.,* **nach Berlin**) 2; **~ Hause** (to go) home 3

der **Nachbar, -n, -n/die Nachbarin, -nen** neighbor 2

nachdem' (*conj.*) after 10

nach•gehen, ging nach, ist nachgegangen to be slow (*said of a clock*)

nachher afterwards 4

der **Nachmittag, -e** afternoon 1

nachmittag: heute ~ this afternoon 1

nachmittags afternoons 3

nach•schlagen (ä), schlug nach, nachgeschlagen to look up

nächst next 4

die **Nacht, ¨e** night 10

der **Nachtisch** dessert 6

nah (näher, nächst) near, close 12

die **Nähe: in der ~** nearby, in the vicinity 11

der **Name, -ns, -n** name 4

nämlich after all 2

die **Nase, -n** nose 9

naß (ä) wet 2

die **Nation', -en** nation

die **Nationalität', -en** nationality

die **Natur', -en** nature 6

natür'lich natural(ly); of course 3

die **Natür'lichkeit** naturalness

N.C. = der Numerus clausus (*Latin*) limited number of students admitted to certain degree programs

neben (+ *acc./dat.*) beside, next to 7

nebenan' next door

das **Nebenfach, ¨er** minor (subject) 4

nehmen (nimmt), nahm, genommen to take 3

nein no E

nennen, nannte, genannt to call; to name 10

nervös' nervous 1
nett nice 1
das **Netz, -e** net
neu new E
das **Neubaugebiet** new housing development
(das) **Neubraun'schweig** New Brunswick
die **Neuheit, -en** novelty
neulich recently 11
(das) **Neuschott'land** Nova Scotia
neutral' neutral
die **Neutralität'** neutrality
nicht not 1; **nicht?** *(tag question)* don't you? isn't it? E; **Sie heißen [Monika], nicht?** Your name is [Monika], isn't it? E; ~ **mehr** no longer 4; ~ **wahr?** isn't that so?; ~ **nur ... sondern auch** not only . . . but also 5
nichts nothing 1; **(es) macht ~** (it) doesn't matter 7; ~ **Besonderes** nothing special 11
nie never 6
niederdeutsch North German; low German
die **Niederlande** *pl.* Netherlands
Niedersachsen Lower Saxony
niedrig low 12
niemand no one 6
der **Nieselregen** drizzle
das **Niveau', -s** level of performance
noch still, in addition 2; ~ **ein** another, additional 4; ~ **einmal** again, once more 11; ~ **immer** still 10
die **Nonchalance'** nonchalance
der **Norden** north 2
nördlich to the north 2
normal' normal
(das) **Norwegen** Norway
die **Notiz', -en** note 4
der **Novem'ber** November 2
die **Nummer, -n** number E
nun now; well *(interjection)* 6
nur only, nothing but, solely, just 2

O je! Oh my! 8
ob *(conj.)* whether, if 5
der **Ober** waiter; **Herr Ober! Waiter!**
das **Oberland** highlands
das **Obst** fruit 3
obwohl' although *(conj.)*
oder or 1
offen open 7
öffentlich public(ly), openly 12
offiziell' official(ly)
öffnen to open 8
oft (ö) often 1
oh oh
ohne *(+ acc.)* without 3
das **Ohr, -en** ear 9
ökono'misch economic
der **Okto'ber** October 2
das **Öl** oil
die **Oma, -s** grandma
der **Onkel, -** uncle 4
der **Opa, -s** grandpa
die **Oper, -n** opera 13
das **Orche'ster, -** orchestra 11
ordnen to put in order
die **Ordnung** order 11
die **Organisation', -en** organization
der **Ort, -e** place (geographical) 9
der **Osten** east 2
(das) **Österreich** Austria 2
österreichisch Austrian *(adj.)* 5
der **Ozean, -e** ocean 2

paar: ein ~ a few 3
das **Papier', -e** paper E
das **Papier'geschäft, -e** stationery store
der **Park, -s** park 7
das **Parlament', -e** parliament
parlamenta'risch parliamentary
die **Paro'le, -n** slogan
die **Partei', -en** (political) party
der **Partner, -/die Partnerin, -nen** partner
die **Partnerschaft** partnership
partout' at all *(French)*
die **Party, -s** party 8
der **Paß, Pässe** passport 5

passen *(+ dat.)* to fit; to suit 8
passiv passive
die **Person', -en** person 10
das **Personal'** personnel
persön'lich personal(ly) 10
die **Persön'lichkeit** personality
pfeifen to whistle
der **Pfennig, -e** 1/100 of a German mark 12
die **Pflanze, -n** plant E
pflanzen to plant 11
pflanzlich plant *(adj.)*
pflegen to care for; to foster
das **Pferd, -e** horse
das **Pfund** *(abbr.* **Pfd.)** pound (= 1.1 U.S. pounds) 3
phanta'stisch fantastic 6
die **Philosophie'** philosophy 4
die **Physik'** physics 4
das **Picknick, -s** picnic 4
das **Pils** pilsener beer
plädie'ren (für) to plead (for)
das **Plakat', -e** poster
der **Plan, ⸚e** plan 5
planen to plan 12
das **Plastik** plastic
die **Platte, -n** record 8
der **Plattenspieler, -** record player 8
der **Platz, ⸚e** space; place; seat 4; ~ **nehmen** to take a seat 12
das **Plätzchen** little place
platzen to burst
plausi'bel plausible
pleite broke (out of money) 7
plötzlich suddenly 10
plump unrefined
(das) **Polen** Poland
die **Politik'** politics, political science
der **Poli'tiker, -/die Poli'tikerin, -nen** politician
poli'tisch political
die **Polizei'** police 7
die **Pommes frites** *(pl.)* French fries 6
das **Pop-Konzert, -e** pop concert
positiv positive

die **Post** postal system; mail
das **Poster, -** poster
praktisch practical(ly) 8
der **Präsident', -en, -en**/die **Präsiden'tin, -nen** president
die **Präzision'** precision
der **Preis, -e** price 12
prima excellent, fine, great
der **Prinzip', -ien** principle
privat' private 4
pro per 10
die **Probe, -n** rehearsal 11
probie'ren to try; to taste 6
das **Problem', -e** problem
produzie'ren to produce
das **Produkt', -e** product 9
professionell' professional(ly)
der **Profes'sor, Professo'ren**/die **Professo'rin, -nen** professor 1
das **Programm', -e** program 11
der **Programmie'rer, -/**die **Programmie'rerin, -nen** programmer 10
das **Programm'kino, -s** art cinema, theater
progressiv' progressive 1
das **Projekt', -e** project
der **Protektionis'mus** protectionism
protestie'ren to protest
das **Prozent', -e** percent 14
der **Prozeß', Prozesse** process
prüfen to examine; to test; **prüfend** quizzically
die **Prüfung, -en** examination 4
die **Psychologie'** psychology 4
der **Pulli, -s** sweater 6
pünktlich punctual(ly) 7
die **Puppe, -n** doll 10
putzen to clean 9

der **Quadrat'kilometer, - (***abbr.* **km²** *or* **qkm)** square kilometer
die **Qualität', -en** quality
quengeln to whine
quietschen to squeal

die **Rabenmutter** unfit mother
das **Rad, ¨er** bike (*short for* **Fahrrad**) 5; wheel; **Rad fahren** to bicycle

das **Radeln** cycling
das **Radio, -s** radio E
der **Rand, ¨er** edge; **am Rande** on the edge
(sich) **rasie'ren** to shave 9
rationalisie'ren to make improvements that increase efficiency
rationiert' rationed
der **Ratskeller, -** town hall restaurant 6
der **Rauch** smoke 7
der **Raum, ¨e** room; space
räumen to clear; to vacate
rauschen to rustle
raus•fahren (ä), fuhr raus, ist rausgefahren to drive out (into the country)
rechnen to calculate; ~ **mit** to count on
recht right 5; **du hast immer ~** you're always right 7; **Ist es dir ~?** Is it all right/O.K. with you? 5; ~ **haben** to be right 7; rather, quite
das **Recht, -e (auf +** *acc.***)** right (to) 13
die **Rede, -n** discussion; speech, talk; **die ~ ist von ...** the topic under discussion is . . .
reden (über + *acc.***)** to talk (about) 7; **Red, wie dir der Schnabel gewachsen ist.** Don't mince your words.
das **Referat', -e** report 4
das **Reform'haus, ¨er** health (food) store
regelmäßig regular(ly)
die **Regelstudienzeit** limit on time spent at university
der **Regen** rain 2
der **Regenmantel, ¨** raincoat 6
die **Regie'rung, -en** government 9
regnen to rain 2
reich rich, wealthy 4
die **Reihe, -n** row; series
rein pure, clean 6
rein (= herein) in
die **Reinheit** purity

die **Reise, -n** trip 4
reisen, ist gereist to travel
reizend charming
die **Rekla'me, -n** advertisement, commercial 6; ~ **machen** to advertise
relativ' relative(ly)
die **Religion'** religion
renovie'ren to renovate, restore
der **Rentner, -/**die **Rentnerin, -nen** retiree, pensioner
die **Reparatur', -en** repair
reparie'ren to repair 8
das **Repertoire'** repertoire
die **Republik', -en** republic
die **Reser've, -n** reserve
der **Reser'vestatus** to be in reserve
respektie'ren to respect
das **Restaurant', -s** restaurant
das **Resultat', -e** result
die **Retrospekti've** retrospective
das **Rheuma** rheumatism
richtig correct, right; real; really 2
die **Richtigkeit** accuracy; correctness
riechen, roch, gerochen (nach) to smell (of) 3
der **Rock, ¨e** skirt 6; rock (music)
die **Rockband, -s** rock band
die **Rockmusik** rock music
rodeln to sled, go tobogganing
der **Rohstoff, -e** raw material 9
der **Rolladen, ¨** shutter, blind
die **Rolle, -n** role 5; **eine ~ spielen** to play a part; to be important 5
rot (ö) red E
rufen, rief, gerufen to call
die **Ruhe** calm; peace and quiet
ruhig calm, easy-going, quiet; **sei ~** be quiet 1
(das) **Rumä'nien** Rumania
rundlich plump
runter down
(das) **Russisch** Russian (language)
(das) **Rußland** Russia

die **Sache, -n** thing 6; *(pl.)* clothes

sagen to say, tell 2
die **Sahne** cream; whipped cream
der **Sakko, -s** sport coat 6
sammeln to collect, gather 10
die **Sammlung, -en** collection
der **Samstag** (*in southern Germany*) Saturday E
samstags on Saturdays 3
der **Sänger, -**/die **Sängerin, -nen** singer
der **Satz, ̈e** sentence 8
sauber clean 7
das **Schach** chess 1
schade too bad; a pity 9
das **Schaf, -e** sheep
die **Schallplatte, -n** record
schätzen to appreciate
schauen to look at
die **Scheibe, -n** pane
scheinen, schien, geschienen to shine 2; to appear, seem 9
der **Schenkel, -** thigh
schenken to give as a gift 5
schicken (nach) to send (for) 14
das **Schiff, -e** ship 5
die **Schiffsreise** ship cruise
das **Schild, -er** sign 14
der **Schilling, -e** Austrian unit of currency
schlafen (ä), schlief, geschlafen to sleep 5
das **Schlafzimmer, -** bedroom 8
schlagen (ä), schlug, geschlagen to hit, slap
die **Schlagsahne** whipped cream
die **Schlange: ~ stehen** to stand in line 13
schlecht bad, badly 1; **mir geht's ~** I don't feel well 1; **mir ist ~** I feel nauseated 9
die **Schleife, -n** sash, ribbon
schließen, schloß, geschlossen to close 3
schließlich finally, after all 7
schlimm bad, terrible 6
der **Schlitten, -** sled; die **Schlittenbahn** toboggan run
das **Schloß, Schlösser** lock; castle 8

schluchzen to sob
der **Schluß: ~ jetzt** that's enough
der **Schlüssel, -** key 8
schmecken (*+ dat. of person*) to taste 6
der **Schmerz, -en** pain 9
schmutzig dirty
der **Schnee** snow 2
schneien to snow 2
schnell fast, quick(ly) 8
die **Schnur, ̈e** rope, line
die **Schokola'de** chocolate 6
die **Schokola'dencreme** chocolate mousse 6
schon already 2
schön nice, beautiful 2
schonen to protect
die **Schönheit** beauty
der **Schrebergarten, ̈** small garden plot on outskirts of city
schreiben, schrieb, geschrieben to write 4; **~ (an + acc.)** to write (to); **~ (über + acc.)** to write (about)
die **Schreibmaschine, -n** typewriter 10; **~ (schreiben) können** to be able to type 10
schreien, schrie, geschrie(e)n to cry; to scream
der **Schriftsteller, -**/die **Schriftstellerin, -nen** writer, author 5
der **Schritt, -e** step 9
der **Schuh, -e** shoe 6
der **Schulabschluß** formal completion of schooling
schuldig: ~ sein (*+ dat.*) to owe
die **Schule, -n** school 4
der **Schüler, -**/die **Schülerin, -nen** pupil
die **Schulwelt** school environment
das **Schürzchen** little apron
schützen to protect against, shelter from
schwach (ä) weak 9
schwarz black E
(das) **Schweden** Sweden
schweigen, schwieg, geschwiegen to be silent

die **Schweiz** Switzerland 2
Schweizer Swiss (*adj.*) 2
(das) **Schweizerdeutsch** Swiss German (language)
die **Schwelle, -n** threshold, sill
schwer heavy; difficult 3
der **Schwerpunkt, -e** emphasis, concentration
die **Schwester, -n** sister 3
schwierig difficult 13
die **Schwierigkeit, -en** difficulty 7
schwimmen, schwamm, ist geschwommen to swim 1
der **Schwindelmeier** (*colloq.*) swindler
schwindeln to fib
der **Schwof** public dance (*colloq.*)
die **Science Fiction** science fiction
der **See, -n** lake 11
die **See, -n** ocean, sea
segeln, ist gesegelt to sail 11
der **Segen** blessing
sehen (ie), sah, gesehen to see 4
sehr very 1
sei (du-*imperative of* **sein): ~ so gut** be so kind, do me a favor; **~ mir nicht böse.** Don't be angry with me. 7
die **Seife** soap 6
sein his; its 2
sein (ist), war, ist gewesen to be 1; **gut dran ~** to be well off
seit (*+ dat.*) since, for [time] 5; **~ wann** how long, since when 4; **~ kurzer Zeit** recently 6
die **Seite, -n** side; page 5
der **Sekretär', -e**/die **Sekretä'rin, -nen** secretary E
selbst oneself, myself, etc. 3
selbständig independent
selbstverständ'lich of course; natural(ly); obvious(ly)
selten seldom, rare(ly) 12
seltsam strange
das **Seme'ster, -** semester 4
das **Seminar', -e** seminar, seminar room 4

die **Seminar'arbeit, -en** seminar report 4

der **Semmelteig** bread dough

der **Sender, -** radio or TV station

die **Sendung, -en** radio or TV program

der **Septem'ber** September 2

die **Serie** series

setzen to set, put 7

seufzen to sigh

das **Shampoo'** shampoo 6

sicher safe; certain(ly) 7

sichtbar visible

Sie you (formal) E

Sie!... (used to get someone's attention) Hey!... 4

sie she, it E; **sie** they 1

die **Silbe, -n** syllable

das **Silber** silver

singen, sang, gesungen to sing 11

der **Sinn, -e** sense; mind; purpose

die **Situation', -en** situation, condition 14

sitzen, saß, gesessen to sit 5

die **Skepsis** skepticism

der **Ski, -er** ski 9

Ski laufen (ä), lief Ski, ist Ski gelaufen; also **Ski fahren (Ski** is pronounced **Schi)** to ski 9

das **Skilaufen/Skifahren** skiing 9

so so, thus, this way 1; ~ ... **wie** as ... as 2; ~ **[ein]** such [a] 4

so was something (like that) 11

die **Socke, -n** sock 6

sogar' even 11

sogenannt so-called

der **Sohn, ⁚e** son 4

solch (-er, -es, -e) such a (sing.); such (pl.) 4

soli'de solid

sollen (soll), sollte, gesollt to be supposed to 4

der **Sommer** summer 2

sondern (conj.) but, on the contrary 5; **nicht nur,** ~ **auch** not only, but also 5

der **Sonnabend** (in northern Germany) Saturday E

die **Sonne** sun 2

der **Sonntag** Sunday E

sonntags on Sundays 3

sonst otherwise 3; ~ **noch (et)was?** Anything else? 3

sonstwie otherwise

die **Sorge, -n** care, worry 12; **Das ist nicht meine** ~. That is not my problem.

sorgen für to care for 10

die **Sorte, -n** sort, kind

soviel so much

die **Sowjet'union** Soviet Union

sozial' social; for the common good

die **Sozial'hilfe** welfare

soziali'stisch socialist

sozusa'gen so to speak

die **Spaghet'ti** (pl.) spaghetti 3

der **Spalt** crack

spalten to split

(das) **Spanien** Spain

(das) **Spanisch** Spanish (language) 10

sparen to save

sparsam thrifty, saving

der **Spaß** fun 7; **es macht** ~ that's fun 7; ~ **an [+ dat.] haben** to enjoy [something] 6; **Späße** (pl.) jokes 7

spät late 1; **Wie** ~ **ist es?** What time is it? 1; **später** later 1

der **Spatz, -en** sparrow

spazie'ren, ist spaziert to take a walk, stroll

spazie'ren•fahren (ä), fuhr spazieren, ist spazierengefahren to go for a pleasure drive 9

spazie'ren•gehen, ging spazieren, ist spazierengegangen to go for a walk 11

der **Spazier'gang, ⁚e** walk, stroll

die **Spezialität', -en** specialty

die **Sphäre, -n** sphere

das **Spiel, -e** game

spielen to play 1

spitze (colloq.) first-rate 13

der **Sport** sport 1; ~ **treiben** to engage in sports 1

die **Sprache, -n** language 7

sprachlich linguistically; as far as the language is concerned 12

sprachlos speechless 8

sprechen (i), sprach, gesprochen to speak 5; ~ **über** (+ acc.) to speak about; ~ **von** to speak of; ~ **mit** to speak to (someone)

der **Sprecher, -/die Sprecherin, -nen** speaker

die **Sprechstunde, -n** office hour

sprichwörtlich proverbial

der **Staat, -en** country, state 2

stabil' stable

die **Stabilität'** stability

die **Stadt, ⁚e** city 2

das **Städtchen, -** little town

städtisch city (adj.)

stark (ä) strong 9

sich **stärken** to fortify oneself

starr blank

statt (+ gen.) instead of 8

der **Status** status

das **Steak, -s** steak 6

stecken to stick, put into 7; to be (inserted) 7

stehen, stand, gestanden to stand 3

stehlen (ie), stahl, gestohlen to steal

steigen, stieg, ist gestiegen to rise

(sich) **steigern** to intensify

der **Stein, -e** stone

die **Stelle, -n** position, job; place 10

stellen to place 7

die **Stereoanlage, -n** stereo system 8

das **Steuer** steering wheel

die **Steuer, -n** tax 9

die **Steuererhöhung, -en** tax increase 14

die **Steuersenkung, -en** tax decrease 14

das **Stichwort, ⁚er** key word

still still, quiet

die **Stimme, -n** voice

die **Stirne** forehead

der **Stock, Stockwerke** floor (of building) 8

stolz proud(ly) 11
stoppen to stop
stören to bother, to disturb 8
der **Strandkorb, ̈e** wicker beach chair with hood
die **Straße, -n** street E
die **Straßenbahn, -en** streetcar 5
der **Strauß, ̈e** bouquet
das **Streichquartett** string quartet
der **Streik, -s** strike 12
streiken to strike 14
der **Streß** stress 11
der **Strumpf, ̈e** stocking
die **Strumpfhose, -n** pantyhose 6
das **Stück, -e** piece 6; theater play 13
der **Student', -en, -en/die Studen'tin, -nen** student E
der **Studen'tenausweis, -e** student identification card
der **Studen'tenjob, -s** job for students
die **Studen'tenkneipe, -n** pub frequented by students
das **Studen'ten(wohn)heim, -e** dormitory 4
die **Studiengebühren** (pl.) tuition
der **Studienplatz, ̈e** available space for student in a course of study
studie'ren to study; to go to college 4
das **Studium** studies 11
der **Stuhl, ̈e** chair E
die **Stunde, -n** hour; lesson 8
der **Stundenplan, ̈e** class schedule 11
der **Stundenzeiger, -** hour hand (of a clock)
subventionie'ren to subsidize
suchen to look for 3
der **Süden** south 2
der **Supermarkt, ̈e** supermarket 3; **in den ~** to the supermarket 3
die **Suppe** soup
surfen to surf 11
süßlich sweet
das **System', -e** system

systema'tisch systematical(ly)
die **Szene, -n** scene

die **Tablette, -n** pill, tablet 3
das **Taftkleid** taffeta dress
der **Tag, -e** day E; **Guten ~!/Tag!** Hello! Hi! 1; **eines Tages** one day 6
täglich daily 6
die **Tante, -n** aunt 4
der **Tante-Emma-Laden, ̈** mom-and-pop store
tanzen to dance 1
die **Tasche, -n** bag; pocket 3
das **Taschenbuch, ̈er** paperback 14
das **Täßchen** small cup
die **Tasse, -n** cup
tatsächlich really
die **Taube, -n** dove, pigeon
das **Taxi, -s** taxi
technisch technical
der **Tee, -s** tea 3
der **Teenager, -** teenager
der **Teil, -e** part, portion 5; **zum ~** in part 9
teil•nehmen (i), nahm teil, teilgenommen (an + dat.) to take part (in) 14; **Ich habe an dem Gespräch teilgenommen.** I took part in the conversation. 14
das **Telefon', -e** telephone E
die **Telefon'zelle, -n** telephone booth
telefonie'ren to telephone 12
die **Telefon'nummer** telephone number E
das **Tempo, -s** speed; **~ 100** speed limit 100
die **Tendenz'** tendency
das **Tennis** tennis 1
der **Termin', -e** appointment 12
die **Terras'se, -n** terrace, patio 8
teuer (teurer, teuerst-) expensive 4
der **Text, -e** text
die **Texti'lien** (pl.) textiles
das **Thea'ter, -** theater 13
das **Thea'terstück, -e** play 13

das **Thema,** pl. **Themen** theme; topic
der **Tisch, -e** table E
das **Tischtennis** table tennis 1
der **Titel, -** title
der **Toast** toast
die **Tochter, ̈** daughter 4
der **Tod, -e** death
die **Toilette, -n** bathroom 8
toll great; fantastic 6
die **Toma'te, -n** tomato
tot dead
total' complete, total
die **Tour, -en** tour, trip 11
der **Touris'mus** tourism
der **Trabant'** brand of car manufactured in the GDR
traditionell' traditional
tragen (ä), trug, getragen to carry; to wear 6
trampen (colloq.) to hitchhike 11
die **Träne, -n** tear
der **Transport', -e** transportation; transport
(sich) **treffen (i), traf, getroffen** meet 7; **ich treffe mich mit Freunden** I'm meeting friends 11
treiben, trieb, getrieben to engage in 1; to drive
die **Treppe, -n** step; stairway
der **Treppenläufer, -** carpet runner
treten (tritt), trat, ist getreten to step
sich **trimmen** to get into shape
trinken, trank, getrunken to drink 4; **Was gibt's zum Trinken?** What's there to drink?
trocken dry 2
die **Trockenheit** dryness
trotz (+ gen.) in spite of 8
trotzdem nevertheless 12
die **Tschechoslowakei'** Czechoslovakia
Tschüß! (informal) So long! Good-by! 1
tun, tat, getan to do 6
die **Tür, -en** door E

der **Türke, -n, -n**/die **Türkin, -nen**
Turk
die **Türkei'** Turkey
türkisch Turkish
der **Türrahmen, -** door frame
die **Tüte, -n** bag
typisch typical(ly) 7

die **U-Bahn** (*abbr. for* **Untergrundbahn**) subway 5
über (+ *acc./dat.*) about; above 3;
by way of
überall everywhere 13
**überfah'ren (ä), überfuhr,
überfahren** to run over
überhaupt' in general; at all 6
überle'ben to survive
(sich) **überle'gen** to reflect, think
about
übermorgen day after tomorrow
überra'schen to surprise 7
überra'schend surprising
die **Überra'schung, -en** surprise
die **Überschrift, -en** headline
überset'zen to translate
die **Überset'zung, -en** translation 9
überzeu'gend convincing
die **Übung, -en** exercise; practice
die **Uhr, -en** clock, watch E; **Wieviel ~ ist es?** What time is it? 1
um (+ *acc.*) around; at 1; **~ zwei
Uhr** at two o'clock 1; **~ wieviel
Uhr?** at what time? 1; **~ ... zu**
(+ *inf.*) in order to 9; **~ Himmels willen** for heaven's sake
die **Umfrage, -n** opinion poll
die **Umgangssprache, -n** colloquial
language
umgekehrt in reverse, backwards
die **Umschulung** retraining
umsonst' gratis, for free, in vain
der **Umstand, ⁻e** circumstance
um•stellen to adjust
die **Umwelt** environment 6
umweltfreundlich good for the environment
die **Umweltverschmutzung** pollution of the environment

der **Umzug, ⁻e** procession, parade
unabhängig independent 9
die **Unabhängigkeit** independence
unbedingt necessarily
und and, plus E; **~ so weiter
(usw.)** and so on, etc. 6
der **Unfall, ⁻e** accident 12
ungarisch Hungarian
(das) **Ungarn** Hungary
ungefähr approximately 8
ungelernt unskilled
ungemahlen unground
ungespritzt unsprayed
ungezwungen uninhibited
unglaub'lich unbelievable 7
das **Unglück** misfortune
die **Universität', -en (die Uni, -s** *colloq.*) university 4
das **Univiertel** university district
unkultiviert uncultured
unleserlich illegible 12
UNO United Nations (Organization)
unordentlich disorganized, disor-
derly
die **Unordnung** disorder
unschuldig innocent(ly); not guilty
14
unser our 2
unsozial socially unjust
unten below, beneath; downstairs
5
unter (+ *acc./dat.*) under; among 7
sich **unterhal'ten (ä), unterhielt, unterhalten** to converse, chat
unterrich'ten to inform; to instruct,
to teach
(sich) **unterschei'den, unterschied,
unterschieden** to distinguish 9
der **Unterschied, -e** difference 4
unverschämt impertinent
der **Urlaub** vacation 12; **in ~
fahren** to go on vacation; **in ~
sein** to be on vacation 12
die **USA** (*pl.*) U.S.A. 7
usw. (= **und so weiter**) etc. (and
so on) 6

der **Vater, ⁻** father 4
Vati daddy
die **Veran'staltung, -en** event; rally
verant'wortlich responsible 14
die **Verant'wortung** responsibility
10
die **Verbes'serung, -en** improve-
ment
verbin'den, verband, verbunden to
connect, associate
verbrei'tet (*p.p. of* **verbrei'ten**)
widespread
verbrin'gen, verbrachte, verbracht
to spend (time) 11
verder'ben (i), verdarb, verdorben
to spoil
verdie'nen to earn 10
der **Verdienst', -e** earnings
verei'nigen to unify
verfau'len to rot
verfüh'ren to seduce
**verges'sen (vergißt), vergaß, verges-
sen** to forget 6
vergeß'lich forgetful 12
der **Vergleich', -e** comparison
**verglei'chen, verglich, verglichen
(mit)** to compare (to/with) 13
das **Vergnü'gen** enjoyment, fun 13;
Viel ~! Have a good time!
vergrö'ßern to increase
sich **verhei'raten (mit)** to marry
verhei'ratet (mit) married (to) 5
verkau'fen to sell 12
der **Verkäu'fer, -**/die **Verkäu'ferin,
-nen** salesperson
das **Verkehrs'mittel** means of
transportation
verkün'den to announce
verkür'zen to shorten
verlet'zen to injure; to violate 8
verliebt' in love
verlie'ren, verlor, verloren to lose
3
verpe'stet polluted
verra'ten to betray
verschie'den different 5
verschwen'den to waste
verschö'nern to beautify

die **Versi'cherung** insurance
verspre'chen (verspricht), versprach, versprochen *(dat. of person)* to promise 12
verständ'lich understandable 12; **sich ~ machen** to make oneself understood
verste'hen, verstand, verstanden to understand 4
verstoh'len furtively
versu'chen to try 5
der/die **Verwand'te** *(noun decl. like adj.)* relative
verweich'lichen to pamper
der **Vetter, -n** cousin *(m.)* 4
das **Videospiel, -e** video game
viel (mehr, meist-) much 1
viele many 3
vielleicht' maybe, perhaps 1
der **Vielvölkerstaat** multi-ethnic state
das **Viertel, -** quarter 1; **~ nach [zwei]** quarter after [two]; **~ vor [drei]** quarter to [three] 1; district 11; **das Stadtviertel** city district 11
die **Vitamin'tablette, -n** vitamin pill
die **Voka'bel, -n** vocabulary word
das **Volk, ̈er** people, folk 5
volkseigen state-owned
das **Volkslied, -er** folk song
die **Volkskunst** folk art
voll full; complete(ly) 10
der **Volleyball** volleyball 1
von *(+ dat.)* from; of 2
vor *(+ acc./dat.)* before 1; in front of 7; **~ allem** above all 7; **~ [einer Woche]** [a week] ago 7; **~ kurzem** recently 5
voraus'•sehen (ie), sah voraus, vorausgesehen to anticipate
vorbei'•kommen, kam vorbei, ist vorbeigekommen to come by 5; **bei mir ~** to come by my house 5

vor•bereiten to prepare 4; **sich ~ (auf + acc.)** to prepare oneself (for) 11
die **Vorbereitung, -en** preparation
vor•gehen, ging vor, ist vorgegangen to be fast *(said of a clock)*
vor•haben, hatte vor, vorgehabt to intend, have in mind 11
vorher before 6
die **Vorlesung, -en** lecture 4
die **Vorlesungsnotizen** *(pl.)* lecture notes
der **Vorname, -ns, -n** first name 7
vor•schlagen (ä), schlug vor, vorgeschlagen to suggest
vor•sehen (ie), sah vor, vorgesehen to call for, anticipate
die **Vorspeise** appetizer
sich *(dat.)* **vor•stellen** to imagine
die **Vorstellung, -en** idea, concept; performance (of a play) 10
das **Vorurteil, -e** prejudice 10
vorwurfsvoll reproachfully
das **Vorzimmer, -** outer office, anteroom

wachsen (ä), wuchs, ist gewachsen to grow 6
das **Wachstum** growth 14
wagen to dare
der **Wagen, -** car 5
die **Wahl, -en** choice; election
die **Wahlveranstaltung, -en** political rally
während *(+ gen.)* during 8; *(conj.)* while, whereas
wahrschein'lich probably 14
der **Wald, ̈er** forest 7
das **Walnußblatt, ̈er** walnut leaf
die **Wand, ̈e** wall E
das **Wanderlied, -er** hiking song
wandern, ist gewandert to hike; to go walking 1
die **Wanderung, -en** hike 11
wann when 1
war *(past tense of sein)* was 2
die **Ware, -n** merchandise; commodity, goods 12

warm (ä) warm 2
warnen (vor + dat.) to warn (against) 12
warten (auf + acc.) to wait (for) 5
warum' why 2
was what 1; **= etwas** something 8; **~ anderes** something different 7; **~ für (ein)** what kind (of) 1; what (a) 2
die **Wäsche** wash, laundry 10
waschen (ä), wusch, gewaschen to wash 9
die **Waschmaschine, -n** washing machine 9
das **Wasser** water 6
Wasserski fahren (ä), fuhr Wasserski, ist Wasserski gefahren to waterski
wechseln to change, switch 10
weg away, gone 5
der **Weg, -e** way 3; **auf dem ~** on the way 3
wegen *(+ gen.)* on account of, because of 8
weg•fahren (ä), fuhr weg, ist weggefahren to leave; to drive away 5
weg•nehmen (i), nahm weg, weggenommen to take away
die **WG, -s** *(abbrev. for* **die Wohngemeinschaft, -en**) group of people sharing an apartment 11
weh tun *(+ dat.)* to hurt 9
weiblich feminine
die **Weide, -n** pasture, meadow
das **Weihnachten** Christmas 7
das **Weihnachtsgeschenk, -e** Christmas present
weil *(conj.)* because 5
der **Wein** wine 3
weinen to cry
die **Weise: auf diese ~** in this way 5
weiß white E
weit far 10
weiter farther; further 2; **und so ~** and so on 6

welch (-er, -es, -e) which E;
  Welche Farbe hat ...? What color
  is . . .? E
die Welt, -en world 5
der Weltkrieg, -e world war 5
der Weltmarkt, ⁻e world market
wem (dat. of wer) (to) whom 5
wenig little, few 3; ein ∼ a little
weniger minus (in subtraction) E
wenigstens at least 14
wenn (conj.) when; if 5
wer who 1
die Werbung advertising
werden (i), wurde, ist geworden to
  become 4
werfen (i), warf, geworfen to
  throw 9
der Werkzeugmacher, -/die
  Werkzeugmacherin, -nen tool-
  maker
der Wert value
wert worth; worthwhile 12
der Westen west 2
das Wetter weather 2
wichtig important 6
die Wichtigkeit, -en importance
widerfah'ren (ä), widerfuhr, ist
  widerfahren to happen to
wie how E; like 2; as 3; ∼ immer
  as always 3; ∼ wär's mit...? How
  about . . . ? 7; ∼ alt sind Sie?
  How old are you? E
wieder again 2
wieder·haben to have back
das Wiedersehen: auf ∼!
  Good-by! 1
Wien Vienna 5
wieviel' how much E
die Wiese, -n meadow
die Wilden (pl.) the wild ones
willkom'men welcome
der Wind wind 2
windsurfen: ∼ gehen to go windsurfing 11
der Winter winter 2
winzig tiny
wir we 1
wirklich really 1

die Wirklichkeit reality 10
wirksam effective
der Wirkstoff, -e ingredient
die Wirtschaft economy 9; ∼, en
  inn, pub, tavern 11
wirtschaftlich economic
die Wirtschaftswissenschaft economics
wischen to wipe
wissen (weiß), wußte, gewußt to
  know (a fact) 4; ∼ über (+ acc.)
  to know about; ∼ von to know
  of
der Wissenschaftler, -/die Wissenschaftlerin,-nen scientist
wo where 2
die Woche, -n week E
das Wochenende, -n weekend 3;
  Schönes ∼. Have a nice weekend.
woher' where from 7
wohin' where to 5
wohl well 9; probably, indeed 7
der Wohlstand affluence
der Wohnblock, -s block of flats,
  apartment building
wohnen (bei) to live, reside (at a
  place) 4
Wohnen: ∼ und Essen room and
  board
das Wohngeld (government) rent
  supplement
die Wohngemeinschaft, -en a
  group of people sharing an apartment 11
das Wohnhaus, ⁻er apartment
  building
die Wohnung, -en dwelling; apartment 7
das Wohnzimmer, - living room 8
wollen (will), wollte, gewollt to
  want to, intend to 4
das Wort, ⁻er word E; das ∼
  haben to have the floor
der Wortprozessor, -en word
  processor 10; mit dem ∼ arbeiten
  to do word processing 1
der Wortschatz vocabulary

das Wunder, - miracle; wonder
wünschen to wish 12
würde (subj. of werden) would 11
die Wurst, ⁻e sausage, lunch meat
  3
das Wurstbrot, -e cold meat sandwich
die Würze, -n spice

z.B. = zum Beispiel for example 4
die Zahl, -en number, numeral E
zahlen to pay 4
der Zahn, ⁻e tooth 9; sich die
  Zähne putzen to brush one's
  teeth
der Zahnarzt, ⁻e/die Zahnärztin,
  -nen dentist
die Zahnpasta toothpaste
der Zaun, ⁻e fence 8
zeigen to show 8; ∼ auf (+ acc.)
  to point to
die Zeit, -en time 6; seit kurzer ∼
  recently 6; zur gleichen ∼ at the
  same time 10; zur ∼(z.Zt.) at the
  time; currently 13
die Zeitschrift, -en magazine
die Zeitung, -en newspaper 9
das Zelt, -e tent
zelten to camp in a tent 5
die Zensur', -en grade, mark 4
zentral' central
das Zentrum, Zentren center
die Zerstö'rung destruction
ziehen, zog, gezogen to pull
das Ziel, -e goal 10
ziemlich quite, rather 6
die Zigaret'te, -n cigarette 12
das Zimmer, - room E
der Zirkel, - compass, divider
zu too 2; ∼ (+ dat.) to, at 3
zueinan'der to each other
zuerst' at first 6
zufrie'den satisfied 13
der Zug, ⁻e train 5
der Zugang access
zugleich' at the same time
zu·hören to listen
die Zukunft future 12

zuletzt' last
zu•machen to close 8
die **Zunge: auf der ~ liegen** to be on the tip of one's tongue
zurecht'•legen to put out
zurück' back, in return 4
zurück'•zahlen to pay back 4
zusam'men together 2
die **Zusam'menarbeit** cooperation
zusam'menhängen, hing zusammen, zusammengehangen to hang together; to be connected

zu•sehen (ie), sah zu, zugesehen to watch
die **Zuverlässigkeit** dependability, reliability
zuviel' too much, too many 4
der **Zuzug** immigration
der **Zwang: sich keinen ~ antun** to feel free
zwar indeed; no doubt
der **Zweck, -e** purpose 13
das **Zweifamilienhaus, ⸚er** two-family house, duplex

zweifeln to doubt
zweit- second
der **Zweite Weltkrieg** World War II
die **Zwiebel, -n** onion
zwischen (+ *acc./dat.*) between, among 7
die **Zwischenprüfung, -en** qualifying exam

English-German Vocabulary

The English-German end vocabulary contains the words included in the active vocabulary lists and the *Erweiterung des Wortschatzes* section of the chapters. Not included from the active lists are numbers, articles, and pronouns. The plural forms of nouns are given. Strong and irregular weak verbs are indicated with a raised degree mark (°). Their principal parts can be found in the Reference section. Separable-prefix verbs are indicated with a raised dot: **mit•bringen.**

able: to be ~ to können°
about über; **to be ~** handeln von
above all vor allem
abroad das Ausland
accept an•nehmen°
accident der Unfall, ⸚e
account: on ~ of wegen *(+ gen.)*
acquaintance der/die Bekannte
(noun decl. like adj.); **to make the ~ of** kennen•lernen
actually eigentlich
addition: in ~ noch
address die Adresse, -n; **What is your ~?** Wie ist Ihre Adresse?
advertisement die Reklame, -n
afraid: to be ~ Angst haben, (sich) fürchten
after nach *(prep.);* nachdem *(conj.);* **~ all** schließlich
afternoon der Nachmittag, -e; **this ~** heute nachmittag
afternoons nachmittags
afterwards nachher
again wieder; noch einmal
against gegen
ago: [ten years] ~ vor [zehn Jahren]
air die Luft
airplane das Flugzeug, -e
airport der Flughafen, ⸚
all alle; **at ~** überhaupt
allowed: to be ~ dürfen°
almost fast
alone allein
also auch
although obwohl
always immer
America (das) Amerika

American *(adj.)* amerikanisch; **~ (person)** der Amerikaner, -/die Amerikanerin, -nen
among unter
and und; **~ so on** und so weiter
angry böse; **don't be ~ with me** sei mir nicht böse
answer die Antwort, -en; **~ [the woman]** [der Frau] antworten; **(to) ~ the question** auf die Frage antworten
anyone jemand
anything: ~ else? Sonst noch etwas?
apartment die Wohnung, -en
apology die Entschuldigung, -en
appear scheinen°; erscheinen°
appointment der Termin, -e
apprenticeship die Lehre, -n
approximately ungefähr
April der April
arise entstehen°
arm der Arm, -e
arrive an•kommen°
article der Artikel, -
artificial künstlich
as als; wie; **~ ... ~** so ... wie; **~ always** wie immer
ask fragen; **~ for** bitten° um
aspirin das Aspirin
assignment die Aufgabe, -n
assume an•nehmen°
astonished erstaunt
at an; auf; **~ (a place)** bei
attic der Dachboden
August der August
aunt die Tante, -n
Austria (das) Österreich

Austrian österreichisch *(adj.);* **~ (person)** der Österreicher, -/die Österreicherin, -nen
author der Autor, -en/die Autorin, -nen
automobile das Auto, -s
autumn der Herbst
away weg
awfully riesig *(colloq.)*

back zurück
bad schlecht; schlimm; **not ~** ganz gut; **too ~** schade
badly schlecht
bag die Tasche, -n
bake backen°
baker der Bäcker, -/die Bäckerin, -nen
bakery die Bäckerei, -en; **at the ~** beim Bäcker; **to the ~** zum Bäcker
balcony der Balkon, -s
ball-point pen der Kugelschreiber, - (der Kuli, -s *colloq.*)
band die Band, -s
bank die Bank
basement der Keller, -
basketball der Basketball
bath das Bad, ⸚er
bathe (sich) baden
bathroom das Bad, ⸚er; die Toilette, -n
be sein°
beautiful schön
because weil; denn; **~ of** wegen
become werden°
bed das Bett, -en
bedroom das Schlafzimmer, -

beer das Bier; ~ **garden** der Biergarten, ̈
before vor; vorher
begin an•fangen°; beginnen°; ~
  the work mit der Arbeit
  anfangen
beginning der Anfang, ̈e
believe glauben
belong to gehören
beside bei; neben; außer;
  außerhalb
besides außerdem; außer
better besser
between zwischen
bicycle das Fahrrad, ̈er
big groß
bike das Rad, ̈er
birthday der Geburtstag, -e; **When
  is your ~?** Wann hast du
  Geburtstag?
black schwarz
blouse die Bluse, -n
blue blau
body der Körper, -; **part of the ~**
  der Körperteil, -e
book das Buch, ̈er
book bag die Büchertasche, -n
bookcase das Bücherregal, -e
bookstore die Buchhandlung, -en
border die Grenze, -n
boss der Chef, -s/die Chefin, -nen
both beide; beides
bother stören
bottle die Flasche, -n
boy der Junge, -n, -n
bread das Brot, -e
break brechen°
breakfast das Frühstück; **for ~**
  zum Frühstück; **to eat ~** frühstücken
bright hell
bring bringen°; ~ **along**
  mit•bringen°
broke (out of money) pleite
broken kaputt
brother der Bruder, ̈; **brothers and
  sisters** die Geschwister *(pl.)*
brown braun

brush: to ~ my teeth mir die
  Zähne putzen
build bauen
bus der Bus, -se
business das Geschäft, -e; **~man**
  der Kaufmann, -leute; **~woman**
  die Kauffrau, -en
busy: to be ~ beschäftigt sein; **to
  keep ~** (sich) beschäftigen
but aber; sondern
butcher der Metzger, -/die
  Metzgerin, -nen
butcher shop die Metzgerei, -en; **at
  the ~** beim Metzger; **to the ~**
  zum Metzger
butter die Butter
buy kaufen
by: ~ [car] mit [dem Auto]

café das Café, -s
cake der Kuchen, -; die Torte, -n
call nennen°; an•rufen; **~ [your]
  home** bei [dir] anrufen
calm ruhig
camp: to ~ in a tent zelten
can können°
capital die Hauptstadt, ̈e
car das Auto, -s; der Wagen, -
card die Karte, -n; **(playing) cards**
  die Karten *(pl.)*
care die Sorge, -n; **(to) ~ for** sorgen für; **(to) take ~ of** sich
  kümmern um
carry tragen°
cassette die Kassette, -n
cassette deck der Kassettenrecorder, -
castle das Schloß, Schlösser
celebration die Feier, -n; das Fest,
  -e
cellar der Keller, -
century das Jahrhundert, -e
certain(ly) bestimmt; sicher
chair der Stuhl, ̈e
change wechseln
cheap billig
cheerful lustig
cheese der Käse

chemistry die Chemie
chess das Schach
child das Kind, -er
chocolate die Schokolade, -n
chocolate mousse die Schokoladencreme
Christmas das Weihnachten
cigarette die Zigarette, -n
citizens' action group die Bürgerinitiative
city die Stadt, ̈e; **old part of the ~**
  die Altstadt
class die Klasse, -n; **German ~**
  die Deutschklasse, -n
classical klassisch
clean sauber; **to ~** putzen; auf-
  •räumen
clear klar
climate das Klima
clock die Uhr, -en
close eng; nah(e)
close: to ~ schließen°; zu•machen
clothing die Kleidung; **article of ~**
  das Kleidungsstück, -e
coat der Mantel, ̈; **sport ~** der
  Sakko, -s
coffee der Kaffee; **for (afternoon)
  ~** zum Kaffee
cola drink die Cola
cold kalt; die Erkältung, -en; **to
  catch a ~** sich erkälten
colleague der Kollege, -n, -n/die
  Kollegin, -nen
collect sammeln
college: to go to ~ studieren; auf/
  an die Universität gehen
color die Farbe, -n; **What ~ is . . .?**
  Welche Farbe hat . . .?
comb: to ~ (one's hair) (sich)
  kämmen
come kommen°; **~ along**
  mit•kommen°; **~ about** ent-
  stehen°; **~ by** vorbei•kommen°
commercial (TV or radio) die
  Reklame, -n
company die Gesellschaft, -en; die
  Firma, Firmen; **have ~** Besuch
  haben

compare (to/with) vergleichen° (mit)

compete konkurrieren

complete(ly) ganz; voll

computer der Computer, -; ~ **science** die Informatik

concept die Vorstellung, -en

concert das Konzert, -e

concerto das Konzert, -e

conservative konservativ

contrary: on the ~ sondern; doch

cook kochen

cool kühl

corner die Ecke, -n

correct richtig

cost kosten

cough husten

could könnte

country das Land, ∵er; der Staat; **in our** ~ bei uns; **in the** ~ auf dem Lande; **out into the** ~ ins Grüne; **to the** ~ auf das Land

course der Kurs, -e

course: of ~ natürlich; klar; selbstverständlich

courtyard der Hof, ∵e

cousin *(female)* die Kusine, -n; ~ *(male)* der Vetter, -n

cry weinen

culture die Kultur

currently zur Zeit

customer der Kunde, -n, -n/die Kundin, -nen

daily täglich

dance tanzen

dangerous gefährlich

dark dunkel

daughter die Tochter, ∵

day der Tag, -e; **one/some** ~ eines Tages

December der Dezember

decide (sich) entscheiden°; beschließen°; **to make a decision (after reflecting on it)** sich entscheiden

decorate dekorieren

demonstration die Demonstration, -en

dentist der Zahnarzt, ∵e/die Zahnärztin, -nen

department store das Kaufhaus, ∵er

depend on ab•hängen von

describe beschreiben°

dessert der Nachtisch, -e

develop (sich) entwickeln

different verschieden; anders; **something** ~ (et)was anderes

difficult schwer; schwierig

difficulty die Schwierigkeit, -en

dining room das Eßzimmer, -

dinner das Abendessen, ; **for** ~ zum Abendessen; **to eat** ~ zu Abend essen

discussion die Diskussion, -en

dishwasher der Geschirrspüler, -

district das Viertel, -; **city** ~ das Stadtviertel, -

disturb stören

divided by [in mathematics] dividiert durch

do machen; tun°

doctor der Arzt, ∵e/die Ärztin, -nen

doll die Puppe, -n

done fertig; **to have something** ~ etwas machen lassen

door die Tür, -en

dormitory das Studentenheim, -e

downstairs unten

dress das Kleid, -er; **to** ~ (sich) an•ziehen°; **I get dressed** ich ziehe mich an

drink trinken°

drive fahren°; **to** ~ **away** weg•fahren°

driver der Fahrer, -/die Fahrerin, -nen

dry trocken; **to** ~ **(dishes)** ab•trocknen

dumb dumm; **something** ~ etwas Dummes

during während

dwelling die Wohnung, -en

each jed- (er, es, e)

ear das Ohr, -en

early früh

earn verdienen

east der Osten

easy-going ruhig

eat essen°

economy die Wirtschaft

egg das Ei, -er

employer der Arbeitgeber, -/die Arbeitgeberin, -nen

employee der Arbeitnehmer, -/die Arbeitnehmerin, -nen

employed berufstätig

end das Ende, -n; **in/at the** ~ am Ende

engage treiben°; ~ **in sports** Sport treiben

engineer der Ingenieur, -e/die Ingenieurin, -nen

England (das) England

English *(adj.)* englisch; ~ **language** (das) Englisch

enjoyment die Lust; das Vergnügen

enough genug

entrance hall der Flur, -e

environment die Umwelt

especially besonders

etc. usw.

even sogar; ~ **if** auch wenn

evening der Abend, -e; **Good** ~! Guten Abend!; **this** ~ heute abend

evenings abends

every jeder

everything alles

everyone jeder

everywhere überall

exactly genau

examination die Klausur, -en; die Prüfung, -en; **comprehensive** ~ das Examen, -

example das Beispiel, -e; **for** ~ zum Beispiel (z.B.)

excellent(ly) ausgezeichnet

excuse die Entchuldigung, -en; ~ **me!** Entschuldigung!

expect erwarten
expensive teuer
experience die Erfahrung, -en
explain erklären
explanation die Erklärung, -en
expressway die Autobahn
extent: to some ~ einigermaßen
eye das Auge, -n

face das Gesicht, -er
fairly ganz; ziemlich
fall der Herbst
familiar bekannt
family die Familie, -n
famous bekannt
fantastic phantastisch; toll
far weit
farmhouse das Bauernhaus, ¨er
farmer der Bauer, -n, -n/die
  Bäuerin, -nen
farther weiter
fascinating faszinierend
fast schnell
father der Vater, ¨
fear die Angst, ¨e; **(to)** ~ sich
  fürchten; **(to)** ~ **for** Angst haben
  um
feast das Fest, -e
February der Februar
Federal Republic of Germany die
  Bundesrepublik Deutschland
  (BRD)
feel sich fühlen; ~ **like** Lust
  haben; **I don't** ~ **like working**
  ich habe keine Lust zu arbeiten; **I
  don't** ~ **like it** dazu habe ich
  keine Lust
feeling das Gefühl, -e
fence der Zaun, -e
fever das Fieber
few wenig(e); **a** ~ ein paar
fight kämpfen
film der Film, -e
finally schließlich
find finden°
fine fein
finger der Finger, -
finished fertig

first erst; **at** ~ zuerst; ~ **of all**
  erst einmal, erstens; ~ **name** der
  Vorname, -n, -n
first-rate Klasse!; Spitze!
fish der Fisch, -e
fit passen
floor der Boden, ¨; ~ **(of a building)** der Stock, *pl.* Stockwerke;
  first ~ das Erdgeschoß
flower die Blume, -n
fluent(ly) fließend
fly fliegen°
food das Essen; die Lebensmittel
  (pl.)
foot der Fuß, ¨e; **on** ~ zu Fuß; **to
  go on** ~ laufen°
for für *(prep.)*; denn *(conj.)*
foreign fremd; ~ **language** die
  Fremdsprache, -n; ~ **worker** der
  Gastarbeiter, -/die Gastarbeiterin,
  -nen
foreigner der Ausländer, -/die
  Ausländerin, -nen
forest der Wald, ¨er
forget vergessen°
forgetful vergeßlich
fork die Gabel, -n
(the) former jen- (er, es, e)
formerly früher
fourth das Viertel, -
France (das) Frankreich
free frei; **for** ~ umsonst
freeway die Autobahn, -en
freezer der Gefrierschrank, ¨e
French *(adj.)* französisch; ~ **(language)** (das) Französisch
French fries die Pommes frites *(pl.)*
fresh frisch
Friday der Freitag
friend der Freund, -e/die
  Freundin, -nen
friendliness die Freundlichkeit
friendly freundlich
from von; aus
fruit das Obst
fuel das Benzin
full voll

fun das Vergnügen; der Spaß;
  that's ~ es macht Spaß
furniture die Möbel *(pl.);* **piece of**
  ~ das Möbelstück, -e
further weiter

garage die Garage, -n
garbage dump die Mülldeponie, -n
garden der Garten, ¨
gasoline das Benzin
general: in ~ überhaupt,
  allgemein
gentleman der Herr, -n, -en
genuine echt
German *(adj.)* deutsch; ~ **(person)**
  der/die Deutsche *(noun decl. like
  adj.);* ~ **(language)** (das)
  Deutsch; **to do** ~ **(homework)**
  Deutsch machen; **I'm doing German** ~ ich mache Deutsch; ~
  Mark D-Mark; ~ **studies (language and literature)** die
  Germanistik; ~ **secondary school**
  das Gymnasium, *pl.* Gymnasien
German Democratic Republic die
  Deutsche Demokratische Republik
  (DDR)
Germany (das) Deutschland
get bekommen°; kriegen; ~ **up**
  auf•stehen°; **to** ~ **together**
  zusammen•kriegen, sich treffen°
gigantic riesig
girl das Mädchen, -
give geben°; ~ **as a gift**
  schenken
glad froh
gladly gern
glove der Handschuh, -e
go gehen°; ~ **by [car]** mit [dem
  Auto] fahren°
goal das Ziel, -e
gone weg
good gut
Good-by! Auf Wiedersehen!;
  Tschüß! *(colloq.)*
government die Regierung, -en
grade die Zensur, -en
grandfather der Großvater, ¨

grandmother die Großmutter, ⁓
grandparents die Großeltern *(pl.)*
gray grau
great toll
green grün
groceries die Lebensmittel *(pl.)*
group die Gruppe, -n
grow wachsen°
growth das Wachstum
guest der Gast, ⁓e; der Besucher, -/ die Besucherin, -nen; ⁓ **worker** der Gastarbeiter, -/die Gastarbeiterin, -nen
guilty schuldig; **not ⁓** unschuldig
guitar die Gitarre, -n

hair das Haar, -e
half die Hälfte, -n; halb
hand die Hand, ⁓e
handbag die (Hand)tasche, -n
hang hängen°
happy froh
hardly kaum
hard-working fleißig
has hat
hat der Hut, ⁓e
have haben°; **to ⁓ to** müssen°; **to ⁓ something done** etwas machen lassen
head der Kopf, ⁓e
headache die Kopfschmerzen *(pl.)*
healthy gesund
heavy schwer
Hello! Guten Tag!; Grüß dich!; Hallo! *(informal)*
help helfen°; **⁓ with [work]** bei [der Arbeit] helfen
here hier; da; **⁓ [toward the speaker]** her; **⁓ you are** bitte sehr
Hey! Du!; He!
Hi! Tag!
high hoch
hike die Wanderung, -en; **(to) ⁓** wandern
history die Geschichte
hitchhike trampen
hobby das Hobby, -s

hold halten°
holiday der Feiertag, -e
home: at ⁓ zu Hause; **(to go) ⁓** nach Hause; **at the ⁓ of** bei
hope hoffen; **I ⁓** hoffentlich; **⁓ for** hoffen auf *(+ acc.)*
horrible furchtbar; fürchterlich
horribly furchtbar; fürchterlich
hot heiß
hour die Stunde, -n
house das Haus, ⁓er
how wie; **⁓ are you?** Wie geht es Ihnen?/Wie geht's?
however aber
human being der Mensch, -en, -en
hunger der Hunger
hungry: to be ⁓ Hunger haben; **to get ⁓** Hunger bekommen/ kriegen
hurt weh tun°

idea die Idee, -n; die Vorstellung, -en; die Ahnung; **No ⁓!** Keine Ahnung!
idle: be ⁓ faulenzen
if wenn; ob; **even ⁓** wenn auch
ill krank
illegible unleserlich
illness die Krankheit, -en
image das Bild, -er; die Vorstellung, -en
immediately gleich
import restriction die Importbeschränkung, -en
important wichtig; **be ⁓** eine Rolle spielen
impression der Eindruck, ⁓e
in(to) in; hinein
independent unabhängig
individual einzeln
industrious fleißig
industry die Industrie, -n
inflation die Inflation
influence beeinflussen°
inhabitant der Einwohner, -/die Einwohnerin, -nen
innocent(ly) unschuldig
in order to um ... zu

in spite of trotz
instead of (an)statt
intelligent intelligent
intend to wollen°
interested: to be ⁓ (in) (sich) interessieren (für)
interesting interessant
invite ein•laden°
is ist; **isn't it?** nicht? *(tag question)*; **Your name is [Monica], isn't it?** Sie heißen [Monika], nicht?

jacket die Jacke, -n
January der Januar
jeans die Jeans *(pl.)*
job der Beruf, -e; der Job, -s; die Stelle, -n; **to have a ⁓** jobben *(colloq.)*
jogging das Jogging
join in mit•machen (bei + *a group*)
journalist der Journalist, -en, -en/ die Journalistin, -nen
July der Juli
June der Juni
just eben; erst; gerade

key der Schlüssel, -
kilogram das Kilo(gramm)
kilometer der Kilometer, -
kind: be so ⁓ sei so gut
kindergarten der Kindergarten, ⁓
kitchen die Küche, -n
knife das Messer, -
know (a fact) wissen°; **⁓ (be acquainted)** kennen°; **to get to ⁓** kennen•lernen

lake der See, -n
lamp die Lampe, -n
land das Land, ⁓er
language die Sprache, -n
large groß
last letzt
late spät; **Until later!** Bis dann!
laundry die Wäsche
lawyer der Jurist, -en, -en/die Juristin, -nen
lay legen

lazy faul
lead führen
learn lernen
least: at ~ wenigstens
leave lassen°; weg•fahren°
lecture die Vorlesung, -en
leg das Bein, -e
leisure time die Freizeit
lend leihen°
lesson die Stunde, -n
let lassen°
letter der Brief, -e
library die Bibliothek, -en
lie liegen°
life das Leben, -
light leicht; **~ (in color)** hell
like wie; **would ~** möchte; **to ~** gern haben; mögen
likewise ebenso; auch
linguistically sprachlich
list die Liste, -n
literature die Literatur
little klein; wenig; **a ~** ein bißchen, ein wenig
live leben; wohnen
living room das Wohnzimmer, -
living standard der Lebensstandard
lock das Schloß, Schlösser
long lang; lange
longer: no ~ nicht mehr
look: ~ at an•sehen°, schauen; **~ like** aus•sehen°; **~ for** suchen; **~ forward to** sich freuen auf
lose verlieren°
loud laut
lounge around faulenzen
love lieben; **in ~** verliebt
low niedrig
luck das Glück; **Good ~!** Viel Glück!; **to be lucky** Glück haben
lunch das Mittagessen; **for ~** zum Mittagessen; **to have ~** zu Mittag essen°
lunch meat die Wurst, ¨e

magazine die Zeitschrift, -en
major subject das Hauptfach, ¨er

make machen
man der Mann, ¨er; **~!** Mensch!
manner die Art
many viele; **how ~** wieviel; **too ~** zuviel
map die Landkarte, -n
March der März
market der Markt, ¨e
marmalade die Marmelade
married verheiratet
marry heiraten
mathematics die Mathematik
matter: it doesn't ~ (es) macht nichts
May der Mai
may dürfen°; **that ~ well be** das mag wohl sein
maybe vielleicht
meal das Essen
mean meinen; bedeuten; **What does that ~?** Was bedeutet das?
meat das Fleisch
meat market die Metzgerei, -en
meet (sich) treffen°; kennen•lernen; **I'm meeting friends** Ich treffe mich mit Freunden
member das Mitglied, -er
merchandise die Ware, -n
merchant der Kaufmann, -leute/ die Kauffrau, -en
merry lustig
milk die Milch
million die Million, -en
mind: to have in ~ vor•haben°
mineral water das Mineralwasser
minor subject das Nebenfach, ¨er
minute die Minute, -n; **Just a ~, please!** Einen Moment, bitte!
miserable elend
Miss Fräulein
modern modern
moment der Moment, -e; **at the ~** im Moment
Monday der Montag
Mondays montags
money das Geld
month der Monat, -e

more mehr; **no ~** kein...mehr; **~ and ~** immer mehr; **~ or less** mehr oder weniger
morning der Morgen; **Good ~!** Guten Morgen!; **this ~** heute morgen
mornings morgens
most of the time meistens
mostly meistens
mother die Mutter, ¨
motorcycle das Motorrad, ¨er
mountain der Berg, -e
mouth der Mund, ¨er
movie der Film, -e; **~ theater** das Kino, -s
movies das Kino, -s; **to the ~** ins Kino
Mr. Herr
Mrs. Frau
Ms. Frau
much viel; **how ~** wieviel; **too ~** zuviel
music die Musik
music lesson die Musikstunde, -n
musical instrument das Musikinstrument, -e
musician der Musiker, -/die Musikerin, -nen
must müssen°

name der Name, -ns, -n; **What is your ~?** Wie heißen Sie?; **to ~** nennen°; **Your ~ is [Mark], isn't it?** Sie heißen [Mark], nicht?
named: to be ~ heißen°
narrow eng
nasty gemein; **what a ~ trick** so eine Gemeinheit
native country die Heimat
nature die Natur
natural(ly) klar; natürlich; selbstverständlich
near bei; **~by** in der Nähe, nah(e)
neck der Hals, ¨e
need brauchen
neighbor der Nachbar, -n, -n/die Nachbarin, -nen

nervous nervös
never nie
nevertheless trotzdem
new neu
newspaper die Zeitung, -en
next nächst
nice nett; schön
night die Nacht, ¨e; **last** ~ gestern abend; **Good** ~! Gute Nacht!
no nein; kein; nicht; ~ **longer** nicht mehr; ~ **more** kein ... mehr
no one niemand
north der Norden
nose die Nase, -n
not nicht; **isn't that so?** nicht?; ~ **at all** gar nicht; ~ **any, no** kein; ~ **only ... but also** nicht nur ... sondern auch
note die Notiz, -en
notebook das Heft, -e
nothing nichts; ~ **special** nichts Besonderes
notice bemerken
November der November
now jetzt; nun
number die Zahl, -en
numeral die Zahl, -en
nursery school der Kindergarten, ¨

observe beobachten
obtain kriegen
occupy beschäftigen
occupied: to be ~ beschäftigt sein
occur (to one's mind) einfallen°
ocean der Ozean, -e
October der Oktober
of von
offer an•bieten°
office das Büro, -s
often oft
oh ach; ~ **I see** ach so; ~ **my** o je; ~ **well** naja
OK okay (O.K.); ganz gut; **it's (not)** ~ es geht (nicht)

old alt; **I'm [19] years** ~ ich bin [19] Jahre alt; **How** ~ **are you?** Wie alt bist du?
on an; auf; ~ **account of** wegen
once einmal; mal; ~ **more** noch einmal
one (pronoun) man; ~ **another** einander
oneself selbst
only nur; erst
open offen; **(to)** ~ auf•machen
opera die Oper, -n
opinion die Meinung, -en; **What's your** ~? Was hältst du davon?
or oder
orchestra das Orchester, -
order die Ordnung; **(to)** ~ bestellen
other andere
otherwise sonst; anders
out of aus
outside draußen; ~ **of** außerhalb
own eigen

page die Seite, -n
paint malen
pale blaß
pants die Hose, -n
pantyhose die Strumpfhose, -n
paper das Papier; die Arbeit, -en
paperback das Taschenbuch, ¨er
parents die Eltern (pl.)
park der Park, -s
part der Teil, -e; **in** ~ zum Teil; **to play a** ~ eine Rolle spielen; **to take** ~ **(in)** teil•nehmen° (an)
participate (in) mit•machen (bei); **I** ~ **in a game.** Ich mache bei einem Spiel mit.
particular besonder-
particularly besonders
party die Party, -s; die Feier, -n; das Fest, -e; die Fete
passport der Paß, Pässe
patio die Terrasse, -n
pay: ~ **for** bezahlen; zahlen; ~ **back** zurückzahlen

peasant der Bauer, -n, -n/die Bäuerin, -nen
pencil der Bleistift, -e
people die Leute (pl.); man
per pro
performance die Vorstellung, -en
perhaps vielleicht
permit lassen°
permitted: to be ~ dürfen°
person der Mensch, -en, -en; die Person, -en
personal(ly) persönlich
pharmacy die Apotheke, -n; **to the** ~ in die Apotheke
philosophy die Philosophie
photograph fotografieren
physics die Physik
piano das Klavier, -e
pick up ab•holen
picnic das Picknick, -s
picture das Bild, -er
piece das Stück, -e
Ping-Pong das Tischtennis
pity: what a ~ schade
place der Platz, ¨e; die Stelle, -n; der Ort, -e
plan der Plan, ¨e; **to** ~ vor•haben°
plant die Pflanze, -n; **(to)** ~ pflanzen
play das Theaterstück, -e; **(to)** ~ spielen
please bitte; **(to)** ~ gefallen°
pleased: to be ~ **(about)** sich freuen (über)
pleasure die Lust; das Vergnügen
pocket die Tasche, -n
police die Polizei
portion der Teil, -e
position die Stelle, -n
possible möglich; **it's (not)** ~ es geht (nicht); **that would (not) be** ~ das ginge nicht
postcard die Karte, -n
potato die Kartoffel, -n
pound das Pfund
practical(ly) praktisch
prejudice das Vorurteil, -e

prepare (for)   (sich) vor•bereiten
(auf)

present   das Geschenk, -e; **(to) give
a** ~   schenken

pretty   ganz schön; ~ **pale**   ganz
schön blaß

price   der Preis, -e

private(ly)   privat

probably   wahrscheinlich

product   das Produkt, -e

profession   der Beruf, -e

professor   der Professor, -en/die
Professorin, -nen

program   das Programm, -e; **TV or
radio** ~   die Sendung, -en

programmer   der Programmierer, -/
die Programmiererin, -nen

progressive   progressiv

promise   versprechen°

proud(ly)   stolz

psychology   die Psychologie

pub   die Kneipe, -n; die Gaststätte,
-n; die Wirtschaft, -en

public(ly)   öffentlich

pullover   der Pulli, -s; der Pullover, -

punctual(ly)   pünktlich

purpose   der Zweck, -e

pure   rein

put   legen; stellen; setzen; hängen

quality   die Qualität, -en

quarter   das Viertel, -

question   die Frage, -n

questionable   fraglich

quick   schnell

quiet   ruhig

quite   ziemlich

radio   das Radio, -s

railroad   die Bahn, -en

rain   der Regen; **(to)** ~   regnen

raincoat   der Regenmantel, ¨

rare(ly)   selten

rather   ziemlich; ~ **than**   lieber als

raw material   der Rohstoff, -e

reach   erreichen

read   lesen°

ready   fertig

real   echt; richtig

reality   die Wirklichkeit

really   wirklich; richtig; echt (slang);
~ **neat**   echt toll

reason   der Grund, ¨e; **for that** ~
daher; darum; aus diesem Grund

receive   bekommen°

recently   vor kurzem; neulich; seit
kurzer Zeit

record   die Platte, -n

record player   der Plattenspieler, -

recover (from)   sich erholen (von)

recuperate   sich erholen

red   rot

refrigerator   der Kühlschrank, ¨e

refugee   der Flüchtling, -e

rehearsal   die Probe, -n

remain   bleiben°

remember (someone/something)
sich erinnern (an + jemand/
etwas)

rent   die Miete, -n; **to** ~   mieten;
vermieten

repair   reparieren

replace   ersetzen

report   das Referat, -e; **(to)** ~   berichten

reporter   der Journalist, -en, -en/
die Journalistin, -nen

request   bitten° (+ um)

responsibility   die Verantwortung,
-en

responsible   verantwortlich

restaurant   das Restaurant, -s; die
Gaststätte, -n; **town hall** ~   der
Ratskeller, -

return: in ~   zurück

reward   der Lohn, ¨e

rich   reich

right   das Recht, -e; **Is it all** ~ **with
you?**   Ist es dir recht? **to be** ~
recht haben; **you're** ~   du hast
recht; **that's** ~   genau; richtig; ~
to   Recht (auf + acc.)

role   die Rolle, -n

roll   das Brötchen, -

room   das Zimmer, -

run   laufen°

running   das Jogging

safe   sicher

sail   segeln

salary   das Gehalt, ¨er

same   gleich; **It's all the** ~ **to me.**
Das ist mir egal.

sandwich   das [Butter]Brot, -e

satisfied   zufrieden

Saturday   der Samstag; der Sonnabend

Saturdays   samstags

sausage   die Wurst, ¨e

say   sagen

schedule   der Stundenplan, ¨e

school   die Schule, -n

seat   der Platz, ¨e

secretary   der Sekretär, -e/die
Sekretärin, -nen

see   sehen°

seem   scheinen°

seldom   selten

sell   verkaufen

semester   das Semester, -

seminar   das Seminar, -e; ~ **room**
das Seminar, -e; ~ **report**   die
Seminararbeit, -en

send   schicken

sentence   der Satz, ¨e

September   der September

serious   ernst; **Are you** ~?   Ist das
dein Ernst?

serve   dienen (+ dat.)

set   setzen

several   einige; mehrere

shampoo   das Shampoo

shave   (sich) rasieren

shine   scheinen°

ship   das Schiff, -e

shirt   das Hemd, -en

shoe   der Schuh, -e

shop   das Geschäft, -e; der Laden, ¨;
(to) ~   ein•kaufen

shopping bag   die Einkaufstasche, -n

short   kurz; ~ **(people)**   klein

show   zeigen

shower   (sich) duschen

sick krank
side die Seite, -n
silly doof
similar ähnlich; gleich
simple einfach
simply einfach
since seit (prep.); da (conj. = because); ~ **when** seit wann
sing singen°
single einzeln
single-family home das Einfamilienhaus, ¨er
sister die Schwester, -n
sit sitzen°
situated: to be ~ liegen°
situation die Situation, -en
ski der Ski, -er; **(to) ~** Ski laufen°, Ski fahren°
skirt der Rock, ¨e
sleep schlafen°
slow(ly) langsam
small klein
smart intelligent
smell riechen°
smile (about) lächeln (über + acc.)
smoke der Rauch
snow der Schnee; **(to) ~** schneien
so so; also; **isn't that ~?** nicht?; ~ **that** damit; ~ **long!** Tschüß!
soap die Seife
soccer der Fußball
sock die Socke, -n
solution die Lösung, -en
some etwas; einige; manch (-er, -es, -e); **to ~ extent** einigermaßen; **at ~ point** irgendwann
someone jemand
something etwas/was; ~ **like that** so was
sometime irgendwann
sometimes manchmal
somewhat etwas
son der Sohn, ¨e
song das Lied, -er
soon bald

sorry: I'm ~ (es) tut mir leid
south der Süden
space der Platz, ¨e
spaghetti die Spaghetti (pl.)
Spanish (language) (das) Spanisch
speak sprechen°
speechless sprachlos
spell buchstabieren
spend (money) aus•geben°; ~ **(time)** verbringen°
sport der Sport; **to engage in sports** Sport treiben°
spring der Frühling
stairs die Treppe, -n
stand stehen°; ~ **up** auf•stehen°; ~/**put upright** stellen
standard German (das) Hochdeutsch
state (in the FRG) das Land, ¨er; ~ **(in the USA)** der Staat, -en
steak das Steak, -s
step der Schritt, -e; die Treppe, -n
steps die Treppe, -n
stereo system die Stereoanlage, -n
still noch; immer noch; noch immer
stomach der Magen
stop auf•hören (mit); halten°
store das Geschäft, -e; der Laden, ¨
story die Geschichte, -n
straight gerade
straighten up auf•räumen
strange merkwürdig
street die Straße, -n; ~ **car** die Straßenbahn, -en
stress der Streß
strike der Streik, -s; **(to) ~** streiken
stroll spazieren
strong stark
student der Student, -en, -en/die Studentin, -nen
studies das Studium
study studieren; lernen; arbeiten; durch•arbeiten
stupid dumm; doof
subject (academic) das Fach, ¨er

subway die U-Bahn
such solch (-er, -es, -e); ~ **a** so ein
suddenly plötzlich
suit (man's) der Anzug, ¨e; (woman's) ~ das Kostüm, -e; **to ~** passen
summer der Sommer
sun die Sonne, -n
Sunday der Sonntag
Sundays sonntags
supermarket der Supermarkt, ¨e; **to the ~** in den Supermarkt
supper das Abendessen; **for ~** zum Abendessen; **to have ~** zu Abend essen
supposed: to be ~ to sollen°
surf surfen
surprise überraschen
swim schwimmen°
Swiss (adj.) Schweizer; ~ **(person)** der Schweizer, -/die Schweizerin, -nen
switch wechseln
Switzerland die Schweiz

table der Tisch, -e
table tennis das Tischtennis
take nehmen°
take along mit•nehmen°
take off sich aus•ziehen° (+ dat.); **I take off my shoes** Ich ziehe mir die Schuhe aus
talk: ~ about reden (über); sprechen°
tall (people) groß
task die Aufgabe, -n
taste schmecken; probieren
tasty lecker
tax die Steuer, -n; ~ **decrease** die Steuersenkung, -en; ~ **increase** die Steuererhöhung, -en
teacher der Lehrer, -/die Lehrerin, -nen
telephone das Telefon, -e; telefonieren; an•rufen°

television das Fernsehen; ~ **set** der Fernseher, -; **color** ~ der Farbfernseher; ~ **program** die Fernsehsendung, -en; **to watch** ~ fern•sehen°

tell sagen; erzählen; **to** ~ **(about)** erzählen (von), erzählen (über + *acc.*)

tennis das Tennis

terrace die Terrasse, -n

terrible schlimm; furchtbar

test die Klausur, -en; **(to) take a** ~ eine Klausur schreiben°

than als *(after a comparison)*

thank danken; ~ **you very much** danke sehr/schön

thanks danke; der Dank; ~ **a lot, many** ~ vielen Dank

that daß; jen- (er, es, e)

theater das Theater, -; **movie** ~ das Kino, -s; ~ **play** das Theaterstück, -e

then dann; da

there da; dort; dahin; ~ **is/are** es gibt

thereby dadurch

therefore also; deshalb; daher; darum

these diese

they sie

thing das Ding, -e; die Sache, -n

think denken°; meinen; ~ **of** halten° von; **What do you** ~**?** Was meinst du?

third das Drittel, -

thirst der Durst

thirsty: to be ~ Durst haben°

this dies (-er, -es, -e)

throat der Hals, ¨e

throw werfen°

Thursday der Donnerstag

thus also

ticket die Karte, -n

tie binden°; **neck** ~ die Krawatte, -n

tight eng

time die Zeit, -en; das Mal; mal; **at this** ~ zur Zeit; **at that** ~ damals; **at the same** ~ zur gleichen Zeit; **for a long** ~ lange; **a short** ~ **ago** vor kurzem, neulich; **What** ~ **is it?** Wieviel Uhr ist es?; **at what** ~**?** um wieviel Uhr?; **Have a good** ~**!** Viel Vergnügen!

times mal; **[three]** ~ [drei] mal

tinker basteln

tired müde; kaputt

to an; auf, in; nach; zu

today heute; **What day is it** ~**?** Welcher Tag ist heute?

together zusammen

tomorrow morgen; **day after** ~ übermorgen

too zu; **me** ~ ich auch

tooth der Zahn, ¨e; **to brush [my] teeth** [mir] die Zähne putzen

tour die Tour, -en

town hall restaurant der Ratskeller, -

trade der Handel

train der Zug, ¨e; die Bahn

translation die Übersetzung, -en

travel fahren°; reisen

tree der Baum, ¨e

trip die Fahrt, -en; die Tour, -en

trousers die Hose, -n

try versuchen; probieren

Tuesday der Dienstag

TV das Fernsehen; ~ **set** der Fernseher, -; ~ **program** die Fernsehsendung, -en

typewriter die Schreibmaschine, -n

unbelievable unglaublich

uncle der Onkel, -

under unter

understand verstehen°

undress (sich) aus•ziehen°; **I get undressed** ich ziehe mich aus

unfortunately leider

union die Gewerkschaft, -en

university die Universität, -en; die Uni, -s

until bis; ~ **now** bisher

up to bis zu

USA die USA *(pl.)*

use benutzen; gebrauchen

vacation der Urlaub; die Ferien *(pl.);* **on/during** ~ in den Ferien; **to go on** ~ in Urlaub fahren°; **to be on** ~ in Urlaub sein°

vain: in ~ umsonst

vegetable das Gemüse

very sehr; ganz; riesig *(colloq.)*

vicinity: in the ~ in der Nähe

video game das Videospiel, -e

village das Dorf, ¨er

visit der Besuch; **(to)** ~ besuchen

visitor der Besucher, -/die Besucherin, -nen

volleyball der Volleyball

wage der Lohn, ¨e

washing machine die Waschmaschine, -n

wait (for) warten (auf)

walk der Spaziergang, ¨e; **(to) take a** ~ einen Spaziergang machen; spazieren; **(to) go for a** ~ spazieren•gehen°

walking: to go ~ wandern

wall die Wand, ¨e

want (to) wollen°

war der Krieg, -e; **world** ~ der Weltkrieg, -e

warm warm

warn (against) warnen (vor)

was war

wash die Wäsche; **(to)** ~ waschen°

watch die Uhr, -en; **(to)** ~ an•sehen°

water das Wasser

way der Weg, -e; die Art; **in this** ~ auf diese Weise; **on the** ~ auf dem Weg

weak schwach; ~ **and tired** schlapp

wear tragen°

weather das Wetter

Wednesday der Mittwoch
week die Woche, -n; **a ~ from**
  [Monday] [Montag] in acht
  Tagen
weekend das Wochenende, -n
welcome: you're ~ bitte (sehr)
well gut; wohl; **I'm not ~** mir
  geht's schlecht; **~** *(interjection)*
  na!, nun!; **~ now, oh ~** na
well known bekannt
west der Westen
wet naß
what was; **~ kind (of), ~ a** was
  für (ein)
when wann; wenn; als
where wo; **~ (to)** wohin
whether ob
which welch (-er, -es, -e)
while während
white weiß
whole ganz
whom wen *(acc. of* wer); wem *(dat.
  of* wer)
why warum
willingly gern

wind der Wind
window das Fenster, -
windsurfing: to go ~ windsurfen
  gehen°
wine der Wein, -e
winter der Winter
wish wünschen
with mit; **~ it** damit; **~ me** mit
  mir
woman die Frau, -en
woods der Wald, ¨er
word das Wort, ¨er
word processor der Wortprozessor,
  -en; **to do word processing** mit
  dem Wortprozessor arbeiten
work die Arbeit; **(to) ~** arbeiten;
  to ~ through durch•arbeiten; **it
  doesn't ~** es geht nicht; **it works**
  es geht
worker der Arbeiter, -/die
  Arbeiterin, -nen; der Arbeitnehmer, -/die Arbeitnehmerin,
  -nen; **foreign ~** der Gastarbeiter, -/die Gastarbeiterin, -nen

world die Welt, -en
worry die Sorge, -n; **(to) ~ about**
  sich kümmern um
worth wert
worthwhile wert
would würde; **~ like** möchte
wow Mensch!
write schreiben°
writer der Schriftsteller, -/die
  Schriftstellerin, -nen
wrong falsch; **What's ~?** Was ist
  los?; **What is ~ with you?** Was
  hast du?

year das Jahr, -e
yellow gelb
yes ja
yesterday gestern
you: (to) ~ dir *(dat. of* du)
young jung
your *(fam. pl.)* euer
youth die Jugend; der/die Jugendliche, -n

Index

Permissions and Credits

The authors and editors of *Deutsch heute, Fourth Edition* would like to thank the following companies and organizations for granting permission to use copyrighted material:

Realia

p. 5: Deutsche Bundespost, Posttechnisches Zentralamt, Darmstadt.

p. 6: Freie Universität Berlin.

p. 6: Volkswagen Aktiengesellschaft, 3180 Wolfsburg.

p. 6: Bayerische Motoren Werke Aktiengesellschaft, München.

p. 7: Süddeutscher Rundfunk, Öffentlichkeitsarbeit, Stuttgart.

p. 8: GRUNDIG Elektrogeräte GmbH, Fürth/Bayern, West Germany.

p. 10: Kalender "Dumme Sprüche für Gescheite," Friedrich W. Heye Verlag, Hamburg/München.

p. 14: Deutscher Paket Dienst GmbH, Unna.

p. 16: Universität Tübingen (Presseamt).

p. 25: Courtesy of Far-Out Disco Bar, Freiburg.

p. 27: Courtesy of Hotel Hohenstaufen, Koblenz.

p. 27: Courtesy of Hotel Ibis, Nürnberg.

p. 27: Courtesy of Hotel Ibis, Köln.

p. 28: Günther Poehling, Hamburger Tennisschule, Hamburg.

p. 31: Polaroid GmbH, Offenbach.

p. 39: © DSB / Sport-Billy Productions 1987.

p. 42: © DSB / Sport-Billy Productions 1987.

p. 46: Eduscho Kaffee GmbH & Co, Bremen.

p. 58: *Zahlenspiegel — Bundesrepublik Deutschland/Deutsche Demokratische Republik: Ein Vergleich,* Bundesministerium für innerdeutsche Beziehungen, 3. Ausgabe, 1985.

p. 60: Presse- und Informationsamt der Bundesregierung.

p. 68: Wertkauf Verwaltungsgesellschaft mbH, Karlsruhe.

p. 73: Levi Strauss GmbH, Heusenstamm.

p. 75: *Eltern* Magazin, Grüner + Jahr AG & Co., Verlagsgruppe München.

p. 79: Courtesy of Musik Wiebach, Berlin.

p. 81: Johannes Sandner, Musik Sandner, Erlangen.

p. 95: Courtesy of Café Melanie, Berlin.

p. 96: Süddeutscher Rundfunk, Stuttgart.

p. 103: Rettet das Watt: Bund für Umwelt und Naturschutz e. V., Kiel.

p. 112: Erwin Nitschke, Alles für das Fahrrad, Hamburg.

p. 116: Courtesy of Kennwort Milch, Centrale Marketinggesellschaft der deutschen Agrarwirtschaft mbH, Versmold.

p. 120: Jazzhaus Freiburg, Vereinigung Freiburger Jazzhaus e. V., Freiburg.

p. 124: Geschichtliches Siegel der Universität Würzburg (mit Wappen des Gründers Julius Echter von Mespelbrunn).

p. 132: Siegel der Universität Hamburg.

p. 142: Tourist Board Basel / Offizielles Verkehrsbüro Basel.

p. 148: Goethe Institut, München.

p. 150: Pizzeria Ristorante "La Stanza".

p. 155: Presse- und Informationsstelle der Universität Heidelberg.

p. 163: Bundeskanzleramt, *Österreich, Tatsachen und Zahlen,* 1986/87, Seite 6.

p. 183: PO & CO, Internationale Plakatkunst, Berlin.

p. 186: Kölner Verkehrsburo.

p. 192: Gottfried Fickl Ges. m.b.H. & Co. KG, Wien.

p. 196: Grosser Kurfürst Gasthaus, Berlin.

p. 200: Mathäser Bierstadt, München.

p. 205: Print-Anzeige, Müsli-Riegelv. Dr. August Oetker, Bielefeld.

p. 206: Courtesy of Henkel KG, Düsseldorf.

p. 207: Bäder- und Kurverwaltung Baden-Baden (Tourism and Convention Center), Baden-Baden.

p. 211: Ford-Werke AG, NH/VMM, Köln.

p. 211: Gesamtverband Deutscher Musikfachgeschäfte, e. V., Bonn.

p. 219: Courtesy of Herr Altvater, Teekanne GmbH, Düsseldorf.

p. 225: Courtesy of Herr Kirmeyer, Biobäcker, Frankfurt am Main-Bockenheim.

p. 229: Die Grünen, Bonn.

p. 463: Süddeutscher Verlag GmbH, Werbeabteilung, München.

p. 464: Uni Pressedienst, Universität Zürich.

p. 480: *Die Zeit*, Nr. 39, 20. September 1987, Seite 1, © Zeitverlag Gerd Bucerius GmbH & Co., Hamburg.

p. 481: *Kölnische/Bonner Rundschau*, Köln.

p. 490: *Kölnische/Bonner Rundschau*, Köln.

p. 495: Courtesy of BRAUN Elektronics USA.

Photos

p. xviii: Beryl Goldberg

p. 5: Kevin Galvin

p. 9: © Ulrike Welsch

p. 17: Uta Hoffman

p. 18: Beryl Goldberg

pp. 20, 32: © Ulrike Welsch

p. 36: Manfred Vollmer

p. 50: Julie O'Neil

p. 66: Palmer & Brilliant

p. 71: Bildarchiv Foto Marburg/Art Resource

pp. 82, 85, 87: Beryl Goldberg

pp. 91, 93: © Ulrike Welsch

p. 94: Manfred Vollmer

p. 111: © Ulrike Welsch

p. 122: Beryl Goldberg

p. 125: left: ADN/Zentralbild; right: Foto Inter Nationes

p. 127: Kathy Squires

p. 130: Beryl Goldberg

p. 133: Kathy Squires

p. 135: Peter Menzel

p. 136: Beryl Goldberg

p. 156: Judy Poe

p. 160: Kathy Squires

p. 162: Wiener Fremdenverkehrsverband

p. 165: Judy Poe

p. 166: Historical Pictures Service

p. 173: Stuart Cohen

p. 177: Judy Poe

p. 185: Diego Goldberg/Sygma

p. 187: Judy Poe

p. 194: Beryl Goldberg

p. 201: Uta Hoffman

p. 204: Hildegunde Kaurisch

p. 206: German Information Center

p. 215: Russel A. Thompson/Taurus Photos

p. 226. German Information Center

p. 232: © Ulrike Welsch

p. 235: Stuart Cohen

p. 237: Kathy Squires

p. 239: © Ulrike Welsch

p. 241: Owen Franken/Stock Boston

p. 259: Manfred Vollmer

p. 268: Stuart Cohen

p. 271: © Ulrike Welsch

p. 275: Palmer & Brilliant

p. 280: Stuart Cohen

p. 283: Peter Dreyer

p. 287: © Ulrike Welsch

p. 302: Judy Poe

p. 304: Uta Hoffman

p. 306, left and right: dpa photoreporters, inc.

pp. 309, 311, 313, 327: Swiss National Tourist Office

p. 340: Jo Röttger/Visum

p. 344: Manfred Vollmer

p. 346: © Ulrike Welsch

p. 352: German Information Center

p. 370: © Ulrike Welsch

p. 375: Kathy Squires

p. 379: from *Zweihundert Bildnisse und Lebensabrisse berühmter deutscher Männer*, Verlag von Georg Wigand, Leipzig, 1870

p. 384: Landesbildstelle Berlin

p. 389, left: German Information Center; right: Foto Inter Nationes/Renate von Forster

p. 402: Anton Steinhart, *Gartentor im Winter*, 1937. Ölgemälde. Courtesy Rainer Zimmermann

p. 403: German Information Center

p. 406: Gerd Ludwig/Visum

p. 412: Mercedes-Benz Foto

p. 414: Manfred Vollmer

p. 417: Erich Hartmann/Magnum

p. 418: Historical Pictures Service

p. 429: German Information Center

p. 433: Dieter Hauswald

p. 438: Theodor Rosenhauer, *Bildnis des Vaters*, 1931. Ölgemälde. Courtesy Rainer Zimmermann

p. 439: Courtesy Werner Schmidli

p. 442: Eastfoto

p. 446: Kathy Squires

p. 447: Verkehrsamt Berlin/Brodersen

p. 450: Eastfoto

p. 457: ADN/Zentralbild/Sindermann

p. 459: ADN/Zentralbild

p. 472: Otto Dix, *Kleine Verkündigung*, 1950. Courtesy Otto Dix Stiftung, Vaduz

p. 473: Foto: Panorama DDR/Barbara Koppe.

p. 478: Fredrik D. Bodin

p. 482: Beryl Goldberg

pp. 484, 485, 496, 499: German Information Center

p. 502: Henning Christoph

Bilder aus der Bundesrepublik Deutschland

p. i, top: Michael Lange/Visum; bottom: German Information Center

p. ii, top: Michael F. Myers; bottom: Hamburg Information

p. iii, top: Erich Hartmann/Magnum; bottom: Manfred Vollmer

p. iv, top: Peter H. Dreyer; bottom: Stuart Cohen

Bilder aus Österreich

p. i, top: Todd Powell; bottom: Fremdenverkehrsamt Wien

p. ii, top left: Suzanne Murphy; top right: Judy Poe; bottom: Judy Poe

p. iii: Damm/ZEFA

p. iv, top: Todd Powell; bottom: Studio Mike/ZEFA

Bilder aus der Schweiz

p. i, top: Judy Poe; bottom: Damm/
ZEFA

p. ii: Swiss National Tourist Office

p. iii, top: Leidmann/ZEFA; bottom:
Kevin Galvin

p. iv, top left: Jaques/Photo
Researchers; top right: Judy Poe;
bottom: Porterfield/Chickering/
Photo Researchers

Bilder aus dem Alltag

p. i: © Ulrike Welsch

p. ii, top left: J. Douglas Guy; top
right: Kathy Squires; bottom, ©
Ulrike Welsch

p. iii: Gradl/ZEFA

p. iv, top: Fredrik D. Bodin/Stock
Boston; bottom left: Beryl
Goldberg; bottom right: J. Douglas
Guy

p. v, top: Manfred Vollmer; bottom:
Tony Freeman

p. vi, top: Uta Hoffmann; bottom:
Carol Palmer

p. vii: Uta Hoffmann

p. viii, top left: Fredrik D. Bodin; top
right: ADN/Zentralbild; bottom:
Uta Hoffmann

*Bilder aus der Deutschen
Demokratischen Republik*

p. i, top: Kathy Squires; bottom:
ADN/Zentralbild

p. ii: ADN/Zentralbild

p iii, left: Wachter/Focus on Sports;
top right: ADN/Zentralbild;
bottom right: ADN/Zentralbild

p. iv, top: J. Douglas Guy; bottom:
ADN/Zentralbild

Illustrations

Proverb illustrations by
Chris Demarest.

All other illustrations by Penny
Carter.